Petrine Theology

Petrine Theology

DOUGLAS W. KENNARD

WIPF & STOCK · Eugene, Oregon

PETRINE THEOLOGY

Copyright © 2022 Douglas W. Kennard. All rights reserved. Except for brief quotations in critical publications or reviews, no part of this book may be reproduced in any manner without prior written permission from the publisher. Write: Permissions, Wipf and Stock Publishers, 199 W. 8th Ave., Suite 3, Eugene, OR 97401.

Wipf & Stock
An Imprint of Wipf and Stock Publishers
199 W. 8th Ave., Suite 3
Eugene, OR 97401

www.wipfandstock.com

PAPERBACK ISBN: 978-1-7252-7116-6
HARDCOVER ISBN: 978-1-7252-7117-3
EBOOK ISBN: 978-1-7252-7118-0

09/20/22

This book is dedicated to
Edwin Blum
For whom an earlier version a part of
this manuscript was prepared decades ago.

Contents

Abbreviations | ix

1. Lost Boy or Foundation for Christian Theology | 1
2. God | 11
3. Christology | 22
4. Peter's Letter Form Presents Intentional Missional Trinity | 51
5. The Holy Spirit | 58
6. God's Word | 61
7. Humanity | 66
8. Christ's Vicarious New Covenant Atonement, Sanctification, Purification, and Redemption | 85
9. Peter's Gospel | 123
10. Exodus Following Jesus to Kingdom Virtues | 137
11. The Household of God | 176
12. Suffering | 215
13. Standing Against Satan and Exorcizing Demons | 225
14. False Teachers | 240
15. The Coming of the Lord | 254

Select Bibliography | 283
Subject Index | 321
Author Index | 323
Scripture Index | 331

Abbreviations

'Abod. Zar.	Rabbinic 'Abodah Zarah
Abr.	On the Life of Abraham
Adv. Gent.	Adversus nationes
Adv. Haer.	Against Heresies
Advice	Advice about Keeping Well
Adv. Jud.	Adversus Judaeos
Aem.	Aemilius Paullus
Aen.	Aeneid
Aet.	On the Eternity of the World
AfO	Archiv für Orientforschung
AfOB	Archiv für Orientforschung: Beiheft
Ag.	Against
Ag. Ap.	Josephus, Against Apion
'Ag. Ber.	'Aggadot Berešit
Agr.	Agricola
Aj.	Ajax
AJT	American Journal of Theology
Alex.	Alexander
Alex. fort.	De Alexander magni fortuna aut virtute
All.	Allegoriae

Anab.	*Anabasis*
AnBib	*Analecta biblica* series
Ancor.	*Ancoratus*
ANEP	Ancient Near Eastern Pictures Relating to the Old Testament. Edited by James Pritchard.
ANET	Ancient Near Eastern Texts Relating to the Old Testament. Edited by James Pritchard.
Ann.	*Annales*
ANRW	*Aufstieg und Niedergang der römischen Welt: Geschichte und Kultur Rom sim Spiegel der neueren Forschung.* Edited by H. Temporini and W. Haase. Berlin.
Ant.	*Antiquities* as in Josephus, Jewish history or Sophicles, history
Ant. rom.	*Antiquitates romanae*
Apoc.	*Apolalypse*
Apoc. El.	*Apocalypse of Elijah* in Hebrew and Coptic
Apocr. Jn.	*Apocryphon of John*
Apol.	*Apology*, as for Plato, *Apology of Socrates* or Justin Martyr, numbered *Apology*
Apos.	*Apostles* as in pseudepigrapha *Epistle to the Apostles*
'Arak.	Rabbinic *'Arakin*
Arist.	*Aristites*
ARN	'Abot de Rabbi Nathan
ARW	Archiv für Religionswissenschaft
Ascen. Isa.	Ascension of Isaiah
As. Mos.	Assumption of Moses
ASTI	Annual of the Swedish Theological Institute
ATJ	Ashland Theological Journal
Att.	*Epistular ad Atticum*
Aul. Gel.	*Aulus Gellius*
B. or b.	Babylonian Talmud

BA	*The Biblical Archaeologist*
BAG	Bauer, W., W. E. Arndt, and F. W. Gingrich. *Greek-English Lexicon of the New Testament and Other Early Literature.* Chicago, 1957.
Bapt.	*Baptism*
Bar	Apocrypha Baruch with number 1 or 2 before
BAR	*Biblical Archaeology Review*
Barn.	*Barnabas*
BASOR	*Bulletin of the American Schools of Oriental Research*
Bat.	Rabbinic *Baba Batra*
BBR	*Bulletin for Biblical Research*
BDB	Francis Brown, S. D. Driver, and Charles Briggs, eds. *A Hebrew and English Lexicon of the Old Testament.* Oxford: Clarendon, 1907.
BECNT	Baker Exegetical Commentary on the New Testament
Bell. Cat.	*Bellum catalinae*
Bell Civ.	*Civil War*
Ben. Is. Jac.	*De benedictionibus Isaaci et Jacobi*
Ber.	Rabbinic *Berorot*
BEvT	Beiträge zur evangelischen Theologie
BHT	Beiträge zur historischen Theologie
Bib	*Biblica*
BJRL	*Bulletin of the John Rylands University Library of Manchester*
BMAP	*The Brooklyn Museum Aramaic Papyri.* Edited by E. G. Kraeling.
BN	*Biblische Notizen*
BR	*Biblical Research*
Bride	*Advice to Bride and Groom*
Brut.	*Brutus* or *De claris oratoribus*

BSac	*Bibliotheca sacra*
BTB	*Biblical Theology Bulletin*
BTZ	*Berliner Theologische Zeitschrift*
BV	*Biblical Viewpoint*
BZ	*Biblische Zeitschrift*
BZAW	*Beihefte zur Zeitschrift für die alttestamentliche Wissenschaft*
C. Ap.	Josephus, *Contra Apionem*
C. Ar.	*Orations against the Arians*
Carn. Chr.	*The Flesh of Christ*
Cat.	*Catechetical Lecture*
CBQ	*Catholic Biblical Quarterly*
CD	Damascus Document also found at Qumran
Cels.	*Against Celsus*
Cherubim	Philo, *On the Cherubim*
Chron.	*Chronicle*
CIJ	*Corpus inscriptionum judaicarum.* Edited by J. B. Frey, Rome, 1936–52.
Cim.	*Cimon*
Claud.	*Claudius*
Clem.	*Clement,* 1 or 2 or a pseudo-Clement manuscript
Cod.	*Codex*
Col. In omnes B. Pauli epist.	*Collection of Commentaries of Pauline Epistles*
Comm. Isa.	*Commentarii in Isaiam*
Comm. Jo.	*Commentarii in evangelium Joannis*
Comm. Rom.	*Commentarii in Romanos*
ConB	Coniectanea Biblica: New Testament Seires
Conf.	*On the Confusion of Tongues*
Consol. Phil.	*Consolation of Philosophy*
Controv.	Seneca the Elder's *Controversiae*

CPJ	*Corpus papyrorum judaicarum*. Edited by V. Tcherikover, Cambridge, 1957–64.
CSEL	*Corpus Scriptorum Ecclesiasticorum Latinorum*. Edited by Filium.
CTJ	*Calvin Theological Journal*
CTM	*Concordia Theological Monthly*
CTQ	*Concordia Theological Quarterly*
Cult. Fem.	*The Apparel of Women*
CurTM	*Currents in Theology and Mission*
C.W.	*On the Civil War*
Cyr.	*Cyropaedia*
DBS	*Dictionnaire de la Bible*: Supplement. Edited by L. Pirot and A. Robert.
Decl.	*Declamations*
Def. Or.	*Defense of Oratory*
Def. orc.	*De defectu oraculorum*
De lib. arb.	*De Libertate Arbitrii*
Dem. ev.	*Demonstration of the Gospel*
Demon.	*Ad Demonicum*
Deus	*That God Is Unchangeable*
Dial.	*Dialogue*
Dial. D.	*Dialogue of the Dead*
Diatr.	*Diatribe (Dissertationes)*
Did.	*Didache*
Diogn.	*Diognetus*
Doctr. chr.	*De doctrina christiana*
Down. J.	*Downward Journey*
DSD	*Dead Sea Discoveries*
Eb.	*Ebionites*
Ebr.	*On Drunkeness*
'Ed.	Rabbinic *'Eduyyot*
Eleem.	*Works and Almsgiving*

Eloc.	*Style*
En.	*Enoch* with number 1 or 2 or 3 before
Ep.	*Epistle*
Eph.	*To the Ephesians*
Eph. Tale	*Ephesian Tale* by Xenophon of Ephesus
Epid.	*Epidemics* or Irenaeus, *Demonstration of the Apostolic Preaching*
Epigr.	*Epigrams*
Ep. More.	*Epistulae morales*
ʿ*Erub.*	Rabbinic ʿ*Erubin*
Esar	Esarhaddon Treaty
Esd	Apocrypha Esadras with number 1 or 2 before
Esth.	*Esther*
Eth. nic.	*Ethica nicomachea*
EvQ	*Evangelical Quarterly*
EvT	*Evangelische Theologie*
ExAud	*Ex auditu*
Exh. Cast.	*Exhortation to Chastity*
Expl. Dan.	*Explanatio in Danielem*
Exp. S. Pauli epist. Ad Rom.	*Exposition of Saint Paul Epistle of Romans*
ExpTim	*Expository Times*
Fac. Dict.	*Factorum ac dictorum memorabilium libri* or *Memorable Deeds and Sayings*
Fid. Grat.	*De fide ad Gratianum*
Fin.	*De finibus*
Fiod. op.	*De fide et operibus*
Flaccus	*Against Flaccus*
Frag.	*Fragment*
Frat. Amor	*De fraterno amore*
Fug.	*De fuga et inventione*
GELNT	*Greek English Lexicon of the New Testament*

Geogr.	*Geographica*
Giṭ.	*Giṭṭin*
Good Person	Philo, *That Every Good Person Is Free*
Gos.	*Gospel* as in pseudepigrapha *Gospel of Peter* or others
Hab. Virg.	*The Dress of Virgins*
Haer.	*Against Heresies*
Ḥag.	Rabbinic *Ḥagigah*
Hall	*The Hall*
HAT	Handbuch zum Alten Testament
Heb.	*Hebrews* as in *Gospel of the Hebrews*
Heir	*Who Is the Heir?*
Her.	*Quis rerum divinarum heres sit*
Herm. Mand.	*Shepherd of Hermas, Mandates*
Herm. Sim.	*Shepherd of Hermas, Similitudes*
Herm. Vis.	*Shepherd of Hermas, Visions*
Hist.	*History*
Hist. Consc.	*How to write History*
Hist. eccl.	*Histora ecclesiastica* or *Ecclesiastical History*
Hist. plant.	*Historia plantarum*
Hom.	*Homily*
HTR	*Harvard Theological Review*
HUCA	*Hebrew Union College Annual* Int *Interpretation*
Ḥul.	*Ḥullin*
Hypoth.	*Hypothetica*
ICC	International Critical Commentary
Inst.	*Institutes* as: Lactantius, *The Divine Institutes* or Quintilian, *Institutio oratorio*
Int	*Interpretation*
Inv.	*De invention rhetorica*
Ioh.	A work on *John*

IRT	Issues in Religion and Theology
Is. Os.	*Isis and Osiris*
JAAR	*Journal of the American Academy of Religion*
JAC	*Jahrbuch für Antike und Christentum*
JAOS	*Journal of the American Oriental Society*
JBL	*Journal of Biblical Literature*
JBTh	*Jahrbuch für biblische Theologie* (Neukirchener)
Jdt	Apocrypha Judith
JETS	*Journal of the Evangelical Theological Society*
JJS	*Journal of Jewish Studies*
JLW	*Journal of Luther's Works*
JNES	*Journal of Near Eastern Studies*
Jos.	*On the Life of Joseph*
Jos. Asen.	*Joseph and Aseneth*
Josh.	Joshua
Jov.	*Adversus Jovinianum libri II*
JRT	*Journal of Religious Thought*
JSJ	*Journal for the Study of Judaism in the Persian, Hellenistic, and Roman Periods*
JSNT	*Journal for the Study of the New Testament*
JSNTSup	*Journal for the Study of the New Testament: Supplement Series*
JSOT	*Journal for the Study of the Old Testament*
JSOTSup	*Journal for the Study of the Old Testament: Supplement Series*
JSP	*Journal for the Study of the Pseudepigrapha*
JTS	*Journal of Theological Studies*
JTSA	*Journal of Theology for Southern Africa*
Jub.	*Jubilees*
Kel.	Rabbinic *Kelim*
Ketab.	Rabbinic *Ketubbot*

Kgdms	Kingdoms in LXX (reflects Hebrew of 1–2 Kgs) preceded by 3 or 4
KTU	*Keilalphabetische Texte aus Ugarit.* Edited by Manfried Dietrich et al.
L.A.B.	*Liber antiquitatum biblicarum Pseudo-Philo*
Lac.	*Respublica Lacedaemoniorum*
L.A.E.	*Life of Adam and Eve*
Lam.	*Lamentations*
LCL	Loeb Classical Library
Leg.	*Leges* or *Laws*: Cicero, *De legibus* or Philo, *Allegorical Interpretation*
Life	Josephus, *The Life*, or Philstratus, *The Life of Apollonius*
LQ	*Lutheran Quarterly*
Luc.	*Luke* or *Lucan*
Lucil.	*Ad Lucilium*
LW	*Living Word*
LXX	Septuagint
Lyc.	*Lycurgus*
m. or *M.*	*Mishnah*
Macc	Apocrypha Maccabees with number 1 or 2 or 3 or 4 before
Magn.	*To the Magnesians*
Mak.	Rabbinic *Makkot*
Marc.	*Against Marcion* or Seneca, *Ad Marciam de consolatione*
Mart.	*To the Martyrs*
Mart. Pal.	*The Martyrdom of Palestine*
Mart. Pol.	*Martyrdom of Polycarp*
Matt.	*Matthew*
Meg.	Rabbinic *Megillah*
Mek.	Rabbinic *Mekilta*

Mem.	*Memorabilia*
Menaḥ.	Rabbinic *Menaḥot*
Mes.	Rabbinic *Metzi'a*
Midr.	Rabbinic *Midrash*
Migr.	*On the Migration of Abraham*
Mil.	*Pro Milone*
MM	Moulton, J. H., and G. Milligan, *The Vocabulary of the Greek Testament*. London, 1930.
Mor.	*Moralia*
Mort.	*The Deaths of the Persecutors*
Mos.	*Moses*
Moses	*On the Life of Moses*
MSJ	*The Master's Seminary Journal*
MT	Hebrew Masoretic Text, reflected in *Biblica Hebraica Stuttgartensia*. Edited by Funditus Renovata et al., 1977.
NAC	New American Commentary
Names	*On the Change of Names*
Narr.	*Narration*
Nat.	*Naturalis historia* of Pliny the Elder
Nat. d.	*De natura deorum*
Naz.	Rabbinic *Nazir*
NCB	New Century Bible
Ned.	Rabbinic *Nedarim*
Neot	*Neotestamentica*
NICNT	New International Commentary on the New Testament
Nid.	Rabbinic *Niddah*
NIDNTT	*The New International Dictionary of New Testament Theology*. Edited by Colin Brown.

NIDOTTE	*New International Dictionary of Old Testament Theology & Exegesis.* Edited by Willem VanGemeren.
NIGTC	New International Greek Testament Commentary
Noc. att.	*Attic Nights*
NovT	*Novum Testamentum*
NovTSup	Supplements to Novum Testamentum
NT	New Testament
NTOA	Novum testamentum et orbis antiquus
NTS	*New Testament Studies*
Num.	*Numa*
Od.	*Odyssey*
Odes Sol.	*Odes of Solomon*
Oec.	*Economics*
Oed. frag.	*Oedipus* fragment
Off.	*De officiis*
'Ohal.	Rabbinic 'Ohalot
Ol.	*Olympian Odes*
Oneir.	*Oneirocritica*
Op.	*Works and Days*
Or.	*Prayer*
Orat.	*Orations*
OT	Old Testament
Paed.	*Christ the Educator*
Pan.	*Refutation of All Heresies*
Part. or	*Partitiones oratoriae*
Pelag.	*Adversus Pelaganos dialog III*
Pesaḥ.	Rabbinic *Pesaḥim*
Pesiq. Rab Kah.	*Pesiqta de Rab Kahana*
Pet.	*Peter* as in *Apocalypse of Peter* or *Acts of Peter*

PG	*Patrologia graeca.* Edited by J.-P. Migne. 161 vols.
Phil.	Ignatius or Polycarp, *To the Philadelphians*
Philops.	*The Lover of Lies*
Phoen.	*Phoenician Maidens*
PL	*Patrologiae cursus completus: Series Latina.* Edited by J.-P. Migne. 221 vols.
Plant.	*On Planting*
P.Lond.	*Greek Papyri in the British Museum.* Edited by F. G. Kenyon et al,. London, 1893.
P.Mich	*Greek Papyri in University of Michigan.*
Pol.	Ignatius, *To Polycarp* or Aristotle and Martial, *Politics*
Post.	*On the Posterity of Caini*
P.Oxy.	*The Oxyrhynchus Papyri.* London, 1898–2010.
Pr Azar	Apocrypha Prayer of Azariah
Praed.	*The Predestination of the Saints*
Praem.	*De praemiis et poenis*
Praep. ev.	*Preparation for the Gospel*
Praescr.	*Prescription against Heretics*
Princ.	*First Principles*
Pr Man	Apocrypha Prayer of Manasseh
Prog.	Theon's *Progymnasmata* in James Butts' translation and treatises on it
Ps.-Arist.	Pseudo-Aristides
Ps.-Jon.	*Targum Pseudo-Jonathan*
Ps.-Phoc.	Pseudo-Phocylides
Pss. Sol.	*Psalms of Solomon*
Pun.	*Punica*
Q	within Qumran manuscript (e.g., 11Q132.2 is read as cave#Qdocument numbers #chapter.#verse)

QE	*Quaestiones et solutions in Exodum*
Qidd.	Rabbinic *Qiddušin*
Quint. Fratr.	*Epistulae ad Quintum fratrem*
Rab.	*Rabbah* often with a biblical book, such as Leviticus (Lev)
RB	*Revue biblique*
RBL	*Review of Biblical Literature*
Res.	*Resurrection of the Flesh*
Resp.	*Republic*
Rev.	*On Revelation*
RevExp	*Review and Expositor*
RHA	*Revue Hittite et asianique*
RHE	*Revue d'histoire ecclésiastique*
Rhet.	*Rhetoric*
R. N.	*De rerum natura*
rom.	*Romanae* as in Dionysis, *Ant. rom.*
Roš Haš.	Rabbinic *Roš Haššanah*
RQ	*Römische Quartalschrift für christliche Altertumskunde und Kirchengeschichte*
RTR	*Reformed Theological Review*
Rust.	*De re rustica*
Šabb.	Rabbinic document *Šabbat*
Sacr.	*De sacrificiis Abelis et Caini*
Sanh.	Rabbinic document *Sanhedrin*
SANT	Studien zum Alten und Neuen Testaments
Sat.	*Satirae*
SB	*Sammelbuch griechisher Urkunden aus Aegypten*. Edited by F. Preisigke et al.
SBL	Society of Biblical Literature
SBLDS	Society of Biblical Literature Dissertations Series

SBLMS	Society of Biblical Literature Monograph Series
SBLSP	Society of Biblical Literature Seminar Papers
Scap.	*To Scapula*
Scorp.	*Antidote for the Scorpion's Sting*
SCS	*Society of Christian Scholars* series (Scholars Press)
Šeb.	Rabbinic *Šebi'it*
Šebu.	Rabbinic *Šebu'ot*
Sedr.	*Sedrach*
Sem.	Rabbinic *Semaḥot*
Šeqal.	Rabbinic *Šeqalim*
Serm.	*Sermon*
Sib. Or.	*Sibyline Oracles*
Sir	Apocrypha Hebrew Sirach/LXX Ecclesiasticus
Smyrn.	*To the Smyrnaens*
SNTSMS	Society for New Testament Monograph Series
Sobr.	*On Sobriety*
Sol.	*Solomon*
Somn.	*On Dreams*
Spec. Laws	*On the Special Laws*
Speech	*Speech in Character*
Str-B	Strack and Billerbeck, *Kommentar zum Neuen Testament*
Strom.	*Miscellanies*
StudBib	*Studia Biblica*
Sull.	*Sulla*
SwJT	*Southwestern Journal of Theology*
Symp.	*Symposium*
t. or *T.*	*Tosefta*

T. 12 Patr.	Testaments of the Twelve Patriarchs
T. Abr.	Testament of Abraham
T. Benj.	Testament of Benjamin
T. Dan.	Testament of Daniel
T. Hez.	Testament of Hezekiah
T. Hos.	Testament of Hosea
T. Isaac	Testament of Isaac
T. Iss.	Testament of Issachar
T. Job	Testament of Job
T. Jud.	Testament of Judah
T. Levi	Testament of Levi
T. Mos.	Testament of Moses
T. Naph.	Testament of Naphtali
T. Sim.	Testament of Simeon
Ṭ. Yom	Rabbinic Ṭebul Yom
T. Zeb.	Testament of Zebulum
Taʻan.	Rabbinic Taʻanit
Tan.	Rabbinic Tanḥuma
TB	Theologische Bücherei: Neudrucke und Berichte aus dem 20. Jahrhundert.
TDNT	Theological Dictionary of the New Testament. Edited by Gerhard Kittel and Gerhard Friedrich.
TDOT	Theological Dictionary of the Old Testament. Edited by G. Johannes Botterweck and Helmer Ringgren.
Test.	To Quirinius: Testomonies against the Jews
Tg.	Targum
Tg. 1 Chr.	Targum of 1 Chronicles
Tg. Isa.	Targum Isaiah as an Early Jewish commentary on Isaiah
Tg. Jon.	Targum Jonathan

Tg. Neof.	*Targum Neofiti*
Tg. Ps.-J.	*Targum Pseudo-Jonathan*
Ṭhar.	Rabbinic *Ṭhearot*
Them.	*Themistocles*
Theoph.	*Divine Manifestation*
Thom.	*Thomas* as in *Gospel of Thomas*
Tim.	Plato's *Timaeus* or Aeschines' *In Timarchum*
TNTC	Tyndale New Testament Commentaries
Tob	Apocrypha Tobit
Top.	*Topica*
TQ	*Theologische Quartalschrift*
Trall.	*To the Trallians*
Tranq. an.	*De tranquillitate animi*
TRev	*Theologische Revue*
Trin.	*Trinity or in Latin, Trinitate*
TrinJ	*Trinity Journal*
TRu	*Theologische Rundschau*
TS	*Theological Studies*
TSK	*Theologische Studien und Kritiken*
TU	Texte und Untersuchungen
TWOT	*Theological Wordbook of the Old Testament.* Edited by R. Laird Harris et al.
TynBul	*Tyndale Bulletin*
USQR	*Union Seminary Quarterly Review*
Val. Max.	*Valerius Maximus*
VC	*Vigilae christianae*
Verr.	*In Verrem*
Vesp.	*Vespasianus*
Vir. ill.	*De viris illustribus*
Virt.	*De virtutibus*
Vis. Isa.	*Ascension of Isaiah*

VT	*Vetus Testamentum*
VTE	*Succession Treaty of Esarhaddon*
VTSup	Supplements to *Vetus Testamentum*
War	Josephus, *Jewish War*
WBC	Word Biblical Commentary
Wis	Apocrypha Wisdom of Solomon
Worse	Philo, *That the Worse Attacks the Better*
WTJ	*Westminster Theological Journal*
WUNT	Wissenschaftliche Untersuchungen zum Neuen Testament
Y. or y.	Jerusalem Talmud
Yad.	Rabbinic *Yadayim*
Yebam.	Rabbinic *Yebamot*
ZA	*Zeitschrift für Assyriologie*
ZAW	*Zeitschrift für die alttestamentliche Wissenschaft*
ZNW	*Zeitschrift für die neutestamentliche Wissenschaft und die Kunde der ältern Kirche*
ZRGG	*Zeitschrift für Religions und Geistesgeschichte*
ZST	*Zeitschrift für systematische Theologie*
ZTK	*Zeitschrift für Theologie und Kirche*

1

Lost Boy or Foundation for Christian Theology

THE EARLY CHURCH CONSIDERED Peter to be the foundation for apostolic Christian tradition. Stating this, J. N. D. Kelley identified, "St. Peter is the starting point of apostolic tradition and the symbol of unity" for the church.[1] For example, the Gospels always list Peter as first apostle (Matt 10:2–4 even uses πρῶτος "first" to refer to Peter; Mark 3:13–19; Luke 6:13–16; Acts 1:13). The Gospels, Acts, and the early church declare Peter to be repeatedly the spokesman for the apostles (Matt 14:28; 15:15; 16:16–19; 18:21; 26:35, 40; Mark 8:29; 9:5; 10:28; John 6:68; Acts 1:15; 2:14; 3:4, 12; 4:8; 5:3, 8; 8:20; 10:9—11:18; 15:7)[2] and one of three within the core disciple band (Matt 17:1; 26:37; Mark 5:37; 9:2; 13:3: Luke 9:28). Paul and Clement of Rome declared Peter to be one of the pillars of the church, along with Jesus' brother James and John Zebedee (Gal 2:9).[3] On the basis of Jesus' commission of Peter in Matt 16 and the record of the book of Acts, much of the early church declared Peter to be the foundation for the church.[4] The Orthodox Church considers Peter as foundation for the church, undergirding apostolic tradition and patriarchy of

---

1. Kelly, *Early Christian Doctrines*, 205.

2. John Chrysostom, *Hom. 2 Tim 3:1* 4; Cyril of Alexandria, *In Ioh.* 1:42; *De trin. dial.* 4; Theodoret, *Quaest In Gen. interp.* 110; *In Ps.* 2.

3. Clement of Rome, *1 Cor* 5.

4. Cyril of Alexandria, *In Ioh.* 1:42; *In Luc* 22:32; Epiphanius, *Ancor.* 9; Maximus the Confessor, *Vita accert* 24; Cyprian, *Ep. Of Cyprian* 54.7; 70.3; 72.11; 74.16; *Treatise of Cyprian* 1.2.

Syria and Rome.[5] This is the starting point that later gets spun in the Roman Catholic Church grounding Peter as the first pope, possessing the keys of the kingdom with Jesus Christ as the foundation, but before that doctrine emerges, many in the church considered Peter to be the foundation. Either way, Peter certainly laid the foundation for the church universal as Ignatius claimed.[6] Didymus declared Peter to be the leader and chief among the apostles.[7] Philip Schaff summarized this sentiment of Peter being the church's chief actor to ground the apostolic tradition, "Peter was the chief actor in the first stage of apostolic Christianity and fulfilled the prophecy of his name in laying the foundation of the church among the Jews and the Gentiles."[8] Mature scholarly biographers of Peter, such as Pheme Perkins concur, "Peter is the universal 'foundation' for all the churches. . . . There is no figure who compasses more of that diversity than Peter."[9] F. J. Foakes-Jackson concluded, "the very fact that Peter was singled out by the unanimous voice of the writers of the N.T. for pre-eminence is sufficient reason why he should demand our serious attention."[10] From this foundational bridge position, Martin Hengel begins to make integrated attempts toward a Petrine theology.[11] Martin Hengel and Larry Hurtado conclude that Peter has a "particular theological competence" to contribute to the field of biblical theology.[12] This book brings together a theological construction to reflect the biblical claims from biblical and early patristic sources expressing Peter's voice.

In later patristics, the historical Peter became less the focus and traditional appropriation of a "Peter of faith" moved to the fore to ground Roman Catholic doctrines, such as the papacy retaining Peter's leadership for the church. With Protestantism taking up Paul as their patron apostle, Peter gets lost behind Roman Catholic tradition. An example is that Martin Luther shifts from loving Peter's spiritual contributions "as the noblest books of the New Testament" to that of hating the Roman Catholic use

---

5. Photius, *PG* 120.800B; Palamas, *Trials* 2.1.38; Meyendorff et al., *Primacy of Peter*.
6. Ign. *Magn.* 10:9.
7. Didymus, *De trin.* 1.30.
8. Schaff, *History of Christian Church*, 1:96.
9. Perkins, *Peter*, 184; Hengel, *Saint Peter*, 79–80, 102; Helyer, *Life and Witness of Peter*.
10. Foakes-Jackson, *Peter*, xii.
11. Hengel, *Saint Peter*, 86–87.
12. Hengel, *Saint Peter*, 35; see Hurtado, "Apostle Peter in Protestant Scholarship," 8.

of a tradition of Peter to support the papacy.[13] To reflect this transition, Gene Green used a metaphor from J. M. Barrie's novel *Peter Pan* to declare Peter as one of the "lost boys" of Christian theology.[14] For example, NT theologies often exclude Petrine theology altogether, namely: Rudolf Bultmann, Udo Schnelle, Adolf Schlatter, and Greg Beale.[15] This neglect of Peter to "neverland" became a motive for Green to try to put together part of a theology for Peter.

With the rise of later biblical criticism, Petrine theology fragmented, and viewed within those fragments it has become viewed as "warmed-over Paulinist," and thus both irretrievable and largely irrelevant. For example, Francis Beare analyzed parallels among Peter and Paul's contributions and concluded that 1 Pet "is strongly marked by the impress of Pauline theological ideas, and in language the dependance on St. Paul is undeniably great. All through the Epistle we have the impression that we are reading the work of a man who is steeped in the Pauline letters."[16] In contrast, Goppelt made a similar analysis and concluded that many of these shared themes actually were from paraenetic sections sharing wisdom that Jesus' teachings or Jewish wisdom, such that he concluded concerning a relationship between Peter and Paul, "there can be no mention of any literary dependence."[17] It is probably better to view Petrine theology as providing a bridge from Jesus' ministry to that of Paul's.

Peter Davids, making major contributions to Petrine theology, mostly described the separate theologies of 1 Pet and 2 Pet, summarizing that many major Pauline themes are missing from 1 Pet:

> Many of the major Pauline themes are missing from 1 Peter. Faith, justification, and works are not an issue for 1 Peter, much less specific "works of the law" such as circumcision and Jewish festivals, which are so important for Paul. First Peter does not use *ekklesia* (ἐκκλησία, "church"), which is also important for Paul. While both Paul and 1 Peter discuss election, the discussion in 1 Pet 2:4–10 is much different than that in Rom

---

13. Luther, "Preface to the New Testament," quoted by Elliott, *1 Peter*, 5; *Luther's Works*, 35.361–62; *Table Talk* (1533) WATR 1:194, no. 445 (*Luther's Works* 54:72).

14. Green, *Vox Petri*, 1; using "lost boys" as those children who fall out of the baby carriages when the nanny is looking the other way. Elliott described this as an "exegetical step-child" (*1 Peter*, 3).

15. Bultmann, *Theology of the New Testament*; Schnelle, *Theology of the New Testament*; Schlatter, *New Testament Theology*; Beale, *New Testament Biblical Theology*.

16. Beare, *First Epistle of Peter*, 44.

17. Goppelt, *1 Petrusbrief*, 4,9 with fuller discussion on 48–51.

11:26–29, nor does Paul ever cite Exod 19:6, which is central to 1 Peter's discussion. When Paul talks about gifts, he associates them with the Spirit, but Peter makes no mention of the Spirit in his discussion about gifts. Finally, the list of terms and ideas that are important to 1 Peter and not found in Paul or important to Paul and not found in 1 Peter is significant.[18]

This provides a warning so that an interpreter should not read Paul onto the text, but rather understand meaning within Peter's context.

Furthermore, splintering Petrine theology fosters so many biblical theologies discussing Petrine attributed works divided into theologies of 1 Pet and of 2 Pet, separated by different vocabulary and expression. Additionally, often one of these sources is considered to not be from Peter, and thus removed from consideration. Rarely is the broad patristic claim considered for Mark within the Petrine corpus which won this Gospel's canonicity. Recently Gene Green has made a valiant case for Mark's inclusion while separating Peter's theology into: 1 Pet, Mark, and Peter imbedded in Gospels and Acts. Green leaves 2 Pet excluded from Petrine theology, though he acknowledged that Peter likely wrote that epistle that claims him as author, that the majority of the global church considers Peter wrote the epistle, and there is not sufficient warrant to reject Peter as author.[19] Additionally, Ralph Martin indicated that, "probably no document in the N.T. is so theological as 1 Peter, if 'theological' is taken in the strict sense of teaching about God."[20] Joel Green extends this thought with "1 Peter is about God and the ramifications of orienting life wholly around him."[21] Occasionally, the Petrine statements from the book of Acts and the Gospels are folded in to inform a theology of Peter, but this approach is more common among those exploring the early history of the church than those who explore biblical theology.

Ferdinand C. Baur and the Tübingen school followed G. W. F. Hegel's concept of evolving religion dividing Christianity into thesis-Peter's Jewish Christianity in Acts, countered by antithesis-Paul's gentile Christianity that becomes synthesized in second-century traditional Christianity (including Petrine epistles seen through Pauline interpretations). My previous critique of Hegel presented Hegel's thesis, antithesis, and synthesis as contradictory and thus unable to be fused into a meaningful

---

18. Davids, *Theology of James, Peter, and Jude*, 111; Elliott, *1 Peter*, 38–39.
19. Green, *Jude, 2 Peter*, 172, 144–45; *Vox Petri*, 97.
20. Helyer, *Life and Witness of Peter*, 105.
21. Helyer, *Life and Witness of Peter*, 105.

synthesis.²² When the Tübingen school followed Baur's lead to develop that Christianity developed from Judaism before it universalized under Paul, early Christianity ended up not following Hegel into the early church tradition, but returning to its Protestant bias for Pauline theology, and cutting adrift selective aspects of Peter for Roman Catholics to prooftext their claims. Peter and Paul were not oppositional in their ministries as Baur developed from Gal 2:7. Thus, when Protestant scholars read 1 Pet they tend to read it through a "warmed-over Paulinist" lens, and Jewish forms of Christianity got lost as an echo of Paul. Of course, Peter is far more complex than Jewish Christianity,²³ since he wins the first gentiles to Christ and writes 1 and 2 Pet primarily to gentile Christians.

Lutz Doering documents recovery of Petrine studies from this anti-Pauline restrictive "bumbler" and from "warmed-over Paulism" to a bridge figure and symbol of unity.²⁴ For example, James Dunn celebrated, "Peter was probably in fact and effect the bridge-man (pontifex maximus!) who did more than any other to hold together the diversity of first-century Christianity."²⁵ Peter serves as the outstanding bridge from the oral apostolic witness to that of the foundational written witness.

The Gospels and Acts were witness expressed through an oral phase, more authoritative than written texts. Perhaps recognizing that the disciples were called to be this oral-witnesses (Luke 24:48; Acts 1:8, μάρτυρες). Such a role of witness is one of memory and testimony from personal experience. As such, the subject matter to which a witness testifies is not likely to be submitted to empirical investigation because the events and statement of views occurred previously as testimony (Matt 8:4; 18:16).²⁶ In a Hebrew trial setting multiple oral witnesses were involved to strengthen credibility (Deut 17:6; 19:15). If the witnesses prove to be contradicted credibly then they were considered a false witness and could suffer the same judgment that they were trying to obtain for the one accused (Deut 5:20; 19:16–18). In the Greco-Roman legal system, a

---

22. Kennard, *Critical Realist's Theological Method*, 70–72.

23. Baur, *Kritische Untersuchungen*; modernized by Goulder, *St. Paul versus St. Peter*, 1–7; but defeated by the complex pictures shown by Grappe, *Images de Pierre* and Bockmuehl, *Remembered Peter*.

24. Doering, "Schwerpunkte und Tendenzen," 203–23.

25. Dunn, "Has the Canon a Continuing Function?," 577; similarly, *Unity and Diversity in the New Testament*, 385–86.

26. Aristotle, *Rhet.* 1.15; Plato, *Leg.* 12; Josephus, *Ant.* 6.66; 1QS 5.24–26.1; Philo, *Spec. Laws* 4.30, 41–44, 59–61; *Jos.* 242; *m. Mak.* 1.6; *m. Roš Haš.* 1.8; *Sifre* on Deut 19:19; *Šeb.* 30a; *Gem. Mak.* 5B; Trites, *New Testament Concept of Witness*.

witness needed to be an adult free male Roman citizen with honorable reputation and not operating for personal gain.[27] Such a witness would make appropriate comments in court as eyewitness testimony he had actually experienced.[28] With legal imagery encouraging the credibility of the role of a witness, Papias found the collective memory of Christian eyewitness testimony to be more valuable than the written texts being produced for as long as available eyewitnesses testified about Jesus' ministry and the early church.

> I shall not hesitate also to put into properly ordered form for you everything I learned carefully in the past from the elders and noted down well, for the truth of which I vouch. For unlike most people I did not enjoy those who have a great deal to say, but those who teach the truth. Nor did I enjoy those who recall someone else's commandments, but those who remember the commandments given by the Lord to the faith and proceeding from the truth itself. And if by chance anyone who had been in attendance on the elders should come my way, I inquired about the words of the elders—[that is] what [according to the elders] Andrew or Peter said, or Philip, or Thomas or James, or John or Matthew or any other of the Lord's disciples, and whatever Ariston and the elder John, the Lord's disciples were saying. For I did not think that information from books would profit me as much as information from a living and surviving voice.[29]

In the second century both Irenaeus and Papias recount that their early memories of the eyewitness testimony took great prominence and were in full accord with the written texts of Scripture.[30] Similar claims for accurate vivid early memories framing later perception were made by Seneca the elder.[31] When such testimony occurred in Christian contexts a corporate memory of tradition could be specifically identified and the

---

27. Pindar, *Ol.* 1.54; Plato, *Apol.* 31c; Gorgias, 27–31, 41E–5E; Demosthenes 58.4; Plutarch, *de Amicorum Multitudine* 2.2.93e; TDNT 4:479.

28. Plato, *Symp.* 179b; Heraclitus, *All.* 34; Sophicles, *Ant.* 515.

29. Eusebius, *Hist. eccl.* 3.39.3–4; Arthur Dewey develops an argument from Rom 10 that the written *torah* supported the authoritative and transformative oral gospel testimony ("Re-Hearing of Romans 10:1–15," 109–27); Bauckham, *Jesus and the Eyewitnesses*, 293–94; Kelber, "Generative Force of Memory," 15–22.

30. Papius recounted in Eusebius, *Hist. eccl.* 5.20.4–7; Irenaeus, *Letter to Florinus*; Bauckham, *Jesus and the Eyewitnesses*, 295.

31. Seneca, *Controversiae*, preface 3–4; Bauckham, *Jesus and the Eyewitnesses*, 295–96; Mackay, *Signs of Orality*; Horsley et al., *Performing the Gospel*; Cooper, *Politics of Orality*; Horsley, *Oral Performance*.

others of the group would provide a resilience to reinforce the accuracy of their corporate memory.[32] Such a pattern mirrors the corporate memory of rabbinic Judaism that began to establish written accounts of their oral discussions beginning around AD 200 with the *Mishnah* and then the two corroborating written accounts of the *Talmud* later around 450 and AD 600. Such Jewish oral tradition and written oral tradition shows very little shift of account except the addition of more recent rabbinic voices.[33] Also, in Judaism there was liturgical retelling of narrative in *rabbah* texts composed during the second to fourth centuries, which resiliently re-tell the biblical narratives for liturgical purposes. The resilience and consistency in the agreement of these written accounts of oral *Torah* or narrative re-telling provide a pattern for how local Jewish-Christian corporate eyewitness memory could be corporately preserved into written texts of Gospels and Acts.

From such eyewitness testimony, Markus Bockmuehl develops *The Remembered Peter* as "arguably the only major player to feature in the ministries of both Jesus and Paul; and on any reckoning he provides a vital personal continuity between them both."[34] Bockmuehl encouraged use of techniques of the Jewish affirming side of the third quest for the historical Jesus and that of the dialog around the new perspective concerning Paul. Bockmuehl anticipated that reflection on Peter will provide significant benefit in understanding the transition from Jesus' exclusive mission to Israel (Matt 10:5–6) to Paul's mission to the gentiles (Acts 9:15; 22:21; 26:17). As such, Petrine theology becomes another planet between Jesus[35]

---

32. Examples of such claims include: Clement of Alexandria, *Strom.* 7.106.4; Eusebius, *Hist. eccl.* 2.1.4; similar claims were made at Qumran (1QS 6.6–8) and by gnostic 2 *Apoc. of James* 36.15–25; Halbwachs, *On Collective Memory*; Assmann, *Das kulturelle Gedächtnis*; Kelber, "Case of the Gospels," 65; "Generative Force of Memory," 15–22; Dunn, *Jesus Remembered*, 239–43; Ricoeur, *Memory, History, Forgetting*; Bauckham, *Jesus and the Eyewitnesses*, 296, 310–57; "Gospel of John," 659; Silberman, *Orality, Aurality and Biblical Narrative*; Dewey, *Orality and Textuality in Literature*; Draper, *Orality, Literacy, and Colonialism*; Kirk, "Social and Cultural Memory," 14–15; Thatcher, "Why John Wrote a Gospel," 82–85; Thatcher, *Jesus, the Voice, and the Text*; Kelber and Byrsog, *Jesus in Memory*.

33. Gerhardsson, *Gospel Tradition*; *Memory and Manuscript*; Bailey, "Informal Controlled Oral Tradition," 34–54; "Middle Eastern Oral Tradition," 363–67; Boomershine, "Jesus of Nazareth," 7–11, 16–17; Jaffee, "Oral-Cultural Context," 27–73; Dunn, *Jesus Remembered*, 197–254; Bauckham, *Jesus and the Eyewitnesses*; Walton and Sandy, *Lost World of Scripture*, 97–101, 105–8, 110, 152–66.

34. Bockmuehl, *Remembered Peter*, 31; Perkins, *Peter*, 13 presents Schillebeeckx as saying the same point.

35. Dunn, *Jesus Remembered*; Wright, *Jesus and Victory of God*; Kennard, *Messiah*

and Pauline[36] studies, with lesser moons such as a theology of James,[37] Heb,[38] and Luke[39] circling.

Though Petrine theology has gone through an era of neglect,[40] Peter has theological expression that both fits his time and makes significant contributions to the field of biblical theology. For example, Martin Hengel declared Peter to be the "Underestimated Apostle."[41] It is time for Peter's voice to be heard.

Most Petrine theology treats the contributing units as independent of each other: a theology of 1 Pet, a theology of 2 Pet, sometimes contributions from Peter in Mark or Acts. However, the field of biblical theology is admitting more honestly to a methodology construct from a point of view.[42] Rarely have these glimpses of Petrine theology been integrated into a unified construct, as the current work before you will attempt to accomplish. Separating Peter into a theology of his sources fragments his theology and diminishes the integrated depth of theology that Peter contributes. Gene Green grants that Peter's voice is contained within Mark and allows the Gospel to continue to contribute to a composite of Peter's theology.[43] However, Green's theology of Peter does not interact with 2 Pet, even though he inclines to accept Petrine authorship, because he considered his engagement to be a large enough task already and the academic disagreement over authorship.[44] Green concluded his synthesis of Peter by recognizing that his unified construct "only skims the surface of the apostle's thought as it has come down to us in the various Petrine sources."[45] Larry Helyer

---

Jesus.

36. Dunn, *Theology of Paul*; Wright, *Paul and Faithfulness of God*; Kennard, "Covenant Pneumaticism," 3:30–161; Moo, *Biblical Theology of Paul*.

37. Eisenman, *James the Brother of Jesus*; Davids, "James," 31–91.

38. Kennard, *Biblical Theology of Hebrews*.

39. Bock, *Theology of Luke and Acts*.

40. Elliott, "Rehabilitation of an Exegetical Step-Child," 243–54; Howe conclude, "No longer 'an exegetical step-child,' 1 Peter has not only been adopted by the biblical studies guild; it continues to receive the attention and recognition it deserves" in her "Review of *Reading First Peter with New Eyes*."

41. Hengel, *Saint Peter*.

42. Johnson, *Constructing Paul*; Boring, "Narrative Dynamics in First Peter," and Bauman-Martin and Webb, "Reading First Peter with New Eyes," 1–40; Petrine sources are justified in Kennard, *Petrine Studies*, chapter on Sources.

43. Green, *Vox Petri*, 32–45, 126–233.

44. Green, *Vox Petri*, 97–98; though I suspect his previous commentary (Green, *Jude, 2 Peter*, which does not have a section engaging theology satisfied his personal study.

45. Green, *Vox Petri*, 417.

extends the synthesis a bit further in recognizing the "heart" focuses on Peter's two epistles as the primary content, but interacting with the leading theme of 1 Pet as it appears in the Gospel of Mark and Peter's speeches in the book of Acts.[46] Helyer added 2 Pet to his Petrine theology, even though he acknowledged many scholars consider it written by someone other than the author of 1 Pet. In both Green's and Helyer's approach the separate epistles, Gospel of Mark, and Peter's speeches contribute separate gems for their collage of theologies of Peter,[47] thus creating a theology of Petrine sources. The construct of the present volume attempts to go further by providing a more detailed engagement integrating each source to unify a Petrine theology as well as interacting with depth and complexity rather than merely skimming the sources.

Kennard's *Petrine Theology* has the basic integrated chapters to reflect the standard biblical theological discussion of Peter's theology, with its many contributions: Peter's Jewish heritage, compatible sovereignty and free will, high Christology, missional Trinity, Hebraic anthropology, Jewish atonement, redemption and new exodus, Gospel as allegiance to Christ, contextual sociological ecclesiology, suffering and spiritual warfare in a narrow virtuous exodus way to kingdom, and nuanced consistent eschatology. However, due to the size of the study, a companion book, *Petrine Studies*, was also composed to discuss: foundational issues (which sources can be demonstrated to be Petrine, and recipients and form of Peter's letters), a brief biography of Peter, Peter's communal revelational testimony and empirical evidentialist epistemology, Markan sociological issues to extend Peter's concept of the church into relevant life concerns (such as tradition, inclusion of gentiles, divorce and wealth), and Markan historical issues concerning Jesus' death and resurrection. Narrative theology contributions are especially provided by chapters developing Peter's biography, the Markan section of "Exodus Following Jesus to Kingdom Virtues," and "Jesus' Historical Death and Resurrection." Originally, both books were composed to reflect a fully integrated Petrine theology, supporting and playing off each other. However, for the reader's ease the work was divided into integrated companion volumes: *Petrine Theology* and *Petrine Studies*. The topic of a Petrine theology entails both volumes, though *Petrine Theology* contains the primary trajectory, with

---

46. Helyer, *Life and Witness of Peter*, 16–17.
47. These sources are justified in Kennard, *Petrine Studies*, chapter on Sources.

Petrine Studies providing important support material to complete a Petrine theology project.

Green expressed the value of such an integrated Petrine theology. For example, he summarized Peter's theology as the grounding for the early church.

> Peter's theology is, in the end very much the theology of the early church. At various points we encounter unique contributions to early Christian theologizing, such as the apostle's discussion of Christian theologizing, such as the apostle's discussion of Christ's proclamation to the spirits in prison (1 Pet 3:18–22) and his affirmation that if Israel repents, "times of refreshing" will arrive "from the presence of the Lord," and then God will "send the Messiah appointed for you, that is Jesus" (Acts 3:19–20).[48]

Green continues to encourage Petrine theology to be valued in prime place.

> Peter stands at the very beginning of Christian theology. May the "lost boy" of Christian theology find his rightful place at the table once again. But if we look closely, we will see that he has been seated at the head of the table all along.[49]

---

48. Green, *Vox Petri*, 417.
49. Green, *Vox Petri*, 418.

2

God

Peter Davids described the theology of 1 Pet as "all of the teaching in the letter is related to God in one way or another. In fact, the core problem in the letter—that is, the suffering of the followers of Jesus—is due to their perceived obedience to God in Jesus."[1]

Peter primarily utilized θεὸς to refer to the divine presence (eighty-three times, 1 Pet 1:2). This is the normal LXX translation of *Elohim* (Acts 2:30; 3:22; 2 Sam 7:12–13; Deut 18:15), conveying "power" (2 Pet 3:5 with verbal power to create everything; 1 Pet 1:5 with power to keep those who are his).[2] Such a powerful God to act positions Peter's understanding of God to be that of Isaiah's "living" God (Matt 16:16; Isa 37:4, 17; 49:18),[3] and thus able to dramatically act within Jewish monotheism. In Peter, about half the time, "God" refers to the "Father" (1 Pet 1:2–3; 2 Pet 1:17). As such, God is described as the great "Majestic Glory" (2 Pet 2:17).

God is the creator of everything through his word[4] (2 Pet 3:5; Acts 4:24), and thus is the sovereign to whom believers are to submit and pray (1 Pet 1:3–5; 5:6; 2 Pet 1:2; 3:18; Acts 4:24, 29). God speaking the creation into being demonstrates his sovereignty and our need to submit.

God established his covenant with his people Israel (Acts 3:25–26). This covenant relation is imposed upon his vasal people as their sovereign

---

1. Davids, *Theology of James, Peter, and Jude*, 157.
2. Quell, TDNT 3:84–86.
3. Kennard, *Biblical Theology of Isaiah*, 44–55.
4. Probably not a reference to John 1, where Christ is the "word," but referring to creation by speaking it into existence as in Gen 1, "God said" and it was so, since context is that of Genesis flood (2 Pet 3:5–6).

in various aspects of this relationship, through the Abrahamic covenant (Acts 3:25), Mosaic covenant (1 Pet 2:9; Acts 3:22), and Davidic covenant (Acts 2:30).[5] God extends these covenantal salvation blessings on to the church, including gentiles who are included through God's mercy (1 Pet 2:9–10).

God is sovereign in action. God's will is established (1 Pet 2:15; 3:17; 4:2, 6, 19). He resists the proud with a mighty hand (1 Pet 5:5–6). God predetermines and foreknows (1 Pet 1:2, 20; Acts 2:23). God chose Christ (1 Pet 2:4; Acts 10:41), raised him from the grave (1 Pet 1:3; Acts 2:24, 32; 3:15, 26; 4:10; 10:40), and made him Lord and Christ by exalting him (1 Pet 3:22; Acts 2:36; 5:31). God knows human hearts and keeps them reserved for judgment at his day (1 Pet 2:4; 3:12; Acts 4:19; 8:21; 10:33). All grace bestowed comes from God (1 Pet 4:10; 5:10, 12). God speaks and the universe was created (2 Pet 3:5). God speaks prophecy (2 Pet 1:21; Acts 2:17; 3:18, 21), and sends prophets (2 Pet 1:21; Mark 1:1–3). Others repeat the definite message from God (1 Pet 1:23; 4:11, 17; 2 Pet 3:5; Acts 4:31; 6:2; 11:1). Whoever God calls to himself believes and experiences the benefits of salvation (1 Pet 2:4; Acts 2:39; 15:7). God possesses a household of people who are his (1 Pet 2:10, 16; 4:17; 5:2). They are kept by the power of God (1 Pet 1:5). When God sets out an action to follow, it is madness to oppose such divine action (Acts 3:19; 5:29; 10:15, 28; 11:9). Such a sovereign being is to be feared (1 Pet 2:17; 1:17; Acts 10:22), trusted (1 Pet 1:21; 3:5), and worshiped (1 Pet 1:3; 2:12; 4:11, 16; Acts 2:47; 3:8–9; 4:21, 24; 10:46; 11:18). In his sovereignty, he is bringing his kingdom to earth (2 Pet 1:11; Mark 4:26, 30; 10:23).

With such an OT emphasis in Petrine theology, the dominant Hebrew name for God, *Yahweh*, gets only a brief cover by the LXX translation κύριος (1 Pet 1:25; 3:12; Acts 2:20–21, 25, 34; 3:22; 4:26; Mark 12:36; Pss 2:2; 16:8; 110:1), which word also covers *Adonai*, blending the two expressions together (Acts 2:34; Mark 12:36; Ps 110:1). This modest presence of κύριος for God is odd since *Yahweh* occurs five times as often as *Elohim* in the OT and only a brief mention in Peter's Gospel statements, with half of these references referring to Christ. Furthermore, the memorial name *Yahweh* sets up the dominant theme of the presence of the *Yahweh* traveling with Israel to facilitate the Exodus and bring them into the promised land (Exod 3:14–15). Such an Exodus theme is strongly developed in Hebrew but the meaning of "*Yahweh* as the present one to

---

5. For an analysis of these covenants see Kennard, *Biblical Covenantalism*.

help"⁶ is absent, leaving κύριος to largely emphasize Jesus' kingship (Acts 2:34–35; Mark 12:35–37). With Jewish divinity assumed, Peter puts his emphasis of κύριος on the supremacy of Christ over all other aspects of Judaism, consistent with the Jewish two powers heresy (1 Pet 1:25; 3:12; Acts 2:20–21, 25, 34; 3:22; 4:26; Mark 12:30).⁷ So Peter's missional trinity launches from Peter's identification with this second divine person called God, developed in the chapter on trinity.

When God is referenced in relationship to the Son Jesus Christ, the title of "Father" appears as describing God (1 Pet 1:2–3; 2 Pet 1:17; Mark 1:11; 9:7) who ordains the Son and impowers him with the Spirit (Acts 2:34–35; Mark 1:11; 12:35–37).

The sovereign Lord (κύριος) or God (θεὸς) and Father is the one to whom Peter primarily prays (Acts 1:24; 4:24, 29; 8:24; 1 Pet 1:17; 2 Pet 2:2), but prayers are also offered to Lord (κύριος) Jesus (2 Pet 1:2). Whatever the Lord establishes is not to be contradicted (Acts 10:14; 11:8). Christians are to submit to authorities for the Lord's sake (1 Pet 2:13). The Lord calls all the saved to himself (Acts 2:39). He is the source of salvation (1 Pet 2:3). He rescues the godly from condemnation because he is patient (2 Pet 2:9; 3:15). He sends the Spirit to minister among the people of God (Acts 5:9). He sent an angel to rescue Peter from prison (Acts 5:19; 12:7, 11) and thus the Lord rescued Peter from prison (Acts 12:17). There is a future eschatological day of the Lord, which comes when the Lord shall come (2 Pet 3:8–10; Acts 2:21). When this occurs, the apostates will be judged (2 Pet 2:11) and refreshment of kingdom will come from the Lord (Acts 3:19).

The "master" (Δέσποτα) is the sovereign Lord and owner of others (2 Pet 2:1; Acts 4:24).⁸ The reference is used in the LXX about forty times as translating *Adonai*, though the first Petrine instance might be a reference to Jesus as Lord through redemption (Δέσποτα, 2 Pet 2:1). The term is used of "god," when one wishes to emphasize power and thus it is regularly used as an address in prayer (Acts 4:24; LXX Gen 12:2, 8).⁹ The word Δέσποτα is also used of powerful masters, who abuse slaves (1 Pet 2:18).

---

6. If one understands the "Yahweh" in Exod 3:14–15 as a qal Hebrew verb, though it could grammatically also be a hiphil verb promising Yahweh's presence to deliver from any future need. In Mark 6:50, Jesus' statement, "It is I" (ἐγώ εἰμι) is how the LXX Exod 3:14 describes "I am who I am" (אֶהְיֶה אֲשֶׁר אֶהְיֶה), so possibly another hint at Jesus' divinity.

7. Segal, *Two Powers in Heaven*.

8. BAG, "Δεσπότης," 175.

9. Rengstorf, "Δεσπότης," TDNT 2:44–49.

God is called the "Shepherd and Guardian" of our souls in the context where Jesus is presented as God's servant and Christians have a past of straying like sheep (1 Pet 2:24–25; Isa 53:6). With believers being the flock of God, the elders serve as shepherds on location under the Chief Shepherd who will reward them for their service (1 Pet 5:2, 4).

God the Father is also called the "Majestic Glory" (2 Pet 1:17). The concept of glory emerges from the idea of "honor" and "radiance," and thus pictures the *shekinah* glory cloud from the tabernacle extended to the transfiguration presence providing Jesus and the cloud around Moses and Elijah with glowing glory (2 Pet 1:17; Mark 9:3, 7). In this manner, Jesus' resurrection and kingdom are referred to as glories to follow and developed metaphorically as "light" (1 Pet 1:9, 11, 21; 2 Pet 1:19). Such glory characterizes Jesus Christ now and forever (2 Pet 3:18). Those who recognized Jesus' glory returned glory to God in praise for the transformative joy that God provides (1 Pet 1:8; 4:14; Acts 3:6, 13; 4:21). Ultimately, believers will glorify God at the return of Jesus Christ (1 Pet 2:12). Peter also calls angels "glories" due to their association with the divine (2 Pet 2:10), and flowers "glories" for their beauty (1 Pet 1:24).

God is holy (ἅγιός) developed from the Hebrew *qadosh*, a positive metaphysical ontological set-apartness rather than Rudolf Otto's negative sociological "wholly other," more reminiscent of Kantian "noumena."[10] Biblical holiness develops the inner nature of God, which manifests itself in his acts. This idea is not primarily the act of separation but rather belonging to the category of the separate. The central passage in Peter that sets the tone for God's holiness is 1 Pet 1:14–16, which quotes Lev 11:44–45; 19:2; and 20:7. God is essentially separate, and he is the one who calls his elect. With the believer being sprinkled with Christ's sanctifying blood, believers are cleansed to an appropriate holy category (sanctified or saint[11]) as defined within the new covenant in the same process as Israel had been with the initiation of the Mosaic covenant (1 Pet 1:2). As the believer enters into a relational prayer life with the Father, she also must maintain a distinctive set apart life demonstrating the godliness of

---

10. Kennard, *Biblical Covenantalism*, 1:259–61; Neusner and Chilton, "Sanders's Misunderstanding of Purity," 205, 208, 211; NIDOTTE 3:877; TWOT 2:786; Kornfeld, TDOT 12:522; Gammie, *Holiness in Israel*, 9–11; Wilson, "Holiness" and "Purity," in *Mesopotamia*; *Sifra Qedošim Pereq* 11.21; *Šemini Pereq* 12.3. 5; contrast with Otto, *The Idea of the Holy*, 6, 25; following Kant, *Critique of Pure Reason*.

11. Peter develops the Spirit "sanctifying" believers but does not refer to believers as "saints" (the normal result of such sanctification), but Luke develops those to whom Peter ministers as "saints" (Acts 9:32, 42).

this relationship, knowing that there will be a day of judgment (1 Pet 1:14–17). To accomplish this growth in holiness, the believer sets Christ apart as Lord of her heart so that she may be ready to give a gentle reverent defense for the hope in her (1 Pet 3:15).

The primary way "holy" is referenced in Peter is by referring to the Holy Spirit. The Holy Spirit proclaims divine prophecy to humans (1 Pet 1:12; 2 Pet 1:21; Acts 1:16). God anointed Jesus Christ with the Holy Spirit and power to accomplish his healing ministry (Mark 1:10–11; Acts 10:38). This prophetic ministry was continued by the apostles who were "filled" with the Holy Spirit to speak boldly about Christ and heal those in need (Acts 2:4; 4:8). In opposition to the Spirit's ministry, Ananias and Saphira were "filled" by Satan, resulting in lying to the Holy Spirit (Acts 5:3). These "fillings" are empowerments to do what the empowering agent is about. The Holy Spirit is God's gift to the believer which brings salvation blessings (Acts 2:33, 38; 5:32; 8:15–19; 10:44–47; 11:15–16; 15:8); whereas, Satan's filling brings deception and is judged by God through Peter (Acts 5:1–11).

Peter also referred to Jesus Christ as the "holy one of God" who captivated Peter's life focus and was opposed by the religious and political leaders of his day (Acts 3:14; 4:27, 30). Though those leaders killed Christ, in such a pious condition Jesus could not remain in the grave because God was with him (Acts 2:27).

God's holiness is shared in a finite way by those associated with him, such as angels (Acts 10:12), prophets (2 Pet 3:2; Acts 3:21), apostles' commandment (2 Pet 2:21), the mountain of transfiguration (2 Pet 1:18), and the whole congregation elected by God to be a holy nation and priesthood (1 Pet 2:5, 9). Holy women, like Sarah, hope in God emphasizing character development in their lives and not external trappings (1 Pet 3:5). Holiness is not identified with morality, but morality is affected by God's holiness (1 Pet 1:17–18).

God is transcendent over creation, not in a Kantian agnosticism of the noumena but that God is marvelously known in many specific ways, which are not bound by space and time. As original creator of the whole universe, God transcends the creation (1 Pet 4:19; 2 Pet 3:5–7; Acts 4:24). God's transcendence is that of an active agent who will judge, destroy, and remake the existing creation into a new heaven and earth showing as in a Jewish monotheism, that God transcends the creation (2 Pet 3:10–13). God's judgment fits the trajectory of his purpose, such that judgment might seem slow in coming but it will accomplish what he sets as his goal (2 Pet 3:8–9).¹²

This transcendent engagement with time is not that of an Augustinian or Boethian concept of contemporaneousness with all-time framing a supertemporal eternity as D. S. Russel claimed,¹³ merely that human assessment of time should not restrict God because God's expressed purposes in time will be eventually accomplished. God is temporally everlasting in his permeation through an unbounded long time (αἰῶνος) in glory and reigning forever without end (1 Pet 4:11; 5:10–11; 2 Pet 3:18),¹⁴ though these qualities are also present now (νῦν) in time (2 Pet 3:18). This everlasting (αἰῶνος) quality also extends to God's works, such as the word of God that grounds the believer's imperishable inheritance (1 Pet 1:3–4; 23–25). Though the word αἰῶνος can also mean "long time" as in "ancient" communication with Abraham, Moses, and Samuel (Acts 3:21).

God has exhaustive prior knowledge without discussing the theoretical concept of omniscience.¹⁵ God knows and reveals knowledge prior to an event in the form of prophecy (1 Pet 1:11; 2 Pet 1:20–21; 3:1–2). However, the term "foreknowledge" used of God reflects a meaning of "prior determining relationship," either of God's relationship with Jesus Christ prior to creation (1 Pet 1:20, Προεγνωσμένου), which intimates aspects of trinity, or of the divine foreknowledge (Προγνώσει) as a synonym for God's predetermined plan (ὡρισμένῃ βουλῇ) for Jewish leadership's heinous sin of killing Christ (Acts 2:23).¹⁶ The divine determinism of Jesus' crucifixion is twice identified (foreknown and predetermined), grounding this sinful event as set by God and then followed by two statements of Jewish leadership culpability in killing Jesus ("you nailed to a cross" and "you put him to death"), that probably best fits a pattern of complementarian divine determinism/human free will, akin to Augustine, Aquinas, and Jonathan Edwards.¹⁷ In this passage, Peter claims this

---

12. Similar statements in *Jub.* 4:30; *1 En.* 91:17; *2 En.* 33.

13. Augustine, *Trin.* 5.2.3; Aquinas, *Of the Truth* 2.12; Anselm, *Proslogium* 13; Boethius, *Consol. Phil.* 5.2.9–8, 22–31; Russell, *Method and Message*, 212.

14. Cullmann, *Christ and Time*; GELNT, "αἰῶνος," 27–28.

15. The concept of omniscience appears early in Christendom, as in *2 Clem.* 9.9.

16. At least since the commentary of Holtzmann, *Die Apostelgeschte*, 34–37, commentators have commented upon the sharp juxtaposition of the human free-will and the divine determinism to kill Christ; Jacobs and Krienke, "Foreknowledge, Providence, Predestination," 1:693.

17. Augustine, *Ep.* 214.2 free-will compatible with determinism of *Praed.* 1.2, 13, 27; Anselm, *de lib. arb.* 3; "Foreknowledge and Freechoice," 205–6; Aquinas, *Summa*

heinous event of sin (killing Christ) was chosen by God, not a claim that every human choice is determined by God. Extending this concept, Mark developed divine hardening through Jesus' parabolic ministry and Isaiah's covenant curse (Mark 4:12; Isa 6:9).[18] Jesus' parables attracted folks because they liked the stories, and these parables were also designed to limit the crowd's perception, a strategy clarified as Jesus quotes Isa 6:9–10 as a *pesher* to identify that God was operating a ministry of hardening in Jesus' day to prevent repentance and forgiveness, so that a new judgment and dispersion might be sent on unresponsive Israel (Mark 4:12). This serves as another sovereign determinism prompting Israel's rejection of Jesus as the Christ. In a broader passage concerning God's determining election of Christ and the church, those who reject Christ "stumble" and "the disobedient" are appointed to "this" neuter singular relative pronoun (ὃ in 1 Pet 2:8 *pesher* launching from Isa 8:14, "'λίθος προσκόμματος καὶ πέτρα σκανδάλου·' οἳ προσκόπτουσιν τῷ λόγῳ ἀπειθοῦντες εἰς ὃ καὶ ἐτέθησαν"). The aorist passive ἐτέθησαν describes an "appointment" that grounds the divine choice of the relative pronoun of this passage (2 Pet 2:8). The singular relative pronoun (ὃ) indicates that each of these persons is appointed by God. Normally, relative pronouns would refer to the nearest antecedent nouns of the same number and gender, namely the parallel neuter singular nouns, "stumbling" and "disobedient" describing unbelievers rejecting the stone from Isa 8:14, which would expand complementarian divine determinism to that of God determining those who continue to reject Christ, namely a double determinism of God actively choosing those he elects to believe and those he rejects to their disobedience. Such disobedience renders those disobedient still culpable for their choice of disobedience, even though God chose this disobedience for them (similar to Acts 2:23 and Mark 4:12), in the same way that believers "received faith" presumably from God (λαχοῦσιν πίστιν, 2 Pet 1:1) in a similar manner to God providing magnificent promises to inform the believer's knowledge (2 Pet 1:3–4), which does not remove the believer's responsibility to continue to increase their faith and knowledge in Christ within their own moral development (2 Pet 1:1, 5). Many interpreters find this complementarian divine determinism too restricting for free human choices, at least regarding one's disposition concerning Christ,

---

Theologica, Pt 1, Q 19, Art. 6 "I answer that" with Q 83, Art. 1, "I answer that"; Edwards, *Freedom of the Will*, 1.2, p. 141; 2.2, pp. 176–77; 2.3, pp, 182–83; 2.4, pp, 186–87; Kennard, *Classical Christian God*, 135–66.

18. Kennard, *Biblical Theology of Isaiah*, 53, 94, 117, 127–29.

so they opt for God merely providing an antecedent outcome of "doom," nowhere mentioned in the passage (1 Pet 2:8). This insertion contrasts with the context of this pericope which is about the elect included as believers valued after the pattern of God electing and valuing Christ (1 Pet 2:4, 7, 9). If the relative pronoun refers to "doom" then the antecedent becomes the implied damnation as outcome of the "stumbling." This last view is grammatically possible, since sometimes relative pronouns do not match the gender and number of the antecedent.[19] However, this libertarian option with more free-will elbow room is concluding for the relative pronoun as selectively referring to an implication of the earlier available antecedent (προσκόμματος, ignoring the nearer antecedent [σκανδάλου], which is also parallel in Isa 8:14 to the one they choose) in the passage importing a meaning into the passage with a trajectory opposite to that of the contextual emphasis of valued elect of the passage. I prefer to follow the available parallel antecedent words in the passage even if it makes for a more difficult view of double determinism, which we have already seen, Peter holds in at least the religious leaders' specific rejection of Christ (Acts 2:23).

Divine election is implemented in time. While God "foreknew" (προεγνωσμένου) Jesus Christ from before the foundation of the world (1 Pet 1:20), God's electing Christ was an in-time choice (ἐκλεκτὸν) by God valuing Jesus as the Christ because it involved human belief or rejection of Christ (1 Pet 2:4, 6–7). This in-time choice could then be extended to the community of faith aligned with Christ as the "chosen" (ἐκλεκτοῖς, ἐκλεκτὸν) by God (1 Pet 1:1; 2:9). The Father "foreknew" (πρόγνωσιν) the elect community, but the Holy Spirit sanctified these believers so that the believers could initially obey and be covenantal holy by Christ's blood (1 Pet 1:1–2; Exod 24:8). With believers initially obeying as part of the election process, the believer's election is implemented in-time.

The Lord knows whatever he needs to know to accomplish his will. Peter quotes from Ps 34 to emphasize that the believer needs to speak and act in a peaceful manner for the purpose of inheriting a blessing. The theological basis for this exhortation is that the Lord is attentive to the situation and prayers of righteous humans (1 Pet 3:12). This attentiveness is graphically portrayed by the anthropomorphism of the Lord's eyes and ears. This attentiveness is extended by God seeing a person's actions and hidden gentle and quiet spirit (1 Pet 3:4; Acts 4:19). With God present to

---

19. Wallace, *Greek Grammar*, 337–38.

raise Christ, God's sovereign power is victoriously conquering death and sin (Acts 2:24). God's presence to protect humble believers is a comfort and deliverance for them, as it was for Noah and Lot (1 Pet 1:5; 2 Pet 2:5, 8-9). Additional anthropomorphism of the Lord's knowledge extends the face or personal presence of the Lord opposed to the proud and those who do evil, as during Noah's flood, and Sodom and Gomorrah (1 Pet 3:12; 2 Pet 2:4-6, 9). Whatever God needs to carry out his will and judge the unrighteous, he knows even to penetrating the hearts of all humans (1 Pet 3:12; Acts 1:24; 15:8-9). God even extends this divine opposition to those who aligned with believers and then apostatized (2 Pet 2:4-9; Acts 5:4-11; 8:20). The certainty of judgment of the unrighteous should motivate believers to fear God as a motive to be faithful (1 Pet 1:17; 2:17; 4:5; 2 Pet 2:4, 6, 9; Acts 5:11). This is part of the reason Peter responded to the Jewish religious leaders that apostles had to obey God, rather than humans commanding them to be silent about Jesus Christ (Acts 4:19-20; 5:29). The other reason is that Christ had commanded them to speak as witnesses (Acts 1:8).

God and Christ have sufficient power to rule as sovereign co-regency forever (1 Pet 4:11; 5:11; 2 Pet 1:11). God sovereignly created everything, and he can sovereignly destroy it all, and has done so at the flood judgment (Acts 4:24; 2 Pet 3:6-7, 10-11). Believers are to humble themselves under the mighty hand of God that he might exalt them in the proper time (1 Pet 5:6). This salvation is accomplished by the power of God, especially at the powerful coming of Jesus Christ (1 Pet 1:5; 2 Pet 1:11, 16). However, God's kingdom is already growing among the disciple band to eventually dominate the landscape (Mark 4:26, 30-32).

God's "will" is described by a few Greek expressions. The dative βουλῇ refers to the "resolute purpose" of God that determines an event to occur (Acts 2:23; 4:28), whereas the present participle βουλόμενός refers to God's "wish" or "desire" that God will try to bring about, such as none perish, even if all will not choose Christ (2 Pet 3:9). Peter uses θέλημα to refer to God's ethical desire for believers to do good and right in contrast to gentiles' immoral desire (1 Pet 2:15; 3:17; 4:2, 19).

Believing prayer is a ramification of God's sovereignty. Because God is sovereign and cares, the believer needs to humble himself under the mighty hand of God in prayer (1 Pet 5:6-7). Peter encourages his readership that God is attentive to the prayers of the righteous and the sovereign one who can effect any situation (1 Pet 3:12). For example, as the disciples replace Judas, Peter led the disciples into prayer: "Lord, who knows the hearts of all men, show which one of these two you have chosen to occupy this ministry and apostleship from which Judas turned aside to go to his own place" (Acts 1:24–25). Their prayer is founded on God's choice and their desire was to know that choice. In response to persecution from the Jewish leadership, the believers prayed to the sovereign Lord, who created everything and prophesied this struggle (Acts 4:23–27; Ps 2:1–2). They acknowledge that the sin committed by the oppressors was guaranteed and will be overthrown by God's predetermined purpose, and as servants to the sovereign God they asked for boldness to continue to proclaim God's message (Acts 4:28–31). God answered affirmatively and the disciples continued to spread the gospel. Furthermore, when Peter blessed the believers in his first letter, the blessing expounded God as manifestly sovereign in salvation and prophecy (1 Pet 1:3–12). When Peter gives benediction of praise to God, these include the ideas of everlasting glory and dominion of God (1 Pet 4:11; 5:11; 2 Pet 3:18). The sovereignty of God is the reason Peter prays. Only a sovereign God can accomplish these ends. Peter appeals to such an effective God, prompting worship of his sovereign.

God judges through righteousness and impartiality (1 Pet 2:23; 4:5). In divine eschatological judgment, God judges according to each human's work (1 Pet 1:17; Acts 10:34–35). This impartiality should motivate each human to fear God and do what is right. However, it is with difficulty that these righteous people are saved because they experience such suffering as God beginning to judge, which eschatologically will damn the godless person (1 Pet 4:17–18; 2 Pet 2:13).[20] Jesus demonstrates an example of what this righteousness looks like (1 Pet 3:18; Acts 3:14). Righteous Christ also substitutionally bore the sins for unrighteous people in his death, so that the believer might live righteously among fellow humans (1 Pet 2:24; 3:18; 2 Pet 1:1). God's righteousness is worked out among believers who live righteously, reminding them to continue and not depart from this righteousness (2 Pet 1:13; 2:21). Peter reminds the religious leaders that their opposition to the gospel is not right and that the apostles must obey God (Acts 4:19). Through these experiences, Peter testified that if a believer suffers for righteousness' sake, then she is blessed (1 Pet 3:14). Such Christians who have been wrongly judged by others will have their judgments reversed by God (1 Pet 4:5–6, 17–19; Acts 12:1–17). Through these sufferings, God is faithful and will deliver them (1 Pet 4:19). God

---

20. This is the judgment side of the argument in Pate and Kennard, *Deliverance Now and Not Yet*.

desires believers to be righteous and God is responsive to their prayers, opposing those who do evil (1 Pet 3:12; 4:19). For example, righteous Cornelius' prayers were heard by God, who included his family among the saved (Acts 10:22). Likewise, righteous Noah and Lot were preserved while the world around them was destroyed under God's judgment (2 Pet 2:5, 7–8). The unrighteous will ultimately suffer destruction and death as their wages (2 Pet 2:13). Ultimately, God's righteousness will be worked out when the new heavens and earth are established as God's righteous kingdom (2 Pet 3:13).

As sovereign, God is the source of "grace" (Χάρις), especially for the humble (1 Pet 5:5, 10; Prov 3:34). Such grace is a synonym for salvation blessings (1 Pet 1:2, 10; 2 Pet 1:2) and for "mercy" (ἐλεος,1 Pet 2:10; Hos 2:23). Grace and mercy provide salvation for all races and genders alike (1 Pet 2:10; 3:7; Acts 15:11; Hos 2:23). Outside of salvation, the gentiles had not received mercy but salvation comes as an expression of God's mercy and grace. The gracious inheritance God provides should motivate believers to stand firm and grow in grace, and to utilize what God has given to serve each other (1 Pet 4:10; 5:12; 2 Pet 3:18).

3

Christology

MANY DISCUSS PETRINE CHRISTOLOGY as primitive, meaning that Peter developed early ideas of Christ apart from later developments.[1] Such a view does not require a low or undeveloped Christology. First Peter emphasized the suffering ministry of Jesus. Second Peter emphasized the ministry of Jesus as the judge. Mark and Peter's sermons in Acts emphasize Jesus as the king who is bringing his kingdom by the Spirit, healing, and forgiveness for those who align with him. The unified person, Jesus Christ is both the sovereign God, co-regent with the Father, and human suffering servant, historically saving and judging.

The name "Jesus" is a transliteration of a common Hebrew name "Joshua," meaning "*Yahweh* saves." Peter only uses the name alone twice, describing Jesus' arrest and resurrection (Acts 1:16; 2:32). Mark usually refers to Jesus with third personal pronoun or implied from the verb, but in narrative contexts with other referents present, he uses "Jesus" to clarify who is doing action in the narrative (Mark 2:5, 19; 3:7; 5:15, 30, 36; 6:4; 9:2; 10:21, 23, 27, 49; 11:7, 29, 38; 12:34–35; 15:15). Jesus' name usually appears with combinations (such as "Jesus from Nazareth,"[2] Acts 2:22; 3:6; 10:38; Mark 1:24; 16:6), and often in narrative is replaced by one of his titles, such as "Christ" or "Lord."

---

1. Davies, "Primitive Christology in 1 Peter," 115–22.
2. The "Nazareth" reference indicates his hometown, no argument is developed to indicate a Nazarite vow, or a messianic "branch" from Isa 11:1, or to explain a prophetic background to which Matthew may have alluded (Matt 2:23), or that this reference came from disciples of John the Baptist (John 1:35).

Several titles refer to an overlapping messianic king presentation. "Christ" or the Hebrew "Messiah" referring to an "anointing," usually identifying Jesus as messianic king, who will rule (Acts 4:26–27; Matt 16:16), but also could refer to the Holy Spirit anointing him with empowerment to accomplish his ministry (Acts 10:38; Mark 1:10, 12). Contextually, Ps 2:2 quoted in Acts 4:26 identifies Christ as the "messiah" anointed by God, who he will protect as he defeats all regal opposition to him. Prophets predicted that Christ would suffer as part of his messianic role (1 Pet 1:11; Acts 3:18). Jesus suffered in his humanity as a sacrificial redemption by giving up his life (1 Pet 1:19; 2:21; 4:1), sufferings observed and shared by Peter (1 Pet 3:16; 4:13–14; 5:1). Peter used "Christ" so frequently that it often does not emphasize a regal messianic meaning but becomes simply part of Jesus name ("Jesus Christ" in contrast to others).

"Lord" (κυρίος) is another title that is used of Jesus. The title involves the concept of a master, possessing others as king, or over others in patronage.[3] As a term it was appropriated by the Caesars (Augustus, Tiberius, Caligua, Nero and Domitian) and the Jewish rulers (Herod the Great, Agrippa I and Agrippa II), so Jesus' use for himself challenges their legitimacy, since he is the ultimate Lord.[4] The LXX uses this word to translate most instances of the Hebrew *Yahweh* and *Adonai*, and Peter retains this use in quotes such as Ps 110:1 (Acts 2:34–35; Mark 12:36). Forty-two percent of Petrine uses of κυρίος are of the Father God, with one instance referring to the Holy Spirit (Acts 5:9). One Petrine use has Sarah calling Abraham "lord" (1 Pet 3:6). About 10 percent of Peter's use refers to an ambiguous divine person, either Father or Christ (2 Pet 2:9, 11; 3:8–10, 15). About a third of Peter's usage of "lord" (κυρίος) refers clearly to Jesus Christ as majestic miracle worker and king to whom Peter prays (Luke 5:8; Acts 1:6, 24).

The "master" (Δέσποτα) is the sovereign Lord and owner of others (2 Pet 2:1; Acts 4:24).[5] The reference is used in the LXX about forty times for translating *Adonai*. Though, most commentators view Peter using the word as referring to Jesus as Lord who redeemed those who aligned with him (2 Pet 2:1). The term is also used of "god," when one wishes to

---

3. BAG, "κυρίος," 459–60.

4. Bietenhard, "Lord, Master," DNTT, 2:511; Cullmann, *Christology of the New Testament*, 197–99; Suetonius, *De Vita Caesarum* 13.2; the title was also used to describe gods (1 Cor 8:5); Deismann, *Light from the Ancient East*, 352–53; Gelardini, "Contest for a Royal Title," 93–106; Williams, "Divinity and Humanity of Caesar," 131–47.

5. BAG, "Δεσπότης," 175.

emphasize power and thus it is regularly used as an address in prayer (Acts 4:24; LXX Gen 12:2, 8).[6]

The discussion of these titles in Christology during the last several centuries is framed by many contributors. In the wake of Immanuel Kant and Friedrich Schleiermacher, David Strauss developed Christianity subjectively as a moral philosophy from Jesus' moralizing.[7] In a milder form of Strauss' view, William Wrede concluded that Mark was presenting a "messianic secret" view, which entailed that Jesus life was not messianic, and his teaching did not reveal himself to be messianic, which meant that Jesus began to be recognized by the early church as messiah only after his resurrection.[8] J. A. T. Robinson extended this further on the basis of Acts 3:20, claiming Jesus would become recognized as Christ only upon his return from heaven to initiate his kingdom.[9] Contrarily, Albert Schweitzer presented Mark as a historical document containing Jesus as self-consciously aware of being messiah, especially in his parables,[10] and unfortunately failing in his attempt to bring about kingdom. Moderating Schweitzer, T. W. Manson agreed that Wrede's view was a "road to nowhere."[11] Ulrich Luz recognized that when Jesus commanded the demons and disciples to keep silent and they did, contributing toward a messianic secret (Mark 1:34; 3:11–12; 8:30; 9:9), but when the healed were commanded to silence, they gave testimony of their healing even more, thwarting any view of a messianic secret (Mark 1:44–45; 7:35–37).[12] James Dunn separated parables (with their kingdom emphasis) as something different than the messianic secret which he recognized can be found in the narrative, similar to Luz.[13] Heikki Räisänen concluded that the messianic secret is of little consequence in Mark, merely dealing with

---

6. Rengstorf, "Δεσπότης," TDNT 2:44–49.

7. Kant, "Critique of Practical Reason," 291–364, and *Religion within the Boundaries of Mere Reason*; Schleiermacher, *Life of Jesus*; Strauss, *Life of Jesus*.

8. Wrede, *Messianic Secret* presents Jesus not living life of messiah (216, 230), Jesus does not reveal he is messiah in his teaching, therefore a secret (80–81, 113–14, 126), thus Jesus becomes known as messiah only after presentation of his resurrection (216–17). Weiss, *Das Urchristentum*, 85–87; Conzelmann, "History and Theology," 181–82; Tuckett, *Messianic Secret*.

9. Robinson, "Most Primitive Christology of All?," 181, 83.

10. Schweitzer, *Quest for the Historical Jesus*, 335, 338–48, 368–95.

11. Manson, "Life of Jesus," 211–21.

12. Luz, "Das Geheimnismotiv und die markinische Christologie," 9–30.

13. Dunn, "Messianic Secret in Mark," 92–117.

the title "Son of God."[14] Jack Kingsburry identified that each of Jesus' titles overlap and in Mark they reveal rather than hide a messianic secret.[15] The high Christology of Murray Harris, Richard Hayes, and Richard Bauckham developed that the leading questions in Mark were not hiding a secret messianism but inviting the reader to see Jesus as deity (Mark 1:27; 2:7; 4:41; 10:18; 12:37; 14:61).[16]

Jewish messianism begins with the royal roles of "anointed" or "Christ," "Son of David," "Son of God," and the "temple builder" grounded in the Davidic covenant, which promised that Israel will have a kingdom in the land, accomplished by *Yahweh* (2 Sam 7:9–10 and 1 Chr 17:8–9 with Gen 12:7; 15:18–21; Deut 28:3–11).[17] David is presented as the Lord's "anointed" (מָשַׁח; ἔχρισεν) to be king over Israel by Samuel with oil and by the Spirit of the Lord coming powerfully upon David (1 Sam 15:1, 17; 16:3, 12–13). Extending Mosaic covenant blessings, David and his lineage on his throne will have rest from his enemies (2 Sam 7:11 with Exod 3:20; 20:11–12; 33:14; Deut 5:14; 12:10; 25:19; Josh 1:5; 21:44; 22:4; 23:1). After the Babylonian captivity, Chronicles promises this Mosaic covenant blessing more forcefully with Israel's enemies being subdued (2 Sam 7:11; 1 Chr 17:10). Additionally, the construction of the temple by the Davidic king draws him into the pattern of Moses, who had given Israel the tabernacle in the exodus—namely Solomon, David's son, will build the temple in Jerusalem (2 Sam 7:13; Exod 25–40).

This transition from David and his lineage to a more ultimate messiah can be seen in the shift from 2 Sam 7 to 1 Chr 17. For example, after Babylonian captivity, Chronicles promises this Mosaic covenant blessing more forcefully with a more ultimate Davidic king or messiah who will subdue Israel's enemies (2 Sam 7:11; 1 Chr 17:10).[18] This Davidic son will have an everlasting kingdom as God's son, which serves as an adoption formula to establish dynastic relationship[19] in God's kingdom enabling him to build the temple house and not be rejected as was Saul

14. Räisänen, *Das "Messiasgheimnis" im Markusevangelium*, 143–68.
15. Kingsburry, *Christology of Mark's Gospel*, 14, 18–21.
16. Bauckham, "Markan Christology," 21–36; Harris, *Jesus as God*; Hayes, *Echoes of Scripture in the Gospels*.
17. Kennard, *Biblical Covenantalism*, 2:25–72.
18. Sir 45.25; 47.11.
19. God is Father to king as Son, ancient Near East examples include from: Egypt: Pharaoh as son of Re, Ugarit and Mesopotamia: Keret is son of El, and Roman: Caesar as Son of God; von Martitz, TDNT 8:336–40; Hengel, *Son of God*, 24; Dunn, *Christianity in the Making*, 14–16; Deismann, *Light from the Ancient East*, 346.

(2 Sam 7:12–15; 1 Chr 17:11–14; 22:10; Pss 2:7; 89:3–4, 26–27, 34–37; 132:11–12; Acts 2:30).[20] For example, as a comfort, in 2 Sam 7:14, *Yahweh* promised the Davidic covenant through an adoption formula[21] of continued light to correct the Davidic son when he sins, "When he commits iniquity, I will correct him with the rod of men and the strokes of the sons of men" (2 Kgs 8:19; 2 Chr 21:7). For the generations of Davidic kings to live in peace and blessing requires each king's faithfulness. For example, the necessity of the Davidic king's compliance with human obligation (2 Sam 7:14; 2 Kgs 8:19; 2 Chr 21:7; Pss 89:30–32; 132:10; possibly 2 Kgs 11:17–18) does not put at risk the Davidic covenant blessing for the Davidic lineage (2 Sam 7:15–16; 2 Kgs 8:19; 1 Chr 17:12, 14; Pss 89:33–36; 132:11).[22] Furthermore, this phrase about discipline is left out of 1 Chr 17 perhaps because the captivity removed the disobedient Davidic kings and probably because there was a growing hope of a grander eschatological king. With the Davidic kings removed from office by the captivity, the promise of the Davidic king not being rejected like Saul becomes hollow without a return to a Davidic king on the throne. With the failures of the Davidic kings and their not being like David (1 Kgs 11:4–8, 33; 14:8; 15:3–5, 11; 2 Kgs 14:3; 16:2; 18:3; 22:2; 2 Chr 7:17; 11:17; 29:2, 25–30; 34:2–3; 35:4, 15), after the Babylonian captivity, the Chronicler looked for a more ultimate Davidic king, who will subdue Israel's enemies (1 Chr 17:10). Furthermore, 2 Sam 7:16 is more oriented to David: "Your house and your kingdom shall endure before me forever; your throne shall be established forever" while *Yahweh* speaks in 1 Chr 17:14, "I will settle him in my house and in my kingdom forever and his throne shall be established forever." The covenant from *Yahweh* to David is binding as a covenant grant forever (2 Sam 7:12–15; 1 Chr 17:11–14; Pss 89:3–4, 34–37; 132:11–12).[23]

While not actually a Davidic king image, Jesus and early Judaism merge the Davidic king with Daniel's "Son of Man." Maurice Casey

20. The Messiah is predicted to be the builder of the temple (2 Sam 7:13; 1 Chr 17:12; Zech 4:7–10; *Sib. Or.* 5.420–33). Additionally, God is portrayed to be the builder of the temple (1 *En.* 90.28–29; Jub 1.17; 2 Bar 4.3; 32.4; 11QTemple 29.8–10; 4QFlor. 1.3, 6; *Midr. Ps.* 90.17; *Mekilta of R. Ishmael* 3).

21. Adoption formula you are "my son" 2 Sam 7:14 parallel to 2 Kgs 16:7; parallel to Hittite treaty between Šuppiluliuma and Šattiwazza as contained in Weidner, *Politische Dokumente aus Kleinasien*, 2:22–26; Weinfeld, "Covenant Grant," 69–102; Kalluveettil, *Declaration and Covenant*, 368–72.

22. Freedman and Miano, "People of the New Covenant," 13–16.

23. The Davidic covenant is also declared to be everlasting in 4QSam 23.5.

proposed that the plural Aramaic instances of "sons of man" frames the ambiguity of the phrase simply as identifying Jesus as a specific human (either of Ps 8:4 or a specific prophet like Ezek 2:1).[24] However, Jesus blends the Daniel context of "Son of Man" with the Davidic king image of Ps 110:1 at his trial (Mark 14:62; Matt 26:64; Luke 22:69; Dan 7:13) and in his Olivet discourse (Mark 13:26; Matt 24:30; Luke 21:27; Dan 7:13), clarifying that Jesus' use of the phrase "Son of Man" means Daniel's divine cloud riding "Son of Man."[25] Daniel 7 concluded the vision of four beasts with the divine Ancient of Days in his throne room, who will conquer all the gentile nations which have stood against God. The MT and Theodotion's LXX present the Son of Man as a distinctive second divine power to the Ancient of Days fostering the Jewish two powers heresy within Jewish monotheism.[26] That is, entering this throne room is the Son of Man riding on the clouds (Dan 7:13-14). Some understand this title to refer to the primordial man who will rule like Ps 8:4 mentions, but most recognize that the cloud-riding identifies the Son of Man as imagery of the king of the Gods,[27] like Marduk or Baal. Yet in Judaism's monotheism the Ancient of Days is clearly the presentation of this monotheistic God. Therefore, this divine one comes up to God and receives his dominion to rule the kingdom. Early Judaism retains this pre-existent Son of Man as a heavenly being with everlasting dominion on the earth.[28] An alternative reading in the Old Greek LXX identifies the Son of Man "as" (ὡς) the Ancient of Days, perhaps as a reaction to this Jewish two-powers heresy.[29] However, Zeigler and Munnich consider that a likely scribal ellipsis of an epsilon before the ὡς would bring the Old Greek in line with the MT and Theodotian's LXX, thus continuing to support two divine participants in

---

24. Casey, "Aramaic Idiom," 3-32; *Solution to the "Son of Man" Problem*; plural in 4Q197 4 1.12; 3.11; 4Q205 2 1.26; 4Q246 2.1; 1QapGen 21.16; 22.21.

25. Adams, "Coming of the Son of Man," 39-61; Hurtado and Owen, "*Who Is the Son of Man?*"; Müller, *Expression "Son of Man"*; singular in MT; LXX; *1 En.* ; *4 Ezra*; *2 Bar*; 1QapGen 20.7; 4Q201 3.14; 4Q202 2.18; several others use Daniel imagery without "Son of Man" phrase.

26. Segal, *Two Powers*; Schreuer, "Midrash, Theology, and History," 230-54; Boyarin, "Beyond Judaisms," 323-65.

27. Sabourin, "Biblical Cloud," 290-311, esp. 304; another option of Son of Man definitions is that of a prophet, following Ezekiel's use, however that is unlikely with the divine, conquest and king imagery with Daniel's Son of man; Casey, *Son of Man*; Burkett, *Son of Man*; Tödt, *Son of Man*; Slater, "One Like a Son of Man," 183-98; Moloney, *Johannine Son of Man*; "Johannine Son of Man Revisited," 177-202.

28. *1 En.* 39.6; 40.5; 48.3, 6; 62.7; *4 Ezra* 13.26, 52; Syriac Bar 29.

29. Old Greek LXX Dan 7:13; Zacharias, "Old Greek Daniel 7:13-14," 454-55.

the throne room as do the other Daniel texts.[30] In Daniel the movement is toward God to receive the kingdom, while early Jewish and New Testament texts describe the cloud-riding Son of Man as coming from God to implement judgment and then establish his kingdom on earth. This Danielic Son of Man is explicitly called "Messiah" in the *Similitudes of Enoch* 46.1; 47.3 and in *4 Ezra* 7.28–29; 12.11; 13.32. Furthermore, the DSS manuscript 4Q246 refers to "the Son of God" in profoundly Danielic language as before the throne of God, and then coming to earth to conquer his enemies and establish his everlasting kingdom. Drawing upon the insights of John Collins (from 4Q246) and N. T. Wright (from Mark 13), Marvin Pate argued that the Danielic Son of Man is portrayed as fighting on behalf of the righteous (Essenes or the disciples of Jesus, respectively), whose enemies include the nation of Israel.[31] However, Judaism generally developed this Son of Man image to be messianic in Israel's favor.[32] This meant that any resistant gentile powers would be generally crushed as the Son of Man rode the clouds to conquer and establish righteous Jews in the messiah's kingdom (Dan 7:17–27). Jesus extended this destruction to include damnation for his betrayer and participants of the Sanhedrin court in Jesus' trial (Mark 14:21, 62, plural "you all" of ὄψεσθε). Jewish tradition also developed a co-regency between God and this Son of Man messiah to reign in the kingdom.[33] However, Jesus' reign as Son of Man would be one in which he demonstrates the model of service (Mark 10:45).

Because Jesus' use of the title "Son of Man" appears to be his favorite self-designation among his disciples, there are several uses that are not obviously alluding to Dan 7:13.[34] The Son of Man has authority to forgive sins (Mark 2:10). The Son of Man is Lord of the Sabbath (Mark 2:28). These two references might still be considered within the Son of Man's reign, once he clarified it. However, Daniel made no allusion to the Son of Man being delivered over to the religious leaders for crucifixion and yet that is how Jesus described himself (Mark 9:31; 10:33). These instances

---

30. Ziegler and Munnich, *Susanna-Daniel-Bel*; Zacharias, "Old Greek Daniel 7:13–14," 454–55.

31. Pate, *Communities of the Last Days*, 127–32.

32. *1 En.* 37–71; *4 Ezra* 13; *Tg. 1 Chr.* 3.24; *b. Sanh.* 38b rabbi Akiva sees it as a messiah reference while rabbi Jose does not.

33. 11Q13; 4Q400–405; 11Q17; *b. Sanh.* 98a; *Num. Rab.* 13.14; *'Ag. Ber.* 23.1, 3; *Midr. Haggadol Gen.* 49.10; Burkett, *Son of Man Debate*, 97–124.

34. Hooker, *Son of Man in Mark*, 81–198.

may be considered a play toward a messianic secret until clarified at Olivet discourse and in Jesus' trial or a hint that though Jesus is going to die, he will eventually reign in his kingdom.

John Collins argued that there are four messianic paradigms in the Jewish inter-testamental literature: 1) "Davidic Messiah" (anointed king)[35] or "Son of God,"[36] 2) priest,[37] 3) prophet,[38] and 4) Danielic "Son of Man."[39] Only the first model, the Davidic messianic king fits the Davidic covenant material. Some texts just focus on divine election of the Davidic covenant hope.

> You have loved Israel more than all the peoples. You have chosen the tribe of Judah and have established your covenant with David that he might be a princely shepherd over your people and sit before you on the throne of Israel forever.[40]

However, the Davidic king and the Danielic Son of Man are often joined to develop the messianic king imagery further. Combining these images, Jewish apocalyptic writings of *1 En.* 37–71; *4 Ezra* 11–12; and *2 Bar* 39–40 develop a coming deliverer who will defeat the enemies of Israel. Qumran joins in with this sentiment. For example, the Qumran Florilegium text 4Q174 interprets 2 Sam 7:11–14 as a promise that there will be a descendant of David to destroy the enemies of God and will

---

35. Davidic king references include: 2 Bar. 70.10; 72.2; *1 En.* 48.10; 52.4; *4 Ezra* 7.28; 12.32; *Pss. Sol.* 17.32; 18.57; *Shemoneh 'Esreh* 14; Sir 47.11, 22; 1 Macc 2:57; CD 7.20; 12.23–13.1; 14.19 (=4Q266 frag. 18, 3.12); 19.10–11; 20.1; 1QS 9.11; 1QSa 2.11–12, 14–15, 20–21; 1QSb 5.20; 1QM 5.1; 4Q161; 4Q252 frag. 1 5.3–4; 4Q381 frag. 15.7; 4Q382 frag. 16.2; 4Q458 frag. 2, 2.6; 4Q521 frag. 2 4, 2.1; 4Q521 frag. 7.3; 4QFlor 1.10–13; 4QPat. 3–4; *b. 'Erub.* 43a; *Yoma* 10a; *Sukkah* 52a; 52b; *Meg.* 17b; *Hagiga* 16a; *Yebam.* 62a; *Ketab.* 1126; *Soṭah* 48b; *Sanh.* 38a; *Gen. Rab.* 97 on Gen 49:10; *Ex. Rab.* 25.12 on Exod 16:29; *Num. Rab.* 14.1 on Num 7:48; Kennard, *Messiah Jesus*, 377–414; *Biblical Covenantalism*, 2:25–72.

36. Messianic Son of God references include: 1QSa (1Q28b); 4Q174 (4QFlor) 1.10–12; 4Q174 1 I.11; 4Q246 1.9; 2.1 and 4Q369 1 II; *Sib. Or.* 5.261; *1 En.* 105.2; *4 Ezra* 7.28–29; 13.32, 37, 52; 14.9; Broadhead, *Naming Jesus*, 116–23.

37. Not a role developed in the Gospels but Heb especially develops this role (Kennard, *Messiah Jesus*, 353–76; *Biblical Theology of Hebrews*, 36–51).

38. Mosaic prophet role is grounded in Deut 18:15–22 and echoed in Acts 3:22–23; 1QS 9.10–11; 4Q175 1.5–8; Kennard, *Messiah Jesus*, 243–68.

39. Collins, *Scepter and the Star*, 3–14, especially 12; Pate (*Communities of the Last Days*, 107–32) follows him in this analysis to an abbreviated fashion.

40. 4Q504 1–2 iv 4–8; 4Q252 5.2–5; Abegg, "Covenant of the Qumran Sectarians," 82; *Pss. Sol.* 17.4.

reign on an everlasting throne. The text refers to a "shoot"[41] which is the Davidic Messiah from Isa 11:1; Jer 23:5; 33:15 and Zech 3:8 and 6:12.

> This passage refers to the Shoot of David, who is to arise with the Interpreter of the Law, and who will [arise] in Zi[on in the La]st Days, as it is written, "And I shall raise up the branch of David that is fallen" (Amos 9:11). This passage describes the fallen booth of David, [w]hom He shall raise up to deliver Israel.[42]

In fact, the sectarian perspective of Qumran means that the Davidic messiah would destroy a portion of Israel that would not align themselves with the Qumran community.[43] This judgment to establish the kingdom is also presented by *1 Enoch* as occurring by Daniel's Son of Man. This kingdom reign of the messiah is more clearly a reign over the whole world.

> On that day all the kings and the mighty and the exalted, and those who possess the earth, will stand up; and they will see and recognize how he sits on the throne of his glory, and righteous are judged in righteousness before him, and no idle word is spoken before him. And pain will come upon them as upon a woman in labor. . . . And pain will take hold of them, when they see that Son of Man sitting on the throne of his glory.[44]

The Qumran manuscript, *Messianic Apocalypse*, identified these Jewish expectations for a kingly messiah who will bring in a kingdom program that meets real needs.[45]

> [the hea]vens and the earth will listen to his messiah, and none therein will stray from the commandments of the holy ones. Seekers of the Lord, strengthen yourselves in his service! All you

---

41. For branch of David texts cf. 4Q161 frag. 7–10.iii.22; 4Q174 frag. 1–3.i.11–12; 4QpIsa. frag. 7–10 iii 22; 4QCommentary on Genesis A 5.3–4; 4Q252 frag. 1 v. 3–4; 4Q285 frag. 5.3–4; frag. 7 lines 3–4; 11Q14 lines 12–13; *Pss. Sol.* 17.4, 21, 27–36; 18.7.

42. 4Q174 3.11–13 translated VanderKam and Flint, *Meaning of the Dead Sea Scrolls*, 265, and endnote 7 of chapter 11 on p. 450.

43. 1QM with 1QS 1:23–24; 2:14–17; 9:16.

44. *1 En.* 62.4–5; and in 52.4 this messiah is called the Anointed One; also in 48.10; 52.4; 84.2 this messiah is ruler of the whole world; 4Q246; 4Q382 frag. 16 2; *4 Ezra* 13; *Sib. Or.* 5; Reynolds, "'One Like a Son of Man,'" 70–80; Collins, "Son of Man in First-Century Judaism," 448–66.

45. 4Q521; Vermes, *Jesus the Jew*; "Qumran Forum Miscellanea I," 303–4; Puech, "Une apocalypse messianique (4Q521)," 475–522. Similar sentiments are echoed by Maimonides, *Thirteen Principles of the Faith*, no. 12; *Yad haHazaqa* contained in Patai, *Messiah Texts*, 323–27.

> hopeful in (your) heart, will you not find the Lord in this? For the Lord will consider the pious and call the righteous by name. Over the poor his spirit will hover and will renew the faithful with his power. And he will glorify the pious on the throne of the eternal kingdom, he who liberates the captives, restores sight to the blind, straightens the b[ent]. And the Lord will accomplish glorious things which have never been. . . . For he will heal the wounded and revive the dead and bring good news to the poor.

This reign of the Lord's anointed one will have heaven and earth obeying him, benefited by him in kingdom and fellowshiping before him forever.[46]

This left Israel with an expectancy for the coming Davidic king. With the failure of the Maccabees and especially Judas Maccabeus in 164 BC, another was expected. Pompey conquered Israel for Rome in 63 BC which fostered a sense that the Davidic king could come at any time, perhaps prompted by reflection on Dan 2 and 7. For example, shortly after Pompey's capture of Jerusalem in 63 BC the *Pss. Sol.* celebrate the expected Davidic messiah.

> Behold, O Lord, and raise up unto them their king, the Son of David, at the time in which you see, O God, that he may reign over Israel thy servant. And gird him with strength, that he may shatter unrighteous rulers, and that he may purge Jerusalem from the nations that trample her down to destruction.[47]

Herod the Great tried to capitalize on this sentiment as he rose to power by killing Judas ben Hezekiah and destroying the Jewish resistance.[48] Despised though Herod the Great was, he tried to realize the expectancy of the messiah as he built his temple construction project (37–34 BC), designed to present himself as the Davidic king. As Herod lay dying Judas ben Sariphaeus and Matthias ben Margalothus pulled down the ornamental eagle from the temple and a revolt was on, only to be crushed by Herod's son Archelaus.[49] Other would-be messiahs fostered peasant movements to bring in the kingdom during this power vacuum before Archelaus put together his power block, namely, Judas son of Ezekias,

---

46. 4Q521 frag. 2, 4.ii.1; 1QSa 2.14-15, 20-21.

47. *Pss. Sol.* 17.23-25.

48. Josephus, *Ant.* 14.158-60, 420-30 which incurred the wrath and denouncement of the Jews (Josephus, *Ant.* 14.172-76; *War* 1.208-15; and from Qumran [*T. Mos.* 6.2-6]).

49. Josephus, *Ant.* 17.149-66, 206-18; *War* 1.648-55, 2.1-13.

Herod's servant Simon, and Athronges.[50] When Archelaus and Antipas each argued in Rome for succession, a Jewish delegation plead for autonomy. During the absence of the would-be rulers, another rebellion took place and twice had to be put down by Varus, king of Syria.[51] Such rebellions have at the core the hope that God would raise his messiah to bring in the kingdom.

Within these waves of turbulence, Mark presents Jesus in the narrative revealed as this blended role: Messiah/Christ, Lord, Son of David, son of God, and Son of Man.[52] Morna Hooker argued that the Markan prologue is the key to Markan Christology as the Davidic king initiating God's kingdom with his authoritative teaching and healing to call disciples to follow him to kingdom (Mark 1:1, 15, 17, 22).[53] The Gospel of Mark begins by clarifying Jesus' messianism because it is about Jesus Christ, the Son of God (Mark 1:1), much as Peter began his epistles with "Jesus Christ" (1 Pet 1:1–3; 2 Pet 1:1–2). Peter's epistles also end with "Lord Jesus Christ" indicating he is messiah (1 Pet 5:14; 2 Pet 3:18).

At Jesus' baptism, Leander Keck identified that the Spirit coming upon Jesus is a divine empowerment akin to the Qumran expectation facilitating messiah with the ability to initiate the kingdom of God (Mark 1:10 with Isa 61:1 in Luke 4:18–21; Acts 2:22 with 2:19–20; 10:37–38; 2:22 with 1 Sam 15:1, 17; 16:3, 12–13; Mark 9:40; Matt 3:16; 12:28; Luke 3:22; 4:18; 11:20; John 1:32–33; 3:2; 9:33; 10:38; 14:10).[54] During Jesus' baptism, the *bath qol* (divine speech, "daughter of a voice") announced Jesus was God's son and that God was pleased to present him in this role (Mark 1:11). Clearly by Jesus' baptism (and in Luke 2:49 in Jesus' childhood), Jesus is aware of his kingly Son of God role in order to proclaim a gospel of the kingdom of God (Mark 1:14–15), but this does not mean Jesus was not Christ before this Spirit anointing.[55]

50. Josephus, *Ant.* 17.7, 10.5–6; *War* 2.4.1.

51. Josephus, *Ant.* 17.250–64; *War* 2.39–50.

52. Even getting to divinity: Geddert, "Implied YHWH Christology of Mark's Gospel," 325–40.

53. Hooker, "'Who Can This Be?,'" 79–99.

54. Keck, "Mark 3:7–12 and Mark's Christology," 349–59 defeating Bultmann's claim that such spirit role points to Hellenistic hero, such as Hercules (*History of the Synoptic Tradition*, 250–51); multiple attestation texts are listed beyond Mark to indicate historicity; *Gos. Hebrews* 2; *Gos. Ebionites* 4:2.

55. Bigg, *Peter and Jude*, 35; Matthew and Luke present Jesus as Christ, Davidic King at and before Jesus' birth (Matt 1:1, 17–18; 2:9–11; Luke 1:17, 32, 52–55; 69–71; 2:11).

CHRISTOLOGY 33

The demonized are the most perceptive in the Synoptic Gospels, recognizing Jesus and identifying him as the holy one of God, the messiah, Son of David, and the Son of God (Mark 1:24, 39; 3:11, 14–15; 5:7; 6:7, 12–13; 8:25–27; Matt 8:29; Luke 4:41; 8:28).[56] The "holy one of God" indicates a unique relationship with God, but it is only taken as messianic in conjunction with these other clearly messianic titles (Mark 1:23–24 with 3:11; Acts 3:14 with 18).[57] Responding to Jesus' casting out demons, questions arose among the crowd, such as "What is this new teaching with authority that casts out demons?" (Mark 1:22, 27).

Many blind people called for Jesus as the Son of David to heal and Jesus healed them (Acts 2:22; 4:12; 10:38; Mark 8:22–25; 10:46–52; Matt 9:27–31; 11:5; 12:22; 15:30–31; 20:34; 21:14–15; Luke 4:19; 11:14; 18:42–43; John 9:11).[58] In kingdom there was an expectation of the paralyzed being healed (Micah 4:6–7). Fulfilling this expectation, Jesus healed lame and paralyzed so they could walk (Mark 2:12; Matt 4:24; 8:13; 9:6–9; 11:5; 15:30–31; 21:14–15; Luke 5:24–26; 7:10; 13:10; John 5:8, 11). The crowd wondered, "What is this?" admitting that they had never seen anything like this, including the Son of Man forgiving sins (Mark 2:12). Lepers came to Jesus and asked for healing to meet their needs and Jesus cleansed them (Mark 1:41; 14:3; Matt 8:2–4; 11:5; 26:6; Luke 5:13; 7:22; 17:14).[59] The lepers gave testimony of their healing, refusing to treat it as a secret (Mark 1:45). When the daughter of Capernaum synagogue leader died, Jesus resurrected her (Mark 5:35, 41; Matt 9:18, 25; 11:5; Luke 7:11–15; 8:45, 51; John 11:43–44). When a deaf-mute was healed, he spread the news widely and the people marveled at how Jesus could heal so effectively (Mark 7:35–37; 9:25; Matt 9:32–34; 11:5; 12:22; 15:30–33; 17:18; Luke 9:42; 11:14).

56. Josephus, *Ant.* 18.63–64 identifies Jesus as an effective healer and miracle worker, thus called "messiah." Babylonian Talmud indicates Jesus is a dangerous heretic because he healed people so effectively (*b. Sanh.* 107b; 104b; 43a; 67b; *b. Soṭah* 47a); *Sib. Or.* 8.206–7; Pilate's letter to Claudius supports Jesus exorcizing of demons contained in *Acts of Peter and Paul* 40–42 and Tertullian, *Apol.* 5.21; Origen, *Cels.* 1.38, 68; 8.9; Lactantius, *Ep.* 45.

57. Broadhead, *Naming Jesus*, 97–100; There is no indication of an Aramaic wordplay fulfilling Nazarene fulfilment of Matt 2:23, contra Mussner, "Ein Wortspiel in Mk 1,24?," 285–86; nor any clear priestly allusion in Mark as argued by Kertelege by comparing Ps 106:16 description of Aaron (*Die Wunder Jesu im Markusevangelium*, 53).

58. Pilate's letter to Claudius contained in *Acts of Peter and Paul* 40–42 and Tertullian, *Apol.* 5.21.

59. *Egerton Gos.* 2; Pilate letter to Claudius contained in *Acts of Peter and Paul* 40–42 and Tertullian, *Apol.* 5.21.

The disciples saw Jesus still a storm that threatened them on the Sea of Galilee, and asked, "Who is this that even the sea obeys him?" because normally stilling storms would be a divine role controlling the sea (Mark 4:41; Pss 65:7; 88:26; 89:8–9, 25; 93:3–4; 106:8–9; 107:23–32; Isa 51:9–10).[60] In another instance, Jesus identifying himself, came to the disciples in the midst of another storm walking on water and they were astonished (Mark 6:45–52; Matt 14:24–33; John 6:16–21).[61] Jewish tradition normally held that God was the one who walked on water (Job 9:8 LXX),[62] and God alone was who rescues from the sea (Exod 14:10—15:21; Ps 107:23–32; Jonah 1:1–16).[63] The fact, that Jesus walked on water and rescued Peter when he sank, identifies Jesus with these divine roles.

Some had firm opinions of who Jesus was. The most common assessment of Jesus' role was that he was a prophet, like Elijah or John the Baptist (Mark 6:14–15; 8:28). Religious leaders rejected Jesus, considering Jesus' healed on the Sabbath, concluding that he did his healings by the power of Satan (Mark 2:27—3:6). Though, some Pharisees sought signs from Jesus as they rejected his supernatural meeting people's needs by healing them (Mark 8:11). In contrast to those who sought and obtained healing from Jesus, his family and hometown thought Jesus had lost his senses (Mark 3:20–21; 6:1–5). King Herod proposed Jesus to be revivified John the Baptist, raised from the grave (Mark 6:14) and subsequently at Jesus' trials, Herod sent Jesus back to Pilate declaring him innocent and having Jesus dressed in a gorgeous robe of royalty (Luke 23:11–12).[64]

---

60. 2 Macc 9:8; 4Q381; Isa 51 describes Yahweh as the one who controls the sea; Ortlund, "Old Testament Background," 325–26; Ps 88:26 describes that God is the one whose "hand is set against the sea"; Kirk and Young, "'I Will Set His Hand,'" 333–40.

61. Multiple attestation biblically and *Odes Sol.* 39.8–13 supports the authenticity of this miracle. Also, Dura Europa third-century AD Christian chapel pictures Peter in this miracle walking on water (Bockmuehl, *Simon Peter in Scripture and Memory*, 40, 72). Jesus' reassuring statement in Mark 6:50, "It is I" (ἐγώ εἰμι) is how the LXX Exod 3:14 describes "I am who I am" (אֶהְיֶה אֲשֶׁר אֶהְיֶה), so possibly another hint at divinity.

62. Also Job 38:16; Ortlund, "Significance of Jesus Walking on the Sea (Mark 6:45–52)," *Neot* 46:2(2012) 319–37, especially 325–26; Kirk and Young, "'I Will Set His Hand to the Sea,'" *JBL* 133:2(2014) 335; also there is no parallel Greco-Roman mythology for walking on water, even though Poseidon and Xerxes are reported to fly in a chariot over water (McPhee, "Walk, Don't Run," *JBL* 135:4[2016] 763–77).

63. Wis 14.2–4; 1QH 6.22–25; *T. Naph.* 6.1–10.

64. *Gos. Pet.* 1.2 and 2.5 has Herod deliver Jesus over to the Jewish people to be killed. However, the *Gos. Pet.* 11.47–48 identifies that Pilate has governance over Jesus' death and tomb.

At the climax of the Synoptic Gospels, Peter identified that Jesus was the Christ (anointed one) to be king, the Son of God (Mark 8:29; Matt 16:16-20; Luke 9:20).[65] In Simon's statement of Jesus' lordship, Peter became a symbol of the personal commitment of a disciple. Simon and his insight[66] become foundational for the movement and thus Jesus changes Simon's name to Peter, "rock man."

Jesus was transfigured before Peter, James and John as a momentary glimpse into Jesus' kingdom (2 Pet 1:11, 16-18; Mark 9:1-10; Matt 16:28—17:9; Luke 9:27-36). Jesus' face and clothes shone as the sun, enabling these disciples to be eyewitnesses of Jesus' majesty. Moses and Elijah appeared talking with Jesus. Out of fear, Peter blurted out that it was good for them to be there and that if Jesus wished, they could make three tabernacles, one each for: Jesus, Moses and Elijah. Perhaps Peter was thinking that the Feast of Tabernacles might be appropriate as kingdom is initiated, since as a festival, it will be celebrated in kingdom (Zech 14:16), and perhaps it was that time of year. Instead, a bright cloud overshadowed them and the *bath qol*,[67] the voice of God (the Excellent Glory) spoke from the cloud, saying, "This is my beloved Son, in whom I am well pleased. Hear him!" In sampling a taste of the kingdom, this voice reassured the disciples that the prophecies of Christ's kingdom will be confirmed further (2 Pet 1:11, 16-19).[68] Then Jesus came alone and touched the disciples, asking them to rise and not be afraid but "Tell the

65. Schweizer affirms such Christological commitments and confession is the core of discipleship (*Lordship and Discipleship*).

66. Peter's *declaration* is likely included within the feminine foundation rock (πέτρᾳ) because it is referred to as "this rock" with the feminine pronoun (ταύτῃ), rather than second person singular masculine "you" referring to Peter, who was described as rock in the masculine (Πέτρος), or first person masculine "me" referring to Christ (Matt 16:18), who is not in this context described as a rock but is only elsewhere described as a rock (which in those other contexts makes good sense) without reference to this text. Caragounis, *Peter and the Rock*, 119. John 1:42 recounts Simon being called the Aramaic "Cephas" ("rock") from early in his discipleship.

67. On the concept and instance of *bath qol*: Dan. 4:31; Josephus, *Ant.* 13.282-83; *Song Rab.* 8.9.3; *b. ʾAbot* 6.2; *B. Bat.* 73b; 85b; *Mak.* 23b; *ʿErub.* 54b; *Šabb.* 33b; 88a; *Soṭah* 33a; *p. Soṭah* 7.5.5; *Pesiq. Rab Kah.* 11.16; 15.5; *Lev. Rab.* 19.5-6; *Deut. Rab.* 11.10; *Lam. Rab.* Proem 2, 23; *Lam. Rab.* 1.16.50; *Ruth Rab.* 6.4; *Qoh. Rab.* 7.12.1; *Sib. Or.* 1.127, 267, 275; Artapanus in Eusebius, *Praep. ev.* 9.27.36; Arrian, *Alex.* 3.3.5; Lucian, *C.W.* 1.569-70; Plutarch, *Isis* 12; *Mor.* 355E; *Mart. Pol.* 9. The *bath qol* was present in Israel before the spirit of prophecy departed (*b. Pesaḥ.* 94a; *Ḥag.* 13a; *Sanh.* 39b) and a few sources give it future ramifications as well (*Lev. Rab.* 27.2; *Pesiq. Rab Kah.* 17.5).

68. The statement does not require a claim for Jesus' divinity, so it does not preview deification contra Burkett, "The Transfiguration of Jesus (Mark 9:2-8)," *JBL* 138:2(2019) 413-32.

vision to no one until the Son of Man is risen from the dead." The disciples kept quiet about what they had seen until later, but they questioned Jesus what rising from the dead meant.

Jesus' triumphal entrance into Jerusalem fulfills the people welcoming Jesus as they might a lead rabbi or potential king of peace riding into Jerusalem (Zech 9:9; Matt 21:5; Mark 11:10 quote of Ps 118:26). The people cried out the ascent *hallel* Ps 118:25–26 to identify that Jesus coming is blessed of the Lord, with anticipation that the Davidic kingdom is impending, a point Jesus also makes (Mark 11:9–10; 12:10–11, 36–37; Pss 118:22, 110:1). The Ps 118 quote is wrapped with the statement "hosanna" which becomes a prayer to God, and perhaps for Christ to "deliver."[69] However, Jerusalem was largely unresponsive and had replaced prayer for commerce in the temple. Jesus warned the people that they had rejected him in their dullness, rebellion, and murder plots; but God's plan kept Jesus at the center, so that they were rejecting him to their peril (Mark 11:18, 27–12:12).

During the Olivet discourse, Jesus clarified for his disciples that "Son of Man" means Daniel's Son of Man (Mark 13:26–27; Dan 7:13). The coming of the Son of Man is not hidden in houses or the wilderness but visible for all to see like lightening flashing across the sky (Mark 13:26; Dan 7:13–14; Matt 24:27, 30; Luke 21:27).[70] Daniel's presentation of the Son of Man as cloud rider coming up to the Ancient of Days to receive his everlasting dominion, is shifted as in early Judaism[71] to describe the Son of Man's cloud riding from the Ancient of Days to come to earth to enforce his kingdom onto the willing and unwilling. Thus, the coming of the Son of Man is a very real visible coming. This is not to be confused with a spiritual or personal coming like the coming of the Holy Spirit,[72] nor a vision at one's death (Acts 1:11; 7:56; 9:4–7). Jesus will re-

---

69. Goldingay, *Psalms*, 3:363. This is a standard psalm sung on the ascent for Passover (*m. Pesaḥ.* 5.7; 9.3; 10.5–7; *t. Pesaḥ.* 8.22; *b. Pesaḥ.* 117a; Keener, *Matthew*, 492. There is no evidence that the LXX statement "ties up the festival cords" is harkening to Sukkot or a festival offering (Goldingay, *Psalms*, 3:364), Mark is more reflective of the MT leaving these themes undeveloped.

70. *Ep. Jer.* 61; 4Q246 2.1–2; *2 Bar.* 53.9. Lightening also occurs with divine theophanies and judgment (Exod 19:16; Pss 18:14; 144:6; Zech 9:14; Philo, *Moses* 2.56; *L.A.B.* 11.4).

71. *1 En.* 37–71; 11Q13; 4Q400–5; 11Q17; *4 Ezra* 13.26, 52; *Bar.* 29; *Tg. 1 Chron.* 3.24; *b. Sanh.* 38b.

72. Though the arrival of the Holy Spirit is an obvious eschatological phenomenon: Joel 2:28–29; Acts 1:6, 8; 2:1–21; 1QS 4.3–4; 8.12–16; *Sib. Or.* 4.46, 189; 2 Macc 7:23; 14.46.

turn bodily from the heavens riding on the clouds, visible for all, revealed as conquering to establish Christ's kingdom is his powerful coming (1 Pet 1:7–8; 2 Pet 1:16, 18; Mark 13:26; Dan 7:13; Matt 24:30; Luke 21:27; Rev 19:11–16)[73] so that no one need be deceived. Christ comes with his kingdom glories to follow (1 Pet 1:11; 4:11; 5:1, 10–11; 2 Pet 1:11, 16, 19).

Preceding the day of Christ's coming there will be cosmic disturbances as evidence of Messiah's coming (Mark 13:24–25; Isa 24:18–23; Joel 2:10, 31; 3:15; Matt 24:29; Luke 21:25; Acts 2:20; Rev 6:12–13; 8:12).[74] The sun and moon will be darkened, and the stars will fall from the sky. Admittedly, this language of upheaval has been used metaphorically in contexts that could be argued as now past (Isa 13:10; 34:4; Ezek 32:7; Amos 5:20; 8:9; Zeph 1:15).[75] Josephus describes some heavenly upheaval as omens of the AD 70 destruction: namely, a star and comet that looked like a sword over Jerusalem and the clouds looking like armies attacking cities.[76] However, when the language is climaxed by the entrance into the everlasting kingdom, as it is here in the Olivet discourse, it remains as a vivid astronomical indicator of when Christ's kingdom will begin (Mark 13:24–30; Joel 2:10, 31; 3:15; Matt 24:28–29, 32–35; Luke 21:25–32; Rev 6:12–13; 8:12). This darkening of the heavens is more supernatural than a natural description of cloud cover because the powers of the heavens are shaken. Likewise, the earthly impact is extreme with dismay, perplexity and men fainting from fear (Luke 21:25–26). All the tribes of the earth will see the Son of Man and mourn their judgment (Matt 24:30).

Mark uses Jewish rhetorical criticism describing the interrogation of rabbi Jesus' acumen to get at the basic issue of Jesus' authority (Mark 11:27–33; 12:13–44).[77] The religious leaders attempt to shame Jesus, but Jesus demonstrated his scribal superiority justifying Jesus has the right to judge his opposition, indicating who the Son of Man will judge. Jewish

---

73. Jub 1.28; *1 En.* 62.3; *T. Mos.* 10.7.

74. 1QH 11.13; *Sib. Or.* 2.194, 200–202; 3.81–93, 796–808; 5.344–50; 7.125; 8.190–92, 233, 413; *1 En.* 80.4–6; *As. Mos.* 10.5–6; *T. Levi* 4.1; *4 Ezra* 5.4–5; *2 Bar* 70; 70.2; *T. Mos.* 10.5; *Apoc. Elijah* 5.7; *b. Sanh.* 99a; this is not to be identified as fulfilled with the rending of the Jerusalem Temple's external veil with stars sown on it as was suggested by Allison (*End of the Ages Has Come*, 33).

75. Besides these times of conquest, *Sib. Or.* 5.152 claims creation was shaken at the appearance of Nero and *4 Ezra* 4.18–19 speak of cosmic disorders at the giving of the Law. On this basis, Wright (*Jesus and the Victory of God*, 354–55) argued that this metaphor then only means "an earth-shattering event!" rather than describing cosmic events.

76. Josephus, *War* 6.5.288–309.

77. Kennard, *Epistemology and Logic*, 76–82 develops rabbinic patterns for assessing scribal ability, within which Jesus excelled; *Messiah Jesus*, 131–35.

Talmudic rhetorical criticism sets four distinct question styles for this examination: 1) *halachic* or scientific questions about the application of Torah to specific situations, 2) nonsense question designed to ridicule a scholar and his interpretations of Scripture, 3) conduct questions larger than any one text, and 4) *haggadic* or contrary question.[78] The Jewish leadership broadly wished to use these rabbinical techniques to trap Jesus and show him deficient and overreaching (Mark 12:13–37; Matt 22:15–46; Luke 20:19–44). Instead, the approach backfired on them, showing Jesus warranted as a superior scribe.

The initial challenge comes from rival Herodians and Pharisees in the form of a scientific question, identified by "is it lawful to give poll-tax to Caesar, or not?" (Mark 12:13–17; Matt 22:15–22; Luke 20:19–26). Herodians held high posts aligning with Roman dominance (Mark 3:6; 12:13; Luke 20:19 with Matt 22:16).[79] The champions of village synagogues, Pharisees were progressive Jews, tending to accept the prophets and writings, and embracing resurrection afterlife (Acts 23:6–10; Dan 12:2).[80] Poll tax demonstrated submission to Rome, so Judas of Galilee led a revolt against this tax in AD 6.[81] If Jesus attacked poll tax, then the Herodians would have him trapped in advocating seditious activity as a zealot, a capital offense under Rome. If Jesus said that the tax was lawful, then Jesus would alienate the Jewish populous and deflate their hopes for him being messiah who removes the Roman oppressors.[82] Jesus responded by asking his accusers whose face and inscription is on the coin. The people responded that the coin identified Tiberius Caesar by head and with its inscription. Jesus responded, "render to Caesar the things that are Caesar's and to God the things that are God's." The religious leaders and the people were amazed at his answer (Mark 12:17; Luke 20:26),[83] while neither aligning himself with Caesar nor being a seditious zealot.

The nonsense question challenge (Mark 12:18–27; Matt 22:23–33; Luke 20:27–40) came from Sadducees (conservative Jews dominating the

---

78. Daube, *New Testament and Rabbinic Judaism*, 158–69; "Rabbinic Methods of Interpretation and Hellenistic Rhetoric," *HUCA* 22(1949) 239–64; Molina and Neyrey, *Calling Jesus Names*, 73–74.

79. M. Menaḥ. 10.3; m. 'Abot 1.3.

80. Josephus, *Ant.* 13.297–98; 18.1.4; *War* 2.8.14, 2.164–66; *Nahum Commentary* on 2.12 (col. 1.4–8); 3.1–4 (col. 2.1–10), 3.6–7 (col. 3.1–8), 3.9b–11 (col. 3.12—14.8); m. 'Abot 1.3.

81. Josephus, *Ant.* 17.204; 18.3.i.1; *War* 2.8.1, para. 118.

82. Tacitus, *Ann.* 2.42.

83. *Gos. Thom.* 100.

high priesthood, only accepting Pentateuch as Scripture, Matt 26:57–65; Luke 3:2; John 18:13; Acts 4:6; 23:6–10).[84] The Sadducees built a theological riddle on the law for Levirate marriage, which provided an inheritance within a family if a husband died without an heir (Deut 25:5).[85] Not believing in resurrection,[86] the Sadducees weave a nonsensical question about Levirate marriage for procreating an heir continuing in the afterlife, and wonder if a wife had seven husbands whose wife would she be in the resurrection afterlife.[87] The absurdity is made particularly acute by conjectures of marriage in resurrection (foreign to the law) and polyandry (foreign to Judaism). Jesus responded that Sadducees were ignorant about the resurrection, which he understands is evident from the Scriptures in a Pharisaic orientation, and God can do it. So, Jesus claimed they were playing with half a deck of Scriptures with too small a God. Jesus instructs that resurrection is not for procreating and levirate marriage, showing Sadducees were out of touch with the purposes of the law. Jesus passed from the manner of resurrection to its fact, populated already by Abraham, Isaac, and Jacob. To demonstrate this, Jesus cites Pentateuch texts which the Sadducees would recognize as Scripture, what God said to Moses in Exod 3:6, "I am the God of Abraham, and the God of Isaac, and the God of Jacob," and then affirmed that God is not the God of the dead but of the resurrected living (Mark 12:27; Luke 16:19–31).[88] The multitude was astonished at Jesus teaching showing Sadducees mistaken (Mark 12:27; Matt 22:33–34; Luke 20:39).

The third challenge came from a Pharisee lawyer as a conduct question (Mark 12:28–34; Matt 22:34–40). The lawyer asked Jesus about the greatest commandment Law priorities. Jesus responds correctly with the *shema* as greatest commandment, "You shall love the Lord your God with all your heart, and with all your soul, and with all your mind." He quickly followed with a second command, "You shall love your neighbor as yourself." These two commands are alike in that the whole Law and prophets

---

84. Josephus, *Ant.* 13.297–98; 18.1.4, 16–17; *War* 2.8.14, 2.164–66; *Nahum Commentary* on 3.8 (col. 3.8–9), 3.9b–11 (col. 3.12–14.8); *m. 'Abot* 1.3.

85. Josephus, *Ant.* 4.8.23; *m. Yebamot*.

86. Josephus, *Ant.* 18.1.4; *War* 2.8.14.

87. Wis 2.1–5; *1 En.* 102.6–11; *m. Sanh.* 10.1; *b. Sanh.* 90b.

88. 4 Macc 7:18–19; 13:17; 16:25; Philo, *Sacr.* 1.5; *T. Abr.* 20.8–14; 50–55; *Qoh. Rab.* 9.5.1; *b. Sanh* 90b; *Ex. Rab.* 1.8; *Deut. Rab.* 3.15; *L.A.B.* 4.11; *T. Isaac* 2.1–5; *T. Benj.* 10.6; *Apoc. Sedr.* 14.3; *3 En.* 44.7.

depend upon them (Luke 10:25–28).[89] When the lawyer affirmed Jesus' answer, Jesus responded to him, "You are not far from the kingdom of God" (Mark 12:34). The Jewish leaders were frustrated at not being able to trap Jesus.

Jesus turned the tables on the Pharisees and asked a contrary question, demonstrating scribal warrant and authority to judge as king (Mark 12:35–37; Matt 22:41–46; Luke 20:41–44). Jesus' question raised the essential issue of authority of the Messiah. "Whose son is the Christ?" The religious leaders answered, "The son of David." Jesus then asked the contrary question, "Then how does David in the Spirit call him 'Lord,' saying, 'The Lord said to my Lord, sit at my right hand, until I put your enemies beneath your feet?' If David calls him 'Lord,' how is he his son?"[90] This contrary question pressed the authority of Christ consistent with rabbinical reasoning beyond the Davidic king (Ps 110:1).[91] No one was able to answer him. Jesus demonstrated his superior scribal ability and that he was also David's Son and Lord, so from that day on no one asked any more entrapment questions. Jesus responded to these religious leaders by judging that they were damned for their abuse of vulnerable people and that their temple would be destroyed (Mark 12:41—13:2).

At Jesus' trial the religious leaders put forward false charges, including the messianic claim that Jesus was going to destroy and rebuild the temple (Mark 14:58; 15:29; Matt 26:61; John 2:19). While Jesus was silent before his accusers (1 Pet 2:23; Mark 14:61), eventually the high priest put Jesus under oath to truthfully tell whether he is the Christ (anointed as the king of the Jews), the Son of God (Mark 15:2; Matt 26:63; 27:11; Luke 20:20; 22:67, 70; 23:2–3; John 18:29–33; 19:7–9).[92] Jesus answered "yes" to these appellations and then identified himself as Daniel's Son of Man who will come in the clouds to judge all and reign. This statement combines phrases from Ps 110:1 and Dan 7:13 like early Jewish

---

89. Akiva, *Sipre* on Lev 19:18; *T. Iss.* 5.2; 7.6; *T. Dan.* 5.3; Aristeas, *Ep.* 229; Philo, *De virt.* 51; 95; *Spec.* 2.63; *Abr.* 208; *T. Naph.* 8.9–10; *Jub.* 7.20; 20.2; 36.7–8; Josephus, *War* 2.139.

90. All these "Lord" references are κύριος but in the Hebrew of Ps 110:1 *Yahweh* speaks to *Adonai*, which in Jesus' and Peter's understanding identified Jesus as God (Ps 110:1; Mark 12:36; Acts 2:34–36).

91. Akiva, *b. Sanh.* 38b; *Gen. Rab.* 85.9; *Num. Rab.* 18.23; *Tg.* on Ps 110.

92. *Gos. Pet.* 3.6–9; 4.7, 11; 11.45–46; 15.32; around AD 200 Serapion discovered that the greater part of the *Gos. Pet.* was in accordance with the historical Jesus, but he rejected its authority, pointing out that there were heretical additions.

eschatological texts had done, putting the Jewish leadership under judgment.[93] The Sanhedrin condemned Jesus to death, but Jesus as Son of Man condemned the religious leaders to damnation and defeat.

Jesus was crucified under the charge "The King of the Jews" (Mark 15:21–39; 1 Pet 2:21; Matt 27:32–54; Luke 23:33–49).[94] In Mark there are six times Jesus is called "king," which challenges the legitimacy of other kings in the book (Mark 15:2–32).[95] John especially emphasizes this charge by mentioning that it was in Hebrew, Latin, and Greek and that the religious leaders took issue with its text, for it actually claimed him to be the king of the Jews, rather than as Jewish leadership desired, that Jesus had wrongly claimed to be such a king (John 19:19–21). However, Pilate kept the text how he wrote it as a slam against the Jews. As Jesus dies on the cross, a centurion overseeing his death confessed "Truly this man was Son of God!" (Mark 15:39).

Peter's sermons in the book of Acts pick up where Mark left off with Peter's post-resurrection assessment. The focus of the gospel message is that Jesus is the king who you will have to deal with in kingdom salvation. Each sermon develops this theme a little differently, but the commonality places the focus on Jesus and whether the audience aligns with him. Peter claims, Jesus is the divinely empowered man who has done many miracles, but the Jewish leadership killed him within God's plan, but God vindicated Jesus by resurrecting him, to which Peter's witness indicates that Jesus is the Davidic king to provide the Holy Spirit for believers empowering them to live eschatological lives unto kingdom (Acts 2:16–36). A special emphasis in this context develops that Jesus is the Davidic king promised (Acts 2:30 quoting 2 Sam 7:12–13) announced as the anointed one to be king by God (Acts 2:36) and functioning in this exalted Christ role as receiving and giving the Holy Spirit (Acts 2:33). While in this context "Lord" (κύριος) stands for Davidic king and deity (Acts 2:34–36). In quoting Ps 110:1, Peter demonstrates Jesus is the Lord (Davidic king and God), much as Jesus had hinted at (Acts 2:34–36; Mark 12:35–37). The concept of "Lord" (κύριος) in Acts 2:36 is elevated by the LXX quote from Ps 110:1 in Acts 2:34 which takes the אֲדֹנִי/Adonai as Lord (κύριος)

---

93. *1 En.* 62.5; *T. Benj.* 10.6; *T. Job* 33.3–9; *Apoc. El.* 1.8; Peter claims that the Ps 110:1 claim is already realizable in Christ's ascension to be seated at God's right hand (Acts 2:33–36; Heb 1:3, 13; 10:13).

94. *Gos. Pet.* 4.2.

95. Herod is called "king" five times (Mark 6:14–27) and plural kings are mentioned once (Mark 13:9); Gelardini, "Contest for a Royal Title," 93–106.

in referring to Christ. However, since in Acts 2:34 the word "κύριος" also translates Ps 110:1 יְהֹוָה/*Yahweh*, this citation draws Jesus' divinity within a Jewish monotheism as part of the gospel as well. Acts 2:33 exaltation of Jesus to sit at the right hand of God affirms Ps 110:1 promise as combined with 2 Sam 7:12 sitting on David's throne (Acts 2:31), thus declaring Jesus to be Davidic messianic (Christ) Lord, as well as divine Lord (Acts 2:34, 36). As Davidic messianic Lord, Jesus received the promise of the Holy Spirit to be bestowed to facilitate his kingdom and he poured out this Holy Spirit empowerment upon believers aligned with him (Act 2:33 with 2:16–18, 38). Jesus is recognized by Peter to be already reigning as Davidic king on David's throne and God, as co-regent because the Spirit has been given for believers to live in the present last days. However, there is a greater stage of Jesus' kingdom when his enemies will be made a footstool for his feet in their utter defeat (Acts 2:35).

In Acts 3, Jesus serves many roles including healer, forgiver, holy and righteous one (Acts 3:14), ἀρχηγὸν (the prince or leader of life, Acts 3:15), the prophet after Moses pattern (Acts 3:22–23; Deut 18:18–22; Mark 8:28), the Abrahamic seed through whom global blessing comes to all families in kingdom (Acts 3:25–26; Gen 12:1–3; 15:1–21; 17:1–8; 22:16–26), and the one who will bring in the kingdom (Acts 3:20–21, 26). The hostile Jewish leaders in their unholiness and unrighteousness demanded the death of the holy and righteous one (Acts 3:14; 4:26–27). Later at one of Peter's trials, Jesus is presented as the only Savior for physical and spiritual healing (use of σωζω in Acts 4:9 and 12). As such, Jesus becomes the Savior who grants repentance to believers (2 Pet 1:1; 3:2; Acts 4:9; 5:31). For a receptive gentile audience, Jesus is presented as the lord and judge of all, who also heals (Acts 10:38, 42). The focus of Peter's gospel statement is the person of Jesus Christ (as the one that they must deal with in their salvation), rather than an event that this person does. Reception of the gospel entails aligning oneself with this Jesus as the anointed King and Savior.

In Acts 3:13 and 26 the word παῖδα refers to Jesus as "son" or "servant." Traditionally, many import vicarious atonement into this text by connecting this term with Isaiah's servant songs.[96] In Acts 3:13 the meaning could be either "servant" or "son," though the context refers to Jesus' death without any development except Israel's culpability. Rather, what is developed in this context, is that God glorified his παῖδα Jesus,

---

96. Pate and I develop this interpretation and my answer here briefly mentioned at length in our book: Pate and Kennard, *Deliverance Now and Not Yet*, 433–81.

whom Israel had culpably killed. God's assessment of Jesus is that he is the holy and righteous one, the prince of life. There is no development of atoning servant (παῖς from Isa 52:13); rather there is regal honor, which would be better associated with a translation of παῖδα as "son" (Acts 3:15, 19–21, 26; Ps 2:2, 12 quoted in Acts 4:25; continuing regal emphasis of Acts 2:25–36; 3:20–23). In Acts 3:26, παῖδα refers to the resurrected one to bless Israel by turning them from their wicked ways. Resurrection is not clearly developed in Isa 53, but there is some ambiguous continuing of the servant so that he could be allotted a portion with the great and divide booty with the strong after the servant's atoning death (Isa 53:12). However, nowhere in this or any other Petrine gospel statement in Acts is there a clear connection of Jesus death as Isaiah's Servant atonement. Here παῖδα can be understood as in Acts 3:13 as better referring to Jesus as God's Davidic son who in his reign will bless Israel in turning Israelites from their wicked ways (Acts 3:26). In fact, if we let the previous Petrine sermon influence our hermeneutical choice, παῖδα should be understood as "son," in that "Jesus is the Davidic messiah" is the core of the previous sermon (Acts 2:22–36). At this point Bruce chimes in and appeals to 1) Phillip's encounter with the Ethiopian eunuch and 2) the Acts 4 prayer.[97] In Acts 4:25 παιδός is often translated as "servant" because David is faithfully providing revelation, but it could be understood as an allusion that he is the king "God's son." The critical παῖδά reference comes in Acts 4:27 as referring to Jesus as "God's son" the king, to whom Ps 2:1–2 refers. Psalm 2:12 defines παιδείας as son, referring to the messianic Christ, rather than connecting it with Isa 53. Thus, the point in Acts 3:13 is the same as the core of the previous Acts 2 sermon and the following prayer παῖδά reference. Namely, that Jesus is glorified as the Davidic king, thus Israel is culpable in their killing of their messiah. Likewise, the elevated role to bless Israel in Acts 3:26 fits wonderfully within this theme of Jesus ascending in honor as the Davidic messiah to bless with salvific blessings like the giving of the Spirit (Acts 2:33–36). Therefore, I understand παῖδα in Acts 3:13 and 26 as referring to "son" in a messianic sense here, since

---

97. Bruce, "Speeches in Acts–Thirty Years After," 60–61. On pp. 61–62, Bruce continues his appeal with the phrase "hanging on a tree" (ξύλου) in Acts 5:30 and 13:29 which he understands must carry a vicarious atonement meaning, but this does not follow from his good point from Deut 21:22 that Jesus' death is an experience of curse by hanging on a tree. Most other individuals who experienced this Deuteronomic curse were criminals with no development of an efficaciousness of death developed. Jesus is certainly viewed by the Jews who killed him as a criminal (guilty of heresy) and thus to be cursed in this way.

there is no near context development for Isaiah's servant imagery, and in both sermons near the context there is evidence for Jesus as Davidic messiah. In a broader biblical theological argument, there is also a dominant emphasis of Jesus as king with which they will have to deal in Petrine and Lukan salvation sermons as well. So once again, neither does Peter, nor Luke, develop any soteriological accomplishment in Jesus' death, rather merely that Israel is culpable. The point here is that Jesus is the anointed Davidic king, with whom believers need to align.

In a section to ground the church, Jesus Christ is the elect of God (1 Pet 2:5–8). Peter presents a scriptural *pesher* using Isa 28:16; 8:14 and Ps 118:22 to discuss Jesus as a "living stone, rejected by men but choice and precious in the sight of God (1 Pet 2:4).[98] The value of Christ's election is accentuated by changing the word for "place" from Isa 28:16 LXX "ἐμβαλῶ" (throw or place) to Peter's use of "τίθημι" (lay or place).[99] Isaiah prepares Jerusalem for judgment by laying in Zion an ambiguous tested cornerstone (MT: *mwsd*, "foundational cornerstone" or LXX: ἀκρογωνιαῖον, "capstone" or the "crowning point") that is other than Yahweh himself (Isa 28:16).[100] In the MT the word describes a stone for the foundation to support walls and roof of a large structure, such as in a temple, and thus the stone is costly, select, valued, and honored. The LXX shifts to "capstone" or the "crowning point" and applies it messianically, as a climax later in the construction process.[101] Perhaps the metaphor shifts from a theological foundation to one of an experiential climax for God building church and kingdom. Both metaphors are valued stones for the construction of the building by Yahweh. If people believe in this tested stone, then their lives can be built without being disturbed by the earthquakes of life and their lives can be focused on Christ bringing climax to church and kingdom. Peter identifies this stone in his context to be Jesus Christ (1 Pet 2:6). Peter expands the rejected beyond the Jewish

---

98. Oss, "Interpretation of the 'Stone' Passages," 181–200.

99. Himes, "Why Did Peter Change the Septuagint?," 227–44; Williams, "Case Study in Intertextuality," 37–55, esp. 43. Kim overpressed the Zechariah identification of son of David with the shepherd king (Zech 9–14) and Davidic stones (Zech 3:8–9; 4:7–10; 6:12–13) because there is no clear allusion in Peter (Kim, "Jesus—The Son of God," 134–48, though a chart on p. 142 nicely summarized his conjecture).

100. The ambiguity of the referent in this passage has fostered views of the cornerstone being: Jerusalem, Hezekiah, a remnant, confidence in the land, and Christ (Young, *Isaiah*, 2:301–3).

101. Elliott, *1 Peter*, 409; Qumran applies Isa 28:16 referring to their community (1QS 8.7–8; and possibly: 1QS 5.5; 4QpIsad 1; 1QHa 6.26–27; 7.8–9).

religious leaders to include any who do not believe. Peter then reminds his readers that Christ as the rejected stone is highly valued by God, and believers share in some of that value in their communal election which molds believers into living stones contributing to God's chosen building of the Church (1 Pet 2:5, 7). Psalm 118 provides praise for a new beginning on an occasion of deliverance, the *Mishnah* describes that Levites sang this psalm during the Passover slaughter of the lambs,[102] and added a discussion of approaching closed gates of the temple to discuss how a rejected stone became valued and used as the head of the corner (Ps 118:22 LXX, ἐγενήθη εἰς κεφαλὴν γωνίας). John Goldingay describes this construction process.

> The builders would look at stones that are available to see which would fit into different stages of the building work. A stone unsuitable at one stage might be exactly what was required later. A nuance of this is the reusing of stones from demolished buildings, which had a practical rationale, but in connection with a temple would also symbolize and embody continuity between a rebuilt temple and its predecessor. A recycled stone might even end up in a key position, perhaps holding together two walls at right angles at the corner of a building, in the building's foundation or at the top of its superstructure.[103]

Finding a new honored place shows the stone to be highly valued. Goldingay claims that the valued place among the targums is to use this whole section (Ps 118:22–29) as referring to God's choice of David.[104] Peter appropriates this verse in the same *pesher* manner as Jesus had done previously, rejecting the Jewish religious leaders in his parable concerning the abusive vineyard tenants rejecting those who came from the lord (1 Pet 2:7; Mark 12:1–12; Ps 118:22). Similarly, Qumran claimed that the Jerusalem leadership were "builders of a rickety wall" who covered up their vulnerability with "whitewash."[105] In contrast, Christ is highly valued in God's building program. Peter cites a separate[106] passage from

---

102. M. Pesaḥ. 5.7; 9.3; 10.5–6.

103. Goldingay, *Psalms*, 3:361; *T. Sol.* 22.7–9; 23.1–4 describes Solomon erecting the cornerstone at the head of the corner.

104. Goldingay, *Psalms*, 3:361.

105. CD 4.19 alluding to Ezek 13:10; 8.12, 18.

106. Peter cites three separate stone passages while Paul conflates Isa 8:14 within 28:16, showing Peter is not dependent upon Paul for these citations (Koch, "The Quotations of Isaiah 8,14 and 28,16," *ZNW* 101:2[2010] 223–40).

Isa 8:14 exploring the destruction of Syria and Samaria by Assyria, so that Ahaz and Judah might trust Yahweh in this threatening time. Ahaz and Judah do not believe, until Hezekiah leads them in faith and they survive the Assyrian flood judgment. However, Isa 8:14 is applied in this new messianic day to a new group of unbelievers, who stumble and damn themselves in their disobedience (1 Pet 2:8). In contrast to God's determining election of Christ and the church, those who reject Christ as "stumbling" and "disobedient" are appointed to "this" neuter singular relative pronoun (ὃ in 1 Pet 2:8 *pesher* launching from LXX Isa 8:14,[107] "'λίθος προσκόμματος καὶ πέτρα σκανδάλου·' οἳ προσκόπτουσιν τῷ λόγῳ ἀπειθοῦντες εἰς ὃ καὶ ἐτέθησαν"). The aorist passive ἐτέθησαν describes an "appointed" that grounds the divine choice of the relative pronoun of this passage (2 Pet 2:8). The singular relative pronoun (ὃ) indicates that each of these persons is appointed by God. Normally, relative pronouns would refer to the nearest antecedent nouns of the same number and gender, namely the parallel neuter singular nouns, "stumbling" and "disobedient" describing rejecting in unbelief from Isa 8:14, God determining those who continue to reject Christ, namely a complementarian double determinism of God actively choosing those he elects to believe and those he rejects to their disobedience. Such disobedience renders those disobedient still culpable for their choice of disobedience, even though God chose this disobedience for them (similar to Acts 2:23 and Mark 4:12), in the same way that believers "received faith" presumably from God (λαχοῦσιν πίστιν, 2 Pet 1:1) in a similar manner to God providing magnificent promises to inform the believer's knowledge (2 Pet 1:3–4), which does not remove the believer's responsibility to synergistically continue to increase their faith and knowledge in Christ within their own moral development (2 Pet 1:1, 5). Many interpreters find this complementarian divine determinism too restricting for free human choices, at least regarding one's disposition concerning Christ, so they opt for God merely providing an antecedent outcome of "doom," nowhere mentioned in the passage (1 Pet 2:8). This insertion contrasts with the context of this pericope which is about the elect included as believers valued after the pattern of God electing and valuing Christ (1 Pet 2:4, 7, 9). If the relative pronoun refers to "doom" then the antecedent becomes the implied damnation as a metonymy of cause, "stumbling," for effect, doom. This last view is grammatically possible, since sometimes relative pronouns do not

---

107. LXX: Aquila, Symmachus, and Theodotion have σκανδάλου, funding Peter's quote.

match the gender and number of the antecedent.¹⁰⁸ However, this option with more libertarian elbow room is concluding for the relative pronoun as selectively referring to an implication of the earlier available antecedent (προσκόμματος, ignoring the nearer antecedent [σκανδάλου], which is also parallel in the contextual quote of Isa 8:14 to the one they choose) in the passage to import a meaning into the passage with a trajectory opposite to that of the contextual emphasis of valued elect of the passage. I prefer to follow the available parallel antecedent words in the passage even if it makes for a more difficult view of double determinism, which we have already seen, Peter holds in at least the religious leaders' specific rejection of Christ (Acts 2:23) and Mark 4:12 presents also governs God's determinative rejection of unbelievers concerning Jesus.

Emerging from Isa 53:5 and 9, servant Jesus is identified as "shepherd and guardian" of the Christian's life (1 Pet 2:25, 22). This royal allusion concretizes Yahweh's kingly shepherd role (Gen 48:15; 49:24; Exod 15:13; Pss 31:4; 44:12; 48:15; 74:1; 77:21; Isa 40:11; 49:9–10; 63:11; Jer 31:10; Ezek 34:12–13; 37:24; Hos 4:16; Mic 2:12; 4:6–8; Zeph 3:19) for his people Israel as God's flock (Pss 74:1; 77:20; 78:14, 52; 79:13; 80:1; 95:7; 100:3; Isa 49:9; 63:11; Jer 13:17; 31:10; Mic 2:12; Zech 9:16; 10:3),¹⁰⁹ much like ancient Near Eastern kings were called shepherds of their own people.¹¹⁰

> The imagery of the shepherd also describes the lovingkindness of Yahweh as the fulfillment of that association with Israel which he established in the beginning. The office of a shepherd as an image of kingship is of course found throughout the Near East, and is ascribed to gods as well as to kings, often in stereotyped forms. This element of the courtly style always has something of an official stamp, as a result of which the characteristics of love and providential care appear simply to be taken for granted as involved in faithfulness to the kingly calling.¹¹¹

---

108. Wallace, *Greek Grammar*, 337–38.

109. 4Q266 frag. 18, col. 5.13; *1 En.* 89.16–24, 51–53; *L.A.B.* 23.12; 30.5; *Sipre Deut.* 15.1.1; *Exod. Rab.* 24.3; *Pesq. Rab.* 9.2; 26.1/2.

110. *Lipit-Ishtar* prologue; *Code of Hammurabi* prologue, 1.50; epilogue; Homer, *Od.* 4.291 with 4.24; Xenophon, *Cyr.* 8.2.14; *Mem.* 3.2.1; Dio Chrysostom, *Oracle Kingship* 4.43.

111. Eichrodt, *Theology of the Old Testament*, 1:236–37; Stuhlmueller, "Yahweh-King and Deutero-Isaiah," 32–33; Brettler, *God Is King*, 65; Kennard, *Biblical Theology of Isaiah*, 28–29.

Moses was Israel's shepherd (Ps 77:20; Isa 63:11).[112] David was Israel's shepherd (2 Sam 5:2; 1 Chr 11:2; Ps 78:70–72; Ezek 34:23; 37:24).[113] Other appointed leaders, such as Ezra were also Israel's shepherd (Num 27:17; 1 Kgs 22:17; Jer 3:15).[114] The anticipated messiah is to be the good shepherd for Israel (Mic 5:4; Jer 23:1–6; Ezek 34:23; Zech 13:7).[115]

This imagery of the shepherd reaches a high point in the book of Isa with Yahweh as the "great shepherd" having brought forth his flock in a new exodus from Egypt (Isa 40:11; 63:11; Pss 23:1–4; 28:9; 74:1–2; 77:20; 78:52; 79:13; 80:1; 100:3; Jer 13:17; 31:10; Ezek 34:11–17; Mic 7:14; Zech 9:16; 10:3).[116] The imagery has compassion and love with provision for all needs: "He tends his flock like a shepherd; he gathers the lambs in his arms and carries them close to his heart; he gently leads those that have young" (Isa 40:11). Goldingay describes this compassionate shepherding role.

> Pasturing the flock and leading the mothering ewes to watering places together (to pasture or feed would not normally imply giving food to the animals, but taking them to where they can find it), as do gathering lambs and carrying them. In each case the second expression heightens the first: the prophet moves from pasturing sheep in general to the ewes' particular need for water and rest, and with respect to the lambs moves from gathering/arm to carrying/bosom. The verse as a whole suggests the personal caring of *Yhwh* for Israel as a flock. While it is always the people as a whole that *Yhwh* is concerned for (the prophet is not individualistic), the caring is one that recognizes and meets the distinctive needs of its many members.[117]

Isaiah applies this shepherding compassion to the new exodus. They will feed beside the roads and find pasture on every hill. They will neither hunger nor thirst nor will the desert heat or the sun beat upon them. He who has compassion on them will guide them and lead them beside springs of water. (Isa 49:9–10) Yahweh is the great shepherd over Israel (Isa 40:11; Ps 80:1) and the nations (Isa 14:30; 34:6; Ps 100:3; Ezek 39:18).

---

112. *1 En.* 89.35; *L.A.B.* 19.3; *Sipre Deut.* 305.3.1; *y. Sanh.* 10.1, para. 9; *y. Soṭah* 5.4; *Pesiq. Rab Kah.* 2.8; *Exod. Rab.* 2.2; 5.20; *Tg. Ps.-J.* on Gen 40:12; 1Q34; 1Qbis frag. 3, col. 2, line 8.

113. 4Q504 4.6–8; *Gen. Rab.* 59.5.

114. *4 Ezra* 5.18; *Mek. Pesaḥ.* 1.162–63; CD 19.8–9.

115. *Pss. Sol.* 17.40; *Tg. Neof.* 1 on Exod. 12:42; 4Q165 frag. 1–2.

116. Sir 18.13; 4Q509 4.24; *1 En.* 89.18; *L.A.B.* 28.5; 30.5; Philo, *Agriculture* 50–51; *b. Ḥag.* 3b; *b. Pesaḥ.* 118a; *Exod Rab.* 34.3; *Lam. Rab.* 1.17, par 52; *Pesiq. Rab.* 3.2.

117. Goldingay, *Message of Isaiah 40–55*, 31.

God is the shepherd enabling his people to pasture safely and even lie down relaxed, knowing that they are protected from any wild beast.

Peter applies this royal messiah and divine shepherd role to Jesus, who cares and protects believers who have left the straying ways and returned to him (1 Pet 2:25). The care Jesus provides beyond his mimetic pattern enables the Christian flock of God to have direction and protection on their exodus way to kingdom. Jesus as shepherd will appear in his second coming and reward those who have traveled to kingdom (1 Pet 5:4). Elders of the household of God are to imitate Jesus' faithful shepherding as the responsibly care for and protect the flock of God under their care.

Jesus is the judge of all, appointed to fulfill this role as the Son of Man at his powerful coming (1 Pet 4:5;[118] Acts 10:42; Mark 13:26–27; 14:62). In fact, since the end of all things is at hand, Christ is ready to judge all humans (1 Pet 4:5, 7). Christ's judgment of forgiveness is already proclaimed for those who believe in him (Acts 10:43). Those who heard the gospel, trusted Christ, and followed Christ in being condemned in their humanity through martyrdom, will be vindicated in God resurrecting them as he had done for Jesus (1 Pet 4:6). In Jesus' resurrection, Jesus has already begun to make pronouncements of judgment upon groups of rebellious demons (1 Pet 3:19).[119] However in the future sent by God, Jesus will return to earth in a powerful coming[120] (2 Pet 1:16; Acts 3:21). This expression of Jesus' coming will bring judgment but also begins the restoration of Israel and kingdom salvation (1 Pet 1:5, 7; 2 Pet 1:11; Acts 1:6–7; 3:19–21).[121] Jesus shall reign gloriously forever (1 Pet 4:11; 5:11; 2 Pet 1:11).

118. "Living" refers to presently alive. In the same way as Christ died in martyrdom in this context, "dead" refers to people who died. There is no support for believers being the "living" and unbelievers being the "dead," that would be more theologically Johannine or Pauline.

119. This discussion is developed in the chapter of Jesus standing against Satan.

120. "Powerful coming" is a hendiadys of 2 Pet 1:16 "the power and coming" of our Lord Jesus Christ. This is not a summary of Jesus first coming in performing miracles (as claimed by Ign. *Phld.* 9.2; Clement of Alexandria, *Strom.* 6.15.128; Mayor, *Jude and 2 Peter*, 195; Green, *2 Peter and Jude*, 83). In this context, the transfiguration prefigures and guarantees this powerful coming, so that they are surer it will take place. Nor should this passage be viewed as realized eschatology, which ignores this future hope (as claimed by Love, "First Epistle of Peter," 82–83).

121. Contrary to the Wright, *Jesus and the Victory of God* view that this judgment took place under Vespasian with kingdom continuing as the church. Christ's reign grows the kingdom, but Christ's kingdom is more dramatic than Vespasian conquering Jerusalem.

The divinity of Jesus Christ in conjunction with the Father is developed in the next chapter on the Trinity. Also the death, atonement, resurrection, and teaching of Christ are placed in other chapters.[122]

---

122. Discussion concerning atonement is present in ch. 8 of *Petrine Theology*. Jesus' teaching, historical death, and resurrection are developed in companion volume, Kennard, *Petrine Studies*.

4

Peter's Letter Form Presents Intentional Missional Trinity

MANY BIBLICAL THEOLOGIANS DO not develop the Trinity in the NT but consider that the doctrine of the Trinity develops in the early church, after the completion of the last NT books. Certainly, the doctrine does develop in the church, but Peter is intentional about developing a missional Trinitarian view in his writings. Ramsey Michaels identified that 1 Pet begins as "trinitarian in form."[1] However, Peter's use of letter form and *pesher* argument develop intentionality in presenting the Trinity.

Form critical studies pioneered by Adolf Deissmann and continuing letter form criticism since show that letters in the Roman Empire generally begin with an author description, followed by a recipient's line, then a short blessing, and more Hebraic letters often added a long blessing.[2] First and Second Peter are broadly recognized to be letters utilizing this letter form.[3] This letter form is utilized by Peter in 2 Pet to clarify the divinity

---

1. Michaels, *1 Peter*, 4, 13 develops this Trinitarian view from 1 Pet 1:2; Kennard, "Doctrine of God in Petrine Theology," presented a fuller missional Trinitarian view; 1 Pet 1:2 draws a brief mention of Trinity by the following: Kistemaker, *Peter and Jude*, 12; Jobes, *1 Peter*, 45, 68.

2. Deissmann, *Light from the Ancient East*, 149–251; Francis, "Form and Function of the Opening," 113–25; Klauck, *Ancient Letters and the New Testament*.

3. von Harnack, *Die Chronologie der altchristlichen Litteratur*, 451–65 was the first to suggest 1 Pet was reworked into a modern analysis of epistolary form though Mayor (*Jude and 2 Peter*, cxv–cxxiii) includes the patristic sources claiming the books are letters from a pre-modern perspective; Beasley-Murray, *Baptism in the New Testament*, 251–58; Elliott, *Elect and the Holy*, 11–13; 1 Pet, 7–12; Kelly, *Peter and Jude*, 2–3, 39; Bauckham, *Jude, 2 Peter*, 131; Dalton, *Christ's Proclamation to the Spirits*, 62–71; Jobes, *1 Peter*, 53–55, 59; Davids, *2 Peter and Jude*, 143; Kennard, *Petrine Studies*, chapter on

of Jesus Christ and the Father. Furthermore, letter form in 1 Pet clarifies different missional roles that each of the Trinitarian members accomplish while emphasizing the divinity of the Father, among the other persons.

The recipient's line in 2 Pet 1:1 identifies that the readers have received a faith "by the righteousness of our God and Savior Jesus Christ." In this instance of the Granville Sharp rule, the article (τοῦ) controls both coordinate nouns (of the same case connected by the conjunction) referring them to the same person, namely the Savior Jesus is God.[4] Ethelbert Stauffer argued against the Granville Sharp rule here by claiming that the pronoun following "God" (θεοῦ ἡμῶν) isolates the trailing noun to indicate two persons are in view.[5] Daniel Wallace compellingly responded that Granville Sharp's rule is in place in this context even with the insertion of a pronoun by developing the parallel "in v 11 of this same chapter (as well as in 2:20 and 3:18), the same author writes τοῦ κυρίου ἡμῶν καὶ σωτῆρος Ἰησοῦ Χριστοῦ, an expression which refers to one person, Jesus Christ."[6] Wallace further developed that over half of the NT texts that fit Sharp's rule have an intervening word, such as a possessive pronoun, between the substantives and yet the construction clearly refers to only one person.[7] A. T. Robertson exhorts, "Why refuse to apply the same rule to 2 Peter i.1, that all admit . . . to be true of 2 Peter i.11?"[8]

In the letter form, this recipient statement is followed by a short blessing of grace and peace from "God and Jesus our Lord" (2 Pet 1:2, τοῦ θεοῦ καὶ Ἰησοῦ τοῦ κυρίου ἡμῶν). In this instance, both "God" and "Lord" retain an article identifying that there are two separate persons sourcing this blessing. So "God" is here another (than Lord Jesus) who in the context would probably be identified as the promise keeping God, Father, Majestic Glory, and source of Jewish prophetic Scripture (2 Pet 1:3–4, 17, 21). However, in first-century letter form those persons itemized as "God" (θεοῦ) or "Lord" (κυρίου) within the short blessing of letter form

---

"Letter Form in the Epistles of Peter."

4. Robertson, *Grammar of the Greek New Testament*, 127, 785–86; Wallace, *Greek Grammar*, 270–77; Bauckham, *Jude, 2 Peter*, 168; Davids, *2 Peter and Jude*, 163; *Theology of James, Peter, and Jude*, 210.

5. Stauffer, "θεος," TDNT 3:106.

6. Wallace, *Greek Grammar*, 277.

7. Wallace develops his point by identifying a few of these texts, namely John 20:17; 2 Cor 1:3; 1 Thess 3:2; 1 Tim 6:15; Heb 12:2; Rev 1:9; P.Lond. 417.1; P.Oxy. 2106. 24–25; *Greek Grammar*, 277.

8. Robertson, "Greek Article and the Deity of Christ," 185.

are expressed as divine.⁹ Which means that though Jesus is described as "Lord," such a reference in this short blessing would include him within the concept of divine, along with the Father. The prayer for grace and peace is requested from both divine persons, Father God and Lord Jesus. Taken together 2 Pet 1:1–2 indicate duality in the Godhead, within a Jewish monotheistic divinity which is reminiscent of the two powers portrayal of Yahweh within Judaism.¹⁰

Furthermore, since "God" (θεοῦ) is normally conceived of as the one to whom prayers are given,¹¹ Petrine prayers may further this two powers divinity. Peter's general discussion of prayer considers believers praying to the Jewish Holy One and recognizing that they are praying to God the Father (1 Pet 1:15–17; Lev 11:44; 19:2; 20:7). The relationship from Father to Son is one of love and honor for the Beloved Son, who is the Father's pleasure (2 Pet 1:17; Mark 1:11; 9:7). However, letter form often included final blessings such as doxology as a prayer.¹² The doxology in 2 Pet 3:18 is a prayer addressed to Christ. The second line addressed the doxology to him (αὐτῷ) referring to the nearest referent, "our Lord and Savior Jesus Christ." Thus, this Christ has "the glory, both now and the everlasting day." Such a reference to glory in a doxology would identify Christ as God for in doxologies "glory" refers to God (as Father: Luke 2:14; Rom 11:36; Eph 3:21; Phil 4:20; Jude 25; Rev 7:12; or Christ: Gal 1:4–5; 1 Tim 1:17; or both: Rev 5:13). In 2 Pet 3:18 Jesus Christ is the divine glory.

Peter also presents Jesus is God through *pesher* re-appropriation of Ps 110:1. Mark 12:36–37 records Jesus' statement and Luke repeats this¹³ as Peter's statement in Acts 2 demonstrating Jesus is the Lord (Davidic King and God). The concept of "Lord" in Acts 2:36 reference is elevated

---

9. Deissmann, *Light from the Ancient East*, 214; Francis, "Form and Function of the Opening," 117; Klauck, *Ancient Letters and the New Testament*, 42, 92–93; "Letter of Emperor Claudius"; O'Brien, "Letters, Letter Forms," 551.

10. Dan 7:13–14; Isa 9:6; Ps 110:1; *1 En.* 46.1; 47.3; 62.7–9 describe Daniel's Son of Man as pre-existent from the beginning; *4 Ezra* 7.28–29; 12.11; 13.32; 4Q346 col. 2 v1; Segal, *Two Powers in Heaven*.

11. Thayer, *Greek-English Lexicon of the New Testament*, 287.

12. Deissmann, *Light from the Ancient East*, 149–251; Francis, "Form and Function of the Opening," 113–25; Klauck, *Ancient Letters and the New Testament*.

13. Luke claims historical accuracy: Luke 1:1–4; Acts 1:1–2; within Hellenistic history accuracy is standard: Dionysius of Halicarnassus, *Ant. rom.* 1.6.1; 7.43.2; Arrian, *Alex.* 6.2.4; Plutarch, *Alex.* 30.7; 31.2–3; Josephus, *Ag. Ap.* 1.50–52; 2.107; Kennard, *Epistemology and Logic*, 97–98.

by the quote from Ps 110:1 in Acts 2:34 and Mark 12:36 follow the LXX in translating אֲדֹנִי as Lord (κυρίῳ) in referring to Christ. However, since the κύριος also translates יְהוָה blending both Lord Christ and the speaking Yahweh to be both divine Lord. By this *pesher*, Peter's statement draws Jesus' divinity within a Jewish monotheism as part of the gospel as well. Additionally, for a receptive gentile audience, Jesus is presented as the Lord and Judge of all, who also heals (Acts 10:38, 42). So, the focus of Peter's gospel statement is the person of Jesus Christ (as the divine one that they must deal with in their salvation), rather than an event that this person accomplished.

Mark developed Jesus as messiah but occasionally more like divinity shines through. In a storm on the Sea of Galilee, the disciples woke Jesus, crying out, "Save us, master;[14] we are perishing!" (Mark 4:35–41). Jesus rebuked the winds and the sea; and it became perfectly calm. The disciples fearfully marveled, saying, "What kind of man[15] is this, that even the winds and the sea obey Him?" Here Jesus takes on the sovereign role of Yahweh, controlling the storm to become as calm as glass (Pss 65:7; 88:26; 89:8–9, 25; 93:3–4; 106:8–9; 107:23–32; Isa 51:9–10).[16] In a later storm, Jesus saw the disciples' boat was in the middle of the sea battered by waves and the disciples strained on the oars against a contrary wind (Mark 6:45–51). His disciples saw Jesus walking on the sea and were frightened. Jesus spoke to them, "Take courage, it is I;[17] do not be afraid." Jewish tradition had it that God was the one who walked on water (Job 9:8 LXX), and Jesus was identifying himself with that divine

---

14. "Master" (ἐπιστάτα) is a unique Lukan term parallel to "lord" (κύριος) and "teacher" (διδάσκαλε), but especially shows his authority and their submission to him (Luke 5:5; 8:24, 45; 9:33, 49; 17:13).

15. Davies and Allison, *Matthew*, 2:70 draws parallels with the Jonah account. Antiochus IV Epiphanes claimed that the sea would obey him but never demonstrated this ability like Jesus did here (2 Macc 9:8). A couple of early Jewish accounts and Greek narratives describe how storms were eased by prayer (*y. Ber.* 9.1; *b. B. Mes.* 59b; Homer, *Hymns* 33.12; Aristides, *Hymn to Serapis* 33), which shows the disciples' culpability for lack of faith in praying about the storm. Likewise, *b. B. Bat.* 73a indicates a tradition that clubs engraved with "I am that I am, Yah, the Lord of Hosts, Amen, Amen Selah" will subdue waves that would otherwise sink a ship. Such rescues are the work of the deity, thus implying Jesus is God.

16. 2 Macc 9:8; 4Q381; Isa 51 describes Yahweh as the one who controls the sea; Ortlund, "Significance of Jesus Walking," 325–26; Ps 88:26 describes that God is the one whose "hand is set against the sea"; Kirk and Young, "'I Will Set His Hand,'" 333–40.

17. Jesus' statement, "It is I" (ἐγώ εἰμι), is how the LXX Exod 3:14 describes "I am who I am" (אֶהְיֶה אֲשֶׁר אֶהְיֶה), so possibly another hint at divinity.

role.[18] Peter blurted out, "Lord if it is you, command me to come to you on the water." When Jesus said "Come," Peter got out of the boat and walked on the water toward Jesus. However, when Peter saw the wind, he became afraid and began to sink, calling out, "Lord save me!" Immediately Jesus grabbed him, saying, "You[19] of little faith, why did you doubt?" In Jewish tradition it is God alone who can rescue from the sea (Exod 14:10—15:21; Ps 107:23–32; Jonah 1:1–16).[20] When they got into the boat, the wind stopped, and they were greatly astonished and worshiped Jesus, saying, "You are certainly God's Son!"

First Peter moves this two powers Jewish divinity into an intentional missional Trinitarian ministry and relationship description of recipients (1 Pet 1:1–2) and the long blessing (1 Pet 1:3–12).[21] After Peter identified himself as the author, the recipient's description emphasizes that they are in the sphere of the elect (1 Pet 1:1, ἐκλεκτοῖς). The first description of their elect condition indicates that the recipients are characteristically temporary residents scattered outside their homeland and within the northern two thirds of Turkey, north of the Taurus Mountains, and perhaps even indicating the route on the Roman roads which this letter traveled. However, the recipient's singular election status was also described according to combined efforts of the Trinitarian persons' missional involvement (1 Pet 1:1–2).[22] Namely, that their election status was according to the foreknowledge of God the Father, by the agency (ἐν) of the Holy Spirit's sanctification resulting (εἰς) in initial obedience and covenantal atonement provided by the death[23] of Jesus Christ. However, this sanctification and atonement results in divine fostering obedience indicative of the initiation of the new covenant (1 Pet 1:2; Ezek 36:24–28; Jer 31:31–33).[24] Following

18. Also Job 38:16; Ortlund, "Significance of Jesus Walking," 319–37, esp. 325–26; Kirk and Young, "'I Will Set His Hand,'" 335; also there is no parallel Greco-Roman mythology for walking on water, even though Poseidon and Xerxes are reported to fly in a chariot over water (McPhee, "Walk, Don't Run," 763–77).

19. These "you" statements are grammatically singular referring to Peter doubting.

20. Wis 14.2–4; 1QH 6.22–25; *T. Naph.* 6.1–10.

21. 1 Pet 1:3–12 is treated as a unit of praise by Elliott, *1 Peter*, viii; Davids, *1 Peter*, 50; *Theology of James, Peter, and Jude*, 122; Jobes, *1 Peter*, 5–6; Keener, *1 Peter*, vii.

22. Michaels, *1 Peter*, 4, 13; Kistemaker, *Peter and Jude*, 12; Jobes, *1 Peter*, 45, 68.

23. The metaphor of sprinkling the people with blood is reminiscent of the initial covenant cleansing in Exod 24:3–8 and the atonement of Isa 52:15 by Yahweh's Servant; Kennard, *Biblical Covenantalism*, 3:190–91, 198; *Biblical Theology of Isaiah*, 202–3; Bigg, *Peter and Jude*, 93; Jobes, *1 Peter*, 72.

24. Kennard, *Biblical Covenantalism*, 3:198; 2:79–89; *Biblical Theology of Isaiah*, 202–3; Selwyn, *1 Peter*, 120–21; Davids, *1 Peter*, 49.

this Trinitarian election, there is a short blessing developed with an optative mood as in prayers to the divine persons funding their election.

The long blessing further rehearsed missional Trinitarian persons as involved in facilitating the rescue unto eschatological salvation (1 Pet 1:3–12).[25] The first person involved in this Trinitarian ministry is God the Father (1 Pet 1:3–5). In this instance of the Granville Sharp rule, the article (ὁ) controls both coordinate nouns (of the same case connected by the conjunction) referring them to the same person, identifying that the Father is God.[26] The mercy of God the Father caused Christians to be born again[27] to a living hope prefigured by the manner of Christ's resurrection. This resurrection elevates all believers to an incorruptible undefiled inheritance reserved in the heavens and that these believers are also guarded by the power of God resulting in (εἰς) a salvation ready to be revealed in the last time. The divine or human agency providing this salvation is through faith or faithfulness (1 Pet 1:5, διὰ πίστεως).

The second Trinitarian Person involved in this missional salvation in this long blessing is Jesus Christ (1 Pet 1:6–9). The eschatological salvation is a cause for joy despite the Christians suffering various trials because the trials serve as a crucible purifying gold by removing dross and proving the believer's faith as genuine. What remains within suffering Christians is tested faith[28] resulting in glory and honor at the second coming of Jesus Christ. The focus of the eschatological salvation is now on Jesus Christ in the blessing. "Although you do not see [Christ] you love him, although you do not see him now, you believe him" (1 Pet 1:8). Such a tested faith amid suffering provokes joy with rejoicing and glory, obtaining the outcome of each believer's tested faith to be his own salvation (1 Pet 1:9).

The third Trinitarian Person involved in the long blessing missional salvation is the Holy Spirit (1 Pet 1:10–12).[29] In Judaism the phrase "Holy Spirit" refers to an extension of the monotheistic God (Ps 139:7; Isa 11:2). The phrase "Spirit of Christ" usually refers to the divine Spirit

---

25. Witherington, *Indelible Image*, 1:332.

26. Robertson, *Grammar of the Greek New Testament*, 127, 785–86; Wallace, *Greek Grammar*, 270–77.

27. 1QH 3.19–23 identify new birth as personal entry into the Qumran community as a new covenant and a new eschatological creation; Jobes, *1 Peter*, 83.

28. Like Sir 2.1–9; Seneca, *Prov.* 5.10; Elliott, *1 Peter*, 340–41; Bigg, *Peter and Jude*, 104

29. Witherington, *Indelible Image*, 1:332.

(Acts 16:6–7; Rom 8:9; Gal 4:6; also likely in Phil 1:19 and 2 Pet 1:21)[30] so the reference is likely to have the same Trinitarian view in 1 Pet 1:11. For Peter the Holy Spirit is a divine (1 Pet 1:11–12; θεοῦ πνεῦμα, 1 Pet 4:14; τῷ θεῷ, Acts 5:3–4) person who empowers Christians and a personal agent to whom lies can be given (1 Pet 1:22; 2 Pet 1:21; Acts 2:17–18, 38; 4:8, 31; 5:3–4; 8:15–18; 10:38; 11:15). Concerning this revealed salvation message prophets made careful search, inquiring concerning the time that the Spirit within them was indicating concerning Christ's sufferings and subsequent glories (1 Pet 1:10–11). So, Christ was the content of the Spirit's missional ministry to the prophets. Furthermore, the Holy Spirit's ministry continues in his agency to foster gospel proclamation, so that the prophetic word might be understood by the combined enablement of accurate communication of the gospel and new covenant Holy Spirit transformation (1 Pet 1:12).

Using the features of letter form (namely: recipients' line, short blessing, long blessing, and final blessing), Peter shows intentionality in presenting a Trinitarian personal missional emphasis of Father, Jesus Christ, and Holy Spirit, especially in 1 Pet. The Trinitarian persons foster recipients' election and are all involved in a believer's eschatological salvation.

---

30. Ign. *Mag.* 8; *Ep. Barn.* 5; Selwyn, *1 Peter*, 135; Best, *1 Peter*, 81.

5

The Holy Spirit

AS IN THE TRINITARIAN discussion, the short and long blessing develop the Holy Spirit involved with missional salvation (1 Pet 1:2, 10–12).[1] In Judaism the phrase "Holy Spirit" refers to an extension of the monotheistic God, onomatopoetically like a rushing "wind," which one can't see even though one can see its effect (*ruach*, LXX πνεῦμα, Ps 139:7; Isa 11:2; 63:10–11; Joel 2:28–32; Acts 2:2, 4, 17–18). In Peter, the word πνεῦμα continues to mostly refer to a divine person, though an occasional reference identifies something related to God, such as angels, the resurrected life, and a divinely prized attitude. The phrase "Spirit of Christ" usually refers to the divine Spirit as he reveals Christ (Acts 16:6–7; Rom 8:9; Gal 4:6; also likely in Phil 1:19 and 2 Pet 1:21)[2] so the reference is likely to have the same Trinitarian view in 1 Pet 1:11. For Peter the Holy Spirit is a divine (1 Pet 1:11–12; θεοῦ πνεῦμα, 1 Pet 4:14; τῷ θεῷ, Acts 5:3–4) person who empowers Christians and a personal agent to whom lies can be given (1 Pet 1:22; 2 Pet 1:21; Acts 2:17–18, 38; 4:8, 31; 5:3–4; 8:15–18; 10:38; 11:15). The Spirit has intellect and gives utterance (Acts 2:4; 4:8, 31; 10:19), some of this speaking includes prophecy about stages of salvation history (1 Pet 1:11; 2 Pet 1:21; Act 1:16). In communicating this prophecy, the prophets are "carried along" by the Spirit much as a strong wind might "drive" a ship (φερόμενοι, 2 Pet 1:21; Acts 27:15–17). Concerning this salvation prophets made careful search, inquiring concerning the time that the Spirit within them was indicating concerning Christ's sufferings and subsequent glories (1 Pet 1:10–11). So, "Jesus as the Christ"

---

1. Witherington, *Indelible Image*, 1:332.
2. Ign., *Magn.* 8; *Ep. Barn.* 5; Selwyn, *1 Peter*, 135; Best, *1 Peter*, 81.

was the content of the Spirit's missional ministry to the prophets. However, the Holy Spirit's ministry continues in his agency to foster gospel proclamation, so that the prophetic word might be understood by the combined enablement of accurate communication of the gospel and new covenant Holy Spirit transformation (1 Pet 1:12).

The Spirit sanctifies or renders a believer ontologically holy through the process associated with Jesus' death viewed as a Jewish sacrifice sprinkling them with Jesus' sacrificial blood, but this sanctifying sacrifice transforms from within so the believer initially obeys Jesus Christ (1 Pet 1:2). This sanctification is the process of implementing God's election. Obviously, sanctification begins the believer being associated with Jesus, it is not a later development in Peter. With people being sprinkled with blood, this sanctification initiated a covenant relationship and exodus, much as Moses had done at Mount Sinai (1 Pet 1:2; Exod 24:1–11). This internally transforming sacrifice should be seen as Peter's way of discussing the initiation of the new covenant that Heb develops more fully.[3]

The Spirit is "poured out upon" believers by Christ facilitating this enablement from his Davidic royal throne as an expression initiating kingdom (Acts 2:17–18, 30, 33; Joel 2:28–32). The Spirit resting upon believers prompted them to prophesy, as indicated in the repetitive addition to the Joel quote "and they shall prophesy" (Acts 2:18 to reinforce Acts 2:17 quote of Joel 2:28). Such prophetic praise of Jesus as the Christ is exampled by Peter's sermon in Acts 2:22–39 and repeated by the gentile believers in Cornelius' household when the Spirit is poured out and fell upon them (Acts 10:44–45; 11:15). This process of the Spirit upon believers is also described as "gave," "received," and "baptized by the Spirit." Though different descriptions are used it is the same event and phenomena to initiate the Spirit enabled life. The Holy Spirit is received by Jews hearing Peter (Acts 2:38). The Holy Spirit cannot be bought, he is "given" by Peter and the apostles laying on their hands or at divine initiative (Acts 8:20; 10:45; 11:17; 15:8). Such divine giving of the Spirit identifies that gentile believers in Christ have the same authentic salvation, including forgiveness as the Jewish believers in Christ before them. Thus, the Spirit is "received" by believers (1 Pet 4:10; 2 Pet 1:9, 17; Acts 1:20, 25; 2:33, 38; 10:43, 47). This is the same experience of believers being "filled" with the Holy Spirit (Acts 2:4; 4:8). This process is also described as being "baptized by the Holy Spirit," which had not happened yet in Acts 1:5 but

---

3. Kennard, *Biblical Theology of Hebrews*, 52–105

occurs at Pentecost and with Cornelius' household faith in Jesus as the Christ (Acts 11:15–17; 2:4, 38). This relationship is also called "resting on," which provides encouragement for persecuted Christians to have the Spirit of glory and of God resting on them (1 Pet 4:14; Acts 1:8). The continuing presence of the Holy Spirit empowers and obligates the believer to obey God as a witness to Christ's resurrection and authority (Acts 1:8; 5:29, 32). Ultimately the humble persevering believer will be glorified.

6

God's Word

GOD AND THE SPIRIT are involved in giving God's word to humans. Peter views the divine word as the oral and written pronouncements of God. Peter uses the phrases, "enduring word of God" (λόγου ζῶντος θεοῦ) to be identical to "the word of the Lord" from Isaiah (ῥῆμα κυρίου, 1 Pet 1:23, 25; 2 Pet 3:1–2; Isa 40:6–8). The words ῥῆμα and λόγος are synonymous and appear interchangeably, meaning "word expression, assertion and subject discussed."[1] Both words mean "word" (1 Pet 4:15; 2 Pet 2:3; 3:2: Acts 2:14, 22; 5:5). Both words are used as the "subject discussed" (2 Pet 1:19; Acts 8:21; 10:37). Both words can be prophesied specifically or more generally of kingdom (1 Pet 1:23–25; 2 Pet 1:19; Acts 11:16). Both words are expressed to mean "gospel" (1 Pet 1:25; 3:1, 15; Acts 5:20–32; 8:21; 10:22; 11:14). The only distinction in Peter is that λόγος is used once to refer to God "speaking" creation into effect (2 Pet 3:5; Gen 1) and more frequently in Peter's written letters while ῥῆμα is used more frequently in Peter's speaking vocabulary.

The description of the word shows its character. As gospel, the word is enduring and imperishable seed, such that it produces an imperishable life identified with imperishable inheritance of salvation (1 Pet 1:4, 23, 25). Isaiah 40:6–8 is quoted to develop this theme of word permanence within the context of the new exodus unto kingdom (1 Pet 1:23–25). The contrast is with the transitoriness of petite fragile flowers that appear in the Near Eastern deserts in a wet spring but last only hours when the hot dry Sirocco wind blows up from the desert. The gospel word is the permanent

---

1. BAG, "λόγος," 478–79; "ῥῆμα," 742–43.

life-causing dependable message from God. It is the same message that if disobeyed condemns one, stumbling over Christ (1 Pet 2:8).

Within this context a different form of λόγος appears, namely λόγικος, meaning, "of the word"[2] and describing the kind of milk for which to desire (1 Pet 2:2). In contrast to deception and treachery (1 Pet 2:1, δόλον), Peter commands believers to long for the "pure" milk of the word (1 Pet 2:2, ἄδολον). Peter used a simile, "as" (ὡς) a newborn baby, not a claim that this is merely for young Christians.[3] Rather as a baby desires milk, believers of any spiritual age should have a "wholistic desire" for the word to frame their thinking and life (1 Pet 2:2 constative aorist). So repeatedly the Scriptures are appealed to as a framework for believer's thinking, speech, and practice.

A prophetic word proclaims divine revelation beforehand that includes foretelling something future (1 Pet 1:10; 2 Pet 1:20–21; 2:16; 3:2; Acts 2:16–18, 30; 3:18, 21–25).[4] God authors true prophecy so that humans are empowered by the Holy Spirit to announce it and record it (2 Pet 1:21). The human prophet can increase their confidence in this prophecy by making careful search and inquiry as to details of the prophecy authored by God (1 Pet 1:10–11). However, prophecy is a process of the Holy Spirit that "bears" the prophet along as a strong wind might force a ship to go in a determined direction (2 Pet 1:21; Acts 27:15, 17). The Spirit determines what is said, though the human prophet has some effect on how it is said. At times only the human is mentioned as giving this prophecy (2 Pet 3:2; Acts 2:25–31).

Prophecy includes Jesus' prophetic ministry (1 Pet 1:11; Acts 3:21), Israel and gentile rejection and opposition to Jesus (Acts 4:11, 25–27), Jesus' sufferings (1 Pet 1:11; Acts 3:21), Jesus' resurrection (Acts 2:25–29), ascension of Christ (Acts 2:34–35), the need to replace Judas (Acts 1:20–22), the reign of Christ of Davidic throne (Acts 2:30), and the glories of Christ's kingdom (1 Pet 1:11; 2 Pet 1:16–19; Acts 3:21). A prophetic

2. BAG, "λόγικος," 477

3. Jobes, "Got Milk?," *WTJ* 63(2002) 1–14 provides a balanced exhortation for all Christians to intake Scripture and frame our lives by it, rather than emphasizing nursing newly converted Christian intake of word of God as developed by Tite, "Nurslings, Milk and Moral Development," 371–400 developed Hellenistic, *Odes Sol.*, and Qumran metaphors. Also, not an initiation rite of baptism as advocated by Beare, (*1 Peter*, 88), nor Cybele milk initiation nor Isis milk imparting immortality (Kelly, *Peter and Jude*, 85). Peter uses the metaphor differently than Paul's young believers who are still carnal (1 Cor 3:1–2).

4. BAG, prophet related words, 730–31.

statement in Scripture guarantees that it will be fulfilled (Acts 1:16). The Holy Spirit foretold by the mouth of David specific statements that take on divine authority in their oral and written form (Acts 1:20). Such an oral statement might convey what becomes a pre-rabbinic oral tradition before composition or its post written *pesher* application to the new situations, such as replacing the fallen disciple Judas by Matthias.

On the day of Pentecost, Peter claims that the Spirit produced tongues is prophecy (addition to LXX within quote of Acts 2:18 within context). Peter identified that the eschatological revelation that Joel 2:28–32 spoke about as occurring when Israel enters kingdom and is no longer shamed, "is that"[5] revelational prophecy occurring already because believers in Christ already live in eschatological days.

The clarity of the Scripture is assumed by Peter, when properly handled (2 Pet 1:20). No prophecy was ever authored by human will, so no interpretation of a human will can take such prophecy captive to a private interpretation (2 Pet 1:21). So, it is first important to understand prophecy in its context, reassuring Peter that kingdom comes with Christ's powerful coming. This shows that Peter presents these prophetic texts from a *pesher* perspective of eschatological reality with the messiah already beginning to realize aspects of the kingdom (2 Pet 1:16; Acts 2:16, 32–36). Thus, Peter's hermeneutic entails eschatology has begun, and the messiah is revealed, which extends beyond Brownlee's development from 1QpHab *pesher* that eschatology is anticipated prompting Qumran for preparation for a war and the coming messiah.[6] Peter's certainty of fulfilment of prophecy, extends Matthew's development[7] of fulfillment presenting *pesher* as a basis for diligence in peaceful pure living (2 Pet 3:14). Bernard Lindars proposed that this *pesher* provides an apologetic to maintain rabbinic framework to supply a Christian boundary for interpretation like that provided by Qumran, but more extensive because messiah had begun eschatology.[8] The prophesied kingdom is thus not

---

5. τοῦτό ἐστιν τὸ is a statement identifying that they experience the same phenomena as Joel prophesied.

6. Brownlee, "Biblical Interpretation," 54–76; *Midrash Pesher of Habakkuk*, 35–36; Schutter, *Hermeneutic and Composition in 1 Peter*, 117, 168–69.

7. Foundational connections were made by Stendahl, *School of St. Matthew*, 190–201.

8. Lindars, *New Testament Apologetic*, 13–15, 33–74, 251–86 extended Ellis work from Paul to apply it to Peter. In a page Davies and Allison, *Matthew*, 2:787 developed this from Matt 16 to include a central place for Peter.

myth but human epistemic confidence in prophecy can be increased.[9] As aspects of the prophesy become fulfilled, the believer should be motivated to understand, hope in the prophesied, zealously pursuing it (2 Pet 1:3–15; 2:4–9; 3:9, 13–14, 17).

Paul wrote his letters within the wisdom of God and Peter considered that they were also Scripture (2 Pet 3:14–16). Thus, the wisdom of God, as provided by the rest of Scripture, provides a framework through which a person can understand Paul's contributions in his letters. Peter admits that some of Paul's concepts were hard to understand[10] but within this wisdom perspective understanding was possible. Peter provides the interpreter with a hermeneutical guide of eschatology and Jesus as messiah to read Scripture considering the rest of Scripture. Peter intimates what one sees practiced in his statements that the continuity of Scripture provides a framework for what Peter teaches, rather than imposing meaning onto the text. Which means that the untaught and unstable are culpable as they distort these meanings for their own ends. The interpreter must be careful not to let her agenda dominate meaning. Perhaps a good hermeneutical guide is whether the biblical text continues to challenge one's own interpretations, and whether we as interpreters modify our traditions to come in line with the near contextual statement of the word of God. Each chapter will explain the meaning and hermeneutical rationale for the concepts in those chapters.

Additionally, the framework for understanding proper boundaries of interpretation is set out for the apostles in an extension of rabbinic scribal assessment: "loosing" the acceptable, and "binding" excluded teaching and practices (Matt 16:19; 18:18).[11] Davies and Allison identify that "the halakic decisions of the community have the authority of heaven itself."[12] Peter is granted this scribal authority by Jesus, which

---

9. Discussed in Kennard, *Petrine Studies*, chapter on Petrine epistemology.

10. Peter does not develop Paul's Hillel hermeneutic as I developed in Kennard, *Epistemology and Logic*, 141–49.

11. These verses can grammatically be treated as future perfect paraphrastics (what you bind shall have been bound) but the narrative context emphasis on privilege and responsibility makes it more natural to read it as indicating real scribal privilege and responsibility of issuing authoritative *halakah* (teaching), as I have indicated above and this is the early Jewish pattern elsewhere (CD 5.24–25; 1QS 5.24–25; 4Q477 frag. 2.1–2; *m. Naz.* 5.1–4; *y. Jom. Tobb* 60.1; 61.1; *y. Oriah* 61.2; *y. Šabb.* 4.1; 6.1; 16.2, 4; *b. Ḥag.* 10a; *b. Meg.* 26.7; *b. Avodah Zarah* 7.1; 39.2; *b. Ber.* 23.1; *b. Sanh.* 100.1; *Tosaphata in Jevam.* cap. 1; *Pesachin*, cap. 4 hal. 5; *Mamrim*, cap. 1, cap 2; Lightfoot, *Commentary on the New Testament*, 2:237–40).

12. Davies and Allison, *Matthew*, 2:787.

would indicate that Petrine theology sets parameters for the discipleship community (Matt 16:19). Then this framework is expanded to the rest of the apostles, in the context of church discipline (Matt 18:18). Of course, such apostolic tradition can be corrected as Peter was granted the rabbinic right to bind and loose in Matt 16, which make his comments authoritative for the church as an apostolic tradition. This rabbinic apostolic authority was expanded to the other disciples in Matt 18. Peter was immediately incorrect about whether Jesus should go to the cross, which shows that apostolic authority may need to be corrected by more accurate truth, such as the instruction Jesus supplied to the apostles (Matt 16:23). Considering this scribal apostolic authority, a person should not develop her own meaning, by pressing a novel meaning onto a text, nor a meaning advantageous to human concerns to the neglect of divine revealed meaning of the text, for such attempts distort the Scriptures leading to destruction (2 Pet 3:16).

The word γραφὴ means "writing," and Peter uses it of the Scriptures. Books of the OT (such as Pss, Isa, and Lev), especially the LXX version are primarily viewed as Scripture (Acts 1:16, 20; 1 Pet 1:16; 2:6–8). But Paul's letters are also seen by Peter to be included within Scripture (2 Pet 3:16, λοιπὰς as "remaining" or "rest of" Scripture). To misinterpret Paul or Peter is likely to misinterpret some of the rest of the Scripture, since the interpretive framework of Scripture progressively builds through divine revelation.

Peter consciously writes Scripture containing part of the prophetic word (2 Pet 1:3–11; 3:1–2). Peter views his own letters with this scriptural authority, since Peter writes God's grace to his readers with divine authority (1 Pet 5:12). He utilized that divine authority to make this letter required for his readers, "stand firm in it!" Peter has a similar statement of authoritative applicability in his second letter (2 Pet 3:1). Here he writes as a reminder that the authoritative message of the prophets, Jesus Christ, and apostles should guide one's faith and practice, because those who mock the message are certainly condemned by God.

7

Humanity

PETER DOES NOT DISCUSS humanity at length, but he utilized a Hebraic conceptual vocabulary and worldview reflected through Greek terms, as evident by Peter's dependance upon OT quotes and allusions, which imply that each human is a multi-faceted unity in relation with others. This approach is a functionalism (because of the redundant descriptions of holistic humanity in the model), which I call a multifaceted unity (of: image of God [from Gen, James and Paul but not in Peter], soul, spirit, body, heart, mind, will, and conscience). However, the concreteness of especially Hebrew descriptive words could also be appealed to in claiming this model as an ontological model because it describes the way we are from the Hebrew biblical perspective, and so we should think about ourselves in this manner.[1] Thus, this view should be thought as ontological and functionalist both, even though this is a novel way for philosophy to conceive of humanity. However, part of the point of this chapter is to call theology and other human disciplines back to being reconfigured by Peter's Jewish biblical theology. For example, within Christendom there are many views of the nature of the human being. Among the most prominent are two views rooted in Platonism which have had long-standing traditions in Christianity. Dichotomists, following the *Epistle to Diognetus*, make a distinction between the material and

---

1. I suspect if an ancient considered this model he would probably consider it to be ontological metaphysics, especially as it is dependent upon concrete Hebrew expression. He would probably add concepts like clean/unclean, holy/common, and life/death to this metaphysic (whole OT and Pauline model Kennard, *Critical Realist's Theological Method*, 365–408 or Isaiah's expression in *Biblical Theology of Isaiah*, 62–77 combined with *Biblical Covenantalism*, 1:244–314, "Hebrew Metaphysic."

immaterial parts of a human, reflective of Plato's soul and body concepts.[2] Theologians adhering to this view argue that soul and spirit are used interchangeably, whereas trichotomists, following Justin Martyr, point out that soul and spirit are distinct.[3] Such a trichotomy view is reflective of the neo-platonic trichotomy view of spirit, soul, and body. In the twentieth century, additional views of humanity emerged including advocates of a holistic model. In the second half of the twentieth century within the descriptive biblical theology movement a model of the human being as a multifaceted unity gained dominance in the discipline. The near unanimity of biblical theologians embracing this model can be seen by the treatment in the theological wordbooks[4] and by the scholarly descriptions of humanity from specialized biblical theologies,[5] which corroborate these word studies of this chapter.

SOUL

The concept of "soul" is wholistic and connects a human with the rest of the creation. That is, the language of the Genesis account identifies that animals and humans are "living souls" (Gen 1:20, 24, 30; 2:7; 9:4–5, 10).[6] The animals pre-modernly described as souls are non-microbial animals (fish, foul, insect, reptile, amphibian, and mammal). Soul has a holistic connotation in that it signifies a complete living being.[7] The words for "soul," *nephesh* in the Hebrew and *psyche* (ψυχὴν) in the Greek, have developed from the idea of breath to mean the whole person who both

---

2. Mathetes, *Epistle to Diognetus*, 499.

3. Justin Martyr, *Apol.* 1.29; van Kooten, *Paul's Anthropology in Context*, which presents a tripartite model especially philosophically, however on pp. 376–77 the Pauline model is presented as more complex akin to the development in this chapter.

4. Kittel and Friedrich, TDNT; Botterweck and Ringgren, TDOT; Brown, NIDNTT; Harris, Archer, and Waltke, TWOT; VanGemeren, NIDOTE.

5. Dunn, *Theology of Paul*, 51–78; Wolff, *Anthropology of the Old Testament*; Kennard, *Critical Realist's Theological Method*, 365–408; *Biblical Theology of Isaiah*, 62–77.

6. Seebass, TDOT 9:510–16; Jacob, TDNT 9:620, 639–40, 648–49, 653; Fredericks, NIDOTTE 3:133; Waltke, TWOT 2:589–91.

7. Wolff, *Anthropology of the Old Testament*, 24–25; Seebass, TDOT 9:510–16; Jacob, TDNT 9:620, 639–40, 648–49, 653; Fredericks, NIDOTTE 3:133; Waltke, TWOT 2:589–91; Dunn, *Theology of Paul*, 76–78; McKenzie, *Dictionary of the Bible*, 839; Rahner and Vorgrimler, *Theological Dictionary*, 442–43; Cooper, *Body, Soul, & Life Everlasting*, 42–43; Murphy, "Human Nature," 22; and Anderson, "On Being Human," 178, 186; 11QTemple 51.19; 54.20;61.12; 1QS 11.13; CD 12.11–12; 1QH 2.2, 24; 3.6; 5.17–18; 9.18; 15.16.

breathes and desires, lives and moves (1 Pet 3:20; 2 Pet 2:14; Acts 2:23, 27; Exod 23:12; Deut 12:12).[8] "Soul" can actually refer to the person as a pronoun (1 Pet 1:22; 2 Pet 2:8; Mark 8:36–37; 14:34). Very few biblical references develop "soul" as a part of a human,[9] and in those cases it refers to the throat or neck, the organ of breathing (Isa 51:23; Jer 15:9; Luke 2:35).[10] In other places, soul stands in the place of a pronoun, indicating living persons (Ps 54:4; Acts 2:41). At times, especially in the Pss, "soul" in Hebrew has a pronominal suffix "his soul" or "my soul," which in these instances is not a part of a person but akin to "my life" (1 Pet 1:9; Mark 8:36–37; Pss 3:2; 6:3). Peter used the word to convey the idea of "life" beneath these other references (1 Pet 2:25; 4:19; Acts 3:28). At times soul is combined in a list with other human descriptors to communicate that all a person must be involved in a task such as loving God (Mark 12:30, 33; Deut 6:4–5; Matt 22:32; Acts 4:32; 1 Thess 5:23). Only rarely is there a verse like Heb 4:12, which indicates that the word of God can separate between soul and spirit, suggesting the two concepts are not identical.

This biblical concept of soul is very different from the philosophical and traditional theological alternatives. For example, Tertullian followed the Stoics in conceiving of the human soul as corporeal, generated with the body, but departs from them in considering the soul to be depraved by sin and renewed by regeneration.[11] Plato reasons that the soul is an eternal form for each human, which as eternal continues from a pre-incarnate existence to a post-incarnate afterlife, while our shadowy bodies are birthed and then decay.[12] While Origen followed Plato's view of soul,[13] Augustine modified the concept in the direction of Neoplatonism, denying eternal pre-existence and affirming a created tripartite quality of each human soul to reflect the Trinity.[14] In contrast, Aristotle and Aquinas proposed a hylomorphic view in which the material human is formed

---

8. Brown, NIDNTT 3:676 and 679.

9. Wolff, *Anthropology of the Old Testament*, 24–25; Jacob, TDNT 9:620, 639–40, 648–49, 653; Fredericks, NIDOTTE 3:133; Waltke, TWOT 2:589–91; Dunn, *Theology of Paul*, 76–78; Pannenberg, *Anthropology in Theological Perspective*, 523.

10. Dihle and Jacob, TDNT 9:609 and 618.

11. Tertullian, *Treatise on the Soul* 4–5, 10–11, 24, 27, 38, 41, 51; De an. 9 in *Against Praxeas*.

12. Plato, *Phaedr.* 245–47; *Phaed.* 103–5; *Leg.* 10.

13. Origen, *Princ.* 2.9.6.

14. Augustine, *City of God* 7.23, 11.23, 13.2, 19.3, 21.3, 22.4 and *Ep.* 166.27.

as soul.[15] René Descartes proposed a radical form of substance dualism in which the soul is akin to a thinking substance that is the real person within the extended substance of body.[16] Karl Barth identified that body and soul are a "concrete monism," both terms describing the unique and singular experience of the person.[17] Nancey Murphy's challenge excludes the concept of soul from theological discussion by advocating humans as nonreductive physicalism.[18]

SPIRIT

In contrast to soul, spirit does not refer to the person as a whole but rather indicates a facet of her being (1 Pet 3:4; Isa 19:3; Dan 7:15; Zech 12:1). It is that aspect of the person as the seat of actions, relationally oriented to God and other spirit beings (1 Pet 3:4).[19] For example, Isa 19:3 indicates that the Lord in his judgment "demoralizes the spirit" of the Egyptians "within them." The spirit describes some of the same features as "heart" in that a gentle and quiet spirit demonstrates a person's submissiveness, which is highly prized by God. Peter uses this imperishable "spirit" to describe the resurrected life, connecting human resurrection with the spiritual realm of God and angels (1 Pet 3:18; 4:6; Mark 1:23, 26–27; 3:11; 5:2, 8; 12:25).[20] Spirit lives beyond this life (1 Pet 3:18; 4:6; Luke 24:37, 39; 1 Tim 3:16), so death is referred to as giving up the spirit (Mark 15:37, 39; Matt 22:50; Luke 23:46; Acts 7:59).[21]

---

15. Aristotle, *Topics* 4.6; *Metaphysics* 5.8; 7.10; 8.3; 12.5; 13.2 and *Soul* 2.1–3; Thomas Aquinas, *Summa Theologica*, Pt 1, Q 3, Art. 1; Pt 1, Q 18, Art. 3, ans and rep 1; Pt 1, Q 51, Art. ,1 rep. 3; Pt 1, Q 70, Art. 3, ans and rep 2; Pt 1, Q 72, Art. 1, rep 1; Pt 1, Q 75–76; Pt 1, Q 97, Art. 3, ans.

16. Descartes, *Meditations on First Philosophy*, 20, 135–36, 208–9.

17. Barth, *Church Dogmatics*, 3/2:393, 517.

18. Brown et al., *Whatever Happened to the Soul?*, 2, 25, 49–72, 99–148; Murphy, *Bodies and Souls, or Spiritual Bodies?*; "Reductionism"; van Gulick, "Reduction, Emergence." A reverse reductionism to see all through the lens of soul is accomplished by Swinburne in *Evolution of the Soul*. The biblical theology movement does neither.

19. Wolff, *Anthropology of the Old Testament*, 36; Baumgärtel et al., TDNT 6:362–63, 367, 370, 375–76, 396–401; VanPelt et al., NIDOTTE 3:1075–77; Payne, TWOT 2:837; Dunn, *Theology of Paul*, 77; Brown, NIDNTT 3:693–94.

20. Tob 6.6; 2 Macc 3:24; *Jub.* 15.31; *1 En.* 60.11; *T. Dan.* 1.7; 5.5; 1 ZS 3.17; 1QM 12.8; 13.10.

21. VanPelt et al., NIDOTTE 3:1074–75.

Several philosophers and theologians conceive of the traditional concept of spirit to be identical to that of soul, often in a dichotomy of spirit or soul and body. For example, Tertullian followed the Stoics in conceiving of the human spirit as corporeal, generated with the body.[22] Plato reasons that the spirit is an eternal form for each human, which as eternal continues from a pre-incarnate existence to a post-incarnate afterlife, while our shadowy bodies are birthed and then decay.[23] While Origen followed Plato's view of spirit,[24] Augustine modified the concept in the direction of Neoplatonism, denying eternal pre-existence and affirming a created tripartite quality of each human spirit or mind to reflect the Trinity.[25] In contrast, Aquinas proposed a hylomorphic view in which the material human is formed as soul which constitutes a spiritual and immortal aspect of life.[26] René Descartes proposed a radical form of substance dualism in which the spirit is akin to a thinking substance that is the real person within the extended substance of body.[27] Paul Tillich conceived of human spirit as an existential fifth dimension extending an Einstinian relativistic metaphysic (of space/time dimensions), which human existence participates along with God.[28] This view permits receiving consciousness and revelation from beyond oneself within the spirit milieu. Wolfhart Pannenberg metaphorically illustrated this relationship of spirit in God and in humanity through Michael Faraday's universal force field which relate the effect of electricity on another dimension, that of magnetism.[29] Many of these views are foreign to the biblical text, though Tillich's and Pannenberg's metaphors may have some relevance if corralled back in ontological and functional directions to reflect the biblical ideas, though complex scientific metaphors may put most people off rather than be an aid to relate significance.

---

22. Tertullian, *De an.* 9 in *Against Praxeas*.

23. Plato, *Crat.* 399–401; *Phaedr.* 245–51; *Min.* 79–83; *Phaed.* 114–18; *Tim.* 40–46.

24. Origen, *Princ.* 2.9.6.

25. Augustine, *City of God* 8.16; 19.

26. Aquinas, *Summa Theologica*, Pt 1, Q 29, Art. 1, rep 5; Pt 1, Q, 75, Art. 4; Pt 1, Q 76, Art. 1, ans; Pt 1, Q 118, Art. 3, ans; Pt 3, Suppl. 79, Art. 1, ans and rep 4.

27. Descartes, *Meditations on First Philosophy*.

28. Tillich, *Systematic Theology*, 3:15–30, 111–61, 297–423.

29. Pannenberg, *Systematic Theology*, 1:382–84; I think the universal ambiguity of Faraday works in Pannenberg's favor of this metaphor rather than extending it to the specificity of Maxwell's equations.

The Hebrew and Greek words for "spirit" (*ruah* and πνεῦμα) refer to air in motion, which one cannot see but one can see its effect (Acts 2:2, 4, 17; Exod 14:21; John 3:6, 8).[30] However, most of Peter's use of "spirit" is of the divine Holy Spirit. This preponderance of uses emphasizes a dimension of existence that is not normally considered, for clearly God and the angels act within the visible world (Acts 12:8–10; 2 Kgs 6:16–17; Dan 10:20–21).[31] At times, this spirit ontological dimension appears in the visible world somewhat like a three-dimensional sphere penetrating a two-dimensional flatland.[32] This actual dimensional spirit goes deeper than the existential dimensionalism by which Tillich described the realm of the spirit. The uninitiated may not be sensitive to spirit presence or be able to explain spirit nature while those who lift their eyes from the four-dimensional world of space and time will find a whole realm racing with activity that affects human existence at every turn. Therefore, since God is spirit, an individual must be spiritually alive to relate to him. Thus, spirit is that avenue through which God and demons encounter the person and through which the individual is most open and responsive to God (1 Pet 3:4; Matt 5:3; Luke 1:45; Rom 1:9; 1 Cor 7:34). James Dunn further delineates the relational aspect of spirit in contrast to philosophical and theological misconceptions.

> The New Testament writers can speak of the (human) spirit as though it was a something possessed by the individual; but this does not mean that they envisioned the spirit of man as a divine spark (the real "I") incarcerated in the physical, "the ghost in the machine" (an anthropology more typical of Greek philosophy). This language is more likely to be simply a natural and easy way of speaking about man in his belongingness to the spiritual realm, the power he experiences in him which relates him to beyond, "the dimension of the beyond in the midst."[33]

Everyone is responsible for diligence in utilizing the knowledge and faith God has given him (2 Pet 1:1, 3–5; John 3:16–18). The combined

---

30. Wolff, *Anthropology of the Old Testament*, 32–33; Kleinknecht et al., TDNT 6:334–35, 360, 368; Payne, TWOT 2:831; Kamlah, NIDNTT 3:690–91.

31. Wolff, *Anthropology of the Old Testament*, 36; Baumgärtel et al., TDNT 6:362–63, 367, 370, 375–76, 396–401; VanPelt et al., NIDOTTE 3:1075–77; Payne, TWOT 2:837; Dunn, *Theology of Paul*, 77; Brown, NIDNTT 3:693–94.

32. Abbot, *Flatland*, v. 68–78, 93–94, 97–100; Tillich, *Systematic Theology*, 3:15–30, 111–61, 297–423.

33. Dunn, NIDNTT 3:694.

effect of the Holy Spirit's agency and the individual's responsibility brings about new birth (1 Pet 1:10-12, 22-25; John 3:3-8). If a person is a knower and believer of some salvific truth, he must work diligently to increase his knowledge and faith, along with other qualities such as goodness, self-control, and perseverance, in order to provide assurance of his eschatological salvation (2 Pet 1:5-11). However, if such a person does not diligently increase these qualities, then he is doubly blind and may be condemned (2 Pet 1:9; 2:1, 18-22; Acts 1:16-20; 8:12, 24). All those chosen by God will not only continue within God's protecting power, but already have their eschatological salvation prepared for them (1 Pet 1:2-5).

BODY

The body describes a human in the physical dimensions and in relationship to others. Plato considered that humans are pure spirit utilizing a body for their existence in world of shadows.[34] Origen and Augustine followed Plato's view of spirit, but they modified the concept of body and things in the direction of affirming creation of bodies as a good, accomplished by the creative act of God.[35] Reflective of his Aristotelianism, Aquinas proposed a hylomorphic view in which the material human is formed as soul, utilizing a body for the person's connectiveness to the world.[36] René Descartes proposed a radical form of substance dualism in which the spirit is akin to a thinking substance that is the real person within the extended substance of body.[37] In contrast, Nancey Murphy, Warren Brown, and Elving Anderson advocate a nonreductive physicalism that considers humans as a "whole complex function, both in society and in relation to God, which gives rise to 'higher' human capacities such as morality and spirituality."[38] However, biblical literature presents a

---

34. Plato, *Phaedr.* 245-50; *Min.* 79-82; *Phaed.* 77-78; 114-15; *Tim.* 40-45.

35. Origen, *De Princ.* 2.9.6; Augustine, *City of God* 8.16; 19.

36. Aquinas, *Summa Theologica*, Pt 1, Q 29, Art. 1, rep 5; Pt 1, Q 75, Art. 4; Pt 1, Q 76, Art. 1, ans; Pt 1, Q 118, Art. 3, ans; 3; Suppl. 79, Art. 1, ans and rep 4.

37. Descartes, *Meditations on First Philosophy*.

38. Brown et al., *Whatever Happened to the Soul?*, 2, 25, 49-72, 99-148; Murphy, *Bodies and Souls, or Spiritual Bodies?*.

balance between these extreme views which see body as either "the totality of man from every aspect,"³⁹ or reduce it to solely the material.⁴⁰

The biblical words for "body" used in the OT and NT reflect that "body" describes a human in the physical dimensions and in relationship to others. For example, Rudolf Bultmann and the descriptive biblical theology movement emphasize that the concept of "body" is holistic of the human person; "man does not have a *sōma*; he is *sōma*."⁴¹ The Hebrew *bśr* is within Ps 16:8-9 quoted by Peter as σάρκα in Acts 2:26 to describe the whole person. In this respect it functions like "soul" to describe the whole person, who rejoices (Acts 2:27). This wholistic concept of σάρκα contains humans within a relationship to all of humanity and life (1 Pet 1:24; Acts 2:17). Death is experienced at the close of earthly life (σάρκα, 1 Pet 3:18; 4:1, 6). Peter primarily utilized σάρκα in a positive wholistic manner as a participant within humanity. Peter also uses σῶμα wholistically to refer to Jesus' body on the cross (1 Pet 2:24). Peter used "tent" to describe one's visible body, especially in its temporary brevity of earthly life, so it sets up Peter's imminent death and exodus theme (2 Pet 1:13-15; like 2 Cor 5:3-4).

In addition, usage of these words indicate that the body contacts its environment and others through various members: the hand acts (Acts 2:23), speaking with the mouth and tongue (1 Pet 2:22; 3:10; Acts 1:16; 2:25; 3:18, 21; 4:25), and empirically seeing with the eye (1 Pet 3:12; 2 Pet 2:14). Peter used "walking" to describe locomotion (1 Pet 5:8) but his emphasis described a moral manner of life (1 Pet 4:3; 2 Pet 2:10; 3:3). To describe false teachers, σάρκα describes "fleshly desires" of non-submission and sensuality (2 Pet 2:10, 18; like Rom 7:5; 8:4-7; Gal 5:19-21; Jude 7).

HEART

The most emphasized concept of biblical anthropology is "heart" (*lb* and καρδία), which stands wholistically for a person thinking and feeling.⁴²

39. Dahl, *Resurrection of the Body*, 121-26.
40. Gundry, *Soma in Biblical Theology*, 156.
41. Bultmann, *Theology of the New Testament*, 1:194; Wolff, *Anthropology of the Old Testament*, 28-29; Bratsiotis, TDOT 2:318, 323-31, esp. 325-28; Baumgärtel et al., TDNT 7:1056, 1058, 1111; Oswalt, TWOT 1:136; Chisholm, NIDOTTE 1:777-78; Dunn, *Theology of Paul*, 56-61; Motyer, NIDNTT 1:233-38; Conzelmann, *Die Kleineren Briefe des Apostels Paulus*, 8:137; Robinson, *Body*.
42. Wolff, *Anthropology of the Old Testament*, 40, 44-55; Baumgärtel et al., TDNT 3:607, 611-13; 9:626-27; Lac, NIDOTTE 2:749; Bowling, TWOT 1:466-67; Song, NIDNTT 2:181-82; McDonald, *Christian View of Man*, 24-25; Calvin, *Calvin's*

Peter cites Ps 16:8–9 in Acts 2:26, translating the Hebrew *lb* with καρδία to indicate the whole person, who is glad. T. Song identifies "*Leb* means less an isolated function than the man with all his urges, in short, the person in its totality (Ps 22:26; 73:26; 84:2)."[43] Walter Eichrodt echoed this sentiment that the heart is "a comprehensive term for the personality, its inner life, its character. It is the conscious and deliberate spiritual activity of the self-contained human ego."[44] Thus, the hidden person of the heart effects all that the person is about (1 Pet 3:4). The heart contains the function of reason (Mark 2:6, 8). Heart fosters morality so evil comes out from a person's heart (Mark 7:21). Sin is conceived in the heart whether Satan fills the heart with deception or the human choses on her own (Acts 5:3–4; 8:22). False teachers have their hearts trained in greed (2 Pet 2:14). Jesus is aware and grieves at a person's heart that is hard or far from Jesus' concerns (Mark 6:52; 7:6). God knows the heart of all humans and can make sovereign decisions with intimate knowledge of the person (Acts 1:24). Jesus scatters the message of the kingdom into the hearts of those who hear him, but Satan can take the message out of her unresponsive heart (Mark 4:15). The heart is divinely cleansed by God when a person believes, enabling her to obey God (Acts 15:9). When the heart rejoices, the whole person rejoices (Acts 2:26).[45] When commands are made that effect the believer's whole being, they include the heart (1 Pet 1:22; 3:4, 15). The believer should not doubt but believe and love from her heart (Mark 11:23; 12:30, 33). Jesus Christ is to rule over a believer's heart, which enables the believer to boldly speak about salvation and do good for others (1 Pet 3:15). When the believer sees the kingdom and Christ's second coming approaching, she should have an increased confidence in the whole of her being, the heart (2 Pet 1:19).

MIND

Philosophical and theological discussions about mind-body relationship between the extremes of Hobbes' materialism[46] and Berkeley's idealism[47]

Commentaries on Deut 29:4; Isa 51:7; Matt 14:24; John 12:40; Rom 2:15; Eph 1:16; 1 Thess 3:13; and Sermon No. 45 on Deut 4:22.

43. Song, NIDNTT 2:181.
44. Eichrodt, *Theology of the Old Testament*, 2:143.
45. Dunn, *Theology of Paul*, 74–75.
46. Hobbes, *Leviathan*.
47. Berkeley, *Human Knowledge* sect 18–20, 50.

would include those who try to relate mind and body. Plato advocated a noninteractive parallelism between mind and body⁴⁸ that is modified by some others, such as Augustine into a divine illuminational occasionalism.⁴⁹ Descartes considered that the mind and body interact on each other.⁵⁰ In contemporary Christianity, Nancey Murphy, Warren Brown, Elving Anderson, and Robert Van Gulick advocate a nonreductive physicalism that considers humans as a "whole complex function, both in society and in relation to God, which gives rise to "higher" human capacities such as morality and spirituality."⁵¹ Other forms of materialism propose different mechanisms. In contrast, Kennard aligns with Tillich in identifying that the mind can follow the spirit into being conceived of as a different dimension that overlappingly interacts with the body.⁵² Additionally, there are a wide variety of functionalisms, where different kinds of constructs yield the same mental event.

Biblically, "mind," more than any other concept is referred to by a number of words which carry approximately the same meaning, including Διανοίας, οἶδά, γινώσκω, and ἐπιγνώσκω.⁵³ They are usually used to describe how people think or commands about how they should think. Mind explores the generation of consciousness in relation to others. The scope includes thought, understanding, assessment, intent and purpose (1 Pet 1:13; Luke 1:51; Acts 20:3; 28:22; 1 Cor 1:10; 7:25, 40; 13:11; Eph 1:18; Heb 4:12; 1 John 5:20; Rev 17:13, 17). Peter used μνησθῆναι and ἀνεμνήσθη to indicate remembering previous information (2 Pet 3:2; Mark 14:72). Sober diligence with insight and purpose is described by ἔννοιαν (1 Pet 4:1). Believers are to be of one mind or harmonious (ὁμόφρονες, 1 Pet 3:8). When a demoniac is made well, they returned to

---

48. Plato, *Timaeus*.

49. Augustine, *Enarrations on the Psalms*, 118; *De peccatorum meritis et remissione et de baptismo parvulorum* 1.25.38; *City of God* 10.2. The medieval church tends to appreciate platonic illuminationism following Augustine until Aristotelian sensibility wins out in the wake of Aquinas.

50. Descartes, *Discourse* 5 and 6, *Meditations* 6, and *Objections and Replies*.

51. Brown et al., *Whatever Happened to the Soul?*, 2, 25, 49–72, 99–148; Murphy, *Bodies and Souls, or Spiritual Bodies?*; "Reductionism," 19–39; van Gulick, "Reduction, Emergence," 40–73.

52. Tillich, *Systematic Theology*, 3:15–30, 111–61, 297–423; Kennard, *Critical Realist's Theological Method*, 403–6: *Biblical Theology of Isaiah*, 74–76.

53. Gilchrist and Wilson, TWOT 1:366, 2:580; Dunn, *Theology of Paul*, 73–74; Goetzmann, NIDNTT 2:616–20; McDonald, *Christian View of Man*, 24–25; Kennard, *Epistemology and Logic*, 121–27.

a sound mind (σωφρονοῦντα, Mark 5:15). The chapter on epistemology explores the range of Petrine knowing within mind.[54]

WILL

One of the subcategories of mind is will. The human will is a mental capacity involved in choice.[55] Greek θέλω suggest desire, purpose, and choice (2 Pet 1:21; Mark 15:14; Acts 12:4; 1 Tim 2:8; Jas 4:4). This suggests that choices made by God or man are authentic in nature and cause events to occur (Acts 2:23). Lived out in daily activity, will is the self's awareness of his responsibility for actions. Self as will plans and initiates responses to her environment.

CONSCIENCE

"Conscience" refers to a second subcategory of mind, entailing a person's fallible personal self-assessment. The Old Testament does not develop a word for self-judgment; God's judgment of human actions through his word comes closest to the NT concept of conscience (Pss 51:10; 119). Emerging through classical Greek, the word for conscience (συνειδήσεως) conveys awareness of personal thought and behavior.[56] In contrast to an external standard or law, conscience is subjective in its assessment of self's attitudes and behaviors (Acts 5:2; 12:12; 14:16; 23:1; Rom 2:15; 2 Cor 4:2). Conscience is not the ultimate standard; God is. Therefore, conscience should not be equated with divine assessment. Due to the human condition, conscience can accuse falsely and result in unfounded psychological guilt. This occurs because conscience can be shaped to be more restrictive or permissive. As the believer re-educates the conscience, it can affirm her godly living. The New Testament concept includes the idea of having a good conscience, in contrast to the classical Greek concept which almost exclusively condemns (1 Pet 3:16, 21; Acts 23:1; 1 Tim 1:4, 19).[57] Peter emphasized that a good conscience is possible for a believer

---

54. Kennard, *Petrine Studies*, chapter on Petrine epistemology and *Epistemology and Logic*, 121–27.

55. Brown, NIDNTT 3:1015; Schrenk, TDNT 3:44–47; Coppes, TWOT 1:4.

56. Brown, NIDNTT 1:349; Friedrich, TDNT 7:904–5; Pierce, *Conscience in the New Testament*; McDonald, *Christian View of Man*, 16–19.

57. Maurer, "συνειδήσις," TDNT 7:907; Hahn, "Conscience," NIDNTT 1:348; Marshall, *Pastoral Epistles*, 217; good conscience also appears in Philo, *Praem.* 79–84; *Spec.*

who is consistently diligent in striving to maintain a good conscience (1 Pet 2:19; 3:16, 21). In fact, an aspect of baptism is a pledge to pursue a good conscience (1 Pet 3:21), that is, a commitment to live obediently, serving God because Christ has been raised. As the commitment to right living finds fruition in one's life, conscience ceases to condemn. Therefore, a good conscience is important for all believers but is essential for Christian leaders.

RELATIONSHIP WITHIN HUMANITY

Humans live in relationship with other humans, and many of the descriptions of humans mentioned so far identify aspects of these relationships. This relation in Peter is a communal commonsense realist social construct that reflects reality and makes sense of it to those who live it.[58] Peter tries to locate human groups to make sense of their fit in this reality. This includes biography and their roles in "an ordering of experience" that is justified and maintained so that one can live within it.[59] Peter achieves this through a symbolic "all-embracing frame of reference"[60] that extends Israel's covenantal framework in the world into a new covenant framework for the church, though Christians must still try to function within first-century Roman constructs, such as their resident alien status.[61]

In Peter's thinking, all humans are either Jewish or gentile, but a new group is emerging which draws from both, those who are believers in Christ. This new group will be discussed in the chapter on the household of God. Peter Davids summarized Peter's view of rebellious Greco-Roman culture.

Laws 1.203; Josephus, *War* 2.582.

58. Using the communal commonsense realist nuance like Plantinga, *Warrant and Proper Function* and *Knowledge and Christian Belief* framing his social constructions rather than the individualist post-Kantian and post-Hegelian dialectic of Berger and Luckmann, *Social Construction of Reality* but applied to positive communal religious concerns by Berger, *Social Reality of Religion* rather than the negative "world" concern applied to Paul by Adams, *Constructing the World*, though the concept of "socio-political alien" and Christian among Judaism or Roman culture would fit Adam's emphasis.

59. Berger, *Social Reality of Religion*, 19 and 29–52; Kennard, *Petrine Studies*, chapters on "The Recipients of the Petrine Letters," and "A Man Called Peter."

60. Symbolism reflective of Berger and Luckmann, *Social Construction of Reality*, 114 within "worldview" construction of 110–46.

61. Developed in Kennard, *Petrine Studies*, chapter on Recipients.

> That culture is "ignorant" (1:14), the nonbelievers are not God's people (2:10) but like sheep going astray (2:25), and pagans live in a "flood of debauchery" (4:3–4). In other words, Peter has nothing positive to say about the culture and life-style of the non-Christian world. His is clearly a "Christ against culture" type of relationship.[62]

While Richard Niebuhr's category of "Christ against culture" has a place in describing the Christian's understanding of the Greco-Roman world surrounding the Christian[63] it does not describe the church's purpose within the world, which is more of a conversionist model as described by Edward Adams.

> For the *conversionist* sect, the world is evil because human beings are corrupt. To be saved human beings must be personally transformed, that is to say, they must undergo a powerful experience of conversion. What is looked for is a change in the heart of individuals, not a change in the objective world (though it is often posited that at some future time objective reality will change to match the subjective sense of salvation).[64]

This "sect" typology appropriated by Adams from R. B. Wilson is helpful to orient minority communities, such as the first-century church; however, it doesn't orient all of society.[65] While Adams used Pauline vocabulary, he more accurately describes Peter's church engagement with the world, as the redeemed Christian of the elect church follows the narrow way of the new exodus unto kingdom salvation, with the possibility of winning some to join them in kingdom.

In Petrine theology, this conversionist model of the church converting part of the Greco-Roman world (1 Pet 2:15; 3:1, 16) was developed especially by John Elliott in a conversation in the literature with David Balch, who argued instead that the church must assimilate to the broader Hellenistic culture to diminish the possibility of them suffering under persecution as the other (a Niebuhrian Christ of culture model).

The unbelieving Jews of Israel in the first century are seen by Peter as guilty of the death of Christ (Acts 2:23, 36; 3:14–15; 4:10; 5:28). This

---

62. Davids, *1 Peter*, 21.

63. Niebuhr, *Christ and Culture*.

64. Adams, *Constructing the World*, 8–9 explains Wilson's category from *Magic and the Millennium*.

65. Critiques made by: Wilson, *Magic and the Millennium*, 27; Adams, *Constructing the World*, 11–12; Horrell, *Social Ethos of the Corinthian Correspondence*, 24–25.

does not present racial antisemitism because Peter is also Jewish but a recognition that in the first half of the first century Jews occupied a perverse generation in rebellion against God (Acts 2:40). This rebellion is evident even more in that the Roman Procurator Pilate wished to release Jesus when the hard-hearted Jewish leadership were set to see him die (Acts 3:13–15). The first-century Jewish sin of killing Christ is emphasized by God reversing it through Christ's resurrection (Acts 4:10). Jesus Christ had been sent to turn them from their wicked ways (Acts 3:26). These Jews were not beyond hope, for while they had participated in the death of Christ, they were ignorant of Jesus significance (Acts 3:17). In ignorance, it was not a high hand sin, but they still needed to repent (Acts 2:38; 3:19). Repentant Jews were welcomed among the new believers in Christ (Acts 2:38–47; 4:32–37). To not repent would exclude them from the remnant who were being gathered for the new exodus to experience the blessing of the Abrahamic covenant, and thus would render them guilty of the Mosaic covenant (Acts 3:22–23, 25–26). Such a position would ultimately bring condemnation upon any unbelieving Jew. The church was not to assimilate to this Jewish rebellion but follow Christ unto kingdom.

There is even less said concerning the gentiles' involvement in sin, though there were some "without the Jewish Law," such as Pilate and Roman soldiers, who were involved in crucifying Christ, and thus guilty (Acts 2:23). The character of Greco-Roman society that Peter's readers lived among had classic gentile vices, namely sensuality, lusts, drunkenness, carousals, drinking parties, and abominable idolatries (1 Pet 4:3). Peter describes this gentile lifestyle as a futile one of lusts inherited from their forefathers (1 Pet 1:14, 18). When the gentile is redeemed by Christ, becoming a Christian, the change from this lifestyle surprised his fellow gentiles in believing gentiles departing from assimilation to Hellenism culture by no longer running with them in these sins (1 Pet 4:4). This indicates that gentile involvement in sin was cause enough to consider all gentiles guilty in sin. Furthermore, since salvation was available through Christ (Acts 4:12), and gentiles came to salvation and the new community of the church in the same manner as the believing Jewish person did (Acts 10:1—11:18; 15:7–11), it was reasonable to view the unbelieving gentile as heading for condemnation. When discussing the certain condemnation of false teachers, Peter utilized illustrations of past condemnations of gentiles in their sin (2 Pet 2:5–9).

Lusts that were expressed through these sins have brought physical death into the world (2 Pet 1:4). This physical death is characterized by corruption that can occur for unreasoning animals (2 Pet 2:5–6, 9, 12, 19). The result of destruction is further implied by the context of Ps 2 (Acts 4:25–28), and that salvation as only available in Christ (Acts 4:12). The implication is that all outside of Christ shall be condemned. Peter does not develop other results of sin for the one who has never believed. However, for those who have believed and then rejected Christ, there is much that Peter says concerning both their sin and their condemnation, as will be developed in the chapter of false teachers. This condemnation of corruption is removed for the believer in salvation. God has provided the believer an incorruptible life, inheritance, and attitude (1 Pet 1:4, 23; 3:4).

The recipients of Peter's letters were a mixed group of Jewish and gentile believers.[66] God redeemed them to become obedient children, but they had been characterized by former lusts (1 Pet 1:14; 2:10; 4:2–4). Such a sinful life is identified with the need for Christ's death to redeem them and the new exodus way to lead them to kingdom salvation. They were continually straying like sheep in their sin, but Christ died for their sin and as the Prince of life leads his followers through a covenantal new exodus to kingdom (1 Pet 2:24–25; 2 Pet 1:3–11; Acts 3:15–26).

Peter writes to believers who live within the patriarchy and feudalism of first-century Roman society, and in his first letter several are vulnerable temporary residents. This raises an important discussion beginning in 1981 with two groundbreaking monographs on 1 Pet. John Elliott set out an ethic for the vulnerable temporary resident believer in Christ, that is funded by his need to do good and perhaps to sacrifice among a corporate priesthood scattered in the community to remove any feature that might antagonize patrons in their lives, and to perhaps win a few converting to Christ by the believer expressing attractive good deeds and integrity (1 Pet 2–3).[67] In the same year, David Balch positioned the domestic code (1 Pet 3:1–7) as within the Greco-Roman pattern of house codes, so that the Christian community might survive among a dominant culture.[68] Part of the issue is does Peter define "good" and "righteousness" by a subjective standard of Hellenistic assimilation to thus not be viewed as the "other" by doing what Hellenism expects through the house codes in order to remove persecution. Rather, Peter defines "good" as qualities evident in works of benefit and generosity (1 Pet 2:12, 18; 3:11). In fact, counter to Hellenistic culture, which permitted those in power to abuse

---

66. Kennard, *Petrine Studies*, chapter on Recipients.
67. Elliott, *Home for the Homeless*.
68. Balch, *Let Wives Be Submissive*.

those under their care, Peter advocates maintaining a good conscience (1 Pet 3:16, 21). Peter models Christian goodness after the traits of God, Jesus, and perhaps caring elders who shepherd the church (1 Pet 4:10; Mark 10:17-18). Likewise, "righteous" may be defined by Peter as that trait of behaving according to the Law (1 Pet 3:12; Mark 2:17). Again, Jesus excels as Peter's model of righteousness in doing good, though Lot's hospitality is righteous as well (1 Pet 2:21-24; 3:18; 2 Pet 2:8-9; Gen 18:28; 19:3, 16). The positions Peter expressed in 1 Pet 2–3 do fit the feudal and patriarchal patterns of Greco-Roman house codes, with very few additional comments, so that the particulars of the ethic expressed reflect the dominant Greco-Roman culture, but that is not what renders them appropriate.[69] Appropriateness in Peter is indicated by God's pleasure, not the culture's (1 Pet 2:15, 19-20). That is, Peter modifies the house code, not developing masters, nor fathers because Peter is working with the underclasses, and Peter develops the wife more than the husband and focused on inner qualities more than female adornments, thus resisting Hellenic patterns to which Balch claims Peter is orienting.[70] John Elliott argued that there were clear distinctions between the Church and the Hellenistic world.

> Nothing in 1 Peter, including its discussion of household duties, indicates an interest in promoting social assimilation. It was precisely a temptation to assimilate so as to avoid further suffering that the letter intended to counteract . . . The letter affirms the distinctive communal identity and seeks to strengthen the

---

69. Elliott, "1 Peter, Its Situation and Strategy," 62-63; Christensen, "Balch/Elliott Debate," 173-93; Weidinger, *Die Haustetafeld*; Schrange, "Zur Ethik der NT Haustafeln," 1-22; Hartman, "Some Unorthodox Thoughts," 219-34; Towner, "Households and Household Codes," 417-19.

70. Full house code treatments include Husband/wife, father/children, and master/slave relations much like in early Judaism (Philo, *Decal.* 165-67; *Spec. Laws* 2.225-27; *Hypoth.* 7.14; Josephus, *Ag. Ap.* 2.199-217) and Christianity (Eph 5:22—6:9; Col 3:18—4:1; Titus 2:2-10; *1 Clem.* 1.3; 21.6-89; *Did.* 4.9-11; *Barn.* 19.5-7; Polycarp, *Phil.* 4.2-3; Ign. *Pol.* 4.1-3), which reflect Hellenistic house codes (Aristotle, *Pol.* 1.2.1; Musonius Rufus, 8; Arius Didymus, *Epit.* 2.7.11d; Christensen, "Balch/Elliott Debate," 173-93), except Peter completely ignores father/children and master relations, and develops the wife more than the husband and focused on inner qualities more than female adornments, thus resisting Hellenism (1 Pet 3:3-4; contra: Clement of Alexandria, *Paed.* 3.11.66; Tertullian, *Or.* 20; *Cor.* 14; *Cult. fem.* 1.6; 2.2.7-14; Cyprian, *Hab. Virg.* 8; Valerius, *Fac. Dict.* 9.1.3; Elliott, "1 Peter, Its Situation and Strategy," 61-78, esp. 65, 68, 70-71; Balch, "Early Christian Criticism," 161-73; "Hellenization/Acculturation in 1 Peter," 79-101; Horrell, "Between Conformity and Resistance," 111-43 following a strategy argued by Scott, *Weapons of the Weak* and *Domination and the Arts of Resistance*; Harland, *Associations, Synagogues, and Congregations*, 195).

solidarity of the Christian brotherhood so that it might resist external pressure urging cultural conformity and thereby making effective witness to the distinctive features of a communal life, its allegiance and its hope of salvation.[71]

As such, Peter emphasized a good conscience is possible for a believer who is consistently diligent in striving to maintain a good conscience (1 Pet 2:19; 3:16, 21), in contrast to the Hellenistic concept of "conscience" which almost exclusively condemns (1 Pet 3:16, 21; Acts 23:1; 1 Tim 1:4, 19).[72] So, Peter's new covenant internalism is a different motivation and strategy for negotiating through the Hellenistic culture than Hellenism encourages, contrary to Balch.

Another issue in the Hellenistic literature is the issue of honor and shame. Philo advocated that in Hellenistic culture, honor was a primary concern, "wealth, fame, official posts, honor, and everything of that sort are the concerns with which the majority of humanity is busy."[73] Plutarch concurred that striving for honor is that which separates humans from animals but goes further reflecting Hellenist culture in claiming that such striving for honor brings us close to the gods.[74] In striving for honor, one should do everything to avoid shame (Prov 10:5; 18:3).[75] Peter encourages his audience to give honor to all men especially those in authority, such as the king (1 Pet 2:17), and a Christian wife should be granted honor as a fellow heir of the grace of life (1 Pet 3:7). Likewise, Peter considered that despising of angelic authorities was a foolish trait of false teachers not granting appropriate honor (2 Pet 2:10–11). However, Peter does not encourage believers in Christ to seek their own honor contrary to the Hellenistic values but following Christ's narrow way Christians should seek to serve others, which in Hellenism would be a demeaning task but in Christ shows true greatness (Mark 10:35–45). While Peter denigrates the seeking of honor from Hellenistic society, he values the honor that God provides at the second coming of Christ for those who continue with tested faith (1 Pet 1:7). Likewise, Peter recognized that persecution

---

71. Elliott, "1 Peter, Its Situation and Strategy," 72–73, 78.

72. Maurer, "συνείδησις," TDNT 7:907; Hahn, "Conscience," NIDNTT 1:348; Marshall, *Pastoral Epistles*, 217; good conscience also appears in Philo, *Praem.* 79–84; *Spec. Laws* 1.203; Josephus, *War* 2.582.

73. Philo, *Abr.* 264.

74. Plutarch, *Who Is the Heir?* 7.3; Dio Chrysostom, *Orat.* 31.37; Isocrates, *Philippus* 134; Campbell, *Honour, Family, and Patronage*, 148.

75. Sir 42.17, 19; Plutarch, *Orat.* 76.4.

of Christians was a cultural dishonor, but it was overshadowed by God's election, adoption, and honoring believers as valued precious stones in God's church now, with eschatological honor to come at Christ's return (1 Pet 2:4–10; 1:7).[76]

Though patriarchy, feudalism, and honor culture are ubiquitous in first century Roman society, Peter's observed ethic fits within his culture but does not advocate this culture. This dissonance raises important concerns, such as how transferable this ethic is to other cultures which are not feudal or patriarchal. It probably means that Peter is not advocating feudalism and patriarchy as universal norms. If Balch's approach is preferred, then the ethic in relationships might be discussed here in a Petrine theology but could be discussed within church as a reminder for believers to maintain contact with society so that they might survive misunderstandings and persecutions. Clarifying Balch, Christianity should not frame itself in manners which society would consider stupid, such as an antivax movement. The fact that Peter discussed internal virtue, good conscience, and sacrifice that could be personally detrimental but could be evaluated by God and the eschatological judgment indicates that Elliott's strategy is more on target in this passage (1 Pet 2:15, 20–21; 3:1, 15–16). Additionally, the rare development of a Christian rationale as fellow heir and effective prayer for husband privilege extends beyond normal house code development within patriarchy, indicating Elliott's development reflects Peter more accurately (1 Pet 3:7). If Elliott's approach of polite resistance as a distinctive community imitating Jesus and motivated by hope to possibly win some to Christ has warrant, then it should be an outgrowth of a church ethic, so primary discussion of these church/society issues occurs within the chapter on "The Household of God" because the expressed rationale frames the orientation for the vulnerable church, living within a feudal and patriarchal Hellenistic culture. The two purpose statements for the household of God provides the framework for evaluating the Christian's relationship within society, namely, is the purpose of evangelism, with testimony and worship, and good deeds being maintained? To maintain these purposes might argue for different practices in a different culture, and Peter expressed what that ethic was in first-century Greco-Roman society for a vulnerable minority population.

Broadly Peter called for believers to understand their culture and to be humble peacemakers, doing good in society (1 Pet 3:8–12). As

---

76. Elliott, *Conflict, Community, and Honor*, 51–80.

such, Peter calls believers to honor all humans (1 Pet 2:17). As Christians excel in this calling some from society might be converted to Christ and kingdom.

8

Christ's Vicarious New Covenant Atonement, Sanctification, Purification, and Redemption

IN PETRINE EPISTLES, CHRIST'S atonement is compared to the corporate atonement pattern of Moses' initial cleansing of the people and tabernacle, which is reflected in the Day of Atonement and Isaiah's servant song (1 Pet 1:2, 18–19; 2:22–24; 2 Pet 2:1; Exod 24; Lev 16; Isa 52:13—53:12; Heb 9:1–28). Like these events, Christ's sacrifice accomplished vicarious corporate atonement for the group in establishing sanctification to be holy and cleansed. Everlasting forgiveness and a life-transforming redemption initiate the new exodus toward kingdom. Jesus' vicarious atonement is further set as a pattern by which the Christian follows Christ in mimetic atonement unto kingdom salvation (1 Pet 2:19–23; 1:6–9; Mark 8:34–38; 10:33–45).[1]

MOSAIC SACRIFICE CONTEXT AS PATTERN FOR PETRINE SANCTIFICATION AND PURIFICATION

In the Mosaic covenant context, sin is divided into unintentional sins where atonement is available (Lev 4:2: 5:1, 15, 20–23; Num 15:27, 29;

---

1. Mimetic atonement is where an example sets a pattern to emulate. Such a view was common in early Judaism and Greco-Roman literature (Pate and Kennard, *Deliverance Now and Not Yet*, 22–71; 2 Macc 6:18–17.42; 4 Macc 10:10; 11:12, 20, 27; 16:24–25; 17:2, 11–12, 18; Wis 3.5–6; 7.14; 11.19; 12.22; deaths of Socrates, Cato, Diogenes, Demonax, and Seneca: Seneca, *Ep.* 24.6–7; Epictetus, 4.1 168–72; Plutarch, *Tranq. an.* 475D-F 1.11; Tacitus, *Ann.* 15.62; Seeley, *Noble Death*).

Acts 3:17) and high-handed rebellion where covenant exclusion (Lev 18:29; 20:2–5, 18; 23:29–30) and death is the outcome (Lev 8:35; 10:1–2; 20:2–5; 22:9; 23:29–30; Num 4:15–20; 15:30–36; 18:22).[2] Often the death risk is an active divine judgment but sometimes it is to be meted out in capital punishment (Lev 20:9–16; 24:10–23; Num 15:32–36). The only hope for defiant sinners is if a mediatory figure stands before Yahweh to seek pardon for the people (Exod 15:25; 17:4; 32–34; Num 11:2, 11; 12:13; 14:13–19; 16:22; 20:6; 21:7). At times intentional sin might not be a high hand rebellion because the sinner repents quickly and brings an appropriate sacrifice (Lev 5:1, 20–26; 6:1–7; Num 5:5–8; 19:21–22).[3] However, sacrificial atonement is a privilege granted by Yahweh alone, not an inalienable right.[4] So any high-handed sin runs the risk of identifying the sinner as a rebel to be killed and excluded from covenant (Num 15:30–36).[5] In these priestly contexts, ritual is never a replacement for righteous acts and reparation; social justice is part of the atonement (Lev 6:5–6; Amos 5:21–24).[6]

Cleansing from such practices require the removal of all idols and rebellion (Gen 35:2; Josh 22:17; Ezek 24:13). Cleansing the tabernacle requires the communal rituals of the Day of Atonement (Lev 16; Heb 9:23–24). Likewise, cleansing and atonement includes recovering the person and the nation as well as the tabernacle for holy service (Lev 16; Heb 9:14, 26–28; perhaps 1 Pet 2:5). This cleansing atonement requires continued alignment in holy living to reflect atonement holiness (Lev 11:44; 16; 19:2; 20:7, 26; 1 Pet 1:16, 18).

In the novel *The Picture of Dorian Gray*, Oscar Wilde's adventurer does not age nor suffer the consequences of his adventures.[7] In a similar manner, Milgrom identified that Israel's sins infect the tabernacle much like the picture of Dorian Gray: "Sin may not leave its mark on the face of the sinner but it is certain to mark the face of the sanctuary; and unless it is quickly expunged, God's presence will depart."[8] By the time of

---

2. Levine, *Leviticus*, 3; Gane, *Cult and Character*, 233; Sklar, *Sin, Impurity, Sacrifice, Atonement*, 11–43; "Sin and Atonement"; "Sin and Atonement," 472–89; Boda, *Severe Mercy*, 68.

3. Sklar, "Sin and Atonement."

4. Gane, *Cult and Character*, 204.

5. Sklar, "Sin and Atonemen."

6. Balentine, *Leviticus*, 59; Boda, *Severe Mercy*, 73.

7. Wilde, *Picture of Dorian Gray*.

8. Milgrom, "Israel's Sanctuary," 390–99.

the prophets, the people and land of Israel were severely polluted by sin caused impurity and thus precariously perched toward captivity (Ps 106:38–39; Isa 24:5; Jer 2:7; 3:9; Hos 5:3; 6:10). Peter warns Jews that rebelling against Christ is a rebellion against God and Christ's Abrahamic and Mosaic blessing which provides repentance from their wicked ways (Acts 3:22–26). John Gammie affirmed Milgrom's construct of Dorian Gray's picture; however Gammie also defends that the purification offerings atoned for the individual and not only for the tabernacle: "Sanctuary and sancta indeed reflected the state of the people's sinfulness precisely because the uncleanness that the former accrued were not removed at every [purification]⁹ offering."[10]

Wherever the blood goes is cleansed and sanctified by purification offerings. In Moses initial cleansing sanctification of Israel, the people are sprinkled with blood and thus cleansed much like the altar is as well (Exod 24:6–8; underlying 1 Pet 1:2). Later instances of applying blood cleanse Aaron and the priests for service (Exod 29:21), an individual leper for recovery (Lev 14:6–7), and the tabernacle on the Day of Atonement (Lev 16:14–19), but none of these later instances sprinkles the people with blood. The nation is brought under required Mosaic covenant obedience with the people being sprinkled with blood (Exod 24:6–8; or in 1 Pet 1:2 new covenant obedience). Emphasizing the initial sprinkling cleansing role as parallel within Petrine sanctification, Ernest Best and Peter Davids understand this "obedience" in 1 Pet 1:2 to be that of initial obedience parallel to Pauline initial faith,[11] whereas many others view the context of the covenant relationship of obedience, which initiates the people into this obedient relationship by being sprinkled with blood.[12] The context does not develop an ending to this obedience, so both views are contextually possible, but perhaps the best option is the second because it subsumes the first within it. In 1 Pet 1:2 Christians are sprinkled with Christ's blood in a new covenant manner that fosters an internal obedience prompted by the internal sanctification work of the Holy Spirit. Peter also addressed "purification" (καθαρισμοῦ) of Christians which initiated our exodus unto kingdom as a "purification of his former sins" (2 Pet 1:9). Thus, all believers have initially been cleansed by Christ's redemptive death, so there is no longer gentile uncleanness, nor Jewish

9. Technically, Gammie used *hatta't* to be explained in this direction in a few pages.
10. Gammie, *Holiness in Israel*, 41.
11. Best, *1 Peter*, 71; Davids, *1 Peter*, 48–49.
12. Bigg, *Peter and Jude*, 93.

uncleanness for believers benefiting from Christ's atonement. Christ's atonement further identifies that Jesus' atonement cleansing removes all separation between Jewish and gentile believers. This atonement cleansing participates within Jesus' kingdom cleansing as evidenced in unclean lepers, the woman with hemorrhage, and the dead being cleansed through kingdom healing (Mark 1:40, 44; 5:34, 42; Matt 8:2–3; 9:22; 10:8; 11:5; Luke 5:12; 7:15, 22; 17:14, 17; John 11:44).

The concept of כִּפֶּר/*kpr* indicates redemption and atonement. For much of the nineteenth and twentieth centuries, כִּפֶּר/*kpr* was identified with Arabic *kafara* "to cover" sin,[13] but meaning is not determined by etymology; meaning is determined by use.[14] Richard Averbeck claims that such an etymology is confused when compared to other options like the Hebrew piel stem and Akkadian D stem.[15] For example, in Gen 32:20 כִּפֶּר/*kpr* does not mean "cover" the face since the face of Esau is immediately seen by Jacob. Instead, כִּפֶּר/*kpr* or *kipper* is probably better related to כֹּפֶר/*kpr* or *kopper* which means "ransom" (Exod 30:12–16; Lev 16:10, 21–22; 17:11; Deut 21:1–9)[16] and also carries the meaning of atonement.[17] Redemption is clearly seen in the use of כִּפֶּר/*kpr* concerning both: 1) census and 2) the law of homicide (but not murder) which permitted a certain amount of money to be paid "to ransom a life" (Exod 21:29–30; 30:12–16; Num 31:50; 35:31–33; while there is a prohibition banning ransoming in response to the sin of adultery, Prov 6:34–35).[18] These are substitutionary payments made as "vicarious atonement," *on behalf of* the beneficiaries within a covenantal relationship. Milgrom develops the substitutionary process as that of Levite guards who "siphon off God's wrath upon themselves when an Israelite encroaches upon the

---

13. Kurtz, *Sacrificial Worship of the Old Testament*, 67–71; Janowski, *Sühne als Heilsgeschehen*, 20–22; Stamm, *Erlösen und Vergeben im alten Testament*, 61–66; Elliger, *Leviticus*, 71.

14. de Saussure, *Cours de linguistique Générale*; Barr, *Semantics of Biblical Language*; Feder, "On *Kuppuru, Kippēr*," 535–45.

15. Averbeck, "כִּפֶּר," NIDOTTE 2:689–710, esp. 692.

16. Hermann, *Die Idee der Sühne im Alten Testament*, 99, 101–2; "ἱλάσκομαι, ἱλασμός," TDNT 3:301–10, esp. 303; Brichto, "On Slaughter and Sacrifice," 19–55, esp. 26–27 and 34–35; Levine, *In the Presence of the Lord*, 67; Schenker, "*kōper* et expiation," 32–46; Milgrom, *Leviticus*, 1:1082–83; Sklar, *Sin, Impurity, Sacrifice, Atonement*, 46–72.

17. Janowski, *Sühne als Heilsgeschehen*, 185–276; Gese, "Die Sühne," 85–106; "Atonement," 93–116.

18. Milgrom, *Numbers*, 370 identifies that atonement prevents Yahweh's wrath. In a similar ransom situation 11QT 21.7–9; 22.15–16 has firstfruits offering to ransom the rest of the crop for common purposes.

sancta"[19] thus being a "vicarious" atonement diffusing the wrath on behalf of Israel (Num 1:53; 8:19; 18:22–23). Extending further, Phineas ransoms Israel through vicarious penal substitution from imminent wrath through capital punishment by killing Baal-worshiping Jews in their sins (Num 25:7–12). The sacrifice was "substitutionary" because the sacrifice was in place of all Israel which were viewed by God as guilty, even though the killed were in the guilty act, thus penal but also personally guilty. Additionally, Israel is ransomed vicariously by slaying Saul's sons for violating the Gibeonite covenant, thus again penal but personally guilty (2 Sam 21:3–6). In contrast, guilty Babylon could not ransom or avert her fate; Babylon was judged under covenant curse (Isa 47:11; see Ps 49:8–9 on a similar individual level).

Through intercession, Moses vicariously ransomed Israel from the sin before the golden calf without a substitute (Exod 32:30–40). Furthermore, the blood at the altar must be drained away to "ransom your lives" Israel (Lev 17:11). Such a vicarious ransom 1) delivers the guilty party, 2) appeases the injured party, 3) avoids penalty, and 4) reestablishes a peaceful relationship between them, 5) including forgiveness, which as a complete idea entails atonement. Such an atonement is substitutionary but there is no development of any penal substitute.

While this atonement is clearly substitutionary in a Jewish sacrificial manner, such Jewish sacrifice is not normally viewed as penal within a Jewish context. Paul Felix claims that Peter develops Christ's atonement as penal substitution in at least 1 Pet 1:18–19 but Dan McCartney developed that substitution in an OT sacrificial pattern has no allusion to penal.[20] In the rest of the article Felix merely assumed that substitution implies penal, but as we have seen that is not the case in the Jewish sacrificial system. To identify something as "penal" (from the Latin *poena*, meaning "penalty") means that covenant judgment is being averted onto the representatives who die in judgment as a substitute judgment (Num 25:7–12; 2 Sam 21:3–6). That is, in penal atonement God's wrath goes upon the guilty or the substitutionary sacrifice.[21] Such a representative

---

19. Milgrom, *Studies in Levitical Terminology*, 28–31; *Leviticus*, 1:1082–83.

20. Felix, "Penal Substitution in the New Testament," 182–83; McCartney, "Atonement in James," 176–89.

21. Justification works within a forensic context: Cicero, *Rhetoricum libro duo* 2.53; Justinian, *Inst.* 1; Martin Luther, *Luther's Works*, 56.379.1–15; Melanchthon, *Corpus Reformatorum*, 421; *Apologia* art. 4 par. 252 and 305; McGrath, *Iustitia Dei*, 211, 457; *Augsburg Confession*, art. 4; Kennard, *Gospel*, 17–18.

ransom is a "substitute" because the representative animal or person atoning takes the place of those under covenantal judgment in death even though the actual place of death on an altar is not where the sinner would die.[22] So, the term "penal" may not be so helpful because such Jewish purification sacrifices are only rarely in such a legal framework to remedy a past crime. Usually describing the sacrifice as a substitute covenantal ransom would clarify the covenantal atonement stipulations better than appeals to legal fines. Only a few of these ransoms are in a forensic framework, such as in a homicide case but these substitute only monetary penalties, rather than blood sacrifice (Exod 21:29–30). However, all ransom is covenantal and any that involve blood and sacrifice fit a covenantal atonement substitution better than describing it as a covenantal substitute with continued covenantal obligations (Lev 1–7; 16). None of these covenantal animal sacrifices are ever described as taking God's wrath upon themselves, so they are not described as penal. That is, all the blood sacrifices ransoming the believer employ a covenantal sacrifice rather than a forensic framework. The issue is that the emphasis is on covenant rather than law, and atonement sacrifice rather than legal substitute. The atonement is a real covenantal recovery to the appropriate holy, righteous, and clean condition in covenant through the appropriate covenantal means. Justification and atonement are not legal fiction but restoration of covenantal relationship. First Peter, Heb, John, Paul and the early church viewed Christ's death through this Jewish covenantal sacrificial model rather than a legal one, so such metaphors are not to be seen as inventions of the new perspective in Paul (1 Pet 1:2, 18–19; 2:24; Heb 9:7–28; John 1:29, 36; Rom 3:25).[23] Which means that in Peter, Christ's

---

22. 4 Macc 4:11–12 the heavenly army's wrath is propitiated; contrary to Finlan, *Paul's Cultic Atonement Metaphors*, 102.

23. *Barn.* 7–8 Jesus' death parallel to Day of Atonement and red heifer cleansing; Justin Martyr, *Dial.* 13.1–9, 40.1–4, 72.1, 111.2–3 develop Jesus' death as parallel to paschal lamb, Day of Atonement, and Isa 53 sacrificial lamb (Markschies, "Jesus Christ as a Man," 332–33, and Baley, "'Our Suffering and Crucified Messiah,'" 378–79; Cyprian, *Test.* 15 Jesus' death is parallel to Jewish sacrifice, Isa 53, and Passover lamb; *Ep.* 63.14.4 in *CSEL*, 3c: 410–11; Origen, *Comm. Jo.* 6.32–38 and Augustine, *Trin.* 4.14 or 19 and *On Forgiveness of Sins, and Baptism* 54–55 identify Jesus' death parallel to Jewish daily sacrifices; Theodoret of Cyrrhus, *Interpretation of the Letter to the Romans* in *PG*, 82; Chrysostom, *Hom. Rom.* 7 11:378; both mentioned in Oden, *Justification Reader*, 62; Origen, *Comm. Rom.* 2:110 cited in Oden, *Justification Reader*, 65; Cyril, *Catechetical Lectures* 13.3 develops Jesus' death parallel to Day of Atonement; Eusebius, *Theoph.* 3.59, *Comm. Isa.* 2.42 on Isa. 53:5–6 and 11–12, and *Dem. ev.* 3.2.61–62 develop Jesus' death as a Jewish sacrifice and sin offering (Markschies, "Jesus Christ as a Man," 305, 308, 312–13); Nazianzen, *In Defense of His Flight to Pontus* 1.3–4 develops Jesus'

death is only penal in that he dies under the legal judgment of death sentence from the Roman official Pilate (Mark 15:15, 26; Acts 2:23; 3:15; 4:27; 10:39), and that is not enough to identify "penal" in the traditional theological sense. There is no penal replacement, for the language of Christ's atonement is described as sacrificially covenantal substitutional (1 Pet 1:2, 19; 2:24; 3:18; 2 Pet 1:9). There is no framework where penal substitution is permitted for capital crimes.[24] If someone else dies in place of the criminal, it is a travesty of justice and the criminal still must suffer the consequences of the law. However, with Peter using the language

---

atonement parallel to Passover; Ambrose, *Fid. Grat.* 3.11.67 parallel to Melchizedek sacrifice; Leo the Great, *Sermons* 55.3; 56.1; 59.5, 7; 68.3 parallel to daily Jewish sacrifice and Passover; *Presbyterian Church of England, The Articles of the Faith, 1890*, Article XIII, "Justification by Faith" in Schaff, *Creeds of Christendom*, 3:918; also the abundance of early church iconography presenting Jesus as a sacrificial lamb show the profusion of Jesus' death conceived through the lens of Jewish sacrifice, for example: a third-century Roman catacomb lamb image for Christ, Jesus as lamb with cruciform halo in apex of dome in the sixth-century church of Ravenna, the sixth-century basilica of Saints Cosmos and Damian in Rome shows the Lamb of God on a rock surrounded by the twelve apostles as lambs indicating mimetic atonement, seventh-century Roman altar portraying the Lamb of God on the altar with the cross, the eighty-second canon of the AD 692 Council of Trullo affirmed Jesus was incarnate in human flesh by banning the very common practice of representing Jesus' death as a lamb, "we decree that henceforth Christ our God must be represented in his human form but not in the form of the ancient lamb." Sanday and Headlam, *Romans*, 122–24.

24. Namely, where wages of sin are death (Rom 6:23; Gen 2:17; 5:5, 11, 17, 20, 27, 31). In Roman law a criminal under death sentence might make an appeal to the whole populous to have banishment substituted for capital punishment in *provocation ad populum* but if granted the criminal would suffer banishment from the community. No evidence of any ancient Near Eastern law provides for an innocent person dying in place of a criminal of a capital crime to legally expunge the criminal's guilt. Though, in some ancient Near East settings a significant fine could be paid by the guilty person to replace capital punishment if the victim's family requested it but such a fine would still be paid by the criminal: Exod 21:29–30; 4Q251 frag. 8.5; Beckman and Hoffner, *Hittite Diplomatic Texts*, 109 #18 B, "Treaty Between Hattusili 3 of Hatti and Ulmi-Teshhup of Tarhuntassa," 1 obv. 7'–14'; p. 119 #18 C, "Treaty Between Tudhaliya 4 of Hatti and Kurunta of Tarhuntassa," 20 ii 95–iii 20; p. 145 #23A, "Letter from a King of Hatti to an Anatolian Ruler," 4 obv. 31–35; Roth, *Law Collections from Mesopotamia*, 82; *Laws of Hammurabi* 5. Probably the closest legal substitute pattern would be the Union Enrollment Act of 1863, statue 731, 37th congress, 3rd session, ch. 75, sec. 13 identifying a drafted person: "or he may pay . . . three hundred dollars . . . for the procuration of such substitute . . . and thereupon such person so furnishing the substitute, or paying the money, shall be discharged from further liability under the draft." *Century of Lawmaking*, 733. If the substitute got killed in the war the person paying the money would still have discharged his draft duty. However, this is not a legal replacement for a capital sentence, it is merely a legal replacement who happens to die.

of covenant sacrifice, atonement has more a future focus of growth in a continuing relationship, than settling a past injustice.

The Mosaic covenant includes atonement as accomplished through purification sacrifice. This means that the concern in the Mosaic covenant is for Israel to be clean, and appropriate considering the relationship that Israel already has with Yahweh. Throughout the ancient Near East the issue of purity identifies and retains a people with their god. Within the Mosaic covenant, Israel is in a clean ontological condition, grounded in the initial cleansing act of sprinkling the people (Exod 24:5–8; 1 Pet 1:2; 2 Pet 1:9; Heb 9:18–22). As such, Israel is not trying to initially obtain this clean condition, rather they are corporately trying to retain and maintain it. To do so, Yahweh instituted a sacrificial system.

The problem which the Jewish sacrificial system addresses is primarily that of the communicable disease of uncleanness. Uncleanness can be transmitted by normal issues of life (like a woman's menstrual period or leprosy Mark 1:40, 44; 5:34, 42; Matt 8:2–3; 9:22; 10:8; 11:5; Luke 5:12; 7:15, 22; 17:14, 17) or by touching something that has touched an unclean thing (Lev 12:2; 15:2–33; Deut 23:10). So, uncleanness is not primarily sin because uncleanness can be transmitted without sin occurring. However, sin can bring about uncleanness and a condition of uncorrected uncleanness is sin.[25] That is, natural defilement can become moral defilement if Israelites do not avail themselves of the available sanctification means for recovering from uncleanness. Many in early Judaism considered gentiles to be sinners,[26] unclean,[27] and excluded from kingdom, unless they converted to Judaism (Acts 11:2–3; 15:1).[28] For Peter's mostly gentile recipients, Peter's sanctification by Holy Spirit and Christ cleanses them and forgives their sin (1 Pet 1:2; 2 Pet 1:9; Acts 10:34–35, 44–48; 11:15–18; 15:8–11).[29] So that whatever the believer had

---

25. Klawans provides an excellent discussion of the full range of this topic in his volume: *Impurity and Sin in Ancient Judaism*. Additionally, two fifths of Rabbinic writings develop the issue of uncleanness, purification, and atonement (*Šeqalim*; *Tamid*; *Yoma*; *Zebahim*; *Menahot*; *'Arakhim*; *Bekhorot*; *Me'ilah*; *Temurah*; *Makhširin*; *Tohorot*; *'Uqsin*; *Kelim*; *Parah*; *Miquaot*; *Tebul Yom*; *Yadayim*; and *Hagigah*).

26. Ps 9:17; Tob 13.6; *Jub.* 33.23–24; *Pss. Sol.* 2.1–2.

27. *Y. Šabb.* 1.3; *b. Šabb.* 17b; *b. 'Abod. Zar.* 36b.

28. Kennard, *Biblical Theology of Isaiah*, 228–32; Rabbi Joshua argues this point from Ps 9:17 in *Tosefta Sanh* 13.2; *'Abod. Zar.* 2b–3a; Kaminsky, "Israel's Election," 17–30.

29. Kennard, *Petrine Studies*, developed further in "Jewish Traditions and Gentile Conversion."

been before (Jew or gentile), going forward they are now among the holy (sanctified) household of God.

As framed in the law, the purification sacrifice articulates the idea of collective responsibility to recover Israelites and the nation from their uncleanness. Uncleanness is overcome, returning the unclean to a metaphysically clean and holy condition through the sacrificial system. For example, a Jewish mother must offer the appropriate sacrifice after the birth of her baby for them to be returned to a condition of cleanness, even if that baby is the sinless messiah (Lev 12:3–8; Luke 2:22–24). So, the Mosaic context involves definite atonement for the group, with the benefits applied to the individual to the extent that their life reflects the covenantal obligation. If the individual Israelite continues to rebel, then the benefits that the group receives are of no effect for the rebel. To the extent that individual Israelites do not continue to purify themselves by living holy lives, the nation needs to purify: 1) itself, 2) the tabernacle, and 3) the land on the Day of Atonement, or God's presence will depart from the nation Israel.

The basic purification offering is the חַטָּאת/*htt't*, which is translated in LXX as "sin offering" (Lev 4:3, חַטָּאתוֹ; and LXX Lev 16:5, 9 ἁμαρτία). As such, most view this sacrifice too restrictively as a sin offering which then means that their idea of Christ's sacrifice is legally dealing only with their sins. However, Jacob Milgrom takes issue with the conception of "sin offering" compellingly re-identifying it as the "purification offering." Milgrom explains:

> This translation is inaccurate on all grounds: contextually, morphologically, and etymologically.
>
> The very range of the *hatta't* in the cult gainsays the notion of sin. For example, this offering is enjoined upon recovery from childbirth (Lev 12), the completion of the Nazirite vow (Num 6), and the dedication of the newly constructed altar (Lev 8:15; see Exod 29:36–37). In other words, the *hatta't* is prescribed for persons and objects who cannot have sinned.
>
> Grammatical considerations buttress these contextual observations. Morphologically, it appears as a *pi'el* derivative. More importantly, its corresponding verbal form is not the *qal* "to sin, do wrong" but always the *pi'el* (e.g., Lev 8:15), which carries no other meaning than "to cleanse, expiate, decontaminate" (e.g., Ezek 43:22, 26; Ps. 51:9). Finally, the "waters of *hatta't* (Num 8:7) serve exclusively a purifying function (Num 19:19; see Ezek 26:25). 'Purification offering' is certainly the more accurate

translation. Indeed, the terse comment of Rashi (on Num 19:19) is all that needs to be said: *hatta't* is literally the language of purification" (cf. also Barr 1963:874).

It is not my intention to investigate the origin of this mistranslation. It can be traced as far back as the LXX, which consistently renders ἁμαρτία, followed by Philo (*Laws* 1.226) and Josephus (*Ant.* 3.230). It is, however, important to note that if the rabbinic sources had been carefully read, the subsequent translations could have avoided this mistake. True, the sage Rabbi Eliezer states unequivocally that "the *hatta't* is brought on account of sin" (*m. Zebah.* 1.1), but his generalization is directed only to chap. 4 (and its parallel, Num 15:22–31), where the *qal*, meaning "to sin, do wrong," indeed is found. All other *hatta't* sacrifices are prescribed for specific physical impurities, such as the new mother, . . . the contaminated Nazirite, and the like; and in these cases, not one sage claims that the afflicted brings this sacrifice because of his sins. Indeed, this idea is vigorously denied (*b. Šebu.* 8a; *Ker.* 26a). Moreover, not only is the *hatta't* unrelated to sin in rabbinic thought, but most authorities deny emphatically that the impurity itself was caused by sin. Even the minority who see a causal connection between sin and affliction argue that the affliction in itself suffices to expiate the sin (*'Arak.* 16a; *b. Nazir* 19a; *Nid.* 31b), and they concur with the majority that the purpose of the *hatta't* is for ritual purification.

The discussion on the parturient is decisive: "But according to R. Simeon son of Yahai who holds that a woman in confinement is a sinner, what can be said (concerning the purpose of her *hatta't*)? The sacrifice she brings is, nevertheless, for the purpose of permitting her to partake of consecrated food and *is not expiatory*" (*Ker.* 26a). Finally, the categorical statement of the Talmudic commentators, the tosafists (on Lev 12:8), leaves no doubt concerning the rabbinic view: "According to the literal meaning of the text her (the parturient's) sacrifice is not brought for sin."

The advantage of freeing the *hatta't* from the theologically foreign notion of sin and restoring to it its pristine meaning of purification is that now it is possible to see this sacrifice in its true ancient Near Eastern setting. Israel was part of a cultic continuum which abounded in purifications both of persons and of buildings, especially sanctuaries. The *hatta't*, I aver, is the key that opens the door to this world.[30]

---

30. Milgrom, *Leviticus*, 1:253–54; in addition to the rabbinic texts cited in the quote *m. Yoma* 3.9; 4.1.

This concept of a purification offering is the basic construct of sacrifice with which Jews operate. In the sacrificial process, wherever the blood is applied is then cleansed. This means that the priest must first inspect the lamb to make sure it is unblemished and spotless, unlike the blemishes and spots of leprosy, so that it is covenantal appropriate as a sacrifice (Num 19:2; 28:3, 9, 11; 29:17). Peter applies this same language to Jesus as an appropriate unblemished and spotless sacrifice (1 Pet 1:19), which in language describing a lamb does not discuss sin, but in a context of futile gentile way of life (1 Pet 1:18) may mean morally that Jesus is impeccable (as in Heb 9:14; 4:15; 7:26–27). From this Jewish atonement framework, Christ's precious blood can be applied, showing the precious value of his death beyond gold. Returning to the Jewish context, "atonement" (כִּפֶּר/*kpr*) vicariously accomplishes cleansing (Lev 12:8; 14:18–21, 31, 53; 15:15, 30; 16:30; Num 8:32; 2 Pet 1:9; Heb 9:18–23).[31] Usually this atonement is returning the tabernacle or altar to a pure condition, but occasionally people are also sprinkled with blood and thus cleansed, and if they have committed sins then these people are forgiven for continued covenantal service (Exod 24:3–8). Such cleansing includes atonement forgiveness for sins committed in ignorance (Lev 4:2, 13, 22, 27; 5:2–4; Num 15:30–31; 2 Pet 1:9; Acts 3:17; Heb 5:2; 9:7). God's forgiveness within the Mosaic covenant everlastingly forgives past sins (Exod 34:6–7; Ps 103:12; Mic 7:18–20). When the object of atonement (כִּפֶּר) is people, then its meaning includes forgiveness, rendering the people cleansed to their appropriate level of holiness and righteous, so that they might live holy within these blessed promises of the newly framed covenant (Exod 24:3–8; 1 Pet 1:2, 16; 2 Pet 2:4).[32] Jacob Milgrom contested that persons are only spoken as indirect objects in sacrifice settings but Roy Gane successfully answered him that the preposition מִן/*mn* indicates consistently a purification (of the people) "from" their sins (that are mentioned following the preposition מִן/*mn*, LXX περὶ) in forgiveness (Lev 4:26; 14:19;

---

31. At times this cleansing is accomplished before כִּפֶּר so that כִּפֶּר is not actually the purification (Lev 12:7–8). At times כִּפֶּר is either synonymous or synthetically parallel with cleansing and consecrations (Lev 16:18–19; Ezek 43:20, 26). So obviously some sense of ceremonial purity is accomplished by כִּפֶּר, especially since some of its uses render clean a house or person when no sin had made them unclean (Lev 14:53; 15:15, 30).

32. The parallel arrangement with forgiveness which is evident in Lev 4:20, 26, 31, 35; 5:10, 13, 18; 6:7; 10:17; 16:30 and Ps 79:9 indicating that forgiveness is included within כִּפֶּר. Additionally, כִּפֶּר deals with people's sins such that forgiveness is included within its semantic field (Lev 16:32–34; Num 15:25, 28; Deut 21:8; Pss 65:3; 78:38; 79:9; Isa 6:7; 27:9; Ezek 16:63). Gane, *Cult and Character*, xx, 47–49, 299; Gammie, *Holiness in Israel*, 39; Büchler, *Studies in Sin and Atonement*, 22, 267, 429.

15:15, 30).³³ Peter mirrors this phrase in Christ dying "for sin" (περί, 1 Pet 3:18). An individual whose sin is atoned (כִּפֶּר) has his iniquity pardoned (Isa 6:7; 27:9), whereas an individual who does not have atonement does not have forgiveness and is thus still under judgment (Num 16:46–47; 25:11–13; 1 Sam 3:14; Isa 22:14; 28:18; 47:11). So vicarious "atonement" (כִּפֶּר) appeases divine wrath of covenant curse, returning them again to covenantal blessings (Deut 32:43; 2 Sam 21:3; Pss 78:38; 79:9).³⁴ Gane summarized his view that purification through the year is primarily personal cleansing and forgiveness, while the corporate cleansing on the Day of Atonement is largely cleansing the tabernacle and corporate forgiveness of the nation.³⁵ Occasionally, in Ezekiel, the LXX refers to this purification offering as "propitiation," dealing with uncleanness, forgiveness of sin, and God's covenant curse (ἱλασμόν; Ezek 43:20; 44:27). That is, even in these eschatological purification offerings there is still appeasement which makes the unclean condition vicariously favorable or atoned (כִּפֶּר) with God (Ezek 45:15, 17, 20). Peter applies this purification offering of Christ to all believers, purifying them from their sins (2 Pet 1:9; also 1 Pet 3:18). This unifies the church in that gentile and Jewish believers are all cleansed, even their hearts are cleansed for new covenant transformation (Acts 10:28, 47; 11:3, 15–18; 15:8–9).

One passage explains that the critical feature to obtain atonement in all the offerings is the life (נֶפֶשׁ/*nps*) that is given, for which the blood stands as an emblem (Lev 17:11). The life (נֶפֶשׁ) offered vicariously benefits our life (נֶפֶשׁ). So, the blood in sacrifice is not magical, for it merely indicates that the offering is given. However, for Peter, Christ's blood stands as a metaphor for Christ's death, and is thus precious as an atonement (1 Pet 1:19). However, there are instances when the offering is completed without any blood and yet vicarious atonement (כִּפֶּר) is accomplished (Exod 21:30; 30:15; Num 31:50; Heb 9:22³⁶). Even in one instance atonement (כִּפֶּר) is accomplished by loving-kindness and truth

---

33. Milgrom, "Preposition מִן in the חַטָּאת Pericopes," 161–63; Gane, "Private Preposition מִן," 209–22; *m. Yom.* 8.8–9 supports Gane's conclusion of people forgiven in atonement provided the sin or guilt offering is accompanied with repentance.

34. *M. Yoma* 8.8–9; Kennard, *Biblical Covenantalism*, 1:151–313.

35. Gane, "Private Preposition מִן," *JBL* 217.

36. Notice that Heb 9:22 acknowledges that "almost" (σχεδόν) always blood is used in cleansing, but this admits that there are instances when other means cleanse, such as an exchange of money, or if the worshiper is poor, a grain offering will suffice as a purification offering (Lev 5:11).

without an offering at all (Prov 16:6).³⁷ This indicates that no deed accomplishes atonement (כִּפֶּר); one's life focus following the narrow way and the divine enablement to this narrow way are important for atonement to be realized through the available means. That is, mimetic atonement is intertwined with vicarious atonement (1 Pet 2:21–24).

Milgrom underscores that, "As shown (Lev 4:13–14), the *hatta't* laws assume that the inadvertent offender becomes aware of his act and feels remorse for it, expressed by the verb *'asam*. Repentance is thus a precondition for the *hatta't*."³⁸ That is, external deeds are not effective without one's personal commitment to follow God's Law. God is an active agent to forgive, and has established this as a feature in relationship; God is not a vending machine.³⁹

The guilt offering (אֲשָׁמוֹ/*'asam* or LXX: ἐπλημμέλησεν) is a special case of purification offering which deals with an individual who feels his guilt (Lev 5:6–7; 6:17; 7:1–7, 37; 19:21–22; Num 18:9). Such an offering atones and propitiates (Num 5:8: כִּפֶּר or in LXX it is ἱλασμόν). That is, this offering is very much like the purification offering, in that the clean Nazarite completes his time of purity with a guilt offering when no sin or uncleanness has rendered him impure (Num 6:12). In such guilt offerings the blood is placed on the altar and if necessary on the one who is to be cleansed, indicating that both sancta and person are to be cleansed in this atonement (Lev 7:5; 14:12–28). Rabbi Rabad claimed that such a guilt offering requires a confession (Num 5:7–8).⁴⁰ At times, such a guilt offering mentions an object taken and requires that it be returned along with 20 percent added before this guilt offering is effective in atoning for the person's sin (Lev 5:15–19; 6:6). However, if no object is mentioned, then the offering is the appropriate response for one who feels his guilt and confesses it before God. Jacob Milgrom summarizes the guilt offering (אֲשָׁמוֹ/*'asam*) as follows:

> In sum, the cultic texts reveal four usages of the root *'sm*, as follows: the noun "reparation" and "reparation offering," and the

---

37. This כִּפֶּר is parallel to the fear of the Lord which keeps one from evil and its ensuing punishment.

38. Milgrom, *Leviticus*, 1:264; 1QS 3.3–6, 8–9; 4.5; 5.13; *b. Šebu* 1.16.2/13A.D; *m. Yoma* 8.8.A; *t. Kippurim* 4.8.A; *m. Sanh.* 6.2.D; Chilton and Neusner, *Classical Christianity and Rabbinic Judaism*, 199–203.

39. Noonan, "On the Efficacy of the Atoning Sacrifices," 285–318.

40. *Sipra. Hobah* 7.3; *Sipre Zuṭa* on Num. 5:5; *t. Menaḥ.* 10.12; Milgrom, *Leviticus*, 1:344–45.

verbs "incur liability [to someone]" and "feel guilt" (without a personal object). These meanings derive from the consequential 'asam, the punishment or penalty incurred through wrongdoing. The fourth meaning, "feel guilt" refers to psychological guilt. These findings are best summarized by citing two passages in which all four meanings appear (indicated by italics): "He shall pay it to its owner as soon as he *feels guilt* (*beyom 'asmato*). Then he shall bring to the priest, as his *reparation* (*'asmato*) to the Lord, an unblemished ram from the flock, or its assessment, as a *reparation offering* (*le'asam*)" (Lev 5:24b–25); and "When that person *feels guilt* (*we'asemâ*), he [lit., 'they'] shall confess the wrong he [lit., 'they'] has done, make *reparation* (*'asamo*) in its entirety, add one-fifth to it, and give it to the one to whom he has *incurred liability* (*le'aser 'asam lo*)" (Num 5:6b–7).[41]

Both purification and guilt offerings vicariously bear the uncleanness or guilt away from the sancta and the one or group for whom they are offered. Each of the purification and guilt offerings accomplishes vicarious "atonement" (כִּפֶּר: Lev 14:18–19; Num 5:8)[42] or "propitiation" (LXX: ἱλασμόν; Num 5:8; Ezek 44:27). For example, in the Day of Atonement, these offerings along with the scapegoat[43] bear the guilt away from the nation (Lev 10:17; 16:22; Heb 9:7). Peter identified that by extension Jesus' vicarious atonement similarly "bore" our sin away expressed in similar manner to the scapegoat (1 Pet 2:24, ἀνήνεγκεν). Through the Day of Atonement, Israel continues with Yahweh in a relationship of peace as evidenced by the continuing Mosaic covenant benefits. If Israelites violate the stipulations of the covenant and don't resolve their uncleanness by these available means, then the Israelite and the nation continue to bear the guilt of their sin (Lev 5:1, 17; 17:16; 20:19; Num 9:13; 14:34).

Corporate national atonement to deal with this continuing uncleanness occurs at the establishment of the Mosaic covenant and its renewal

---

41. Milgrom, *Leviticus*, 1:345.

42. M. *Yoma* 8.8–9.

43. The scapegoat ritual is similar to the Hittite substitution ritual where the uncleanness and sin is sent away from the cult and people but in the Hittite situation it is sent to a designated region of the offended god and there is no clear biblical teaching that a demon Azazel is being placated but rather the focus is on the removal of the iniquities to an undesignated wilderness location (Lev 16:8, 20–22), and there is greater variety of animals used in this pattern by the Hittites (van Brock, "Substitution rituelle," 117–46; Kümmel, "Ersatzkönig und Sündenbock," 289–318; Gurney, *Some Aspects of Hittite Religion*; Wright, *Disposal of Impurity*; Hoffner, "Hittite-Israel Cultural Parallels," xxxii.

at the Day of Atonement. Moses established Israel as clean in the ritual of cleansing initiating the Mosaic covenant, and likewise Christ's atonement initiates the new covenant as developed in Heb (Exod 24; 1 Pet 1:2; Heb 9:7). Within the Mosaic covenant, Yahweh demands that Israel be kept clean and holy (Lev 11:44–45). If Israel does not deal with their uncleanness, then it becomes a sin. Ultimately, sins defile Yahweh's holy name and bring covenant curse as was previously developed (Deut 28:15—29:29; Ezek 43:7–8). For Israel to ignore this mandate and to become unclean defiles the tabernacle and puts Israel at risk to be cut off in covenant curse (Lev 15:31; Num 19:13). This defilement of tabernacle includes the holy place and altar as well (Lev 16:16, 18; Num 19:20). For example, high-handed unrepentant sin (such as refusing to purify oneself after touching a dead body) defiles both tabernacle and holy place (Num 19:13, 20). Likewise, believers in Christ are to cultivate holiness, since the Holy Spirit and Jesus' sanctification (ἁγιασμῷ) has initially placed them into such a holy condition (ἅγιον; 1 Pet 1:2, 15–16). New covenant obedience is the appropriate Christian response going forward.

ISA 53 AND SERVANT AS SACRIFICE

Eschatological atonement was expected through the messiah in his priestly ministry.[44] One possibility of this eschatological atonement was through the concept of Isaiah's "servant of the Lord."

44. 1QS text 7 1.19; 11QMelch 12.7–8; 4Q541; *1 En.* 39.4–6; 41.2 (much like Rom 8:28–30; Col 3:1–4); 48.1–4; 51.4–5; 61.4; 62.14; *T. Levi* 18; Kennard, *Messiah Jesus*, 302–5; Pate and Kennard discuss other possible allusions Paul may have made to Isa 52–53 (*Deliverance Now and Not Yet*, 173–76). Some of these claimed allusions (such as Rom 4:25 "justification" as reflecting Isa 53:11, "justify") only work on the level of Vulgate or English text, neither the MT nor the LXX have any similarity in phrase or theology to that of Paul. For an explanation of and an apologetic for this "Isaac Typology," see Wood, "Isaac Typology in the New Testament," 583–89; Daly, "Soteriological Significant," 45–75; Gubler, *Die Frühesten Deutungen des Todes Jesu*, 336–75. Rosenberg, "Jesus, Isaac and the Suffering Servant," 381–88; Riesenfeld, *Jesus Transfiguré*, 86–96; Strack and Billerbeck, *Kommentar zum Neuen Testament*, 3:746; Vermes, *Scripture and Tradition in Judaism*, 193–97; 217–27; Schoeps, *Paul*, 141–49. An important issue that emerges is whether pre-Christian Judaism expected a suffering messiah. Those who say yes include Cullmann, *Christology of the New Testament*, 55–56, 60; Lohse, *Märtyrer und Gottesknecht*, 104–6; Jeremias, "παῖς θεοῦ," TDNT 5:677–717. The last-mentioned author summarizes the evidence for the messianic interpretation of the Isaianic servant in Palestinian Judaism: (1) this interpretation was confined to Isa 42:1; 43:10; 49:1–2 and 6–7; and 52:13—53:12; (2) in relation to Isa 42:1 and 52:13—53:12, the messianic understanding is "constant from pre-Christian times"; (3) the messianic interpretation of the passion sayings of Isa 53 can be traced back at least with a high

Differing interpretations of the suffering servant in Isa 53 are reflected in the translations, however David A. Sapp and Otto Betz present convincing cases for the following development: (1) MT-The servant's afflictions and death are portrayed as vicariously atoning, (2) the LXX tones down the servant's suffering (he does not die, but is divinely rescued), almost to the point of being representative atoning, (3) while *Targum Jonathan* to the prophets transposes suffering from the servant/messiah to Israel's enemies.[45] This reinterpretation makes Israel's enemies become the sacrifice of atonement. There is perhaps an "Isaac Typology" (based on Gen 22:1–14) that lies behind Isa 53, and its influence is to be seen in the Inter-testamental period and throughout the NT where the motif of suffering and death in an atoning and vicarious sense emerges.[46]

---

degree of probability to the pre-Christian period though not with the same certainty (παῖς θεοῦ). Those who do not think pre-Christian Judaism gives evidence of a suffering Messiah expectation include: Hooker, *Jesus and the Servant*, 56–67; Str-B, 2:273–74; Menard, "*Pais Theou* as a Messianic Title in the Book of Acts," 83–92; especially 84–85; Longenecker, *Christology of Early Jewish Christianity*, 105; Fitzmyer, *Luke*, 2:156–66. The latter summarizes the evidence for this view: The notion of a suffering messiah is not found in the OT or in any texts of pre-Christian Judaism. Str-B, 2.273–99 says that the "Old Synagogue" knew of "a suffering Messiah, for of whom no death was determined, i.e. the Messiah ben David" and a "dying Messiah, of whom no suffering was mentioned," the Messiah ben Joseph (Str-B, 273–74). Yet when it cites the passages from Rabbinic literature (Str-B, 282–91) that speak of the suffering Messiah ben David, they are all drawn from late texts, which scarcely show that the expectations of such a figure existed among Palestinian Jews in or prior to the time of Jesus. The same must be said of the texts about the dying Messiah ben Joseph (Str-B, 292–99). Str-B rightly rejects the implication found at times in Christian commentators that Mark 8:31; Matt 16:21 refer to a "suffering Messiah," and the latter is not a "messianic" title without further ado. Where in pre-Christian Judaism does one find a "Son of Man" as an agent of Yahweh anointed for the salvation, deliverance of his people? True, in *Tg. Jonathan* the "servant" of Isa 52:13 is identified as "the Messiah": "See, my servant, the Messiah, shall prosper; he will be exalted, great, very mighty," and 53:10c is made to read, "They will look upon the kingdom of their Messiah, many sons and daughters will be theirs." Yet no use of "Messiah" is made in the crucial verse, 53:12. It is not surprising that the "Servant" of Isa 52–53 was eventually identified with a messiah in the Jewish tradition; but it remains to be shown that this identification existed in pre-Christian Judaism or in Judaism contemporary with the NT (Fitzmyer, *Luke*, 2:156–66; Wright, *Jesus and the Victory of God*, 591).

45. For numbers 1 and 2 see Sapp, "LXX, 1QIsa, and MT Versions," 170–92; while Betz treats the *Targum*, "Jesus and Isaiah 53," in Bellinger, *Jesus and the Suffering Servant*, 70–87, esp. 73.

46. For an explanation of and an apologetic for this "Isaac Typology," see Wood, "Isaac Typology in the New Testament," 583–89; Daly, "Soteriological Significant," 45–75; Gubler, *Die Frühesten Deutungen*, 336–75. Rosenberg, "Jesus, Isaac and the Suffering Servant," 381–88; Riesenfeld, *Jesus Transfiguré*, 86–96; Strack and Billerbeck, *Kommentar zum Neuen Testament*, 3:746; Vermes, *Scripture and Tradition in Judaism*,

The term "servant" is used several ways throughout Isaiah but in the four servant songs it refers to a spiritually instructed individual amid a sinful and blind nation (Isa 40:2; 42:1, 19; 53:9).[47] This servant as an individual trusts Yahweh throughout discouragement and suffering for other's sins, of which he is innocent (Isa 42:1; 49:4; 53:4–6, 9–11), whereas Israel corporately is spiritually deaf and dumb, doubting Yahweh in discouragement and suffering for their own sins (Isa 40:2, 27; 42:19). This concept of servant is one who is chosen for a special ministry by God. Regal description "prohibits an understanding of "servant" as slave or lackey but determines its meaning as "trusted envoy" or "confidential representative.""[48] Qumran noticed these features and even changed aspects in 1QIsa and 4Q541 from the MT to be more messianic regarding offering Himself as an atonement for humanity.[49] Peter extends this messianic application to Jesus (1 Pet 2:22 quoting Isa 53:9).

In summary form, the servant songs convey a good overview of the servant's role. As a humble prophet Yahweh's servant will bring salvation and the proper order to the earth (Isa 42:1–4). Yahweh, through the new covenant, guarantees his servant's mission for accomplishing salvation (Isa 42:5–9). The servant, called by Yahweh, rejected by his own people, will bring salvation to the gentiles and at the proper time restore Israel to the land and to Yahweh (Isa 49:1–13). The righteous servant declares that by his being rejected while trusting Yahweh, he learned to comfort the weary (Isa 50:4–9). Yahweh applies the lessons from his servant's experience to others by reminding believers to live by faith, while unbelievers are warned about judgment (Isa 50:10–11). Yahweh promises to exalt his servant because he voluntarily provided a "substitutionary atonement," having died as a vicarious sacrifice on behalf of guilty people to cleanse and save them (Isa 52:13–15). Israel responds in a confession of their sin and belief in the servant's atoning death (Isa 53:1–9; Zech 12:10–11). Israel's confession probably takes place as the servant is honored in kingdom. This confession fits the pattern of the servant offering himself as purification and guilt offering on their behalf, thus "vicarious

---

193–97; 217–27; Schoeps, *Paul*, 141–49.

47. Kennard, *Biblical Theology of Isaiah*, 194–212.

48. Williams, "Poems About Incomparable Yahweh's Servant," 75.

49. 1QIsa 52:14 replaces the MT "marring" (מִשְׁחַת) with a Qal singular "I have anointed" indicating that God established the sacrifice role for his messiah, and 1QIsa 51:5 replaces the MT first-person "My righteousness" with a third-person "His arm" also indicating Messianism, also 4Q541 9.1.1.2 "he will atone" (Hengel and Bailey, "Effective History of Isaiah 53," 101, 103, 108, 146).

atonement." Because of the effectiveness of the covenantal "guilt" (MT) or "sin" (LXX) offering (Isa 53:10) by the servant, the servant will be blessed with a continuing inheritance (Isa 53:10–12).

The theological meaning of the servant's death is carried by the sacrificial terminology. The servant atones for many nations and Israel in their sin through the pattern of covenantal atonement (purification or guilt offering). In his marred appearance, he is identified as "he will sprinkle many nations" (Isa 52:14–15; יַזֶּה/*yzh*). Expanding the concept of corporate sprinkling beyond mere Israel in Mosaic covenant to all ethnicities in new covenant and the atonement forgiveness which accompanies initiating this relationship (Exod 24:8; Heb 9:13; 1 Pet 1:2). Such corporate atonement is like the scapegoat at the Day of Atonement (Lev 16:20–22 vicarious but not developed as penal sacrifice; Isa 51:17, 22; 53:4). The sins of the people are confessed upon the scapegoat to bear them away into the wilderness (Lev 16:22). This vicarious "bearing" of the people's sin is what the Servant accomplishes (Isa 53:4, 10; perhaps reflected in 1 Pet 2:24). The Servant's death is to deal with our corporate iniquities, that is, to bring atonement and peace with God for a future going forward. Such atonement and reconciliation are what one would expect as benefits from a *guilt offering* (Isa 53:10 MT identifies אָשָׁם/*'sm* "guilt offering," though the LXX identifies it as a purification or "sin offering," LXX: δῶτε περὶ ἁμαρτίας). There is no object taken, so no reparations are required, only Israel's conscious confession of their sin, which is in fact the voice of Isa 53:1, "Who has believed our message?" Likely, Peter echoes this Jewish testimony as the church accompanies their own sacrifice of obedience and suffering with verbal praise and testimony "proclaiming the excellencies of God who called you out of darkness into marvelous light" (purpose statements for the church combine 1 Pet 2:9, "proclamation," with "offering spiritual sacrifices" in 1 Pet 2:5). Isaiah presents this confession of corporate Israel as in the future kingdom era (Isa 52:7–10; 54:1–17). Presumably, individual Israelites could confess their sin earlier than that expression of kingdom and have the atonement benefits of the servant applied to them. John Oswalt describes this substitution sacrifice from Isa 53:4–6, 10–12.

> It is here and in vv. 10–12 that the issue of the substitutionary suffering of the servant, and thus his capacity to deliver his people, comes to the fore. He does not suffer merely as a result

of the people, but in the people. He suffers *for* them, and because of that, they do not need to experience the results of their sins.[50]

As has been shown, the servant's substitutionary sacrifice is informed especially by the language of the cult, not a courtroom situation (especially Lev 5:1, 17; 10:17; 16:22; 17:16; 20:19; and Num 9:13; 14:34).

The NT refers to Isa 53 directly in several places (Matt 8:17; Luke 22:37; Acts 8:32–35, Rom 10:16; 15:21) but only 1 Pet 2:22 indicates that Jesus atoned silent before his accusers as a mimetic[51] atonement pattern for the Christians to follow (quoting Isa 53:9). Only 1 Pet adds in the context that Jesus "bore our sins in his body on the cross," with imagery of the Christians having strayed like sheep (1 Pet 2:24–25 probably alluding to Isa 53:4–6, 10). So at least Peter probably recognized that Isa 53 describes Christ's death as vicarious substitutionary atonement such as a guilt offering (Isa 53:10), though his emphasis in the context is on instruction for servants suffering to follow Jesus in silent mimetic atonement (1 Pet 2:18–23). Additionally, with no clear statement using Isa 53 in the NT for vicarious atonement, the synoptic and Acts pattern identifies more with mimetic atonement (Mark 8:31; 9:12, 31; 10:42–45; Matt 16:21–28; 20:22–28; Luke 9:22–27; 18:31–33; Acts mirrors Luke twice with James and Stephen dying while Peter is rescued and Paul coming to near death with shipwreck and snake bite before coming to Rome).

In *1 Enoch* and some Qumran texts, the teaching about the Isaianiac suffering servant combine[52] with *merkabah*[53] mysticism, and a combina-

50. Oswalt, *Isaiah*, 3:385, and for contextual development 386–87, 401; for a discussion on a range of interpretations of Isa 53 see Pate and Kennard, *Deliverance Now and Not Yet*, 92–96.

51. Mimetic atonement is where an example sets a pattern to emulate. Such a view was common in early Judaism and Greco-Roman literature (Pate and Kennard, *Deliverance Now and Not Yet*, 22–71; 2 Macc 6:18–17.42; 4 Macc 10:10; 11:12, 20, 27; 16:24–25; 17:2, 11–12, 18; *Wis.* 3.5–6; 7.14; 11.19; 12.22; deaths of Socrates, Cato, Diogenes, Demonax, and Seneca: Seneca, *Ep.* 24.6–7; Epictetus, 4.1 168–72; Plutarch, *Tranq. An.* 475D–F 1.11; Tacitus, *Ann.* 15.62; Seeley, *Noble Death*).

52. Pate and Kennard (*Deliverance Now and Not Yet*, 75–77) follow Nickelsburg (*Resurrection, Immortality, and Eternal Life*, 71–72) in connecting these imageries in contrast to Sjöberg's (*Der Menschensohn im ältiopischen Henochbuch*, 116–39) contentions.

53. Or Jewish divine chariot presentations of a real divine temple in heaven, simultaneous to that of God inhabiting the temple on earth. That is, both the heavenly and earthly temples are real and different things may be occurring in these different realities. For example, the heavenly temple is normally thought to be where God's presence dwells (Isa 6:4) but the amazing thing is that with the cleansed tabernacle God dwells on earth, with the ark of the covenant serving as his throne (Exod 40:34–38). However,

tion of vicarious and mimetic atonement, such as found in 1 Pet. *First Enoch* joins mainstream Judaism in announcing the afflictions of the righteous are to be seen as mimetic atonement, especially at the culmination of the messianic woes.[54] In this context, the Son of Man as Messiah[55] employs a vicarious representative role of suffering on behalf of the elect, who join in the messianic woes.[56] That is, the heavenly Son of Man appropriates to himself the afflictions of the elect so that the elect on earth may enjoy in heaven the glory of the Enochian Son of Man. This glory already exists in heaven[57] but the public resurrection of the elect will vindicate them before the wicked.[58]

However, meanwhile the teacher of righteousness viewed himself as Isaiah's suffering servant providing vicarious atonement for his community.[59] Thus to be associated with him is to experience divine forgiveness.[60] After the teacher of righteousness died, his followers recalculated that deliverance to occur at the end of forty years would entail their mimetic

---

the uncleanness of the earthly temple dislodges the divine presence from the earthly temple, while it remains in the heavenly temple (Ezek 1:4-28; 11:22-25). The different conditions of the pure heavenly temple and the occasionally unclean earthly temple show that they are both real in this multidimensional Hebraic framework rather than the idealism of the earthly shadows, that a Platonism would portray (*1 En.* 14; 37-71; *2 En.* 15-17; *4 Ezra* 9.26—10.59; 13.35-36; *2 Bar.* 4.2-7; 6.9; 32.4; Gal 4:26; Heb 12:22; Rev 3:12; 21:2, 10; *Asc. Isa.* 9; *Adam and Eve* 37; *Apoc. Ab.* 29; *Exod. Rab.* 43.8; *m. Hag.* 2.1; *b. Hag.* 14a; 15a; *Hek. Rab.* 20.1; *b. Sanh.* 38b; Pate and Kennard, *Deliverance Now and Not Yet*, 98-103; Sholem, *Jewish Gnosticism*; Lincoln, *Paradise Now and Not Yet*, 9-32, 169-95; Dean-Otting, *Heavenly Journeys*; Gruenwald, *Apocalyptic and Merkavah Mysticism*, 29-72; Schafer, *Kehhalot-Studien*; Chernus, "Visions of God in Merkabah Mysticism," 123-46; Isaacs, *Sacred Space*, 59-61; Koester, *Hebrews*, 97-100).

54. *1 En.* 43.4; 47.1-2; 48.6; 103.9—104.8.
55. *1 En.* 46.1-7; 48.2-10; 52.4.
56. *1 En.* 39.6; 48.1-4; 51.4-5; 61.4; 62.14.
57. *1 En.* 39.4-5; 41.2 much like Rom 8:28-30; Col 3:1-4.
58. *1 En.* 62.14-16.
59. 1QH 15.8-27 especially 15.18 and 16.4—17.36; 11QMelch. 6-25. The Teacher of Righteousness probably understood himself to be on the verge of exaltation in Jerusalem (1QH 14.28-36; 15.24-28). However, the Damascus Document suggests that the Teacher of Righteousness died before he could deliver on his promises (CD 19.34-35; 20.13-16). Deliverance was recalculated to be forty years later (CD 20.13-16; 11Q Melch.; 1QS 8.1-16).
60. Especially 1QH 15.18 and 11Q Melch. 9-25.

suffering to fill up what was lacking from the teacher's sufferings.⁶¹ However, after the forty years came and went with no rescue, the Qumran covenanters reinterpreted their deliverance mystically to mean that they were caught up to heaven in the worship setting with and because of the teacher of righteousness' vicarious atonement.⁶²

Additionally, because of Qumran's separation they also considered that the community itself mimetically atoned for its members through a sacrifice of humility, prayer, and mystical community worship, provided the member repents of sin and submits to community discipline (Pss 51:17; 141:2);⁶³ nonmembers remained unclean as sinners. 1QS identified God's merciful justification occurs at the eschatological judgment for those who reflect the narrow way from their heart.⁶⁴ Actually, the *Babylonian Talmud* considered that confessional prayer and the study of *torah* was more effective in atoning than animal sacrifice, so those practices replace burnt offerings for atonement.⁶⁵

Furthermore, mimetic atonement is celebrated among Jews. For example, Sir considers that a virtuously righteous life atones.⁶⁶ Additionally, Maccabean and other Jewish martyrs were seen to propitiate the sins of the people as mimetic deaths and suffering redeem Israel from the domination of foreign powers.⁶⁷

With the destruction of the Jerusalem temple in AD 70 and AD 135 some forms of early Judaism continued to offer purification sacrifices including those of the Day of Atonement in synagogues⁶⁸ and in alternative Jewish temples such as Onias temple in Leontopolis in the Nile delta or the Jewish Elephantine temple (near the Aswan high dam in Egypt).⁶⁹

---

61. The Teacher of Righteousness probably understood himself to be on the verge of exaltation in Jerusalem (1QH 14.28–36; 15.24–28).

62. 1QH 11.19–38; 15.26–36.

63. Prayer: 1QS 3.8; 5.6–7; 8.5–6, 10; 9.4–5; 1Q34 1+2; 4Q400 frg. 1 lines 15–16; 4Q508 frg. 2 2–3; 22+23; 4Q509 frg. 16 3; 5–6 ii, 7; 11Q5 27.2–11; *Jub.* 5.17–18; 34.18–19; *Festival of Prayers*; *Pss. Sol.* 3.8; 9.6; Philo, *Mos.* 2.23–24; *Spec.* 2.196 esp. within 193–203; *Leg.* 306; *L.A.B.* 13.6; *b. Ber.* 26b; mystical worship: *1 En.* 14.8–25; *T. Levi* 3.4–5; *Songs of the Sabbath Sacrifice*; 1QH 11.19–38; 15.26–36.

64. 1QS 11.2–3, 12,13–15; 4QMMT C.31.

65. *B. Ber.* 32b; *b. Menaḥ.* 110a.

66. Sir 3.3, 35.5–6, 9.

67. *1 En.* 43.4; 47.1–2; 48.6; 103.9—104.8; 4 Macc 6:29; 17:21–22; 4Q171 frg. 1–10 ii 8–11.

68. Philo, *Mos.* 2.23; *Seder 'Abodah*; *b. Meg.* 31a.

69. Josephus, *Ant.* 13.62–68; *War* 7.426–32; Porten, *Archives from Elephantine*,

Several other Jewish frameworks without a functioning Jewish temple practiced modified purification sacrifices and Day of Atonement sacrifices from their synagogues.[70] While these approaches were acknowledged, Yoḥanan ben Zakkai additionally proposed (similar to Prov 16:6) that acts of mercy and loving kindness remained as an effective atonement to cleanse and forgive on the basis of Hos 6:6.[71] Philo identified that confession atones,[72] as does repentance,[73] affliction,[74] and prayer.[75] Pinḥas ben Yair drew all these categories together as a narrow way of salvation unto everlasting life for holiness, cleanness, righteousness.

> Heedfulness leads to [physical] cleanness, cleanness to purity, purity to separateness, separateness to holiness, holiness to humility, humility to the shunning of sin, the shunning of sin to saintliness, saintliness to the Holy Spirit, the Holy Spirit to the resurrection of the dead.[76]

Obviously, Christianity takes things into a messianic sacrifice and kingdom.[77]

128–33, 279–82, 311–14.

70. The Jewish practice would have sacrifice complete the reconciliation process (Lev. 1–7; *Ep. Aristeas* 170–71; *Sir.* 34.18–19; 35.12; Philo, *Spec.* 1.236–37). Continuing this practice, Matthew 5:23–24 and Acts 18:18; 21:23–27 support Jewish Christian participation in Jewish sacrifices. In contrast, *Gos. Eb.* 7 as recorded by Epiphanius, *Pan.* 30.16.4–5 has Jesus condemn such practice of Jewish sacrifices. Of course, the law prescribes the Levitical sacrifices for Israel (Lev 1–7, 16:1—17:9). Additionally, the OT describes the kingdom era under the Messiah as continuing to practice these sacrifices that atone (Jer 33:18; Ezek 43:18—46:24), though Heb 10:1–8 ceases the sacrifices for now for any new covenant people who would be disturbed by their reminder, and *Lev. Rab.* 9.7, written four centuries after the destruction of the temple (fifth century AD), ceases the ritual sacrifices in the messianic kingdom.

71. *The Fathers according to Rabbi Nathan* cited by Neusner, *Idea of Purity*, 68.

72. Philo, *Post.* 70–72.

73. Philo, *Spec. Laws* 1.188.

74. Philo, *Leg.* 3.174; *Congr.* 107.

75. Philo, *Mos.* 2.24.

76. *M. Soṭah* 9.15; *y. Šeqal.* 3.3.

77. For further discussion see Kennard, *Messiah Jesus*, 107–56 for Jesus' development of Law and traditions concerning cleansing and sacrifice, and 293–332 for Jesus' messianic sacrifice, and 377–414 for Jesus' messianic rule.

PETRINE SANCTIFICATION AND PURIFICATION AS BORN AGAIN

After Peter identified himself as the author, the recipient's description emphasizes that they are in the sphere of the elect (1 Pet 1:1, ἐκλεκτοῖς). The first description of the elect is characterized as temporary residents scattered outside their homeland and within the northern two thirds of Turkey, north of the Taurus Mountains (1 Pet 1:1–2).[78] Their election status was according to the foreknowledge of God the Father, by the agency (ἐν) of the Holy Spirit's sanctification resulting (εἰς) in initial obedience and covenantal atonement provided by the death[79] of Jesus Christ. However, this sanctification and atonement results in divine fostering obedience indicative of the initiation of the new covenant (1 Pet 1:2; Ezek 36:24–28; Jer 31:31–33).[80] Spirit-initiated obedience serves to balance the human responsibility side of continuing to be faithful within this divine work which is noticeable in the mind of the believer. Such obedience is then like an Edwardsian religious affection and thus provides reassurance for Jesus' atonement sanctification.[81]

Peter ties Jesus' sacrificial death with the Jewish sacrifice concept in Isa 53 (1 Pet 1:2; 2:22–25; Isa 52:15; 53:5–6, 9). In such Jewish sacrifices there is no development of a penal aspect. Which means for Peter the only clear penal aspect of Jesus' death is that Jesus dies as a criminal, with death sentence pronounced by the Roman official Pilate, under the charge that Jesus is the king of the Jews (Mark 15:15, 26). Therefore, Jesus is the pure covenantal sacrifice who died for redemption of humanity (developed previously). However, this redemption accomplishment emphasizes a life transformation "that we might die to sin and live to righteousness" (1 Pet 2:24). Such is the life healing that Jesus' atonement provides which transforms the believer from her "straying like sheep" condition to that of following Jesus in mimetic atonement, with suffering if necessary (1 Pet 2:24–25, 20–23). Furthermore, in Jesus' sanctified purity and just character, Jesus died for we who are unjust so that Jesus

---

78. Michaels, *1 Peter*, 4, 13; Kistemaker, *Peter and Jude*, 12; Jobes, *1 Peter*, 45, 68.

79. The metaphor of sprinkling the people with blood is reminiscent of the initial covenant cleansing in Exod 24:3–8 and the atonement of Isa 52:15 by Yahweh's Servant; Kennard, *Biblical Covenantalism*, 3:190–91, 198; Bigg, *Peter and Jude*, 93; Jobes, *1 Peter*, 72.

80. Kennard, *Biblical Covenantalism*, 3:198; 2:79–89; Selwyn, *1 Peter*, 120–21; Davids, *1 Peter*, 49.

81. Edwards, *Religious Affections*.

might bring us to God through the resurrection which he initiated, and we participate within (1 Pet 3:18, 4:6). Likewise, redemption includes purification from their former sins utilizing καθαρισμοῦ which is normally taken as a "purification" or sin offering which cleanses and provides atonement as recovering from leprosy or the flow of blood (2 Pet 1:9, 22; Mark 1:44; Luke 2:22; 5:14; LXX: Exod 29:36; 30:10; Neh 12:45).

Based on this purification (ἡγνικότες),[82] Peter calls believers in Christ to fervently love one another from the heart (1 Pet 1:22). This command is grounded upon two foundational reasons. The first reason is that believers have in obedience to the truth purified themselves, which is the kind of cleansing occurring in covenantal sanctification and sprinkling with blood (1 Pet 1:2; 22). The second reason to love applies a *pesher* from Isa 40:6–8 which identifies that the exodus word preached in the gospel is an imperishable word (1 Pet 1:23–25). This imperishable gospel word is a seed that is alive to create imperishable people who believe this exodus message with a resurrection hope of imperishable inheritance (1 Pet 1:3–4, 23, 25). Such a new imperishable outcome is akin to being born again, thus also grounding the command to live loving the brethren.

PETRINE REDEMPTION ATONEMENT

Because of atonement, Petrine redemption is Christ's work setting people free from their previous lifestyles, much like the initiating atonement did when Israel received the law (Exod 20:1—24:8; 1 Pet 1:2, 18). Peter does not use Paul's exhaustive redemption concept, which includes features such as justification, forgiveness, and the ultimate resurrection departure from the sinful body (Rom 3:24; 8:23; Eph 1:7, 14), nor Luke's eschatological kingdom concept of redemption (Luke 1:68–69; 2:38; 24:21; also in Old Greek LXX Dan 4:34). Rather Peter's concept of redemption emphasized a changed life "from your futile way of life" to initiate a new meaningful exodus way of life (1 Pet 1:18).

The concept of redemption is the exchanging of ownership, often by paying a price either in a market or on a battlefield. Initially the concept of redemption is grounded in the exodus with Yahweh's rescue and release of Israel to inherit the land and serve the living God (Deut 7:8; 9:6; Pss 74:2; 77:15). Passover commemorates this redemption with a redemption sacrifice that sanctifies all, especially the first born (Exod 12:1—13:16).

---

82. Such "purifying" (ἡγνικότες) is as in cleansing for temple (Acts 21:24, 26; 24:18).

Emerging from the exodus, the first born were to be redeemed by the Levites vicariously replacing them in living service and a payment to be made to Aaron (Num 3:11–51). By extension, any Israelite entangled in debt and selling himself into slavery was to be redeemed by those family members around him, since such slavery was inappropriate for those whom Yahweh had redeemed (Lev 25:25–27; 47–49). Peter expressed this thought with two words. First, ἐλυτρώθητε means "to set free, redeem or rescue" and often includes paying a ransom (1 Pet 1:18; LXX Ps 118[119]:134; Isa 44:22–24; Hos 13:14).[83] The second word, ἀγοράσαντα, emphasizes the market imagery of purchasing goods or people (2 Pet 2:1; 1 Cor 6:20; 7:23).[84] In such an exchange the goods or people are set free from the seller, usually to be possessed by the purchaser. Both Greek words for redemption are used to describe purchasing of slaves resulting in either enslavement to a new owner or to be set free.[85] Furthermore, these words express the idea of ransom, wherein a conqueror may free prisoners by defeating their master in battle.[86] In such an example, the one redeemed exchanges allegiance to the previous dominating power for allegiance to the one bringing about the redemption. However, the redemption of people does not require the one redeemed to have a new owner; the person may simply be set free.

The purchase price of the redemption Peter talks about was the death of Christ. Jesus died as a substitution on behalf of others.[87] Peter develops this theme by first designating what the price of redemption was not and then identifying what it was (1 Pet 1:18–19). For example, the price was not perishable (φθαρτοῖς), that which is subject to corruption or destruction.[88] Additionally, silver and gold are mentioned as dross compared to the extreme value of the actual price paid. In contrast, the actual price paid is the precious blood of Christ. The imagery of the blood refers to Christ's death in a Jewish sacrificial lamb pattern (1 Pet 1:2, 19, 21; Acts 1:19; 5:28), not a Bengelian effusion (draining Christ dry in order to obtain his blood as the imperishable material substance of value).[89]

---

83. BAG, 484; 1 Macc 4:11; *Pss. Sol.* 8.30; 9.1.

84. BAG, 12; 1 Macc 13:49; Josephus, *War* 2.127.

85. Both words used this way in Deissmann, *Light from the Ancient East*, 328, 333.

86. Büchsel, "λύτρον," TDNT 4:344; Moulton and Milligan, *Vocabulary of the Greek Testament*, 4:383.

87. Büchsel, "λύτρον," TDNT 4:343.

88. Harder, "φθαρω," TDNT 9:103–4.

89. Contra Bengel, *Gnomon of the New Testament*, 4.474; Human martyr blood as

Thus, Christ's death is characterized by a simile: Christ's blood shed was like that of the sacrificial lamb: unblemished and spotless, indicating the required purity of the sacrifice in a priestly covenantal context.

There is no description of a price being paid to another, neither to God nor to Satan, for Peter describes redemption in the OT pattern of Yahweh delivering Israel from bondage and captivity (Exod 6:6; Isa 52:3; 2 Pet 2:1). Additionally, by this time among the Jews the concept of ransom had become identified with vicarious sufferings and martyrdom of the righteous without giving anyone a payment because the martyrs lives were just spent on the battlefield.[90] The situation would be analogous to those whereby slain soldiers of a conquering army accomplish the freeing of slaves through the shedding of soldiers' blood in a decisive battle that wins a war.

The accomplishment of Petrine redemption is that of freeing people from their previous futile sinning and straying ways of life (1 Pet 1:18; 2:24–25). A prior lifestyle was characterized by ματαίας, which means "idle, empty, fruitless, useless, powerless, lacking truth."[91] This futile lifestyle was inherited from the forefathers as the worthless commitments of a pagan.[92] For example, this prior lifestyle was composed of ignorant lusts (1 Pet 1:14), diverse evil actions (1 Pet 2:1) and gentile dissipation (1 Pet 4:3–4). No doubt there were Jews among those with such lifestyles since in 1 Pet so many Jewish imageries are used. These Jews, however, either had a milder former lifestyle or else ran in the same gentile excesses. In either case their lives before the redemption through Christ had been futile (1 Pet 1:18). Now Christ had freed from (ἐκ) such futility. They no longer needed to be involved in their previous lifestyles. As such, Petrine redemption is an act that focuses on requiring the redeemed to live differently. For example, the repeated commands throughout 1 Pet remind believers of their obligation. The act of Christ redeeming them must be followed by their own action. However, Petrine redemption does not extend through the believer's life with any continual monergistic enablement. The continued soteriological enablement described by Peter is identified with other soteriological motifs, such as the continued presence

---

redemption during battle (4 Macc 17:22) and the priest's prayer for that redemptive victory outcome (4 Macc 6:29); Hughes, "Blood of Jesus,) 99–109; Jewett, *Romans*, 286.

90. Human martyr blood as redemption during battle (4 Macc 17:22) and the priest's prayer for that redemptive victory outcome (4 Macc 6:29).

91. BAG, 496.

92. Bauernfeind, "ματαίας," TDNT 4:521–24.

of the Spirit upon the believer (1 Pet 4:14). Petrine redemption then is a definite act wherein Christ initially frees a person from his former futile way of life and thus renders him under obligation to obey synergistically in his new changed lifestyle with the enablement of the Holy Spirit.

Petrine redemption is not equated with Petrine salvation. In Peter, "salvation" is a present process (1 Pet 3:21; 4:18; σῴζω, whereas Mark 5:29 uses it of "healing," and Acts 4:9 combines salvation with healing) that is not complete until one enters kingdom in the end times (Acts 2:21, future indicative σωθήσεται; 1 Pet 1:5, 9; 2 Pet 3:15). In contrast, Petrine redemption is a past fact, fully accomplished by Christ when the life is initially transformed (1 Pet 1:18; 2 Pet 2:1). Peter never describes salvation as a past fact. Things can be presently soteriological, however, if they normally lead to the future salvation. Additionally, Petrine salvation focuses on freedom from judgment and obtaining kingdom within a gracious strictured two ways framework in contrast to apostasy (1 Pet 1:3–9; 2 Pet 1:2–11; 2:1–22). Petrine redemption focuses on the past transformation of futile lifestyle to vital righteous living, so it initiates the new exodus much as the first Passover initiated Israel's first exodus. In Peter, one can be soteriologically redeemed without having been saved in the same manner as much of Israel was redeemed by the first Passover but died before they ever got into the promised land. While Peter includes redemption with the total process of salvation, he indicates by extent of redemption that the redemption of an individual does not guarantee that she will be ultimately saved. Calvin floated this view of previously non-saved knowers of the truth apostatizing.[93]

Petrine redemption is not actually bringing Israel out of Egypt (a mere historical parallel), because 2 Pet is written to a mixed group of Christians, some of whom have come from gentile backgrounds. Most notably, in 2 Pet 2:1 "the people," who should be understood as Israel,[94] were distinguished from the recipients of Peter's letter. That is, Israel had false prophets; the present recipients of Peter's letter will be harassed when false teachers rise from among them.

The context of 2 Pet develops soteriological concerns regarding "divine nature."[95] For example, the recipients of the letter have the same

---

93. Calvin, *Calvin's Commentaries*, 22:393; Bauckham, *Jude, 2 Peter*, 240–41, 274–81.

94. Strathmann, "λαός," TDNT 4:50–57.

95. Parallel to 2 Pet, Jude develops a similar common salvation (Jude 3), judgment (Jude 5–16) and exhortations to guarantee salvation (Jude 17–23), and the security

kind of faith as apostle Peter (2 Pet 1:1). After a short blessing (2 Pet 1:2), the recipients have been granted everything pertaining to life and godliness through the true knowledge of Christ (2 Pet 1:3). These magnificent promises provide the believers each individually with everlasting life by obtaining immortality of the divine nature (2 Pet 1:4 reflecting the change between plural verb and individual nouns and adjectives).[96] Terrance Callan proposed that 2 Pet 1:3–4 includes a genitive absolute introduced by ὡς serving as a protasis for a conditional sentence[97] in which 2 Pet 1:5–7 is the apodosis.[98] "For this reason" (2 Pet 1:5, καὶ αὐτὸ τοῦτο) references the previous 2 Pet 1:3–4 protasis as realized and introduces the apodosis to follow.[99] Divine power and promises serve as the foundation upon which virtues show we are kingdom bound.

"Divine" (θείας) as an adjectival description of "divine" power to facilitate the promises and "divine" nature as the outcome of the promises (2 Pet 1:3–4). "Nature" (φύσεως) describes the whole condition of a person. When these words are combined in Jewish contexts of "corruption" (φθορᾶς), they often have the sense indicating incorruptibility or immortality of the resurrection body after death (2 Pet 1:4).[100] Such a condition is not realized until the individual escapes corruption of mortality and lusts to participate in the resurrection nature, so this will be discussed among Petrine exodus and eschatology (2 Pet 1:4, aorist of ἀποφυγόντες; 2 Pet 2:19–20).

Upon this foundation of promises unto resurrection, Peter develops a narrow way of virtues unto everlasting kingdom (2 Pet 1: 5–11).[101] Beginning with the faith granted, Christians are to apply moral excellence, knowledge, self-control, perseverance, godliness, brotherly kindness, and love in their lives as they pursue the kingdom (2 Pet 1:1, 5–6, 11). By living into these virtues in an increasing manner, the Christian reassures

---

from Christ the Savior (Jude 24–25).

96. Echoed by 2 *Clem.* 5.5.

97. Like 1 Cor 4:18 except protasis is contrary to fact; 1 Pet 4:1 and 1 Thess 3:6–8 have similar construction without ὡς; Sir 1.1–6 protasis for 1.7–14 apodosis; Callan, "Syntax of 2 Peter 1:1–7," 636–37.

98. Callan, "Syntax of 2 Peter 1:1–7," 632–40.

99. Like: Lucian, *Icaromenippus* 2; Josephus, *Ant.* 10.11.6, sec. 257; Cassius Dio, *Hist.* 78.25.3; Aelius Aristides, *To Plato: In Defense of Oratory* 455–56; Rom 13:6; 2 Cor 5:5; 7:11; Gal 2:10; Callan, "Syntax of 2 Peter 1:1–7," 639–40.

100. 4 Macc 18:3; Wis 2:23.

101. This narrow way of virtues will be developed in the chapter "Exodus Following Jesus to Kingdom Virtues" in contrast to *theosis*.

herself that her election and entrance unto kingdom is ensured (2 Pet 1:8, 10–11). Such assurance of election evidenced by one's growing transformed virtues is especially developed within Reformed tradition.[102] In this perspective, Peter's view frames an experiential assurance, which in a Methodist tradition is later identified with William Perkins' "temporary faith" from 2 Pet 1:10 or Richard Rogers' believing heart in contrast to an "unbelieving heart" from Heb 3:12,[103] whereas, in a Reformed tradition, Calvin described apostates from previously non-saved knowers of the truth.[104] Either way, a two ways soteriological strategy of virtues in Christ is set up, in contrast to their temptation to depart from new covenant benefits, much like Heb developed.[105] These virtues growing in the believer's life become the synergistic evidence for them having been elected by God and that they will be in kingdom. Following this, Peter guarantees that kingdom salvation shall be fulfilled by appealing to earlier stages of the prophecy that have already occurred, such as the transfiguration (1 Pet 1:16–19).

In contrast to the traditional individual reformation soteriology of the Reformed, Lutheran or Arminian traditions, Peter paints within a communally covenantal background. We need to be careful applying modern constructs of individualism on a text. A better strategy is to notice the constructs available in the historical-cultural context and allow them to evidence something of the range of the possible views. Then more specifically, we should prefer those constructs that the text floats as models it identifies as setting up the foundation for the teaching it develops. And of course, in this, any clear statement in the text takes priority over these inclinations of the possible and the likely.

Those who do not pursue such kingdom virtues shall be severely judged and miss salvation (2 Pet 1:9; 2:2–9). Some have escaped such defilement through this knowledge of Christ only to be re-entangled which results in being worse off than at first (2 Pet 2:20–22). That is, these scoffers shall be condemned while the beloved shall be saved (2 Pet 3:3–15).

102. This point is developed in the Reformed tradition: Calvin, *Calvin's Commentaries*, 22:376–78 on 2 Pet 1:10; *Institutes of the Christian Religion* 3.15.8, "judged by their fruits," and especially by Edwards, *Religious Affections*.

103. Perkins, *Workes of Mr. William Perkins*, 1:125, 358, 3:271; Rogers, *Seven Treatises*, 102, 109, 136, 243, 298, 308, 322, 401; Rogers also advocates "temporary faith" in *Doctrine of Faith*, 10; Kendall, *Calvin and English Calvinism to 1649*, 69, 81–82.

104. Calvin, *Calvin's Commentaries*, 22:393; Bauckham, *Jude, 2 Peter*, 240–41, 274–81.

105. Kennard, *Biblical Theology of Hebrews*, 66–137.

The temporal deliverances of Noah and Lot during temporal judgments are subsumed under the greater soteriological concerns (2 Pet 2:5, 7, 9). These deliverances are not developed to make the great judgment day seem less. Rather, they reinforce the fact that since God has judged previously, he will certainly do so again in this greater future judgment when he also saves those who are his.

The buying (ἀγοράσαντα) is best seen as soteriological redemption. Even though ἀγοράσαντα does not translate OT words for soteriological redemption, the word always means soteriological redemption in the NT when it refers to people as the object of the purchase (1 Cor 6:20; 7:23; Rev 5:9; 14:3–4). Furthermore, the context clearly develops soteriological issues. Within this development there is a major emphasis on lifestyle, which is quite appropriate to Petrine redemption. For example, those who have knowledge of Christ are to abundantly appropriate in their lives with virtues of faith, moral excellence, knowledge, self-control, perseverance, godliness, brotherly kindness, and love (2 Pet 1:2–7). This meaningful way of life assures the believer that she shall bear fruit and enter the everlasting kingdom (2 Pet 1:8–11). This meaningful way is the reverse of the pre-redemptive futile sinful way of life (1 Pet 1:18; 2 Pet 1:9). So ἀγοράσαντα here is best seen as soteriological redemption. The lack of a mentioned price is no reason to overthrow this soteriological meaning since half of the NT soteriological meanings of this word omit any mention of a price (2 Pet 2:1; Rev 14:3–4).

The master (δεσπότην) who is denied by the false teachers is Jesus Christ (2 Pet 2:1). First, since the redemption accomplished by the master is soteriological (2 Pet 2:1) and Peter described only Christ as the one who soteriologically redeems people (1 Pet 1:18–19), then Christ is the master of whom Peter speaks in 2 Pet 2:1. Second, Christ is the master because the context emphasizes soteriological concerns. For example, Peter elsewhere uses δεσπότην of the sovereign creator (Acts 4:24). However, the sovereign creator is an unlikely reference in 2 Pet 2:1 since creator is only a minor element in 2 Pet, subservient to the greater concern of eschatological salvation and judgment (2 Pet 3:4–7). Additionally, Peter elsewhere used δεσπόταις of earthly slave masters (1 Pet 2:18). However, there is no indication of earthly masters and their slaves in 2 Pet. In fact, the false teachers are free with the human freedom to pursue a multitude of different actions inappropriate for slaves, most notably their own licentious living. Third, 2 Pet is broadly parallel to Jude and Jude 4 uses δεσπότην to refer to Christ within a context of common salvation in which the false teachers are denying the only master and Lord, Jesus Christ.

It is inappropriate to appeal to a hypothetical redemption in 2 Pet 2:1, patterned after Luke 14:15–24 in a manner as A. Chang maintained such a hypothetical purchase.[106] But Chang nullified his position by arguing that the statements of purchase are outright lies. He argued for false statements of actual purchase rather than true statements of hypothetical purchase. Such an argument better supports the view of charity, calling someone something that they call themselves, even though it is false. However, I. H. Marshall developed the hypothetical nature of the purchase in Luke. In that case "the purchase may well have been arranged on the condition of later inspection and approval" where the reference to necessity (ἀνάγκην in Luke 14:18) "implies the legal obligation of the purchaser to complete the sale."[107] However, this Lukan example is in the middle of an actual transaction and does not develop the effect of a rejection of a completed purchase such as Peter develops in 2 Pet 2:1. The meaning of Petrine redemption as actual or hypothetical is then not determined by an appeal to Luke but by the context of 2 Pet.

A contextual appeal to 2 Pet surfaces three groups who have experienced the change of life normally resulting from Petrine redemption. The first is that body of believers who are growing in the qualities of salvation (2 Pet 1:4–6). For example, this group escaped lusts through moral excellence and godliness. Second, the theoretical possibility of a second group is admitted by Peter in the context, those who have begun with these changed qualities and then left them, having forgotten their purification from their former sins (2 Pet 1:9–11). Peter condemns these apostates as doubly blind, unfruitful, and in danger of missing the kingdom. Peter then develops this theoretical group as two actual groups: the false teachers, and those who barely escape lusts, only to be enticed back into their former lifestyles (2 Pet 2:18–22; Simon of Acts 8:13, 20).[108]

---

106. Chang, "Second Peter 2:1," 55–56.

107. Marshall, *Luke*, 589.

108. Two groups are indicated because the accusative of 2 Pet 2:18 cannot be identified with the subject, the false teachers who entice them (contra Jerome, *Jov.* 2 n. 3 and Augustine, *Fid. op.* 45). Simon Magnus is an example of such a false teacher who had believed, been baptized, and aligned with believers (Acts 8:13) but upon seeing the power of the bestowal of the Holy Spirit is warned by Peter about Simon's precarious situation of impending damnation (σὺν σοὶ εἴη εἰς ἀπώλειαν, Acts 8:20, similar to Theodotion LXX Dan 2:5; 3:96 and Old Greek LXX Dan 2:18; 6:23) due to his root of bitterness and bondage to iniquity (Acts 8:20, 23). Justin Martyr later identified that

These two groups experience the lifestyle change that the knowledge of Christ produces. For example, those who barely escape from the ones who live in error still actually escape for a time (2 Pet 2:18). The repetition of ἀποφυγόντες in 2 Pet 2:18 and 20 identifies the possibility of some people barely escaping, only to be overcome again. The context of verse 20 is primarily to do with the false teachers who are the third group. This is demonstrated contextually since the false teachers are those who entice the vulnerable escapees by fleshly desires, promising freedom while they themselves are slaves overcome[109] by judgment[110] (2 Pet 2:18–19). Furthermore, the use of γάρ in 2 Pet 2:19–20 connects this immediately preceding material with what follows, so that false teachers remain the primary subject.[111] The false teachers are indicated as the subject through the repetition of "overcome" emphasizing the judgment that "overcomes" the false teachers (2 Pet 2:20 ἡττῶνται; 2:19 ἥττηται). Since verse 20 primarily has to do with the false teachers, they also had escaped the defilements of the world by the knowledge of Christ. They have experienced the change of life normally resulting from Petrine redemption (1 Pet 1:18; 2 Pet 2:20).

The false teachers have been redeemed soteriologically under Peter's concept of redemption. 1) They have been redeemed soteriologically because Christ has bought them in a soteriological manner (2 Pet 2:1). 2) The soteriological redemption was not hypothetically applied but accomplished, since the false teachers experienced the results of Petrine redemption: a changed life (2 Pet 2:20). Thus, where the results of the work have been present one should consider the work of redemption as having been accomplished. 3) Redemption results were accomplished by the knowledge of Christ, which further identifies the redemption as having

---

Simon Magnus did not repent, and he died trying to perform a miracle that would lead others astray and was therefore damned (*1 Apol.* 26.3; 56.2). Bock, *Acts*, 333–36.

109. As in a battle, those overcome are slaves of their enemy; Bauckham, *Jude, 2 Peter*, 277.

110. The use of φθορᾶς refers to the divine judgment (2 Pet 2:12) and its mortality (2 Pet 1:4). The word is not used by Peter for moral corruption (Harder, "φθορω," TDNT 9: 104 and Köster, "φύσις," TDNT 9: 275).

111. Perhaps in the focus on the false teachers the enticed ones barely escape (ἀποφεύγοντας; 2 Pet 2:18) and are warned of a similar fate by the repetition of ἀποφυγόντες in 2:20. However, the conceptual relationship between verse 18 "enticed by fleshly desires" and verse 20 "the defilements of the world" is not significant for the argument because there is no verbal connection (as with the false teachers in 2:10). Since the context emphasizes the false teachers as the subject, any conceptual appeal should maintain this emphasis.

been soteriologically accomplished. For example, the divinely-given, true knowledge of Christ is within the precious and magnificent salvation promises (2 Pet 1:3–4). This soteriological knowledge is a commitment to truth that leads to salvation and kingdom (2 Pet 1:8–11; 3:18). So, the one who diligently continues in soteriological knowledge shall arrive at kingdom salvation. It is then best to see the false teachers as actually having begun by Petrine soteriological redemption, which resulted in their transformed lives through Christ's death.

The false teachers have in turn exchanged their knowledge and moral living for an ignorant life of rampant sin and certain condemnation. Having come to know (ἐπεγνωκέναι) the way of righteousness and experiencing (ἐπιγνοῦσιν) it, they have then rejected it (2 Pet 2:21), which in turn has plunged them into an ignorant life (2 Pet 2:12 ἀγνοοῦσιν). Such ignorance is akin to the unbeliever's condition of practicing sinful lust and persecuting Christ (Acts 3:17; 1 Pet 1:14; 2:15). These false teachers are worse off than if they had remained unredeemed ignorant unbelievers (2 Pet 2:21). 1) They know the commandment that they must live righteously. In being overcome by the entanglements of the world they know judgment will follow their disobedience. 2) Their true bent demonstrates clearly that they are fools (2 Pet 2:22). Proverbial statements such as "a dog returning to its vomit and a washed sow returning to the mire" recall the contextual use in Proverbs 26:11 signifying a fool returning to his folly. These false teachers cannot say they never knew better. They have committed high-handed sin, knowingly rejecting both Christ and the way they must live. Such an unrighteous life will be kept by the Lord under impending punishment for the day of judgment (2 Pet 2:9).

Such a concept renders Petrine redemption superabundant rather than impotent. First, the elect are redeemed, accomplishing for them a transformation of life that leads toward their guaranteed salvation (1 Pet 1:1–5, 18). In Peter's terminology salvation is identified with the resurrection and the kingdom (1 Pet 1:5, 9–10). Things can be considered presently soteriological, however, if they normally lead toward that salvation even if they do not fully accomplish it (1 Pet 3:21; 4:18; 2 Pet 3:15). Redemption as a soteriological work of Christ is effective in its transformation of the lives of the elect on their journey toward salvation. Second, redemption is no less effective where it accomplishes its full work of life transformation among some, like the false teachers who are not recipients of other soteriological works, which are needed if they would be saved. One should not fault a work of Christ that does more than is soteriologically necessary. A work of Christ may go beyond the limits of the elect to benefit others for a time. This redemption is not, however, universalism because it is applied to all who are transformed. Thus, Petrine redemption is not equated with prevenient grace either, because it definitely effectively initially transforms the group broader than the elect, whose lives are transformed, in order for some non-elect to depart from this past redemption. Petrine redemption should then be conceived of as a limited redemption, which nevertheless extends beyond the limits of the elect. It also includes all who experience the transformation of life by means of Christ's death, even for a time.

MIMETIC ATONEMENT ESPECIALLY IN MARK

Hellenistic biography presents the "supreme indicator" of a person's character to be the way a person faces his own death,[112] which shows why the Gospel of Mark ends with Jesus' martyrdom, accentuating mimetic atonement. Jesus' death in Mark is developed largely through a simple retelling of the historical event.[113] In this passion narrative, no development of atonement occurs.

Additionally, Jesus predicts his death that he must suffer many things from the elders, chief priests and scribes, and be condemned to death (Mark 8:31, 34–38; 9:12, 31; 10:33–34; Matt 16:21; 17:12, 22–23; 20:18; Luke 9:22, 44; 17:25; 18:31; 22:22).[114] In the Synoptics, Jesus does not explain why his death must happen. These wicked religious leaders were simply following in the foolish way to kill the righteous man who showed up their evil ways.[115] However, Jesus' death frames a future for the disciples to imitate him in mimetic atonement. This mimetic atonement (Mark 8:34–38; 10:35–45 giving your whole life in service) reflects Peter's emphasis primarily developing mimetic atonement (1 Pet 2:21–24, servants follow Jesus' example of silent suffering).

Jesus sets his resolve like flint to suffer (Isa 50:6–7) because He realized that the kingdom is only obtainable by going through the Messianic woes (Dan 9:24–27). It is these Messianic woes that begin his martyrdom

---

112. Bond, *First Biography of Jesus*, 68.
113. Kennard, *Messiah Jesus*, 279–86.
114. *Acts of Pilate* 4.3; Justin, *Dial.* 106.
115. Pattern of Wis 2.12–20.

and the potential martyrdom of his disciples. Albert Schweitzer developed this briefly as follows:

> In order to understand Jesus' resolve to suffer, we must first recognize that the mystery of this suffering is involved in the mystery of the kingdom of god, since the kingdom cannot come until the [tribulation] *peirasmos* has taken place. . . . The novelty lies in the form in which [the sufferings] are conceived. The tribulation, so far as Jesus is concerned, is now connected with an historical event: He will go to Jerusalem, there to suffer death at the hands of the authorities. . . . In the secret of His passion which Jesus reveals to the disciples at Caesarea Philippi the pre-Messianic tribulation is . . . concentrated upon Himself alone, and that in the form that they are fulfilled in His own passion and death at Jerusalem. That was the new conviction that had dawned upon Him. He must suffer for others . . . that the kingdom might come.[116]

These predictions of Jesus' crucifixion, provide a call to the cost of discipleship within mimetic atonement context. The main contextual implication for Jesus' death in these predictive comments is an undergirding of the cost of discipleship; since Jesus is heading for crucifixion, the true disciple must follow him by taking up their cross in impending martyrdom as well (Mark 8:34–37; Matt 10:38–39; 16:24–26; Luke 9:23–26; 14:27).[117] That is, the disciple must be ready for the possibility that those who would kill Christ, may kill them as well (Acts 7:54–60; 12:1–6).[118] This mimetic atonement view was common in Jewish,[119] Greek, and Roman literature.[120]

Specifically, in Mark 10:35–45, Mother Zebedee asked for her sons to sit at Jesus' right and left in the kingdom (also Matt 20:18–24). Jesus

---

116. Schweitzer, *Quest for the Historical Jesus*, 384–90; for an expansion of this perspective see Pate and Kennard, *Deliverance Now and Not Yet*.

117. This emphasis is in line with that of scholarly commentators on these verses. Davies and Allison, *Matthew*, 2:222–23, 670–671; Senior, *Passion of Jesus in Matthew*, 40–45; Gundry, *Mark*, 452–54; Bock, *Luke*, 1:850–57, and 2:1286–87; Beck, "Imiatio Christi and the Lucan Passion Narrative," 28–47.

118. Nero's persecution of Christians, Tacitus, *Ann.* 15.44; *1 Clement* 6; *Did.* 16.3–5.

119. 1 Macc 2:27–28; 2 Macc 6:12–17.42; 4 Macc 1:8–11; 6:27–30; 7:8–9; 9:23–24; 10:10; 11:12–27; 12:16–18; 16:16, 24–25; 17:2, 11–22; 18:1–5; Wis 2.12–20; 3.5–6; 4.18–15.14; 7.14; 11.19; 12.22; *T. Mos.* 9–10.10; Pate and Kennard, *Deliverance Now and Not Yet*, 29–71; Seeley, *Noble Death*; Green, *Death of Jesus*, 168.

120. Seneca, *Ad Lucilium Epistulae Morales*, 24.4–7; 98.12–14; Silius Italicus, *Punica*.

responds to the Zebedee boys and mother, that they do not know what they are asking. "Are you able to drink the cup that I am about to drink?"[121] The Zebedee boys do not realize that Jesus is likely alluding to God's cup of wrath poured out for Jesus' martyrdom. However, they say, "we are able." To which Jesus responds, "My cup you shall drink,"[122] fulfilling their disciple role of being like their master in martyrdom. James Zebedee dies under the zeal of Herod to persecute the church (Acts 12:2), and John Zebedee dies exiled to Patmos after boiling in oil under Domitian persecution and survived till Nerva's reign.[123] Bear in mind that if the disciples partake of the cup of God's wrath in mimetic atonement, then Jesus' experience as developed in this context is not a unique vicarious atonement. It is better to see neither the disciples' nor Jesus' cup taking developed in this context as depicting a vicarious atonement than to fund a conjectured vicarious atonement off the martyrdom of the disciples and Christ, because mimetic atonement coheres within early Judaism.

However, the role of sitting on Jesus' right or left is not Jesus' but for the Father to designate. Jesus then deals with the deeper issue in their lives. Greatness in the kingdom is not the goal of lording over others but of serving others (Mark 10:42–45; Matt 20:25–28). It is in this context that Jesus says, "The Son of Man did not come to be served, but to serve, and to give his life as a ransom for many" (Mark 10:45; Matt 20:28).[124] Here Jesus' life given includes his death (through the cup imagery) but he emphasizes his life spent in service as the example of true kingdom greatness which his disciples are to follow. That is, mimetic atonement has Jesus' servanthood life as the price of ransom ($\lambda\acute{\upsilon}\tau\rho o\nu$) rescuing the

---

121. This mimetic atonement suffering is additionally supported by Jesus' metaphor of baptism within an OT concept of suffering by submersion (2 Sam 22:4–7, 17–18; Pss 18:4–6, 16–17; 32:6; 42:7; 69:1–2, 13–17; 124:1–5 [repeated liturgically as a song of ascent]; 144:7–11; Job 22:11).

122. Jesus' cup refers to his impending death (Mark 14:33–34; Matt 26:37–38), perhaps after the pattern of the "cup of wrath" (Pss 11:6; 75:8; Isa 51:17, 22; Jer 25:15, 17, 27; 49:12; 51:7; Rev 16:1—18:6).

123. Irenaeus, *Haer.* 3.1.1; Eusebius, *Hist. eccl.* 3.34.13; Lightfoot, *Apostolic Fathers*, 513–31.

124. A defense of the authenticity of this statement: Feuillict, "La coupe et le baptême," 356–91; Howard, "Did Jesus Speak," 515–27; Casey, *Aramaic Sources of Mark's Gospel*, 206; Sanders, *Jesus and Judaism*, 147; McKnight, *Jesus and His Death*, 356–58 conjectures that Mark reflects Isa 53. However, in Pate and Kennard, *Deliverance Now and Not Yet*, 316–18, 328–32, we explore the possibility of Isa 53 lying beneath these verses, examining the alternatives and concluding that the near-context emphasis should not be overruled by the pendulum swing of plausible academic conjecture.

many from an ambiguous bondage into his kingdom way. If λύτρον is defined by the other synoptic references, such ransoming has to do with God's raising up a Davidic king to deliver Israel from their enemies (Luke 1:68–69; 2:38; 24:21), not a vicarious atonement for sin. This follows the Jewish pattern where a martyr's death ransoms the covenant people Israel from the sins of the nation.[125] For example, in 4 Macc 6:29 a prayer is uttered by those on the battlefield, "Make my blood their purification, and take my life in exchange for theirs." The speaker goes on to exhort others to "imitate me" in remaining faithful on the battlefield even if martyrdom is their lot.[126] Fourth Maccabees 17:20–22 goes on to praise the martyrs for becoming "a ransom for the sin of our nation and through the blood of those devout ones and their death as an atoning sacrifice, divine Providence preserved Israel." In early Jewish Greek manuscripts of mimetic atonement, this atonement is conveyed by words like: "through" (διά), "example" (ὑπόδειγμα), and the contextual pattern imitative death.[127] George Nickelsburg explains this early Jewish mimetic atonement option from passages in 2 Macc 6:18—7:44, 1 Macc 2 and the *T. Mos.* 9. Each instance recounts the event which the respective author interprets as the catalyst that turns God's wrath from Israel and brings release from the persecution. Each is a story about parent and sons who are ready to die rather than transgress the Torah. Written in the heat of persecution, *T. Mos.* anticipates an apocalyptic denouement in which God will avenge the innocent blood of his servants, notably Taxo and his sons (*T. Mos.* 9:7; 10:2 interpretation of Deut 32:43). For the pro–Hasmonean author of 1 Macc, Mattathias' zealous deed stays God's wrath (Num 25:8, 11). The Maccabean victories are an answer to the dying patriarch's appeal to execute judgment on the Syrians (1 Macc 2:66-68; Deut 32:43). The version of the story in 2 Macc 7 takes cognizance of the fact that it was Judas Maccabeus who turned back the Syrian armies and brought deliverance to Israel. However, although Taxo's prediction has not been fulfilled as stated, our author nevertheless espoused in part the ideology of the *T. Mos.* The innocent deaths of the martyrs and their appeal for vengeance before and after death (2 Macc 7:37; 8:3) contribute to turn God's wrath to mercy (2 Macc 8:5) and facilitate the Maccabean victories that are

---

125. 1QpHab. 8.1–3; 2 Macc 6:30; 7:9, 11, 14, 16–17, 22–23, 29, 30–38; 4 Macc 6:27–29; 9:23–24; 17:21–22.

126. 4 Macc 9:23–24.

127. 2 Macc 6:31; 4 Macc 17:20–22.

recounted through the rest of the book.[128] However, in this Markan context, battlefield service is not in view but rather serving through humility as Jesus provides the example. However, gaining kingdom is the goal in both Maccabean and Jesus' humble service. Jesus repeatedly called his disciples to take up their cross and follow him in this mimetic atonement (Mark 8:34–38; Matt 10:38; 16:24–27; Luke 9:22–26; John 12:24–25).

In Mark 10:45 Jesus said, "The Son of Man did not come to be served, but to serve, and to give his life a ransom for many." Notice first, this ransom (λύτρον) provides an example of Jesus serving others that the disciples are to follow. "The many" (πολλῶν) is the new covenant people, whom Jesus is gathering around him. Such a kingdom meaning fits delightfully in this passage that acknowledges Jesus as the King in his kingdom but not like other kings (Mark 10:42; Matt 20:21, 25). This ransom is "for" (ἀντὶ) the many in this Gospel context (Mark 10:45). That word ἀντὶ has the sense of substitution, "on behalf of" or "in place of." In this case both could apply. Jesus shows his greatness as King in taking the place of servants and serving on their behalf throughout his kingly life on earth and as supremely exampled in his death with God's wrath. The point of the passage is not vicarious atonement in a death event but by contextual emphasis this passage shows that disciples are also to be servants after Jesus' pattern of serving others for his whole life. As such, this passage follows the Jewish mimetic atonement pattern.[129]

The Gethsemane prayer also develops Jesus' cup imagery with his impending death (Mark 14:33–34; Matt 26:37–38). Jesus' request that this cup pass from him is best developed in Heb 5:7 as praying for resurrection.[130] The Passover cup statement also alludes to Jesus' impending martyrdom, as Jesus' blood of the new covenant is poured out for many (Mark 14:24 and Luke 22:20, ὑπέρ, "for"; Matt 26:27–28, περὶ, "concerning"). In Matt 26:28, Jesus' death is explained as for (εἰς) or to the outcome of forgiveness of sins. This last reference might return to vicarious atonement, within the synoptic emphasis of mimetic atonement, the same emphasis Peter had in 1 Pet 2:18–25.

128. Nickelsburg, *Jewish Literature*, 119–20.

129. 1 Macc 2:27–28; 2 Macc 6:12—17:42; 4 Macc 1:8–11; 6:27–30; 7:8–9; 9:23–24; 10:10; 11:12–27; 12:16–18; 16:16, 24–25; 17:2, 11–22; 18:1–5; Wis 2.12–20; 3.5–6; 4.18—15.14; 7.14; 11.19; 12.22; 1Q5 5.6; 1QS 9.4–5; 1Q34 bis 3.1, 5; 4Q508 1.1; 4Q513 frag. 2.2.4; 11Q10 (*Tg. Job*) 38.2; *Sipre Deut. Pisqa* 333.5; *T. Mos.* 9.1—10.10; cf. Pate and Kennard, *Deliverance Now and Not Yet*, 29–71; Gundry, *Mark*, 869.

130. Blaising, "Gethsemane a Prayer of Faith," 333–43; Kennard, *Biblical Theology of Hebrews*, 49–51.

9

Peter's Gospel

PETER PREACHED THE GOSPEL as the message that focused on Jesus is Lord and everyone needs to align with him (1 Pet 1:12, 25; 4:6). Peter expressed that the gospel (εὐηγγελίζω) is grounded in the imperishable word, causing imperishable life unto resurrection (1 Pet 1:12, 23—25; 4:6). This gospel was what Peter and others announced to his readers by the empowerment of the Holy Spirit (1 Pet 1:12). This proclamation was accomplished while the listeners were alive, though many of these believers had died by the time of Peter's writing the letter (1 Pet 4:6). The appropriate response to gospel was to obey the gospel message (1 Pet 4:17). Of course, Peter believed that Jesus died for our sins and says so, but he does not identify that fact as the gospel (1 Pet 2:24). Jesus' life and ministry is Peter's gospel in the Gospel of Mark and the book of Acts.

Peter provided the material from his repeated statements about Christ for the Gospel of Mark. Using the expression of "good news" or "gospel" is an indication of biography. For example, the *Priene Inscription* 2.81-82 used the word "good news" (εὐαγγελίου) twice identifying a narrative describing Augustus' life up until the time when he began to rule as Caesar.[1] The Gospel of Mark utilized the term in the same biographical manner (Mark 1:1), which in the context identifies the good news of the narrative of Jesus Christ and his kingdom message (εὐαγγέλιον, Mark 1:14–15; 8:35; 13:10; 14:9; 16:15; Matt 4:23; 9:35) which is repeatedly proclaimed by the apostles (εὐαγγέλιον, Matt 24:14; 26:13; Byzantine addition of Mark 16:15). However, Mark's emphasis is that Jesus has

---

1. *Priene Inscription* 105; similarly emperor Septimius Geta in *Inscriptiones Grecae* 3.1081; Dihle, "Gospels and Greek Biography," 361–86.

authority to heal and meet the needs of the people beyond other lords like Caesar. Jesus offers the kingdom of God (Mark 1:14–15) as an alternative to the Herodians' kingdom or Caesar's kingdom, so the gospel could be summarized as "Jesus is Lord."

The gospel can also be summarized as the narrative account of Jesus as he repeatedly heals and meets needs. The patristics concluded that there were four such authoritative Gospels that contain these legitimate accounts about Jesus and that each of the four were authoritative salvific Gospel, including Mark's summary of Peter's sermons.[2]

Such biographical accounts set up not only a belief in the authoritative Lord but a narrow way to follow exampled by the Lord's virtues. Hellenistic biography intentionally has virtues for the disciple and reader to imitate[3] as they "follow" the model for discipleship (Mark 1:17; 2:14; 8:34). For example, Quintilian folds qualities of the person in the narrative to be illustrated by the person's works.[4] Often the origin story indicates who the person will be like.[5] In Luke's example, Jesus is predicted to be the messiah to bring in the Abrahamic and Davidic covenants elevating the poor in eschatological reversal of his reign and destroying the opposition (Luke 1; 3:23–34), whereas Mark begins anticipating Jesus to be a new Moses leading his people through a new exodus event as Son of God (Mark 1:1–3 citing Isa 40:3).

However, these Hellenistic biographies regard the "supreme indicator" of a person's character to be the way one faces his own death,[6] which shows why Mark ends with Jesus' martyrdom, with no development

---

2. Irenaeus, *Haer.* 3.1.1–2; 3.10.5; 3.11.9; Ign. *Smyrn.* 1.1.1–2; John Chrysostom, *Hom. Matt.* 1.7; Justin, *1 Apol.* 66; *Dial.* 10.2; 103.19; 106; Eusebius, *Anti-Marcionite Prologue*; *Hist. eccl.* 2.15.1–2; 3.39.14–15; 5.20.6; 6.14.5–7; Tertullian, *Adv. Haer.* 4.2.2; 4.4–5; 4.5.3; Origen, Frag. in *Comm. in Matt.* 1.1–20; *Comm. Jo.* 1.5, 7–9; Gregory of Nazianzus, *Carmida dogmatica* 1.12.6–9; Theodoret, *Dialogs* 1; Jerome, *Vir. ill.* 7–9; Bauckham, *Jesus and the Eyewitnesses*, 300–305.

3. Philo, *Moses* 1.158; Josephus, *War* 1.4–8, 13–16; *Ant.* 1.1–2; Plutarch, *Aem.* 1.1, 5; Tacitus, *Agr.* 1; Dionysius, *Ant. Rom.* 8.56.1; Bond, *First Biography of Jesus*, 68, 168; Kurz, "Narrative Models for Imitation," 171–89; Fiore, *Function of Personal Example*, 26–44; de Boer, *Imitation of Paul*; Crouzel, "L'imitation et la 'suite' de Dieu et du Christ," 7–30; Cothenet, "Imitation du Christ," 7:1536–1601; Gutierrez, *La Paternité spirituelle selon S. Paul*; Pate and Kennard, *Deliverance Now and Not Yet*, 369–72; Trompf, *Idea of Historical Recurrence*, 97–101; Talbert, "Biographies of Philosophers and Rulers," 1643; Fornara, *Nature of History*, 104–20.

4. Quintilian, *Inst.* 3.7.10–22; 5.10.24–31.

5. Quintilian, *Inst.* 3.7.12; Ps. Hermogenes, *Prog.* 15–17.

6. Bond, *First Biography of Jesus*, 68.

concerning his resurrection. Such a biographic style further underscores discipleship and mimetic atonement.

Jesus called his disciples to follow him (Mark 1:17; 2:14), which is an invitation to follow the Father's will (Mark 3:35) in the same pattern as Jesus followed the Father's will (Mark 14:36). Such a life calls disciples to believe in this gospel (εὐαγγελίῳ, Mark 1:15). This believing life is alert to dangers but trying to follow Jesus in fervent prayer and forgiving others (Jesus: Mark 1:35; 2:5; 6:46; 14:32–36; disciples: 11:23–25; 14:38). Likewise, as Jesus has come to serve, his disciples are to serve others (Mark 9:35–41; 10:42–45). Because of the contextual emphasis on service, Jesus gave his whole life (not merely his death) in service ransoming the many, such as Jesus rescuing the blind men after he calls his disciples to serve (Mark 10:45–52; Matt 20:28–34).[7] Furthermore, Jesus sent out his disciples to imitate his kingdom ministry to meet real needs and call others to repent to the narrow way unto kingdom (Mark 4:11; 6:7–13; 11:10; 15:43). Amid the difficulties of persecution, the disciples are to continue to follow and confess Christ even to their death (Mark 8:29, 34–38; 13:9–13). If a disciple does not continue but is ashamed of Christ and his words, then "the Son of Man will also be ashamed of him when he comes in the glory of his Father with the holy angels" (Mark 8:38). However, those who endure "to the end will be saved" (Mark 13:13).

Peter's gospel message is also contained repeatedly in the book of Acts as that Jesus is the Lord who will eschatologically judge, so align with him.[8] Luke describes Peter and Paul's salvation messages in Acts as gospel (εὐαγγέλιον, Acts 15:7; 20:24).[9] Dibelius describes these sermons as follows: "An introduction suggested by the actual situation is normally followed by the kerygma of Jesus' life, passion and resurrection, usually with the disciples' witness; to this is subjoined a scriptural proof and an exhortation of repentance."[10] Peter clearly remains within an exclusivist strategy for salvation (Acts 4:12). N. T. Wright captures the essence of this gospel as, "Jesus the crucified and risen Messiah, is Lord."[11] The vicarious atonement is not developed in Luke's statements of gospel. Martin Luther identified that "the gospel is a story about Christ, God's and David's Son, who died and was raised and is established as Lord. This is the gospel in a

7. Kennard, *Messiah Jesus*, 275–77.
8. Kennard, *Messiah Jesus*, 439–70.
9. Stuhlmacher, *Gospel and the Gospels*, 22.
10. Dibelius, "Speeches in Acts," 165.
11. Wright, *What Saint Paul Really Said*, 46.

nutshell."[12] The Petrine emphasis of gospel proclamation in Acts may be summarized as follows:[13]

1. The focus of gospel messages is that Jesus is the Davidic King (Lordship), who you will have to deal with in end times judgment.
2. The core salvation benefits have to do with the kingdom being realized now in: forgiveness, and the Spirit being poured forth. However, additional kingdom benefits also ensues: healing, Jubilee, eschatological reversal, special Spirit manifestations and freedom from one's previous entanglements of the Law or idolatry.
3. Jesus' death provides an example for Jesus' disciples to imitate, and it shows the responsibility of rebellion, it is never referred to as a vicarious atonement.
4. Jesus' resurrection shows God's vindication identifying that Jesus is the Davidic King.
5. Every gospel sermon appeals to evidence to confirm the message, such as prophecy and miracles.
6. Repentance is what Jews in rebellion need to do, while gentiles need to come to faith (Acts 2:38; 3:19; 5:31; 10:43; 11:17; 15:7).
7. Baptism is tightly connected to this initial salvation response (1 Pet 3:21; Acts 2:38, 41; 8:12, 36–38; 9:18; 10:47–48; 11:16).
8. This salvation message brings the converts into the way of salvation extending Jesus' way unto kingdom (2 Pet 1:1–11; Acts 9:2; 13:10; 16:17; 18:25–26; 19:9; 22:4; 24:14, 22).

---

12. See "A Brief Instruction on What to Look For and Expect in the Gospels," in Luther, *Luther's Works*, 35:118.

13. Conzelmann, *Acts*, xliv, and Schweizer, "Concerning the Speeches in Acts," 208–16, esp. 210 have similar lists affirming my numbers: 1, 6, and 7 (Conzelmann's "Christological kerygma"). Their lists make more of stylistic rhetorical devices like connecting the speech with the situation and the role for OT quotes as beginning and demonstrating the message (Conzelmann's call for a hearing from miracle or prophecy, connection with the situation, use of OT quotation, *kerygma* attempted to be scripturally proven), supporting my #6. Conzelmann's response is more strongly slated toward "repentance the condition for salvation (where appropriate)." Instead see my more balanced assessment in my #7. McKnight placed the focus of the Acts sermons on the narrative of Jesus life and ministry as a miniature of the Gospel of Luke (*King Jesus Gospel*, 113–31, 166–75), though the life and ministry emphasis in Acts sermons mainly serve as a forum to recount Jesus confirming miracles (#6 on list) and to connect with the audience's awareness of Jesus' ministry. Earlier studies include: Stanley, "Conception of Salvation," 231–54; Guilbert, "Message of Salvation," 406–17; Jones, "Christology of the Missionary Speeches."

This topic is usually studied in more microscopic detail.[14] As such, it is rather rare for works to explore and compare the gospel speeches as a group, but this has been done before by a few.[15] Marion Soads has the best summary as follows:

> When one views the speeches together, one observes a remarkable coherence. The consistency occurs in terms of the forms and the contents of the speeches. There are 1) regularly repeated elements-for example, the manner of address, the tendency to speak beyond the immediate situation, the declaration of truth claims, the use of the past in explanation or support of the claims made, and the act of offering God's now-available salvation to the hearers for acceptance or rejection; 2) regularly repeated motifs-for example, divine necessity, a Christological contrast scheme, the Holy Spirit, the early Christian witness, and salvation; and 3) regularly repeated basic vocabulary. . . . What is "the meaning to be attributed to the speeches in the work as a whole"? One finds that the speeches unify the Acts

---

14. Usually, each feature of the respective sermons is mentioned verse by verse in a commentary, but occasionally closer looks of a particular sermon are undertaken such as: Dibelius, "Speeches in Acts," 138–85; Hemer, "Speeches in Acts II," 239–59; Porter, "Thucydides 1.22.1," 121–42 re-evaluated the issue in favor of Bruce's previous works; Schubert, "Final Cycle of Speeches," 1–16; Zehnle, *Peter's Pentecost Discourse*; Padilla, "Speeches in Acts," 171–94.

15. Soards, *Speeches in Acts* is the most profitable here in analyzing content with a special sensitivity to rhetorical device but he does not correlate the speeches; Ridderbos, *Speeches of Peter in Acts* nicely summarizes the content in each speech, especially with a focus on: eschatology apostolicity, Christology (especially my point #1), and paraenesis; Schweizer, "Concerning the Speeches in Acts," 208–16; Dodd, *Apostolic Preaching and Its Developments* mostly develops a continuity of the gospel through the whole NT, with a few pages on the Spirit, messianism and eschatological nature of the gospel *kerygma*, and a nice overview chart covering the whole NT gospel statements; which gems are foreshadowed in "Framework of the Gospel Narrative," 396–400 which primarily examines the Gospel of Mark; Cadbury, "Speeches in Acts," 1:402–26; Bruce, *Speeches in the Book of Acts* and "Speeches in Acts," 53–68, and Kennard, *Messiah Jesus*, 439–70 and *Gospel*, 117–46 survey the speeches in Acts with an emphasis on showing the gospel particulars, and *Epistemology and Logic*, 101–20 analyzed the epistemic and logical concerns of the gospel sermons. Luke responsibly handled these sermons after the pattern of the historian Thucydides; Hemer (*Book of Acts*, 75–79, 415–27) and Kennard (*Epistemology and Logic*, 86–101) defend the historicity of the speeches by comparing them to other Greek historians and the surrounding Acts context; Horsley ("Speeches and Dialogue in Acts," 609–14) primarily shows that Acts is consistent and more generous with the placement of speeches in Greek classical narrative; Kennedy (*New Testament Interpretation*, 114–40) surveys the speeches in Acts for some of the gems through rhetorical criticism; a narrative approach is framed by McKnight, *King Jesus Gospel*, 113–31, 166–75 and Kuhn, "Kingdom Story through Speech," 147–78; White, "Apostolic Preaching of the Lord Jesus," 33–51.

account, and through them Luke advances his theme of divinely commissioned unified witness to the ends of the earth.[16]

Luke recorded four of Peter's gospel presentations in Acts, and I have correlated these to surface the Petrine pattern of the gospel (Acts 2:14–39; 3:12–26; 4:8–12; 10:34–43). It is amazing how similar the pattern is in light of these messages emerging from very different situations, with different amount of time, and being heard by rather different groups. This demonstrates that Peter was consistent with his presentation of gospel, especially since there is great overlap with the Gospel of Mark. The chart on a following page summarizes these sermons.

The Gospel begins with an introduction transitioning from the circumstances at hand to the person of Jesus. These circumstances are as varied as the Spirit has poured out, or a man has been healed or they are on trial or the fact of Jewish exclusivity, when a gentile requests Peter's salvation message. This introduction with its variety bridges to the person of Jesus.

The focus of the gospel message is that the person of Jesus is the one who you will have to deal with in kingdom salvation. Each sermon develops this theme a little differently, but the commonality places the focus on Jesus and whether the audience aligns with him. For example, Acts 2 develops that Jesus is the Davidic king promised (Acts 2:30, quoting 2 Sam 7:12–13) announced as the anointed one to be King by God (Acts 2:36), and functioning in this exalted Christ role as receiving and giving the Holy Spirit (Acts 2:33). While in this context "Lord" (κύριος) stands for Davidic king and deity, as a term it was also appropriated by the Caesars (Augustus, Tiberius, Caligua, Nero, and Domitian) and the Jewish rulers (Herod the Great, Agrippa I and Agrippa II).[17] Contrary to these others, Acts 2 demonstrates Jesus is the Lord (Davidic king and God). The Lord concept of this Acts 2:36 reference is elevated by the quote from Ps 110:1 in Acts 2:34 which takes the אֲדֹנִי/Adonai as Lord (κύριος) in referring to Christ. However, since in Acts 2:34 the κύριος also translates Ps 110:1 יְהוָה/Yahweh, which draws Jesus' divinity within a Jewish monotheism as part of the gospel as well, whereas in Acts 3 Jesus serves many roles including healer, forgiver, ἀρχηγὸν (the prince or leader of life), the prophet after Moses' pattern, and the one who will bring in the kingdom.

---

16. Soards, *Speeches*, 14.

17. Bietenhard, "Lord, Master," NIDNTT 2:511; Cullmann, *Christology of the New Testament*, 197–99; Suetonius, *De Vita Caesarum* 13.2; the title was also used to describe gods (1 Cor. 8:5); Deismann, *Light from the Ancient East*, 352–53.

For a more hostile audience, on trial Jesus is presented as the only Savior for physical and spiritual healing (use of σώζω in Acts 4:9 and 12). For a receptive gentile audience, Jesus is presented as the Lord and judge of all, who also heals (Acts 10:38, 42). The focus of Peter's gospel statement is the person of Jesus Christ (as the one that they must deal with in their salvation), rather than an event that this person does. Reception of the gospel entails aligning oneself with this Jesus as King and Savior.

The kind of salvation that Peter offers the Jews is forgiveness of their sins and the gift of the Holy Spirit, with the outcome that the kingdom would then come[18] (Acts 2:38; 3:19–21). This retains the kingdom relationship that John the Baptist and Jesus maintained of kingdom, forgiveness, and the Spirit. The main sin that Peter identified that these first century Jews were involved with is that of disowning and killing Christ (Acts 2:23; 3:18–19). Disowning Christ is the very sin that Peter had done in his denial, and like him they must turn from this denial or Jesus would deny them before the Father and his angels (ἠρνήσασθε, Acts 3:13; ἠρνήσατο, Luke 22:34, 57, 61; 12:9; Matt 10:32–33). Presumably, it is this sin of denying and killing Christ that they must repent from as they align themselves with Christ. When they repent, Luke reports that they believe the message (Acts 4:4).

When the Jewish leaders are addressed by Spirit filled Peter, they are offered a salvation that includes physical as well as spiritual salvation (use of σώζω in Acts 4:9, 12). This also identifies Peter's gospel with the kingdom message that Jesus had maintained in Luke's Gospel. Applying Ps 118:22 in a *pesher* as Jesus had done: Jesus was rejected by the religious leaders as the builders, but God has chosen him as the precious foundational stone for kingdom (Acts 4:11; 1 Pet 2:7; Matt 21:42).

Salvation offered to the gentile proselytizers in Cornelius household had the same outcome of forgiveness and the Holy Spirit (Acts 10:43–44). However, no specific sin was mentioned so they are not called to repent, but rather to believe in Jesus as the Christ. As contrast, Luke's record of Peter's preaching reserves repentance for those who had shown some rebellion previously, while those, like Cornelius who are heading toward God, responsive to his revelation, are called to believe in the gospel message that helps them to know it a bit more specifically.

---

18. For the defense of the interpretation of this clause see: Kennard, *Classical Christian God*, 202.

Peter's Gospel Sermons in Acts

	Made to Jewish populace		To Jewish leaders	To gentiles
	Acts 2:14–40	Acts 3:12–26	Acts 4:8–12	Acts 10:28–43
Introduction	Spirit poured forth	God healed the man	If on trial for healing	Neither God nor I am partial
Focus	Jesus is declared to be Davidic King	Jesus is the healer, forgiver, prince or leader, the prophet, and the One Who brings in kingdom	Jesus is Savior (physical and spiritual healing)	Jesus, the Lord and Judge of all, enabled by Spirit did good and healed all sick
Attestation	God attested to Jesus by signs and predetermined His death	God glorified Servant by miracle	Miracle done in Jesus' name	God anointed Him with powerful Spirit to do miracles
Death	You Jews killed Jesus by Lawless (Romans) men	You Jews ignorantly disowned him to death	You Jews crucified him	Jews killed him
Resurrection	God raised him	God raised him	God raised him	God raised him
Evidence	Prophecy required Jesus' resurrection because he is the Davidic king	All prophets spoke of Jesus suffering and reign in kingdom, which includes healing	Prophecy of your Jews rejection and God's choosing him	Prophets witness to salvation thru Jesus and we witness to the fact of his resurrection
Salvation	Repent for forgiveness of sins and the gift of the Spirit, and each be baptized	Repent so kingdom may come Cut off by Sadducees and temple guard	Salvation only in the name of Jesus	Believe and receive forgiveness of sins Cut off by Spirit and salvation

These salvation messages do not develop any efficaciousness of the death of Christ for sins. Rather, in Peter's gospel presentations the death of Christ is a historical fact of which many in the audience are aware and it also shows the culpability of the Jews of that generation as killing Christ (Acts 2:23; 3:14–15, 17; 4:10; 10:39). Notice that I am not saying that Peter does not believe Jesus' death to be efficacious for sins, he clearly does (1 Pet 2:24), however he does not see the need to mention this fact in his statement of the gospel as Luke and Mark have repeatedly shown. This means that the "efficaciousness of the death of Christ" is not an essential component to be mentioned when the gospel is described (for Peter and Luke do not mention it). They treat the death of Christ as indicating Jewish culpability. In Acts 2:23 there is an admission that "Lawless men" were involved in Christ's death, which probably shows culpability as violators of the Law but probably alludes to Roman involvement (Mark 15). Also, God determined Christ's death as well.[19] Additionally, in Acts 3:17 Peter identified that the Jewish people and their rulers acted in ignorance, not knowing Jesus to be the prince of life, whom they will have to deal with in their salvation. However, this ignorance does not remove their culpability for their rebellion and killing of Christ. Notice that I am not saying the anti-Semitic statement that all Jews of all time are Christ killers; I am merely saying that a particular group of a generation of Jews is clearly indicated to be culpable for their rejection and killing of Christ. Peter sees that this is an important thing to say in all of his gospel statements which Luke records, even when Peter is not talking to Jews (Acts 10:39).

In Acts 3:13 and 26 the word παῖδα refers to Jesus as "son" or "servant." Traditionally, many import vicarious atonement into this text by connecting this term with Isaiah's servant songs.[20] In Acts 3:13 the meaning could be either "servant" or "son," though the context refers to Jesus' death without any development except Israel's culpability. Rather, what is developed in this context, is that God glorified his παῖδα Jesus, whom Israel had culpably killed. God's assessment of Jesus is that he is the holy and righteous one, the prince of life. There is no atoning servant (παῖς from Isa 52:13) development; rather there is regal honor, which would be better associated with a translation of παῖδα as "son." In verse 26, παῖδα

---

19. At least since the commentary of Holtzmann, *Die Apostelgeschte*, 34–37, commentators have commented upon the sharp juxtaposition of the human free will and the divine determinism to kill Christ; Jacobs and Krienke, "Foreknowledge, Providence, Predestination," NIDNTT 1:693.

20. Pate and Kennard, *Deliverance Now and Not Yet*, 433–81.

is referred to as the resurrected one to bless Israel by turning them from their wicked ways. Resurrection is not clearly developed in Isa 53, but some ambiguous continuity of the servant so that he could be allotted a portion with the great and divide booty with the strong after the servant's atoning death (Isa 53:12).²¹ However, nowhere in this or any other Petrine gospel statement in Acts is there a clear connection of Jesus death as Isaiah's servant atonement. Here παῖδα can be understood as in verse 13 as better referring to Jesus as God's Davidic "son" who in his reign will bless Israel in turning Israelites from their wicked ways (Acts 3:26). In fact, if we let the previous Petrine sermon influence our hermeneutical choice, παῖδα should be understood as "son," in that "Jesus is the Davidic messiah" is the core of the previous sermon (Acts 2:22–36). At this point F. F. Bruce chimes in and appeals to: 1) Phillip's encounter with the Ethiopian eunuch, and 2) the Acts 4 prayer.²² In Acts 4:25 παιδός is often translated as servant because David is faithfully providing revelation, but it could be understood as an allusion that he is the king "God's son." The critical παῖδά reference comes in Acts 4:27 which refers Jesus as "God's son" the king, to whom Ps 2:1–2 develops. Psalm 2:12 defines παιδείας as "son," referring to the messianic Christ, rather than connecting it with Isa 53. Thus, the point in Acts 3:13 is the same as the core of the previous Acts 2 sermon and the following prayer παῖδά reference. Namely, that Jesus is glorified as the Davidic king, thus Israel is culpable in their killing of their messiah. Likewise, the elevated role to bless Israel in Acts 3:26 fits wonderfully within this theme of Jesus ascending in honor as the Davidic messiah to bless with salvific blessings like the giving of the Spirit (Acts 2:33–36). Therefore, I understand παῖδα in Acts 3:13 and 26 as referring to "son" in a messianic sense, since there is no near context development for Isaiah's servant imagery, and in both sermons there is near context evidence for Jesus as Davidic messiah. In a broader biblical theological argument, there is also a dominant emphasis of Jesus as king with which they will have to deal in Petrine and Lukan salvation sermons as well.

21. Kennard, *Biblical Theology of Isaiah*, 194–212.
22. Bruce, "Speeches in Acts," 60–61. On pp. 61–62, Bruce continues his appeal with the phrase "hanging on a tree" (ξύλου) in Acts 5:30 and 13:29 which he sees must carry a vicarious atonement meaning, but this does not follow from his good point from Deut 21:22 that Jesus' death is an experience of curse by hanging on a tree. Most other individuals who experienced this Deuteronomic curse were criminals with no development of an efficaciousness of Christ's death developed. Jesus is certainly viewed by the Jews who killed him to be a criminal (guilty of heresy) and thus to be cursed in this way.

So once again, neither does Peter, nor Luke develop any soteriological accomplishment in Jesus' death, rather merely that Israel is culpable.

The statements of Christ's death are quickly followed by a resurrection statement vindicating Jesus as the Christ, for God raised him up (Acts 2:24–32; 3:13, 15; 4:10; 10:40). Taken together, Jewish culpability shows their rebellion and God's victory through resurrection shows that this generation of Jews are in a very precarious condition of cursing themselves under the Abrahamic and Mosaic covenants (Acts 3:22–26).[23]

Each of Peter's gospel statements is also accompanied by two forms of evidence to prompt faith, that of 1) the Spirit orchestrated healings and 2) the prophetic fulfillment for Jesus. The Spirit orchestrated healings include the recollection of the miraculous attestation from Jesus' ministry (Acts 2:22; 10:38–39) as well as the continuing empowerment of healing among the apostles (Acts 3:1–12, 16; 4:9). This healing from Jesus' ministry is taken to be an aspect of the fulfillment of prophecy (the repetition τέρατα [from LXX of Joel 3:3 (English: Joel 2:30)] and σημεῖα [not in the LXX of Joel but added by Peter or Luke in their quoting of Joel] in Acts 2:19, 22). However, the fulfillment of prophecy extends to a range of other evidence including 1) that Jesus would be the Mosaic prophet and the Davidic king, 2) Jesus would be rejected by the Jewish leadership, 3) Jesus would resurrect, 4) the Spirit would be poured out and cause the tongues phenomena at Pentecost, and 5) the whole world would be blessed by Jesus kingdom ministry (Acts 2:16–22, 24–36; 3:21–25; 4:11; 10:43). There is no gospel statement that Peter mentions without including a mention of both healings and fulfillment of prophecy.

A favorable response to the gospel message is shown not just in faith or repentance, but also in immediately being baptized if one is able (Acts 2:41; 10:47). This follows the pattern of proselytizing into Judaism[24] and John the Baptist's baptism for repentance and the identification with a Judaism aligned with the kingdom (Mark 1:5–8; Luke 3:3–6). In the gospel presentation of Acts 3 Peter and John were taken captive by the temple guard, so that this response does not occur. In fact, in Acts 2:38 Peter develops the response to the gospel as follows: 1) you all repent

---

23. Pate and Kennard develop this Deuteronomistic curse on Israel in the first century and in the Great Tribulation in *Deliverance Now and Not Yet*.

24. Josephus, *War* 2.150; *Ant.* 14.285; 18.93–94; 18.117; *T. Levi* 2.3.1–2; *Sib. Or.* 4.162–70; Epictetus, *Dissertationes* 2.9.19–20; *Apoc. Moses* 29.6–13; *b. Yebam.* 46a–48b; *Midrash Sifre Num.* 15.14; *m. Ṭhar.* 7.6; *t. Yoma* 4.20; *t. Pesaḥ.* 7.13; 1QS 3.3–9; 4QTLevi ar; *m. Para* 8.10; S.v. "βαπτίζω," NIDNTT 1:144–45; Witherington, *Acts*, 155.

(μετανοήσατε, second-person plural), 2) each be baptized (βαπτισθήτω, second-person singular) in the name of Jesus Christ,[25] 3) for your all forgiveness of sins (εἰς ἄφεσιν τῶν ἁμαρτιῶν ὑμῶν, second person plural) and 4) you all shall receive the Holy Spirit (λήμψεσθε, second person plural). The order leaves it quite clear that their human responsibility is to repent and be baptized as they identify with Jesus and this gospel. The third and fourth features are divine benefits given to them in response to their repentance and baptism. The εἰς clause indicates that baptism also heads toward the outcome of their forgiveness of sins. That is, the first two are their responsibility and the second two are the divine benefits. However, the fact that the first, third, and fourth are plural, while the command to "be baptized" is singular, tends to pull the plurals together as referring to the same thing: repent for forgiveness and the Holy Spirit. The second-person singular of the command to "be baptized" makes this feature an attending circumstance to these others: indicate your repentance and involvement with this salvation by baptism. Additionally, the statements come in pairs: the first command is the essence but it is seen or evidenced in the second command. So, repentance is seen in a person's baptism. Likewise, their forgiveness is evidenced in the manifestation of the Spirit of God upon them. In Cornelius' household, Peter calls them to believe for their reception of forgiveness, and the Spirit manifests the kind of tongues that he had done at Pentecost. This Spirit manifestation shows that they had embraced the authentic salvation (Acts 10:43–46; 11:14–17). It follows then from this fact that they were authentically saved, that baptism is not critical like a work to obtain forgiveness, for Cornelius' household already were divinely blessed with forgiveness and the Holy Spirit, but Peter had them quickly baptized as a further evidence of their faith. So, whether baptism occurs before or after salvation begins is not as critical as to keep it close to this beginning. Luke records another instance in which Phillip had expressed the gospel and the people of Samaria had believed and been baptized identifying them with this gospel message, but these Samaritans did not receive the Holy Spirit until Peter came and laid hands upon them (Acts 8:12–17). In these instances, the baptism of the Holy Spirit evidences the authentic salvation included

---

25. Water baptism in the name of Jesus is not contradictory to Matthew's baptism into the name of the Father, Son, and Holy Spirit (Matt 28:19). Everything for Peter in Acts is accomplished in the name of Jesus Christ, including: prayer (Acts 1:24), healing, (Acts 3:6; 4:10), salvation (Acts 4:12), and suffering (Acts 5:41).

them, while their water baptism pictures this inclusion as an act of obedience identifying them with the authentic salvation.

Peter discussed baptism as a "pledge" or "prayer" and not the effect of water washing believers (1 Pet 3:21). The Noahic flood illustrated how deliverance can be obtained through water. Baptism is somewhat like the flood in that salvation is an ongoing process for the one who has been baptized. The present ongoing nature of the salvation process is emphasized by the "now" (νῦν) and the present indicative (σῴζει) surrounded by past events largely characterized by the aorist tenses. Peter makes it clear that there is nothing magical about the immersion in water providing external washing that would remove dirt. Rather, the external act is an emblem for the internal "appeal" (ἐπερώτημα), which is either or both a "request" in prayer or a "pledge" to God,[26] for God to facilitate a good conscience within Christ's narrow way for the believer (1 Pet 3:21).[27] There is no evidence that prayer accompanies baptism, though it could be appropriate. The emphasis in the context is that a good conscience is the believer's human responsibility, so a pledge toward this consistency with resurrection as the goal, makes good sense of how baptism functions for Peter (1 Pet 2:19; 3:16 with 3:21).[28] By the end of the second century baptism was being viewed as a contract repudiating immoralities of paganism and Satan to pledge acceptance of the Christian way of life.[29] Baptism becomes a pledge of obedience to living the rest of one's life for God's desires (1 Pet 4:2), and is essentially the visible outworking of repentance (Acts 2:38; 5:31).

In the Petrine portion of Acts, the narrow way continuing toward salvation is anecdotally present, unlike the clear statement of the way toward salvation and the reverse way toward damnation in 2 Pet 1:5–11 and 2:1–22, the two ways. On the positive side Peter refers to Jesus as the ἀρχηγὸν, the role of "pioneer" or "prince," who leads the way and blazes the trail for others to follow into salvation life (Acts 3:15).[30] However, in the Petrine section of Acts this two ways or *imitatio Christi* salvation way is more apparent through the broad way of curse. For example, Peter's

---

26. BAG, "ἐπερώτημα," 285; Richards, "1 Peter 3:21," 77.

27. Crawford, "'Confessing God from a Good Conscience,'" 23–37.

28. Reicke, *Disobedient Spirits*, 182–85.

29. Kelly, *Peter and Jude*, 163; Justin, *1 Apol.* 61.2; Tertulian, *Spect.* 5; Cyril Alexandria, *Hom. Pasch* 30.3; Ps. Oecunenius, PG, 119:560.

30. Elsewhere in the NT in this same way in Heb 2:10; 12:2; Lampe, "Lucan Portrait of Christ," 167; Bruce, "Speeches in Acts," 61.

curse of Judas with two imprecatory psalms in Acts 1:20 is best seen as an apostasy on Judas' part toward damnation (Luke 22:22; also the passing of Judas portion [κλῆρον] to Matthias in Acts 1:17, 26; Mark 14:21; Matt 26:24–25; and his association with Satan in John 13:27). Likewise, Ananias and Saphira apostatized to the love of money and personal honor rather than practically loving others and the Spirit killed them (Acts 5:1–11). In this perspective, these three (Judas, Ananias, and Saphira) did not continue toward salvation but were damned. Similarly, Peter threatened Simon the magician with damnation when he tried to buy the power to bestow the Holy Spirit (Acts 8:20 where Peter says "May your silver and you go to hell," (τὸ ἀργύριόν σου σὺν σοὶ εἴη εἰς ἀπώλειαν).[31] This last situation adds an interesting spin since Simon is said by Luke to believe and be baptized (Acts 8:13), and yet here Peter threatened him with destruction. This view is even more acute if Ireneaus' and Hippolytus' traditions of Simon are true, since in these extra-biblical traditions Simon opposes Peter and the gospel and Simon dies trying to show that he could also bring himself back from the dead.[32] The narrow way quality for Peter's gospel will be developed further in the next chapter on Exodus unto kingdom.

In speaking to Israel, Peter authentically offers the kingdom restoration and the refreshing benefits of the Abrahamic, Mosaic, and Davidic covenants, if they would repent and embrace Jesus as their messianic prophet and king (Act 3:19–26).[33] Already kingdom benefits are being realized by believers in forgiveness and the new covenant bestowal of the Holy Spirit. However, Peter offers the era of Israel restoration in which Jesus is the new Moses leading Israel into the prophetically predicted kingdom era, if Israel would repent (Act 3:19–23). In fact, Jesus as God's son would provide Israel with this internal repentance and obedience, if Israel was open to this possibility (Act 3:24–26). This authentic offer would move the timing up concerning kingdom, is Israel repented. Unfortunately, Israel as a nation did not repent (Acts 4:21; 5:40; 7:54, 58; 12:2–3) and the kingdom era has not come yet in its fullest restoration form, where Israel's enemies are utterly defeated (Acts 2:35; Mark 12:36; Ps 110:1).

Peter's gospel is essentially, "Jesus is Lord, align with him."

---

31. Bruce, *Acts*, 184n37.

32. Justin, *1 Apol.* 26; 56; *2 Apol.* 15; *Dial.* 120.6; Irenaeus, *Haer.* 1.23.1–5; Hippolytus, *Haer.* 4.51.3–14; 6.7–20; 10.12; *Homily of Clement* 7.9; *Acts of Peter* 4–28.

33. Kennard, *Biblical Covenantalism*, esp. 2:221–47; *Gospel*, 117–36.

10

Exodus Following Jesus to Kingdom Virtues

ANYTIME THAT ISRAEL IS not in covenant faithfulness and blessing in the land, Yahweh holds open to them to be led on a new exodus journey unto kingdom.[1]

Ulrich Simon summarizes the continuity between Israel's exodus from Egypt and the new exodus into kingdom.

> God's providential care for Israel overrules foes and adversities in history. The first Exodus manifested the order of redemption. Then God appointed Moses to lead the oppressed people from Egypt through the Sea to the desert; the covenant of Sinai sealed the liberation. In the second Exodus YHWH raises up his conqueror, his second Moses, who represents the new covenant; he gathers up Israel, scattered in the desert, and leads the exiles back to their land. Therefore, God banishes fear from Israel by doing again what he has done before; the new Exodus differs slightly in the sequence of events and surpasses the first in scale.[2]

The premiere new exodus passage of Isa 40:1–11 is quoted in Mal 3:1 and Mark 1:2–3. In this Isa passage, God speaks comfort to his people for Israel's new exodus to the land (Isa 40:1).[3] This exodus launches be-

---

1. Lund, *Way Metaphors*, 38, 145; Stock, *Way in the Wilderness*; Kennard, *Biblical Theology of Isaiah*, 213–22.

2. Simon, *Theology of Salvation*, 97.

3. In MT God speaks, in contrast to 1QIsa identifying priests as speakers, or Targums identifying a prophet as speaking. Qumran expressed this statement as a *pesher* encouraging their distinctive community as those to be comforted while they prepared

cause God ends Israel's hard labor of covenant curse and her iniquity is removed.[4] The compound subject in Isa 40:3 of "voice calling" probably indicates multiple individuals along the way announcing preparation for Yahweh's way to travel this exodus.[5] The imagery is as though people down the way call out, perhaps as the group is about to pass they will sing the *hallel* psalm ascending for festival, "blessed is he who comes in the name of the Lord" (Ps 118:26; further realized in Jesus' entrance into Jerusalem in Mark 11:9–10). The construction imageries of straightening and smoothing the rough to become a plain and removing the hills to fill in valleys and removing steep grades to become level all point to Yahweh's aid in facilitating the exodus way (Isa 40:3–4; 43:19; 49:11).[6] Isaiah described these hills as winnowed and pulverized by Yahweh to make the way smooth (Isa 41:15–16). Early Judaism utilized this imagery to describe the hope of obliteration of evil and transformation under a messiah as the Maccabean revolt occurs, as the Qumran community enlarges, and then as Roman dominance tightens.[7] During this new exodus, the wilderness will be marvelously transformed. As the exodus transpires, the weighty glory of Yahweh will be seen by all flesh (humans and animals) along the way for God's mouth has spoken this as real comfort (Isa 40:5; Mark 1:3). Those who watch and travel the exodus way will hear the announcement that they can count upon,[8] that as flesh they are as vulnerable as grass before the hot desert *sirocco* wind or the judging breath of Yahweh, while God excels in goodness as the flowers in their field (Isa 40:6–8). In contrast to human vulnerability, God's word remains binding and encouraging forever (1 Pet 1:23–25; Isa 40:8). With such profound generosity coming with God, those announcing[9] Yahweh's procession

---

the new exodus way (Isa 40:1 cited in 4Q176 frag. 1, col. 1 4–8; 1QS 8.12–16; CD 7.10–13; 13.24—14.1; Brooke, "Isaiah 40:3," 117–32; Sawyer, *Fifth Gospel*, 24). Israel is the people comforted rather than people comforting others as in the Vulgate and Jerome considering "people" as in vocative address.

4. The three *ki* clauses are essentially equal in meaning, Watts, *Isaiah*, 2:605.

5. Kautzsch and Cowley, *Gesenius' Hebrew Grammar*, 146b; *qwl* is neuter and *qwr'* is masculine but both are singular.

6. Isa 40:3 new exodus re-gathering of Israel is echoed in Bar 5.6–9 and *Pss. Sol.* 11.4–6, though *Pss. Sol.* 8.17 understands Isa 40:3 as referring to coming of Pompey.

7. Jdt 16.15; Sir 16.18–19; Bar 5.6–9; 1QS 8.12–15; 9.18–21; 4Q 176; 11QMelch 2.15–16, 24–25; *T. Mos.* 10.4; *Gen. Rab* 50.9; *Num. Rab.* 1.2; *Lev. Rab.* 1.15; David, *Name and Way of the Lord*, 72–87.

8. Isa 40:7–8 perfect tenses express a gnomic or proverbial sense, Waltke and O'Connar, *Introduction to Biblical Hebrew Syntax*, 488.

9. *Mbssrt* is feminine gender "herald," which may hint at female heralds or Mrs.

should position themselves so their voices will carry from the hilltops because they have a comforting message to remove fear by announcing the presence of God; declaration of "Here is your God" follow the exodus travelers (Isa 40:9). There is none to stop Yahweh, for Adonai Yahweh will come with power fostered by his weapon wielding arm ruling for him, each bringing about God's work in his presence (Isa 40:10). Yahweh provides sight, light, and guidance on the new exodus way as his presence had guided Israel before through the wilderness toward the promised land (Isa 42:16). Such imagery presented visual light guidance as the pillar of fire did in the exodus (Isa 42:16; Exod 13:21; 14:24; 33:9; Num 14:14). As Yahweh proceeds through the exodus, he brings Israel as his hired personnel with him.

In *1 En.* 1.6–7 and *T. Mos.* 10.4, an eschatological interpretation of this new exodus into the kingdom of God replaced the hope for the return of Jewish exiles.[10] This eschatological exodus quoting Isa 40:3–5 is used by the Qumran community to describe their own self-designation as a kingdom bound community.[11]

Mark explicitly quotes Isa 40:3 and fuses it with language from the Mal 3:1 restatement to identify another dispersed Jewish community of repentant and forgiven, kingdom oriented Jews (Mark 1:2–4). This exodus imagery continues to extend beyond the re-gathering after the Babylonian captivity because rabbinic interpretations continue to make self-defining appeals to this passage for the new exodus in the wake of Roman dispersions.[12] The new exodus following Jesus defines a new family.[13]

John the Baptist understood his own role was preparing the exodus way for Messiah Jesus (Mark 1:1–4; Matt 3:3; Luke 3:4–7; John 1:22–27). John would have been the Elijah, who prepared Israel for Jesus, if the people had accepted his testimony about Jesus being their coming king. Malachi predicted, "Behold, I am going to send you Elijah the prophet before the coming of the great and terrible day of the Lord. And He will restore the hearts of the fathers to their children, and the hearts of the

---

Isaiah, or be a generic term like "teacher" (*qhlt*), though it is reflected in LXX by a male gendered term, ὁ εὐαγγελιζόμενος; Goldingay, *Message of Isaiah 40–55*, 28; Goldingay and Payne, *Isaiah 40–55*, 86–87.

10. Pao, *Acts and the Isaianic New Exodus*, 43.

11. Isa 40:3–5 quoted in 1QS 8.13–16; 9.9, 16–21; 10.21; Brooke, "Isaiah 40:3," 117–32; Charlesworth, "Intertextuality," 197–224.

12. Teugels, "Consolation and Composition," 433–46.

13. Santos, "New Family of Jesus," 542–601.

children to their fathers, lest I come and smite the land with a curse" (Mal 4:5–6 [3:23–24 MT]). Judaism anticipated Elijah to come at the end of the age to prepare Israel for the coming kingdom.[14] The angel Gabriel identified John as this Elijah, who will turn back many of the sons of Israel to the Lord their God and it is John who will go as a forerunner before Jesus in the spirit and power of Elijah, to turn the hearts of the Fathers back to the children, and the disobedient to the attitude of the righteous; so as to make ready a people prepared for the Lord (Luke 1:16–17). Responding to his birth, Zacharias identified his son John "will be called the prophet of the Most High; for [John] will go before the Lord to prepare his ways; to give his people the knowledge of salvation by the forgiveness of their sins" (Luke 1:76–77). God mercifully provided a revelatory entrance for John to "guide our feet into the way of peace" (Luke 1:79). Jesus also identified John as this greatest prophet, Elijah, by quoting the Malachi text above (Matt 11:7–11; 17:10–12; Luke 7:24–28). However, Jesus identified that John would be Elijah conditioned upon the people accepting John's testimony.

Luke records that John's ministry took place beginning AD 25 and continuing until AD 29 (Luke 3:1–2).[15] John came to the wilderness district of the Jordan dressed like Elijah, in a poor man's camel's hair robe, with a rope as a belt.[16] John came in an Elijah like role preaching a baptism of repentance for forgiveness of sins (2 Kgs 1:8 LXX; Mark 1:2–11; Matt 3:1–17; 11:14; 17:11–13; Luke 3:2–22).[17]

14. Sir 48.10; 2 Esdr. 6.26; Kennard, *Messiah Jesus*, 73–76.

15. The beginning date of AD 25 is indicated by the fifteenth year of Tiberias Caesar, whereas, the ending date of John's ministry would be AD 29, since Jesus needs to emerge in AD 28 and establish his ministry before John is killed (Matt 14:1–12; Mark 6:14–29; Luke 9:7–9; Josephus, *Ant.* 18.116–19). Agreeing with these dates: Wright, *Jesus and the Victory of God*, 147; Meier, *Marginal Jew*, 1:372–433.

16. This is the common Bedouin rough desert clothing, Epiphanius, *Haer.* 30.13, 4–5; Josephus, *War* 1.480. Likewise, his diet of locusts is kosher and a common Bedouin food (Lev 11:21–22; *Ḥul.* 3.7; *Šabb.* 9.7; *Ber.* 6.3).

17. Jewish tradition expected Elijah to precede the Messiah and still does (Mal 3:23–24; Sir 48.9–11; *b. Sanh.* 97b; *Pes. Rab.* 161a; *Eccl. Rab.* 4.1; *Yalqut Shim'oni*, par. 771; *m. 'Ed.* 8.7; *b. Menaḥ.* 45a; *Maharil, Hilkbot Shabbat*, end; *Ma'ase diR. Y'hosu'a ben Levi*, BhM 2.49–50, 125; *Seder 'Olam Rabba*, [identified by the Talmud to be second century], ch. 17; *Yemenite Midrash*, 349–50; Yitzaq Ber, *Seder 'Avodat Yisrael*, 310–11. Sometimes Jewish tradition develops Elijah as doing those things normally associated as Messianic, while not being the Messiah, like: 1) providing manna and oil (*Mekh. diR. Yism'el*, p. 80), 2) awakening the dead (*m. Soṭah* 9.15; *y. Sheql* 47c bot.; *Ma'ase Daniel in Y'huda Ibn Sh'muel*, *Midr'she G'ula*, 225–26), and 3) redeeming the kingdom people (*b. Sukkah* 52b; *Pes. Rab.* p. 13a; *Mid Haser w'Yater*, 16, 42; *Rashi ad Lev.* 26.42). Jewish

Jesus extends this offer of forgiveness to the paralytic and encouraged his disciples to forgive everyone (Mark 2:5; 11:25). While the leaders are disturbed about Jesus forgiving others, prophets have a right to forgive sins[18] and disciples are to be bringing people to forgiveness. In a later context, where Jesus commands his disciples to forgive everyone, Peter asks to what extent should they forgive (Matt 18:15–22).[19] Peter realized that church discipline requires forgiving his brother (whether it is Andrew or another kingdom family member). Peter thought maybe a magnanimous seven times of forgiving was sufficient, but Jesus virtually says to continue to forgive an indefinite number of times without counting (which is the meaning of seventy times seven). Then Jesus told a kingdom parable about forgiveness (Matt 18:23–35). The kingdom may be compared to a certain king who wished to settle accounts with his slaves. One slave owed ten thousand talents[20] or virtually the national debt (since a talent is about 58–80 pounds of precious metal, such as gold). This slave did not have the means to repay so the lord commanded that he, his wife, his children and all that he had be sold to recoup a slight part of the loss. The slave fell, prostrating himself before his lord saying, "Have patience with me, and I will repay you everything." The lord of the slave felt compassion and released him and forgave him the debt.[21] The slave went out and found a fellow slave who owed him a hundred denarii, or roughly a hundred days wage for a day laborer, and seized him. Putting a choke hold[22] on him, he said, "Pay back what you owe." So, his fellow slave fell and began to entreat him saying, "Have patience with me and I

---

tradition retains a sense that many will not recognize Elijah when he comes (*Mid. Zuta, Shir haShirim* 2.8; *Seder 'Olam Rab.* ch. 17) and unfortunately that was true of John.

18. Josephus, *Ant.* 6.92; Hägerland, "Prophetic Forgiveness in Josephus and Mark," 125–39; Martin, "It's My Perogative," 67–74.

19. Corroborated by *Gos. Nazareans* 10 as reported by Jerome, *Pelag.* 3.2 though Jerome has Peter asks if he should forgive "seven times in a day."

20. Ten thousand is the largest single number Greek could express and talent is the largest unit of currency (Keener, *Matthew*, 458). Josephus, *Ant.* 12.175–76 describes a tax farmer as offering to collect for Ptolemy up to 16,000 talents. Jerome gives the revenue from Egypt to Ptolemy to be 14,800 talents. Darius tried to purchase peace from Alexander the Great for ten thousand talents (Plutarch *Mor.* 180B; *Alex.* 29). So, this servant is probably a highly placed political appointment or an outrageous amount to make an exaggerated point (like the cutting off hands or eyes; Matt 18:8–9). Davies and Allison, *Matthew*, 2:798. The combined annual tribute of Galilee and Perea just after the death of Herod the Great was two hundred talents (Josephus, *Ant.* 17.318).

21. The parable in *Ex. Rab.* 31.1 also recounts a lender who forgave a large debt.

22. Same action described in *B. Bat.* 10.8 and *b. 'Abod. Zar.* 4a.

will repay you." The first slave was unwilling, however, and instead had him thrown in prison until he should pay back what was owed. Such a debtor's prison does not pay the debt; it merely removes the person from being able to earn money so that family and friends might step forward to pay his debt. His fellow slaves were deeply grieved over what had happened so that they reported it to their lord. The lord summoned the slave, saying, "You wicked slave, I forgave you all that debt because you entreated me. Should you not also have had mercy on your fellow slave, even as I had mercy on you? His lord, moved with anger, handed him over to the torturers[23] until he should repay all owed him, which of course is an everlasting torment in debtor's prison, since there is no way possible that he could pay the equivalent of the national debt (or tax collected by Rome on eastern half of their empire). We sometimes think how inappropriate the lord is in forgiving and re-obligating a slave for this debt, but in the ancient Near East such a master has the right to do this. Forgiveness is not primarily resolving the past; forgiveness re-establishes a relationship going forward. The shocking thing about this parable is not what the individuals do in the parable, but what Jesus says in the next verse. "So shall My heavenly Father also do to you, if each of you does not forgive his brother from your heart." Jesus developed that everlasting destiny of being relationally forgiven by the Father is contingent upon being forgiving people.[24] Evangelicals who tend to see things from a positional justification standpoint tend to doubt that Jesus is committed to the everlasting forgiveness of God being patterned on our having the virtue of forgiving others, as is stated in the Lord's Prayer (Matt 6:12, also 14–15) and in Sir 28.2–5. So, divine forgiveness is patterned after and to the same extent "as" (ὡς) our human forgiving of others (Matt 6:14–15, third-class conditional clause). Jesus said, "For if you forgive men for their transgressions, your heavenly Father will also forgive you. But if you do not forgive men, then your Father will not forgive your transgressions" (Matt 6:14–15). Such forgiveness involves everlasting destiny as the parable made clear, therefore it is necessary that we be forgiving people.

---

23. Herod the Great employed torture (Josephus, *War* 1.548). Such torture was a practice cruel rulers used to extort money from tarty officials (Josephus, *War* 2.448; Livy 3.13.8; 25.4.8–10; 39.41.7; 43.16.5; Appian, *Hist. rom.* 2.8.2; Aul. Gel. 16.10.8).

24. Polycarp, *Phil.* 2.3; 6.2; Clement of Rome, *1 Clem.* 13.1–2; Clement of Alexandria, *Strom.* 2.18.91; Meier, *Marginal Jew*, 2:301; Theissen and Merz, *Historical Jesus*, 263; Aune, "Forgiveness Petition," 66, 70–71.

Within this generosity, Luke and early Judaism record that John the Baptist's offer of salvation is for all flesh, presumably gentiles[25] (Luke 3:6; Isa 40:5). John called Jews to repent for the kingdom is at hand, which as a ministry focus prepares or makes Israel ready for Jesus' ministry to follow,[26] by turning the hearts of each generation to the other (Mal 4:6; Luke 1:15; 16:16).[27] This was a ministry that John identified as preparing for the new exodus from dispersion to re-gather into the kingdom (Isa 40:3 in 40:1–31 context; John 1:23). To facilitate kingdom, John predicted Jesus is the Messiah to bring in this new exodus (Mark 1:1–4).

Public confession was to occur among the people and in better times it did occur (Lev 5:5; 16:21; 26:40; Num 5:6–7; Ps 32:5; Prov 28:13; Neh 9:2–3). When Jews confessed their sins, then they were baptized by John in the Jordan River and many came for baptism (Mark 11:32; Matt 21:26; Luke 7:29; 20:6). When the religious leaders came out to investigate, John called the whole group to the Jewish approach which taught that right conduct is the expectation for God's acceptance of their repentance (Matt 3:8–10). This included that much of Israel is already under sentence of judgment, with the axe at the root of the tree, ready to be cut down and be thrown into the fire (Mark 4:12). John emphasized that the way unto kingdom was to be described instead by virtues of generosity and social justice (Luke 3:10–14). God was just in judging Israel through John the Baptist, because 1) the religious leaders and many of the people rejected him as having a demon and 2) Herod had him imprisoned and killed for calling down Herod's sin (Mark 6:14–29; 11:30–33; Matt 2:3–12; 11:18; 21:25–27, 32; Luke 3:19–20; 7:33).

Utilizing the Jewish framework of two ways, the prophet John the Baptist pointed toward Jesus as the Son of God. John's prophetic voice extends the announcement of Isa 40:3 as a call to a new exodus which defines John's preparatory ministry for Jesus' to follow (Mark 1:2–3; Matt 3:3; Luke 3:4–6). Jesus' ministry comes with a distinctive baptism which will immerse the kingdom bound people in the Spirit, while immersing the unrepentant in judgment fire of damnation.[28] Thus, Jesus' baptism

25. This is a Lukan emphasis (Luke 2:32). However, the *Mishnah* identifies that Elijah will act as judge to settle all remaining disputes and resurrect the dead (*m. Ed.* 8.7; *m. Sotah.* 9.15).

26. The MT Isa 40:3 "prepares," whereas all the Gospels follow the LXX "make ready," even John's self-description in John 1:23.

27. Sir 48.10.

28. Notice that in the context, fire is clearly that of judgment (not an allusion to Pentecost "tongues of fire," Acts 2:3), so that Jesus' baptism brings about the two ways

will effect the outcome in both of the two ways. Only one of the two ways saves (that which eschatologically identifies with the Holy Spirit [Ezek 36:25–27; Joel 3:1–5]),[29] the other way damns. Jesus' ministry extends John's, Jesus submitted to John's baptism, identifying with the kingdom way and "to fulfill all righteousness," not because he had any sins to repent from.[30] That is, Jesus submitted to the total will of God as the righteous messiah (Jer 23:5–6; 33:15; Zech 9:9).[31]

God indicated approval of Jesus in a series of ways at his baptism: Scripture was affirmed (Isa 40:3; Mark 1:2–3; Matt 3:3; Luke 3:4–6), the prophet John was affirmed (Matt 3:10–12; Luke 3:9, 16–17; John 1:6–8, 30–34; 5:33; 10:41), with heavens opened the Spirit descended and the heavenly voice approved Jesus (Mark 1:10–11; Matt 3:16–17; Luke 3:21–22). The description of the heavens opening reflects biblical language of God's revelation and eschatological deliverance which then affirms Jesus as the divinely approved (Isa 64:1 [LXX 63:19]; Ezek 1:1; Hag 2:6, 21; Job 14:12 LXX; Ps 102:26).[32] Craig Keener understands the dove presentation of the Spirit to be a harbinger of the new era, as after the flood.[33] However, the Spirit's presence upon Jesus empowers his ministry for prophecy and kingship (Isa 11:1–5; Luke 1:15; 4:1). Finally, an early Judaism replacement to prophecy, the heavenly voice, the *bath qol* (daughter of a voice), joins with John's and Jesus' prophetic voice to affirm the intimate relationship and divine approval of Jesus with God.[34]

---

outcomes (Matt 3:10–12; Luke 3:9, 16–17): Spirit empowerment blessing (Acts 2:16, 38; 4:8, 31; 5:3; 8:15–18; 10:45; 11:15–17; 15:8) or fire as the traditional Jewish instrument of eschatological judgment (Matt 3:10, 12; Luke 3:9, 17; Isa 66:24; Joel 2:30; Mal 4:1; Jdt 16.17; 4 Macc 9:9; *Jub.* 9.15; 1QpHab. 10.5, 13; *1 En.* 10.6; 54.1–2; 90.24–25; 100.9; *Pss. Sol.* 15.4–5; *Sib. Or.* 3.53–54; *4 Ezra* 7.36–38; 13.10–11; *2 Bar* 37.1; 44.15; 59.2; *T. Zeb.* 10.3; *Apoc. Abr.* 31). In fact, fire and water combine in Jewish literature to become an eschatological flood of fire (Ps 66:10–12; Isa 30:27–28; 43:2; 66:15–16; Dan 7:10; Rev 20:10–15; *Sib. Or.* 2.196–205, 252–54; 3.54, 84–87, 689–92; *1 En.* 17.5; *2 En.* 10.2; *4 Ezra* 13.10–11; Josephus, *Ant.* 1.70; *T. Iss.* 5.21).

29. Jub 1:23; 1QS 4.21.

30. The biblical texts indicating Jesus submits to John's baptism are corroborated by *Gos. Ebionites* 1–4 (frag. 3) as recorded by Epiphanius (*Panarion* 30.13.3–6; 30.14.3), unlike *Gos. Nazareans* 9 (frag. 2) as reported by Jerome (*Pelag.* 3.2), which has Jesus protest to John that he has not done any sins so that a baptism for the remission of sins would be inappropriate.

31. *Pss. Sol.* 17.26–34; *T. Jud.* 24.1; *Pesiq. Rab.* 36.

32. *Sib. Or.* 3.82; 8.233, 413; *2 Bar.* 22.1; *T. Abr.* 7; *Herm.* 5.1.1.4; *Apocr. Jn.* 1; *Asen. Isa.* 14.2/3; Virgil, *Aen.* 9.20–21.

33. Keener, *Matthew*, 132–33; Gen 8:8–12; *4 Bar.* 7.8.

34. On the concept and instance of *bath qol*: Dan. 4:31; Josephus, *Ant.* 13.282–83;

Jesus extended and replaced John's ministry by preaching the gospel of God in Galilee, namely, the kingdom of God is at hand and all should repent and believe this gospel (Mark 1:14–15; 4:11, 26, 30; 9:47; 10:14–15, 24–25; 13:8; 14:25). This kingdom anticipation is echoed by disciples, a pious scribe and Joseph of Arimathea also confessing the coming kingdom of God (Mark 11:10; 12:34; 15:43). While many do not believe Jesus (Mark 11:31; 15:32), those who came to Jesus in faith received healing (Mark 2:5; 5:34; 10:52), prompting Jesus to express amazement at the disciples' lack of faith (Mark 4:40; 9:23–29; 11:22–24).

Such an origin story shows disciples what they are to be about, imitating Jesus' discipleship traits.[35] Specifically, Jesus began to call individuals, such as Simon and Andrew to "Follow me and I will make you fishers of men" (Mark 1:16–20). This calls the disciple to first follow and imitate Jesus. With Mark recording Peter's biography of Jesus, the virtues that Jesus exemplified and taught become virtues that a disciple is to imitate.[36] For example, Jesus exemplified the virtues of the narrow way unto kingdom that Jesus' sermons call his disciples to embrace as they follow him (Mark 1:17; 2:14; 3:35; 8:34–35; 10:28–30).

The Jewish concept of disciple is that of a responsive learner. Thus, disciple-making would exclude those who do not accept the message of the mentor. Fernando Segovia develops that discipleship entails "the 'teacher'/'disciple' relationship with all its accompanying and derivative terminology (for example, 'following' or 'on the way')."[37] As such, early

---

Song Rab. 8.9.3; *b. 'Abot* 6.2; *B. Bat.* 73b; 85b; *Mak.* 23b; *'Erub.* 54b; *Šabb.* 33b; 88a; *Soṭim* 33a; *p. Soṭim* 7.5.5; *Pesiq. Rab. Kah.* 11.16; 15.5; *Lev. Rab.* 19.5–6; *Deut. Rab.* 11.10; *Lam. Rab. Proem* 2, 23; *Lam. Rab.* 1.16.50; *Ruth Rab.* 6.4; *Qoh. Rab.* 7.12.1; *Sib. Or.* 1.127, 267, 275; Artapanus in Eusebius, *Praep. ev.* 9.27.36; Dionysius Halicarnassus, *Ant. rom.* 1.56.3; 5.16.2–3; 8.56.2–3; Arrian, *Anab.* 3.3.5; Lucian, *C.W.* 1.569–70; Plutarch, *Is. Os.* 12; *Mor.* 355E; *Mart. Pol.* 9. The *bath qol* was present in Israel before the spirit of prophecy departed (*b. Pesah.* 94a; *Ḥag.* 13a; *Sanh.* 39b) and a few sources give it future ramifications as well (*Lev. Rab.* 27.2; *Pesiq. Rab. Kah.* 17.5).

35. Narrative purpose: imitate the hero (Quintilian, *Inst.* 3.7.12; Ps. Hermogenes, *Prog.* 15–17).

36. Philo, *Moses* 1.158; Josephus, *War* 1.4–8, 13–16; *Ant.* 1.1–2; Plutarch, *Aem.* 1.1, 5; Tacitus, *Agr.* 1; Dionysius, *Ant. rom.* 8.56.1; Quintilian, *Inst.* 3.7.10–22; 5.10.24–31; Kurz, "Narrative Models for Imitation," 171–89; Fiore, *Function of Personal Example*, 26–44; de Boer, *Imitation of Paul*; Crouzel, "L'imitation et la 'suite'," 7–30; Cothenet, "Imitation du Christ," 7:1536–1601; Gutierrez, *La Paternité spirituelle selon S. Paul*; Pate and Kennard, *Deliverance Now and Not Yet*, 369–72; Trompf, *Idea of Historical Recurrence*, 97–101; Talbert, "Biographies of Philosophers and Rulers," 1643; Fornara, *Nature of History*, 104–20.

37. Segovia, *Discipleship in the New Testament*, 2.

Judaism thought of following Moses or Torah as within a discipleship relationship.[38] For example, the Pharisees consider the Sadducees' disbelief of the prophets as calling into question and in some instances actively excluding the Sadducees from being a disciple of the sages and Moses (Matt 6:33; John 9:28–29).[39] So it is important to listen and follow the disciple-maker to obtain the offered covenantal blessing in the land as kingdom (Exod 33:14) with that of wisely living a blessed life now. A disciple is a "student" (μαθητης). This concept is built off the verb μαθητευω which means "to instruct or to teach" (Matt 13:52; 27:57; 28:18–20; Acts 14:21). The basic pattern of the disciple is to be a student of a living rabbi or group such as John the Baptist or the Pharisees or Jesus (Matt 11:2; 22:16; Mark 2:18; 6:29; Luke 5:30, 33; 7:18–19; 11:1; John 1:35, 37; 3:25).[40] Martin Hengel underscores that this pattern of a charismatic leader teaching his students is what is meant by "discipleship."[41] In early Judaism, this practice of discipleship to Moses evidences "following" God. Upon this foundation, most of the NT references speak of disciples being Jesus' students. Jesus' disciples receive instruction in an interactive format asking questions (Mark 4:34; 7:17; 10:10; Matt 5:1; 9:37; 11:1; 13:10, 36; 19:23; 23:11; 24:3; Luke 6:20; 8:9; 11:1; 12:1, 22; 16:1; 17:1, 22; 20:45; John 9:2; 16:17–29). An important aspect of this discipleship relationship to Jesus is to listen to his teaching and pursue him with questions appropriate to his teaching (Mark 4:10). These questions that they would ask served as an indicator of their interest and maturity. Jesus would answer their questions but he would also direct the instruction through his kingdom teaching.

The twelve disciples are Jesus' primary students, namely:[42] Peter, Andrew, James and John Zebedee, Philip, Bartholomew, Thomas,[43]

---

38. Philo, *Spec. Laws* 1.345; 2.88; *b. Sanh.* 11a, bar.; *Soṭah* 48b; *Song Rab.* 8.9.3; ARN 26.54; *Qoh. Rab.* 11.6.1.

39. Wis 1:1; *Jub.* 1.15; 21.2; 1QS 1.1–2; 5.9, 11; CD 1.10; 6.6; 4Q185 frg. 1–2, col. 1, lines 8–12; 4Q416 frg. 2 (with 4Q417), col. 3, lines 12–14; *b. Yoma* 4a; also of Abraham (*m 'Abot.* 5.19).

40. Meye (*Jesus and the Twelve*, 93–99) has a good discussion of the basic discipleship words and their fit in the rabbinic and Markan context.

41. Hengel (*Charismatic Leader and His Followers*) wished to distance this model from eschatological prophet (like Elijah) and established rabbi (John the Baptist).

42. Lists of disciples were a common Jewish convention (*m. 'Abot* 2.8). One rabbinic document (*b. Sanh.* 43a) claims "Jesus of Nazareth had five disciples: Mattai, Maqai, Metser, Buni and Todah." Perhaps this statement corroborates Matthew and Judas as disciples. However, the document does not limit the number to only five disciples. No Jewish source corroborates Peter as a disciple of Jesus.

43. Meaning "twin," also called Didymus (John 11:16; 20:24; 21:2).

Matthew, James of Alphaeus, Thaddaeus, Simon the zealot,[44] and Judas Iscariot[45] (Mark 3:16–19; Matt 10:2–4; Luke 6:14–16; Acts 1:13). These disciples were to listen to Jesus explain the word of God and to do what it demands. In this obedience, they mark themselves as primary family of Jesus (Mark 3:33–35; Matt 12:48–50; Luke 8:21).[46] As such, the disciples become Jesus "household," prefiguring Petrine ecclesiology (οἶκος; Mark 3:25; 10:29; 1 Pet 2:5).[47] Stephen Barton says, "The language of kinship functions as a way of expressing fundamental allegiances and commitments and the transfer from one set of allegiances, beliefs and society to another."[48] Such an intimate discipleship family tie subsumes one's allegiance to biological family relations as a lower allegiance (Mark 3:33–35; 10:28–31; Matt 10:35–39; 12:48–50; 19:27–29; Luke 8:21; 12:52–53; 14:26; 18:28–30).

These twelve were also called "apostles" or "sent men," after the Jewish pattern of a commissioned agent sent forth in another's name or authority.[49] In such a pattern, the one sent becomes like the sender.[50] The ministry of the apostles was to include proclamation of the kingdom of God is at hand to reign on earth through his messiah (Matt 10:7; Luke 9:2). This is the same message as proclaimed by John the Baptist (Matt 3:2) and Jesus (Mark 1:15; Matt 4:17, 23; 9:35). All opposition shall be judged but those who repent and align with God's kingdom will experience the benefits of kingdom, including deliverance from sickness, death, and demons. The disciples were to go and proclaim this message

44. "Cananaean" (Matt 10:4 and Mark 3:18) does not derive from Canaanite but from the Aramaic word *qan'ān* meaning "enthusiast" or "zealot" (as Ζηλωτὴν in Luke 6:15; Acts 1:13); eventually this group developed political opposition to Rome (Josephus, *War* 2.8.1; *Ant.* 18.1.1).

45. Probably a region in Judea (Josh 15:25; Jer 31:24 LXX [48:24]; Luce, *Luke*, 318; Schürmann, *Lukasevangelium*, 318n51), rather than other options of "false one," "dagger man," and "dyer."

46. Similar subsuming of biological family to those aligned with God's plan occurs in early Judaism description of heroes (Philo, *Her.* 276–83; *Mos.* 1.150; 2.142; *Virt.* 53–65; *Spec. Laws* 4.70; Josephus, *Ant.* 1.222–25, 234; 5.263–66; Barton, *Discipleship and Family*, 23–47).

47. Best, *Following Jesus*, 226–29 expresses this idea from Mark more tentatively than does the study of Matt by Crosby, *House of Disciples*.

48. Barton, *Discipleship and Family*, 32; Philo, *Her.* 276–83.

49. *M. Qidd.* 2.1; *m. Giṭ.* 3.6. In Matt, Mark, and John, "apostle" (meaning "sent one") is mentioned once, usually around this list, whereas in Luke and especially Acts the word is amplified as they go as sent.

50. John 13:14–16; Josephus, *Ant.* 17.11.1; *m. Ber.* 5.5; *m. Roš. Haš.* 1.3; 4.9; *m. Yoma'* 1.5; *Mek. on Ex.* 12:41.

to Israelites who would listen (Mark 6:7–13; Matt 10:1–42; Luke 9:6), and eventually the message was to be proclaimed to gentiles as well (Mark 13:10; Matt 24:14; 28:18–20; Luke 24:47–49; Acts 1:8).[51]

Of this group of disciples, there was an inner circle of three who are occasionally given special access to Jesus, namely Peter and the Zebedee brothers (Mark 9:2; 14:33; Matt 17:1; 26:37; Luke 9:28). The inner group of three and Andrew are always listed first in all the lists. However, the privileged status of Jesus' disciple extends beyond the twelve to a multitude of students (Matt 8:21; Luke 19:37).

Jesus' disciple must use Jesus' teaching to resist temptation as Jesus accomplished (Mark 1:12–13; 14:32–41). A prime example of Jesus proclaiming the kingdom of God to resist temptation is expressed in the parable of the Sower (or the parable of the soils, since that is the issue on which it focuses; Mark 4:3–20; Matt 13:1–9, 18–23; Luke 8:5–15).[52] Mark placed this parable as a defining feature for the narrative to follow, much like the other Gospels utilized the sermon on the mount or plain. Jesus addressed the multitude with this parable from a boat and then interpreted the parable later to his disciples, who asked what it meant. This approach of public discourse followed by private explanation is a common Jewish method enabling the disciples to go further.[53] In the parable, the sower is unidentified. The seed is the message of the kingdom, which should be understood as largely defined by Jesus' previous kingdom teaching. There are some who hear the word of the kingdom but they do not understand it, and the evil one takes the word away.[54] Even though these may contemplate the kingdom message ("in his heart"), the kingdom message is no longer accessible to them. There are others who hear the word and receive it with joy but because it gained no root in its rocky environment, when persecution came the outcome was stumbling (σκανδαλίζεται), which in Mark's and Jesus' terminology is damnation in everlasting hell

---

51. The Byzantine addition of Mark 16:15 concurs.

52. Similar parables are told in: *m. 'Abot* 5.10–15 [especially verse 12 which describes four kinds of hearers: 1) slow to hear and swift to lose, 2) slow to hear and slow to lose, 3) swift to hear and swift to lose, and 4) swift to hear and slow to lose]; *Pesikta Rab.* 11.2; ARN 40.9; Davies and Allison, *Matthew*, 2:386; but *Gos. Thom.* 9 does not add an interpretation like the biblical texts; Justin, *Dial.* 125.1; *1 Clem.* 24.5.

53. This is a similar pattern to that of first century teacher Johanan ben Zacchai; Daube, "Public Pronouncement and Private Explanation," 175–77.

54. Jesus' identification of the birds with Satan (Matt 13:19) comports with Jewish tradition that reflects Azazel manifesting himself as an unclean bird (*Apoc. Abr.* 13; *Jub.* 11.11).

(Mark 9:42–49; Matt 11:6; 13:41–42; 18:7–9). There are others caught up in the worry of the world and the deceitfulness or pleasures of riches. The message of the kingdom is not received but gets choked out by these cares so that the message remains "unfruitful" (ἄκαρπος). This imagery of unfruitfulness remains ambiguous in not defining where the person is between those of a clearer life of good or bad fruit, who can clearly be delineated as included or excluded from Jesus' kingdom (Matt 7:17–18). Luke may imply further ambiguity by the description that the fruit "does not bring about maturity" (τελεσφοροῦσιν; Luke 8:14). This ambiguity raises a lack of clarity about whether these will make it to the kingdom or not. The final soil is good in that this man hears the word of the kingdom, understands it and the person himself epitomizes this message so that he (not merely the word) brings forth the abundant fruitfulness,[55] which clearly identifies these people with the kingdom. Jesus concludes the parable with the exhortation for his audience to understand, and thus to join the last group of kingdom-responsive people. That role of being a fruitful disciple has been given them by the Father (Mark 4:11).

The Lukan and Markan context spins the parable of the soils into the parable of the lamp (Mark 4:21–25; Luke 8:16–18). Oil lamps lit are used to shine light to their environment, not to be under a basket (Matt 5:14–15; Mark 4:21; Luke 8:16; 11:33).[56] Mark used the parable more as a warning that anything secret will become known. This use further pressed the exhortation of the parable of the soils to be careful to listen and apply the kingdom message because whoever possesses the kingdom benefits will have more given to them. In contrast to the one who does not have, even what he thinks he has will be taken away from him.[57] In this way, then, the parable of the Sower comes to function as an apologetic, even a sort of theodicy, explaining the evil that has befallen Israel (Mark 4:12).[58] Those unwilling to recognize Jesus authority and become disciples are sovereignly excluded by keeping the unresponsive listeners merely entertained by Jesus' parables, not prompted to repent and be forgiven (Mark 4:11–12 and Luke 8:10; while fuller quote of Isa 6:9–10 within Matt 13:13–16 is more explicit for sovereign exclusion).

---

55. Varro, *Rust.* 1.42.2 claims that seed in Syria could yield a hundredfold: *Sib. Or.* 3.263–64; Theophrastus, *Hist. plant.* 8.7.4; Strabo 15.3.11; Pliny, *Nat.* 18.21.94–95.

56. The same point is made in *Gos. Thom.* 33b.

57. The same point is made in *4 Ezra* 7.25; *Gos. Thom.* 41; *b. B. Qam.* 92a.

58. Concealment of kingdom to the outsider as blind and deaf (4Q416 2.iii.18; 1QS 4.11; 11.8–7; Davies and Allison, *Matthew*, 2:375).

A basic quality for disciples is to follow Christ. Anselm Schultz, Hans Deiter Betz, Fernando Segovia, and James Dunn underscore that discipleship in early Judaism and Jesus' ministry is all about following and imitating the mentor.[59] Jesus repeated his call to discipleship so that they will respond to follow Jesus into a deeper extended commitment (John 1:41–42; Matt 4:19).[60] One might claim to be a disciple based on hearing Jesus a few times but unless one follows Jesus in his itinerant ministry one would barely be a disciple (Matt 8:21). Dallas Willard developed that such discipleship would eventually identify one's total life with that of the mentor.

> The secret of the easy yoke, then, is to learn from Christ how to live our total lives, how to invest all our time and our energies of mind and body as he did. We must learn how to follow his preparation, the disciplines for life in God's rule that enabled him to receive his Father's constant and effective support while doing his will. We have to discover how to enter into his disciplines from where we stand today-no doubt, how to extend and amplify them to suit our needy cases.[61]

The backdrop for Jesus' disciples is his command to "Follow Me and I will make you fishers of men" (Matt 4:19). When Jesus gave this command, Jesus' disciples followed him (Mark 2:15; 3:7; 6:1; 8:10; 10:46; Matt 8:23; 9:19; 12:1–2; Luke 7:11; John 2:2, 12; 3:22; 18:1). Jesus fleshes out his exodus kingdom way, so that following him is following him unto kingdom salvation. For example, Andrew announced to his brother Simon, "We have found the messiah" and he brought Peter to Jesus. Jesus revealed the newcomer's heart, "You are Simon the son of John; you shall

---

59. Schultz (*Nachfolgen und Nachahmen*) has a thorough examination of the verb "to follow" and related terminology in the Jewish sources and the NT, followed by a similar examination of the concept of "imitation" and related terminology in Greek and Jewish sources as well as in the NT. Likewise, Betz (*Nachfolge und Nachahmung*) divides his discussion into three parts: 1) the concept of "following" Jesus in the Gospels, 2) the concept of "imitation" in the ancient Mediterranean world, and 3) the role of "imitation" in the theology of Paul. Segovia (*Discipleship in the New Testament*) underscores *imitatio Christi* nuance on discipleship from each Biblical author's perspective. Dunn, *Jesus' Call to Discipleship* unpacks this commitment to master around the Sermon on the Mount and its implications for the church. Wright also champions that discipleship is about following Jesus (*Following Jesus*).

60. See "following" in *Pesiq. Rab Kah.* 18.5 and more deeply "adherent" in 6.4.

61. Willard, *Spirit of the Disciplines*, 9.

be called Cephas" (in Aramaic) or Peter (in Greek). Here, Peter is seen as a foundational rock disciple (John 1:40–42).[62]

Following this encounter, Jesus called some of the same group again from fishing, and they left their nets, boats and father to follow him (Matt 4:18–22; Mark 1:16–20; Luke 5:1–11). Luke recorded that Peter and Andrew had a boat near the Zebedee boat. Jesus asked Simon to put out from shore so that he could teach the crowds. As Jesus finished his sermon, he asked Peter to put out into deep water to let his nets down for a catch of fish. Peter explained to the "master"[63] that they had labored all night when one expected to catch fish and did not catch any, but at Jesus bidding, Peter and Andrew in the boat will let down the nets. When they had done this, the catch enclosed so large a quantity of fish that their nets began to break. They signaled to their partners in another boat to come help them. So many fish were pulled into both boats from this catch that both boats gunnels were near the water line. Either this is a miracle of knowledge (Jesus knew where the fish would be) or it is a miracle of creation (Jesus created the fish to be there). The fishermen, Peter, and James and John Zebedee, were so amazed at the extensive catch that Peter fell at Jesus' feet saying, "Depart from me, for I am a sinful man, O Lord!" Jesus called them to discipleship, "Do not fear, from now on you will be catching men." They brought their boats to land and left everything with father Zebedee and his hired men, and followed Jesus. Probably this is the same event as in Matt 4:18–22 and Mark 1:16–20, however, these accounts do not supply Jesus' teaching and miracle, which provide the context through which to see this discipleship call. So it could be that they are called again. Either way, they have repeated callings to discipleship that prompt them out of their vocation of fishing, to follow Jesus. In these calls, Jesus said, "Follow me and I will make you fishers of men." Peter and Andrew left their nets, boat and follow Jesus. James and John, left their father Zebedee mending the nets with the hired men, to follow

---

62. John developed Andrew and Peter as from Bethsaida (John 1:44), perhaps indicating origination or where they might have either done some of their fishing or sold their fish, while the Synoptics place Peter's home and main fishing port in Capernaum (Mark 1:16, 21, 29). Bethsaida is a little east of Capernaum on the north shore of the Sea of Galilee. Bethsaida would be an unlikely invention for a fellow fisherman fishing out of Capernaum, so it is likely accurate (Mark 1:19–21).

63. Master (ἐπιστάτα) is a unique Lukan term parallel to teacher (διδάσκαλε) but especially shows his authority and their submission to him (Luke 5:5; 8:24, 45; 9:33, 49; 17:13).

Jesus. In the Markan account (without the miracle preceding their being called), Jesus' word to call them is presented as powerful and effective.

Directly following a time of Jesus' teaching in which Jesus healed and forgave the paralytic, Jesus called Matthew from his tax booth to follow him (Mark 2:13–14; Matt 9:9; Luke 5:27–28).[64] Matthew left everything and followed Jesus. Another call event occurred after Jesus spent an evening in prayer, when he chose twelve disciples to be in the core of his following (Mark 3:13–19; Matt 10:1–4; Luke 6:12–16). Jesus called the twelve to be with him and that he might send them out to preach (Mark 3:14). This time of calling ushered into extensive healing and instruction that weeded out those unwilling to follow in true discipleship (John 2:11, 17, 22; 12:16). Craig Keener developed that such teaching challenged Jesus' followers to a difficult commitment.

> Jesus sometimes made it difficult for would-be disciples to follow him; sometimes he thrust them aside (Q material in Matt 8:19–22; Luke 9:57–62), especially if they held high worldly status (Mark 10:21–22; Matt 19:21–22; Luke 18:22–23).[65] In the same way, the Johannine Jesus is particularly hard on Nicodemus and the wealthy official Antipas (3:3, 10; 4:48) and to a lesser extent on members of his family (2:4; 7:6–8)-on those who would be most likely to assume their right of access to him (contrast his inviting treatment toward the Samaritan woman). But Jesus probably thrusts aside or made matters difficult for prospective disciples for the reason other ancient popular teachers did: to test the would-be student's real willingness to become a learner, challenging a disciple to recognize the need to sacrifice.[66]

The Synoptics portray a similar difficult level of commitment as is evident by Jesus' statements to the rich young ruler (Mark 10:17–30; Matt 19:16–30; Luke 18:18–30).[67]

---

64. Matthew's call is also corroborated by the *Gos. Pet.* 14.60 and *Gos. Eb.* 5 as reported by Epiphanius (*Panarion* 30.13.2–3) and in "frag. 4" in *New Testament Apocrypha*, 1:170.

65. As Shammai, schematically contrasted with the gentle Hillel in rabbinic tradition, is said to have done with prospective converts (the later tradition, dominated by Hillel's followers (*t. 'Ed.* 2.3), naturally viewed this negatively, though Shammaites earlier predominated (*t. Šabb.* 1.16; *b. Beṣah* 20a).

66. Keener, *John*, 1:472.

67. Developed in Kennard, *Petrine Studies*, esp. chapter entitled "Mark 10:17–31: Standard and Poor."

Peter becomes the exemplar for a normal disciple's commitment confessing Jesus as the Christ (Mark 8:27–29; Matt 16:16–20; Luke 9:20).[68] Jesus asked who the people thought the Son of Man to be, and the disciples respond with revivified prophets like John the Baptist, Elijah, or Jeremiah. However, Peter identified that Jesus was the anointed one to be king, the Son of the living God. Eduard Schweizer affirmed such Christological commitments and confession is the core of discipleship in his volume about lordship and discipleship.[69] In Peter's statement of Jesus' lordship, Peter became a symbol of the personal commitment of a disciple. Jesus called Simon blessed as a son of Jonah,[70] perhaps because he could see the Messianic outcome after the Jonah sign miracle (Matt 16:4, 17). Simon is blessed with a personal beatitude[71] in that this insight defines him here as informed from the Father, rather than his own human agency.[72] Simon and his insight[73] becomes foundational and thus Jesus changes his name to "Peter" (Πέτρος) and explains that it is he with his insight confession that will become foundational rock (ταύτῃ πέτρᾳ) upon which Jesus will build his church.[74] Other disciples following Jesus should likewise affirm Jesus as the Messiah. This assembly of people already begun and being built up by Jesus is the growing disciple band, which will become Jesus' universal church. This very group (as church) will take the aggressive charge of attacking the gates of Hades (the place of the dead; Isa 38:10;

---

68. Hummel, *Die Auseinandersetzung zwischen Kirche*, 59–64; Kähler, "Zur Form- und Traditionsgeschichte," 40; Damgaard, *Rewriting Peter*, 37–56.

69. Schweizer, *Lordship and Discipleship*.

70. Remember biologically that John is his father (John 1:43; 21:15–17; *Gos. Heb.* frag. 9). Jonah (*iona*) is not the abbreviation of John (*yehonan*), it is *yoḥai* (Williams, "From Shimon to Petros," 34).

71. Other personal beatitudes toward recipients include: Matt 13:16 = Luke 10:23; John 20:29; *4 Ezra* 10.57; and *Jos. Asen.* 16.14.

72. "Flesh and blood" reflects the rabbinic sense of human agency (Davies and Allison, *Matthew*, 2:623).

73. Peter's confession is likely what is meant by the feminine foundation rock (πέτρᾳ), with the feminine pronoun (ταύτῃ), rather than second-person singular masculine "you" referring to Peter, who was described as rock in the masculine (Πέτρος), or first-person masculine "me" referring to Christ (Matt 16:18), who is not in this context described as a rock but is only elsewhere described as a rock (which in those other contexts makes good sense) without reference to this text. Caragounis, *Peter and the Rock*, 119.

74. Peter's confession as foundational rock is not maintained in other contexts. For example, 1 Pet 2:4–8 and Hermas, *Sim.* 9.12.1 develop Christ as the rock, upon which the church is built.

Pss 9:13;107:18; Job 38:17 LXX "gatekeepers").[75] Hades' gates will fall, so that the dead will be rescued from Hades' clutches. With the Jonah resurrection sign in view, this aggressive rescue from Hades extends beyond evangelism and kingdom miracles to resurrections from Hades, which Jesus leads the way and Peter's insight shows the way to resurrect unto kingdom. With this understanding, Peter becomes a scribe of kingdom, complete with the scribal sign of keys to the kingdom. This concept of church triumphing over the gates of the walking dead, shows that in time the household of God will likely be in a different condition from temporary resident development in 1 Pet. Additionally, from Peter being granted the role of scribe unto Jesus' kingdom, Petrine theology as a loosed perspective should frame the acceptable forms for biblical theology and its continued embrace and application in the church. Petrine theology is thus foundational for Christian theology and practice. To deny or exclude significant aspects of Petrine theology is done to one's peril.

Extending further, from the insight of Jesus' kingship, Peter is here granted a scribal role that the whole disciple band, as church, is later also granted (Matt 16:19; 18:18; John 20:23). If Peter and the disciples "bind" a teaching or practice or a person as excluded from kingdom it is excluded with reference to heavenly salvation and life practice,[76] whereas, if Peter and the disciples "loose" a teaching or practice as permitted or a person as included in kingdom, then it is included with reference to heavenly salvation. If these scribal actions entail forgiving, then as the disciples forgive, divine forgiveness will be meted out unto kingdom.

With the disciple's realization that Jesus is the messiah, Jesus begins to predict his coming death and resurrection. Following Jesus' way to Jerusalem and the cross means that the disciples are to follow Jesus, perhaps to their own death, and thus to kingdom.[77] Peter responds with a comment that rejects Jesus' predictions so much so that he becomes

---

75. Wis 16.13; 3 Macc 5:51; *Pss. Sol.* 16.2; Cullman, *Peter*, 208.

76. These verses can grammatically be treated as future perfect paraphrastics (what you bind shall have been bound) but the narrative context emphasis on privilege and responsibility makes it more natural to read it as indicating real scribal privilege and responsibility of issuing authoritative *halakah* (teaching), as I have indicated above and this is the early Jewish pattern elsewhere (CD 5.24–25; 1QS 5.24–25; 4Q477 frag. 2.1–2; *m. Naz.* 5.1–4; *y. Šabb.* 4.1; 6.1; 16.2, 4; *b. Ḥag.* 10a; *b. Meg.* 26.7; *b. Avodah Zarah* 7.1; 39.2; *b. Ber.* 23.1; *b. Sanh.* 100.1; *Tosaphata in Jevam.* cap. 1; *Pesachin*, cap. 4 hal. 5; *Mamrim*, cap. 1, cap 2; Lightfoot, *Commentary on the New Testament*, 2:237–40; Bornkamm, "Authority to 'Bind' and 'Loose,'" 83–97).

77. Best, *Following Jesus*, 15.

emblematic of Satan's interests and puts Jesus at risk for damnation, with Peter as a stumbling block (σκάνδαλον; Matt 16:23).[78] Such a context raised the cost of discipleship. With the risk of Jesus impending death, the cost of discipleship stiffens. Jesus began to instruct the disciples that he was going to be killed and that would put their own lives at risk through mimetic or imitative atonement (Mark 8:33–38; Matt 16:15–28; Luke 9:20–27, 57–58).[79] With the stakes increasing on each side for and against Christ, the cost of discipleship stiffens further. Jesus will be killed by elders, chief priests, and scribes. "If anyone wishes to come after Me (a synonym for following in discipleship), let him deny himself and take up his cross and follow me." Since discipleship to Christ is following Christ and Christ is heading toward his death, disciples in this time of persecution must head for their deaths as well. As Bonhoeffer tells us, "When Christ calls a man, he bids him come and die."[80] To follow Jesus on the level that he is identifying becomes the essence of discipleship. Thus, carrying one's cross brings shame of rejection and death. Since Jesus is heading for this shame rejection and death, the disciple must as well. Discipleship is not trying to affirm, hold onto or save your own life, for such a tactic of control wastes one's life and it is then lost, departing from the kingdom way toward damnation. True discipleship is zealously living full out for Christ.[81] Discipleship is spending out your life for Christ's sake, for in such an identification of your life with Christ you find your life. Discipleship is not being ashamed of Christ and his words, even if this commitment would result in the world shaming the disciples. This has implications that all of Christ's disciples will not die in such a heinous death as on the cross. However, the disciple does not have a choice in the matter; if they are to be Jesus' disciples in such an extreme time then their lives must be lived under the foreboding shadow of the possibility of their own persecution and death on a cross. There is no profit in gaining even the whole world materially only to lose one's life as damned. Real profit is not in material gain but in the rewards which the Son of Man gives recompensing every man according to his deeds. Some of the disciples were

78. At places like this exemplar of Satan, and Peter's denials, Gundry argued that Peter was an exemplar of false discipleship and apostate (*Peter: False Disciple and Apostate*; similarly, Stock, "Is Matthew's Presentation of Peter Ironic?," 64–69). However, as a whole it is better to see Peter as both an exemplar of discipleship as well as a warning of potential apostasy (continuing discussion: Ridlehoover, "Matthean Peter," 729–44).

79. Kennard, *Messiah Jesus*, 275–79.

80. Bonhoeffer, *Cost of Discipleship*, 7, 89.

81. A helpful tract exploring this zeal: MacDonald, *True Discipleship*, 26–28.

encouraged as they saw the transfiguration expression of the kingdom, reassuring them that kingdom rewards will come. Jesus repeated the stiffened cost of discipleship, pressing difficult implications of loyalty into the lives of his disciples (Luke 14:15–35). Excuses of family and material gain that keep one from zealously involving oneself with the kingdom, damn the reticent. The kingdom will be filled with the willing needy ones who enter without excuse. Which meant Jesus must be placed first in one's life to the extent that disciples must hate all their family members in order to be a disciple of Christ (Matt 10:37; Luke 14:26).

Jesus exemplified this commitment by not being dissuaded by his family when they tried to collect him (considering him mentally off), when Jesus was passionate toward kingdom (Mark 3:31–35; 6:4; Matt 12:46–50; Luke 8:19–21). Instead, Jesus considered that his disciples are his family.[82] That is, no family member can be permitted to persuade you from kingdom involvement, as Jesus did not let his own family dissuade him from his kingdom ministry,[83] whereas rallying to the cost, as Peter claims for the disciples, nets big rewards. "We have left everything and followed you; what then will there be for us?" (Matt 19:27). Jesus responds to the disciples, encouraging them that the gain is increased privilege, responsibility, and everlasting life in the resurrection. Truly I say to you, that you who have followed me, in the regeneration when the Son of Man will sit on his glorious throne, you also shall sit upon twelve thrones, judging the twelve tribes of Israel. And everyone who has left houses or brothers or sisters or father or mother or children or farms for my sake shall receive many times as much and shall inherit everlasting life (Matt 19:28–29).

Discipleship requires alertness and praying, because there is always threat of temptation (Mark 4:5–19; 13:33, 37; 14:38; 1 Pet 1:13–15; 4:7; 5:9). Jesus exemplified this alertness and cultivated a relationship with God in prayer (Mark 1:35; 6:46; 14:32–36).

Discipleship entails consistent relationship and service. When mother Zebedee asked for her sons to sit at Jesus' right and left in the kingdom (Mark 10:35–41; Matt 20:18–24), Jesus responded to the Zebedee boys and mother, that they do not know what they are asking. "Are

---

82. Synoptic Gospels corroborated each other and by the *Gos. Eb.* 6 as reported by Epiphanius, *Panarion* 30.14.5; Santos, "New Family of Jesus," 542–601.

83. Like rabbinic thought which ranked the master above family, next to that of heaven itself (*m. Abot* 4.12).

you able to drink the cup that I am about to drink?"[84] The Zebedee boys said, "we are able." To which Jesus responded, "My cup you shall drink," fulfilling their disciple role of being like their master in martyrdom: James dies under Herod's persecution of the church (Acts 12:2), and John dies exiled to Patmos.[85]

Greatness in the kingdom is not that of lording over others but by serving others (Mark 10:42-45; Matt 20:25-28).[86] It is in this context that Jesus said, "The Son of Man did not come to be served, but to serve, and to give his life as a ransom for many" (Mark 10:45; Matt 20:28).[87] Here Jesus' life given includes his death (through the cup imagery) but he emphasizes his life spent in service as the example of true kingdom greatness which his disciples are to follow. That is, mimetic atonement has Jesus' servanthood life as the price of ransom (λύτρον) rescuing the many from an ambiguous bondage into his kingdom way. If λύτρον is defined by the other synoptic references, such ransoming has to do with God's raising up a Davidic king to deliver Israel into kingdom excluding their enemies in defeat (Luke 1:68-69; 2:38; 24:21), not a vicarious atonement for sin. This follows the Jewish pattern where martyr's death ransoms the covenant people Israel from the sins of the nation.[88] For example, in 4 Macc 6:29 a prayer is uttered by those on the battlefield: "Make my blood their purification, and take my life in exchange for theirs." The speaker goes on to exhort others to "imitate me" in remaining faithful on the battlefield even if martyrdom is their lot.[89] Fourth Maccabees 17:20-22 goes on to

---

84. This mimetic atonement suffering is additionally supported by Jesus' metaphor of baptism within an OT concept of suffering by submersion (2 Sam 22:4-7, 17-18; Pss 18:4-6, 16-17; 32:6; 42:7; 69:1-2, 13-17; 124:1-5 [repeated liturgically as a song of ascent]; 144:7-11; Job 22:11).

85. Irenaeus, *Haer.* 3.1.1; Eusebius, *Hist. eccl.* 3.34.13; Lightfoot, *Apostolic Fathers*, 513-31.

86. Bermejo-Rubio, "Did Jesus the Galilean Redefine," 51-82; like: Dio Cassius 63.13; Plutarch *Otho* 15.3-4; Euripides, *Phoen.* 963-69; Lucian, *Bell Civ.* 2.380-83; Hutchison, "Servanthood," 53-68.

87. A defense of the authenticity of this statement, Feuillict, "La coupe et le baptême," 356-91; Howard, "Did Jesus Speak," 515-27; Casey, *Aramaic Sources of Mark's Gospel*, 206; Sanders, *Jesus and Judaism*, 147; McKnight, *Jesus and His Death*, 356-58 conjectures that Mark reflects Isa 53. However, in Pate and Kennard, *Deliverance Now and Not Yet*, 316-18, 328-32, we explore the possibility of Isa 53 lying beneath these verses, examining the alternatives and concluding that the near context emphasis should not be overruled by the pendulum swing of plausible academic conjecture.

88. 1QpHab. 8.1-3; 2 Macc 6:30; 7:9, 11, 14, 16-17, 22-23, 29, 30-38; 4 Macc 6:27-29; 9:23-24; 17:21-22.

89. 4 Macc 9:23-24.

praise the martyrs for becoming "a ransom for the sin of our nation and through the blood of those devout ones and their death as an atoning sacrifice, divine Providence preserved Israel." In early Jewish Greek manuscripts of mimetic atonement, this atonement is conveyed by words like: "through" (διά), "example" (ὑπόδειγμα), and the contextual pattern of imitative death.[90] George Nickelsburg explains this early Jewish mimetic atonement option from passages in 2 Macc 6:18—7:44, 1 Macc 2 and the *T. Mos.* 9. Each instance recounts an event which the respective author interprets as the catalyst turning God's wrath from Israel and bringing release from persecution. Each is a story about a parent and sons who are ready to die rather than transgress the Torah. *T. Moses* 9:7 and 10:2 anticipates an apocalyptic denouement in which God will avenge the innocent blood of his servants, notably Taxo and his sons. For the pro-Hasmonean author of 1 Macc, Mattathias' zealous deed stays God's wrath (Num 25:8, 11). Second Maccabees 7 recognized that Judas Maccabeus turned back the Syrian armies and brought deliverance to Israel. However, although Taxo's prediction has not been fulfilled as stated, *T. Mos.* 7:37; 8:3, 5 recorded those innocent deaths of martyrs and their appeal for vengeance contribute to turn God's wrath to mercy and facilitate the Maccabean victories.[91] However, in this synoptic context, battlefield service is not in view but rather serving through humility as Jesus provides the example. Gaining kingdom is the goal in both the Maccabean and in Jesus' humble service. Jesus had repeatedly called his disciples to take up their cross and follow him in this mimetic atonement (Mark 8:34–38; Matt 10:38; 16:24–27; Luke 9:22–26; John 12:24–25). In the synoptic passages, "the many" is the new covenant people, whom Jesus gathers around himself. Such a kingdom meaning fits delightfully in this passage that acknowledges Jesus as the king in his kingdom but not like other kings (Mark 10:42; Matt 20:21, 25). This ransom is "for" (ἀντί) the many in this gospel context. That word ἀντί has the sense of "on behalf of" or "in place of." In this case both could apply. Jesus shows his greatness as king in taking the place of servants and serving on their behalf throughout his kingly life on earth and as supremely exampled in his death. The point of the passage is not vicarious atonement but by contextual emphasis this passage shows that disciples are also to be servants after Jesus' pattern. As such, this

---

90. 2 Macc 6:31; 4 Macc 17:20–22.

91. Nickelsburg, *Jewish Literature*, 119–20.

passage follows the Jewish mimetic atonement pattern.[92] The main point is that disciples should be servants as Jesus shows that he serves others.

Jesus' triumphal entrance into Jerusalem fulfills the exodus return to Jerusalem that the gospel began with (Mark 11:1–11 fulfilling a return from 1:2–3 quoting Isa 40:3). The people welcome Jesus as they might a lead rabbi or potential peaceful king riding into Jerusalem (Zech 9:9; Matt 21:5; Mark 11:10, quote of Ps 118:26). The people cried out the ascent *hallel* Ps 118:25–26 to identify that Jesus coming is blessed of the Lord, with anticipation that the Davidic kingdom is impending (Mark 11:9–10). The psalm quote is wrapped with the statement "hosanna" which becomes a prayer to God, and perhaps for Christ to "deliver."[93] However, Jerusalem was largely unresponsive and had replaced prayer for commerce in the temple. Jesus cursed the fig tree as a warning of Jerusalem's rebellion and excluded temple commerce to call them back to practicing prayer in his Father's house (Mark 11:12–25). Jesus warned the people that they had rejected him in their dullness, rebellion, and now murder plots. However, God's plan kept Jesus at the center, so that they were rejecting him to their peril (Mark 11:18, 27; 12:12). In the religious leader's attempts to shame Jesus with tough questions as an inadequate scribe, Jesus demonstrated his scribal superiority and shamed them instead (Mark 11:27–33; 12:13–44).[94]

Jesus' final Passover and upper room discourse provides a level of relationship between Jesus and the disciples that indicate the master is allowing his disciples to be intimately included as he serves them (Mark 14:17–31; Matt 26:20–29; Luke 22:14–34; John 13:1—16:33). Those preparing the meal should have arranged for this foot washing service, to remove the dust and refuse from their feet, for dining comfort.[95] How-

92. 1 Macc 2:27–28; 2 Macc 6:12–17.42; 4 Macc 1:8–11; 6:27–30; 7:8–9; 9:23–24; 10:10; 11:12–27; 12:16–18; 16:16, 24–25; 17:2, 11–22; 18:1–5; Wis 2.12–20; 3.5–6; 4.18–15.14; 7.14; 11.19; 12.22; 1QS 5.6; 1QS 9.4–5; 1Q34 bis 3 1, 5; 4Q508 1,1; 4Q513 frag. 2 2.4; 11Q10 (*Tg. Job*) 38.2; *Sipre Deut. Pisqa* 33.5; *T. Mos.* 9–10.10; Pate and Kennard, *Deliverance Now and Not Yet*, 29–71; Gundry, *Mark*, 869.

93. Goldingay, *Psalms*, 3:363. This is a standard psalm sung on the ascent for Passover (*m. Pesaḥ*. 5.7; 9.3; 10.5–7; *t. Pesaḥ*. 8.22; *b. Pesaḥ*. 117a; Keener, *Matthew*, 492. There is no evidence that the LXX statement "ties up the festival cords" is harkening to Sukkot or a festival offering (Goldingay, *Psalms*, 3:364), Mark is more reflective of the MT psalms, leaving these themes undeveloped.

94. Kennard, *Epistemology and Logic*, 76–82 develops rabbinic patterns for assessing scribal ability, within which Jesus excelled; *Messiah Jesus*, 131–35.

95. Thomas, *Footwashing in John 13*, 27–40, 115; tradition has it that Jerusalem's streets were swept daily (*b. Pesaḥ*. 7a); but foot washing was still of benefit: Rohrbaugh,

ever, Jesus girded himself with a towel and poured water into a bowl and began to wash the disciples' feet. When Jesus came to Peter, he protested, "Lord, never shall you wash my feet." Jesus answered him, "If I do not wash you, you have no part with me." To which Peter overreacted, "Lord, not my feet only but also my hands and head." Jesus responded, "He who has bathed needs only to wash his feet, but is completely clean; and you-all[96] are clean, but not all," meaning Judas, the betrayer is not clean. After washing their feet, he reminded them that if he their Lord, Teacher, Master, and Sender washed their feet, then they ought to wash one another's feet, "for I gave you all an example that you also should do as I did to you all." By serving in this way you are blessed if you do them.

Returning to the table Jesus told his disciples that he earnestly desired to eat this Passover with his disciples (Mark 14:22–25; Matt 26:26–29; Luke 22:14–22; 1 Cor 11:23–26). While they were eating,[97] Jesus took some bread, blessed it, broke it, and gave it to his disciples saying "Take, eat this is my body."[98] Jesus then took the fourth cup (or a second third cup[99]) of the Passover.[100] Jesus gave thanks and gave it to his disciples to drink saying, "This cup is the new covenant in my blood, shed on behalf of many for forgiveness of sins." Each Gospel is enigmatic but when these statements are combined, they add to a covenantal atonement model: Luke adds "the new covenant," Mark adds "for the many," and Matthew "for the forgiveness of sins." The statement of "covenant in blood" is

"Pre-industrial City in Luke-Acts," 135; Avi-Yonah, *Hellenism and the East*, 124.

96. The southern "you-all" reflects a second-person plural in this context, meaning the disciple band is addressed.

97. Passover had four cups (*m. Pesaḥ.* 10; Marshall, *Luke*, 797–98; Bahr, "Seder of Passover," 181–202). The third cup would be preceded by the paschal lamb and discussion of the exodus events recounted, then after the third cup there would be dessert of bread and sometimes salty items which were open to tailor the conversation to particulars like this novel appropriation by Jesus.

98. Most accounts have bread first then cup (Matt 26:26–27; Mark 14:22–23; *m. Pesaḥ.* 103), but Luke 22:17–20 has the meal begin with a cup, bread then cup again, which 1 Cor 10:16 and *Did* 9:1–4 takes as the order of cup then bread. Historically, the likely order is the bread then cup, which is a second instance of the third cup, or a fourth cup (Luke 22:20 "after dining") with the kind of blessings of the third cup.

99. The third cup of Passover usually has the benediction blessing said over it (*m. Pesaḥ.* 10.7).

100. After this cup he does not drink again, so maybe the fourth cup (Luke 22:19 mentions "after eating") or a second instance of the third cup, on the basis of the blessing (Luke 22:18; *m. Pesaḥ.* 10.7) and the parallel of vows in Luke 22:15 and 17; Plummer, *Luke*, 495; Bock, *Luke*, 2:1722. The use of a common cup is unusual for Passover but not unprecedented (*t. Ber.* 5.9; *m. Ber.* 8.8; Jeremias, *Eucharistic Words of Jesus*, 69).

reminiscent of Exod 24:8 (especially in Matthew and Mark, commemorated in discussions from especially the second or third cup). Luke provided the lens of the new covenant of Jer 31:31 (Luke 22:20), with its forgiveness (themes common to the fourth cup, which sometimes looks toward the kingdom), and perhaps a hint of Isa 53:12 death "for many." Jesus then identified that he would not drink wine again until he did so in the kingdom of God, which would likely be the final (or fourth) cup of the Passover, unless he left Passover unfinished.

Jesus then raised the issue that one disciple would fail in temptation and would betray him (Mark 14:10-11, 17-21; Matt 26:14-16, 20-25; Luke 22:3-6, 21-23; John 13:21-30). The fact that Jesus had just washed all their feet and eaten with them serves as irony to the Scripture fulfilling quote, "He who eats my bread has lifted up his heel against me" (Ps 41:9; LXX 40:10; John 13:18; 17:12).[101] He identified his betrayer discretely by dipping bread with him and giving it to him in the fashion one might do as a favor for a guest, but perhaps the bitter herbs in the sauce might indicate curse.[102] Jesus identified that Judas was not one he had chosen for kingdom; as a "son of destruction," Judas was an apostate destined for damnation (John 17:12; 2 Thess 2:3; Rev 17:8).[103] Peter later concurred that Judas left his place of apostleship service, home and lot desolate (Acts 1:17-21, 25). The disciples responded strangely to this news of betrayal, for a repeated dispute arose among the disciples concerning which one of them would be the greatest (Mark 9:33-34; 10:35-41; Matt 18:1; 20:20-24; Luke 22:24; 9:46). Jesus responded as he characteristically did (except without placing a child before them): "Kings of the Gentiles lord it over them, but among you all, let the greatest be as the servant. For who is greater, the one who serves or the one who reclines? I am among you-all as the one who serves. Just as my Father has granted me a kingdom, I grant that you-all may eat and drink at my table in my kingdom, and that you all may sit on thrones judging the twelve tribes of Israel" (Luke 22:25-30).

Peter protested that he would be faithful and die if needed, to which Jesus responded that Peter also would fail, prompted by Satan's sifting

---

101. The same quote was used by Qumran's Teacher of Righteousness to complain of his suffering (1QH 5.22-24).

102. As a favor: Hunter, *John*, 137; as a curse citing Deut 29:18-19: Stauffer, *Jesus and His Story*, 116.

103. *Jub.* 10.3; 15.26; *Sib. Or.* 16.9; CD 6.15; 8.14, 20.

the whole disciple band,[104] so that before morning Peter would deny Jesus three times (Mark 14:27–31; Matt 26:30–34; Luke 22:31–34; John 13:36–38).[105] Matthew and Mark have this comment coming in response to Jesus predicting, on the basis of Zech 13:7, that with Shepherd Jesus killed, they will all flee. Matthew adds that they were all insisting that they would not deny Jesus. John has these comments coming out of Jesus statements that he was going away and that they could not follow him, whereas Luke comments about this from Jesus' compassion to inform them that Satan had demanded to sift the disciples, but Jesus had prayed that Peter's faith would not fail and that after he had turned that he should strengthen his brethren.

Undoing these denials, Peter is reminded after Jesus' resurrection that love for Christ should motivate feeding Jesus' followers (John 21:15–17). After breakfast Jesus questioned Peter to help him articulate his supreme love. Jesus repeated Simon's name in a very formal pattern reiterating that what followed was significant. The question was aimed at discerning Peter's supreme loyalty.[106] This question was asked three times. Each time Peter answered in the affirmative. With the third time, Peter is annoyed probably because it becomes clear that this parallels Peter's three denials before men, and thus serves as a time of Peter's recovery. Jesus responded to each answer with a command reiterating Peter's responsibility to care for the flock owned by Jesus, the Great Shepherd

---

104. Luke 22:31–34 frames the temptation by Satan's sifting to occur to the whole disciple band (plural "you all," ὑμᾶς) who reclined at table: "Satan has demanded to sift you all [ὑμᾶς] like wheat; but I have prayed for you [remaining 'you' statements are singular, σοῦ] Peter, that your faith may not fail and you, after you have turned again, strengthen your brothers"; Bourke, "Peter in the Gospel of Luke," 120–21.

105. At places like this denial and when Peter is an exemplar of Satan in Matt 16:22–23, Gundry argued that Peter was an exemplar of false discipleship and apostate (*Peter: False Disciple and Apostate*; similarly, Stock, "Is Matthew's Presentation of Peter Ironic?," 64–69). However, as a whole it is better to see Peter as both an exemplar of discipleship as well as a warning of potential apostasy (continuing discussion: Ridlehoover, "Matthean Peter," 729–44).

106. The question "Do you love Me more than these?" has three possible meanings. Perhaps, because Peter had previously professed a greater loyalty than the others (Matt 26:33; Mark 14:29; John 13:37; 15:12), Jesus asked "Are you more loyal than they?" Maybe Jesus asked if Peter loved Jesus more than he loved these other disciples. That is, Peter had remained with his friends when they all forsook Christ. Perhaps Jesus asked Peter if he was more loyal to Jesus than to these things of fishing (his old occupation). The text appears to be ambiguous in discerning between these options, but the commonality between them all is a discernment of Peter's supreme loyalty for Christ (Morris, *John*, 870–71).

(John 21:15–17, "my sheep"; 1 Pet 5:4).[107] Jesus did not give the flock over to Peter, but Jesus delegated to Peter the task of shepherding his flock. At this point, Luke adds some redundant instruction on what to take in their sent role and the extent of the cost of discipleship (Luke 22:35–38).

In the book of Acts the concept of disciple continues to be a committed follower of Christ in his kingdom way but become "apostles" or "sent ones" to continue to bring others into this kingdom way.[108] The disciples are a community of committed believers (Acts 1:15; 9:19, 38; 14:20, 22, 28; 16:1; 18:23, 27; 19:1; 20:1, 30; 21:4, 16). The exodus imagery continues to develop the character of the generous community of the people of God.[109] The disciples are following Christ's way (Acts 9:2; 13:10; 16:17; 18:25–26; 19:9, 19, 23; 22:4; 24:14, 22). This is the narrow way of truth and righteousness in contrast to the broad way of judgment (2 Pet 2:2, 15, 21; Matt 7:13–23).[110] Part of the continuing exodus in Acts is the expansion of the itinerary of the word as Peter and others preach the gospel (Acts 2; 3; 4:1–12; 10).[111] The disciples are called Christians because they live like Christ (Acts 11:26). These disciples sometimes have conflict, but they work it out for the furtherance of the gospel (Acts 6:1–7; 15:10; 19:30). These disciples are persecuted and die for their faith in Christ (Acts 4:1–22; 5:17–42; 6:9—8:3; 9:1; 11:19; 14:19; 16:19-34; 21:30—26:32). These disciples remain obedient to Christ in the face of the threat of persecution (Acts 9:10, 19, 25–26). Additionally, the disciples were generous to meet needs of others (Acts 2:44; 4:32–37; 11:29). Apostleship then becomes a sub-category of discipleship associated with the twelve and a very few others who have been directly called by Christ and have seen him in the resurrection. For example, Peter held to a definition that an apostle was a sent one with the personal experience of Jesus ministry from Jesus' baptism to the resurrection (Acts 1:21–22). Because Judas had vacated his portion of this ministry there was a felt need to

---

107. The different ways of speaking in this passage are probably not significant. For example, Jesus asked if Peter loves him with ἀγαπᾷς the first two times and φιλεῖς the third time. Peter answered "Yes" to each of the questions and then added that he loved (φιλῶ) Jesus. The result of this is that Peter loves Jesus with both ἀγαπαω and φιλενω. Likewise, the reiteration of "feed" or "tend" and "lambs" or "sheep" is also not significant except that Peter is given the shepherding responsibility over Jesus' whole flock (Brown, *John*, 1102–6).

108. Pao, *Acts and the Isaianic New Exodus*.

109. Pao, *Acts and the Isaianic New Exodus*, 167–76.

110. 1QS 3.13–14.26; *Barn.* 18–20; *Did.* 1–5; *1 Clem.* 35.5.

111. Pao, *Acts and the Isaianic New Exodus*, 150–67.

replace him to make twelve again. Discipleship in the NT is a student who follows Christ into his kingdom way with continuing obedience. To really be Christ's disciple one needs to keep Christ first in all relationships and decisions. Such discipleship is deeply relational with Christ. As such, discipleship to Christ may be very costly even to martyrdom but it is profoundly rewarding in everlasting life.

As Peter sees the vision in Joppa and brings the gospel to Cornelius' household, it becomes progressively clear that this exodus way unto kingdom also includes gentiles. The giving of the Holy Spirit with similar manifestation as at Pentecost confirm God's full acceptance of gentiles with kingdom salvation (Acts 10:44–48; 11:1–18; 15:7–11). The Jerusalem council of the early church agreed that gentile believers in Christ were equally accepted by God's grace (Acts 15:7,19–20, 28–29). The gospel message brings gentiles and Jewish believers into the way of salvation exodus extending Jesus' exodus way unto kingdom (2 Pet 1:1–11; Acts 9:2; 13:10; 16:17; 18:25–26; 19:9; 22:4; 24:14, 22).[112]

Several commentators develop parallels concerning the new exodus in 1 Pet and Heb, trying to deepen the theme in 1 Pet by comparison.[113] While Heb continues the message for Jewish Christians, 1 Pet expands these exodus themes for his largely gentile audience (1 Pet 1:18; 4:3–4). Parallels developed by these commentators between 1 Pet and Heb regarding these new exodus plans include the following:

1. Believers are ransomed by blood of spotless lamb. 1 Pet 1:18–24; Heb 9:12, 14; 10:10
2. Believers are sprinkled by Christ's blood. 1 Pet 1:2; Heb 12:24
3. Believers are strangers and aliens. 1 Pet 1:1; Heb 2:11
4. Believers are heading toward heavenly inheritance. 1 Pet 1:4; Heb 9:15; 12:17
5. Believers have an undefiled inheritance. 1 Pet 1:4; Heb 7:26; 13:4
6. Believers are in suffering to test them. 1 Pet 1:6–8; Heb 2:9–18
7. Prophets predict Christ's suffering. 1 Pet 1:10–12; Heb:1–2
8. Angels look into salvific things. 1 Pet 1:12; Heb 1:4, 14

---

112. Developed further in Kennard, *Petrine Studies*, chapter entitled "Jewish Traditions and Gentile Conversion."

113. Grässer, "Der Hebräerbrief, 1938–63," 138–236; Moffatt, *Introduction to the Literature of the New Testament*, 440; Masterman, *1 Peter*, 36–38; L. D. Hurst, *Hebrews*, 126–30; Martin, *Metaphor and Composition in 1 Peter*, 131, 143–267 put in chart form by Bauman-Martin, "Speaking Jewish," 163.

9. Believers must discipline themselves toward goal. 1 Pet 1:13; Heb 12:1
10. Believers are to hope in grace. 1 Pet 1:13; Heb 11:1–30
11. God's people are ignorant and erring. 1 Pet 1:14; 2:25; Heb 5:2; 9:7
12. Believers pray with fear through Exodus. 1 Pet 1:17; Heb 4:1; 10:30; 12:7–9
13. Believers should love and be kind to strangers. 1 Pet 1:22; 4:9; Heb 13:1
14. Believers have living word. 1 Pet 1:23; Heb 4:12
15. The community of believers is a "house." 1 Pet 2:5; Heb 3:6
16. Believers are a "holy and royal priesthood." 1 Pet 2:5, 9; Heb 7:1, 26
17. Believers are to offer spiritual sacrifices to God. 1 Pet 2:5, 9; Heb 7:1, 13:10

From this summary of their points, the thrust of Hebrews' pilgrimage works within a two ways framework that reflects the consistent Christian model as articulated by 1 Pet. Once again, the exodus is a Christian framework evidencing the two ways one can live, emphasizing the narrow way of virtues following Christ unto kingdom.

Several of the above exodus parallels ground themselves within Petrine redemption and cleansing, as the exodus initiated in the Passover redemption (1 Pet 1:18–19; Exod 12:1–20).[114] Within a context of positional atonement, election, and efficacious new birth (which all guarantee a believer's eschatological salvation), Peter presents a way of virtues which can reassure an individual of salvation and divine usefulness as opposed to the way of vice that the false teachers exemplify. That is, Peter's view is more complex than the two ways but he subsumes the two ways view within his view (perhaps as Reformed salvation with a prominent role of Edwardsian religious affection framing his affirming salvific way in contrast to the broad way of damnation). Peter's use of redemption and cleansing enables the believer along within a two ways perspective. Christian responsibility and consequences showcase the value of tested faith and urgency for Christians to continue toward eschatological salvation.

Divine choice is built off the choice of Christ as precious and extended to the community or chosen race being built up in him (1 Pet 2:4, 6, 9). The choice is implemented by the foreknowledge of the Father through a preparatory sanctifying work of the Spirit to bring about the

---

114. Kennard, "Petrine Redemption," 399–405.

effect of the individual's initially obeying Jesus Christ and being sprinkled with his blood (1 Pet 1:1–2).

Jesus Christ performs the role of priest offering up a sacrifice, which he is as the spotless lamb that sacrificially dies to redeem (1 Pet 1:19; 2:24). The sprinkling of the people with blood identifies not only an atonement sacrifice but an initiation of a covenant after the pattern of the Mosaic covenant initiated at Mount Sinai (1 Pet 1:2; Exod 24:1–11).

The new birth is fertilized with imperishable seed of the living and abiding word of God (1 Pet 1:23–25). This imperishable word was the gospel which Peter's readers had preached to them. From this proclamation the Father caused them to be born again to a living hope after the pattern of Christ's resurrection (1 Pet 1:3–5). That is, Christ already raised from the dead to his inheritance calls the believers to realize that they have an inheritance which is imperishable, undefiled, reserved in heaven for them and that they are protected by the power of God through faith to receive that salvation that is ready to be revealed in the last time.

For Peter, redemption is Christ's work, setting people free from their previous lifestyles. Peter does not use Paul's redemption concept, which includes features such as forgiveness and ultimate departure from sinful body (Rom 3:24; 8:23; Eph 1:7, 14), nor Luke's redemption concept which speaks of Davidic kingdom conquering all enemies (Luke 1:68–71). Petrine redemption sets up a divinely sourced framework through which Christian virtues should be pursued as a new exodus unto kingdom.

To initiate these virtues, Peter's readers received from God the same kind of faith as Peter the apostle (2 Pet 1:1). This faith was given by God and "received" by the believers from God, much like the lot to determine Judas' replacement "was received" from God (2 Pet 1:1, λαχοῦσιν after the pattern of same verb in Acts 1:17).[115] That is, faith is a gift of God, though the human is also responsible (2 Pet 1:1, 3–6; Acts 3:19, 26: 5:31). Part of the process was that Peter's readers were informed of the true knowledge of magnificent promises which enable them to know God and develop life beyond corruption (2 Pet 1:2–4). Peter identified that upon these magnificent promises his readers might become partakers or partners of the divine nature, having escaped the corruption that is in the world by lust" (2 Pet 1:4). At this point, one's personal eschatology frames the Christian virtues as heading toward a goal, but what goal is this?

---

115. BAG, "λαγχάνω," 382; Hanse, "λαγχάνω," TDNT 4:2.

Especially in the Eastern Church and Roman Catholicism, Petrine discipleship is characterized from 2 Pet 1:4 as *"Theosis."* Grounded not in atonement but in the incarnation of Christ, where Jesus takes human nature upon himself so that he might mystically transform humans to become divinized as immortal.[116] Part of this process is to provide humans with divine light so that we would take on immortal knowledge.[117] When the divine nature of Christ fused with our fallible human nature, the divine nature became a consuming fire to eradicate the evil within our human nature.[118] Athanasius also considered that this divinization process should be called "god adopting believers as sons."[119] Aquinas proposed that God infused justification beginning with an event of God's grace infused into a person, initiating a process to transform her toward faith and away from sin.[120] This divine action facilitates the believer growing in the narrow way toward being like Christ, and ultimately God will eschatologically forgive the believer's sin. Morna Hooker defended this approach as "interchange in Christ" whereby "Christ became what we are, in order that we might become what he is."[121] Believers are transformed to reflect the exemplar Christ until in kingdom we will all be like him.

Scott Hafemann provides a good trajectory though 2 Pet 1:3–11.[122] "Nature" (φύσις) is "wholistic being." An ontological view of "nature" has led to four interpretations of the phrase "Become partners of the divine nature" (γένησθε θείας κοινωνοὶ φύσεως; 2 Pet 1:4). Hafemann summarized the interpretation views of this passage.

---

116. Irenaeus, *Haer.* 4.33.4; Athanasius, *De incarn.* 9; Gregory of Nyssa, *Great Catechism* 25, 37; *Ag. Eunomius* 5.5; Augustine, *Trin.* 3.4; *Doctr. chr.* 1.22.16–17; Leo the Great, *Sermons* 23.5; 24.1–5; 26.2.

117. Clement, *Hom.* 1.4; *1 Clem.* 36.2.

118. Gregory of Nyssa, *Ag. Eunomius* 5.4; Ign. *Smyrn.* 6; *Ep. Eph.* 20.2 "breaking one bread, which is the medicine of immortality, the antidote against death which gives eternal life in Jesus Christ"; Irenaeus, *Haer.* 4.18.4–6; Gregory of Nyssa, *Great Catechism* 37; Cassiodorus, *Exp. S. Pauli epist. Ad Rom* (*PL* 68:417B); Sedulius Scotus, *Col. In omnes B. Pauli epist* (*PL* 103:42D); Hugh of St. Victor, *De sacramentis* 1.9.2; Lossky, "Redemption and Deification" 97–98; Bettenson and Maunder, *Documents of the Christian Church*, 81–82.

119. Athanasius, *C. Ar.* 1.38; 3.25, though he considered the Spirit to divinize believers (*De decret.* 14).

120. Aquinas, *Summa Theologica* Pt 2.1, Q 113, Art. 5–A8; Matthew of Aquasparta, *Quaestiones disputatae de gratia* q. 2.

121. Hooker, *From Adam to Christ*, 13–26; summarizing Irenaeus, *Haer.* 5 preface.

122. Hafemann, "'Divine Nature' in 2 Pet1,4," 80–99; sources in quote reflect Hafemann's notes: "Salvation in Jude 5," 339–42, 480–82.

[1] as a reference to partaking in divine immortality, permanence, and incorruptibility as a result of escaping the transient and corrupt existence of this material world, either at death or at the Parousia (a primary dualistic reading focused exclusively on the future);[123] [2] as a reference to participating in God's/Christ's immortality or incorruptibility, either at death or at the Parouisia, as well as referring to taking on God's or Christ's moral character now (cf. 1:3 with 1:5–7), both of which take place as a result of escaping the moral corruption of this world (an inaugurated-eschatological reading);[124] [3] as a reference to experiencing God's presence and/Christ's moral character now as a result of already escaping the moral corruption of this world in this life (an experiential and/or ethical reading focused fundamentally on the present).[125] [4] as covenantal "partners of Deity" in God's covenant as a result of having been acquitted of the corruption of the fallen world brought about through sinful desire.[126]

The concept of divine nature among these views range across: Platonic permanent essence, immortal in kingdom, mystical *perichoresis*, and synergistically partnering in God's new covenantal exodus program. Hafemann and I prefer the last view as best reflecting Petrine theology and this text in context.

Peter's concept of God reflects his OT quotes and metaphors as an active personal being to accomplish creative and redemptive ends (see chapter on God). A quick survey of the near context reminds of these descriptions of God. God is the active Savior (2 Pet 1:1). God's glory and excellence are descriptions that prompt God's active call to believers, initiating a recovery program of kingdom for us (2 Pet 1:3, 17). This recovery program initiates prophecy and a messianic Savior Jesus, who becomes king in kingdom (2 Pet 1:1, 17, 21). The knowledge of God is personal, calling with magnificent promises funding our human role (2 Pet 1:3–4). The promises from Jesus' prophecy can be very specific and include Peter's impending death (2 Pet 1:14). Jesus' prophesied promise includes Jesus' apocalyptic powerful coming to bring kingdom (2 Pet 1:16–19). This near

---

123. Käsemann, "Apologia for Primitive Christian Eschatology," 179–80; Smith, *Petrine Controversies in Early Christianity*, 95–96; Bauckham, *Jude, 2 Peter*, 181.

124. Calvin, *Calvin's Commentaries*, 22:330; Schreiner, *1, 2 Peter, Jude*, 290–94; Starr, *Sharers in Divine Nature*, 49, 65, 185, 189, 215, 220, 232–33.

125. Mayor, *Jude and 2 Peter*, 190; Danker, "2 Peter 1: A Solemn Decree," 71.

126. Quotes from: Hafemann, "'Divine Nature' in 2 Pet 1,4," 81–82; view from Wolters, "'Partners of the Deity,'" 28–46; "Postscript to 'Partners of the Deity,'" 418–20; Reese, *2 Peter & Jude*, 133, 135.

context initiating faith toward kingdom compares favorably to 1 Pet which initiated a covenant sanctification to redeem believers for meaningful living of tested faith unto kingdom (1 Pet 1:2, 5, 18).

This active deity like the OT concept of the covenant God is very different than Platonism static mysticism or Neoplatonic staging toward a demiurge. God can be known, and is not a mystical other, beyond knowledge (2 Pet 1:2). This God provides magnificent promises to practically work out this knowledge through his program (2 Pet 1:2–3). To turn this passage into the teaching for deification, in which humans participate in the very life and being of God mystically, one would have to read the Jewish resurrection in a very Neoplatonic idea but that would transform humans into gods,[127] which is foreign to the Jewish metaphors throughout 2 Pet. Additionally, other forms of Hellenism, such as a nonpersonal nature of deity does not fit with such active divine agency to save, communicate and bring in a glorious kingdom (2 Pet 1:1–4, 14, 17, 21). Though, Philo utilizes Stoic natural law or transcendentalism to convert Mosaic Law into universally applicable laws guiding human nature,[128] Peter shows no evidence of this natural law, because Peter places faith and obedience on personal and covenantal promises from God to those he called (2 Pet 1:3–4; 1 Pet 1:2). Not everybody has those specific promises. Furthermore, Peter's virtue list fits within established Jewish virtues instead of Hellenistic lists, evidencing that the Jewish framework of exodus is a better model to fit Peter's narrow way within than a Hellenistic *theosis*.[129]

The word "nature" (φύσις) is a verbal noun related to the verb φύω "to grow," thus designating "nature in what it grows" or "nature producing character."[130] The word "nature" (φύσις) can refer to whole nature of the "creature" (James 3:7; Eph 2:3; Phil 2:7)[131] or Jewish monotheistic God (Phil 2:6).[132] However, the phrase θεία φύσις can be naming the biblical

---

127. *Pseudo-Phocylides* 103–4 fuses Jewish resurrection transforming humans into Hellenistic divine deities like Josephus, *Ag. Ap.* 1.232 and Plutarch, *Def. orc.* 10; *Mor.* 415C; whereas Philo, *QE* 2.29 develops this Platonic idea with humans undergoing angelification without becoming Yahweh; *Abr.* 144; *Conf.* 154; Origen, *Comm. Jo.* 13.25; thus Bauckham, *Jude, 2 Peter*, 180–82 and Bigg, *Peter and Jude*, 255–56 argue against deification here.

128. Philo, *Ebr.* 37; *Spec. Laws* 2.129; 3.137; *Migr.* 128; *Moses* 2.216.

129. 1QS 4.2–6; Wis 6.17–20; 8.7; Philo, *Sacr.* 27; *Leg.* 1.64; *m. Sot.* 8.15 rather than Seneca, *Ep. Mor.* 85.2; Cicero, *Leg.* 1.7.23.

130. Hafemann, "'Divine Nature' in 2 Pet 1,4," 84–85.

131. 3 Macc 3:29; Wis 13.1; Plato, *Tim.* 42c; *T. Dan* 3.5; *T. Naph.* 3.4–5.

132. 4 Macc 5:25: God gives law according to his nature; God's nature acts in the

God (likely in 2 Pet 1:4), similar to Josephus and Philo's use.¹³³ In fact, Philo, *Opif.* 21, 23 described θεία φύσις as "creative Jewish monotheistic divine nature" with impressive θείας δυνάμις "divine power," much like 2 Pet 1:3–4 description. As in 2 Pet 1:4, θεία φύσις "creative Jewish monotheistic divine nature" is specifically utilizing θείας δυνάμις "divine power" to ground moral development upon the near context emphasis of magnificent promises (2 Pet 1:3–4).

The word κοινωνοί refers to "partnering" with others. The Zebedee sons were "partners" (κοινωνοί) with Simon in their fishing venture (Luke 5:10). In Matt 23:30 the religious leaders were "partners" (κοινωνοί) with previous Israel in shedding the blood of the prophets. In Heb, believers were "partners" (κοινωνοί) in sharing persecution (Heb 10:33). When employed with a personal noun in the genitive case, κοινωνός can mean "partner," metaphorically referring to God rather than "partaker" referring to eating from the altar (1 Cor 10:18).¹³⁴ Thus, the issue of eating meat sacrificed to idols can involve believers in "partnering" with idolatry and pagan deities. So, in 2 Pet 1:4, believers "partner" with the Jewish monotheistic God in synergistically participating in the magnificent promises for life and godliness.

The ἵνα clause is best understood as indicating purpose with an instrumental διὰ τούτων "by these" referring to the antecedent "these promises" (ἐπαγγέλματα ... τούτων, both in neuter plural; 2 Pet 1:4). Thus, participating in these promises identifies human synergistic activity with God's prophesied kingdom plan. That is, God gave faith, knowledge, calling, promises, and the believer is to reciprocate with moral virtues that identify them for kingdom (2 Pet 1:1–4). Such a covenant partnering with God eschatologically results in escaping the world's corruption (ἀποφυγόντες τῆς ἐν τῷ κόσμῳ ἐν ἐπιθυμίᾳ φθορᾶς, καὶ αὐτὸ τοῦτο ... ἀρετήν) through the virtues identified with God's exodus unto kingdom (2 Pet 1:4–5). That is, the virtues evidence the reason for synergistically participating in God's new covenant kingdom. These virtues become the new exodus of virtue soteriology unto kingdom.¹³⁵ The following support

---

best interest of his people (4 Macc 5:8–9; 13:27; 15:13; 16:3; Philo, *Fug.* 172; *Moses* 2.65; *Migr.* 139; *Spec. Laws* 1.318 where φύσις refers to "the Lord your God of Deut 14:1).

133. Josephus, *Ant.* 8.107; Philo, *Spec. Laws* 3.178; *Abr.* 144; *Let. Aris.* 288.4.

134. Hafemann, "'Divine Nature' in 2 Pet 1,4," 83.

135. Reuschling, "Means and End in 2 Peter 1:3–11," 275–86; not a "gnostic intrusion" or "gnostic retardation" of Charles, *Virtue amidst Vice*, 32 following Goppelt or 97 following Käsemann.

coming from Jewish sources demonstrates the continuation of a Jewish new covenant virtue program (especially regarding virtues emphasized in Judeo-Christianity: faith, endurance, brotherly affection, and love),[136] but the appeal to Hellenistic sources demonstrates that there is also a fit for this way of virtues within the familiar Hellenistic context of these largely gentile believers, even though several of these virtues are not driven by this Hellenism.[137]

Because believers have been provided abundantly in faith and knowledge and the threat of corruption in the world is because of lust, Peter urges his readers to apply all diligence in pursuing the way of virtue (2 Pet 1:1, 3, 5; likewise, faith in gospel content Acts 15:7). "Abundant supply" is urged and actively promised from the patron, who "abundantly supplies" kingdom (χορηγήω, 2 Pet 1:5, 11).[138] Such words of active participation in 2 Pet are like Josephus' description of Sanballat making every effort to obtain peace for his land and the Athenian inscription of the society of Soteriastai praising generosity.[139] Joining God's generous covenantal provision identifies how believers synergistically become partners with their divine benefactor.[140]

The way of virtue begins by trusting God as the apostles have, but this faith could also be seen as faithfulness (2 Pet 1:1, 5; 1 Pet 1:21; Mark 2:5; Acts 6:7; 10:43).[141] Faith and faithfulness are first place as a primary Jewish-Christian virtue,[142] rather than a Hellenistic virtue. Disciples must grow beyond their faithlessness (Mark 4:40) to develop consistency of

---

136. Wis 6.17–20; 1QS 4.9–11; Philo, *Sacr.* 5.27; *m. Soṭ* 9.15 list includes eagerness leads to cleanness to purity to self-control to fear of sin to holiness to Holy Spirit to resurrection from the dead; Matt 5:1–12; Gal 5:22–26; Rom 5:1–5; 2 Cor 6:6–7; Eph 6:14–17; Phil 4:8; Col 3:12–14; 1 Tim 3:2–3; 6:11; Titus 1:7–8; 3:1–2; James 3:17–18.

137. Aristotle, *Rhet.* 1366B; Rufus, *Frag.* 17; Quintilian, *Inst.* 3.7.15; Seneca, *Ep. More.* 85.2; 95.65; Cicero, *Leg.* 1.7.23; J. Daryl Charles argues for stoicism (*Virtue amidst Vice*, 85–132).

138. Χορηγήω is a term of benefaction in LXX: 1 Kgs 4:7; 5:1; Jdt 12:2; 1 Macc 14:10; 2 Macc 3:3; 4:49; 9:16; 3 Macc 6:30, 40; 7:18; and 1 Pet 4:11; 2 Cor 9:10; Dionysius of Halicarnassus, *Ant. rom.* 10.54; Green, *Jude & 2 Peter*, 190.

139. Josephus, *Ant.* 11.8.4, sec. 324; 20.9.2, sec. 204; Didodorus Siculus, *Hist. Library* 1.83.8; 18.34.4; Polybius, *Universal Hist.* 1.18.11; 21.29.12; Danker, *Benefactor Epigraphic Study*, 459; Deissmann, *Bible Studies*, 361, 364; *Light from the Ancient East*, 318 n1.

140. Danker, *Benefactor Epigraphic Study*, 460; Green, *Jude & 2 Peter*, 188.

141. Sir 1.27; 45.4.

142. Isa 7:9; 12:2; 26:3–4; 1 Cor 8:7; 2 Tim 3:10; *Herm. Vis.* 3.8.7; *Mand.* 6.1.1; 8.9; *Sim.* 9.15.2; *Barn.* 2.2; 1 *Clem.* 62.2.43; *Acts John* 29; *Acts Paul and Thecla* 17.

faith and faithfulness (Mark 2:5; 5:34; 10:52; 11:22: Acts 3:16).[143] Faith provides forgiveness (Acts 10:43), the Holy Spirit (Acts 11:17), authentic salvation inheritance (1 Pet 1:5, 9; Acts 11:17; 15:7, 9), and heart cleansing (Acts 15:9). The value in this virtue is especially in continuing as "tested faith" through the crucible of trials, much like gold is purified by heating it and scraping the dross away (1 Pet 1:7). Such tested faith confirms reward, and thus is precious, when Jesus comes establishing kingdom (1 Pet 1:7, 9; 2 Pet 1:1, 5, 9–11; 3:9; Acts 2:34–38; 3:19–21; 10:43; 15:7). Such faith with expectancy is hope in one's own resurrection future based on God initiating the resurrection by resurrecting Christ (1 Pet 1:3, 21; 3:15; Acts 2:26).

Believers are to supply "virtue" or "goodness" (ἀρετῇ)[144] with diligence in their faith. Such "moral excellence" is that which can stem the tide of lust that corrupts the world (2 Pet 1:4–5). In their moral excellence, "practical knowledge" is to be provided informed by these promises (γνωσιν, 2 Pet 1:6; 3:18; and cognate ἐπίγνωσιν, 2 Pet 1:2–3, 8; 2:20). This knowledge is a practical understanding of God's promises and how to live; there is no hint of mystery religious knowledge.

The person who has not initiated salvation in faith is ignorant (1 Pet 1:14), as are those who persecuted Christ or Christians (1 Pet 2:15; Acts 3:17). To have known this way of righteousness and then to depart from it returns the individual to such a way of ignorance (2 Pet 2:12, 21). Peter had been on this apostatizing precipice, departing from the sphere of knowledge in his denials (Mark 14:68, 71; Matt 26:70–74; Luke 22:34, 57, 60), but Jesus recovered him (John 21:15–17) and Peter proclaimed Christ. However, for those who lack these qualities, not continuing this exodus way, there is divine action bestowing "forgetfulness" (2 Pet 1:9). When Peter used the term λαμβανω, he means "received" (1 Pet 4:10; 2 Pet 1:17; Acts 1:20, 25; 2:33, 38; 10:43). Such deficient ones who do not continue with this character development "receive forgetfulness" (λήθην λαβὼν) from God concerning purification of his former sins (2 Pet 1:9). Such is a doubly blind condition, leaving one to stumble off the way (2 Pet 1:8–9).

---

143. Bowes, "Faith-Language, Jesus's Disciples," 767–84.

144. Echoing 2 Macc 15:12; 3 Macc 6:1; 4 Macc 1:2, 10, 30; 10:9; 13:24; Wis 8.7; Phil 4:8; Philo, *Sacr.* 27; 1QS 4.2–6; 2 *Clem.* 10.1; *Herm. Mand.* 1.2; 6.2.3; 12.3.1; *Sim.* 6.1.4; 6.2.3; 8.10.3; *m. Sot.* 8.15 though this one also appears in Hellenistic lists: Herostratus was hailed for his faith, virtue, righteousness, godliness, and diligence (Danker, *Benefactor Epigraphic Study*, 72; Deissmann, *Light from the Ancient East*, 318).

However, in continuing in the way of faith, moral purity, and knowledge, this exodus following Christ is possible. In such knowledge, supply "self-control" of appetites and sexual desires, like that of an athlete who controls his body for his set goal (ἐγκράτειαν, 2 Pet 1:6).[145] It is this self-control that brings the strictures into life from the believer's well thought out moral excellence. Such self-control in not asceticism within a Platonic dualism as Philo and the Patristics understood it,[146] but that of continuing in Jesus' exodus way focused on the kingdom goal. With self-control setting the lived parameters unto kingdom, "endurance" enables believers to stand their ground and endure by keeping going in difficulties and trouble (ὑπομονήν, 2 Pet 1:6; 1 Pet 2:21–23).[147] Such a self-disciplined enduring life is also described by Peter to be the obedient sober life, realizing that God is ready to judge all at his time (1 Pet 1:2, 13–14; 4:1–7). Such endurance is against pressures of temptation and depression prompted by persecution. Endurance is facilitated by hope that Christ's resurrection guarantees our role in kingdom (1 Pet 1:3–4). The Holy Spirit is also given to those who obey Christ (Acts 2:38; 5:32; 10:43–44), and those associated with the Holy Spirit reflect his character in holiness and integrity. Such a self-disciplined life must continue to persevere.

In such perseverance, believers are to apply a practical awareness and frank manifestation of God's moral character in their life (εὐσέβειαν, 2 Pet 1:6–7).[148] Within this godliness believers are to supply a warmth of affection with other believers, reassuring each other of their close family connection grounded in their relationship to God the Father through Jesus Christ (φιλαδελφίαν, 2 Pet 1:7).[149] This born-again life, purified

---

145. Acts 24:25; Gal 5:23; 1 Cor 7:9; 9:25; 2 Tim 3:3; Sir 18.30; Philo, *Worse* 27, sec. 101–3; Josephus, *Ant.* 2.120; 8.8.5, sec. 235; *War* 2.120; *T. Naph.* 8.8; 4 Macc 5:34; *Let. Aris.* 277–78; 1 *Clem.* 62.2; 64.1; 2 *Clem.* 15.1; Hermas, *Vis.* 3.8.7; *Mand.* 6.1.1; *Sim.* 9.15.2; *Barn.* 2.2; *Acts verc.* 2; also present in Hellenistic virtues: Aristotle, *Eth. nic.* 7.1.6; Socrates gave self-control a central place (Xenophon, *Mem.* 1.5.4–5).

146. Grundemann, TDNT 341; *Herm. Man.* 1.2; 8.1–9, 11–12; 6.1; *Sim.* 5.1–5; 9.15.2; *Visions* 1.2.4; 2.3.2; 3.8.4; Clement of Rome, *1 Clem.* 4.3; 15.1; *Ep. Barn.* 2.2; Polycarp, *Ep. Phil.* 4.2; 5.2.

147. Luke 21:19; Rom 5:3–5; 2 Cor 1:6; 6:4; Col 1:11; 2 Thess 1:4; 1 Tim 6:11; Titus 2:2; Heb 12:1; Jas 1:3–4; Rev 2:2–3; 4 Macc 1:11; 7:9; 9:30; 17:4, 12, 23; *T. Jos.* 10.1; *1 Clem.* 62.2; *Herm. Mand.* 8.9; *Barn.* 2.2; in Platonic Hellenism "courage" replaces this virtue (Plato, *Gorgias* 507B; Philo, *Names* 36 sect 197), while "resignation" or "detachment" replaces it in Stoicism (Seneca, *Ep. Mor.* 67.10).

148. 1 Tim 6:11; *1 Clem.* 1.2; Hellenism turns this virtue to "duty" (Bauckham, *Jude, 2 Peter*, 187).

149. Judaism and Hellenism encourages this fraternal love within the family unit

in obedience to the truth has the foundation to "fervently love" one another, which is what Peter commands believers to do (1 Pet 1:22–25, φιλαδελφίαν ἀνυπόκριτον). Within this brotherly kindness they should supply generous action of love on behalf of others, even beyond the bounds of Christian believers (ἀγάπην, 2 Pet 1:7; 1 Pet 1:8, 22; 4:8).[150]

Those who have these qualities in an ever-increasing manner (πλεονάζοντα), have assurance of usefulness, God's election of them, and eschatological salvation (2 Pet 1:8, 10; 3:18). That is, the growth (ὑπάρχοντα) of the person corresponds to the growth (πλεονάζοντα) of these qualities. With such personal and community growth the believers are encouraged about their usefulness and fruitfulness for life and ministry. The one who lacks these qualities is doubly blind (2 Pet 1:9). There is no discussion of possessing these qualities in a stagnant form. They are either growing or absent. If absent, the person should be warned, since she has no authentic assurance of God's authentically choosing her (2 Pet 1:10). As one develops a character of vice (instead of virtue), the person is departing from Jesus' narrow way and following the broad way that leads to destruction (2 Pet 2:15). God's election for the believer was God's choice but the assurance of this election is provided by diligent growth in the way of virtues.[151] This implies that the growing believer will never seriously "stumble" as false teachers are "destroyed" (2 Pet 1:10, Πταίσητέ comparable to 2 Pet 2:1, ἀπώλειαν)[152] and that her entrance[153] into the everlasting kingdom will be abundantly supplied (2 Pet 1:10–11; Mark 9:47; 10:15, 23–25). The one who abundantly supplies (ἐπιχορηγήσατε, 2 Pet 1:5) diligence in these virtues, enabling these qualities to grow, will have her entrance into Christ's kingdom abundantly supplied

---

exclusively (4 Macc 13:23, 26; 14:1; Philo, *Embassy* 12.87; *Sacr.* 27; Josephus, *Ant.* 4.2.4 sect 26; Plutarch, *Frat. Amor.*; Hierocles, *On Duties* 4.27.20). Though, 2 Macc 15:14 and the NT expands this to be a broader community of believers (Rom 12:10; 1 Thess 4:9; Heb 13:1; 1 Pet 1:22; Mark 3:32–35; Matt 23:8).

150. Deut 6:5; Lev 19:18; Mark 12:28–31; Matt 19:19; 23:34–40; Luke 10:25–37; 1 Cor 13; Rom 5:1–5; Gal 5:22; 2 Cor 6:6; 8:7; Eph 4:2; 2 Thess 1:3; 1 Tim 4:12; 6:11; 2 Tim 2:22; 3:10; Titus 2:2; Rev 2:19; *1 Clem.* 62.2; *Herm. Sim.* 9.15.2; *Vis.* 3.8.7; *Act. Verc.* 2; Ign. *Eph.* 14.1. Hellenistic culture only uses this virtue to describe benefactors (Danker, *Benefactor Epigraphic Study*, 461–62).

151. Edwards, *Religious Affections*.

152. Everlasting ruin Jude 24, like falling in battle (Josephus, *Ant.* 7.4.1, sec. 75; Herodotus, *Hist.* 9.101; Diodorus Siculus, *Hist. Library* 15.33.1).

153. Kingdom entrance granted Matt 5:20; 7:21; 18:3; 19:23–24; 23:13; Luke 18:17, 25; John 3:5; Acts 14:22; 1 Sam 29:6; Ps 120:8; *Ep. Aris.* 120; Philo, *Unchangeable* 28 sec. 132.

(ἐπιχορηγηθήσεται, 2 Pet 1:11). Kingdom benefits for the believer appear to be proportional to the growth of these qualities in one's life. Therefore, the object of the salvation process is an ever-increasing development of these qualities in one's life.

The contrast of the broad way of the false teachers is marked by a lack of these virtues in forgetful blindness (2 Pet 1:9). The false teachers are illustrated in Peter with examples that surface two ways: the narrow way that leads to life and the broad way that leads to judgment.[154] This two ways orientation is reflected in Peter's summary statement, "the Lord knows how to rescue the godly from temptation, and to keep the unrighteous under punishment for the day of judgment" (2 Pet 2:9). For example, God knows how to destroy sinning angels housed in Tarturus and ungodly humans in flood, while he preserved Noah a preacher of righteousness (2 Pet 2:4–5). Likewise, God condemned the sensually oppressive cities of Sodom and Gomorrah to ashes while he rescued righteous Lot (2 Pet 2:6–8). Additionally, Balaam of the flesh[155] stands out as the protype for false teachers, leaving the narrow right way for the broad way[156] and seeking financial gain[157] but such people will be judged in wages of unrighteousness (2 Pet 2:15). Peter continued to organize his two ways exhortations calling his readers to confidently trust Christ's coming in kingdom by cultivating holy conduct and godliness, rather than the scoffing judgment deniers who will be condemned by God (2 Pet 3:3–11). Even Peter's final exhortation rings out of two ways: "therefore beloved knowing this beforehand, be on your guard lest, being carried away by the error of unprincipled men, you fall from your own steadfastness, but grow in the grace and knowledge of our Lord and Savior Jesus Christ" (2 Pet 3:17–18).

---

154. This pattern in 2 Pet is a contrast to Jude's use of three examples for every point, with two ways idea receding to background landscape (judged false teachers versus common salvation).

155. Βοσόρ has overwhelming textual evidence in its favor over the closest rival "son of beor." However, Βοσόρ is an untranslatable word most likely as a transliteration of Hebrew *basar*, meaning "flesh."

156. The word "way," which is used twice in 2 Pet 2:15, is also in the LXX discussion of Balaam literally (Num 22:23) and metaphorically (Num 22:32). This "road" or "way" supports the idea of Balaam's prototypical role leaving the narrow way to join the broad way of destruction as presented by Peter.

157. Jude 11 used Balaam in the same manner, coupling him with Cain, who is a pattern of departing into sin, and those who perished in the rebellion at Korah, a pattern of condemnation in apostasy.

11

The Household of God

THERE ARE THREE MAIN imageries developing the symbolic social construct[1] of the corporate body of believers in Peter. The "household of God" is the most prominent. Peter emphasized the privileged position, enablement, and mutuality of service within God's household. Intertwined with the household imagery is that of the priesthood. This motif is often presented with a Reformation interpretation reacting against Roman Catholicism, but Peter presented it instead as an extension of Judaism's covenant program into gentile Christianity. Peter's motif is concerned with declaring the excellencies of God and demonstrating them in personal life. A special emphasis within these motifs has to do with the believers' relationship to the various fabrics of society, largely through testimony, evangelism, and good works, as John Elliott developed.[2] An additional imagery, the "flock of God," developed Peter's view of leadership within the church as caring shepherds. This motif accentuates the need for all believers to live humbly under the leadership of God's shepherds.

---

1. As was developed in the chapters concerning epistemology (in Kennard, *Petrine Studies*) and humanity (in *Petrine Theology*), a communal commonsense realist nuance like Plantinga (*Warrant and Proper Function* and *Knowledge and Christian Belief*) frames Peter's social constructions rather than the individualistic post-Kantian and post-Hegelian dialectic of Berger and Luckmann (*Social Construction of Reality*, 110–46) and Berger's (*Social Reality of Religion*) socially positive rather than the negative "world" concern applied by Adams (*Constructing the World*). Peter develops a positive social construct of the church (Plantinga-Berger) and a negative construct of Christ against and converting the Greco-Roman world (Niebuhr, *Christ and Culture*; Adams, *Constructing the World*, 8–9; and Wilson, *Magic and the Millennium*).

2. Elliott, *Home for the Homeless*; *Elect and the Holy*.

Peter's primary imagery for the church is that of the household of God (1 Pet 2:5; 4:17). The concept of household is further developed by the repetition of the οἶκος root contained in other words within Peter.³ The word "household" (οἶκος) emphasized ownership, oversight, and a sense of community within a group. The word οἶκος can mean a "dwelling," "a household of people," "a trade guild," "a clan," "a nation," and "one's possessions."⁴ The household pattern is used for various levels of society that require management. Within Greco-Roman cities the "household" (οἶκος) was reserved for hereditary resident estates owned and resided in by citizens.⁵ Peter used οἰκία with this meaning referring to a physical building (Acts 10:6, 17, 22, 30; 11:11–13) and to people within the household (Acts 10:2; 11:14; 1 Pet 4:17). Cornelius valued his household, so they all had an opportunity to hear the gospel from Peter (Acts 10:2; 11:14). Within a house, the household maintained a commonality of purpose and some opportunities that demonstrated their unity. This means that in Asia Minor, foreigners and temporary residents did not qualify as οἶκοι,⁶ they were an excluded "other" not belonging in society. So, Peter makes a bold claim for resident aliens (1 Pet 1:1), that though they may fear their vulnerability as alien in broader Greco-Roman society and need to be on their best behavior (1 Pet 1:17; 2:11), the Christian church as God's "household" (οἶκος) and "kingdom" (βασίλειον) provides believers in Christ with a community in which they belong (1 Pet 2:5, 9).

This broader household idea emerges from the LXX following the MT in indicating that the nation of Israel was drawn out of Egypt's "house of slavery" (Exod 13:3, 14; 20:2; Deut 7:8; Acts 7:10) redeemed to become a new chosen nation, as the "house of Israel" (Ezek 36:22, 32, 37; 45:6; to which Peter and Stephen concur, Acts 2:36; 7:42, 46). Within the Mosaic covenant blessing, Israel was promised to be a household kingdom of priests as a holy nation (Exod 19:6; Lev 20:26).⁷ Both a national household and priesthood emerge from the Exod 19:4–6 Mosaic covenantal blessing if Israel would be faithful. Yahweh elected Israel into covenant

3. Παροίκους, οἰκονόμοι, οἰκοδομεῖσθε, οἰκοδομοῦντες, συνοικοῦντες, and οἰκέται.

4. BAG, "οἰκία" and "οἶκος," 559–60, 562–63; Elliott, *Home for the Homeless*, 171–81; Celsus called Christian gatherings to be like "trade guilds" and thus made up of lower social classes (Origen, *Cels.* 3.55;1.62); Poland, *Geschichte des griechischen Vereinswesens*, 114; Meeks, *First Urban Christians*, 51.

5. Demosthenes 44.33–42; Lacey, *Family in Classical Greece*, 90–91; Verner, *Household of God*, 28.

6. Verner, *Household of God*, 28.

7. *Mek. to Ex* 20.17; *Midrash Tan.* Deut 5:21.

relationship with himself as king through a framework of suzerainty treaty. From the fire on the mountain, Yahweh clarified that he has carried Israel to himself for this purpose of covenant relationship with them (Exod 19:4–5).[8] In this clarification there is obligation to comply with obedience to the terms of the revealed covenant. If Israel would obey the Mosaic covenant then they would have great privilege as the special people and possession of God. Through it all, God has the right to make this decision because the whole world is his possession.

Within this covenantal relationship, Israel will be blessed to become Yahweh's household of kingdom priests as a holy nation (Exod 19:6).[9] The emphasis of this statement is on the positive blessings of election by Yahweh. However, the consequence of curse is implied by the awesome presence of Yahweh on the mountain that affected all of Israel with deep fear (Exod 19:16). If the vassal obeys, blessings are promised; if disobedience occurs, then curses shall ensue (Lev 26; Deut 28–29). The curse warnings begin for those who violate the mountain or who disobey the stipulations (Exod 19:12; 20:5). Throughout the ancient Near East, in the case of a breach of covenant, the Great King would certainly come against the vassal, but the curses and blessings in the treaty texts are primarily treated as the actions of the gods who insure the covenant. In Exodus, these fuse together, since God, who guarantees the covenant, is the Great King who ensures compliance. Within this issue, some scholars take gods as guaranteeing covenant to imply that the stipulations are primarily suggestions (perhaps in recognition that the stipulations develop further from covenant to royal correspondence perhaps in reading this covenant through the lens of Syrian treaties, which are more reserved in their curses and usually end with the boundary indicator, *kudurru*).[10] However, the binding nature of the suzerainty treaty stipulations is evident by the diplomatic correspondence which follows a disobedience to the treaty

---

8. The rabbinics claim that torah was offered to others but Israel alone accepted it (*Mek.* 2.234–35; *Pesiq. Rab Kah.* 2.17a; *Sifre Deut. Berakah* 343. 142b) but instead Exod places the issue on Yahweh's active election of Israel (Kennard, *Biblical Covenantalism*, 1:104–243).

9. This promise of covenant blessing is parallel to that in Lev 20:36. Early Judaism echoes this sentiment that draws all Mosaic material into the same Mosaic covenant (*Jub.* 16.18; 33.20; Greek frag. *Levi* 11.4–6; 2 Macc 2:17; Philo, *Sobr.* 66; *Abr.* 56; *Mek. to Exod* 20:17; *Midrash Tan. to Deut* 5:21).

10. McCarthy, *Treaty and Covenant*, 112, 122. For example, the Assyrian treaties have a different structure than the Suzerainty treaty (Kennard, *Biblical Covenantalism*, 1:161–87).

stipulations with threatening devastation for the vassal from the Great King, if the vassal does not quickly comply with what the suzerainty treaty demanded in the stipulations section. For example, the "Letter from Hattusili 3 of Hatti to Kadashman-Enlil 2 of Babylon" threatens Babylon with severe military campaign if they do not swiftly comply with the terms of the suzerainty treaty.[11] The analog for such diplomatic correspondence in the OT is either Moses' interaction with Israel about their sin at the golden calf (Exod 32), or the prophets calling Israel back based on the suzerainty treaty statements of Exod and Deut. Thus, in choosing to write a portion of Exodus in the genre of suzerainty treaty, Yahweh communicates that Israel is required and able to obey the terms of the Mosaic Covenant. Rabbinic Judaism agreed, recognizing that torah blessing provided an elect framework in which there is conditionality for Israel to obey and be blessed.[12] Likewise, the reverse is also true, for if Israel rebelled in disobedience they would then be cursed. From this context of exodus and conquest, Yahweh presses his election will upon his people Israel as a suzerain in a bestowal of the Mosaic Covenant as it is formed in the pattern of an international treaty (Exod 19—Lev 27; Deut; Josh 24).[13] The major point of this suzerainty treaty is that Yahweh is declared to be king and Israel is mandated to remain loyal under allegiance to this reigning God. Yahweh is identified as the author of this covenant in Exod 3 and 19. Now that Yahweh brought Israel to the mountain after an extended exodus narrative which clarified their rebellious character, the treaty statement of the author (Exod 20:1) and historical prologue (Exod 20:2) are brief, fitting the previous exodus narrative. The repeated testing and failure of Israel within this covenant does not remove the binding nature of covenant stipulations upon Israel. Nor does Israel's failure abrogate the terms of the covenant, for there is a pattern evident in some Hittite suzerainty treaties whereby the vassal is described in the historical

---

11. An example is the "Letter from Hattusili III of Hatti to Kadashman-Enlil II of Babylon," see no. 23, in Beckman and Hoffner, *Hittite Diplomatic Texts*, 138–39.

12. 1 Macc 2:50; *Ex. Rab.* 30.23; 32.5; *'Abot* 3.5; *Num. Rab.* 13.2.

13. McCarthy (*Treaty and Covenant*, 243–76) argued that Exod 19–24, and 34, Deut (in pp. 157–205), Josh 24 (in pp. 221–42) and 1 Sam 12 (in pp. 206–21) are also in a Suzerainty treaty format; Exod–Lev is also seen to be suzerainty treaty in Baltzer *Das Bundesformular*, 4, 37–38, 48–52; *Covenant Formulary*, 9–93; and Mendenhahall, "Covenant Forms in Israelite Tradition," 63–67; *Law and Covenant*, 5–41; Durham, *Exodus*, 279; *Mek. to Exod* 20:17; *Midrash Tan. to Deut* 5:21. This suzerainty treaty framework stands strongly against the form-critical approach of Mowinckel (*La décalogue*, 114–60), which ties this covenant to the Babylonian Akitu or New Year's festival.

prologue as having rebelled and the vassal is still obligated through the suzerainty treaty. For example, Sunashshura of Kizzuwatna is recorded to have rebelled within the treaty that Tudhaliya 2 of Hatti imposed on him but he is still bound to obey his suzerain in this treaty.[14] Likewise, Niqmaddu 2 of Ugarit is recorded to have rebelled against Suppiluma 1 of Hatti within the historical prologue of his suzerainty treaty, but is also obligated to obey his suzerain, Suppiluliama.[15] So, Israel is defined and bound by the terms of the Mosaic covenant. However, if Israel is faithful, Israel is also to be blessed by this Mosaic covenant to become a people and kingdom elected and thus valued by God as his people and possession (Exod 19:6; Deut 4:20; 7:6; 10:15; Isa 43:20; Acts 2:36). The Jewish war approached as an expression of a return of this covenant curse upon Israel (Acts 3:23). However, Peter held out an offer for Israel to continue and to return to experience covenant blessing in Christ's kingdom, if they would align with Jesus as the Christ in kingdom blessing (Acts 3:19–26). This statement is not a supersession, rather it is extending the Mosaic covenant offer to Israel for blessing into kingdom blessing with Christ at the center of this blessing. Perhaps this covenantal context for Israel supplies the emphasis for the exodus of the elect Christian believers need to obey their king, Jesus Christ on the way toward eschatological kingdom (1 Pet 1:1–2, 9; 2 Pet 1:3–11; Heb 3:1–6; 1 Tim 3:15).[16] However, believers as God's household suffered a purging judgment preparing them for this future kingdom salvation (1 Pet 4:17–18).

In early Judaism there is also a "temple" meaning for οἶκος. As Moses oversaw the construction of the tabernacle and as David was covenanted by God to have the temple built by Solomon, the structure became known in LXX and MT as the "house of the Lord your God" (Exod 23:19: 34:26; 2 Sam 7:7, 13; 1 Kgs 6:1; Jer 7:11 cited in Mark 11:16–17; Acts 7:47, 49). John Elliott claimed that the NT used οἶκος as temple only in OT quotes and allusions.[17] However, within the Davidic covenant the people of the nation of Israel under the Davidic kings were called a "house" either "of

---

14. "Treaty Between Tudhaliya 2 of Hatti and Sunashshura of Kizzuwatna": rebellion 3–6 (A 1.8–29); obligation 13–64 (A 1.60–64.66); Beckman and Hoffner, *Hittite Diplomatic Texts*, 18–25, no. 2.

15. "Treaty Between Suppiluliama 1 of Hatti and Niqmaddi 2 of Ugarit": rebellion 1 (A obv. 1–8); obligation 3–6 (B obv. 3–23; A rev. 1–15); Beckman and Hoffner, *Hittite Diplomatic Texts*, 34–36.

16. Elliott, *1 Peter*, 419.

17. Elliott, *1 Peter*, 415.

David" (2 Sam 7:11, 18, 29)[18] or as they return from captivity and the messianic expectation elevates "of God" with messiah on God's throne (1 Chr 17:14). Qumran considered the Hasmoneans in rebellion and thus departed from the temple and mainstream Judaism; the Qumran community replaced the Jerusalem temple, with the view that their Qumran community of believing people was the new spiritual temple, a holy house, the true successors to the sons of Zadok.[19] Such views are not of supersession, but rather viewing the Qumran community as the faithful remnant of Israel. Paul extends this community idea as God's temple in a similar meaning to that of Peter but only utilized the term ναος to do so, whereas Peter used οἶκος (1 Cor 3:16–17; 6:19; 2 Cor 6:16; Eph 2:21). There is no "temple" idea when Paul used οἶκος to describe believers as household of God (1 Tim 3:15).

Using *pesher*, Peter extends this Jewish corporate communal view of believers as "house" (οἶκος) under Jesus, the Davidic king (1 Pet 2:5; 4:17), thereby challenging the Greco-Roman understanding of "household." Peter is not replacing Israel with a supersessionism[20] of the church either, because he still maintains that the Abrahamic blessing have fused with the Mosaic and new covenant blessings such that Jesus Christ blesses Israel as the new Mosaic prophet bringing in kingdom blessing for Israel (Acts 3:13–26). So, Israel's role continues eschatological kingdom if they repent, believe, and obey Jesus as the Christ. That is, Israel's blessing in kingdom is an extension of the covenantal blessing from Abraham, Moses, and Davidic covenants. Jews that gain "kingdom" (οἶκος) are part of that faithful remnant, including Peter and other Jewish Christians (the sense of Heb 8:8; 10:1, 21). So that while the church does not supersede Israel, unbelieving Israelites show themselves as a distinct continuing entity heading for destruction from God in their disobedience and rejection of Jesus as Mosaic prophet (Acts 3:23); they exclude themselves from being included among the remnant of God's elect people. The household

---

18. *T. Levi* 2.4–6.

19. 4Q174 1.1–19; 1QS 5.1–10; 8.4–6; 9.3–5; 1QpHab 12.1–3; CD 10.3.21—24.3; Helyer, *Life and Witness of Peter*, 192; though early Judaism also envisioned an eschatological temple (*1 En.* 91.13; 4QEnochg; *Jub.* 1.17).

20. The 1 Pet 2:9 citation of Exod 19:6 is broadly recognized to define the church and Israel respectively with the same passage. Contra: supercession of Danker, "1 Peter 1:24—2:17," 93–102, and Bauman-Martin, "Speaking Jewish," 144–77, or Sibley ("You Talkin' to Me?," 59–75), who argued that 1 Pet is written to Jewish Christians in an attempt to show that this is not supersessionism but most recognize the audience of 1 Peter are gentile Christians primarily.

of believers is elected, owned, and managed by God, thus providing a corporate community of belonging and their purpose. Writing to primarily a gentile Christian audience, with a substantial part being temporary residents outside their homeland, Peter extends these covenantal privileged blessings, belonging, and roles for the whole Christian community as the continuing remnant of the elect of God (1 Pet 2:5, 9–10; 4:17). So instead of supersessionism, Peter expands the concept of the elect of God to now include a multi-ethnic church (gentile and Jew) with Christ's kingdom salvation, while not denying that a remnant of Israel will also participate in Christ's kingdom to fulfill the prophesied roles for Israel.[21] The church becomes God's new elect "household" and we belong to him.

The structure of 1 Pet 2:4–10 yields important relational implications toward understanding the concept of the household of God. John Elliott's explanation of the structure is helpful but selectively simplistic.[22] He compares the repetition of words through the section and concludes that verses 4–5 are parallel with verses 6–10, and that there are three sections of verses: 4–5, 6–8, and 9–10.[23] I recognize the parallel as demonstrated by the verbal repetitions in the chart on the following page, but I prefer to keep verses 6–10 together to complete the parallel structure (when comparing column parallels, such as stone and chosen). When repetitions occur in both columns and within the column (such as stone) the impact is to present 1 Pet 2:4–10 as a cohesive whole. Generally, repetitions which occur in verse 5 describing the household tend to occur in verses 9–10. Each section develops the character of Christ and then the nature of the household of God, so much of this was previously developed in the chapter on Christology as the church is to reflect much of Christ's character as living stone, elect, and valued by God. The second section, verses 6–10 develops the imagery of the first but in fuller detail. That is, this framework holds together Peter's contributions to understanding the household of God. One such contribution is that of understanding οἶκος interposed with a synonym βασίλειον (1 Pet 2:5, 9).[24] That is, the household of God is as though they are a new nation with the identity of being the people of king Jesus Christ. Another contribution will be the explaining of the offering up of spiritual sacrifices as an act of doing and proclaiming the excellencies of God (1 Pet 2:5, 9).

21. Kennard, *Biblical Theology of Isaiah*, 222–32.
22. Elliott, *Home for the Homeless*, 17–23, 129–45.
23. Elliott, *Home for the Homeless*, 18.
24. Elliott, *1 Peter*, 416; also Philo used both terms synonymously (*Praem.* 123).

Verbal Relationship Within 1 Pet 2:4–10

Idea	Verses 4–5		Verses 6–10	
Stone	4a	λίθον	λίθον	6b
	5a	λίθοι	λίθος	7b
			λίθος	8a
Living	4a	ζῶντα		
	5a	ζῶντες		
Rejected	4b	ἀποδεδοκιμασμένον	ἀπεδοκίμασαν	7b
God	4b	θεῷ		
	5b	θεῷ		
Chosen	4b	ἐκλεκτὸν	ἐκλεκτὸν	6c
			ἐκλεκτὸν	9a
Precious	4b	ἔντιμον	ἔντιμον	6c
			τιμὴ	7a
Believe			πιστεύων	6c
			πιστεύουσιν	7a
			ἀπιστοῦσιν	7b
Building	5a	οἰκοδομεῖσθε	οἰκοδομοῦντες	7b
Stumbling			προσκόμματος	8a
			προσκόπτουσιν	8b
House	5a	οἶκος	One meaning of βασίλειον	9b
Spiritual	5a	πνευματικὸς		
	5a	πνευματικὰς		
Priesthood	5a	ἱεράτευμα	ἱεράτευμα	9b
Holy	5a	ἅγιον	ἅγιον	9b
People			λαὸς	9c
			λαὸς	10a
			λαὸς	10a
Mercy			ἠλεημένοι	10b
			ἐλεηθέντες	10b

While the word βασίλειον is formally an adjective, the context indicates that it functions as a substantive (as it is in LXX Exod 19:6 and Rev 1:6; 5:10).[25] That is, usually the noun occurs before an adjective but in this instance,[26] the substantival adjective "kingdom" occurs before "priesthood" (1 Pet 2:9). Also, there is a nice rhythmic pattern of Greek word order that argues for βασίλειον being substantival with the order a noun then an adjective (race chosen), two nouns (kingdom priesthood), a noun then an adjective (nation holy), and then two nouns (people of own possession).[27]

The word βασίλειον is a synonym for household (οἶκος), emphasizing the believing community has a new national status (1 Pet 2:5, 9). The only other instance of the word in the NT means the "kings house" or "royal residence" (LXX Esther 1:9; 2:13; Luke 7:25).[28] Hellenistic usage of the term βασίλειον refers broadly to kingdom, as in kingdom of God (3 Kdgms 5:1; 14:8; 4 Kgdms 15:19; similar to "house," 1 Chr 17:14)[29] or Davidic kingdom (LXX 2 Sam 7:12–16 much as "house," 2 Sam 7:11, 18, 29).[30] Ernest Best prefers to identify the meaning of this as "kingship lineage" of David.[31] Alan Stibbs extended this meaning with attraction to Rom 8:17 to claim that "Christians are here described as sharing with Christ in kingship or sovereignty,"[32] but there is no evidence that the royal household motif develops a claim for a future Christian reign. Instead, Peter extends the Qumran idea of οἶκος as remnant elect people of God[33] into the Jewish-gentile church as the true God indwelt temple and ethnic community. Similarly, Best prefers to frame βασίλειον with God's house the temple, which God inhabits after the pattern of Exod 40:34,

---

25. Not only does LXX treat βασίλειον as a substantive but so do Armenian, Coptic, Peshitta, and Old Latin versions; also these citations: 2 Macc 2:17; *Jub.* 16.18; Philo, *Sobr.* 66; *Abr.* 56; a number of Targums as well (Best, "1 Peter II.4–10," 288).

26. Blass *et al., Greek Grammar of the New Testament*, no. 270, p. 169; also Peter's usual pattern (Best, "1 Peter II.4–10," 288).

27. Contrary to Blinzer, "IEPATEYMA," 62; Cerfaux, "Vestiges d'un florilège," 24–25 who argues because of rhythm, βασίλειον is an adjective.

28. Selwyn, *1 Peter*, 165–67; Stibbs, *1 Peter*, 103–4; Strabo, *Geogr.* 12.2.7, 12.5.2.

29. *Jub.* 16.18; 33.20; 2 Macc 2:17; *T. Levi* 11.6 (Greek frag. 67); Philo, *Sobr.* 66; *Abr.* 56; Best, "1 Peter II.4–10," 290.

30. *T. Levi* 2.4–6.

31. Best, "1 Peter II.4–10," 291, from a discussion on p. 288 of 2 Macc 2:17.

32. Stibbs, *1 Peter*, 104.

33. 4Q174 1.1–19; 1QS 5.1–10; 8.4–6; 9.3–5; 1QpHab 12.1–3; CD 10.3.21–24.3; also 1 Tim 3:15; Helyer, *Life and Witness of Peter*, 192; though early Judaism also envisioned an eschatological temple (*1 En.* 91.13; 4QEnochg; *Jub.* 1.17).

38 and Philo's use.³⁴ However, for Peter (parallel to that of the Qumran idea of οἶκος) the term βασίλειον describes a present reality characterizing the corporate identity of the people of the church in the time of Peter's writing as remnant elect people of God rather than a temple imagery, though Peter might have a "national household" emphasis mixed with the metaphor of the "temple" being constructed with living stones. The Petrine use of βασίλεια as Christ's everlasting kingdom indicates the continuum of the corporate group of Christian believers into a future reign of Christ (2 Pet 1:11). However, there is no distinction in Peter of Christians taking part in the ruling even though they are included within this kingdom. Blinzler concluded that βασίλειον means "temple," since it refers to the king's house and God is the king.³⁵ However, Peter does not identify βασίλειον with any structure (such as a temple); it identifies the believing people (1 Pet 2:9). No king is identified in this context, though if one takes Peter as a whole, Christ and not God would probably be more likely the king identified (1 Pet 4:11; 5:10–11; 2 Pet 1:11). This kingdom is neither identified as a temple, nor a future reign of Christians but instead describes the present corporate body of believers identified with Christ. The broader context of "household of God" is identified in 1 Pet 4:17 with people who can be rebellious and judged by God. Similarly, the parallel structure of 1 Pet 2:4–10 identified "household" with other similar concepts such as: chosen race, kingdom, priesthood, holy nation, and God's people.

God's "household" (οἶκος) provides communal meaning and belonging especially for the "temporary resident" (παροίκους, 1 Pet 1:17; 2:5, 11).³⁶ The recipients of 1 Pet are literally scattered temporary residents (1 Pet 1:1, 17; 2:11). These individuals made up the working class who produced the goods for society. They had little rights and no house of their own. Many obtained their lodging and opportunities within

34. Philo, *Sobr.* 66; *Abr.* 56; Best, "1 Peter II.4–10—A Reconsideration," *NovT* 11.4(1969) 289.

35. Blinzer, "IEPATEYMA, Zur Exegese von 1 Peter 2,5 u. 9," *Episcopus*, 59 reasoning from Philo, *Sobr.* 66, but Philo identifies βασίλειον with people, Shem's descendants and not a structure or temple.

36. Contra Volf who considers "alien" to be the controlling metaphor for postmodern society from 1 Peter ("Soft Difference: Theological Reflections on the Relation between Church and Culture in 1 Peter," *ExAud* 10(1994) 16, 21) though this metaphorical use by Christians does not occur until *Ep. Diognetus* 5.1–5 (Kennard, *Petrine Studies*, chapter on Recipients); contra Achtemeier who considers "Israel" the controlling metaphor (*1 Peter*, 69); "household" is closer to Schutter's view that the controlling metaphor is "Temple-community" (*Hermeneutic and Composition in 1 Peter*, 176–77).

contexts in which they were abused. For example, resident aliens had few rights to defend themselves if accused with a crime or slandered, which was a common occurrence (1 Pet 2:12). The name "Christian" was used to accuse believers of being disloyal to Caesar and society as they associate with a condemned criminal named Jesus (Acts 11:26; 26:28; 1 Pet 4:14–16),[37] and others claimed they were atheists.[38] Even Tacitus writes that Christians were "loathed because of their abominations."[39] John Elliott applied a social-scientific perspective to argue that actual resident aliens were in social estrangement in a foreign land and thus prone to be taken advantage of in persecution and suffering,[40] thus, it is better to view such suffering as occurring to a Christian not officially because one is a Christian, but rather mostly occasional local and sporadic persecutions.[41]

When Christians departed from their previous life (commitments, idols, and divinations) those around them could view them as antisocial and levy accusations (1 Pet 4:3–4; Acts 16:16–34; 19:23–41). Peter urged the believers to own the title "Christian" in a positive manner defining their identity, no longer characterized by human lusts but characterized by allegiance to Christ as evident by righteous gospel living and doing good (1 Pet 4:2–16).[42] Many of the temporary residents in Asia Minor were menial and domestic laborers, clerks, tradesman, teachers, and doctors.[43] To combat their vulnerable condition, Franz Poland argued from early inscriptions that laborers would often band together into trade

37. John 19:12; associating with Jesus is an association with a criminal; such was the charge of many Christians later who did not offer incense to Caesar; Cassius Dio, 52.36.2; Minucius Felix, *Octavius* 12; Suetonius, *Nero* 16.2; Pliny, *Ep.* 10.96–97; Lucian, *Alex.* 25, 38; *De morte Peregr.* 11–13, 16; Josephus, *Ant.* 18.64; Wilken, *Christians as the Romans Saw Them*, 62–67; Horrell, "Label Χριστιανός," 361–81.

38. Acts 15:29; this was especially the case after Jerusalem fell and the temple was destroyed; Cicero, *On the Nature of the Gods* 3.5–9; *Divination* 2.148; *Laws* 2.18–22, 26.

39. Tacitus, *Ann.* 15.44.

40. Elliott, *Home for the Homeless*, 48 provides a nice summary; *1 Peter*, 101–3, 312–16, 457–62, 476–83.

41. Van Unnik, "Teaching of Good Works in 1 Peter," 95–109; Elliott, *Home for the Homeless*, 78–82; Achtemeier, *1 Peter*, 33–36; Harland, *Associations, Synagogues, and Congregations*, 188–89; Kennard, *Petrine Studies*, in chapter on "Source Material for Petrine Theology."

42. Ignatius follows Peter's lead as the first church father to frequently employ "Christian," and used within Peter's positive meaning of characterized by allegiance to Christ (*Eph.* 11.2; 14.2; *Magn.* 4.1; 10.1, 3; *Trall.* 6.1; *Rom.* 3.2–3; *Pol.* 7.3; *Phld.* 6.1; *Mart. Pol.* 3.2; 10.1; 12.1–2; *Diogn.* 1.1; 2.6, 10; 4.6; 5.1; 6.1–9).

43. Broughton, "Roman Asia Minor," 4:631–32, 840.

guilds called "households" (οἶκος).⁴⁴ John Elliott developed that such guild members lived and worked in the same vicinity often for the same goals, providing mutual benefits.⁴⁵ Dill described these trade guilds as a "home for the homeless" as they provided cheerful conversation, fellowship, goodwill, and mutual relief.⁴⁶ Peter, Paul, and Luke described the corporate gathering of believers in these same terms, meeting in households (1 Pet 2:5; Acts 10:2; 11:14; 16:15, 31–34; 18:8; Rom 16:10, 14; 1 Cor 1:11, 16; 16:15; Phil 4:22). These scattered temporary residents have no home; even though these same residents remain aliens. Their inclusion into a household with others of a similar condition whom God has chosen provided a meaningful sense of belonging and mutual purpose. The fabric of society may exclude them or persecute them as was done to Christ, but they have each other for an intimate purposeful community.

The household of believers is a chosen people. Election is the experiencing of divine value and honor. Peter emphasized that the concept of God's choice was through his preeminently valuing of Jesus Christ (1 Pet 2:4–9). For example, Christ is held in precious "honor" (ἔντιμον) by God, yet this "precious value" (τιμή) is for believers (1 Pet 2:4, 6–7). So, God's election of Christ extends to God's election of Christians. Christ is the capstone that holds the Christian's corporate household experience together. This concept of elect household can function as a locally present chosen household in Rome (1 Pet 5:13) or the chosen household of Asia Minor (1 Pet 1:1; 2:5, 9) or as a universal church everywhere there are Christians (1 Pet 4:17; Matt 16:18).

In the Mosaic covenant, Israel had been chosen as the "holy covenantal people" (Exod 19:6),⁴⁷ separated from unholy gentiles. With parallel imagery, Peter identifies in the sanctification of believers with Christ's blood that the Christian community becomes elect and consecrated holy as a distinctively new community of God (1 Pet 1:2; 2:9). All sanctified by Christ in election join the holy household of God (1 Pet 1:2; 2:5, 9).

God's choice of a household of believers is described by a *pesher* application of Hosea 1:6, 9–10; 2:1, 23. Hosea spoke to God's people Israel about their impending captivity from God's rejection from being

---

44. Celsus called Christian gatherings to be like "trade guilds" and thus made up of lower social classes (Origen, *Cels.* 3.55;1.62); Poland, *Geschichte des griechischen Vereinswesens*, 114; Meeks, *First Urban Christians*, 51.

45. Elliott, *Home for the Homeless*, 180–81.

46. Dill, *Roman Society*, 266–67.

47. *Jub.* 16.17–18; 22.10–12; 33.20

his people and subsequent merciful reinstitution as the people of God after the Babylonian captivity. Peter's extension addressed the church including gentiles who never had received mercy as God's people until their becoming believers in Christ, mercifully chosen as believers within the people of God (1 Pet 2:10). In this experience believers will not be ultimately put to shame, as Israelites experienced during Babylonian captivity, whereas any who oppose Jesus Christ as framing the Christian experience will be shamed and destroyed, as they are excluded from kingdom (1 Pet 2:7-8; Acts 3:23). Peter selectively lifts phrases from Hosea and adds his own words mortaring them together to emphasize the point that Christians were mercifully chosen by God to be included within this household privilege. They had been previously excluded in darkness but now are included within God's light, the place of privilege and blessing.

Peter used the word ἱεράτευμα to describe the believers as "corporate functioning priests" (1 Pet 2:5-9). First, the word refers to believers as actual priests rather than merely an abstract concept of a priesthood. For example, the root word ἱεράτευς means "priest." The longer form ἱεράτευμα reflects the plural idea of "a body of priests" from the Hebrew *khnm* (comparing MT with LXX Exod 19:6; 23:22).[48] Furthermore, the selection of ἱεράτευμα over the more abstract sense of priesthood (ἱεράτευμα) used elsewhere in the LXX, emphasizes a concrete sense of "a body of priests."[49] Peter utilized this idea by indicating that actual believers are priests (1 Pet 2:9). Additionally, the suffix (-ευμα) adds the quality of "functioning" as priests.[50] Peter reflects the thought by immediately following the mention of the priests with the function which they perform (1 Pet 2:5-9). Peter's priests are a corporate group as indicated by the plurals (1 Pet 2:9, Ὑμεῖς). This Petrine priesthood has the same corporate sense as do each of the following: chosen race, kingdom, holy nation, and God's people (1 Pet 2:9-10). This corporate sense is not to be individualized as was done in the Reformation[51] and as Paul does

---

48. 2 Macc 2:17.

49. This is after the analogy of στράτευμα (army); Hort, *1 Peter*, 110; Eliott, *Elect and the Holy*, 64-70 and *1 Peter*, 420 extends this analogy from these additional terms: βούλευμα (council session), ποίτευμα (corporate civil body), πρεσβευμα (delegation), and τεχνίτευμα (body of craftsman).

50. Hort, *1 Peter*, 110, λάτρευμα is a rare word in tragedians which has both concrete and functioning senses.

51. Luther removed the division between spiritual and secular by individual believers being priests who can hear and forgive confession (Martin Luther, *To the Christian Nobility of the German Nation*, Weimar Ausgube 6:407, lines 19-25; 6:564, lines 6-14;

with ἱερουργοῦντα in Rom 15:16. Ernest Best described Peter's corporate nature of priesthood of believers.

> They are a body of priests; such is a priest but never a priest in and by himself; it is only as a member of the corporate priesthood that he is such and he can only exercise his priesthood within the corporate existence of the church: the conception is not individualistic.[52]

A primary implication of this corporate functioning priesthood is its identification with the household in 1 Pet 2:5 since both describe the elect corporate body of believers. That is, the household should not then be viewed as a temple through which the priesthood ministers. Both household as kingdom and the priesthood are divinely declared to be an identical group of holy people functioning for the priestly task of offering up sacrifices (1 Pet 2:5, 9). Another implication of this divinely declared corporate functioning priesthood is that it exists as a priestly body whether it is offering up sacrifices.[53]

Comparing and contrasting Petrine priesthood to that of John and Heb further illustrates the Petrine present corporate functioning role. First, Peter's priesthood is a present role of the corporate body of believers, much like in Rev 1:6. However, John also develops a future role of believers being priests in the kingdom that Peter does not include (Rev 5:10; 20:6). Furthermore, the priesthood in Heb was centered on Christ (Heb 4:14—5:10; 7:1—10:18),[54] while Peter maintained the focus on God and believers (1 Pet 2:9). Additionally, Heb maintained a heavenly priesthood (Heb 8:1, 5; 9:24), while Peter develops an earthly one (1 Pet 2:5, 9). Furthermore, Heb focused on Jesus Christ's mediatorial priesthood (Heb 8:6; 9:15), while Peter nearly ignores it, mentioning instead Christ's role as sacrifice "bearing" our sin (1 Pet 2:14, ἀνήνεγκεν). In contrast to Heb, where Christ's priesthood involves the believers in priestly tasks of offering up service and praise, while doing good (Heb 12:28; 13:15–16), Peter developed believers as the priesthood without reference to any Christological priest,[55] but there is overlap with Peter's priest's tasks: praising,

---

LW 30:1–145; 36:3–126; 40:3–44; 44:115–217; Nagel, "Luther and the Priesthood," 283–84.

52. Best, *1 Peter*, 108; Elliott, *Elect and the Holy*, 50–128; *1 Peter*, 420.
53. Contra Blinzer, "IEPATEYMA," 55.
54. Kennard, *Biblical Theology of Hebrews*, 36–105.
55. Contra Torrance, *Royal Priesthood*, 22.

doing good, obeying, and if necessary suffering persecution as a mimetic sacrifice (1 Pet 2:5, 9, 12, 14–15, 18–23; 3:1–2, 5, 16). Unlike Heb where the Christological priesthood is distanced from the Mosaic covenant (Heb 7:4—10:18), Peter's priesthood is a divinely declared reality expressing *pesher* blessings from the Mosaic covenant (1 Pet 2:9; Exod 19:6). This Mosaic relationship shall be developed in greater detail within the significance of God's household.

Peter refers to a "spiritual" house and to "spiritual" sacrifices which raises the issue concerning how πνευματικὸς should be understood (1 Pet 2:5). The word πνευματικὸς means "pertaining to the spirit," as in "spiritual" or "caused by the Holy Spirit."[56] The word is not used as a figure of speech, spiritualizing a hermeneutic.[57] Nor does the word take on a Hellenistic Platonic meaning of "immaterial, nonexternal or heavenly."[58] "Spiritual" is meant in a Hebraic sense of being in the realm of the spirit or the characteristic product of the Holy Spirit, especially their sanctification (1 Pet 2:5; 1:1–2). Paul maintains similar meanings within the realm of the spirit that which is the product of the Holy Spirit and thus the characteristic product of the Spirit (Rom 7:14 with verse 6; 15:27 with verse 30; Eph 1:3; 6:12).[59] Paul's teaching from the Spirit produces a quality of life with the characteristics of the Spirit in contrast to the flesh (1 Cor 2:13–15; 3:1; 14:3; Gal 6:1; Col 1:9). For example, spiritual gifts, spiritual songs, and resurrected spiritual body are all expressions of what the Spirit produces (Rom 1:11 with verse 9; 12:1; 14:1; 15:44–46; Eph 5:18–19; Col 3:16). Paul even declares that Israel on the exodus ate real spiritual food and drank real spiritual drink from a spiritual rock which was Christ (1 Cor 10:3–4), whereas Peter develops the believer's sanctification by Jesus' blood in a Jewish pattern of sacrifice is an accomplishment of the Holy Spirit rendering believers to be a holy people (1 Pet 1:2).

Peter develops a *pesher* metaphor identifying Christ as the rock λίθον), as a metonymy of cause for effect; Christ is the cause for an inanimate rock being characterized by the Spirit (1 Pet 2:4–9). This development echoes "rock man" (Πέτρος) Peter's confession of "Jesus is the

---

56. BAG, "πνευματικὸς," 685.

57. Niebecker, *Das allgemeine Priestertum der Gläubigen*, 90 and Elliott, *Home for the Homeless*, discuss that πνευματικὸς does not mean a spiritualizing hermeneutic in Peter or the rest of the NT.

58. Contra Bigg, *Peter and Jude*, 128; Beare, *First Epistle of Peter*, 96–97; Holzmeister, *Petri et Iudae*, 1:242.

59. John also uses πνευματικὸς as within the realm of the spirit (Rev 11:8).

Christ" as the rock statement (πέτρᾳ), upon which confession statement Christ will build his church (ἐκκλησίαν), victorious over the gates of the city of the spiritually dead (Matt 16:18). In the original contexts of 1 Pet 2 quotes from Isa and Pss, the citations provided sustenance and protection to Israel. Then LXX Isa 28:16 applied the stone allusion to refer messianically.[60] Peter's citations expand the application for all stone passages to refer to the election of Jesus as the Christ and thus highly valued by God, as a dependable stone foundation (1 Pet 2:4–8). The effect of this "rock confession" message is that believers also become divinely elected living stones as spiritual building materials for the household of God (1 Pet 2:5, 9). The parallel relationship of verse 5 and 9 identify that the choosing of the believing people results in Spirit produced characteristics (1 Pet 2:5, 9; 1:1–2). Perhaps, this mirrors providing divine insight for Simon Peter's confession that "Jesus is the Christ," marking him out as the "rock man" and allowed the church to be built upon this confession "rock statement" (featured in Matt 16:17–19 more than Mark 8:29). Additionally, the Spirit produced the salvation message that has imparted life to the believers (1 Pet 1:10–12, 23–25). This new life and the vitality of the corporate community of believers are Spirit-produced phenomena. The household is then obligated to provide real Spirit-produced sacrifices through their role as priests, so actions identified as these sacrifices are described as "acceptable" or "approved" by God (1 Pet 2:5, 20; 3:16).

Following descriptions of the household, Peter developed two purpose statements for God's house as a combined missional purpose. The first purpose statement in 1 Pet 2:5, introduced by εἰς, "to," explains the priestly role of offering Spirit-produced sacrifices. The second purpose statement in 1 Pet 2:9 introduced by ὅπως, "so that" and followed by the subjunctive, explains that the divinely chosen are to proclaim God's excellencies. Furthermore, the parallel structure of 1 Pet 2:5 and 9 identify the two purpose statements as one compound activity: verbal praise accompanied by sacrificial deeds. That is, in the same way that the parallel structure identified the household priests with the chosen kingdom priests, the two parallel purpose clauses are to be seen as one activity. This does not rule out their distinctive emphases within that purpose. For example, in one of the priest descriptions, the concept of "choice" makes a significant contribution. The distinctive contribution within the sacrifice motif is twofold: it is produced by the Spirit and it is suffering done for God as acceptable to him. The

60. Elliott, *1 Peter*, 409; Qumran applies Isa 28:16 referring to their community (1QS 8.7–8; and possibly: 1QS 5.5; 4QpIsad 1; 1QHa 6.26–27; 7.8–9).

distinctive contribution within the proclamation motif is that of a verbal statement about God. Maintaining these distinctives, both motifs as a compound purpose statement contextually expressing the past salvific accomplishment of God which the believer is responsible to communicate.[61] Since these purpose statements immediately precede the house code, the purpose statements present that the household of God engages Hellenistic culture with mimetic atonement and worshiping perspective very different than Hellenism would (1 Pet 2:5, 9).

Spiritual sacrifices are the Spirit produced offerings resultant from the Spirit produced household of corporately functioning priests. First the word θυσίας refers to "sacrifices" in the broadest sense.[62] The basic sense of θυω meaning "to smoke" conveys a sacrifice as in the animal sacrifices of the OT converted into smoke to be acceptable and pleasing to God (Gen 8:21; Lev 1:3, 13; 2:2, 12; 3:5, 16; 4:31; 5:13; Num 28:6–7). The fact that Peter identified that these sacrifices are to be "acceptable to God" excluded pagan sacrifices as a pattern (1 Pet 2:5). Peter's allusions to Isa 53 identify the model sacrifices are Jewish sacrifice similarly provided by Isaiah's servant (1 Pet 2:19–25). Though the word θυσίας can refer to other costly sacrifices as in Ps 51:17 including both "sin offering" and the sacrifice of a contrite heart or Rom 12:1 offering of one's human body as a continuing expression of worship, Peter identified that the sacrifices he had in mind as Spirit produced sacrifices (πνευματικὰς θυσίας) much like the Spirit producing a life of obedience in the believer's initial sanctification process and continuing empowerment to live a set apart life, even in a context of suffering (1 Pet 1:2, 12, 15–16; 4:14; Acts 5:29–32). To identify the specific sacrifices Peter has in mind in this context look for the phrases repeatably emphasized such as: household action accomplished within belief in elect Christ (1 Pet 2:4–5), and submissive good works acceptable to God (1 Pet 2:5, 13, 15–17, 19; 3:4, 9, 12, 17). So unlike Rom 12:1 sacrifice of a whole life of an individual believer, Peter has in mind specific communal sacrifices accomplished by the scattered group which demonstrate the Spirit's transformative character with which God is pleased. There is no evidence to connect Peter's view with offering material gifts as in Phil 4:18. Likewise, there is no evidence for these sacrifices being the eucharist,[63] rather the contextual emphasis

---

61. Ps 107:22 serves as a pattern for this compound purpose combining sacrifice (LXX: θυσίαν) and proclamation (ἐξαγγειλάτωσαν).

62. Hort, *1 Peter*, 112.

63. Contra Justin Martyr, *Dial.* 41.7; 116.3; 117.1; Irenaeus, *Haer.* 4.18; Casel, "Die

determines the sacrifices. So, mediation of the communal priesthood is not here in Peter as direct from the church to God in prayer or a worship service,⁶⁴ these Petrine spiritual sacrifices are the submissive good works and if necessary, suffering persecution⁶⁵ that is acceptable to God, which the society can notice and sometimes understand, prompting some to conversion unto kingdom (1 Pet 2:15, 20; 3:1, 9, 14–17). Many of these features express an acceptance of the ubiquitous feudal patriarchal culture for missional purposes, but not all, for David Balch recognized a "selective acculturation" of "differentiated acceptance and rejection of the surrounding culture."⁶⁶ Such an approach raises an evaluative framework through which to evaluate aspects of acceptance and aspects of Christ against culture.⁶⁷ However, instead of Balch's "Christ of culture" assimilating the church into Hellenistic patriarchy, Elliott provided a strategy of "Christ converting culture," or more technically, Christians following the purposes of the church possibly converting some within this patriarchal culture (1 Pet 2:12, 3:1). Peter invites continuing applicability in any culture when Peter differentiates practices from the dominant culture he works within. Peter writes within a patriarchal era of feudal patronage, providing specific acts that often accept that context, but if the context changes for his readers then the goals of these purpose statements (1 Pet 2:5, 9) are to be realized as the church's mission even if the new context might significantly alter the specific practices to accomplish these purposes.⁶⁸ For example, requirements of patriarchal feudal patronage might

---

λογικὴ θυσία der antiken Mystik," 37–47; Brown, "Sacrifice," NIDNTT 3:435.

64. Some follow Martin Luther in identifying the priesthood of believers with confession, prayer, and worship as sacrifices prompts from Rev 8:3–4 as in Lutheranism (Althaus, *Theology of Martin Luther*, 314–15). Some following Heb 13:5 argue that praise was at times sacrifices once the temple was destroyed (LXX 2 Chr 29:31; 2 Macc 10:7).

65. Only part of the sacrifices are suffering identified with the suffering servant but these reflect mimetic atonement (1 Pet 2:5, 21–24), as Torrance maintained in *Royal Priesthood*, 61, 82, 84, 87; practices in the context acceptable to God are broader than this.

66. Balch, *Let Wives Be Submissive*, 36.

67. Berger (*Social Reality of Religion*) permits positive acculturation, while Adams eschews negative aspects of the Greco-Roman world (*Constructing the World*).

68. Allowing the purpose statements to take precedence over the specifics that follow identify that the author aligns with Elliott against Balch (Elliott, "1 Peter, Its Situation," 62–63; Christensen, "Balch/Elliott Debate," 173–93). Peter's use of house code language reflects the ubiquitous nature of feudal and patriarch culture across the Roman empire, and not a Christian assimilation to Hellenism (contra Balch, *Let Wives Be Submissive*; "Early Christian Criticism," 161–73; "Hellenization/Acculturation in 1

be irrelevant in a context of full citizenship where slavery is excluded. The following discussion emphasizes the purpose statements for which the church provides guidance; these purpose statements are to be what is to be realized. Specific commands will be discussed but if they reflect house codes of the patriarchal feudal patronage then that will be shown in the notes and that becomes a flag for considering applicability in other settings. For example, I do not believe in slavery and Peter does not address masters of slaves to free them, so Peter provided survival and excelling council for those within such a feudal patronage, not a final word on slavery. It would be inappropriate in a Petrine theology to develop the removal of slavery because Peter does not do that. A theology for the vulnerable lower classes must think through practices which fit within the setting in which they live. Since Peter addressed this engagement with culture in several places, those sections will be drawn in where appropriate. So, to evaluate such contextual changes one could ask questions to determine the mission of these sacrifices is to establish and what practices would be included within these sacrifices: Do the deeds accomplish good, benefitting others (1 Pet 2:12, 14–16; 3:1, 16)? Do the deeds show an alignment with God and Christ (1 Pet 2:16; 3:15)? Is God pleased with the deeds (1 Pet 2:19–20)? Do the deeds fit the new context's social expectations (1 Pet 2:13–17 and 3:16 in context)? Are people drawn to Christ in conversion or repulsed (1 Pet 2:12; 3:1–2)? For the most part these motives are very different than those oriented by Hellenistic patriarchal and feudal culture. So, while Peter advocates good deeds and honoring people in a manner that fits within Hellenistic culture, the manner, motives, and levels of assessing Peter's engagement with culture present a radically different framework than the ambience of Hellenism.

The other purpose statement for the corporate priesthood is that of proclaiming God's excellencies (1 Pet 2:9). God's excellencies would either be God's character or actions such as in this context God's mercy to elect believers in Christ as valued by God (1 Pet 2:6–10). These excellencies especially transform the believers from their previous darkness into marvelous light (1 Pet 2:9).[69] So verbal praise focusing on God and thankful testimony of God's salvific accomplishments before others of what God has already accomplished for them. Thus, the proclamation

---

Peter," 79–101; Harland, *Associations, Synagogues, and Congregations*, 195).

69. Like Ps 34:9; 1QS 1.9–10; 3.17–14.1; 1QH 4.5, 6, 23; 1QM; *Jos. Asen.* 15.13; Luke 16:8; John 3:19; 8:12; 9:5; 12:36; Acts 26:18; 1 Thess 5:5; Eph 5:8; Col 1:12–13; *1 Clem.* 36.2; 59.2.

of God's excellencies and a defense of the hope that Christians have in expressing gospel would be included within these statements (1 Pet 2:9; 3:15; Acts 4:1–22; 5:27–42; 10:22–43). The settings would include official interrogations (Acts 4:1–22; 5:27–42) as well as informal requests (1 Pet 3:15; Acts 10:22–43; as well as Peter's failure in Mark 14:66–72).

To make a proper defense of salvific hope, one needs to first set Christ apart as Lord of one's heart and fear God (1 Pet 3:15). That is, Christ must be acknowledged as sovereign especially over the believer's emotions; in contrast to fearing the intimidation of others, the believer is not to fear in the manner that humans would normally fear (1 Pet 3:14). Peter quotes Isa 8:12–13 as the exhortation because it addressed Israel's fear from Ephraim, Syria, and Assyria when Israel was not sufficient, but God was.[70] That is, Israel was not to fear the judgment of humans; they were to fear the Lord of Hosts because they are to view him as holy. In the same manner, believers are to regard Christ as holy allowing for fear of God to motivate obedience, rather than cowering under the fear of humans (1 Pet 1:17; 2:17; 3:14–15).

The second thing one needs to make a proper defense is to always be prepared (1 Pet 3:15). Such preparation extends beyond one's emotional attitude of trusting God instead of fearing humans. Such preparation includes a "readiness" (ἕτοιμοι) of what needs to be said to defend one's hope as God is "ready" to reveal the kingdom salvation (ἑτοίμην, 1 Pet 1:5; 3:15). For the kingdom is a presently existing inheritance with enduring qualities that are reserved for the right moment. Likewise, the believer should have her salvific defense ready for whenever anyone would ask.

Thirdly, the believer is to defend the salvific hope with meekness, gentleness, humility, courtesy, and considerateness (πραΰτητος, 1 Pet 3:16 Greek, but often in 3:15 English).[71] This pleasant friendliness is a calm humility, even accepting injustice done to them, as opposed to roughness.[72] This attitude is the same "gentle quiet spirit" that Peter develops for Christian wives, while Paul applies it to all Christians (1 Pet 3:4; 1 Tim 2:2, 12). The believer's defense of his salvific hope is to be done without defiance or contentiousness.

Finally, the defense is to come from a context of a good conscience which guarantees good deeds. Much like early Judaism, Ps 34:12–16 is quoted by Peter to remind his readers of a wisdom perspective that by

70. Kennard, *Biblical Theology of Isaiah*, 176–85.
71. BAG, "πραΰτητος," 705.
72. Hanck and Schulz, "πραΰτης," TDNT 6:646–47, 650.

zealously doing good they would likely convince many who wish them harm to quit such efforts so that the believers inherit a blessing in this life (a wisdom theme) and maybe more blessing at Christ's return (1 Pet 3:9–14).[73] The believer is to guarantee by his good behavior that he is not at fault in any area of his own life, especially with regards to anything in which he is slandered by his abusers (1 Pet 3:16). Such a firm commitment to do good, maintaining a good conscience, should characterize the believer from his initial commitment onward (1 Pet 3:21). While the maintenance of a good conscience primarily has to do with doing good (1 Pet 3:16; 2:12–16) it may also require suffering unjustly (1 Pet 2:19). The purpose for maintaining a good conscience is that those who treat the believer "wrongly" or "slanderously"[74] might be put to shame (ἐπηρεάζοντες, 1 Pet 3:16). That is, without a case, they might be shamed into silence so that they cease such abuse (1 Pet 2:15).

Such a verbal defense is supported by the other purpose statement of the priesthood household of God offering sacrifices, namely of submission to all authorities and good deeds to all (1 Pet 2:5, 9, 12; 3:16). For example, believers are to keep their behavior excellent among gentiles for the "purpose" (ἵνα) of the gentiles becoming convinced by believer's good deeds and the coming of Christ (1 Pet 2:12). That is, when God comes to judge the gentiles, they will be glorifying God, demonstrating that they are among believers since in Peter glorifying God is a characteristic of the believer (1 Pet 1:8; 2:9; 4:16). Additionally, submissiveness is required in this patronage setting for the purpose (ἵνα) of those to whom one submits being "won over" or "converted" to Christianity without a word (κερδηθήσονται, 1 Pet 3:1).[75] That is, submissive good works are to be done by believers to motivate the surrounding unbelievers to come to faith, thereby extending the household of God. This is the conversionist purpose for the church in the world.[76]

73. Sir 4.12; 14.14; 41.13; 1 Macc 10:55; Esth 9:22; Christensen, "Solidarity in Suffering and Glory," 335–52, esp. 343.

74. ἐπηρεάζοντες has more of an emphasis of wrong treatment in the NT and more the idea of malicious speaking with false accusations in classical Greek (MM, 232).

75. Not that believers are to marry nonbelievers but that sometimes women were converted while already married (1 Cor 7:12–15, 39; 2 Cor 6:14; Josephus, *Ant.* 18.344–45, 349; 20.145–46; *Jub.* 30.7; 1 Esd 8.68–96; 9.7–9; Tob 4.12; 2 Bar 42.4; *T. Jud.* 11.3–5; *b. Quidd.* 68b; *Gen. Rab.* 65.2; *Pesiq. Rab Kah.* 17.6). Actions speak louder than words (1 John 3:18; Philo, *Ios.* 86; John Chrysostum, *Hom. Heb.* 19.1).

76. Peter develops a positive social construct of the church purpose in converting some of the world (Berger, *Social Reality of Religion*; Niebuhr, *Christ and Culture*, Adams, *Constructing the World*, 8–9; Wilson, *Magic and the Millennium*).

"Submission" (Ὑποτάγητε) and "obedience" (ὑπακοὴν) are primary characteristics for those of the household of God (1 Pet 1:2; 2:13, 18; 3:1, 5, 22; 5:5). Peter's emphasis is in "submission," which reflects a perspective for lower social classes, whereas Hellenistic emphasis reading house codes is on "rule" and "obedience,"[77] so again Peter is resisting an element of Hellenism as was developed in chapter on humanity.[78] Such submission is not to be restricted to simply avoiding controversial issues or subversive activities for these are positive concepts of obeying and not a negative concept of not disobeying.[79] However, this emphasis identified that most of Peter's readers are likely underclasses. In this, believers are to be subject to every human institution, such as king or governor, who have a role to reward or punish in society (1 Pet 2:13, 17).[80] Elliott claims Peter positions such governments as standing between God and society, more optimistically than the book of Revelation and more pessimistic than Paul (1 Pet 2:13, 16; Rom 13:1-7; 1 Tim 2:1-3; Titus 3:1-2), for Peter recognized that sometimes these authorities make wrong judgments, such

---

77. Aristotle, *Pol.* 1.6.1255b; 1.7.1255b; Polybius, *Hist.* 6.17.1; Dio Cassius, *Hist. rom.* 1.5.12; Marcus Aurelius, *Medit.* 7.31; 1QS 5.23; m. 'Abot 3.12; *Gen. Rab.* 98.2; Elliott, *1 Peter*, 507; Keener, *1 Peter*, 166.

78. I prefer Elliott's approach over Balch because there are several unique features (like this emphasis on submission rather than Hellenistic emphasis on obedience) that resist Hellenism (Elliott, "1 Peter, Its Situation," 61-78) among a genre broadly appropriating part of house code language common among Hellenism (Aristotle, *Pol.* 1.2.1; Musonius Rufus, 8; Arius Didymus, *Epit.* 2.7.11d; Christensen, "Balch/Elliott Debate," 173-93; Weidinger, *Die Haustafeld*; Schrange, "Zur Ethik der NT Haustafeln," 1-22; Hartman, "Some Unorthodox Thoughts," 219-34), except Peter completely ignores father/children and master relations, and develops the wife more than the husband, with focus on inner qualities more than female adornments, thus further resisting Hellenism (1 Pet 3:3-4, contra Clement of Alexandria, *Paed.* 3.11.66; Tertullian, *Or.* 20; *Cor.* 14; *Cult. fem.* 1.6; 2.2.7-14; Cyprian, *Hab. Virg.* 8; Valerius, *Fac. Dict.* 9.1.3; Elliott, "1 Peter, Its Situation," 61-78, esp. 65, 68, 70-71; Balch, *Let Wives Be Submissive*, however Balch was more cautious, stating, "the ultimate origin of the ethic is to be found in Greek political thought, but I cannot draw firm conclusions about the immediate source of the code in 1 Peter" (p. 120); "Early Christian Criticism," 161-73; "Hellenization/Acculturation in 1 Peter," 79-101, however, this is not "the termination of past family ties" (p. 88) as Balch wrongly claims Elliott advocates; Horrell, "Between Conformity and Resistance," 111-43 following a strategy argued by Scott, *Weapons of the Weak* and *Domination and the Arts of Resistance*; Harland, *Associations, Synagogues, and Congregations*, 195).

79. Sleeper, "Political Responsibility," 281-85; contra Reicke, *James, Peter, and Jude*, xxxvii-xxxviii, 73, 89, 96-97, 99-100, 105, 107-8, 115, 119, 125.

80. The words ἀνθρωπίνῃ κτίσει refer to a human creation and not a divinely created entity, contrary to Hort, *1 Peter*, 139-40. These words are not as broad as all human relations.

as ignorantly killing Christ and persecuting Christians (1 Pet 2:15; Mark 8:31; 9:12, 31; 14:53—15:37; Acts 3:17; 4:19–20; 5:29; 12:7–11). However, Peter urged Christians "as free people" to generally submit to authorities as part of our slavery toward God (morally free submission,[81] even though many are slaves to others in the context as well, 1 Pet 2:16, 18). Peter wrote to a group of temporary residents which present a concern in Roman society of not fitting in[82] but there were likely some in Peter's readers who were longer-term residents but also vulnerable; all his audience needs to act "as if" they were vulnerable temporary residents (1 Pet 2:11, ὡς παροίκους καὶ παρεπιδήμους). As a good deed with the possibility of converting some authorities, Christians are to submit to the authorities in their lives. Those who live dominated by flesh are enslaved in their soul as aliens in war against themselves, bringing about a self-centered perspective which makes it difficult to submit to authority (1 Pet 2:11).[83] The military imagery draws the flesh vice impact into the repeated use of warfare against Satan and the demons (1 Pet 5:8; Mark 5:9). Any difference can draw "slander" (καταλαλοῦσιν), but the only leverage one has is to be known for "good deeds," which is a Hellenistic strategy (1 Pet 2:12, 15; 3:16).[84] Climaxing this section, the wisdom perspective of Ps 34:12–16 provides good deeds as a means of inheriting the blessing

---

81. Moral freedom (ὡς ἐλεύθεροι) usually meant no ruler above them, except God (1 Esd 4.49, 53; 1 Macc 14:26; 2 Macc 2:22; 3 Macc 2:6; Josephus, *Ant.* 2.281, 290, 327, 329; 3.19–20, 64; 12.304, 433; 18.6; 6.86; *T. Mos.* 3.14; *Sipre Deut.* 305.2.1) and released from slavery (Lev 19:20; Sir 7.21; 33.26; 3 Macc 3:28), though Philo used term as a neo-platonic freedom from flesh passion, perhaps closer to 1 Pet 2:11 (Philo, *Leg.* 3.17; *Heir* 271).

82. Kennard, *Petrine Studies*, chapter on Recipients; Cicero, *Mil.* 37.101 recognized that virtue was the only protection for exiles (Balch, *Let Wives Be Submissive*, 65–80, 118; Keener, *1 Peter*, 163–66), though virtuous people live generously beyond their social strictures as citizens of heaven (Eph 2:19 which extends beyond the claim in 1 Pet 1:17; Paul's idea of citizen of heaven is supported by: Philo, *Creation*, 165; *Heir* 267–68; *Conf.* 77; Bede, *Commentary on the Seven Catholic Epistles*, on 1 Pet 1:1; Keener, *1 Peter*, 149–50) but it is imposed as a foreign idea in Peter who is more missional than cosmological (Elliott, *Home for the Homeless*, 39–48; *1 Peter*, 461).

83. Hellenistic philosophers agree: Sallust, *Bell. Cat.* 2.8; Philo, *Creation*, 165; *Heir* 267–68; *Confusion* 77; Arius Didymus, *Ep.* 2.7.10e, but so does an early Jewish and Christian perspective (4 Macc 1:32; Wis 9.15; Josephus, *Ag. Ap.* 2.203; Jas 1:13–15; Rom 7:5–25; *Did.* 1.14), so the issue is not joining the Stoics or Platonists to remove passion (contra Keener, *1 Peter*, 151–53) but to remove flesh dominance from one's life (1 Pet 1:18; 4:1–5; 2 Pet 2:10, 18; Gal 5:16, 19–21; Rom 13:14; Eph 2:3; 1 John 2:16).

84. Van Unnik, "Teaching of Good Works in 1 Peter," 95, 108–9; Balch, *Let Wives Be Submissive*; "Early Christian Criticism," 161–73; "Hellenization/Acculturation in 1 Peter," 79–101; Harland, *Associations, Synagogues, and Congregations*, 195.

THE HOUSEHOLD OF GOD   199

of continued good days in which evil might be turned away from others, because God watches and protects the righteous person (1 Pet 3:9–12).[85]

Elliott points out that Peter is the only NT author who fuses public duty of submission together with the domestic submission duties within the family.[86] For example, Peter encouraged honoring the king but left this description undeveloped except to remind that possibly by doing right, the Christian might silence foolish criticism (1 Pet 2:13–17). There is no Petrine development that Christians are praying for these kings, as Paul does (1 Tim 2:1–2), which becomes part of the second-century apologetic.[87] Furthermore, after developing submission to king and governor, Peter wrote believing slaves[88] are to submit to their masters in a patronage culture,[89] even if they are unreasonable, forcing the slaves to suffer unjustly[90] (1 Pet 2:18–19). Keener reminded, "The basis for enduring unjust treatment is not that it is just, but that one expects reward from

---

85. Jobes, "'O Taste and See,'" 241–51; Woan, "Psalms in 1 Peter," 213–29, esp. 223.

86. Elliott, *1 Peter*, 507, 510 part of the "*oikonomia* tradition" following a pattern found in Aristotle, *Oec.* 2.1.1 and Cicero, *Off.* 2.22–23, which Goppelt (*1 Peter*, 162–79) called "station codes." Keener identified that it was "familiar rhetorical form" to extend an argument on the same topic (submission) to additional groups (*Rhet.* 4.47; Keener, *1 Peter*, 178).

87. Tertullian, *Apol.* 32.1; 30.4–5; such a prayer for emperor health and peace is contained in *1 Clem.* 60.4—61.3; joining the Jewish practice (Josephus, *Ag. Ap.* 2.68–78; *War* 2.195–98, 409–16).

88. οἰκέται fits within the concept of "household slave," so cities are likely the readership (which excludes slaves from mines, agriculture, and galleys) and in this house code pericope it contributes to the emphasis of the "household" (οἶκος) theme. In the Roman empire, at times (after conquests) about a third of the population were slaves and they cannot escape on their own, so their situation was precarious (Cicero, *Verr.* 2.1.33.85; Quint. *Fratr.* 1.2.4.14; P.Oxy. 5.3617; 51.3616; Dio Chrysostom, *Or.* 66.2; Plutarch, *Alex.* 42.1; Josephus, *War* 3.373). Slave masters are not addressed, probably because there were very few since Christianity mostly multiplied among the lower classes.

89. Since submission to one's master is the requirement for slaves, virtue is rarely developed for slaves, and Seneca concluded that virtue was rarely found in slaves (*Lucil.* 32.11; Sevenster, *Paul and Seneca*, 185–89).

90. Slaves were often beaten (Prov 29:19; Sir 42.5; *Deut. Rab.* 3.2; Plautus, *Mem.* 966–77; Cicero, *Fin.* 4.27.76; Quintilian, *Inst.* 1.3.13–14; Martial, *Epigr.* 2.66.1–8; 8.23; Juvenal, *Sat.* 6.474–85, 490–91; Tacitus, *Ann.* 16.19; Varro, *Rust.* 1.17.5; Vedius Pollio, *On Anger* 3.40; Seneca, *On Mercy* 1.18; Saller, *Patriarchy, Property and Death*, 102; Bradley, *Slaves and Masters*; Tracy, "Domestic Violence in the Church," 279–96). Hadrian jabbed an eye out of a slave and bruised slave's hands, branding was a common extreme indignity rather than the norm, and slave women and boys often suffered sexual abuse from the patriarch and sons (Keener, *1 Peter*, 185–86, 193; Plutarch, *Nic.* 29.1; Artemidorus, *Oneir.* 1.8; Seneca, *Controv.* 4. Pref. 10; Lucian, *Down. J.* 11; *Sat.* 29; Tacitus, *Ann.* 14.60; Xenophon of Ephesus, *Eph. Tale* 2.5; 3.12; Aeschines, *Tim.* 16; Valerius Maximus, *Mem.* 8.1).

God, or as Peter puts it, one's conscience before God."[91] So, Christians are called by God to recognize Jesus as a virtuous model for mimetic atonement, silent nonretaliatory suffering waiting for God's reward (1 Pet 2:21–23; 3:9).[92] Likewise, Peter addressed wives directly as moral agents (instead of having the instruction come through her husband as is common in house codes[93]) to submit to their husbands with a gentle and quiet spirit within a patriarchal culture after the pattern of holy women of old, like Sarah (1 Pet 3:1–5).[94] However, Peter identified that those Christian wives become the offspring of Sarah by following her habit of doing what is right without fear, which as a Jewish-Christian motive is very different than Hellenism (1 Pet 3:6). Karen Jobes explained wife submission for community protection and mission.

> Peter's concern that Christian wives continue to submit to their own husbands not only shields Christianity from the accusation that it is a social evil but is clearly motivated by evangelistic intent. The unbelieving husband observes virtues in the wife's good demeanor that are motivated by her relationship with Christ, virtues not inferior to those motivated by Greek moral

---

91. Keener, *1 Peter*, 192.

92. Echoed by *1 Clem.* 16.17; 33.8; Polycarp, *Phil.* 8.2.

93. Elliott, *1 Peter*, 554; 1 Cor 14:34–35; Eph 5:22–33; Aelius Aristides, *Def. Or.* 129–30; Suetonius, *Claud.* 25.5. In fact, to develop a lengthier section for wives than for husbands is unusual in house codes, thus Peter resisted Hellenism here (Elliott, *1 Peter*, 554; Christensen, "Balch/Elliott Debate," 186).

94. Sarah called Abraham "lord" in Gen 18:12 and *T. Abr.* 224–38, with a pattern of obedience (Gen 16:2, 6; 21:12; Josephus, *Ag. Ap.* 2.200–201). In Roman patriarchal culture female submission to the patriarch was expected (Plutarch, *Advice* 140.19) and often taught by pointing to an ideal role model as Peter has done (Xenophon, *Oec.* 7.1–10.13; Plutarch, *Advice* 48), countered only by a few Isis advocates defending egalitarianism (P.Oxy. 1380.145–48; Meeks, *First Urban Christians*, 25). A "gentle" or "meek" wife is valued in patriarchal culture (1 Tim 2:9, 15; Musonius Rufus, 3, p. 40.17–18, 20; 3, p. 42.26; 4, p. 44.16–18, 22; Dio Chrysostom, *Or.* 32.56; Lucian, *Hall* 7; *Sent. Sextus* 237; Libanius, *Speech* 18.3; *Thesis* 1.13.26–27; *Narr.* 37; Euripides, *Oed.* frag. 545; *1 Clem.* 21.7), but meekness also describes Jesus (Matt 11:29; 21:5; 2 Cor 10:1) and is a male virtue (Ps 36:11; Matt 5:5; Gal 5:23; Eph 4:2; Col 3:12; Titus 3:2). A quiet wife is valued in a patriarchal culture (1 Tim 2:11; Sir 26.14; Philo, *Spec. Laws* 3.174; Sophocles, *Aj.* 293; Aristotle, *Pol.* 1.5.8. 1260a; Valerius Max., *Fac. Dict.* 3.8.6; Plutarch, *Lyc. Num.* 3.5), but quiet is also a virtue for males in such a feudal culture (2 Thess 3:12; 1 Tim 2:2). Often the virtues of gentleness and quiet are combined (1 Pet 3:4; 1 Tim 2:2, 11; *1 Clem.* 13.4; *Barn.* 19.4; *Herm. Man.* 5.2.3; 6.2.3; 11.8; funerary descriptions from Lefkowitz and Fant, *Womens' Life in Greece and Rome*, 104–5, 209).

philosophy. Observing this, the man himself may be won to Christ "without words."[95]

There is no discussion of wives enduring domestic violence as there had been for slaves, because wives enduring domestic violence would not be seen in this patriarchal culture as a virtue.[96] Peter encourages Christian husbands to live with their wife in an understanding manner as a fellow-heir of the grace of life (1 Pet 3:7).[97] However, Peter only samples part of the house code[98] aimed at slaves and wives, to develop submission of these more vulnerable in a patriarchal context, leaving the impression that most of Peter's readers are from lower classes of patronage. Then he adds a brief comment for Christian husbands to fill out the house code a bit within the patriarchal context (1 Pet 3:7). Later Peter returns perhaps as an extension beyond the house codes discussion to urge "young men" to submit to the elders of the household of God much like in a synagogue (1 Pet 5:2–3, 5).[99]

With Christianity present only among such a vulnerable minority, issues of egalitarianism for women and slaves and social justice issues were not championed by Christians of the first century, except on the periphery (such as Philemon or female patrons of a local assembly). The agenda Peter has is the preservation of Christianity unto kingdom and

95. Jobes, *1 Peter*, 204; female virtues are encouraged in the house codes (Prov 31:30; Aristotle, *Oec.* 3.1; Xenophon, *Oeconomicus* 7.43), which stand in contrast to adornments which are usually seen as instruments of seduction (Philo, *Virtues* 7.39; Plutarch, *Advice* 30). However, Peter contrasts the inner quality of Christian virtue as opposed to being known for one's adornments, which is not an argument for plainness or rejection of adornments (1 Pet 3:3–4; contra Clement of Alexandria, *Paed.* 3.11.66; Tertullian, *Or.* 20; *Cor.* 14; *Cult. fem.* 1.6; 2.2.7–14; Cyprian, *Hab. Virg.* 8). Peter joins Hellenistic house codes in censoring Valerius Maximus' view considering women as mentally inferior, inclines Valerius to justify women should focus on female adornments (*Fac. Dict.* 9.1.3).

96. DeSilva, "1 Peter," 33–52, esp. 39; Jobes, *1 Peter*, 206; Dossey, "Wife Beating and Manliness," 3–40, esp. 10–13; Reeder, "1 Peter 3:1–6," 519–39.

97. Developed in Kennard, *Petrine Studies*, chapter on "Marriage, Not Divorce," along with Mark's discussion of Jesus teaching concerning divorce.

98. Full treatments include husband/wife, father/children, and master/slave relations much like in early Judaism (Philo, *Decal.* 165–67; *Spec.* 2.225–27; *Hypoth.* 7.14; Josephus, *Ag. Ap.* 2.199–217) and Christianity (Eph 5:22—6:9; Col 3:18—4:1; Titus 2:2–10; *1 Clem.* 1.3; 21.6–89; *Did.* 4.9–11; *Barn.* 19.5–7; Polycarp, *Phil.* 4.2–3; Ign. *Pol.* 4.1–3), which reflect Hellenistic house codes (Aristotle, *Pol.* 1.2.1; Musonius Rufus, 8; Arius Didymus, *Ep.* 2.7.11d).

99. Elders in synagogue (Josephus, *Ant.* 13.297–98; 18.12–15) were occasionally connected with house codes (*1 Clem.* 1.3; 21.6, 8; Polycarp, *Phil.* 4.1–6.1 [wives 5.3, young 5.3, elders 6.1]).

the potential conversion of non-Christians. This evangelistic priority was not to be put at risk by such important social concerns. Peter's agenda priority warns subsequent generations to not so closely associate Christianity with social agendas that will drive a rejection of Christianity, such as anti-intellectualism, prohibition, anti-abortion, rejecters of the other, and aligned with a particular political party. The issue is priority. Social issues are important but not to the extent that it puts Christianity at risk or hindered. Christians are to be generally known as those who work within societal norms for good. Peter does not address legislative issues for Christian citizens, but Peter's priority should serve as a warning for privileged Christians later.

Submission permeates all these various relationships to the extent that this is the superior graded absolute. However, within this feudal patronage culture, if there is a higher authority it is right to obey the higher authority even if this obedience means disobedience to a lesser authority. For example, Jesus' or God's direct command takes precedence over other absolutes. Peter demonstrates that when religious-civil authorities forbid evangelism (the very purpose for household submission) that the believer must obey God and Jesus in evangelizing, rather than obey humans (Acts 1:8; 4:19–20; 5:29; 12:7–11). However, when Christians disobeyed human authorities (resisting assimilation), Peter explained his allegiance to God and defended his Christian hope. Peter enumerated five reasons for resisting assimilation by obeying God rather than the conflicting human rulers. First, Peter must side with God, Israel's true heritage, who raised and exalted Christ (Acts 5:30–31). Second, Peter must oppose the killers of Christ (Acts 5:30). Third, Peter must side with the Prince and Savior through whom salvation (including healing) comes (Acts 4:9–10; 5:31). Fourth, Peter must continue to obey God because the Holy Spirit is given to those who obey him, thus implying their need to continue in obedience where Spirit empowerment inclines (Acts 5:29, 32). Fifth, Peter and others were eyewitnesses and must say what they saw (Acts 5:32). Additionally, when necessary, Peter even suffered punishment at the hands of these authorities for his disobedience to them as he submitted to God (Acts 5:40). However, provided with an opportunity to escape punishment and continue to evangelize, Peter took advantage of it, submitting to God, and then to the lesser human authority (Acts 12:7–11). This hierarchy of submission is to be motivated by the believer's fear of God and respect for human authorities. Believers are not to fear the human authorities and their intimidation (1 Pet 3:6, 14) because all they can do is cause suffering and death. Believers are instead to fear God, showing him their ultimate allegiance because he is the judge who rewards those who fear him, even with resurrection life (1 Pet 1:17; 2:17; 3:15; 4:6). However, believers are to respect all humans,[100] especially the higher authorities, such as the king (1 Pet 2:17). Such respect is simply a lesser form of fear because these authorities have the right to punish those who disobey (1 Pet 2:14, 18, 20). Peter advocated a hierarchy of submission based on a hierarchy of fear. However, instead of feudal fear being the norm to one's patron, in a theocracy God is the superior authority to obey (Prov 24:21).

The household of God is also to do good deeds. Good is that which is excellent, beneficial, and generous (1 Pet 2:12, 18; 3:11).[101] Peter does not define "good" and "righteousness" by a subjective standard of Hellenistic assimilation to attempt not being viewed as the "other" by doing what Hellenism expects through the house codes to remove persecution. In fact, counter to Hellenistic culture, which permitted those in power to abuse those under their care, Peter advocates maintaining a good conscience (1 Pet 3:16, 21). Peter models Christian goodness after the traits of God, Jesus, and perhaps caring elders who shepherd the church (1 Pet 4:10; Mark 10:17–18). Likewise, "righteous" may be defined by Peter as that trait of behaving according to the law (1 Pet 3:12; Mark 2:17). Again, Jesus excels as Peter's model of righteousness in doing good, though Lot's hospitality is righteous as well (1 Pet 2:21–24; 3:18; 2 Pet 2:8–9; Gen 18:28; 19:3, 16). Peter utilizes these concepts to indicate people, things, and actions which are excellent (1 Pet 2:12, 18; 3:10–21a; 4:10). From this base, "good deeds" and "righteous deeds" are the actions which realize this excellence. Peter uses this concept of good deeds to include those actions which are universally recognized as right and favorable by human and God (1 Pet 2:14–15, 20; 3:6, 17; 4:19).[102] For example, such good deeds are rewarded by political officials, the opposite of deeds which are punished (1 Pet 2:14; 3:13). Perhaps by such good deeds the patrons could be won to faith in Christ as some wives had done for their husbands instead of the norm of all in the household embracing the religion of the

---

100. Πάντας refers to "all" and not to merely all the other groups listed in the verse (Blass et al., *Greek Grammar*, 172, no. 336 [21]).

101. Grundmann, "ἀγαθος," TDNT 1:10; Beyreuther, "Good," NIDNTT 2:102–3.

102. *Ep. Aris.* 18, 272; *Sib. Or.* 1.126; 2:313; 3:220; Philo, *Sacr.* 53; 3 Bar 15.2; *T. Reu.* 4.1; *T. Benj.* 5.3; Josephus, *Ag. Ap.* 2.230; *T. Naph.* 8.5; *m. 'Abot* 1.12; *'Abot Rab Nat.* 24.49; Epictetus, *Diatr.* 2.11.25; 3.3.1; 4.8.24.

patriarch (1 Pet 2:12; 3:1).[103] Therefore, the needy are not the recipients in focus but the believer's superior, who has the power to make the believer suffer (1 Pet 2:20). For example, when a superior insults or abuses the believer, the believer is to respond with verbal blessing and peaceful deeds (1 Pet 2:12, 18–23; 3:6, 9, 17). There is no discussion of merits of sacramental acts of humiliation, nor cleansing from post-baptismal sins as discussed by the early church.

There are seven reasons for doing good works in 1 Pet. First, Peter presents the doing of good works as a command by God, binding on all believers (1 Pet 3:8–9, 16). Secondly, believers demonstrate their identification with previous believers by doing good without fear (1 Pet 3:6). Thirdly, the foolish who accuse believers are silenced in shame by the believer's good deeds (1 Pet 2:15; 3:16). Fourth, some may be converted by experiencing good deeds (1 Pet 2:12; 3:1–2). Fifth, doing good deeds tends to minimize believer's suffering (1 Pet 3:10, 13). In fact, sixth, doing good deeds tends to increase the believer's longevity when believers are a minority community (1 Pet 3:10). These last two reasons for good deeds are ultimately attributable to God as a blessing from him. So, opposite Van Unnik's claim, good deeds are not to be viewed as the Greeks did in simply enabling societal life to continue.[104] That is, while peaceful behavior tends to smooth one's own way, even greater than that, God is attentive to the prayers of those who do good, while he opposes evil doers. The ultimate expression of this divine work and seventh reason to do good is that God saves gospel-obeying good-doers as an extension of the believer's life of trust in God (1 Pet 4:17–19). This last reason closely fits with the Jewish concept of the righteous living hereafter, for Peter quotes Prov 11:31, developing this OT concept of everlasting salvation within a first-century Christian framework (1 Pet 4:16–19), and Ps 34:15–16 developing how the believer will inherit a blessing from the Lord in the wake of living the narrow way of doing good (1 Pet 3:9, 12).[105]

For Peter, submission and good deeds perform a vital role in providing an overarching canopy which integrates the household of God to the

---

103. Josephus, *Ant.* 20.34 describes the conversion of the royal house of Adiabene through the king's harem known for good deeds.

104. Van Unnik, "Teaching of Good Works in 1 Peter," 95, 108–9; in Ps 34:9, 11, 16 the fear of the Lord motivates these good deeds and quote in 1 Pet 3:10–12 climaxes with this point in Ps 34:16; 1 Pet 3:12.

105. Contra Van Unnik, "Teaching of Good Works in 1 Peter," 108–9.

rest of society.[106] Submission and good deeds especially structure Hellenistic society for believers since most early believers outside of Israel came from lower classes (slaves, women, and children, Acts 16:11–18; 17:34; 18:1–8; Eph 5:22—6:9; Col 3:18–25).[107] David Balch argued that utilizing the house codes meant that the author of 1 Pet stressed "the importance of Christians seeking peace and harmony in their household relationships and with society."[108] As developed, Peter modified the house codes by selectively excluding parts and developing a higher motive than assimilation for what he does develop. To reflect these, John Elliott argued that "the household code was used to promote both the internal solidarity of the sectarian movement and its external distinction from gentile motives and manners."[109] Believers from these groups have clear obligations in God's household as she lives in society, and some of those deeds are different than what society requires. Peter develops these specific groups in their vulnerability in society.

Contextually connecting to this evangelism through submission and good deeds, Peter adds that husbands should "likewise" or "in the same way" (ὁμοίως) "live with your wives in an understanding way" (1 Pet 3:7). It is an expected comment from the house code but the role is no longer the vulnerable one under the patriarch but the patriarch himself. Patriarchy still frames the role as evident by the explanation, "as with a weaker vessel,"[110] which is at least a reference to general male physical superiority[111] for tasks of physical exertion (like hunting or labor) but in first-century patriarchy "weaker vessel" could be referring to weakness of human nature or morality.[112] Peter does not clarify what kind of

---

106. Religion performs this role for any society; Berger et al., *Homeless Mind*, 79.

107. Tertullian, *Apol.* 3; Julian, *Against the Galileans* 206a; Origen, *Cels.* 3.44.

108. Balch, *Let Wives Be Submissive*, 105.

109. Elliott, *Home for the Homeless*, 231, 115, 140, 229; which is not merely an internal resistance of motives contra Carter, "Going All the Way?," 14–33.

110. "Vessel" refers to wife as valued fragile one, as in pottery (like b. *Meg.* 12b; *Midr. Esth.* 1.11) without clarifying what the vessel held, not a reference to "one's own body" as Paul used the word in 1 Thess 4:4 to make a claim that one's wife is one's own body as some might take Paul's argument in Eph 5:28–29. Paul doesn't say that either. He said loving one's wife is also a love of one's own body; the husband is benefitted by loving his wife.

111. Xenophon, *Lac.* 3.4; Livy, *Hist.* 25.36.9; 28.19.13; Cicero, *Mil.* 21.55; Virgil, *Aen.* 12.52–53; Musonius Rufus, 4, p. 46.8–23; Silius Italicus, *Pun.* 1.445; Dio Chrysostom, *Or.* 2.29; Aulus Gellius, *Att.* 17.21.33; Lucian, *Dial D.* 414; *Lam. Rab.* 4.19.22.

112. Female moral or human weakness is developed broadly (1 Tim 2:14; 4 Macc 15:5; Sir 33.20; 4Q416 frag. 2 4.2–9; PLond. 971.4; Dio Chrysostom, *Or.* 3.70; Clement

weakness he means. In fact, Peter's use of "as" (ὡς) does not make a claim that women are weak but that a husband should try to live with her in an understanding manner "as if she was weak," that is differentially valuing her perspective. The word "live with" (συνοικοῦντες) often in LXX has reference to sexual intercourse but here it is more broadly referencing all of life together as is developed in early Jewish wisdom.[113] Such life together is to be informed by knowledge (γνῶσιν), and thus informed sensitivity because she is a woman. Here patriarchy is upended because the husband's informed perspective "should honor his wife as a fellow heir of the grace of life" (ἀπονέμοντες τιμὴν ὡς καὶ συγκληρονόμοις χάριτος ζωῆς). That is, while in Roman feudal patriarchy only rarely would a woman would inherit, in Christian marriage a husband should consider his wife an equal heir of God's generous life. This honor goes beyond Roman patriarchy honoring the spouse to avoid infidelity,[114] to include a partner of mutual respect.[115] However, Peter goes further identifying that a Christian husband should consider his wife equal in salvation inheritance (1 Pet 3:7 approaches Paul's sentiment of Gal 3:28). So, the ideal for Christian marriage illustrates the harmonious, sympathetic, compassionate, and humble lifestyle that a Christian should excel in society. However, there is an additional benefit for a Christian husband being this way with his wife, because if he is not his prayers may be hindered (1 Pet 3:7).

Peter lived what he taught, traveling missionary journeys with his wife (1 Cor 9:5).[116] Clement of Alexandria presented Peter and his wife as an example of blessed Christian marriage, each collaborating on the mission, controlling their feelings even in deeply emotional settings, such as martyrdom.[117] Ignatius and Clement of Alexandria discussed that during Peter's mission, Peter's wife was forced to follow Christ in martyrdom, with Peter encouraging his wife to resign to her martyrdom and anticipate

---

of Alexandria, *Paed.* 2.10.107; Plutarch, *Bride* 33; *Mor.* 142E; Quintilian, *Decl.* 327.2; *Gen. Rab.* 22.6; *b. Beṣah* 32b) but so is ungendered human weakness broadly developed (Rom 5:6; 6:19; Heb 4:15; 5:2; 1 Cor 8:7–13; Plato, *Leg.* 6.781b; *Resp.* 5; 455d; 451c–56a; *Meno* 71c–73c Philo, *On God* 80; *Spec.* 1.293–94; Clement of Alexandria, *Strom.* 2.15.62; 2.16.72; 7.3.16; *Paed.* 3.12.86).

113. Sir 25.8.

114. Plutarch, *Bride* 36, 47; *Mor.* 143, 144F–45A.

115. Porphyry, *Marc.* 2.21; *Sent. Sextus* 238; Ps.-Arist., *Oec.* 3.2.

116. Clement of Alexandria, *Strom.* 3.52.1–2, 4; 3.52.5 = Eusebius, *Hist. eccl.* 3.30.1; *Acts of Peter* 7; *Acts of Philip*; *Pseudo-Clementine Recognitions* 7.25.3; 7.36.1; 9.38; *Homiline* 13.1.1; 13.11.2; Hengel, *Saint Peter*, 125–27.

117. Clement of Alexandria, *Strom.* 3.53.3; 7.11; Hengel, *Saint Peter*, 125–27.

kingdom.[118] Later Nero crucified Peter upside down in Rome.[119] So, both Peter and his wife gave priestly sacrifices of their lives in martyrdom to point others toward Christ's kingdom.

House codes sometimes transition to synagogue and church as an extended household.[120] Within this believing community, the household is to develop and function within love and stewardship, whether gathered or scattered. Love is the primary command above all others (1 Pet 4:8). Within the community, love had two main expressions: covering sins and hospitality. Believers must decide to cover one another's sins with forgiveness and unified recovery (1 Pet 4:8). This verse develops from Proverbial wisdom, "hatred stirs up strife but love covers all transgressions" and "he who covers a transgression seeks love, but he who repeats a matter separates intimate friends" (Prov 10:12; 17:9; 1 Pet 4:8). Love also expressed itself through hospitality without grumbling, patrons hosting the church in their own homes, much as pioneer synagogues had done (Acts 4:23; 10:48; 12:12; 16:13, 40; Rom 16:15; 1 Cor 16:19; Col 4:15). Also, with limited inns, resident aliens could have their basic needs for food and shelter met by a hospitable host, as Peter had (Acts 9:43; 10:48; Matt 25:35; Luke 7:44–47; 11:5–10; 14:12–14; Rom 12:13; Heb 13:2; 3 John 5–8).[121] Hospitality was to be provided as a demonstration of eager concern for one's fellow believer. Thus, any uneasy feeling, perhaps from the shock of sharing one's privacy, needed to be restrained so that there was no grumbling. Both these expressions of love have a commonality of silence within caring behavior. Only if gossip and grumbling were silenced could the community flourish within the household. Everything is to be characterized by a humble sharing of mind and affection (1 Pet 3:8–9). Empathy humbly joins the other in her sufferings (1 Pet 3:8; 5:5–6). Humility begins by decisively giving God all one's concerns in a recognition that he cares for all believers (1 Pet 5:6). Humility extends to a proper respect of elders (1 Pet 5:5) and for all humans (1 Pet 3:8).

---

118. Ign. *Phld.* 4; Clement of Alexandria, *Strom.* 7.11.

119. Ign. *Tarsians* 3; *Apoc. Pet.* 14.4–6; *Martyrdom Isa.* 4.3; Tertullian, *Scap.* 15; *Apol.* 5; *Praescr.* 36; *Muratorium Canon*, line 37; Lactantius, *De Mortibus persecutorum* 2; Eusebius, *Theoph.* 5.31; *Dem. ev.* 3.5.65; *Hist. eccl.* 2.25.5; 3.1.2; *Acts of Pet.* 9.37.8–38.9; Bauckham, "Martyrdom of Peter," 539–95.

120. 1 Tim 2–3; 5:1—6:2; Titus 1–2; *1 Clem.* 1.3; 21.6, 8; Polycarp, *Phil* 4.1—6.1 (wives 5.3, young 5.3, elders 6.1).

121. *1 Clem.* 10.12; *Herm. Mund.* 8.10.

Fostering community within the household (οἶκος) of God is the believer's stewardship (οἰκονόμοι) of all that God provides (1 Pet 4:10). As a steward operates through a household office so every Christian is to serve in whatever capacity God gives them. Peter applies this stewardship in two primary areas: peaceful speech and generous aid for others (1 Pet 4:11). The one who speaks needs to speak responsibly as if it were words of God which are provided for him. The "as" (ὡς) indicates that direct revelation is not in view but that the person is responsible for what he says but the statement should reflect what God has said on the subject, as Peter has accomplished in this letter repeatedly applying OT quotes into new settings in Christian's lives. Those who serve should serve as from the strength God abundantly provides (1 Pet 4:10). Many of the expressions of stewardship service would reiterate the same concerns which Christians should have as he loves others. Finally, speaking or doing, the ultimate purpose of all Christian stewardship is to glorify Christ. The believer's motive should not be for his own glory or purposes. The glory belongs to Christ forever. Christian service is accomplished within an arrangement where Christian stewards are responsible in all respects to Christ as king. The everlasting king is to receive everlasting glory.

The local church appropriates the synagogue pattern in the middle of the first century. Many consider that the idea of synagogue originated during the Babylonian captivity with Ezekiel's "little temple" or "dwelling place" (Ezek 11:16; Ps 90:1).[122] Perhaps these local Jewish worship sites were a proliferation of what began as alternative Jewish temples in Dan and Bethel (tenth to eighth century BC, which the Samaritan temple replaced in 330–28 BC), Elephantine (fifth to first century BC), and Onias' in Leontopolis (165 BC–AD 73). The synagogue provided worship that imitated temple practices for those who didn't pilgrimage for temple worship days.[123] Additionally, the synagogue was where the Sabbath worship and meal were served.[124]

Early Pharisaic Judaism developed Moses as inventing the idea of the assembly of Israel in covenant reading and practice.[125] Within this Jewish perspective the LXX translated Hebrew assembly words to reflect Moses'

---

122. *b. Meg.* 29a; Levine, *Ancient Synagogue*, 21.

123. *Tosef. Ta'an.* 1.10; *Pesik.* dRK 136b.

124. Josephus, *Life* 279; There is even one statement of a synagogue referred to as the "Sabbath place" (σαββατεῖον, Josephus, *Ant.* 16.6).

125. Philo, *Creation* 128; *Moses* 2.215; Josephus, *Ag. Ap.* 2.175; *Ant.* 16.43–44; *y. Meg.* 75a.

gathering the whole assembly (συναγωγὴν) at the tabernacle to celebrate Passover, read the Scriptures, grieve Israel's sin, make atonement, and worship together (LXX Exod 12:3; 24:7; 36:1, 4; Lev 3–4; Num 14:7; Deut 5:1, 22; 31:11) under the leadership of elders (LXX Exod 3:16–18; 4:29; 12:21; 17:5–6; 18:12; 19:7; 24:1, 9, 14; Lev 4:15; 9:1; Num 11:24–25, 30; 16:25; Deut 5:23; 27:1; 29:10; 31:9, 28). Yahweh judged the assembly of Israel by the law.[126] These synagogues also became associated as a trade guild, but while other trade guilds or *collegia* were sometimes banished, Judaism was legally protected as a long-established group, except when Claudius banished them and Christians from Rome to be resident aliens in "another city not their own."[127]

The Pharisees were most associated with the leadership and development of village Judaism with synagogues to develop obedience to the Law and the teachings of the elders (Mark 8:31; 11:27; 14:43, 53; 15:1; Acts 4:5, 8, 23).[128] This form of early Judaism leadership overlaps with Hellenistic leaders governing a city and specific trade guild leadership also being called "elders."[129] Peter draws these ideas together to continue this elder oversight and the need for the household to submit to these elders overseeing the church (1 Pet 5:2–3, 5; Acts 11:30; 15:2, 4, 6, 22–23). John Lightfoot explains this extension of governance.

> It was not unnatural therefore that, when the Christian synagogue took the place by the side of the Jewish, a similar organization should be adopted.... With the synagogue itself [the Christian congregations in Palestine] would naturally, if not necessarily, adopt the normal government of a synagogue, and a body of elders or presbyters would be chosen to direct the

---

126. Sir 46:14; Deismann argued that LXX reflected Ptolemaic Alexandrian idiom (*Bible Studies*, 154–56).

127. Meeks, *First Urban Christians*, 35, 38; Claudius, *Epist.*

128. 2 Macc 14:37; Jdt 6.16; 1QS 6.8–9; Josephus, *Ant.* 4.186, 218, 220, 224, 255–56; 13.166, 297–98; 18.12–15; *War* 7.412; Philo, *Migr.* 168; *Moses* 2.153.

129. In Jewish leadership priests played a prominent role over elders but elders oversaw city and synagogue (1QS 6.3, 8–9; 8.1; 1QM13.1; CD 10.4–10; Josephus, *War* 2.144–49; *m. 'Or.* 2.5, 12; *m. 'Arak* 9.4; *m. Sota* 9.5–6), whereas, in Hellenism just the city governance was overseen by the elders, religious leadership was in the hands of the pagan priests (Aristotle, *Pol.* 2.7.5, 1272a; Diodorus Siculus, *Libr. Hist.* 21.18.1; Dionysius of Halicarnassus, *Demosth.* 3), and Alexandrian miller trade guild leadership and overseeing farm leadership of pagan temple owned land were also called "elders" (Strack, "Die Müllerinnung in Alexandrien," 213; Merkle, *Elder and Overseer*, 24–65; Keener, *1 Peter*, 355).

religious worship and partly also to watch over the temporal well-being of the society.[130]

Each Jewish town would have at least one synagogue building or they might meet in a house or in the open (Luke 7:5; Acts 16:13, 16, 40),[131] though many larger cities would have synagogues for special groups including an Essene synagogue "where the young sit ranked in rows under the elders,"[132] freedman synagogue (Acts 6:9), and Jewish Christian synagogue (James 2:2; also called "church" [ἐκκλησίας] in 5:14). Presumably, early synagogues would either meet in homes or in the open, much like early churches did setting up rival Christian gatherings (Acts 10:48; 12:12; 16:13, 40; Rom 16:15; 1 Cor 16:19; Col 4:15).[133]

Synagogues and churches meeting in a patron's house or in the open do not leave a distinguishing footprint for archeology. The earliest synagogue ruin found so far is at Delos (from second century BC) but several synagogue ruins[134] remain in Israel from the first century AD, including Gamla, Magdala, Herodion, Masada, and Horvat Ethri, though there were also those synagogues in a patron's house, as there were house churches when fewer people gathered. The structure of a synagogue building was known as a συναγωγὴν (assembly place) or a προσευχαι (prayer place, LXX Isa 56:7; 1 Kgs 8:22).[135] Perhaps the "prayer place" emerged from the Jewish practice of praying near water (Acts 16:13).[136] Synagogue buildings would usually have windows where the columns would support an elevated roof portion, and stadium seating on three walls with additional seating on some wooden chairs and reed mats in the center.[137] There was a centralized small table to roll out a scroll (the best is at Magdala) and a "seat of Moses" for the head elder to govern the service (the best is at Chorizim; Matt 23:2; Luke 8:41), and some raised seating from which to teach (Matt 23:6). For the first two centuries, churches met in homes (Acts 1:13, 15–16; 2:46; 5:42; 12:12; 20:7–8), perhaps renting

---

130. Lightfoot, *Philippians*, 96, 192. Peter does not engage the discussion in Pauline studies concerning spiritual giftedness for eldership.

131. *M. Ned.* 5.5.

132. Philo, *Good Person* 81–82.

133. Blue, "Architecture, Early Church," 92; *m. Šabb.* 1.4.

134. Meyers and Chancey, *Alexander to Constantine*, 204–27

135. Josephus, *Life* 277; *t. Sukkah* 4.6; *Mdr. On Ps* 93; Juvenal, *Satires* 3.296; Meyers and Chancey, *Alexander to Constantine*, 204; Strange, "Ancient Texts," 27.

136. Philo, *Flaccus* 14; Josephus, *Ant.* 14.10.23.

137. *Y. Meg.* 73; Meyers and Chancey, *Alexander to Constantine*, 204–38.

rooms.[138] There are no known church buildings of the first century but as churches grew in the third and fourth centuries, they built buildings which they also called "churches." Among the earliest church remains are the octagonal church over Peter's house, Dura-Europos of Syria, and the Aula Ecclesiae of Rome.[139]

Such first century Christian liturgy includes modifications of synagogue practice including: 1) communal filling by the Spirit, 2) wise Apostolic teaching Jesus' message, 3) singing psalms, hymns, and spiritual songs, 4) prayer, 5) thankfulness to God in Jesus' authority, 6) mutual submission to each other, 7) sharing for edification, and 8) admonishing one another, 9) meeting needs, 10) communal meals, with eucharist every meeting replacing yearly Passover (Acts 2:42; 4:24–37; 16:13, 16, 40; Col 3:16–17; Eph 5:18–21; 1 Cor 6:4; 14:12, 16, 26–33; Heb 2:12). As in synagogue culture, men in the church, especially leadership, should be known for praying for others (Acts 2:42; 4:24–37; 6:4; 1 Tim 2:8). Furthermore, as synagogues celebrate God of the Exodus, so churches celebrate a communal meal of the Lord's Supper commemorating Jesus' new covenant initiated in his death and proclaiming his coming and kingdom (Acts 2:42; 1 Cor 11:18, 22). This communal meal was a simple example of church generosity to meet all the needs of any vulnerable who identify within the community (Acts 2:43–46; 4:34–37; 6:1–6; 1 Tim 4:16).

A group of elders are those older wiser men who have oversight over the household of God as they did over synagogues, with believers as subordinate (1 Pet 5:1–5; Mark 7:3; Acts 8:31; 11:27; 14:53; 15:1; 20:17; 1 Tim 5:1, 17–22; 2 John 1; 3 John 1).[140] This involves sensitive care and willing service, demonstrating an example for the congregation to follow (1 Pet 5:3–4). Such oversight is facilitated if the younger men subject themselves to the leadership of the elders (1 Pet 5:5). As in synagogues, "elders" (πρεσβυτέρους) oversaw the flock of God as a shepherd with prayer, teaching, leading, correcting, restoring, and protecting fellow believers (1 Pet 5:1–5, 14; Acts 15:22; 20:17, 28; 1 Tim 3:1–7; 5:17–20; Titus

---

138. Blue, "Architecture, Early Church," 92; P.Oxy 1129, 1036, 1037, 1038, 2190, and P. Mich. Inventory 319.

139. Blue, "Architecture, Early Church," 94–95.

140. Josephus, *Ant.* 13.297–98; 18.12–15; *Eph.* 1.3; 4.1; *Magn.* 2.1; 3.1; 6.1; 7.1–2; 12.2; 13.1; *Trall.* 1.1–2; 7.2; 13.2; *Phld.* 1.1; 7.1–2; 10.2; *Pol.* 6.1; *Smyrn.* 8.1–2; Polycarp, *Phil.* 5.3; 6.1; *1 Clem.* 1.3; 3.3; 21.6; 44.5; 47.6; 54.2; 57.1; *Herm. Vis.* 2.4.2–3; 3.1.8; Elliott, "Elders as Leaders," 549–59.

2:2; James 5:13–15).[141] Their role reflects that of Peter, who as a "fellow-elder" (συμπρεσβύτερος) was attempting to shepherd Jesus' sheep, feeding and tending them as a love relationship with Christ (1 Pet 5:1; John 21:15–17). Perhaps there is an emerging hierarchy of Peter as apostle with authority over but among elders as a fellow elder (1 Pet 1:1; 5:1; 2 Pet 1:1). There is no evidence of a hierarchy of bishops over elders in Peter, for the earliest evidence of this increasing hierarchy is from Ignatius concerning the bishop of Antioch in Syria.[142]

Elders are warned not to serve for sordid gain of money or power (1 Pet 5:2–3). Elders regularly would be handling money for the church, and they need to do so with accountability (Acts 4:34; 6:1–3; 11:29). Likewise, some elders were even paid but this should not be the reason to seek such service (1 Pet 5:2–3; Acts 20:33; 1 Cor 9:7–14; 2 Cor 12:13–18; 1 Tim 5:17). Elders should serve with sensitive reasonable care and not lording it over as a power trip (1 Pet 5:3, 5; Mark 10:42, 35–45; 1 Tim 3:3, 8; Titus 1:7, 11).[143] The example of Simon Magus seeking power to obtain and give the Spirit demonstrates the wrong kind of people to be elders and Peter was right to refuse him this role (Acts 8:18–20). Peter points to himself as an example as a fellow elder and to Jesus Christ as the chief shepherd modeling how an elder should govern well (1 Pet 5:1, 3–4).

The central practice of each synagogue and church focused on a knowledgeable person as "messenger" (*hazzan*= ἀγγέλῳ), often an elder reading the Scriptures and explaining it in the accepted traditional manner of that community, though others could also explain interpretations (Luke 4:16; Acts 15:21; 13:15; 1 Tim 5:17; Rev 2:1, 8, 12, 18; 3:1, 7, 14).[144]

---

141. Josephus, *Ant.* 13.297–98; 18.12–15.

142. Ign. *Rom.* 2.2.

143. *Did.* 15.1; Polycarp, *Phil.* 5.2; 11.1; Elliott, "Ministry and Church Order," 367–91, esp. 374.

144. Philo, *Spec. Laws* 2.62; *Prov.* 80–83; *Embassy* 156; Josephus, *Ag. Ap.* 1.42; 2.175; *Ant.* 16.43–44; *War* 2.292; *Life* 280; m. *Soṭah* 7.7–8; Theodotos Inscription CIJ 2.1404 "the synagogue for the reading of the Law and for teaching of the commandments"; tract. *Meg.* 3.1–3; 4.6; Ryan, *Role of the Synagogue*, 42–50), fulfilling a similar practice as reading the law in the temple (m. *Yoma* 7.1; m. *Soṭah* 7.7–8; m. *Meg.* 4.4). Additionally, Sabbath biblical literacy instruction would be provided for boys to prepare them for Jewish adulthood (Josephus, *Ant.* 13.289; m. *'Abott* 1.18; 5.17; y. *Meg.* 4.74a; y. *Pe'ah* 2.17a; b. *Šabb.* 17a; b. *Giṭ.* 60b; b. *Yoma* 28ab). An extension of this *torah* focus is that the synagogue and the elders who oversaw the synagogue would fulfill a judicial function of instructing appropriate behavior ("loosed"), disciplining even with scourging to recover individuals, and excluding behavior beyond appropriate ("bound") (Mark 13:9; Matt 10:17–18; 23:34; Luke 12:11–12; 21:12; John 9:13–34; Acts 22:19; Sus 28; Josephus, *Ant.* 14.235, 259–61, 117; *Ag. Ap.* 237, 261; m. *Mak.* 3.12; Ryan, *Role of the*

This "messenger" of the synagogue would lead the congregation in reciting public prayers,[145] which was a role continuing into the local church (Acts 1:14; 4:24; 12:12; Rev 2:1, 8, 12, 18; 3:1, 7, 14). Peter and the elders continue this role of instructing, binding, and loosing of accepted Christian practices in the church (Matt 16:19; 18:15–19; Acts 5:11; 8:20–24; 11:2–18; 15:1–30; 1 Pet 5:5).

In early Judaism such "assembly" of Israel would also be called ἐκκλησίας ("called out" or "church"; all references in this paragraph are of this word). Stephen considered that Moses during the Exodus was with Israel as such an assembly, but that Israel was repeatedly rebellious (Acts 7:38). David called all Israel to assemble to witness the moving of the Ark of the Covenant LXX 1 Chr 13:2, 4). David and other kings called all Israel to gather at the tabernacle/temple in worship (including sacrifices) and praise to Yahweh with temple singers and trumpets sounding (LXX 1 Chr 29:1, 20; 2 Chr 1:3,5; 6:3; 29:28–38; 3 Kgdms 8:22, 65; Pss 21:26; 34:18; 39:9; 88:6; 106:32; 149:1).[146] Jehoshaphat prayed to Yahweh before all Israel in the temple and the spirit came down upon Levites to foster prophecy (LXX 2 Chr 20:5, 14).[147] All Israel celebrated Passover in the temple with the king (LXX 2 Chr 30:2, 13, 23–25). Peter recognized that the believing household of God was the church affiliated with Jesus as the Christ (1 Pet 2:5–8; Matt 16:16–18).

Jesus announced his kingdom message in Jewish synagogues by reading from the scroll, such as Isa 61 and identifying in his teaching that the kingdom miracles anticipated are being realized in his healing ministry (Luke 4:16–21).[148] Jesus demonstrated his kingdom authority by healing all presented to him, including casting out demons, even on Sabbath which was permitted within generous "loosed" Hillel Pharisaic

---

Synagogue, 49–50). This reading law and judicial role of synagogue also emerges from the concept of the elders deciding appropriate practice and judging at the city gate (Deut 17:5; 22:15, 24; 25:7; Ruth 4:1; 1 Sam 18:4; 19:8; Levine, *Ancient Synagogue*, 19–41). The gate also became an important place to read and explain the law (Neh 8).

145. *m. Roš Haš.* 4.9; *Tosef.* 4.12; in this prayer service, an elder would lift a kerchief to indicate in the liturgy when the congregation was to say "amen" (*t. Sukkah* 4.6; *y. Sukkah* 5.I.555 a–b; *b. Sukkah* 51b).

146. Esdr B 15:13; Sir 21:2; 31:11; 39:10; 44:15.

147. Wisdom was shared in the assembly (Sir 21:17). Ezra and all Israel confessed their sin weeping in the temple (Esdr B 10:1, 12, 14). A judgment seat was set up in the temple assembly (Sir 38:32–33).

148. Ryan, *Role of the Synagogue*, 125–263.

practice (Mark 1:21–28; 3:1–5; Matt 12:9–13; Luke 6:6–10; John 9:1–11).[149] Unfortunately, at times the synagogue audience and elders rejected this message and Jesus' authority, because they held a restricted "bound" Shammai Pharisaic view restricting Sabbath healing, and considered Jesus to be dangerous in leading people astray (Mark 1:6; Matt 9:14–37; Luke 4:22–29; 6:11; John 9:12–34).[150] Jewish leadership killed Jesus and put others out of their synagogues as "bound" (John 9:34; 12:42).[151] Those who followed Jesus became his disciples.

Christians developed synagogues (συναγωγὴν; James 2:2) or churches (ἐκκλησίας; Matt 16:18; Acts 2:47; 15:4, 22) aligned with Jesus as the household of God. The church was seen by Christ as a universal and local gathering or household of believers aligned with Messiah Jesus that Jesus was growing up to be his community and kingdom to take captive the walking dead world for Jubilee kingdom (1 Pet 2:4–10, 12; 3:1; 16; Matt 13:30–33, 41–43; 16:16–18; Acts 2:47; Heb 12:23). The core message that Jesus is Messiah serves as the point of inclusion as "loosed" unto kingdom, as well as the breaking point by which "bound" damned are excluded (Matt 16:19; 18:18). Jesus institutes church discipline to recover straying disciples so that they might be included in kingdom rather than excluded by the church and God (Matt 18:12–19). For example, embezzlement goes too far and through Peter the Spirit killed Ananias and Sapphira (Acts 5:11). Church ethical practices come with authority (1 Cor 7:17; 10:32; 11:16) but can be different for different communities provided they edify the whole community to become like Christ (Rom 13–14; 2 Cor 8–10).

Since Peter and all Christians are to serve each other in ministry, the role of deacon emerged as part of this service in Peter's ministry (1 Pet 4:10; Mark 10:43–45; John 21:16–17; Acts 6:1–5). However, Peter makes no comment about deacons being an official servant leader role under elders to meet needs, as developed in Paul and the early church (Rom 16:1; 1 Tim 3:8–13).[152]

---

149. Josephus, *Ant.* 18.63; *b. Sanh.* 107b; 104b; 43a; 67b; *b. Soṭah* 47a; *Sib. Or.* 8.206–7.

150. Josephus, *Ant.* 18.63; *b. Sanh.* 107b; 104b; 43a; 67b; *b. Soṭah* 47a; *Sib. Or.* 8.206–7.

151. Josephus, *Ant.* 18.64.

152. Ign. *Magn.* 6.1; *Trall.* 7.2; *Phld.* 4.1; 7.1; *Pol.* 6.1.

12

Suffering

ONE OF THE MOST prominent themes in 1 Pet is the Christian in suffering (1 Pet 1:6–7; 2:19–20; 3:9, 14, 17; 4:1, 13, 15, 19; 5:9–10) within the pattern of Christ suffering (1 Pet 1:11; 2:21–23; 3:18; 4:1, 13). In fact, it is so prominent that Floyd Filson considered suffering to be the center of 1 Pet.[1] The variety of other well attested themes prevent suffering from becoming the center of Petrine theology. However, suffering is too prominent a concern to be subsumed under another topic. For example, suffering is addressed by Peter with respect to Christ, salvation, the household, and eschatology. No one category of Petrine thought encompasses all that Peter says about suffering. It then should be treated separately as a significant theme within the message of Peter.

The approach to suffering reflects Peter's practical emphasis. Karen Jobes described this practical emphasis.

> When God's call to holiness (1 Pet 1:15) conflicts with the values and morals of social practice, Christians devoted to that call may expect to experience verbal abuse, slander, malicious talk, and other forms of persecution that Peter summarizes as "to suffer grief in all kinds of trials" (1 Pet 1:6).[2]

The present treatment on suffering begins by hinting at the sociological context of suffering. The Petrine perspective of suffering is developed by the words for suffering and the practical pattern for Christians

---

1. Filson, "Partakers with Christ," 410.
2. Jobes, 1 Peter, 45.

to follow in suffering. These two sections serve as the core of Peter's development of suffering.

Peter is not interested in defending which persecution and form of suffering the Christians experienced but in an earlier chapter the suffering was described as the unofficial universal persecution so endemic to the ancient world.[3] For example, the apostles and their followers suffer at the hands of Jewish leaders (Acts 5:40; 6:8—8:3), rulers (Acts 12:1–6; 16:19–24), and mobs (Acts 9:23–25; 14:5, 19; 19:23–41; 23:11–21). The unofficial universal persecution is further justified because three of the mob persecutions occurred in the regions which are addressed by Peter. Additionally, if 1 Pet was authored around AD 62–64, then there would probably be a recent increase of Christians scattering across Asia Minor as resident aliens fleeing persecutions such as the one by which James was killed. Finally, the descriptions of the suffering in 1 Pet fit best with an unofficial form of persecution emerging from society and household. That is, there may be some slandering of Christians before government officials based on mere foolish ignorance (1 Pet 2:12, 15). However, there is also the unjust suffering of slaves meted out by unreasonable masters (1 Pet 2:18–21). Perhaps there is even the potential of wife abuse upon Christian wives from unbelieving husbands (1 Pet 3:6).[4] Additionally, from almost any quarter of society there could be insults, slander, and scoffing (1 Pet 3:9, 16 with 15; 2 Pet 3:3). For example, the gentiles are surprised and malign Christians when the Christians no longer continue in the gentile's lustful practices (1 Pet 4:3–4).

THE WORDS FOR SUFFERING

Peter's words for this ongoing suffering portray his basic perspective of Christian's suffering. The most common word in Peter for "suffering" (πάσχω) has the basic meaning "of experiencing something from without, usually in a negative manner."[5] Jesus Christ's death serves as the supreme example of this kind of suffering (1 Pet 2:21, 23; 3:18; 4:1; Acts 3:18 with 15). As such, Christ suffered once substitutionally in the realm of his flesh, referring to his death (1 Pet 3:18). However, Jesus' suffering

---

3. Kennard, "Recipients of the Petrine Epistles"; a recognition in Jewish and Christian wisdom: Ps-Phoc. 27; 1 Cor 10:13.

4. DeSilva, "1 Peter," 33–52, esp. 39; Jobes, *1 Peter*, 206.

5. Michaelis, "πάσχω," TDNT 5:904; Gärtner, "suffer," NIDNTT 3:719.

also includes the reviling and the time of silent abuse before his death (1 Pet 2:21, 23). However, most Christian suffering does not result in death.[6] Of this kind, Christians are not to suffer as an evil doer (1 Pet 4:15, 19; 5:10); Christians are to be righteous and endure unjust suffering if needed (1 Pet 2:19-20; 3:14, 17).

The phrase "suffered in the flesh" (παθὼν σαρκὶ) should be taken broadly as human sufferings (1 Pet 4:1). For example, in Christ's case it was broader than his death though it ended in his death. Additionally in the Christian's case, it cannot be restricted to martyrdom because the believer being addressed by Peter lives on for more time in the flesh after he has so suffered (1 Pet 4:2).[7] The phrase "he who has suffered in the flesh has ceased from sin" is understood to mean that the one who has suffered demonstrates his allegiance and has stopped doing sinful acts.[8] The aorist "suffered" (παθὼν) with the perfect "has ceased" (πέπαυται) indicates that Peter treats the suffering as a whole that has left the continuing characteristic lasting results of not sinning.[9] This verse doesn't mean that the sufferer is purified by the persecution process,[10] like a case could be made for this point from 1 Pet 1:7 illustration of a crucible over fire being used to purify gold, extended by Peter to develop the Christian's "tested faith" of various trials. Because Peter only used ἁμαρτία of "acts of sin" it is better to understand "has ceased" (πέπαυται) as a middle voice, indicating that he has stopped doing sinful acts and not that he was delivered from the power or guilt of sin, which themes would be better developed in Paul.[11]

The second most common word for suffering in Peter, πάθημα has the same meaning of an experience of "suffering," with a little more emphasis on the involvement of emotions.[12] This word also has reference to Christ's death since these Christological sufferings were prophesied and observed (1 Pet 1:11; 5:1). The Christian experience of this suffering is

---

6. Michaels, "πάσχω," TDNT 5:912-22.

7. Contrary to the church fathers who understood that this phrase meant martyrdom which atoned for sins; Best, *1 Peter*, 151.

8. Contrary to those who say baptism is sharing in Christ's sufferings, for which there is no evidence in Peter (Beare, *First Epistle of Peter*, 153).

9. A similar point to 1 Cor 5:5; 2 Macc 6:12-16; 2 Bar 13.10; 18.6; Sir 2.11.

10. Contrary to Selwyn, *1 Peter*, 209.

11. Contrary to those who say that Christ's death is the finality of sin (Stibbs, *1 Peter*, 147-48), because sins are still occurring for Peter to address these concerns, and Christ never sinned.

12. Michaels, "πάθημα," TDNT 5:930; Gärtner, "Suffer," NIDNTT 3:719.

conceived of as sharing in Christ's suffering (1 Pet 4:13; Mark 8:34–38). However, with reference to Christians, παθήμα probably does not mean death since it includes degrees within it, some of which are common among Christians permitting them to continue to rejoice (1 Pet 4:13; 5:9). Both words extend Christ's suffering and death into the Christian experience. However, the way this is accomplished does not support claims that 1 Pet is a paschal liturgy.[13] That is, the Christian's suffering is real, common, and not discussed in a hypothetical manner, occasioned by the celebration of the effects of Christ's death.

Extending this experience of suffering, λυπέω emphasizes the grieving, pain, and sorrow that results from such experiences of suffering.[14] The aorist λυπηθέντες indicates that such sorrow was not a future or hypothetical possibility but an ongoing experience of distress with which the believer grappled. That is, sorrow is a normal condition of life from suffering and is not overcome when joy is present.[15] While the sorrow is not alleviated, the suffering believer should bear up under the sorrow (1 Pet 2:19). That is, God evidences his favor for such endurance by mandating this endurance amid the sorrow.

Peter also describes suffering through three words which emphasize the nature of a trial or temptation. Peter's word, πειρασμοῖς, has the basic idea of "tested."[16] Such a test is not for the believer's education or development, rather the test demonstrates the condition of the one being tested. This can be seen first in that Peter used the verbal form (πειράζω) as something humans do to God. For example, Ananias and Sapphira put God to the test by their sin of embezzlement (Acts 5:9). Additionally, Peter warned the Jerusalem council not to test God by denying gentile converts whom God had approved (Acts 15:10). God did not need to be educated by these human efforts, but he demonstrated his true righteous character by killing those who tested him (Acts 5:9). Secondly, the Christian experience of this suffering trial comes from unbelievers and not God. Therefore, it is an opportunity for the Christian to demonstrate her true character; it is not an experience primarily for her to learn from God or develop in character. For example, in 1 Pet 1:6 the various trials

---

13. Kennard, "Form in the Epistles of Peter," chapter in *Petrine Studies*; contra Thornton, "1 Peter, a Paschal Liturgy?," 20–26.

14. BAG, "λυπέω," 482–83.

15. deVilliers, "Joy in Suffering in 1 Peter," 70.

16. Seeseman, "πειρα," TDNT 6:22, 30; Haarbeck, "Tempt, Test, Approve," NIDNTT 3:798, 802.

from without evidence the condition of the believer's faith. Christian's suffering under trials is a common enough experience so that he should not be surprised when they come (1 Pet 4:12). Peter gave Lot as an example of these trials, for Lot was severely tortured[17] by the lawless deeds of unbelievers about him (2 Pet 2:8–9). The role God performs in Peter with reference to Christian suffering is not one of orchestrating the sufferings but delivering Christians from them ultimately in the day of judgment.

The second word δοκιμαζω is like πειρασμοῖς. It comes from the root for watching (δοχη) and has developed the meaning of "proved, tested, reliable and genuine."[18] The opposite of this idea is the Jewish leader's "rejection" (ἀποδεδοκιμασμένον) of Jesus Christ. They threw Christ out as unworthy, reflecting more on their unbelief than on Christ's character (1 Pet 2:4, 7). However, for believers experiencing trials, their faith can be shown to be genuine (1 Pet 1:7). Here δοκιμιον does not designate a means of testing but the positive results after being tested.[19] That is, these believers have genuine faith. The pattern is illustrated by "genuine" gold. The suffering Christian is not described by Peter as a refining process where improvement can be made; in Peter suffering is a revealing process evidencing the true nature that is present in the believer.

The third word, πυρὸσις, draws out more the excruciating intensity of the testing experience with a passive idea of being burned.[20] It is derived from the basic root πυρ meaning "fire." Peter used the word to describe fire-tested gold, which is analogous, though greatly inferior, to suffering tested faith (1 Pet 1:7). This same "fire" (πυρ) shall be ultimately utilized by God in "destroying" the elements of heaven and earth (2 Pet 3:7, 12 πυρούμενοι). However, this divine judgment is still future to Christian suffering. Present Christian suffering is characterized as a fiery test (1 Pet 4:12).[21] This fiery test of Christian suffering now, demonstrating "tested faith," also indicates that God's judgment has begun with Christians so that they will not be included in the eschatological suffering (1 Pet 4:14–16). This fits within what Marv Pate and Douglas Kennard championed as "consistent eschatology" in the Petrine material, namely Jesus' disciples have not escaped experiencing the crucible of the messianic woes, so that contemporary suffering now is an expression of

17. BAG, "βασάνιζω," 134.
18. Grundmann, "δοκιμος," TDNT 2:255.
19. Grundmann, "δοκιμος," TDNT 2:259.
20. Lang, "πυρὸσις," TDNT 6:951.
21. BAG, "πυρὸσις," 738.

mimetic atonement following Christ through the messianic woes, and those who follow Jesus will not experience the eschatological suffering of divine judgment but will experience the joys of kingdom.[22] Therefore, these three testing words should not be viewed in an apocalyptic manner[23] because when they are used apocalyptically God is the agent causing the test,[24] whereas when God does not cause the test they are being used non-apocalyptically with reference to the ongoing suffering of this present life. For example, such common testing can come from unbelievers, Satan or even oneself (Heb 3:8–9; Luke 4:13; 1 Tim 6:9). In Peter the test is emphasized as coming from unbelievers (1 Pet 4:12–16; 2 Pet 2:9) but Peter admits that there is a greater adversary, the devil, behind such testing orchestrating them.

Peter's words for suffering approach the same experience from different perspectives. The shades of meaning include the suffering experience, the resultant sorrow, and the trying nature of suffering that demonstrates the character of the life present. Each of these words combine repeatedly in the passage, evidencing that while this suffering can be viewed from different angles, it is still the same suffering. Therefore, the remainder of the chapter will treat the descriptions of suffering together.

The first factor that a Christian should manifest in suffering is the lack of surprise, because suffering was a common experience. That is, Peter commands the believers to not be surprised at the fiery ordeal among them (1 Pet 4:12). The verb "surprise" (ξενίζεσθε) does not mean paralyzing shock but rather perplexity and astonishment as the readers experience the suffering themselves.[25] For example, the verb simply means "strange and surprising."[26] In the same manner that gentiles were surprised (ξενίζονται) when these believers no longer run with them in their gentile lusts, the believers were surprised (ξενίζεσθε) when persecution came (1 Pet 4:4, 12). The believers should not be surprised because such suffering was not a strange (ξένου) occurrence for believers (1 Pet 4:12). In fact, believers suffering was a common occurrence (1 Pet 5:9). That is, wherever believers were in the world there was a similar suffering occurring there also.

---

22. Pate and Kennard, *Deliverance Now and Not Yet*, 301–400.

23. Contra Holdsworth, "Sufferings in 1 Peter," 226–31.

24. 1 Cor 3:13; Rev 3:10; 18:8–9, 18 and perhaps Matt 6:13 and Luke 11:4.

25. deVilliers, "Joy in Suffering in 1 Peter," 80; contra Beare, *First Epistle of Peter*, 163.

26. BAG, "ξενος," 550.

The Christian should suffer as a Christian and not as an "evildoer"[27] (1 Pet 3:17; 4:15). As such, they should not do evil or sin (1 Pet 2:1, 19–20; 3:11). If suffering is necessary, then they should suffer unjustly (1 Pet 2:19–20). Some of these believers had done evil in the past and may be tempted to use their freedom as a cover for future evil (1 Pet 2:1, 16). For example, Simon's act was evil when he attempted to buy the ability to bestow the Holy Spirit (Acts 8:22). If suffering is unavoidable, then believers need to suffer in a manner that keeps evil out of their lives completely, even from any retaliatory word or deed (1 Pet 3:9–10). The motive for not suffering for evil is twofold: God is against all who do evil (1 Pet 3:12) and civil rulers rightfully punish evildoers (1 Pet 2:14). So, the Christian may be slandered as an evildoer, but his good deeds must demonstrate otherwise (1 Pet 2:12; 3:16). Specific kinds of evil are singled out by Peter to emphasize specific actions that the believer should stay clear of to prevent suffering for evil. For example, the Christian should not suffer for sin but if suffering comes their way, they should suffer unjustly (1 Pet 2:19–20). Additionally, the Christian should not suffer as a thief (1 Pet 4:15). Perhaps an example of a similar act would be Ananias and Sapphira's embezzlement for which they were condemned (Acts 5:3). Furthermore, the Christian should not suffer as a meddler in other matters that don't concern him (1 Pet 4:15). This word "meddler" (ἀλλοτριεπίσκοπος) has at least four areas in which the Christian should not meddle.[28] First, he should not have his eye on other's possessions, picking up the idea of thief in the context (1 Pet 4:15). Secondly, highlighting the stewardship of slaves in the context, he should not be an unfaithful guardian of goods committed to him (1 Pet 2:18–20; 4:15). Third, he should not be a busybody as the slanderers were (1 Pet 2:12; 3:9–10, 16; 4:15). Finally, he should not be a spy or informer as Judas had been (Acts 1:16–17; 1 Pet 4:15). Instead of these evil deeds, the Christian should suffer if necessary as a Christian as they have identified with Jesus Christ (1 Pet 4:16). Such Christian suffering means that the believer suffers after the example of Christ. That is, the suffering is not to be earned, only coming upon the believer who does what is right (1 Pet 2:19–23; 3:14, 17–18). The Christian can be reviled in the name of Christ, but he needs to refrain

---

27. BAG, "κακοποιός," 398. The word means "evildoer; it does not mean "magician" or "sorcerer" from Latin "maleficus" which is only one form of such evil (Tertullian, *Scorp.* 12.3; Cyprian, *Text.* 3.37; Lactantius, *Inst.* 2.16.4; Jerome, *Expl. Dan.* 2.2; Theodosius, *Cod.* 9.16.4).

28. Beyer, "ἀλλοτρι(ο)επίσκοπος," TDNT 2:621–22.

from reviling back to his abusers as Christ was silent before his accusers (1 Pet 2:19–23; 4:14). Christian suffering may even require martyrdom; some have followed Christ's example as martyrs (1 Pet 4:6). Peter's life provides a demonstration of the practice he is commanding these believers to follow. For example, Peter suffered trials and flogging for healing a man and evangelizing in the temple (Acts 4:1–22; 5:12–40). Peter's opponents could find no fault with him except that he persisted in being identified with Christ by proclaiming the gospel. In the wake of James Zebedee's martyrdom, Peter was imprisoned to be martyred but an angel released him (Acts 12:1–11). On Peter's missionary journeys, Peter's wife was martyred.[29] Later in Rome, Peter became aware that his martyrdom was approaching quickly, which motivated him to write his final letter, to stir the disciples to continue toward salvation (2 Pet 1:14).[30]

The Christian should suffer with joy. Not that suffering becomes the cause of joy, for suffering evidence that believers will be partakers of salvation, which salvation results in joy (1 Pet 1:6–7). That is, in 1 Pet 1:6 the ἐν ᾧ is best taken as neuter, referring to the whole of what preceded. God is not the subject of the relative clause because that reference is too distant in the text. The "last time" is not the subject because in the NT ἀγαλλιᾶσθε always takes God's help as the subject[31] and the last times provide merely a time frame for God's help to be realized. The joy is then on account of the imperishable salvation ready to be revealed. The suffering is not a cause for joy. Selwyn understands the ἐν ᾧ with "become distressed" (λυπηθέντες) in a proleptic manner as in 1 Pet 2:12; 3:16 and 4:4.[32] The resultant view is that believers rejoice because their sufferings test them, refining them after the pattern of Jas 1:2. However, there is no contextual support for this view in Peter. Instead, suffering causes "sorrow" (λυπεω) in the context (1 Pet 1:6), which is the opposite of joy. Additionally, an appeal to James to develop a pattern is unreasonable because this word for "joy" (ἀγαλλιᾶσθε) is not even in James. There is a better pattern from Jesus' words to the effect that a particular

29. Ign. *Phld.* 4; Clement of Alexandria, *Strom.* 7.11.

30. Ign. *Tarsians* 3; *Apoc. Pet.* 14.4–6; *Martyrdom Isa.* 4.3; Tertullian, *Scap.* 15; *Apol.* 5; *Praescr.* 36; *Muratorium Canon*, line 37; Lactantius, *Mort.* 2; Eusebius, *Theoph.* 5.31; *Dem. ev.* 3.5.65; *Hist. eccl.* 2.25.5; 3.1.2; *Acts of Pet.* 9.37.8–38.9; Bauckham, "Martyrdom of Peter," 539–95.

31. For example, Peter quotes David as rejoicing because God has helped him (Acts 2:26); Bultmann, "ἀγαλλιαομαι," TDNT 1:20.

32. Selwyn, *1 Peter*, 127; H. Conzelman, "χαιρω," TDNT 9:368; contra deVilliers, "Joy in Suffering in 1 Peter," 71–72.

kind of suffering demonstrates the partaker to be a future partaker or salvation, namely, "Blessed are you when men cast insults at you, and persecute you, and say all kinds of evil against you falsely, on account of me. Rejoice and be glad, for your reward in heaven is great, for so they persecuted the prophets who were before you" (Matt 5:11–12). So, the believer's joy is present amid the suffering because the joy is based on the divine aid of salvation that will come (1 Pet 1:6). Furthermore, the joy is identified with the present causal participle "obtaining" (κομιζόμενοι) in 1 Pet 1:9 which provides the expectation of salvation as the reason for the believer's joy (1 Pet 1:8). This pattern is further developed in 1 Pet 4:13, to the degree that a believer shares in the sufferings of Christ they are to continue to rejoice because these rejoicings shall be realized at the revelation of Christ's glory. Peter was consistent with this practice in his life. He did not rejoice because he suffered but because his suffering demonstrated him as worthy (Acts 5:41). This worthiness demonstrated that Peter and the apostles will be partakers of salvation. Likewise, the person who suffers for the name of Christ should consider himself blessed because it evidences that the Spirit associated with glory rests upon him (1 Pet 4:14). In such a condition there is no need for shame (1 Pet 4:16). Such a condition merely evidences that the sufferer is one of the righteous that God is saving (1 Pet 4:1, 17–18). For these believers, the suffering is only temporary and then God himself will perfect, confirm, strengthen, and establish them in their salvation (1 Pet 5:10).

Judaism permitted such suffering to atone for personal[33] and corporate sins[34] but there is no evidence that Peter expressed such a view in his mimetic atonement after Jesus' pattern (1 Pet 2:21–23; Mark 10:43–45). The Christian's priestly sacrifices included suffering for doing good that God is pleased with (1 Pet 2:5, 12, 18–23; 3:1, 14; 4:15–19), none of this is developed by Peter to have Jewish atonement value. While Christians that suffer should follow Jesus' pattern of silence, nonretaliation and prayer, Peter develops that Jesus' atonement provides an additional atonement accomplishment that Christian suffering does not accomplish (1 Pet 2:24–25).[35]

---

33. *Sipre Deut.* 32.5.2, 5; *b. Ber.* 5ab; 17a; *b. 'Erub.* 41b; *Gen. Rab.* 96.5; *Pesiq Rab.* 22.5; Bonsirven, *Palestinian Judaism*, 114–16; Keener, *1 Peter*, 39.

34. 1QS 8.3–4; *Sipre Deut.* 311.1.1; *b. Ta'an.* 8a; *y. Sanh.* 11.5.4; *Gen. Rab.* 96.5; *Pesiq Rab Kah.* 24.9; 26.11; Sup. 2.7; Bonsirven, *Palestinian Judaism*, 111; Keener, *1 Peter*, 39.

35. Developed in chapter on Christ's atonement and redemption.

The Christian sufferer should prayerfully appeal to God for protection. The word "entrust" (παρατιθέσθωσαν) has the sense of entrusting someone to the care and protection of another.³⁶ That is, the one who suffers in the Christian manner, righteously following God's declared will, should entrust himself and his protection to God, who is faithful (1 Pet 4:19). However, the one who does evil should not expect his petitions to be answered by God (1 Pet 3:7, 12). Additionally, the requests should be asked of God from a sober mindset because petitioning him is serious business (1 Pet 4:7). Furthermore, such prayerful appeals to God should include all the believer's concerns and anxieties (1 Pet 5:7). The aorist tense of "casting" (ἐπιρίψαντες) signifies that the believer should give God all his concerns, not trying to take them back. That which can motivate such trust in God is the recognition that God cares for his believers. In fact, he has declared that his eyes are on the righteous and his ears are attentive to their prayer (1 Pet 3:12). The prayer of the righteous includes requests for continuation in a good peaceful life (1 Pet 3:10–12). The faithfulness of God in such prayers is something Peter has counted on repeatedly in his life (Acts 4:25–31; 12:5–17). However, this is no guarantee that God will prevent martyrdom. If this cost is required, and in some instances, it was, then it is appropriate to petition God for one's ultimate well-being and vindication (1 Pet 2:23; 4:6).

The pattern for Christian suffering appropriates several factors. Since Christian suffering was common, the believer should not be surprised when it comes. However, he should not suffer for evil. Instead, he should suffer for righteousness after Christ's example. Such Christian suffering should be accompanied by joy concerning the recognition that it evidences one's salvation, and petition concerning one's protection and ultimate well-being.

---

36. BAG, "παρατίθημι," 628.

13

Standing Against Satan and Exorcizing Demons

AN ALTERNATIVE TO THE vicarious atonement sacrificial death of Jesus and mimetic atonement following Jesus in the narrow way unto kingdom, is that of a victorious redemption that facilitates a new exodus for humanity from bondage under: Satan, idolatry, impurity, and lawlessness.[1] This redemption approach presents Yahweh as a warrior to redeem Israel from an enemy, which threatens them so that Israel might enter kingdom (Isa 49:23; 52:2).[2] Eschatological salvation banishes illness through kingdom healing (Isa 35:3-6; 53:5; 61:1-2).[3] Similarly, the military image describes a messianic figure, such as Son of Man, who engages ungodly powers and redeems his people from them.[4] Jesus utilizes a bit of military imagery in casting out demons that oppressed them, especially regarding "legions" of angels or demons (Mark 5:9, 15;

---

1. Altereatio, *Simonis et Theoophili* 6.24; Tertullian, *Carn. Chr.* 17; Irenaeus, *Haer.* 3.18.6; 3.21.1; 3.23.1; 4.33.4; 5.17.2; 5.21.3; Epiderxis 37; Cyril of Jerusalem, *Cat.* 13.1; Gregory of Nazianzus, *Or.* 30.20; Hilary, *C. Ar.* 1.35; Augustine, *Trin.* 13.11-15, 18; Luther, *Luther's Works*, 22:24; 26:267; 52:156; Aulén, *Christus Victor*, 48; Gutiérrez, *Theology of Liberation*; Martyn, *Theological Issues in the Letters of Paul*, 298-99, 142-44; Ruether, *Introducing Redemption in Christian Feminism*.

2. Wis 5.16-23; Sir 35.22-36.17; 1QM 12.10-14; 19.2-8; *As. Mos.* 10.

3. *Jub.* 23.29-30; *T. Zeb.* 9.8; 2 Bar 73.2; 4 Ezra 13.50.

4. Kennard, *Petrine Studies*, chapter on "A Man Called Peter," and in *Petrine Theology*, "Exodus Following Jesus to Kingdom Virtues"; *Pss. Sol.* 17.23-39; 2 Bar 39-42, 72-74; *1 En.* 37-71; 4 Ezra 12.31-34; 13; Philo, *Praem.* 16 (91-97); 1QSb 5.27; 1QSa 2.11-13; 4QpIsaa.

Matt 26:53; Luke 8:30; Acts 10:38)[5] and that the demons have a ruler, Satan, who must be defeated (Mark 3:22, 27; Matt 9:34; 12:24, 29; Luke 11:15, 22; 1 Pet 5:8). Irenaeus claimed that the gospel is God's message of redemption unto victory defeating the devil and all his henchmen.[6] This redemption includes a new exodus in which the people are set free and forgiven by God.[7] Such redemption sets up a two ways salvation model in the same manner as the exodus initiated the narrow way unto the Promised Land (Exod 12–19; 2 Pet 1:3–11; Heb 3–4).[8] In the wake of Christ's resurrection, Christ announced judgment upon spirits now in prison, showing the exodus way was secure for believers who purpose in their baptism to maintain a renewed conscience unto kingdom resurrection (1 Pet 3:18–21). Beyond Peter, Paul utilized metaphors from Roman victorious redemption celebration "leading captive a host of captives" providing the church with gifts from Christ's spoils of victory (Eph 4:8–13; 2 Cor 2:14–17).[9]

Many angels are aligned with Christ as God's messengers (Acts 5:19–20, 23; 10:3–7, 30–33; 12:6–19). These angels are similar in nature to resurrected humans, at times appearing with human form and shining garments (Mark 12:25; Acts 10:3–7, 30–33). These angels join the prophets in being concerned about how the salvation program works out, watching it intensely (1 Pet 1:12). Some of these angels are more powerful than humans and yet they submit to Christ's authority (2 Pet 2:10–11). After Christ survived Satan's temptations, angels ministered to Christ (Mark 1:13). In one instance, an angel woke Peter up while he was chained between two guards; with the chains falling off, the angel led him out through locked cell and jail, into the street before the angel vanished (Acts 12:6–19). Peter followed this rescuing angel, defeating the Roman attempt to kill Peter. Ultimately Christ will return as the Son of Man and an army of angels will come with him, as he conquers the opposition and gathers those who are his into kingdom (Mark 8:38; 13:27, 32).

---

5. *T. Sol.* 11; Jesus' story repeated by *Epistula Apostolora* 5 in *N.T. Apocrypha* 1.253; later Jesus recounts that he has twelve legions of angels available to defend himself (Matt 26:53).

6. Irenaeus, *Haer.* 5.26.1; frag. 50.

7. Irenaeus, *Haer.* 3.23.1; 5.17.2.

8. Irenaeus, *Haer.* 3.18.6.

9. Kennard, *Gospel*, 188–89.

SATAN

"Satan" (Σατανᾶς) is a transliteration of Hebrew, *hasatan*, "the adversary" or "the enemy of God." Satan is a personal spirit being leading opposition against Christ in the spirit realm and effecting people to take up satanic characteristics, such as deception and destruction (Acts 5:3; Mark 3:23, 26). Satan tempted Jesus as he began his ministry and steals the word of the kingdom from the lives of the unresponsive (Mark 1:13; 4:15). Another name, "the devil" (Διάβολος), reflects his characteristic as the "liar" and "slanderer" to destroy people, especially prompting slander reviling the believing community (1 Pet 2:12; 3:9, 16; 4:14; 5:8). Using these techniques, the slanderer operates as in the arena with Satan as a roaring lion seeking believers to devour and destroy (1 Pet 5:8).[10] Satan is described as the Christian's "opponent" (ἀντίδικος, 1 Pet 5:8). It is important as a believer in Christ to not contribute in any way toward this deception and slander because the devil is the opponent to God and the Holy Spirit (1 Pet 5:5–8; Acts 5:3; 10:38). He afflicts people as ruler of demons, but this will be developed under demonism (Acts 10:38). Jewish religious leaders accuse Jesus of being in league Satan through another title, namely "Beelzebul" or "lord of the flies" or "the ruler of demons" (Βεελζεβούλ).[11] This discussion appears in the next section since it provides Jesus' clarification concerning his exorcism ministry (Mark 3:20–30; Matt 12:22–45; Luke 11:14–32). Satan prompts lies and Peter repeatedly fell prey to these deceptions (Matt 16:22; Luke 22:31). Others did as well (Acts 5:3; 10:38). Satan can only be resisted by humbly drawing on the strength that God supplies (1 Pet 5:8; Acts 10:38).

---

10. Lions were regularly utilized at the Roman games, and were known for tearing bodies apart and feasting on them (Aulus Gellius, *Noct. att.* 5.14; Martial, *Ep.* 8.55; *Pol.* 12.2; Dio Cassius, 60.13.4; Paschke, "Roman *ad bestias* Execution," 489–500; Horrell et al., "Visuality, Vivid Description," 697–716.

11. Similar titles as "ruler of demons" (1QM 17.5–6; *Jub.* 10.8; 48.15; *T. Dan.* 5.6; *T. Sol.* 2.8–3.6; 6.1–11; John 14:30; Eph 2:2; *b. Pesah* 110a). Which means that Satan has a kingdom (4Q286 10.ii.1–13; 4QAmram frag. 2; *T. Dan.* 6.1–4). The title Beelzebul roots in the Canaanite god Baal, perhaps meaning "exalted one," but the English comes from Latin referring to Baal-Zebub, the Philistine god of Ekron in a derisive term "lord of the flies" (1 Kgs 1:2–3, 6, 16; Bock, *Luke*, 2:1074). At this point, Hollenbach concludes, with *b. Sanh* 107b, that Jesus' exorcisms prompt the authorities to consider him dangerous and thus lead to his execution ("Jesus, Demoniacs, and Public Authorities," 567–88), however this is extreme since Jesus' death does not occur for some time and this exorcism is not included among the listed charges brought by the false witnesses.

DEMONS

The Markan emphasis of this theme contains Jesus repeatedly casting out demons[12] (Mark 1:25–28, 39; 3:11; 5:1–20; 9:25–26) and instructing the disciples how they can do the same (Mark 1:25–27; 3:22–30; longer detailed description of 5:1–20 shows process; 6:7, 13; 9:17–29). Jesus exorcises these demons by his own authority without tools of incantation.[13] Repeatedly, in these power encounters Jesus' authority is emphasized! Thus, Jesus' exorcisms do not have a pejorative quality.[14] That is, Judaism knew that demonic power would be crushed by the messianic age and Jesus' exorcism of demons fit within the beginning of the eschatological expulsion of cosmic powers.[15] Mark especially summarizes Jesus' ministry to be that of preaching the kingdom and casting out demons in fulfillment of these Jewish expectations (Mark 1:39; 3:14–15; 6:7, 12–13). Thus, the demons and sick call out to Jesus as the "Messianic Son of David" (Mark 3:11; 5:7; Matt 8:29; Luke 4:41; 8:28).[16] Jesus silences their declarations (Mark 1:34), maybe because they confuse the issue, since he is not challenging Rome and he prefers his works to testify of him (Luke 7:18–23). All the healings attract crowds which eventually force Jesus to minister further and further away from cities, out in the wilderness. Perhaps he also urges silence because he wished that the clear voice of his deeds would not be prematurely excluded to the fringes of Judaism. While he

---

12. "Demons" (Mark 5:12; Ps 91:6; *1 En.* 19.1) are "unclean spirits" (Zech 13:2; *Jub.* 10.5; 11Q5 19.15; 4Q444 1.4, 8; 4Q511 1.6; *T. Benj.* 5.2; Matt 5:13; Luke 7:21), and occasionally some verses combine these terms as referring to the same beings (Mark 5:12–13; Luke 4:33).

13. The *Babylonian Talmud* preserves a tradition that probably associated with Jesus of Nazareth, accusing him of sorcery, or using paraphernalia to perform healings (*b. Sanh.* 43a; 67b). Such focus on his authority raised suspicions from later rabbis about Jesus' orthodoxy in his use of miracle to support his authority (*b. B. Mes.* 59b). Smith extends the Babylonian Talmud to view Jesus as a magician (*Jesus the Magician*). However, Jesus does not use the tools of a magician in the Bible, such as incantation, he does his works of power by his own authority (Aune, "Magic in Early Christianity," 1507–57; Segal, "Hellenistic Magic," 349–75). The NT is aware of the term "magician" (Acts 8:11; 13:6, 8; 19:19) but never applies it to Jesus. The term "magician" is first applied to Jesus by Justin Martyr (*1 Apol.* 30.1; *Dial.* 69.7).

14. Arnobius, *Adv. Gent.* 1.43.

15. *1 En.* 10.4–5; 15–16; 55.4; *Jub.* 10.8–9; Philo, *Plant.* 61; *T. Levi* 18.12; *T. Zeb.* 9.8; *T. Moses* 10.1; *Apoc. Ab.* 14.5; *Tg Ps-J Leb* 16.72; Moscicke overplays the scapegoat parallel because there is no evidence of scapegoats being killed before the *Mishnah* ("Gerasene Exorcism," 363–83).

16. Also some manuscripts of Mark 1:34.

was teaching in the synagogue of Capernaum on the Sabbath the people were amazed at the authority of his teaching, beyond the scribes with which they were familiar (Mark 1:23-28; Luke 4:31-36).[17] A man with an unclean spirit or demon blurted out, "What do we have to do with you, Jesus of Nazareth? Have you come to destroy us? I know who you are-the Holy One of God!"[18] Jesus rebuked him, saying, "Be quiet, and come out of him!" The demon threw him down in their midst and cried out with a loud voice but came out of him. Everyone was amazed at the authority of Jesus' new teaching, having power over demons.

Arriving at the East side of the Sea of Galilee in the Gadarenes[19] region, two "demonized" (δαιμονιζόμενοι) men came out of the tombs to confront Jesus as the Son of the Most High God, and he casts the demons out of them (Mark 5:1-20 more developed than either Matt 8:28-34 or Luke 8:26-39).[20] These extremely strong violent men did not challenge Jesus directly for they asked if they were to be tormented before their time. At the same time, Jesus "had been commanding" (Mark 5:8, iterative imperfect[21] ἔλεγεν, "had been saying," indicates repeated statements in contrast to other verbs in the context) the demons to "come out" of them (the aorist ἔξελθε, "come out," treats the rescue exorcism command as a whole), but the demons were resistant (implied by the imperfect). Instead, the military legion[22] of demons begged not to be sent to the abyss before their time (alluded to in 2 Pet 2:4)[23] but to be sent into a herd of swine,[24] perhaps to defeat Jesus' ministry in the region. With Jesus'

17. Multiple attestation supports the authenticity of this miracle.

18. Perhaps this statement affirms Jesus as a prophet for it is a similar statement to that of the demons in the traditional Elijah context (3 Kgdms. 17.18 LXX; description of Elisha 4 Kgdms. 4.9 LXX; Num 16:3-5; Ps 105:16 LXX; Sir 45.6; CD 6.1; Rev 22:6; Domeris, "Office of Holy One," 35-38).

19. "Gerasenes"(Mark 5:1) is a larger and more powerful city about thirty miles from the lake than "Gadarenes" (Matt 8:28) which is only six miles from the lake but smaller, so it is accurate to describe the miracle in both regions.

20. Multiple attestation supports the authenticity of this miracle.

21. Wallace, *Greek Grammar*, 546-47. This indicates that demons might not leave with only one command under Jesus' authority, which also fits with the author's experience repeatedly having to command demons to leave in exorcism.

22. A legion (a Roman company of four to six hundred men) describes military numbers of demons here and in *T. Sol.* 11; this Mark 5 account is repeated in *Epistula Apostolorar* 5 in *N.T. Apocrypha* 1.253.

23. Judaism saw the deep as the judgment depository of demons (*Jub.* 5.6-7; *1 En.* 10.4-6; 18.11-16; Jude 6).

24. For Jews, pig keeping is prohibited (*m. Qam.* 7.7; 82b) and eating pork also (Lev

permission they ran the swine down into the sea drowning them. The herdsmen told the city, and many came out to find the previously demonized men sitting, clothed, and in their right mind, healed and listening to Jesus. The city folk implored Jesus to leave their region, perhaps because it had already cost them dearly. However, the healed were sent by Jesus to testify to their friends, so they announced it throughout the whole Decapolis region.[25]

In Capernaum a "demonized" (δαιμονιζόμενον) man who could not speak or maybe even hear[26] was brought to Jesus and Jesus healed him (Matt 9:32–34; perhaps Mark 3:22 or 2:12). The multitudes marveled saying, "Nothing like this was ever seen in Israel." The opposition to Jesus did not discount the healings, they denied the source as divine. That is, the Pharisees tried to shame Jesus by claiming he was casting out the demons by the ruler of demons (Mark 3:22–30; Matt 9:34; 12:24; Luke 11:15; John 7:20; 8:48, 52; 10:20).[27] A "demonized" (δαιμονιζόμενος) man who was blind and dumb was brought to Jesus and Jesus healed him, so that the man spoke and saw (Matt 12:22; Luke 11:14).[28] The entire multitude was astonished and began publicly wondering if Jesus was the Davidic messianic king. The Pharisees wished to squash considering Jesus as messiah and instead shamed Jesus by claiming, "This man casts out demons only by Beelzebul the ruler of demons" (Mark 3:22).[29]

Jesus clarified that his exorcisms were by the power of God and not that of Satan. Jesus knew what they were thinking so he countered their reasoning, showing a commitment like that of the religious leaders will end up damning these religious leaders (Mark 3:20–30; Matt 12:22–45; Luke 11:14–32).[30] Jesus' argument goes as follows: 1) The

---

11:7; Deut 14:8), but the decapolis region housed the Roman tenth legion, with a pig mascot (on coins in Jerusalem Rockefeller Museum).

25. The population of the region was mixed Jew and gentiles (Josephus, *War* 3.51–58).

26. κωφός can mean deaf (as in Matt 11:5) or dumb (as in Matt 12:22) or both.

27. Justin, *Dial.* 69; *b. Sanh.* 43a.

28. Multiple attestation supports the authenticity of this miracle.

29. Satan has a kingdom (4Q286 10.ii.1–13; 4QAmram frag. 2; *T. Dan.* 6.1–4). The title "Beelzebul" derived from the Canaanite god Baal, perhaps meaning "exalted one," but the English comes from Latin referring to Baal-Zebub, the Philistine god of Ekron in a derisive term "lord of the flies" (1 Kgs 1:2–3, 6, 16; Bock, *Luke*, 2:1074). At this point, Hollenbach concludes, with *b. Sanh* 107b, that Jesus' exorcisms prompt the authorities to consider him dangerous and thus lead to his execution ("Jesus, Demoniacs, and Public Authorities," *JAAR* 49(1981) 567–88).

30. Multiple attestation supports the authenticity of this discussion.

religious leader's accusation makes no sense, for any kingdom divided against itself will be destroyed. So, if Satan is casting out Satan then he is divided against himself and his kingdom will be defeated. 2) Jewish exorcisms were common enough and they did so by the power of God (Mark 9:38; Luke 9:49; Acts 19:13–16).[31] So the religious leaders' Jewish disciples[32] who exorcize demons will judge the Pharisees for their unbelief. 3) God's kingdom has come because Jesus victoriously casts out demons by the Spirit[33] of God. Graham Twelftree champions the conclusion "that Jesus saw his miracles-and hence at least a large part of his mission-as primarily a battle with the demonic and, concomitantly, an expression of the realization of the kingdom of God in the face of the defeat of Satan."[34] 4) The only way to plunder a strong man's property (like releasing the demonized) is to first bind the strong man, which means that Satan is bound from Jesus' exorcisms (which is the contextual emphasis here, but grammatically it could also mean that the demons are bound (thus rabbinically damned), releasing the demonized.[35] This is similar to early Judaism's eschatological priest, who binds Beliar, so that the priest's eschatological children will tread upon evil spirits, preparing the eschatological judgment to come upon the bound.[36] 5) In the midst of such conflict, there is no middle ground; Jesus clarifies, "He who is not with me is against me; and he who does not gather with me scatters." Either people join Jesus in gathering into kingdom or they will lose the harvest by scattering Israel into dispersion.[37] 6) To attribute the Spirit's empowerment in such healings to Satan is to blaspheme[38] the Spirit, and

---

31. 4Q242 frags. 1–3.2–5; Josephus, *Ant.* 8.2.5; *Text* 20.11–12; 69.6–7; *Pr. Jos.* 9–12; *T. Sol.* 2.8–3.6; 6.1–9; 18.15–16; *b. Git* 68a; *Num. Rab.* 16.24; *b. Ber.* 34b; Justin. *1 Apol.* 54–58; Augustine, *City of God* 10.16; 22.10; Meier, *A Marginal Jew*, 2:581–88 for a discussion of the healings by Honi the Circle drawer and Hanina ben Dosa.

32. "Sons" as disciples (Matt 22:13–14; 23:9–13).

33. Luke 11:20 has "finger of God."

34. Twelftree, *The Miracle Worker*, 263.

35. As in Tob 8.3 and *Jub.* 10.7–9.

36. *T. Levi* 18.12; *1 En.* 10.4–6; Rev 20:1–3; Ellis, *Luke*, 167.

37. Like *Pss. Sol.* 17.18.

38. Early Judaism maintained that magicians performed their acts through the help of spirit agents (*1 En.* 65.6; *L.A.B.* 34.2–3; *Ascen. Isa.* 2.5; *Sib. Or.* 1.96). Furthermore, blaspheming in the first century appears to be broader than the *Mishnah*'s narrow definition that requires the name of God to be used (*m. Sanh.* 7.5), and other texts speak of three ways to blaspheme: 1) speaking ill of Torah (*Sipre 112 on Num.* 15:30 [=Neusner, *Sifre to Numbers*, 2.168—70]), 2) engaging in idolatry (*Sipre 112 on Num.* 15:31 [=Neusner *Sifre to Numbers*, 2.170]), or 3) bringing shame on Yahweh's name (*b.*

such a statement as this betrays a damnable alliance against God, since such a statement will not be forgiven in this age, or the eschatological age to come (Matt 12:31–32).[39] This fits with the Jewish sense that blaspheming would damn. However, it shows the generosity of the Son of Man[40] in his incarnation that he will forgive those who blaspheme against him, perhaps because of his embodiment confuses many about his deity, or he is modeling how we should be forgiving humans, or he is just generous. 7) Their judging words demonstrate that the Jewish religious leaders are evil. Metaphorically, fruit shows what kind of tree it is, either good or evil. The heart and treasure of a person supplies them with what they say. Considering this, the Jewish religious leaders' speech shows that they are shamed as an evil brood of vipers. Matthew 12 emphasizes five times that every careless word brings such a hypocritical judge into eschatological condemnation, so the religious leaders are strongly condemned.

The scribes and Pharisees wished to show that they were not culpable by demanding a sign from Jesus. However, Jesus had been providing abundant miraculous healings to meet needs, not to be judged by unbelieving critics.

Jesus responded to them, showing their eschatological culpability remained because the kingdom of God is present. This means that those who are truly blessed are those who hear this word of God and observe it (Mark 4:20; Luke 11:28). In contrast, the others who see the signs remain culpable for the signs done in their midst, even if they hypocritically seek more signs, only to discount them (Mark 8:11–21; Matt 16:1–12).

> An evil and adulterous generation craves for a sign; and yet no sign shall be given to it but the sign of Jonah the prophet; for just as Jonah was three days and three nights in the belly of the sea monster, so shall the Son of Man be three days and three nights in the heart of the earth. The men of Nineveh shall stand up with this generation at the judgment and shall condemn it because they repented at the preaching of Jonah; and behold something greater than Jonah is here. The Queen of the South shall rise with this generation at the judgment and shall condemn it, because she came from the ends of the earth to hear the wisdom of

---

Pesaḥ. 93b); Bock, *Blasphemy and Exaltation in Judaism*.

39. Jub. 15:34; 1QS 7.15–17, 22–27; P. Ḥag. 2.1.9; Gos. Thom. 44.

40. Mark 3:28–29 has the plural "sons of men" as the potentially blaspheming and damned rather than the ambiguous title of Jesus like Matthew and Luke have. *Gos. Thom.* 44 describes that they would be forgiven for blaspheming Father and Son but not the Spirit; blasphemy of Spirit damns.

Solomon; and behold, something greater than Solomon is here. (Matt 12:38–42; cf. Mark 8:11–12).

That which is greater than Jonah and Solomon is Jesus and the kingdom of God. In early Judaism, exorcism was viewed as casting Satan or demons out of their house.[41] Using this exorcism metaphor, the religious leader's rejection of kingdom means they run the risk of descending into greater demonization and eschatological judgment as evil. For Jesus describes the way demons work, bringing greater culpability upon this evil generation.

> Now when the unclean spirit goes out of a man, it passes through waterless places,[42] seeking rest, and does not find it. Then he says, 'I will return to my house from which I came'; and when it comes, it finds it unoccupied, swept, and put in order. Then it goes and takes along with it seven other spirits more wicked than itself, and they go in and live there; and the last state of the man becomes worse than the first. This is the way it will be with this evil generation (Matt 12:43–45; cf. Luke 11:23–26; exampling 2 Pet 2:20).

This instance of Jesus casting demons out and religious opposition becomes parabolic for the nations' condition at this time: precarious to being judged. It is not enough that king Jesus drive the demons out with his expression of kingdom, but if the people of this generation do not embrace his message and fill their lives with God, then the demons will return, and they will be even more demonized and judged by God as evil.[43]

Withdrawing from the threat of Jewish leaders, Jesus was in the region of Tyre when he healed the daughter of a Canaanite woman (Mark 7:24–30; Matt 15:21–28).[44] This Syrophoenician woman persistently

41. B. Giṭ. 52a; b. Ḥul. 105b.

42. Early Judaism saw the desert as a haunt of demons (Tob 8.3; 2 Bar 10.8; T. Sol. 5.11–12).

43. Irenaeus, Haer. 1.16.3 declares that Israel did not heed this warning and was judged by God.

44. Meier (Marginal Jew, 2:714–26) defends historicity because of multiple attestations, discontinuity, and embarrassment. However, he concludes that the healing of the Canaanite woman's daughter of demons, the Capernaum centurion's son, and the son of the governmental official in Cana are all the same miracle, mostly on the assumption that Jesus did not talk with gentiles. This is a faulty assumption, and each Gospel contributes to the theme of gentile inclusion into kingdom. I view them as three separate miracles based on their unique features: different requester's genders and station, requested in different places, different infirmities, healed in different places, different genders, healed, and different things said to each by Christ. Additionally, Matthew has

called after Jesus saying, "Have mercy on me, O Lord, Son of David; my daughter is cruelly demonized" (δαιμονίζεται). Jesus did not answer her prompting the disciples to wish to send her away. Jesus replied[45] that He was sent only to the lost sheep of the house of Israel. However, she fell at his feet and kept asking him to send the unclean spirit away. Jesus responded, "Let the children be satisfied first, for it is not good to take the children's bread and throw it to the small pet dogs" (κυναρίοις).[46] She accepts her secondary status and replied, "Yes, Lord, but even the small house dogs (κυνάρια) feed on the children's crumbs which fall from the master's table." Jesus answered her, "Your faith is great; be it done for you as you wish." Her daughter was healed at once and the demon departed. Returning home, she found her daughter healed on her bed. Such long-distance miracles were especially counted as miraculous.[47]

Coming down from the mountaintop experience of the transfiguration, Jesus is confronted with a father's only[48] son, who because of demons was dumb, deaf, and epileptically[49] suicidal, throwing him into fire or water (Mark 9:14–29; Matt 17:14–20; Luke 9:38–42).[50] The dad was distraught because he had brought his son to Jesus' disciples but they were unable to heal him even though they had cast many demons out before (Mark 3:15; 6:7, 13; Matt 10:1, 8; Luke 9:1–2). Jesus berated the disciples and the people for their unbelief, since he wouldn't be with them for long. In the wake of his disciples' failure reflecting upon him, Jesus encouraged the father saying, "All things are possible to him who believes" (Mark 9:23–24). The father cried out, "I do believe; help me in my unbelief." Seeing that a crowd was running together to him and wanting this miracle done in private, Jesus rebuked the deaf and dumb demon,

---

all three as different miracles and Mark and Luke each have two of these miracles. Such multiple attestation and multiple accounts argue for these separate miracles.

45. Jesus did not consider it beneath him to talk with a woman, unlike the Jewish tradition (*m. 'Abot* 1.5).

46. Both Jesus and the woman refer to κυνάρια, which is the diminutive word for pet dog. Jesus opens the door with a more familiar image (pet dog), testing her with the fact that she is not a Jew.

47. Bultmann, *History of the Synoptic Tradition*, 225; *b. Ber.* 34b; Lucian, *Philops.* 16; Diogenes Laertius 8.67.

48. Luke normally mentions this "only" (μονογενής) child detail (Luke 7:12; 8:42; 9:38).

49. Literally in Matthew "moonstruck" or "lunatic" (σεληνιάζεται; Matt 17:15), however Luke describes convulsive seizures with foaming at the mouth that looks like epilepsy (Luke 9:39).

50. Multiple attestation and embarrassment confirm the authenticity of this miracle.

making it hear by his authority, and immediately the boy was cured. The boy was temporarily placid, like a corpse, which is common in such reports of effective exorcisms.[51] However, the boy could hear and speak and was free from the demonization. Then the disciples asked, "Why could we not cast it out?" Jesus responded in Mark 9:29 that this kind of demon only comes out by prayer, that is, the disciples will not be effective in this kind of exorcism unless they pray, whereas in Matt 17:20, perhaps getting to the root cause of why they didn't pray, Jesus answered the disciples, "Because of the littleness of your faith; for truly I say to you, if you have faith as a mustard seed, you shall say to this mountain, 'Move from here to there,' and it shall move; and nothing shall be impossible to you."

Jesus sends the twelve and the seventy out to cast out demons as an expression of their kingdom ministry (Matt 10:8; Luke 10:17–20).[52] The disciples were effective in such an exorcism to such an extent that it was one of the most memorable expressions of their kingdom ministry (Luke 10:17–20). Jesus' authority continued to cast out demons and to judge those aligned with demons through the ministry of the disciples (Acts 5:16; 8:7, 20–24; 10:38; 13:8–11; 16:16–19; 19:12). In fact, Jesus' authority to cast out demons was so effective in exorcism of demons that some Jews who were not Jesus' disciples cast out demons in Jesus' name (Mark 9:38–40; Luke 9:49–50; Acts 19:13–20). When the disciples found out they tried to hinder them, but Jesus responded in one instance, "Do not hinder him, for there is no one who shall perform a miracle in my name, and be able soon afterward to speak evil of me, for he who is not against us is for us" (Mark 9:39–40).[53] However, when the demons found out that these exorcists were not disciples of Jesus, the demons did not always comply. Exorcism in Jesus' name also involves a relationship with Jesus, for it is not magic; it is an expression of emerging kingdom.

DESCENT INTO HELL

Peter's concept of descent into hell conveys an element of Jesus' victory over the forces of death. The apostolic fathers' tradition emerging in the

---

51. Josephus, *Ant.* 8.49; Philstratus, *Life* 4.20; Bonner, "Violence of Departing Demons," 334–36.

52. Multiple attestation supports the authenticity of this miracle; also the Byzantine text of Mark 16:17.

53. This proverbial statement is the reverse of the one Jesus says when accused of casting out demons by the power of Satan (Matt 12:30; Luke 11:23).

Apostles Creed raised two points about Jesus' descent into hell: 1) Jesus experienced the fullest extent of death (Acts 2:24; Rom 10:7; Rev 1:18) and 2) Christ brought a evangelistic victory for some of those dead when he preached to them in hell (claiming the following for support: 1 Pet 3:18; 4:6; Eph 4:8–9; Rev 1:18).[54] Both aspects are within the patristic teaching but some of the Fathers emphasize the bringing of salvation victory more. Certain Reformation dogmaticians pointed out that the postdeath evangelism of Jesus was not the lowest expression of death and hell, thus separating this aspect as victory from death, hell, and Satan.[55]

This issue of proclamation in 1 Pet 3:19 hinges upon a series of issues: identification of the spirits, where, who, when, how, and what was said. The options proposed as to who these spirits are include: men (Noah's contemporaries, OT believers, or all men), angels (elect, fallen, particular fallen angels involved in the climactic sin prior to the flood), and the offspring of men and angels. The options as to where the proclamation took place include the earth, the realm of the dead, and a special prison for some angels. Views as to who, when, and how this proclamation took place combine in the following more common configurations: the Spirit of Christ preached through Noah in the days before the flood, the pre-existent Christ preached in the time of Noah, Christ proclaimed the message in the depth of his death, Christ proclaimed the message after his resurrection, Christ proclaimed the message after his ascension, and Enoch went to proclaim to the spirits.[56] Views of the content of the proclaimed message include: an offer of salvation, an announcement of good tidings to those already saved, or an announcement of the certainty of

---

54. I understand the sense of the *Apostles Creed* "descended into hell" as mentioned by the patristics to be a full experience of death, but some follow an interpretation of 1 Pet 3:19 and 4:6, placing the emphasis on claiming that Christ proclaimed the gospel to some dead before he rose from the dead (*Gos. Pet.* 41–42; *Ep. Apost.* 27 [38]; Justin, *Dial.* 72.4; *Herm. Sim.* 9.16.5–7; *Sib. Or.* 8.310–12; Ign. *Magn.* 9.2; Irenaeus, *Haer.* 3.20.4; 4.22.1; 4.27.2; 4.33.1; 5.31.1; *Epid.* 78; *Dial.* 72.4; Hippolytus, *Ben. Is. Jac.* 7; Clement of Alexandria, *Strom.* 2.9.44.1–2; 6.6.445–52; Origen, *Cels.* 2.43; *Matt. serm.* 132); *Ascen. Isa.* 9.16–18; *Odes Sol.* 42.11–20.

55. Quenstedt, *Theologia didactio-polemica Polemica*, 3.373; Hollaz, *Acromaticum Universam Theologiam*, 778.

56. This last option was proposed by Bowyer in 1763 but has gained some support based on *1 Enoch* and the emending of the Petrine text (Harris, "Further Note," 346–49; Goodspeed, "Enoch in 1 Peter 3:19," 91). This view should be rejected for the following reasons: 1) there is no Petrine textual evidence for the view, 2) the text is not incomprehensible as it stands, which is required if one proposes a conjectural emendation, and 3) the intelligibility of the text is not improved by the addition.

condemnation. Each view takes one[57] item from each of the above categories. For example, the "descent into hell" view of the *Apostles' Creed* was proposed by Clement of Alexandria and Origen envisioning the crucified Christ before his resurrection offering salvation to Noah's contemporaries in the realm of the dead.[58] Perhaps the most comprehensive works analyzing this issue are William Joseph Dalton's *Christ's Proclamation to the Spirits* and Chad Pierce's *Spirits and the Proclamation of Christ*.[59]

In 1 Pet 3:18–20, Christ died in the realm of the flesh (earthly human life visible through one's body).[60] Likewise, in 1 Pet 4:6 martyred believers are described also as dying in the realm of the flesh, though vindicated by God in the realm of the spirit (that is, resurrected).[61] Following Christ's death, "he was made alive" (ζῳοποιηθείς) identifying that the description which follows is describing the resurrected Christ (1 Pet 3:18).[62] So that it is not in a Platonic sphere of spirit by which Jesus proclaims but within a historical state of resurrection vindicating Christ in the wake of his historical death. The ἐν ᾧ, "in which," refers to the sentence subject Christ in his condition of resurrection (1 Pet 3:18–19). Within this resurrection condition, Jesus went[63] and made proclamation to the spirits now in prison (1 Pet 3:19). While the word "spirits" (πνεύμασιν) can refer to humans in resurrection (1 Pet 3:18–19; 4:6, πνεύματι), it also regularly

---

57. Rarely do more than one feature from each list get included. One of the rare exceptions is Bo Reicke (*Disobedient Spirits and Christian Baptism*, 90–91, 109), who permits that men, angels, and their offspring are each offered the possibility of salvation around Christ's context of death and resurrection.

58. Clement of Alexandria, *Strom.* 6.6.38–39; Origen, *Prin.* 2.5.

59. Dalton, *Christ's Proclamation to the Spirits*; Pierce, *Spirits and the Proclamation of Christ*.

60. Dalton, *Christ's Proclamation to the Spirits*, 127–34.

61. Since σαρκὶ and πνεύματι are both datives this argues strongly for the sphere of operation, within "embodied humanity" and within "resurrection"; Funk, *Greek Grammar*, 232, no. 447 (5). Thus, the gospel being preached (in the past) to those who are dead (in the present) best means that they either weren't dead when they had the gospel preached to them so that their present resurrection condition is a vindication of their martyrdom or that they are of the walking dead when the gospel was preached to them and then after coming to Christ they were martyred and then vindicated by God resurrecting them. First Peter 4:6 does not mean that dead get a postmortem opportunity to hear the gospel and be saved.

62. The word ζῳοποιηθείς is elsewhere used of resurrection (John 5:21; 6:63; Rom 4:17; 8:11; 1 Cor 15:22, 36, 45; including ζῶσι in 1 Pet 4:6).

63. The word for "going" (πορευθείς) is a non-technical general word for "going," rather than the technical "descending" (κατέβη; Matt 11:23; Luke 10:15; Rom 10:7; Eph 4:9).

refers to evil angels or demons (Mark 1:23, 26–27; 3:11; 5:2, 8; Matt 8:16; 12:45; Luke 10:20; 11:26).[64] The "spirits" that had something to do with sins around Noah's flood which Peter and early Jewish sources identify as in prison are those angels that did not keep their proper abode (1 Pet 3:19–20; 2 Pet 2:4).[65] The other earthly rebels (like humans) before the flood were killed by the judging waters of the flood. However, these sinning angels from the flood context are held in dark pits within Tartarus prison (2 Pet 2:4–5; Jude 6),[66] these angels are kept within this prison under a certainty of future judgment and condemnation. Remember that in the Roman and Jewish context "prison" (φυλακῇ) is not the punishment but a temporary holding place of men or angels until judgment is ready to be carried out (Mark 6:27; Matt 14:3, 10; Acts 5:19, 21; 16:22–40; 22:4; 23:1—26:10; Rev 20:1–3, 7). The "proclamation" (ἐκήρυξεν, 1 Pet 3:19) would be an "open announcement" as in a town crier, rather than that of a "gospel proclamation" (εὐαγγέλιον) which is not in this passage, though it is in 1 Pet 4:6 (εὐηγγελίσθη). While ἐκήρυξεν can refer to gospel being proclaimed if the context explains the message to be the gospel,[67] the message may also be that of a very different sort (Luke 12:3; Rev 5:2). With this proclamation in 1 Pet 3:19 going to condemned angels held in prison, the appropriate proclamation must be consistent with their certain condemnation,[68] so a content of salvation is excluded from the resurrected Christ's proclamation. In the context, after Christ's resurrection and before his ascension there is a message mentioned that was communicated to angels that they need to submit in subjection to the Son, for Christ ascends "after angel's authorities and powers had been subjected to Him" (1 Pet 3:22). So, Christ's message of proclamation could be that demand for angel submission or the announcement of his victory which would have the ramification that these demons' doom was sealed. In such a setting, these spirits would be subjected to the victorious Christ.

In 1 Pet 4:6, the gospel having been "preached" (aorist, in the past) to those who are dead (in the present) best means that they either weren't

64. Tob 6.6; 2 Macc 3:24; *Jub.* 15.31–32; *1 En.* 15.8b–8; 60.11; *T. Dan.* 1.7; 5.5; 1ZS 3.17; 1QM 12.8; 13.10–12; 4Q510 frg. 1 5.

65. Additionally described in Jude 6; 4Q203 frag. 8 6–12; 1QapGen. 0.2–1.25; *1 En.* 6.1–3; 7.1–2; 8.2; 10.4–6, 12–14; 13.1; 14.5; 18.14–16; 21.6, 10.

66. *1 En.* 10.4–6, 12–14; 13.1; 14.5; 18.14–16; 21.6, 10.

67. Mark 1:38; 3:14; Matt 11:1; Rom 10:14; 1 Cor 1:21; 9:27.

68. This fits with *1 En.*, where fallen angels petition God for forgiveness (13.4–5) and God responds with judgment proclamation, "Say to them, you have no peace" (16.4).

dead when they had gospel preached to them so that their present resurrection condition is a vindication of their martyrdom (aorist, bodily condemned in the past) or that they are of the walking dead when the gospel was preached to them and then after coming to Christ they were martyred and thereby vindicated by God resurrecting them (present subjunctive "to live" in resurrected spiritual realm). First Peter 4:6 does not mean that dead get a postmortem opportunity to hear the gospel and be saved. The traditional view underlying the *Apostle's Creed* must be demonstrated out of 1 Pet 3:19 or extrabiblical material for it to be maintained. Likewise, Eph 4:8–9 does not address postmortem gospel either, but the passage does explain Christ as descending (κατέβη) into the lower parts of the earth (where humans live) to capture and lead captive a host of captives, who Jesus then turned around and gave these humans ministering as gifts to the church (Eph 4:11–12). Revelation 1:18 does not address postmortem gospel but shows that Christ who died and resurrected has "the keys of death and of Hades," thus Christ is victorious over Satan, demons, and death.

14

False Teachers

SECOND PETER 2:1 PRESENTS false teachers as "coming in the future," whereas Jude 4 describes them as present ungodly persons. Peter discussed a group that has experienced some salvation benefits of redemption and thus is growing from within the community of believers, for the false teachers "will be there" among them (2 Pet 2:1, future ἔσονται).[1] However, Jude described ungodly persons who slipped in stealthily from the outside[2] without any mention of their received benefits (Jude 4). After these differences, the two letters are complementary demonstrating the similar character and certain condemnation of false teachers. The different descriptions of the false teachers set up distinct ways in which believers should respond. Believers should be aware of the character and certain condemnation of the false teachers so that the believers can protect themselves from being taken in by the false teachers (2 Pet 3:17). That is, Peter urges no evangelistic effort among the false teachers, fully aware that the false teachers had previously rejected a commitment they had made to Christ and his redemption. However, with Jude's false teachers coming from outside of Christianity, believers should evangelistically contend for the faith against the ungodly because these false teachers lack a previous commitment and rejection concerning Christ, implying that some may be able to be snatched from their impending judgment (Jude 3, 22–23). Therefore, this theological exposé of 2 Pet will not often appeal to Jude in the text of the chapter but will interact mostly in the footnotes. The Christians follow Christ's narrow way of truth and righteousness,

---

1. BAG, "παρεισάγω," 630; future παρεισάξουσιν, "will introduce" heresies.
2. BAG, "παρεισέδυ(ν)ω," 630; aorist παρεισέδυσαν, "crept stealthily in from outside."

while the false teachers pursue the broad way of judgment (2 Pet 2:2, 15, 21; Matt 7:13–23; Acts 9:2; 13:10; 16:17; 18:25–26; 19:9, 19, 23; 22:4; 24:14, 22).³

Peter's discussion of the false teachers exists as a tapestry wherein specific themes are surfaced repeatedly and interwoven. There are five different hues interwoven to describe false teachers to explain Peter's thought: false teaching, prideful despising of authority, sensuality, greedy exploitation, and judgment. This order is set by the order of emphasis in 2 Pet (as indicated on the chart 1, 2, 3 . . .) reflecting what precedes the other, with some of the topics deeply connected to another (indicated by –) and others receiving emphasis (indicated by !).

2 Pet	False Teaching	Prideful Despising Authority	Sensuality	Greed	Judgment
2:1	1!–	–3			2, 4
2:2–3	7		5	6	8
2:4–10a		11	10		9!
2:10b–13a	13–	–12!			14
2:13b–16			15!–	–16!	
2:17	17		18		19
2:18–22	20–	–20	21		22
3:1–7	23–		24		25!
3:16	27		26		28

Second Peter begins by surfacing all five themes within the introductory section of verses 1–3. False teaching is emphasized in 2 Pet 2:1 but is repeatedly tied to judgment and expresses itself in prideful despising of the master. Then Peter described sensuality, greed, and judgment of false teachers (2 Pet 2:2–3). The next sentence (2 Pet 2:4–10a) emphasized

---

3. 1QS 3.13–14.26; *Barn.* 18–20; *Did.* 1–5; *1 Clem.* 35.5.

the false teachers' judgment but ends with a mention of sensuality and despising authority. Second Peter 2:10b–13a emphasized despising authority but expressed itself in false teaching and results in judgment. The next section (2 Pet 2:13b–16) begins by emphasizing sensuality and then emphasized greed. Second Peter 2:17 touched on false teaching, sensuality and judgment. Second Peter 2:18–22 begins by prideful false teaching and develops sensuality and judgment. Second Peter 3:1–7 developed false teaching and sensuality as interwoven which works up to an extended discussion of judgment. Finally, 2 Pet 3:16 also interweaves false teaching and sensuality, concluding by a mention of judgment and a warning. The order of the following discussion is established by the order of emphasis (!): false teaching, judgment, prideful despising authority, sensuality, greedy exploitation, and judgment. However, since "judgment" is emphasized twice and it most often follows characteristics with which it is associated it will be discussed last. Peter reflects the interrelation between false teaching and prideful despising of authority, which draws these descriptions together. There is also a close connection between false teaching and sensuality, which would place sensuality as the third topic. Additionally, there is an interrelation with sensuality and greedy exploitation which further established the following order of treatment. Finally, Peter emphasized judgment as the certain outcome on these who have these qualities.

The false teachers among the believers are characterized by secretly introducing false destructive heresies from an ignorant and unstable life. The falsehoods characterize the false teachers (2 Pet 2:1). Contrary to Clement of Alexandria's claim, the false teaching is not gnostic doctrine of Carpocrates[4] because there is no special salvation knowledge developed in Peter's description of the false teachers and all evidence for Gnosticism developed after Peter in mid-second century with diverse frameworks.[5] Jerome Neyrey proposed that this false teaching was likely Epicureanism because it denied judgment.[6] However, such a denial of divine judgment is more broadly represented since the serpent denied it in the garden

---

4. Clement of Alexandria, *Strom.* 3.2.sub fin. Identified the false teachers prophesied by Jude and 2 Pet, whereas some modern writers claim these are not prophetical but descriptive (Bertram, "ἐμπαιγμονη," TDNT 5:636).

5. Plummer, *James and Jude*, 390.; Goguel, *The Birth of Christianity*, 422.

6. Neyrey, *2 Peter, Jude*, 128, 202, 231 citing: Cicero, *Nat. Deor.* 1.9.51; Plutarch, *Adv. Colotem* 1114A; Oenomaus of Gadara cited in Eusebius, *Praep. ev.* 5.19; Origen, *Celsum* 6.78; however, Epicurean circle of life provides an impersonal judgment of one's life (Epicurus, frag. 374; *Letter to Herodtus*, 37, 50; Diogenes Laertius, *Lives of Eminent Philosophers*, 10.33).

of Eden (Gen 3:4), and even Neyrey identified that this theme "may be found frequently" in other philosophies of the day.[7] Gene Green considered Epicurean views were possible since it denied prophecy[8] and Peter develops an extended argument for the effective confidence Christians should have from Judeo-Christian prophecy for the coming kingdom (2 Pet 1:11, 16–21). However, nothing of the core of Epicurean philosophy is developed in 2 Pet, namely sensations to build a mental reserve of pleasure through conversations with friends to buoy one up in life distresses.[9] Neyrey also admits that scoffing was common in other forms of Judaism that denied some prophecy and judgment, namely among Sadducean and antinomian forms.[10] From Peter's prophetic confidence, 2 Pet described the characteristics of the prophesied and future false teaching as emerging from the "ignorant" of sufficient teaching to interpret Scripture correctly (1 Pet 2:15; 2 Pet 3:16). Such ignorance results in "ignorant" behavior[11] like reviling angels (2 Pet 2:11–12). Such ignorance is usually associated with unbelievers who have never come to a knowledge of Christ (Acts 3:17; 1 Pet 1:14), whereas these false teachers are willfully rejecting this Christian knowledge to return to their ignorant position. An additional characteristic of "instability" (ἀστήρικτοι) leads them to distorted views (2 Pet 3:16). Instability makes them exceedingly vulnerable to enticement, as a fish is lured and caught by bait (2 Pet 2:18).[12] Thus, the false teachers and those enticed by them are both unstable (2 Pet 2:14). This vulnerability is increased as the false teachers syncretize false teaching alongside the true teaching in a secret and malicious manner (2 Pet 2:1).[13] This secret maliciousness was a similar charge against

---

7. Neyrey, *2 Peter, Jude*, 231 citing Aristotle, *Caelo* 1.12 282 a 25; Philo, *Aet.* 7, 10, 12, 20, 69, 93; *Somn.* 2.283.

8. Green, "As for Prophecies, They will Come to an End," *JSNT* 82(2002) 107–22; *Jude & 2 Peter*, 213 citing Cicero and Plutarch.

9. Epicurus, frag. 374; *Letter to Herodotus* 37, 50; Hicks, *Epicurus Principle Doctrines*, 23; Diogenes Laertius, *Lives of Eminent Philosophers*, 10.33; Kennard, *Epistemology and Logic*, 128.

10. Neyrey, *2 Peter, Jude*, 128 citing *m. Sanh.* 10.1; 13. 4–5; *m. 'Abot.* 2.14; *b. Roš Haš.*17a.

11. BAG, "ἀγνοεω," 11; the same behavior is identified by Jude 10 with οὐκ οἴδασιν.

12. BAG, "δελεάζω," 173; the word is used from fishing imagery of catching with bait, a practice Peter knows (Matt 17:27), though Xenophon, *Mem.* 2.1.4 described "hooked with gluttony."

13. BAG, "παρεισάγω," 630; "secretly entering a city," Polybius, 1.18.3; 2.7.8.

Socrates, Orpheus, and the rise of heresy in early Christianity.[14] In this the false teachers invent false teaching of their own to suit their purposes. For example, by false "fabricated"[15] words they exploit others for their own financial gain (2 Pet 2:3). This contrasts with Peter and the apostles who did not use erroneous myths and statements about God, life, or the future as the false teachers were doing (2 Pet 1:16). One primary manner through which the false teachers created myths and fabricated words was through the distortion or twisting[16] of Scriptures for their purposes when the Scriptures do not say what the false teachers claim (2 Pet 3:16). Such teaching is characteristically of opinions that lead to destruction. That is, the pernicious aspect is not that the teaching is sectarian[17] or opinion, but that these false teachings lead to everlasting destruction (2 Pet 2:1, 3; 3:7, 16). As such, the false teachers follow in the same pattern as Israel's false prophets; both introduced falsehoods and were condemned (2 Pet 2:1).

The false teaching that Peter identified as characteristic of these false teachers focused on three areas: Christ, living, and judgment. First, the false teachers deny Christ (2 Pet 2:1). Peter used the word "denial" (ἀρνούμενοι) to refer to that precarious state that a person is in when they ignore the truth which is available about Christ and identify oneself with the opposition against Christ (Acts 3:13–14). Such denial can take the verbal expression of claiming that one does not know Christ or does not have allegiance to Christ.[18] An example of this is the denial, from which Peter grievously repented (Mark 14:68, 70; Matt 26:70, 72; Luke 22:57; John 18:25, 27). However, denial of Christ, in Peter's expression includes asking for Jesus to die as was done by the Jewish mob, as well as maintaining a lifestyle that rejects Christ's redemptive work. The redeemed false teachers had done this last form of denial by their licentious living. The whole concept of denying Christ, in whatever form is accomplished, has as a backdrop Christ's words, "whoever denies me before men, I will deny him before my Father" (Matt 10:33; Luke 12:9). Thus, ongoing denial of Christ results in condemnation, which is what was rapidly approaching

---

14. Plutarch, *Alex. fort.* 328D; Diodorus of Sicily 1.96.5; Eusebius, *Hist. eccl.* 4.22.5; Neyrey, *2 Peter, Jude*, 190.

15. BAG, "πλαστος," 672.

16. BAG, "στρεβλοω," 778.

17. "Sect" need not be negative since it is used of Christians as the sect of the Nazarenes (Acts 24:5, 14; 28:22), also Pharisees are the strictest "sect" of mainstream Judaism (Acts 26:5).

18. Neyrey, *2 Peter, Jude*, 188–89 with examples illustrated from Ps 9.

for false teachers (2 Pet 2:1). Additionally, the false teachers promised freedom in life while they can't deliver it because they are entangled as slaves, "overcome"[19] by "destruction"[20] (2 Pet 2:19). Peter reinforced this undesirable condition of the false teachers by developing this truth pictorially. "Springs without water"[21] signified that the false teachers were totally unsatisfying because their lifestyle and promises can never provide refreshing freedom (2 Pet 2:17). Additionally, the allusion to "mists" (ὁμίχλαι) probably refers to a haze which heralds dry weather and is quickly dispersed by wind, rather than a refreshing damp mist.[22] This illustration reiterates a redundant empty promise because it looks so appealing yet is so impotent. Furthermore, Peter develops this image to emphasize the false teacher's instability and inability to prevent an externally empowered driving of the false teachers toward judgment. That is, the mists are forcefully driven to judgment of black darkness before fierce gusts of wind such as are found in a hurricane or whirlwind.[23] Within this headlong rush to judgment, the false teachers mock the coming of Christ and the judgment he brings upon them (2 Pet 3:3–7).[24] Within this description, their scorn and scoffing is emphasized by the pleonastic Hebraism "mockers mocking" (2 Pet 3:3). They were "dishonoring" the way of truth.[25] Ultimately, their mockery is aimed at denying universal judgment, including their own. Ironically, the false teachers mocking is the very evidence of what they deny. That is, such mockers scoffing about

---

19. As in a battle those overcome are slaves of the enemy, that is, judgment; Bauckham, *Jude, 2 Peter*, 277.

20. The use of "destruction" (φθοράν) refers to divine judgment (2 Pet 2:12) and its mortality (2 Pet 1:4); the word is not used by Peter for moral corruption.

21. Jude 12 illustrates the same truth by waterless clouds and barren trees that are uprooted in their worthlessness.

22. Similar metaphor used by Aristotle, *Meteor* 1.346B; Theophrates, *De signis* 4; Wis 2.4; Sir 43.22.

23. BAG, "λαῖλαψ," 463–64; Peter's term for wind is much more forceful than Jude's generic word for "wind" (ἀνέμων). That is, Jude 12 used wind to indicate external empowerment, whereas Peter's more forceful term also indicates the unstable headlong rush to judgment.

24. Some see the mockers as a separate group from the false teachers, but it is better to see them as the same group because 2 Pet is one letter with a continuing context including both descriptions together, with the same lusts (2 Pet 2:18; 3:3) and Jude 18 combines the mockers as false teachers.

25. Βλασφημηθήσεται is best understood at this time as "dishonor" rather than a technical blasphemy which develops in the wake of the *Mishnah* (Neyrey, *2 Peter, Jude*, 193; Bock, *Blasphemy and Exaltation in Judaism*).

the coming of Christ signify the very presence of the last days within which both Christ and judgment shall come.²⁶

The false teachers despise authority, especially spiritual authority, as seen in their contempt, scorn, disregard, and lack of fear (2 Pet 2:10).²⁷ The more active forms of despising authority are spoken against by Peter, such as denying their master Jesus Christ (2 Pet 2:1). It is in this sense that "authority" (κυριότητος) should probably be understood, since Christ is repeatedly called the Lord (κύριος) throughout the context (2 Pet 2:10–11, 20).²⁸ The false teachers also revile condemned angelic glories even when powerful godly angels²⁹ don't revile these condemned angels. In this, the false teachers are like irrational³⁰ instinctive³¹ animals (2 Pet 2:10). That is, such reviling is from ignorance. The result of despising authority renders the false teachers to be destined for destruction as occurs to a captured animal. Additionally, the false teachers speak arrogant vain words to entice others to follow them in fleshly lusts (2 Pet 2:18). Such speech is characterized as haughty or bombastic and pictured by something unnaturally swollen to an excessive size (2 Pet 2:16).³² The flip side of such speech is that it is empty, fruitless, useless, powerless, and lacking truth. That is, such speech is as futile as the gentile unbeliever's life regarding salvation (1 Pet 1:18). Therefore, the promises of freedom by the false teachers are a prideful disregard for their place and spell their certain condemnation (2 Pet 2:18–19).

The false teachers are characterized by sensual lusts. Their sensuality³³ is the licentiousness which is common among gentiles (1 Pet 4:3; 2

---

26. Jude 19 further describes the mockers as soulishly minded (ψυχικοί) without the Spirit and causing divisions, which is the opposite of Peter's description of the believer: sober for God's purposes, fervent in love, and with the Spirit resting upon them (1 Pet 4:7–8, 14).

27. BAG, "καταφρονοῦντας," 421; Jude 8 utilized the synonym ἀθετοῦσιν in a similar way.

28. 2 Pet 2:1 and Jude 4 include κύριος (Lord) along with δεσπότην (master) as a title for the denied Christ. Additionally, Jude 15–16 describes the ungodly persons as speaking harsh things against Christ by grumbling and finding fault.

29. Peter speaks about angels in general, whereas Jude 9 specifies the instance of Michael disputing with the devil over Moses' body which is contained in Jewish tradition (*As. Mos.*, Clement of Alexandria, *Adumb. In Ep. Judae* and Origen, *Princ.* 3.2.1).

30. ἄλογα means without reason or irrational, not contrary to reason.

31. BAG, "φυσικός," 877.

32. BAG, "ὑπέρογκος," 849; Jude 16 describes this arrogance as flattering people for the sake of gaining an advantage over them.

33. BAG, "ἀσελγεία," 114.

Pet 2:2, 13). For example, the unrighteous and lawless sensual conduct of unprincipled men was common in Sodom and Gomorrah (2 Pet 2:7, 9).[34] Their desires[35] are those corrupt polluting[36] desires common among the gentile world (1 Pet 4:2–3; 2 Pet 1:4; 2:10, 18). These are the same lusts which the Christians had departed from in their redemption (1 Pet 1:14, 18). In the same process, the false teachers had departed from these defilements[37] by the knowledge of the Lord Jesus Christ in their redemption (2 Pet 2:1, 20). However, the false teachers had gone back into following their previous lusts, thus giving up the purifying effects of their redemption (2 Pet 2:20, 3:3).[38]

Peter provides two examples of the false teacher's sensuality. They deceptively[39] revel[40] in the pleasure of the daytime, while feasting together in the common meals (2 Pet 2:13). So probably the false teachers feasted and got drunk during the day only to join the believers in their eucharistic meal also. As such, the common meal of believers was blemished[41] by the false teachers' presence among them. Additionally, the false teachers entice unstable individuals into sensuality through the allurement of fleshly lusts as bait (2 Pet 2:14, 18).[42] Jerome Neyrey favorably compares Peter and Philo's use of these concepts.

---

34. Jude 4 described the ungodly persons as turning God's grace into sensuality.
35. BAG, "ἐπιθυμία," 293.
36. BAG, "μιασμος," 522.
37. BAG, "μιάσμος," compared with "μίασμα," 522.
38. Jude 16 and 18 also point out that they follow their own lusts.
39. ἀπάταις, meaning "deceptions," is the best textual critical reading of the text. There is no compelling reason to change this word to ἀγάπαις in order to parallel Jude 12 "love feasts." Furthermore, there is no evidence that the love feast was a daylight meal until later, to avoid scandal (Clement of Alexandria, *Strom.* 7; Hippolytus, *Apostolic Trad.* 26). Additionally, ἀπάταις and τρυφήν are naturally associated together (Hermas, *Mand.* 11.12; *Sim* 6.2.1–2, 4; 6.5.1. 3–4, 6).
40. Τρυφήν can mean "delight" (2 *Clem.* 10.4; *Herm. Sim.* 6.5.7) but it usually means "self-indulgence" consisting of reveling in sensuality and drunkenness (*Herm. Mand.* 6.2.5; 8.3; 12.2.1; *Sim.* 6.5.5).
41. "Stains" (σπίλοι) and "blemishes" (μῶμοι) are parallel in 2 Pet 2:13, resulting in a distasteful spoiling of the believer's feast with the spoiling nature of false teachers among believers. The point is not as in Jude 8 where dreamers defile their flesh. Neither should σπίλοι be read as "hidden reefs" paralleling Jude 12 where these revilers endanger believers.
42. The word "entice" (δελεάζοντες) is an extreme metaphor from catching fish by bait (a practice Peter knows, Matt 17:27); Xenophon, *Mem.* 2.1.4 described "hooked with gluttony."

The basic verb means to bait and catch, as in fishing. It is commonly used in a moral sense as enticement by vice. Philo, for example, regularly speaks of "enticement" by (a) pleasure: *Opif.* 166; *Agr.* 102; *Migr.* 29 (see James 1:14); (b) sexual charms: *Ebr.* 50; *Heres* 274; *Congr.* 77; *Virt.* 40; and (c) gluttony: *Spec. Leg.* 4.100. This connection fits 2 Peter 2:14 and 18, where the author describes his opponents as themselves led by "adultery" (v14) and dissipation at feasts (v13). In 2:18 he describes them as enticing with debauchery and desires of the flesh.

Philo also associated "enticement" with deception and delusion (*Heres.* 71; *Somn.* 23.101; *Fuga* 189; see Josephus, *War* 5.120). Something which is outwardly pleasing is inwardly corrupt and defiling. Hence, it conveys a sense of "pollution" for the author. Finally, in a suggestive passage, Philo speaks of enticement to a certain kind of freedom: "You entice this multitude with the hope of liberty, and then have saddled it with the greater danger which threatens its life" (*Mos.* 1.171). Philo's usage can enlighten our interpretation of 2:17–18, where first the opponents are said to "entice with debauchery" (v17) and immediately to "promise freedom," which is really slavery to vice (v18).[43]

The implication is that in taking the bait, one becomes hooked within sensuality. Such was the case for these sensually enslaved heading for destruction even as they promise freedom.

Peter develops four results from the false teacher's sensuality. First, many among the church will follow the false teachers in their sensuality resulting in the defamation of the way of the truth as the proper Christian life (2 Pet 2:12). Second, the false teachers are entangled and overcome by sensuality (2 Pet 2:20). Their entanglement is as a sheep who is caught in thorns and cannot easily be set free.[44] Their being overcome is as those who are defeated in battle, only the false teachers are overcome[45] by divine judgment[46]; they have no escape from condemnation (2 Pet 2:12, 19–20). Third, the false teachers know the commandment to righteous living and thus know that they are condemned in their disobedience (2 Pet 2:21). Thus, the false teachers in their awareness of condemnation are worse off than an unbeliever who disobeys, ignorant of his

---

43. Neyrey, *2 Peter, Jude*, 215.
44. BAG, "ἐμπλέκω," 256.
45. Bauckham, *Jude, 2 Peter*, 277.
46. Peter only used φθοράν of divine judgment and its mortality (2 Pet 1:4; 2:12); the word is not used by Peter for moral corruption.

condemnation. Fourth, the false teacher's awareness of condemnation amid continued disobedience demonstrates that they are fools (2 Pet 2:22). That is, proverbial statements such as a dog returning to its own vomit and a washed sow returning to the mire recall the contextual use in Proverbs 26:11 signifying a fool returning to his folly. The false teachers are then condemned without excuse in their high-handed sin.

Peter itemized greedy exploitation of believers as a primary character trait of the false teachers (2 Pet 2:3). Their greed is literally an insatiable desire to have more.[47] This greed so characterizes the false teachers that Peter describes them as training their heart by repeatedly "exercising"[48] greed (2 Pet 2:14). Such a mindset is in contrast to the athlete who trains himself physically, the believer who disciplines himself in wholistic essential qualities (2 Pet 1:5–7), and the elder who should eagerly shepherd the church without consideration of any financial gain (1 Pet 5:2). The exploitation which expresses this greed is a commercializing of buying and selling religion (2 Pet 2:3).[49] From the false teachers it largely consists of fabricated and false words[50] which can be sold to an audience to satiate the false teacher's greed (2 Pet 2:3).

Such greed results in false teachers' apostasy. They are led astray, leaving the right way, by their greed (2 Pet 2:15). Peter emphasized this greed with a two ways view of salvation, though Jude's use of multiple imagery more broadly makes the point that all forms of apostasy are condemned by God. For example, Balaam "of the flesh"[51] stands out as the protype for false teachers leaving the narrow right way for a broad way[52] seeking financial gain[53] (2 Pet 2:15). Balaam tried to sell out God's

47. BAG, "πλεονεξία," 673.

48. BAG, "γυμνάζω," 166.

49. BAG, "ἐμπορεύομαι," 265.

50. BAG, "πλαστός," 672; Jude 16 specified flattery as one form of the false words motivated by greed.

51. Βοσόρ has overwhelming textual evidence in its favor over the closest rival "son of beor." However, Βοσόρ is an untranslatable word that most likely serves as a transliteration of the Hebrew *basar*, meaning "flesh."

52. The word "way," which is used twice in 2 Pet 2:15, is also in the LXX discussion of Balaam literally (Num 22:23) and metaphorically (Num 22:32). This "road" or "way" supports the idea of Balaam's prototypical role leaving the narrow way to join the broad way of destruction as presented by Peter. The Targums on Num 22:30 described Balaam as on the broad way of deception, while *Deut Rab.* 1.2 describes way as one of flattery and Philo, *Mos.* 1.293–99 as the way of sexual immorality based on his counsel to seduce Israel (Neyrey, *2 Peter, Jude*, 211).

53. Jude 11 used Balaam in the same manner coupling him with Cain, who is a

message in his attempt to curse Israel (Num 22–24). Balaam's donkey spoke in a human voice, complaining of the ill treatment of being beaten when it would not go any further.[54] Then the angel rebuked Balaam for his foolishness in attempting to curse Israel. Ultimately, Balaam changed his tactic but remained true to his greedy way by suggesting the downfall of Israel by immorality, the way of the flesh (Num 25). Peter characterized Balaam's whole greedy apostasy as "insanity,"[55] because it is a selective love for the wages of unrighteousness (2 Pet 2:15–16). That is, he desired the financial gain while ignoring the others around him and all other consequences. Jesus established the standard of loving God and one's neighbor as oneself, with the treat of damnation for the wealthy man who was instead turned to love his money.[56] Such consequences are extremely dangerous, as demonstrated by the resultant deaths of Ananias and Saphira (Acts 5:1–11) and Peter's threat of impending condemnation upon Simon (Acts 8:18–24).[57] These individuals placed themselves in these precarious situations when they desired their own gain (financial, prestige, or power) and ignored the consequences.

The feature that Peter most emphasized concerning the false teachers is the future divine judgment that destroys them. All the other motifs point out the characteristics whereby one can recognize the false teachers,[58] whereas this motif developed the unseen outcome of the false teachers. Additionally, all the previous false teacher motifs are interwoven with descriptions of the impending destruction on the false teachers. Thus, to the extent that someone can be described by the previous characteristics, they should be aware of this destruction.

---

pattern of departing into sin, and those who perished in the rebellion at Korah, a pattern of condemnation in apostasy. Though Num 22:16–19 briefly mentions Balak's gold, Balaam becomes known traditionally for greed (Philo, *Mos.* 1.267–68; *Cherubim* 33–34; *Num. Rab.* 10.7, 10).

54. In Num 22:21–35 the donkey's rebuke for striking her does not have to be a rebuke of Balaam's whole course of action as expressed by *Targums on Num.* 22:30, namely, *Targum Neofiti* and *Targum Pseudo-Jonathan*, nicely quoted by Davids, *2 Peter and Jude*, 256.

55. BAG, "παραφρονία," 628.

56. Kennard, *Petrine Studies*, chapter "Mark 10:17–31: Standard and Poor."

57. Irenaeus, *Haer.* 1.23.1–5 described Simon Magus as further in apostasy (originating Gnosticism) and condemned (which further highlights the urgency of Peter's threat).

58. The use of ἐλέγξω in Jude 15 further identified the ungodly by revealing them and their deeds.

Peter utilized a multitude of words to describe the false teacher's destruction. The most common word simply means "the ruining waste of destruction" (2 Pet 2:1).[59] It is used of the divine conflagration that will consume the ungodly with the heaven and the earth (2 Pet 3:7; Acts 8:20). This destruction is not asleep; God is aware of the need and the destruction is at work (2 Pet 2:3). In fact, the destruction is swiftly approaching for those who propound the heresies and twist the Scriptures (2 Pet 2:1; 3:16). Additionally, these false teacher's practices are so identified with their certain outcome that the practices themselves are called destructive, for they bring on the destruction. A second word highlights the decision of a judge including the subsequent action.[60] Peter used this word once showing that angels don't make reviling decisions against demons as the false teachers do (2 Pet 2:3).[61] However, when Peter describes the false teacher's judgement, the word is used synonymously with destruction,[62] emphasizing the resultant conflagration which shall be carried on the appropriate day (2 Pet 2:3–4, 9; 3:7). A related word, condemnation in Peter also emphasized the completed destruction of Sodom and Gomorrah as reduced to ashes (2 Pet 2:6), though elsewhere it can mean simply the pronouncement of a sentence. A fourth word meaning "ruin, destruction or corruption," emphasized the divine judgment that kills lustful humans and unreasoning animals (2 Pet 1:4, 2:12, 19).[63] This form of ruin has an ultimate expression in conflagration, but it also has another expression through human mortality (2 Pet 1:4). A fifth word meaning "to punish" is specifically utilized regarding the continuing interim punishment which God brings upon the unrighteous until the eschatological day of judgment (2 Pet 2:9). Contextually this punishment would include the false teacher's temporal entanglements, death, and their captive torment in the conscious realm of the dead (2 Pet 2:4–9, 12, 19–22). Therefore, the false teachers are already under the beginning stages of punishment which will heighten with their death ultimately devastating them with divine conflagration of the heavens and earth.

59. In Peter the word ἀπώλεια could mean "annihilation" as well but the word does not require it and certain non-Petrine verses argue against this sense (Matt 25:41, 46; 2 Thess 1:9); BAG, "ἀπώλειαν," 103.

60. BAG, "κρίμα," 451–52; "κρίσις," 453–54; Schneider, "κρίμα," NIDNTT 2:362; F. Buchsel, "κρίμα," TDNT 2:942.

61. Jude 9.

62. This synonymous sense is evident in the parallel construction in 2 Pet 2:3 and 3:7; Jude 6, 15.

63. BAG, "φθορα," 865; Harder, "φθείρω," TDNT 9:104.

The ultimate judgment of the false teachers is also emphasized by three figures of speech. The divine judgment that kills these lustful men expresses itself as the wages of their wrongdoing (2 Pet 2:12–13). As such, the false teachers suffer wrong[64] which is the proper resultant wage for their doing wrong. Such destruction is a wage which the false teachers ignore as they follow Balaam greedily seeking in their wages gain by exploitation of others (2 Pet 2:15). Peter's play on words indicates that the false teachers earn far more than they bargained for. The second figure, "accursed children," also indicates the false teachers are identified with their outcome of condemnation that they can be presently called accursed (2 Pet 2:14). This figure serves as a dramatic contrast to the believers described as "obedient children" as they head toward salvation (1 Pet 1:14). The third figure described the false teachers as those for whom the black darkness has been reserved (2 Pet 2:17). Peter used the concept of "darkness" to refer to that realm of judgment outside of God's salvation blessings (1 Pet 2:9; Acts 2:20).[65] Additionally in the context Peter used a synonym ζόφος to graphically indicate the "gloomy dark" imprisonment of the for the sinning angels in Tartarus (2 Pet 2:4; Jude 6). The impending darkness which is reserved for the false teachers shall exclude them from divine blessings of salvation even though they may have expressed some benefits in the past.

Temporal judgments and deliverances demonstrate that God will continue to punish the unrighteous and rescue the godly. The conditional nature of 2 Pet 2:4–9 indicates that the conclusion in verse 9 is guaranteed, because God has judged and delivered many times before, but most notably surrounding the flood, and Sodom and Gomorrah.[66] The unrighteous will continue to experience punishment and ultimately the day of judgment.

---

64. "Suffering injustice" (ἀδικούμενοι) is externally preferred reading and as a commercial metaphor is used to indicate the "suffering of wrongdoing" by Papias, *Elephant* 24, 27; Skehan, "Note on 2 Peter 2,13," 69–71; contra Bigg, *Peter and Jude*, 281. However, no colon should be placed after ἀδικούμενοι (contra Skehan) because the play on words is too great to break up: suffering wrong for doing wrong. The theological implication that God does wrong to wrongdoers is a way of expressing the injurious effect of God's righteous destruction of the false teachers (Isa 45:7).

65. There is no need to appeal to Jude 13 for Peter's lack of describing the meteors that flame out and disappear, for 2 Pet 2:17 is not dependent on Jude 13.

66. Unlike Jude's penchant for threes, the condemnation and benefit pattern in 2 Pet 2:4–9 groups the examples into the two ways outcome. The examples in Jude 5–7 indicate the certain condemnation of the false teachers which Peter also emphasized, but Peter's two ways also provide comfort for the godly.

The false teachers are characterized by their false teaching, prideful despising of authority, sensual lusts, and greedy exploitation. As a result of this unrighteous behavior, they will be presently under God's punishment until the conflagration on that ultimate day of judgment. Such an awful outcome is certain upon all who continue in such practices.[67] Believers should be aware of the false teacher's character and outcome, which should motivate believers to protect themselves from joining with similar false teachers.

---

67. It may be possible for some to repent and return to Christ as Simon may have done when Peter threatened him with a similar unconditional warning (Acts 8:20–24; Kennard, *Petrine Studies*, chapter on "The Man Called Peter"). However, the early church considered that Simon Magus did not repent but continued to try to lead people astray until Peter bested him in competition, ending in Simon's death and damnation (Justin, *1 Apol.* 26; 56; *2 Apol.* 15; *Dial.* 120.6; Irenaeus, *Haer.* 1.23.1–5; Hippolytus, *Haer.* 4.51.3–14; 6.7–20; 10.12; *Homily of Clement* 7.9; *Acts of Peter* 4–28.). The false teacher's life commitments show what their outcome will be, and Christians can read such life commitments and respond accordingly.

15

The Coming of the Lord

MANY DIFFERENT END TIME views are claimed for Peter's theology; however, E. G. Selwin made an argument that Petrine eschatology is "thoroughly integrated" with the teaching of 1 Pet as a whole, "both in the mind of the author and in the life and thought of the Christian whom he addresses."[1] Examining Peter's sermons in Acts, F. F. Bruce indicated that Peter might express the most primitive eschatology of the NT.[2] Dom Gregory Dix affirmed that Peter's eschatology reflects Jewish Pharisaism and Edwin Selwyn agreed.[3] Examining the same Acts sermons, Henry Cadbury concluded that Peter's gospel statements are the "most fully-developed" eschatological expression in the book of Acts, separating resurrection from ascension and living in eschatological time.[4] Ernst Käsemann rejected that Peter expressed primitive eschatology, arguing that the eschatology of 2 Pet abandoned a primitive Christian eschatology and re-established a form of apocalyptic familiar in the Gospel of Mark.[5] Following Oscar Cullmann, Henry Cadbury affirmed this same apocalyptic perspective with Peter expressing immanence and urgency of apocalypticism within Peter's sermons in Acts.[6] This claim for apocalypticism often comes with a recognition of abundant figures (such as

---

1. Selwyn, "Eschatology in 1 Peter," 394–401.
2. Bruce, "Speeches in Acts," 68.
3. Dix, *Jew and Greek*, 99; Selwyn, "Eschatology in 1 Peter," 399.
4. Cadbury, "Acts and Eschatology," 300–321.
5. Käsemann, "Eine Apologie der urchristlichen Eschatologie," 283, 285.
6. Cadbury, "Acts and Eschatology," 316 claims he is indebted to Cullmann, *Christ and Time* for this insight.

Son of Man, kingdom salvation, evil being finally defeated, and suffering heading toward glory) and a claim for reduced ethical exhortations, but as was shown in the chapter on the exodus 2 Pet emphasizes the role of ethical virtues for salvation. Additionally, the eschatology claims, especially the Petrine epistles and Peter's sermons repeatedly spin toward ethical exhortations. Furthermore, the figures of speech in 2 Pet are simple, straightforward, and non-extended evidencing a passionate colorful writing style befitting Peter's last exhortations before his death and thus fit within allusions to apocalypticism of the Gospels' use of the Son of Man imagery, rather than a full apocalyptic genre, foreign to Peter, and in the NT only found within the Revelation of John. Following Rudolf Bultmann, John Snyder claimed that 2 Pet does not present an end time coming of Christ but rather a realized eschatology evidenced in his life with the certainty of the judgment of sin,[7] but this neither fits 2 Pet, nor the rest of the Petrine corpus. Chester and Martin argued the reverse, that the false teachers had embraced realized eschatology, but Richard Bauckham disagreed.[8] Bauckham considered that eschatology is essential to 2 Pet, in that the believer is to grow in grace through the messianic woes (2 Pet 1:3–11; 3:11–18), with fervent hope motivating godliness (2 Pet 1:12–21; 3:1–10), which is why the false teachers denial of Christ and judgment, and licentiousness forfeit God's kingdom (2 Pet 2:1–22; 3:1–9), so Peter reestablished that the coming of Christ will take place so that believers will continue on the way of righteousness (2 Pet 3:10–18). In the Petrine material there is a highly developed eschatology extending from the OT, such as Isaiah, and Pharisaic teachings prompting an eschatological salvation and transformation ethic. Helmut Millauer argued that the OT, early Judaism, and Petrine theology presented an elect community that suffered now to purge them so that they might rejoice in the future kingdom.[9] Independently, Mark Dubis argued from early Judaism and 1 Pet that the believer as temporary resident presently experiences the messianic woes in dispersion identifying them as the divinely protected eschatological temple where God designed eschatological deliverance to be realized.[10] Simultaneously, Marv Pate and Douglas

---

7. Snyder, *Promise of His Coming*, 118–31.

8. Chester and Martin, *James, Peter and Jude*, 140–57; Bauckham, *Jude, 2 Peter*, 154–57.

9. Millauer, *Leiden als Gnade*, 15–59, 105–33, 135–44, 165–79; *T. Mos.* 1.18; *T. Jud.* 23.15; *T. Dan.* 6.4; *b. Sanh.* 97b–98a; Acts 3:19–21.

10. Dubis, *Messianic Woes in First Peter*, 48–55, 62–129, 142–91.

Kennard championed "consistent eschatology" in the Petrine material; namely, Jesus' disciples have not escaped experiencing the crucible of the messianic woes, so that contemporary suffering now is an expression of mimetic atonement following Christ through the messianic woes, and those who follow Jesus will not experience the eschatological suffering of divine judgment but will experience the joys of kingdom.[11] Kelly Liebengood framed 1 Pet through a substructure of Zech 9–14 in order to frame the shepherd image as Davidic king with Israel scattered, needing to experience a new exodus to be regathered and renewed into God's new covenant and universal reign including Christians.[12]

The coming of the Lord takes a central place in Peter's eschatology. "Coming" (Παρουσία) in order to be present is a normal concept to describe a hidden deity or a king visiting a province.[13] Peter utilized the concept exclusively as the coming of the Son of Man divine ruler to establish his kingdom. In 2 Pet 1:16 the coming refers to the Lord Jesus Christ, whereas in 2 Pet 3:4 and 12 he refers ambiguously to God as coming. These references to God's coming are developed as an eschatological event which brings the OT day of the Lord to an ultimate judgment and salvation (2 Pet 3:4–7, 10–13). The reference to Christ's "powerful coming"[14] permits but does not require Christ to be the main player in the day of the Lord's coming. The phrase "day of the Lord" means "eschatology" in most places of the OT and all of Peter's use. The fact that Peter has seen a powerful glimpse of this powerful coming at the transfiguration of Christ provided great assurance that Christ will come as prophecies predicted (2 Pet 1:16–19). Early Judaism connected the future coming with an eschatological rising of the morning star,[15] but Peter placed reassurance of the coming kingdom subjectively within the hearts of believers as they see the kingdom coming close (2 Pet 1:19). Furthermore, Christ

---

11. Pate and Kennard, *Deliverance Now and Not Yet*, 301–400.

12. Liebengood, *Eschatology of 1 Peter*, 206–9 summarizes her view but she overpressed the Zech connection and admits it especially in the shepherd role which she regularly reframes by appealing to Isa 53 (pp. 89–103).

13. Braumann and Brown, "Present, Day, Marantha, Parousia," NIDNTT 2:898; BAG, "Παρουσία," 635.

14. In 2 Pet 1:16, "τὴν τοῦ κυρίου ἡμῶν Ἰησοῦ Χριστοῦ δύναμιν καὶ παρουσίαν," the first article in the accusative governs both accusatives (δύναμιν and παρουσίαν) through the Granville Sharp rule to refer to the same event, and thus "powerful coming," while the genitive clause identifies this as "our Lord Jesus Christ's" coming.

15. Num 24:17 LXX is interpreted messianically in *T. Levi* 18.3; *T. Jud.* 24.1; 1QM 11.6–7; 4QTest. 9–13; CD 7.18–20; Rev 22:16.

has already received dominion over all forever which is associated with his coming as king and the bestowal of the Holy Spirit in kingdom (1 Pet 3:22; 4:11; 5:11; 2 Pet 1:11; Acts 2:17–21, 30, 33–36; 10:36, 45). So, Peter counts on the church living within the last time within which God operates dramatically, preparing the way for the Lord's coming (1 Pet 1:20; 4:7; Acts 2:16–17).

The Olivet Discourse in Mark provides a description of evidence for the powerful coming of Jesus Christ (Mark 13; 2 Pet 1:16), though it is a more blatant theme in Matthew (Matt 24:3 asks the question).[16] The Olivet Discourse emerged out of the context of the rejection and judgment of the Jewish leadership and the contrasting majesty of the temple (with beautiful stones and votive gifts) associated with this Jewish leadership (Mark 12:38—13:2; 14:58; 15:29; Matt 23:1—24:1; Luke 19:44; 20:45—21:5; John 2:19; Acts 6:14).[17] Josephus states that, "The temple was built of hard, white stones, each of about 32 feet in length, 12 feet in height and 18 feet in width."[18] These huge ornate white marble stones (decorated with gold) prompted the disciples' comments about the temple's dazzling beauty.[19] This refurbishment of the temple began in 19 BC under King Herod's reign and was finally completed in AD 63–64, a few years before the city and temple were destroyed.[20] Jesus' prediction emphasized the certainty of the destruction of the temple without any stone left upon another, which will not be torn down.[21] Technically, the temple stones were dislodged in two steps. First the fire in the temple destroyed the temple and Josephus describes how on August 5, AD 70, some Romans dislodged the stones to get at the gold that was melting off them.[22] Then, Titus ordered the city to be razed to quarter the tenth legion, leaving the three towers on the Northwest corner of the city to

---

16. For broader discussion context: Kennard, *Messiah Jesus*, 243–67; Pate and Kennard, *Deliverance Now and Not Yet*, 301–25, 401–67.

17. *Gos. Thom.* 71.

18. Josephus, *Ant.* 25.11.3.

19. Josephus, *War* 5.5; *Sukkah.* 41b; *Baba Bathra* 4a; Tacitus, *Hist.* 5.8.

20. Bock, *Luke*, 2:1660.

21. Mark 13:2 and Matt 24:2 emphasize the destruction by the double negative οὐ μή with aorist passive subjunctive. Jesus' prediction of the destruction of the temple follows the pattern predicted by Habakkuk (*Liv. Proph. Hab.* 12; 2 Bar 6.7–9). Additionally, *T. Levi* 10.3 predicts that the external curtain of the temple will be torn so that their sins would no longer be concealed, which predicts the temple curtain judgment that happened during Jesus' death (Mark 15:38; Matt 27:51; Luke 23:45).

22. Josephus, *War* 6.220–70.

remain standing. N. T. Wright claims that Jesus identified the temple's destruction as the definitive proof of his role as prophet.

> As a prophet, Jesus staked his reputation on his prediction of the Temple's fall within a generation; if and when it fell, he would thereby be vindicated. As the kingdom bearer, he had constantly been acting. . . . in a way which invited the conclusion that he thought he had the right to do and be what the Temple was and did, thereby implicitly making the Temple redundant. The story he had been telling, and by which he ordered his life, demanded a particular ending. If, then, the Temple remained forever, and his movement fizzled out (as Gamaliel thought it might), he would be shown to be a blasphemer. But if the Temple was to be destroyed and the sacrifices stopped; if the pagan hordes were to tear down stone by stone; and if his followers did escape from the conflagration unharmed, in a reenactment of Israel's escape from exile in doomed Babylon—why then he would be vindicated, not only as a prophet, but as Israel's representative, as (in some sense) the "son of man."[23]

This destruction of the temple refers to at least the destruction of the second temple ordered by Titus and carried out by the legions of Rome in AD 70. However, in AD 118 Hadrian was initially open for Jews to rebuild the temple but then refused and began to reconstruct the city into a gentile city named Aelia Capitolina. During the three years of the Bar Kochba rebellion (AD 133–35), the high priests with Rabbi Akiva controlled the temple grounds and regularly sacrificed to the Jewish God.[24] The resulting Roman conquest included a leveling of the temple court by Hadrian in AD 135 and the remaking of the site into a temple of Jupiter, placing his own equestrian statue on the site of the Holy of Holies.[25] The fact that the temple was destroyed (by Titus and Hadrian) as Jesus' claimed demonstrated that Jesus is the definitive prophet and includes some form of preterism within an interpretation of this passage.

Mark and Luke render the destruction of Herod's temple to be the judgment issue tied to Christ's coming: 1) for the discussion emerges from description of the abuses of devouring widow's households through

---

23. Wright, *Jesus and the Victory of God*, 362.
24. Dio Cassius, *Hist.* 69.12.1–14.3.
25. For AD 70 destruction see: Josephus, *War* 7.1.1; for the destruction after AD 135 and Hadrian's making of the temple site into a temple of Jupiter, see Dio Cassius, *Hist.* 69.12.1–14.3. This remaking of Jerusalem included siting a temple to Aphrodite where the Christians venerated Golgatha and Jesus' tomb.

temple giving, and 2) and Mark and Luke do not extend the contextual development to establishing kingdom, as does Matthew (Mark 12:40—13:2; Luke 20:47—21:7; Matt 24:1-2 contrasted with Matt 24:30—25:46). So, for Mark and Luke judgment of the temple is the major issue setting for the Olivet Discourse. Forsaking of the temple, Jesus pictorialized the divine rejection of the temple (Matt 23:38; 24:1-2). Following this comment, Jesus and the disciples continue to discuss this topic as they move across the Kidron Valley to ascend the Mount of Olives (Mark 13:3; Matt 24:3; Luke 21:37). From the Mount of Olives with the sun setting over the temple, the disciples ask when these things would occur and what would indicate when all this destruction would take place (Mark 13:4; Luke 21:6-7, 37).[26]

Matthew extends this sign question to include Jesus' coming and the end of the age judgment to establish kingdom (Matt 24:3).[27] Since the disciples were asking about Jesus' coming and he is already there, this question has in view Jesus' coming out as king to establish his kingdom. The disciples are not thinking about Jesus leaving them for a couple millennia, they are anticipating he will come and establish his kingdom soon (Acts 1:6), and thus the authentic offer of kingdom if Israel repents and aligns with Jesus as the Christ (Acts 3:18-26). That is, instead of focusing this judgment on a preterist historically past Roman conquest as advocated by Marcus Borg[28] and N. T. Wright,[29] or the scholarly consensus of focusing this judgment eschatologically (following Johannes Weiss[30] and Albert Schweitzer[31]) into eschatological kingdom realities not realized within preterism), the textual data and the early Jewish context indicates that both are in view. As early as Ephrem the Syrian this view of "already and not yet" was expounded concerning Jesus' interpretation from this passage including the historical punishment of Jerusalem and simultaneously referring to the end of the world before his kingdom.[32] Such an

26. The plural ταῦτα does not refer to several questions but to the plurality of temple stones destroyed or the expansiveness of the temple destruction (Mark 13:4; Matt 24:3; Luke 21:6-7).

27. The article governs the two substantives connected with the conjunction, pulling "coming" and "end" together into the same question.

28. Borg, *Conflict, Holiness and Politics*, scholarly version, and the popularized version, *Jesus: A New Vision*.

29. Wright, *Jesus and the Victory of God*.

30. Weiss, *Jesus' Proclamation of the Kingdom of God*.

31. Schweitzer, *Quest of the Historical Jesus*.

32. Ephrem, *Comm. Diat.* 18.14 follows the Jewish pattern that earlier events characterize a later time (Dan 9:27; 11; Jub. 23.11-32).

idea had been described by *4 Ezra* and *2 Baruch*, which used the lens of Jerusalem's first destruction as a model of the contemporary events of its second destruction. The answers given by Jesus to these two questions provide information, especially in Matthew, to indicate simultaneously when the Roman destruction of the temple would occur and when eschatologically Jesus will come for kingdom reign. Whereas, in Mark and Luke the destruction of Herod's temple is primarily in view, in Matthew the same answers refer to two separate times. In all the Synoptics, the discussion climaxes in the powerful coming of the Son of Man for his judging of the earth, but Matthew blatantly extends this coming further into the Son of Man's coming kingdom reign, while Mark hints at the coming kingdom.

Mark and Matthew identify that some of the answer predicted is merely the beginning of birth pangs (Mark 13:8; Matt 24:8).[33] The metaphor "birth pangs" is used repeatedly in Jewish literature as a metaphor of painful events and for those events which precede the messianic kingdom (Isa 13:8; 26:17-18; 66:7-9; Jer 4:31; 6:24; 13:21; 22:23; 49:22; 50:43; Hos 13:13; Mic 4:9-10; John 16:20-22; 1 Thess 5:3; 2 Thess 2:1-12; Rev 4-19).[34]

The first evidence toward temple destruction and the establishment of kingdom is that some claim to be messiah and the Mosaic prophet (Mark 13:5-6; Matt 24:5, 23-24; Luke 21:8).[35] In Jesus' evaluation, these are attempts to deceive his disciples. Before this prophecy was spoken, several in the Herodian family claimed to be the king of the Jews and argued their claim in the Roman senate: Herod the Great,[36] Archelaus, and Antipas.[37] Others are claimed to be messianic king by their followers: namely, Judas son of Ezekias, Herod's servant Simon, Athronges,[38]

---

33. 1QH11 indicates that among similar birth pangs as here are included a messianic baptism and temptation time reminiscent of Mark 1:9-13.

34. 1QH 3; 1QM; *1 En.* 99.1-100.6; *Sib. Or.* 2.153-73; 3.538, 635-51; *Jub.* 23.11-25; *4 Ezra* 4.51-55.13; 6.17-24; 13.29-32; 15.1-16.78; *2 Apoc. Bar.* 27.1-15; 48.31-41; 70.1-10; *Apoc. Ezra* 3.11-15; *b. Sanh.* 97a; 98ab; *b. Šabb.* 118a; *b. Ketub.* 11a; *Gen. Rab.* 42.4.

35. *Apoc. Elijah* 3.1 claims that the son of Lawlessness will say "I am the Christ."

36. Josephus, *Ant.* 14.158-60, 420-430 which incurred the wrath and denouncement of the Jews (Josephus, *Ant.* 14.172-76; *War* 1.208-15; and from Qumran [*T. Mos.* 6.2-6]).

37. Josephus, *Ant.* 17.149-66, 206-18; *War* 1.648-55, 2.1-13.

38. Josephus, *Ant.* 17.7, 10.5-6; *War* 2.4.1.

Tholomaeus,[39] Theudas,[40] Judas the Galilean and his two sons Jacob and Simon,[41] Eleazar ben Deinaeus and Alexander,[42] Menahem, son of Judas, the Galilean and Simon bar Giora or "the proselyte,"[43] Vespasion,[44] and Simon ben Kosiba of the Bar Kokhba rebellion.[45] All of these claimed messiahs came and went as moments of Jewish rebellion against their Roman overlords. Many of these same individuals are heralded by their followers to be the Mosaic prophet and to bring in the kingdom, which Matthew treats as a synonymous role as messiah. For example, from the mid-forties till the uprising of the Jewish war in the mid-sixties all of these claimed to bring in this kingdom: Tholomaeus,[46] Theudas,[47] Judas the Galilean and his two sons Jacob and Simon,[48] Eleazar ben Deinaeus and Alexander,[49] and an unnamed "imposter" who had promised his followers "salvation and rest from troubles."[50] They were all executed for the separate rebellions that they led. During this time, several other brigand bands also fostered rebellion and were crushed. Then as the Jewish revolt rose in AD 66, several others claimed to be Messiah and prophet.[51] Again in the AD 133–35 Jewish rebellion, Bar Kochba claimed to be Messiah as "a luminary who came down to them from heaven and was magically enlightening those who were in misery."[52] However, Matthew emphasized

39. Josephus, *Ant.* 20.5.

40. Josephus, *Ant.* 20.97–99; Acts 5:36 may identify this event in the company with movements led by Judas the Galilean and Jesus of Nazareth.

41. Josephus, *Ant.* 18.1.1; 20.102.

42. Josephus, *War* 2.253.

43. Josephus, *War* 2.17.8.

44. Josephus, *War* 6.5.4.

45. Dio Cassius, *Hist.* 59.13.3; Justin Martyr, *1 Apol.* 31.6 identifies that during the Bar Kochba rebellion, rabbi Akiva demanded that Christians deny Jesus as Messiah to affirm Simon as messiah; *y. Ta'an.* 68d; Eusebius, *Hist. eccl.* 4.6.2; luminary is used metaphorically of 'king' by Themistius, *Orationes* 16.204c; a Jewish letter dated 6 Nov. AD 135 describes "Simon bar Kosiba, the Prince of Israel" to be in the third year of his reign; coins also identify him as lawful ruler. After the defeat, some punned his title as Simon bar Kozeba, "son of disappointment."

46. Josephus, *Ant.* 20.5.

47. Josephus, *Ant.* 20.97–99; Acts 5:36 identifies this event in the company with movements led by Judas the Galilean and Jesus of Nazareth.

48. Josephus, *Ant.* 20.102.

49. Josephus, *War* 2.253.

50. Josephus, *Ant.* 20.188.

51. Josephus, *War* 6.5.2; 7.11.1; *Ant.* 20.5.1.

52. Eusebius, *Hist. eccl.* 4.6.2; luminary is used metaphorically of "king" by Themistius, *Orationes* 16.204c.

that this characteristic of messianic pretenders would especially occur in the eschatological expression of great tribulation (Matt 24:21–24).[53]

So, if the Olivet discourse is not strictly preterist, it is possible that there will be other false prophets in the future (Matt 7:15; 24:24). Apart from the previous declared messiahs or Mosaic prophet, there are other preterist false prophets not known as messiah. For example, around AD 36 an unnamed Samaritan convinced the population to follow him to Mt. Gerizim to find the temple implements but none were found,[54] in the fifties AD an Egyptian prophet is identified in this role claiming that Jerusalem walls would collapse at his command but they did not (Acts 21:38).[55] There are also some that remain unnamed as prophets promising salvation to those who followed them into the wilderness but some of their promises like crossing the Jordan on dry land went unfulfilled.[56] One of these unnamed prophets in August of AD 70 promised the Jews fleeing into the temple courts that they would receive "tokens of their deliverance" and "help from God" but the Romans still conquered them.[57] It is possible that there will be such false prophets in the eschatological future before Christ would return as well (2 Pet 2:1; Rev 13:11–17).

Early birth pains for Jesus' powerful coming to destroy opposition and establish his kingdom includes potentially frightening wars and rumors of wars, as evident by nations and kingdoms at war with each other (Mark 13:7–8; Matt 24:6–7; Luke 21:9–10). At this time, Paul claims that there will be those who promise "peace and safety" (1 Thess 5:3) but will be overwhelmed by war. Perhaps this will be like the Pax Romana at the end of a Roman lance, as Tacitus recounts: "To plunder, to butcher, steal, these things they misname empire; they make a desolation and call it peace."[58] For example, throughout Jesus' ministry and Pontus Pilate's procuratorship (AD 26–36), N. T. Wright identifies seven local rebellions which Pilate crushed.[59]

---

53. *Did.* 16 concurs in keeping this as an eschatological quality.
54. Josephus, *Ant.* 18.85–87; Barnett, "Jewish Sign Prophets," 679–97.
55. Josephus, *Ant.* 20.168–72; *War* 2.261–63; Eusebius, *Hist. eccl.* 2.21; perhaps *b. Sanh.* 67a.
56. Josephus, *Ant.* 20.167–68, 188; *War* 2.259.
57. Josephus, *War* 6.285–86.
58. Tacitus, *Agr.* 30.
59. Wright, *New Testament and the People of God*, 174.

1. Pilate tried to bring Roman standards into Jerusalem but backed down after a mass protest.⁶⁰
2. He used money from the temple treasury to build an aqueduct and crushed the resistance that this action provoked.⁶¹
3. He sent troops to kill some Galileans while they were offering sacrifices in the temple, presumably because he feared a riot.⁶²
4. He captured and condemned to death the leader of an uprising that had taken place in Jerusalem, involving murder; he then released the man as a gesture of goodwill during the Passover feast.⁶³
5. At the same Passover, he faced a quasi-messianic movement, having some association with two ordinary revolutionaries.⁶⁴
6. He provoked public opinion by placing Roman votive shields, albeit without images, in the palace at Jerusalem, which according to Philo annoyed Tiberius almost as much as it did the Jews.⁶⁵
7. Finally, he suppressed with particular brutality a popular (and apparently non-revolutionary) prophetic movement in Samaria. For this he was accused before the Roman legate in Syria, who had sent him sent back to Rome.⁶⁶

---

60. Josephus, *Ant.* 18.55–59; *War* 2.169–74. A similar incident occurred when Vitellius was sent to fight Aretas in AD 37: see *Ant.* 18.120–23.

61. Josephus, *Ant.* 18.60–62; *War* 2.175–77; Eusebius, *Hist. eccl.* 2.6.6–7.

62. Luke 13:1.

63. Luke 23:19–25 description of Barabbas' activities (committing murder during an insurrection in the city) reads just like a sentence from Josephus.

64. Wright (*New Testament and the People of God*, 174) writes "On Jesus of Nazareth see vol. 2. Josephus' account in *Ant.* 18.63–64 is notoriously controversial (see the discussion in Schürer, *History of the Jewish People*, 1.428–41), but it seems to me that some parts of it at least are likely to be original. The crucial sentence *ho christos houtos en* does not mean, as is usually supposed, 'this man was the Messiah,' but, because of the position of the article, 'the Messiah was this man.' The implication is that Josephus expects his readers to have heard of someone who bore, almost as a nickname, the title '*ho christos*' (cf. Suetonius, *Claudius* 25, *impulsore Chresto*), and is simply identifying this person with the one he is now describing. On Jesus' followers: it is highly likely that some at least of Jesus disciples believed themselves to be involved in a movement of national liberation. The title of one of them, Simon *ho Kananaios* (Mark 3:18) or Simon 'called *Zelotes*' (Luke 6:12) probably indicates known revolutionary tendencies."

65. Philo, *Leg.* 299–306; Wright suggests that there were probably many more of these events that Josephus probably passed over.

66. Josephus, *Ant.* 18.85–89.

Additionally, there was a near rebellion in Judea and Alexandria provoked by Caligula's contemptuous disregard of Jewish concerns during the reign as emperor (AD 37–41). Through wars Claudius I incorporated into the Roman Empire the kingdoms of Mauritania in AD 42, Lycia in AD 43, Trace in AD 46, and Britain during the 40s. Additionally, Nero put down an uprising under Queen Boudicca in Britain during AD 60–61. Then the war finally came to Judea during the Jewish revolt of AD 66–73, bringing the conflict to the people Jesus addressed. Again, Jews brought Roman conquest to themselves in the Bar Kochba rebellion (AD 133–35). Perhaps, the potentially frightening words would argue for literal detail going beyond the one frightening war in Judea to several eschatological wars which will cause fright in Judea. Later in Luke's account, as Jesus carried his cross, He announced that there would be a horrible time of fear to be hid by the mountains and hills (Luke 23:28–31). Such eschatological wars were a Jewish–Christian expectation (Isa 66:16; Rev 6:4).[67] Ultimately an eschatological holy war will occur between God and Satan (Rev 12; 19; 20:7–10).[68]

In contrast to these wars, the kingdom era would be known as a time of universal and lasting peace (Isa 9:6; Mic 5:5; Nah 1:15; Zech 9:10).[69]

In the wake of these wars there were often famines. Prophecies of famines often accompanied military destructions in the ancient Near East (Jer 15:2; Ezek 5:17; 14:13; Acts 11:28). However, there were also famines more commonly in Judea than merely in the wake of war (Acts 6:1; 11:28–29). Perhaps, Luke's combining plagues with famines helps to expand these famines from warfare to be ultimately signs from heaven (Luke 21:11). Mark and Luke indicate that these are earthly signs showing their divine source (Mark 13:4, 8; Luke 21:11). Certainly, eschatological judgments would expand these famines and plagues many times over (Rev 6:5–8; 18:8).[70]

An additional birth pang is the earthquakes in various places (Mark 13:8; Matt 24:7; Luke 21:11). When Jesus died, an earthquake shook the temple, splitting some stones and tearing the veil (Matt 27:51–54).

---

67. Sir 39.30; Wis 5.20; *Jub.* 9.15; 23.16; *1 En.* 56.7; 62.12; 63.11; 90; 91.11–12; 100.1–2; *Pss. Sol.* 15.8[7]; *Sib. Or.* 3.797–99; 4.174; *4 Esra* 6.24; 9.3; *2 Bar* 27.4, 6; 40.1; 48.32, 37; 70.3–8; 1QM; 1QH 11.34–36; 14.29–35; *b. Sanh.* 97a; *b. Meg.* 17b; *m. Soṭah* 9.15.

68. 1QM 15.12–16.1; 17.5–8; 11QMelch. 13–14; 1QH 11.34–36; 14.29–35; 4QFlor; 1QSb 5.20–29; *T. Levi* 18.12.

69. *Sib. Or.* 2.29; 5.780; *1 En.* 10.17.

70. *4 Ezra* 6.22; *2 Bar* 27.6; 70.8; *L.A.B.* 3.9; *Apoc. Abr.* 30.6; *b. Sanh.* 97a.

Additionally, a local earthquake came in answer to Peter and the apostles' prayer for the Spirit's empowerment so that Christians might be bold witnesses (Acts 4:31). The only record of earthquakes just before Jerusalem was destroyed are those in Laodicea during AD 17[71] and Jerusalem during AD 67–68.[72] Remember the earthquakes of Cyprus in AD 76 and Pompeii during AD 79 occur after Jerusalem's destruction but would be relevant for the Bar Kochba rebellion of AD 133–35.[73] Additionally, Josephus reports that one of the omens for the AD 70 destruction was a very local shaking and a *bath qol* voice from the temple saying, "Remove hence."[74] Certainly eschatological judgments include earthquakes with devastating consequences many times over (Isa 5:13–14; 13:6–16; 29:6; Jer 4:24; Ezek 38:19–20; Joel 2:10; Hag 2:6; Zech 14:5; Hab 3:3–6; Rev 6:8, 12; 8:5; 11:13, 19; 16:18).[75]

Jesus warns his disciples about impending persecution and an opportunity to demonstrate the gospel of the kingdom. Mark 13:9 warns the disciples to be on "your guard" with the second person plurals (through the account) pressing these impending events into the lives of disciples. Matthew calls this persecution of the disciples "tribulation" (θλῖψιν). That is, the disciples go through this tribulation (Matt 24:9). Those who deliver the disciples to tribulation include: Jewish leaders,[76] gentile kings and governors,[77] and family members and friends.[78] This persecution will be an expression of their hatred, arresting, flogging and killing the disciples on account of Jesus (Mark 13:12–13; Matt 24:9; Luke 21:12, 16–17;

---

71. Pliny, *Nat.* 2.86.

72. Josephus, *War* 4.4.5; Andreas of Caesarea, *Rev.* 6.12.

73. Tacitus, *Ann.* 14.27; 15.22.

74. Josephus, *War* 6.5.288–309.

75. *1 En.* 1.6–7; 102.2; 1QH 3.12–13; *As. Mos.* 10.41; *T. Mos.* 10.4; *4 Ezra* 5.8.1; 6.13–16; 9.3; *2 Bar.* 2.7; 27.7; 70.8; *T. Levi* 4.1 LAB 3.9; *Sib. Or.* 3.714; *Apoc. Abr.* 30.6, 8ff; *b. Sanh.* 97a.

76. Since they will deliver the disciples over to synagogues (Luke 21:12) and they are a major opposition in the context (Mark 12; 14:53–65; Matt 22–23; 26:57—27:10; Luke 20; 22:47–71; Acts 4; 5:12–42; 6:8—8:3; 9:2; 13:45; 14:2–5, 19; 17:5–9; 18:6, 12–17; 21:27—23:16; 24:5–9; *Mart. Pol.* 17.2;—Bar Kokhba ordered the execution of Christians [Justin Martyr, *1 Apol.* 31.6]).

77. Mark 13:9; 15; Matt 27:11–66; Luke 21:12; 23; Acts 12; 24–26; Nero's persecution of Christians, Tacitus, *Ann.* 15.44; *1 Clement* 6; *Did.* 16.3–5; Christians no longer welcome under the protection of Judaism as a traditional religion were accused and martyred for not offering to Caesar (Pliny, *Ep.* 10.96; *Mart. Pol.*).

78. Mark 13:12; Luke 21:16; John 9:20–23; *Jub.* 23.16, 19; *1 En.* 56.7; 70.7; 99.5; 100.1–2; *4 Ezra* 5.9; 6.24; *2 Bar* 70.3, 7; *b. Sanh.* 97a; *b. Soṭah* 47b.

Acts 7:60—8:1; 12:1–2; Rev 6:9–11).[79] It also leads to an opportunity for a testimony where the gospel of the kingdom will be proclaimed in the whole world as a witness to all the nations (Mark 13:9–11; Matt 24:14; Luke 21:13–15).

Jesus urged the disciples not to prepare to defend themselves nor be anxious beforehand about what they are to say, for utterance of what to say will be given you in that hour (Mark 13:11; Matt 10:19; Luke 21:15). Luke records that Jesus will give them utterance and wisdom which none of the opponents will be able to refute, whereas Mark explains that the Holy Spirit will provide in that hour what they will speak. Peter and the disciples found this promise of Spirit words and empowerment to be proven in their lives (Acts 4:1–22; 5:12–42; 7:22–26).

Luke reassures the disciples that they would not die (Luke 21:18), while all the Synoptics clarify that some of them would die (Mark 13:12; Matt 24:9; Luke 21:16). Perhaps Matthew's greater eschatological emphasis has him develop that falling away damns (σκανδαλισθήσονται; Matt 24:10–12; 18:7–9).

Matthew further explained that many false prophets will arise[80] and mislead many and because of the increased lawlessness,[81] most people's love will grow cold. There may be some evidence of this coldness of love late in the first century (1 John 2:18–23; Rev 3:15–16)[82] but this seems to have more eschatological proportions (2 Thess 2:1–12; Rev 13). All the Synoptics remind the disciples that within the two ways perspective, the one who endures to the end will be saved (Mark 13:13; Matt 24:13; Luke 21:19). After all this the end will come (Matt 24:14).

Further warnings are given to the disciples surrounding the event of abomination of desolation, which Daniel spoke about (Mark 13:14; Dan 8:13; 9:27; 11:31; 12:11; Rev 9:27; Matt 24:15; Luke 21:20). Daniel described an eschatological event of a seven-year period by a covenant between Israel and a gentile messiah. In the middle of this period (three and a half years in) the Jewish sacrifices and grain offerings will be

---

79. Josephus, *Ant.* 20.200–201; Justin Martyr, *1 Apol.* 31.6 identifies that during the Bar Kochba rebellion, Rabbi Akiva demanded that Christians deny Jesus as messiah to affirm Simon as messiah.

80. Corroborated in the first and second centuries by Josephus, *Ant.* 20.5, 97–99, 102, 188; *War* 2.253; 7.11.1; Eusebius, *Hist. eccl.* 4.6.2; maybe 2 Pet 2:1 but more likely false prophets among Jewish people previously as in OT.

81. Lawlessness in eschatological days: 2 Bar 41.3; 48.38; *m. Soṭah* 9.15; *b. Sanh.* 97a.

82. 1QpHab 2.1–10; *1 En.* 90.22–27; 91.7; 93.9 *Jub.* 23.14–17; 4 Ezra 5.1–2.

stopped, and the pinnacle of the summit of the temple will be defiled by an abomination that makes desolate (Dan 9:27; 12:11).

However, Daniel also predicts a similar abomination of desolation which Antiochus Epiphanes desecrated the sanctuary and cut off the regular Jewish sacrifice (Dan 8:3; 11:31). In this defiling, Antiochus settled his score with high priest Jason who had dethroned Menelaus as high priest. In 168–67 BC, Antiochus killed thirty thousand Jews, suppressed Jewish religion, suspended sacrifices for about three years, and later set up an altar and a statue of Zeus Olympus in the temple over the altar of burnt offering, upon which he then sacrificed a pig.[83] First Maccabees 1:54–56 described this desecration as "a desolating sacrifice." The Maccabean response to this was to stand firm even at the expense of their lives. For a few years the Jews wrenched Israel out of foreign control.

When Israel was re-conquered, Gaius tried to erect a statue of himself in the temple, and the Jews reaction echoed that of the Maccabees.[84] Some also see that this abomination might refer to Caligula's attempt to desecrate the temple in AD 40 by having his own statue set up in the Holy of Holies.[85] However, especially Luke makes it clear that the abomination of desolation that is referred to here is during a siege as in the Jewish revolt, which would exclude Caligula's attempt from being included (Luke 21:20).

Presumably, Jesus' teaching to the disciples gives the possibility for another historical abomination of desolation occurring in the Jewish revolt of 66–73, where the Romans surrounded and took Jerusalem and ruined the temple. During the rebellion, Josephus describes that the Zealots defiled the temple by occupying it, allowing criminals to plunder and roam freely in the Holy of Holies, and perpetrated murder within the temple itself.[86] Upon taking the temple, the tenth legion further abominated the temple by sacrificing to their standards standing in the Holy of Holies. Perhaps also the marble statue of a pig (the tenth legion mascot) at the south gate of the temple also contributes to this abomination. The Jewish revolt against Rome ended in the destruction of the temple and capture of Jerusalem in the year AD 70 by Emperor Titus' decision to demolish the entire city except for the western wall and three towers.[87]

83. 1 Macc 1:54–64; 6:7; 2 Macc 6:1–5; 8:17.

84. Josephus, *Ant.* 18.257–309.

85. Eusebius, *Dem. ev.* 8.2; Jerome, *Comm. Matt.*; Theissen, *Lokalkolorit und Zeitgeschichte in den Evangelien*, 132–76; Eisler, *Messiah and John the Baptist*, 314–15.

86. Josephus, *War* 4.3.7, 10; 4.5.4; 5.13.6; 6.2.1; 1QpHab 11.17–12.10.12.

87. Josephus, *War* 7.1.1; Eusebius, *Hist. eccl.* 3.5.4.

Then, Jerusalem was established as a Roman city with the Tenth Legion occupying the city and over eight hundred retired Roman soldiers were brought in by Titus to repopulate the city of Jerusalem.

In AD 132, Bar Kochba led a revolt reacting to these Roman measures. In the wake of this later revolt the temple site was further abominated by turning it into a temple to Jupiter with an equestrian statue to Emperor Hadrian established on the site of the Holy of Holies.[88] Perhaps, these continuing Roman measures should be viewed as continuing stages of the abomination of desolation.

With several abominations of desolation already having occurred, it is possible that there may yet be future expressions to realize this metaphor in the eschaton after the pattern and chronology of Daniel (Mark 13:14; Dan 8:13; 9:27; 11:31; 12:11; Rev 9:27; Matt 24:15; Luke 21:20). That is, an abomination of desolation three and a half years after an international treaty with Israel and three and a half years before the climactic expression of the kingdom begins.

Jesus exhorts those in Judea who see Jerusalem surrounded by armies to flee to the mountains quickly, not bothering to gather up goods from the house or cloak from the field (Mark 13:14–17; Matt 24:15–19; Luke 17:26–35; 21:20–23). Such a flight from wickedness is underscored by Jewish eschatological response (Isa 15:5; Jer 16:16; 49:8; Ezek 7:16; Amos 2:15–16; Nah 3:18; Zech 14:5; Matt 3:7; Rev 12:6).[89] Such flight during threatening time repeatedly saved the lives of those who left quickly (2 Sam. 23–24).[90] Luke repeatedly emphasized that the disciples were to swiftly flee without reservations, even warning them of what happened to Lot's wife. The third-person statements probably indicate the special circumstances for flight that each in the disciples' lifetime may face: some being on rooftops, some being in the field, and some being pregnant.[91] Because of this warning, Christians during the Roman siege of Jerusalem fled to Pella in the Decapolis region rather than the caves in the mountains which were the traditional hideout of the area (Mark

---

88. Dio Cassius, *Hist.* 69.12.1–14.3; Eusebius, *Chron.* "Hadrian, year 19"; *Dem. ev.* 6.13.

89. 1 Macc 2:28; 2 Macc 5:27; *T. Mos.* 9.6; *Ps. Sol.* 17.16–17; *Liv. Proph. Jer.* 15; *Asc. Isa.* 4.13; *Apoc. Elijah* 4.21.

90. 1 Macc 2:28; 2 Macc 5:27; Josephus, *War* 5.10.1; Epiphanius, *Pan.* 29.7; 30.2; *De Mens. et pond.* 15.

91. Eusebius, *Hist. eccl.* 3.5.3; *Sib. Or.* 2.190–92 and 2 Bar 10.13–14 also describes pregnant women and the suckling of kids as a hindrance in that day.

13:14; Ezek 7:16; Matt 24:16; Luke 21:21).[92] The fact that Jesus' prophecy recommends flight to the mountains and the historical destination of Christians was in the foothills of the Jordan Valley confirms that these statements were written predicatively rather than after the fact. The third-person statements may also refer to Daniel's prediction concerning the urgency of Judean inhabitants and disciples to flee the eschatological abomination of desolation. The first-century disciples (and presumably the eschatological ones also) should pray beforehand that their flight may not be in winter (perhaps because of a lack of provisions in the fields[93] or the tendency for winter rains[94]), nor on a Sabbath (which would limit distance traveled by the traditions), thus hindering escaping safely.

"Then" (τότε, Matt 24:16, 21, 23) in those days (Mark 13:19; Luke 21:22–23) there will be a great tribulation (θλῖψις μεγάλη)[95] such as has not occurred since the beginning of the world until now, nor ever shall. This indicates that Jesus is especially describing the eschatological climax abomination of desolation greater than these historical past expressions of the abomination of desolation (Mark 13:19; Matt 24:21).[96] Mark identified the tribulation as the most severe since creation, while Matthew identified this abomination of desolation as the greatest tribulation of all time for the Jews. That is, greater than such extreme persecutions as the Holocaust and the Assyrian conquest of Israel, so I see this "great tribulation" as still future in the eschaton.

Luke personalizes these vengeful days as great distress (ἀνάγκη μεγάλη) for Israel's land, with wrath (ὀργὴ) to the Jewish people (Luke 21:23–24). The expression of this wrath against Jews has many falling by edge of the sword and being led captive into dispersion among many other ethnic groups (ἐθνῶν). During this dispersion Jerusalem will be dominated by gentiles until the times of the gentiles are fulfilled. John the Baptist and the Essenes at Qumran believed themselves to be living at the brink of the

---

92. Eusebius, *Hist. eccl.* 3.5.3; Gundry, *Mark*, 774–75.
93. Schweizer, *Good News according to Mark*, 273.
94. Josephus, *Ant.* 18.8.6.
95. Eschatological imagery from *Sib. Or.* 3.185–90; also Rev 7:14.
96. Mark 13:19 drops the adjective "great" and adds that the tribulation is the most severe since God created the world. The greatness of difficulty of those end times is underscored (Jer 30:7; Joel 2:2; Rev 16:18; 1QM 1.9–14; 1 Macc 9:27), but some authors use similar language to describe tribulation now behind Israel (Josephus, *War* 1.12; *T. Mos.* 8.1). Similarly, Eusebius (*Hist. eccl.* 3.7.2) uses "great tribulation" to describe the conquest of Jerusalem during AD 70.

coming of the eschatological wrath (Matt 3:7, 12; Luke 3:7, 17).[97] This Lukan description better fits the first- and second-century conquests which brought on the dispersion of Jews and gentile domination of Jerusalem which has lasted until recent times in the history of Israel.

However, all the Synoptics draw the account into the eschatological context. Matthew and Mark point out that unless those days had been cut short, no life would have been saved; but for the sake of the elect those days shall be cut short (Mark 13:20; Matt 24:22).[98] The elect are disciples of Jesus alive on earth during this great tribulation gathered by the Son of Man into his salvation (ἐσώθη; Mark 13:20, 22, 27; Matt 24:22, 24, 31). These righteous sufferers have the glory and the dominion of Adam restored for them in salvation (Rom 5; 8:17–25; 2 Cor 4:7—5:21).[99]

To enable this elect to come into kingdom, the gospel of the kingdom will be preached to all ethnic groups before the end shall come (Mark 13:10; Matt 24:14). If the "all nations" is seen as with reference to the Roman context then the extensive spread of gospel during the first century fulfills this statement from the Indus valley to Spain and from northern Gaul to southern Ethiopia. This gospel spread began at Pentecost with many ethnicities represented (Acts 2:8–11). Wherever disciples traveled, they fulfilled aspects of this promise. If the "all nations" is taken in a more extensive manner, then it should fund missionary activity to fulfill the Great Commission, to all ethnicities before Jesus returns to establish his kingdom. Through this means the end-time promise of gentile salvation will be realized (Isa 45:15; 60:15–17; Mic 4:13).[100] It also indicates that this Olivet discourse looks beyond a preteristic coming of Christ to destroy Jerusalem, to include an eschatological coming to establish his kingdom.

These elect believers are vulnerable to deception so the time will be cut short (Mark 13:20, 22, 27; Matt 24:22, 24, 31). This attempt to deceive is especially evident in claims by false christs and false prophets that the Christ is at some place (Mark 13:21–23; Matt 24:23–26). Though great signs and wonders are used to deceive, the disciples are warned not to believe these false claims about Christ.

---

97. 1QH 11.18, 28.

98. Sir 36.8; 4Q385 frag. 3; *L.A.B.* 19.13; 2 Bar 20.1–2; 54.1; 83.1; *2 Esdr* 2.13; *Barn.* 4.3; *Apoc. Abr.* 29.13; *Trimorphic Prot.* 44.16; Davies and Allison, *Matthew*, 3:351.

99. 1QS 4.22–23; CD 3.18–20; 4.18; 6.10; cf. 1QH 4.15 with 2.16; 3.17–21; 2 Bar 15.7–8, 14; 25–27; 32; 48.29–47, 70–74; 51.3–11; *4 Ezra* 7.48 with 7.113–23; this is not to be identified with the cutting short of the rainy season (as in *1 En.* 80.2), which is a judgment on sinners' crops.

100. *T. Jud.* 24.5–6; *T. Levi* 18.9.

The coming of the Son of Man is not hidden in houses or the wilderness but visible for all to see like lightening flashing across the sky (Mark 13:26; Dan 7:13–14; Matt 24:27, 30; Luke 21:27).[101] Daniel's presentation of the Son of Man as cloud rider coming up to the Ancient of Days to receive his everlasting dominion, is shifted in early Judaism[102] and the NT to now describe the Son of Man's cloud riding from the Ancient of Days to come to earth to enforce his kingdom onto the willing and unwilling. Thus, the coming of the Son of Man is a very real visible coming of conquest and establishment of Christ's kingdom. This is not to be confused with a spiritual or personal coming like the coming of the Holy Spirit,[103] nor a vision at one's death (Acts 1:11; 7:56; 9:4–7). Jesus will return bodily from the heavens riding on the clouds, visible for all, conquering to establish his kingdom is his powerful coming (2 Pet 1:16, 18; Mark 13:26; Dan 7:13; Matt 24:30; Luke 21:27; Rev 19:11–16)[104] so that no one need be deceived.

It is recognizable as the coming of the Son of Man like the location of a dead animal in the desert can be recognized by the vultures flying over it (Matt 24:28).[105] Luke especially recognized that the Jewish people had ability to analyzing the weather, which makes them even more culpable in analyzing the age (Luke 12:54–59). It is like a farmer reading the coming of summer by noticing the signs in the leafing out of a fig tree (Matt 24:32–33).[106] This generation that experiences this evidence will not pass away until all is accomplished (Matt 24:34). It is guaranteed to happen because Jesus' words will not pass away (Matt 24:35; Luke 21:33). This certainty of Jesus' words is described in the same manner as that of the divine word (Ps 119:89, 160; Isa 40:8; 55:10–11).[107] That is, when these events take place, Christ's coming is eminent, and thus the need to watch

---

101. *Ep. Jer.* 61; 4Q246 2.1–2; 2 Bar 53.9. Lightening also occurs with divine theophanies and judgment (Exod 19:16; Pss 18:14; 144:6; Zech 9:14; Philo, *Vit. Mos.* 2.56; *L.A.B.* 11.4).

102. *1 En.* 37–71; 11Q13; 4Q400–405; 11Q17; *4 Ezra* 13.26, 52; Bar 29; *Tg. 1 Chron.* 3.24; *b. Sanh.* 38b.

103. Though the arrival of the Holy Spirit is an obvious eschatological phenomenon: Joel 2:28–29; Acts 1:6, 8; 2:1–21; 1QS 4.3–4; 8.12–16; *Sib. Or.* 4.46, 189; 2 Macc 7:23; 14:46.

104. Jub 1.28; *1 En.* 62.3; *T. Mos.* 10.7.

105. Davies and Allison, *Matthew*, 3:355–56 surveys eight views and concludes that this is the consensus of recent commentators and is also supported by *Apoc. Pet.* E 1.

106. Ethiopic *Apoc. Pet.* 2 allegorized fig tree to be Israel branching with martyrs.

107. Bar 4.1; Wis 18.4; *4 Ezra* 9.36–37.

the signs and be alert. Christ comes with his kingdom glories to follow (1 Pet 1:11; 4:11; 5:1, 10–11; 2 Pet 1:11, 16, 19).

Preceding the day of Christ's coming there will be cosmic disturbances as evidence of Messiah's coming (Mark 13:24–25; Isa 24:18–23; Joel 2:10, 31; 3:15; Matt 24:29; Luke 21:25; Acts 2:20; Rev 6:12–13; 8:12).[108] The sun and moon will be darkened, and the stars will fall from the sky. Admittedly, this language of upheaval has been used metaphorically in contexts that could be argued as now past (Isa 13:10; 34:4; Ezek 32:7; Amos 5:20; 8:9; Zeph 1:15).[109] Josephus describes some heavenly upheaval as omens of the AD 70 destruction: namely, a star and comet that looked like a sword over Jerusalem and the clouds looking like armies attacking cities.[110] However, when the language is climaxed by the entrance into the everlasting kingdom, as it is here in the Olivet discourse, it remains as a vivid astronomical indicator of when the kingdom will begin (Mark 13:24–30; Joel 2:10, 31; 3:15; Matt 24:28–29, 32–35; Luke 21:25–32; Rev 6:12–13; 8:12). The fact that these cosmic disturbances continue to be used to describe the eschatological circumstances after the Jerusalem conquest had occurred shows that the biblical writers expect them to really occur in the sky (Rev 6:12–13; 8:12). This darkening of the heavens is more supernatural than a natural description of cloud cover because the powers of the heavens are shaken. Likewise, the earthly impact is extreme with dismay, perplexity, and men fainting from fear (Luke 21:25–26). All the tribes of the earth will see the Son of Man and mourn their judgment (Matt 24:30).

Jesus will come powerfully sending forth his angels to gather his elect from all over the world (Mark 13:26; 2 Pet 2:16, 18; Matt 13:41; 16:27; 24:30–31; 25:31; Luke 21:27–28; Rev 14:15–19).[111] The sound of a

---

108. 1QH 11.13; *Sib. Or.* 2.194, 200–202; 3.81–93, 796–808; 5.344–50; 7.125; 8.190–92, 233, 413; *1 En.* 80.4–6; *As. Mos.* 10.5–6; *T. Levi* 4.1; *4 Ezra* 5.4–5; *2 Bar* 70; 70.2; *T. Mos.* 10.5; *Apoc. Elijah* 5.7; *b. Sanh.* 99a; this is not to be identified as fulfilled with the rending of the Jerusalem Temple's external veil with stars sown on it as was suggested by: Allison, *The End of the Ages has Come*, 33).

109. Besides these times of conquest, *Sib. Or.* 5.152 claims creation was shaken at the appearance of Nero and *4 Ezra* 4.18–19 speak of cosmic disorders at the giving of the Law. On this basis, Wright (*Jesus and the Victory of God*, 354–55) argues that this metaphor then only means "an earth shattering event!" rather than actually describing cosmic events.

110. Josephus, *War* 6.5.288–309.

111. Angels often accompany a theophany (Deut 33:2; Isa 6:2–7; Ps 68:17). Angels aid in the gathering of damned and elect (Jer 51:53; *1 En.* 1.6–9; 54.6; 62.11; 63.1; *Apoc. Elijah* 3.4; *Asc. Isa.* 4.14; *4 Ezra* 4.26–37; 9.17; *2 Bar* 70.1–2; *b. B. Mes.* 83b; *Midr. Ps.* on

trumpet or *šophar* horn will signal their gathering (Joel 2:1; Zeph 1:16; Zech 9:14; 1 Cor 15:52; 1 Thess 4:16)[112] much like it called Jews to gather for Sabbath or other sacred occasions (Num 10:10; Josh 6:5; 1 Kgs 1:34; Ps 81:3; Isa 27:13; Jer 4:5).[113] This gathering is presented in similar language as the Jews being gathered from dispersion to fund a new exodus (Isa 27:12–13).[114] This visual and audible coming indicates that redemption is near.

In the same way as before the impending Noahic judgment, no change in lives was made (Matt 24:37–39). Like Noah's flood, when the Son of Man comes all the people not among the protected elect will be taken away in judgment (Matt 24:39–41; 2 Pet 2:6; 3:5–7; Jude 7; Luke 17:26–30).[115] Men and women will be carrying on their normal occupation and then many will be taken away in judgment[116] (not in rapture) while others beside them are left to go into the kingdom (as in Matt 13:30, 42–43, 49–50; 24:51; 25:10–13, 30). The kingdom is already planned but only part of these plans is revealed to God's faithful now (Dan 2:28, 44).[117] The fact that no one knows the day or hour (except the Father) increases the need for Jesus' disciples to be alert (Mark 13:32; Matt 24:36, 44; Acts 1:7). This inability to identify the exact time could be called "imminence" and prompt alertness for disciples.

Therefore, the disciples are to be alert, watchful and prepared (γρηγορεῖτε) for they do not know which day our Lord is coming and all

---

8:1). Additionally, Gabriel blows the *šophar* for gathering into kingdom (*Quest. Ezra* B 11; *Gk. Apoc. Ezra* 4.36).

112. *Ps. Sol.* 11.1; *Did.* 16.6; *Apoc. Abr.* 31.1; *Shemoneh Esreh* benediction 10; *Quest. Ezra* B 11.9; *Gk. Apoc. Ezra* 4.36; Davies and Allison, *Matthew*, 3:363.

113. *T. Sukk.* 4.11–12; 1QM; *Par. Jer.* 4.2; *Roš Haš.* 26a.

114. Bar 4.36–37; *1 En.* 57.2; *Pss. Sol.* 11.3; this is not just a re-gathering from the Assyrian and Babylonian captivity as Brant Pitre proposed (*Jesus, the Tribulation*, 4, 35–130), but of the continuing dispersion under any gentile domination, including Greek, Roman, and more recent as well.

115. The flood is an eschatological image: 2 Pet 2:5; Isa 24:18; *Jub.* 20.5–6; 1QH 11.14, 29–36; *Sib. Or.* 3.689–91; Josephus, *Ant.* 1.2.3; 1.72–76; *1 En.* 14.1–16, 19; 17.5; 67.10–13; 93.4; *4 Ezra* 13.10–11; *2 En.* 10.2; *Apoc. Adam* 3.3; *3 En.* 45.3; *Mek. on Ex.* 18.1; *b. Sanh.* 108a; Luke 17:26–30; 2 Pet 2:6; Jude 7 adds Sodom as another judgment metaphor along with *Jub.* 16.6; 22.22; 36.10; Greek *Apoc. Ezra* 2.18–19; 7.12.

116. In Matt 24:40 the "then" (τότε) connects verses 40–41 with the prior verse 39. Thus, the phrase "took them all away" (Matt 24:39; ἦρεν ἅπαντας, οὕτως ἔσται) which means judgment should be taken as a synonym for the phrase "will be taken" (Matt 24:40–41; παραλαμβάνεται), indicating that they will be taken away in judgment, not rapture.

117. 1QpHab 7.4–5, 8; 1QS 3.23; 1QM 3.9; 1QH 12.23; *1 En.* 9.6; 103.2; *4 Ezra* 14.5.

that has been said will come upon those who dwell on the earth (Mark 13:33–37; Matt 24:42; Luke 21:34–36; Acts 1:7).[118] This alertness is extended in a practical way of praying in order that they might escape all these things when they take place, so the disciples might stand before the Son of Man. This alertness is illustrated by Mark with a parable of a man taking a journey, who left his slaves in charge with tasks, commanding the doorkeepers to stay on the alert. "Therefore be on the alert-for you do not know when the master of the house is coming, whether in the evening, at midnight, at cockcrowing, or in the morning, lest he come suddenly and find you asleep. And what I say to you, I say to all. Be on the alert!" (Mark 13:35–37). This alertness is a common theme among Jewish parables as well.[119] Matthew recounts several parables on the alertness theme but the most pointed develops a faithful householder who would prevent his house from being broken into by a thief as a parallel to the disciples' alertness to be ready for the coming of the Son of Man (Matt 24:42–44). Luke had earlier presented this same parable to emphasize the disciples need to be ready in a full commitment to the kingdom (Luke 12:37–40). The Gospel of Thomas tells this parable twice, first in verse 21 to teach this alertness theme, and then again in verse 103 to indicate an alert person will be blessed. First Peter 5:8 extends Christian alertness as a quality within a sober spirit, resisting the devil.

The imminence of the Lord's coming is balanced in 2 Pet between God's timing and human participation. This "Lord's coming" may be the same "coming of the Son of Man" to which the Olivet discourse and Christ's powerful coming developed in 2 Pet 1:16–19. Peter emphasized that Christians beloved by God need to remember that God's time is different than the way humans count time; "with the Lord one day is as a thousand years, and a thousand years as one day" (2 Pet 3:8). This different divine time is not an argument for a chiliastic or thousand-year kingdom as developed in Rev 20 and early Judaism and Christianity.[120] In fact, Peter's statements argue the opposite of a known time frame for he points out that one cannot calculate when these events will occur. Neither

---

118. *Mek. on Ex.* 16:32; *Der Eres Rab.* 10; *Ps. Sol.* 17.21; *2 Bar* 21.8; 48.3; 54.1; *4 Ezra* 4.52.

119. A similar parable on this alertness theme is in *Tos. Soṭah* 15.7.

120. *2 En.* 32.1–33.2 text J which is not included in text A; two Arabic manuscripts of *Apoc. Bar.* 27.1–15; Akiva, *Pes.* 68a, *Ber.* 34b, *Sanh.* 91b, 97a–b; 99a; *Šabb.* 63a, 113b; *Abod. Zar.* 9a; *Sifre* [Deut 310]; *Tanch. 'Ekeb* 7; *Ep. Barn.* 5.4; Irenaeus, *Haer.* 5.23.2; 5.28.3; Strack and Billerbeck, *Kommentar zum Neuen Testament*, 3:826; Helyer, "Necessity, Problems, and Promise," 606–9.

does the verse mean that God is contemporaneous with time[121] because Peter still describes God as experiencing time as days and years. Furthermore, God's counting of days and years as being different than human assessment does not mean time is meaningless. God's time as with God's attributes are measured on a vaster scale than a human normally considers. The fact that God's timing has not been reached yet provides no grounds for viewing it as slow, which would raise a concern of God's indifference or impotence (2 Pet 3:9). Presumably some had regarded it as slow, but Peter exhorts believers to regard it as an expression of God's compassionate patience in bringing in salvation for them and others who would repent (2 Pet 3:9, 15). However, to those who mark God as impotent or indifferent, judgment will come quickly when they are not ready (2 Pet 3:4, 9–10). God's timing hinges on his accomplishing a salvific goal rather than an arbitrary date.

Peter exhorts his audience to look for and to hasten the coming of the day of the Lord (2 Pet 3:12). The first word (προσδοκῶντας) describes an expectant "waiting" and observing, with hope and perhaps fear about what will take place. The second word (σπεύδοντας) describes "zealous, industry to hasten" the coming.[122] This concept is not hastening toward the coming, for that would require a preposition but by our zealous industry moving up the calendar day sooner through developing zealous holiness and godliness (2 Pet 3:11–12) and perhaps also repentance and proclaiming the gospel (Acts 3:19–21). Peter offers Israel the refreshing kingdom blessings of the Abrahamic, Mosaic, and Davidic covenants (Acts 2:30–38; 3:13–26), if they would repent and embrace Jesus as their messianic prophet and king (Acts 3:19–21).[123] Both ways to move up the timing of Christ's kingdom would be a postmillennial aspect within the divinely controlled coming of the Lord (a premillennial framework, or more technically, a pre-kingdom framework, since Peter does not develop the millennium as does Rev 20).

When the day of the Lord arrives, God judges the earth by means of a cataclysm which destroys the present heavens and earth (2 Pet 3:7, 10, 12). The "elements" (στοιχεῖα) that are destroyed are the heavenly bodies, such as the sun, moon, stars, and earth (2 Pet 3:7, 10, 12; Joel 2:10;

---

121. Contra *Jub.* 4.30; *Apoc. Abr.* 28; *1 En.* 91.17; *2 En.* 33.
122. BAG, "σπεύδω," 769; Juza, "Echoes of Sodom and Gomorrah," 227–45, esp. 241–42.
123. See discussion in chapter on "Peter's Gospel."

Mark 13:24–26; Rev 6:12–13).[124] Several words describe the destruction process, evidencing that Peter is straining his vocabulary to show the intensity and exhaustiveness of the cataclysm. The heavenly bodies will burn up, consumed by heat in a "fiery end" (καυσούμενα, 2 Pet 3:10, 12; πυρί, 3:7, 12). In this fire, the bodies will melt in "destruction" and "disappear" (τήκεται and λυθήσονται, 2 Pet 3:12; παρελεύσονται, 2 Pet 3:10). The process of the destruction will be with a hissing, crackling sound and a "great sudden roar" (ῥοιζηδόν, 2 Pet 3:10). All the heavenly bodies will "be found" (εὑρεθήσεται)[125] to be included in the process of destruction (2 Pet 3:10). Until that time, the heavenly bodies will be reserved "for fire" (dative of πυρί) by God's word (2 Pet 3:7).

Peter reminds those who mock this word of judgment, that it is the word of God (through prophets, the Lord Jesus, and apostles) that predicted that they mock (2 Pet 3:2–3, 5, 7). This same word of God spoke the heavens and earth into creation (2 Pet 3:5). God who spoke this word has judged before (2 Pet 3:6–7), so it is certain that the heavenly bodies will be reserved for a fiery cataclysm by God's word.

This conflagration is not like that in Stoicism, within which a nonpersonal quasi-divine orchestrates a fire conflagration of the heavens and earth in order to leave them in an earlier stage setting up an endless cycle of conflagrations after thousands of years.[126] Rather, in Judeo-Christianity's linear time, the personal God creates and judges the world by fire in order to personally re-create a new heaven and earth once as a destination of the restoration era of kingdom under Christ's reign (2 Pet 3:5, 10–11; Gen 1–2; Acts 3:21).

---

124. The elements should not be seen here as elementary substances as in Stoicism because such elements of earth, water, air, and fire are foreign to the text. Additionally, it is impossible for fire to consume fire as an element. There is also no evidence that these elements refer to spirits.

125. Metzger, *Textual Commentary*, 636 identifies that the reading is a difficult D reading but concludes for "being found" whereas the fifth revised edition of the Aland, *Greek New Testament*, 781 improves the reading to a C reading by negating the εὑρεθήσεται, thus, "not found." Either way one takes the textual criticism, the text still speaks of complete destruction either in "finding" that the items have been destroyed or because they have been destroyed, they cannot "be found." Wolters, "Worldview and Textual Criticism," 405–13; Davids, "Textual Criticism of 1 Peter 3:10."

126. Stoic destruction of earth with fire occurs naturally from within (Cicero, *Nat. d.* 2.46.118; Lucretius, *R. N.* 5.381–410; Philo, *Her.* 228) in order to begin again in endless cycles (Seneca, *Marc.* 26.6–7; Philo, *Spec. Laws* 1.208; *Mos.* 2.65; *Aet.* 9, 47, 76, 107; Arius Didymus in Eusebius, *Prep. ev.* 15.18; Neyrey, *2 Peter, Jude*, 241.

The goal of this judgment is primarily one of destruction of ungodly humans and not merely heavenly bodies (2 Pet 3:7). Apparently, the destruction of the existing heavens and earth is the extreme cost it takes to judge ungodly humans. The person who considers this message should be zealously holy and godly, identified with the way of salvation and secluded from the way of judgment (1 Pet 1:13–16; 2 Pet 1:5–6, 11; 3:11). The believer should live her life in such a way as to be recognized by God who judges, as identifying herself with Christ's spotless and blameless character (1 Pet 1:19; 2 Pet 3:14) and far from the false teachers' character of blots and blemishes (2 Pet 2:13). Furthermore, any length of time it takes for the cataclysm to come about should be considered as the Lord's patient salvation work and not an opportunity for sin.

Christ reigns currently in his everlasting kingdom but there is a future expression of this reign in the restoration of all things. As with the exhortation to look for the coming of the Lord, Peter describes himself and his readers as in the condition of looking for (προσδοκῶντες) the new heavens and earth (2 Pet 3:12–14). They are expectantly waiting and observing with hope and perhaps fear about God's bringing into existence this remarkably new order which serves as the salvific goal, completely characterized by righteousness. The newness of these heavens and earth evidence that the new order is not merely a remaking or refurbishing of the present order but rates a whole new order of authentically offering the kingdom restoration and the refreshing benefits of the Abrahamic, Mosaic, and Davidic covenants, if Israel would repent and embrace Jesus as their messianic prophet and king (Act 3:19–26).[127] Already kingdom benefits are being realized by believers in forgiveness and the new covenant bestowal of the Holy Spirit. However, Peter offers the era of Israel restoration in which Jesus is the new Moses leading Israel into the prophetically predicted kingdom era, if Israel would repent (Act 3:19–23).

The restoration of all things is another description of either the same age or an earlier stage approximating the new kingdom order (Acts 3:21). The word for "restoration" (ἀποκαταστάσεως) refers to a restoration of everything either to a previous state (as Isa 11 indicated a return to the garden of Eden, or Isa 60–63 indicate the glories of Solomonic trade with other nations)[128] or to perfection.[129] Such a restoration in Judaism took a teleological framework as the designed climax within linear

127. Kennard, *Biblical Covenantalism*, esp. 2:221–47; *Gospel*, 117–36.
128. Kennard, *Biblical Theology of Isaiah*, 223–27.
129. Albrecht Oepke, "ἀποκατάστασις," TDNT 1:389–90.

history, rather than cycles of endless recurrence in Egyptian or Babylonian cyclical history. The concept of restoration includes restoring Israel back into the land after the exile (Jer 16:15; 23:8; 24:6). The restoration eschatologically raises Israel to its full former glory (Ezek 16:55). In this restoration, the prophet Elijah restores all things (Mal 4:6; Mark 9:12; Matt 17:11). The objective restoration of all things for Peter begins when Jesus Christ returns from heaven to earth (Acts 3:20–21). The prophets spoke about the coming of Christ beginning the restoration; it is characterized as the time when the Abrahamic blessings will be realized by repentant humanity, and Christ functions as the Mosaic mediatorial prophet on earth (Acts 3:21–26). The fact that the non-repentant are excluded from these blessings of restoration indicates that this restoration is not a universal salvation.[130] This indicates that the restoration is a state of perfection, excluding the unrepentant that expresses a continuum with the best of the past but excels it. Peter does not limit this kingdom to a thousand years but leaves it as an opened everlasting kingdom to realize all the glorious predictions that the prophets have left to be fulfilled.

This objective restoration is identified with the subjective times of "refreshing" (ἀναψύξεως, Acts 3:19 in English but 20 in Greek). With the aorist verb and the relationship with the noun "time" (καιροὶ), times of refreshing cannot be merely personal, nor corporate breaks in end-time affliction;[131] it needs to be seen as the overarching age of refreshment. The concept of ἀναψύξεως includes "breathing space," "relief," "relaxation," "refreshment," and of course here as the "messianic kingdom age of rest." The definitive age of restoration and refreshing objectively begins together when Christ returns to the earth. However, Peter develops a subjective effect of when that might be. Since Peter makes an authentic offer for the messianic kingdom, the Jews' repentance, providing them with forgiveness, serves as a condition enabling the divinely purposed messianic age of rest to come (as an age, and not merely an individual experience).[132] This means that while the age begins with Christ's coming, the repentance of these Jews (and maybe other non-Christians) influences when Christ will come to initiate this age. That is, perhaps compatibilist responsiveness in repentance and maybe evangelism within God's plan might bring the messianic age of rest sooner than might otherwise be the case. In

---

130. Contra Origen, *Princ.* 1.6.1–4; 2.3.1–5; 3.6.1–9 and any universalists that follow him.

131. Albert Dihle, "ἀνάψυξις," TDNT 9:664.

132. Based on the purpose clause with the aorist subjunctive and previous note.

fact, Jesus as God's son would provide Israel with this internal repentance and obedience, if Israel was open to this possibility (Act 3:24–26). This authentic offer would move the timing up concerning kingdom, if Israel repented. Unfortunately, Israel as a nation did not repent (Acts 4:21; 5:40; 7:54, 58; 12:2–3) and the kingdom era has not come as of yet in its fullest restoration form, where Israel's enemies are utterly defeated (Acts 2:35; Mark 12:36; Ps 110:1).

Through this radical restoration of a new kingdom, Peter emphasized the eschatological nature of personal salvation, reflective of pharisaic resurrection into kingdom.[133] While Christ is already raised, believers will join in participating in a similar resurrection experience. Robert Webb lists expressions of this eschatological personal salvation from 1 Pet as follows:[134]

1.3		a living hope
1.3		the resurrection of Jesus Christ from the dead
1.4		an inheritance . . . kept in heaven for you
1.5		a salvation ready to be revealed in the last time will receive praise, glory, and honor when Jesus Christ is revealed

---

133. *1 En.* 58.3; 62.14–16; 91.10; 92.2; 108.11–14; *2 Bar.*[Syriac] 30.1–5; 2 Macc 7:9–14, 22–23; 14:43–46; 4 Macc 7:19; 16:25; *4 Ezra* 7.32; *Sib. Or.* 4.180; *T. Ben.* 10.6–8; *T. Levi* 18; *T. Jud.* 24; *T. Hos.* 6:2 interpret this text to be resurrection whereas the text speaks of the reviving of Israel on the third day; *Tg. Jon.* on Isa 27:12–13 describes salvation as being accomplished on the third day; *b. Sanh.* 90b where Gamaliel claims that God would give the resurrected patriarchs land, not merely their descendants, and *Johanan Numbers* 18:28 the portion of YHWH given to Aaron is taken that he will be alive again, likewise Num 15:31 is claimed that the remaining guilt of the offender will be accountable in the world to come; 91b–92a; *B. Ta'an.* 2a; *B. Ketub.* 111; *m. Sanh.* 10.1, 3; *T. Mos.* 10.8–10; *Gen. Rab.* 14.5; 28.3; *Lev. Rab.* 14.9; *Messianic Apocalypse* adds resurrection to a modification of Ps 146:5–9 as a Messianic expectation to be done to others; *T. Jud.* 25.4 claims this Messianic resurrection would begin with Abraham, Isaac, and Jacob; *T. Benj.* claims that after these are raised the whole of Israel will be raised; *Pss. Sol.* 3.11–12; 4Q521 frag. 2, col. 2.1–13; frags. 7 and 5, col. 2.1–7; 1QH 14.29–35; 19.10–14; *Targum Songs* 8.5; the benediction in the *Amidah*, the *Shemoneh Esre*. However, Wis 3.1; 8.19–20; 9.15 and Josephus' description of the Pharisees (*Ant.* 17.152–54; 18.1.3–5; *War* 2.151–53; 2.8.14; *Ap.* 2.217–18) follow more a Platonic immortality of the soul view, but even here, departing from Platonism, the soul eventually is given a body to match (Wis 9.15; Josephus, *War* 2.163). Also, the biblical authors (Mark 12:18–27; Matt 22:23–33; Acts 23:6–7) and the *Eighteen Benedictions* present the Pharisees as believing the bodily resurrection of the dead; Gillman, *Death of Death*, 101–42; Wright, *Resurrection*, 129–206 for the post-biblical Jewish view. The early church from patristic through medieval eras embraced bodily resurrection instead of Platonic immortality of the soul with regard to personal eschatology (Bynum, *Resurrection of the Body*; Wright, *Resurrection*, 480–552).

134. Webb, "Intertexture and Rhetorical Strategy," 82–83.

1.9	receive your salvation
1.10	prophets prophesied concerning this salvation
1.11	prophets inquire into . . . the subsequent glory
1.12	angels long to look into these things (i.e., the subsequent glory)
1.13	the grace that Jesus Christ will bring when he is revealed
1.20	Christ was revealed at the end of the ages
1.21	God raised Christ from the dead and gave him glory
1.21	your hope is set on God
2.2	grow into salvation
3.7	wives (along with husbands) are also heirs of the gracious gift of life
3.9	called to inherit a blessing
3.15	the hope that is within you
3.18	Christ was made alive (i.e., resurrected)
3.21	the resurrection of Jesus Christ
3.22	all the spiritual forces of evil are subject to Christ
4.6	believers who have died will experience resurrection life
4.7	eschatological salvation is imminent
4.13	will be joyous when Christ's glory is revealed
4.18	the righteous will be saved
5.1	the author is able to share in the glory to be revealed
5.4	when the chief shepherd appears the elders will win the crown of glory
5.6	God will lift you up in due time
5.10	God has called you to his eternal glory
5.10	God will restore, establish, strengthen, and settle you

In this eschatological salvation, God, Christ, believers, and faithful elders all receive glory in kingdom. Such an abundant eschatological salvation fosters the believer with substantial hope.

Additionally, the Sadducees nonsense question provided Jesus with the opportunity to identify that resurrection begins for believers when they die (Mark 12:18–27; Matt 22:23–33; Luke 20:27–40).[135] The Sadducees built a theological riddle on the law for Levirate marriage, which provided an inheritance within a family if a husband died without an heir (Deut 25:5).[136] The Sadducees wove a nonsensical question about Levirate marriage for procreating an heir continuing in the afterlife, and wonder if a wife had seven husbands whose wife would she be in the resurrection

---

135. Josephus, *Ant.* 13.297–98; 18.1.4; 18.16–17; *War* 2.8.14; 2.164–66; *Nahum Commentary* on 3.8 (col. 3.8–9), 3.9b–11 (col. 3.12–14.8); *m. 'Abot* 1.3.

136. Josephus, *Ant.* 4.8.23; *m. Yebamot*.

afterlife.[137] The absurdity is made particularly acute by conjectures of marriage in resurrection (foreign to the law), and polyandry (foreign to Judaism). Jesus responded that Sadducees were ignorant about the resurrection,[138] which he understands is evident from the Scriptures in a Pharisaic orientation, and God can do it. So, Jesus claimed they were playing with half a deck of Scriptures with too small a God. Jesus instructs that resurrection is not for procreating and levirate marriage, showing Sadducees were out of touch with the purposes of the law. Jesus passed from the manner of resurrection to its fact, populated already by Abraham, Isaac, and Jacob. To demonstrate this, Jesus cites Pentateuch texts which the Sadducees would recognize as Scripture, what God said to Moses in Exod 3:6, "I am the God of Abraham, and the God of Isaac, and the God of Jacob," and then affirmed that God is not the God of the dead but of the resurrected living (Mark 12:27; Luke 16:19–31).[139] Such a affirmation of immediate resurrection upon death is an encouragement for any who know gospel believers who have been persecuted and martyred, for God vindicates them in spirit resurrection (1 Pet 4:6).

Peter presents a highly developed OT eschatology by letting the light of it shine through a series of small windows. The end-time events of the day of the Lord, cataclysm, and restoration follow in the wake of the coming of Jesus Christ as Daniel's Son of Man. This pre-restoration view fits within a modern concept of premillennialism but broader than this as pre-kingdom, since for Peter kingdom is not developed as a thousand years. It also includes features normally associated with amillennialism as Christ is currently the Davidic king in heaven reigning overall, and dead believers are currently alive in resurrection life in the realm of the spirit. This pre-restoration view also includes a postmillennial feature in bringing the restoration sooner by human effort of being zealous in holiness and godliness, and perhaps Israel's repentance to evangelism. The issue and timing of rapture is nowhere developed in Petrine theology. Would that we could make room for Peter's thought forms in our theology and practice his exhortation to alert peaceful pure living in our lives.

---

137. Wis 2.1–5; *1 En.* 102.6–11; *m. Sanh.* 10.1; *b. Sanh.* 90b.

138. Josephus, *Ant.* 18.1.4; *War* 2.8.14.

139. 4 Macc 7:18–19; 13.17; 16:25; Philo, *Sacr.* 1.5; *T. Abr.* 20.8–14; 50–55; *Qoh. Rab.* 9.5.1; *b. Sanh* 90b; *Ex. Rab.* 1.8; *Deut. Rab.* 3.15; *L.A.B.* 4.11; *T. Isaac* 2.1–5; *T. Benj.* 10.6; *Apoc. Sedr.* 14.3; *3 En.* 44.7.

Select Bibliography

Abbot, Edwin. *Flatland: A Romance of Many Dimensions*. London: Seeley, 1884.
Abegg, Martin G. "The Covenant of the Qumran Sectarians." In *The Concept of the Covenant in the Second Temple Period*, edited by Stanley Porter and Jacqueline deRoo, 81–98. Leiden: Brill, 2003.
Abraham, William J. "The Epistemology of Jesus: An Initial Investigation." In *Jesus and Philosophy: New Essays*, edited by Paul Moser, 149–68. Cambridge: Cambridge University Press, 2009.
Abrahams, Israel. *Studies in Pharisaism and the Gospels*. 1st Series. Cambridge: Cambridge University Press, 1917.
———. *Studies in Pharisaism and the Gospels*. 2nd Series. Cambridge: Cambridge University Press, 1924.
Achtemeier, Paul. *1 Peter*. Hermenia. Minneapolis, MN: Fortress, 1996.
Adams, Edward. "The Coming of the Son of Man in Mark's Gospel." *TynBul* 56.2 (2005) 39–61.
———. *Constructing the World: A Study in Paul's Cosmological Language*. Edinburgh: T. & T. Clark, 2000.
Adams, Robert. "The Problem of Total Devotion." In *Rationality, Religious Belief, and Moral Commitment*, edited by Robert Audi and William Wainwright, 169–94. Ithaca: Cornell University Press, 1986.
Aland, Barbara, et al. *The Greek New Testament*. Stuttgart: Deutsche Bibelgesellschaft, 2014.
Aland, Kurt. *The Authorship and Integrity of the New Testament: Some Recent Studies*. Theological Collections 4. London: SPCK, 1965.
Allison, D. C. *The End of the Ages Has Come*. Philadelphia, PA: Fortress, 1985.
Alston, William. *Perceiving God: The Epistemology of Religious Experience*. Ithaca: Cornell University Press, 1991.
Althaus, Paul. *The Theology of Martin Luther*. Minneapolis, MN: Fortress, 1966.
Anderson, A. A. *The Book of Psalms. Volume 1 Psalms 1–72*. Grand Rapids: Eerdmans, 1972.
Anderson, Gary. *Charity: The Place of the Poor in the Biblical Tradition*. New Haven: Yale University Press, 2013.
Anderson, Hugh. *The Gospel According to Mark*. Edinburgh: Oliphants, 1976.

Anderson, R. Dean. *Glossary of Greek Rhetorical Terms Connected to Methods of Argumentation, Figures and Tropes from Anaximenes to Quintilian*. Leuven: Peeters, 2000.

Anderson, Ray S. "On Being Human: The Spiritual Saga of a Creaturely Soul." In *Whatever Happened to the Soul? Scientific and Theological Portraits of Human Nature*, edited by Warren Brown et al., 40–73. Minneapolis, MN: Fortress, 1998.

Anselm. "Foreknowledge and Freechoice." In *Readings in Medieval Philosophy*, edited by Andrew Schoedinger, 203–8. New York: Oxford University Press, 1996.

Applegate, J. K. "The Co-Elect Woman of 1 Peter." *NTS* 38 (1992) 587–604.

Aquinas, Thomas. "Summa Theologica." In *Aquinas: Great Books of the Western World*, 19:1–826; 20:1–1085. Chicago: Encyclopaedia Britannica, 1952.

Assmann, Jan. *Das kulturelle Gedächtnis: Schrift, Erinnerung und politische Identität in frühen Hochkulturen*. Munich: C. H. Beck, 1992.

Augustine. *Great Books of the Western World*. Vol. 18, *Augustine*. Chicago: Encyclopaedia Britannica, 1952.

Aulén, Gustav. *Christus Victor: An Historical Study of the Three Main Types of the Idea of Atonement*. New York: Macmillan, 1969.

Aune, David. "The Forgiveness Petition in the Lord's Prayer: First Century Literary, Liturgical and Cultural Contexts." In *Jesus, Gospel Tradition and Paul in the Context of Jewish and Greco-Roman Antiquity*, 66–71. Tübingen: Mohr Siebeck, 2013.

———. "Magic in Early Christianity." *Principat* 23/2; *vorkonstantinisches Christentum. Vchaeltnis zu roemischem Staat und heidischer Religion. Aufstieg und Niedergang der Roemischen Welt: 2*, edited by Wolfgang Haase, 1507–57. New York: Walter de Gruyter, 1980.

Austin, John. *How To Do Things with Words*. Oxford: Oxford University Press, 1976.

Avi-Yonah, Michael. *Hellenism and the East: Contacts and Interrelations from Alexander to the Roman Conquest*. Jerusalem: Institute of Languages, Literature and the Arts, Hebrew University, University Microfilms International, 1978.

Ayayo, Karelynne. "Magical Exectations and the Two-Stage Healing of Mark 8." *BBR* 24.3 (2014) 379–91.

Bahr, G. J. "The Seder of Passover and the Eucharistic Words." *NovT* 12 (1970) 181–202.

Bailey, K. E. "Informal Controlled Oral Tradition and the Synoptic Gospels." *AJT* 5 (1991) 34–54.

———. "Middle Eastern Oral Tradition and the Synoptic Gospels." *ExpTim* 106 (1995) 363–67.

Balch, David. "Early Christian Criticism of Patriarchal Authority: 1 Peter 2:11—3:12." *USQR* 39 (1984–85) 161–73.

———. "Hellenization/Acculturation in 1 Peter." In *Perspectives on First Peter*, edited by Charles Talbert, 79–101. Macon, GA: Mercer University Press, 1986.

———. *Let Wives Be Submissive: The Domestic Code in 1 Peter*. SBLMS 26. Chico: Scholars, 1981.

Baldwin, Joyce. *Daniel: An Introduction & Commentary*. Downers Grove: InterVarsity, 1978.

Balentine, Samuel. *Leviticus: Interpretation*. Louisville: Westminster John Knox, 2002.

Baley, Daniel. "Our Suffering and Crucified Messiah' [*Dial.* 111.2]: Justin Martyr's Allusions to Isaiah 53 in His Dialogue with Trypho with Special Reference to the New Edition of Marcovich." In *The Suffering Servant: Isaiah 53 in Jewish and Christian Sources*, edited by Bernd Janowski and Peter Stuhlmacher, 324–417. Grand Rapids: Eerdmans, 2004.

Baltzer, Klaus. *The Covenant Formulary in the Old Testament*. Philadelphia, PA: Fortress, 1971.

———. *Das Bundesformular. Seine Ursprung und Seine Verwendung im A.T. Wiss. Monograph 2*. A. und N.T. 4. Neukirchen: Neukirchen-Vluyn, 1964.

Bammel, Ernst. "Markus 10:11f und das jüdische Eherecht." *ZNW* 61 (1970) 95–101.

Barclay, William. *The Gospel of Matthew*. Philadelphia, PA: Westminster, 1975.

Barnett, P. W. "The Jewish Sign Prophets." *NTS* 27 (1980) 679–97.

Barr, James. *The Semantics of Biblical Language*. London: Oxford University Press, 1961.

Barrett, C. K. *A Critical and Exegetical Commentary on the Acts of the Apostles*. 2 vols. London: T. & T. Clark, 1994.

Barth, Karl. *Church Dogmatics*. Edinburgh: T. & T. Clark, 1956.

Barton, Stephen. *Discipleship and Family Ties in Mark and Matthew*. Cambridge: Cambridge University Press, 1994.

———. "Memory and Remembrance in Paul." In *Memory in the Bible and Antiquity: The Fifth Durham-Tubingen Research Symposium (Durham, September 2004)*, edited by Stephen Barton et al., 333–34. Tübingen: Mohr Siebeck, 2007.

Bauckham, Richard. "The Gospel of John and the Synoptic Problem." In *New Studies in the Synoptic Problem, Oxford Conference, April 2008*, edited by P. Foster et al., 658–85. Leuven: Uitgeverij Peeters, 2011.

———. "James, Peter, and the Gentiles," In *The Missions of James, Peter, and Paul: Tensions in Early Christianity*, edited by Bruce Chilton and Craig Evans, 91–142. Leiden: Brill, 2005.

———. *Jesus and the Eyewitnesses: The Gospels as Eyewitness Testimony*. Grand Rapids: Eerdmans, 2006.

———. *Jude, 2 Peter*. WBC 50. Waco: Word, 1983.

———. "Markan Christology According to Richard Hays: Some Addenda." *Journal of Theological Interpretation* 2.1 (2017) 21–36.

———. "The Martyrdom of Peter." *ANRW* 2.26.1 (1992) 539–95.

Bauer, Walter. *Orthodoxy and Heresy in Earliest Christianity*. Minneapolis, MN: Fortress, 1971.

Bauman-Martin, Betsy. "Speaking Jewish: Postcolonial Aliens and Strangers in First Peter." In *Reading First Peter with New Eyes: Methodological Reassessments of the Letter of First Peter*, edited by Robert Webb and Betsy Bauman-Martin, 144–77. London: T. & T. Clark, 2007.

Bauman-Martin, Betsy, and Robert L. Webb. "Reading First Peter with New Eyes." In *Reading First Peter with New Eyes: Methodological Reassessments of the Letter of First Peter*, edited by Robert Webb and Betsy Bauman-Martin, 1–40. London: T. & T. Clark, 2007.

Baur, Ferdinand. "Die Chrisuspartei in der korinthischen Gemeinde, der Gegensatz des paulinischen und petrinischen Christentums in der altesten Kirche, der Apostel Petrus in Rom." In *Tübinger Zeitschrift für Theologie*, 61–206. Tübingen: Friedrich Fucs, Fahrgang, 1831.

———. *Kritische Untersuchungen über die kanonischen Evangelien, ihr Verhältniss zu einander, ihren Charakter und Ursprung*. Boston: Wentworth, 2018.

Beale, G. K. *A New Testament Biblical Theology: The Unfolding of the Old Testament in the New*. Grand Rapids: Baker, 2011.

Beare, Francis. *First Epistle of Peter*. Oxford: Basil Blackwell, 1970.

Beasley-Murray, G. R. *Baptism in the New Testament*. London: Macmillan, 1963.

Beck, Brian E. "*Imiatio Christi* and the Lucan Passion Narrative." In *Suffering and Martyrdom in the New Testament*, edited by William Horbury and Brian McNeil, 28–47. London: Cambridge University Press, 1981.

Beckman, Gary A., and Harry A. Hoffner. *Hittite Diplomatic Texts*. 2nd ed. Writings from the Ancient World 7. Atlanta, GA: Society of Biblical Literature, 1999.

Bede the Venerable. *Commentary on the Seven Catholic Epistles*. Translated by David Hurst. Kalamazoo, MI: Cistercian, 1985.

Beiringer, Reimund, and Didier Pollefeyt. *Paul and Judaism: Crosscurrents in Pauline Exegesis and the Study of Jewish-Christian Relations*. Library of New Testament Studies 463. London: T. & T. Clark, 2012.

Bell, Harold. *Jews and Christians in Egypt: The Jewish Troubles in Alexandria and the Athanasian Controversy, Illustrated by Texts from Greek Papyri*. London: British Museum, 1924.

Bellinger, William, and William R. Farmer. *Jesus and the Suffering Servant: Isaiah 53 and Christian Origins*. Atlanta, GA: Trinity, 1998.

Bengel, J. A. *Gnomon of the New Testament*. Philadelphia, PA: Sheldon & Co., 1864.

Ber, Yitzhaq ben Arye Yosef. *Seder 'Avodat Yisrael*. New York: Schocken, 1937.

Berding, Kenneth. *Polycarp and Paul: An Analysis of Their Literary and Theological Relationship in Light of Polycarp's Use of Biblical and Extra-biblical Literature*. Boston: Brill, 2002.

Berger, Adolf. *Encyclopedic Dictionary of Roman Law*. 2 vols. in 1. Philadelphia, PA: American Philosophical Society, 1953.

Berger, Peter. *The Social Reality of Religion*. London: Faber & Faber, 1969.

Berger, Peter, and Thomas Luckmann. *The Social Construction of Reality: A Treatise in the Sociology of Knowledge*. London: Penguin, 1967.

Berger, Peter, et al. *The Homeless Mind: Modernization and Consciousness*. New York: Vintage, 1973.

Berkeley, George. "Principles of Human Knowledge." In *The Great Books of the Western World*, edited by John Locke et al., 35:403–50. Chicago: Encyclopaedia Britannica, 1952.

Berkowitz, Luci, et al. *Thesaurus Linguae Graecae Canon of Greek Authors and Works*. New York: Oxford, 1990.

Bermejo-Rubio, Fernando. "Did Jesus the Galilean Redefine the Concept of Kingship? Apologetic Agendas from Ancient Texts to Modern Scholarship." *Annali di Storia dell'Esegesi* 35.1 (2018) 51–82.

Best, Ernest. *1 Peter*. NCB. Grand Rapids: Eerdmans, 1971.

———. "1 Peter II 4–10—A Reconsideration." *Nov Test* 11.4 (1969) 270–93.

———. *Following Jesus: Discipleship in the Gospel of Mark*. Sheffield: JSOT, 1981.

Bettenson, Henry, and Chris Maunder. *Documents of the Christian Church*. Oxford: Oxford University Press, 1999.

Betz, Hans Dieter. *Nachfolge und Nachahmung Jesu Christi im Neuen Testament*. BHT 37. Tübingen: Mohr/Siebeck, 1967.

Bigg, Charles. *A Critical and Exegetical Commentary on the Epistles of St. Peter and St. Jude*. Edinburgh: T. & T. Clark, 1978.

Bird, Michael F. "Salvation in Paul's Judaism?" In *Paul and Judaism Paul and Judaism: Crosscurrents in Pauline Exegesis and the Study of Jewish-Christian Relations*, edited by Reimund Beiringer and Didier Pollefeyt, 15–40. Library of New Testament Studies 463. London: T. & T. Clark, 2012.

Blaising, Craig. "Gethsemane a Prayer of Faith." *JETS* 22 (1979) 333–43.

Blakley, J. Ted. "Incomprehension or Resistance? The Markan Disciples and the Narrative Logic of Mark 4:1—8:30." PhD diss., University of St. Andrews, 2008.
Blass, Fredrich, et al. *A Greek Grammar of the New Testament and Other Early Christian Literature*. Chicago: University of Chicago Press, 1961.
Blenkin, G. W. *The First Epistle General of Peter*. Cambridge: Cambridge University Press, 1914.
Blinzler, Josef. "ΙΕΡΑΤΕΥΜΑ, Zur Exegese von 1 Peter 2,5 u. 9." In *Episcopus: Studien über das Bischofsamt. Festschrift für Kardinal Michael von Faulhaber*, edited by the Theologische Fakultät der Universität München, 49–59. Regensburg: Gregorius, 1949.
Blue, Bradley. "Architecture, Early Church." In *Dictionary of the Later New Testament and Its Developments*, edited by Ralph P. Martin and Peter H. Davids, 91–95. Downers Grove, IL: InterVarsity, 1997.
Blum, Edwin A. "1 Peter." In *The Expositor's Bible Commentary*, edited by Frank Gaebelein, 12:209–56. Grand Rapids: Zondervan, 1981.
———. "2 Peter." In *The Expositor's Bible Commentary*, edited by Frank Gaebelein, 12:257–92. Grand Rapids: Zondervan, 1981
Bock, Darrell. *Acts*. BECNT. Grand Rapids: Baker, 2007.
———. *Blasphemy and Exaltation in Judaism: The Charge Against Jesus in Mark 14:53–65*. Grand Rapids: Baker, 2000.
———. *Luke*. Grand Rapids: Baker, 1996.
———. *Proclamation from Prophecy and Pattern: Lucan Old Testament Christology*. JSNTSup 12. Sheffield: JSOT, 1987.
———. *A Theology of Luke and Acts*. Grand Rapids: Zondervan, 2012.
Böckh, August, and Johannes Franz, eds. *Corpus Inscriptionum Graecarum*, Vol. 2. Olms: Hilgesheim, 1977.
Bockmuehl, Markus. *The Remembered Peter in Ancient Reception and Modern Debate*. Tübingen: Mohr Siebeck, 2010.
———. "Simon Peter and Bethsaida." In *The Missions of James, Peter, and Paul: Tensions in Early Christianity*, edited by Bruce Chilton and Craig Evans, 53–90. Leiden: Brill, 2005.
———. *Simon Peter in Scripture and Memory*. Grand Rapids: Baker, 2012.
Boda, Mark. *A Severe Mercy: Sin and Its Remedy in the Old Testament*. Winona Lake, IN: Eisenbrauns, 2009.
Boismard, M. E. *Quatre Hymns baptismales dans la Première Epître de Pierre*. Paris: Latour-Maubourg, 1982.
———. "Une liturgie baptismale dans la Prima Petri." *RevBib* 63 (1946) 182–208; 64 (1957) 161–83.
Bond, Helen. *The First Biography of Jesus: Genre and Meaning in Mark's Gospel*. Grand Rapids: Eerdmans, 2020.
Bond, Helen, and Larry Hurtado. *Peter in Early Christianity*. Grand Rapids: Eerdmans, 2015.
Bonhoeffer, Dietrich. *The Cost of Discipleship*. New York: Macmillan, 1963.
Bonner, Campbell. "The Violence of Departing Demons." *HTR* 37 (1944) 334–36.
Bonsirven, Joseph. *Palestinian Judaism in the Time of Jesus*. New York: Holt, Rinehart & Winston, 1964.
Bonz, Marianne. *The Past as Legacy: Luke-Acts*. Minneapolis, MN: Fortress, 2000.
Boobyer, G. H. "The Indebtedness of 2 Peter to 1 Peter." In *New Testament Essays: Studies in Memory of Thomas Walter Manson 1893–1958*, edited by A. J. B. Higgins, 34–53. Manchester: Manchester University Press, n.d.

Boomershine, Thomas. "Jesus of Nazareth and the Watershed of Ancient Orality and Literacy" In *Orality and Textuality in Early Christian Literature*, edited by Joanna Dewey, 7–17. Atlanta, GA: Society of Biblical Literature, 1995.

Booth, R. P. *Jesus and the Laws of Purity*. JSNTSup 13. Sheffield: Sheffield Academic, 1986.

Borg, Marcus. *Conflict, Holiness and Politics in the Teaching of Jesus*. Lewiston: Edwin Mellen, 1984.

———. *Jesus: A New Vision*. London: SPCK, 1993.

Borgen, P. "Jesus Christ, the Reception of the Spirit and a Cross-National Community." In *Early Christianity and Hellenistic Judaism*, edited by P. Borgen, 253–72. Edinburgh: T. & T. Clark, 1996.

Boring, M. Eugene. "Narrative Dynamics in First Peter: The Function of Narrative World." In *Reading First Peter with New Eyes: Methodological Reassessments of the Letter of First Peter*, edited by Robert Webb and Betsy Bauman-Martin, 7–40. London: T. & T. Clark, 2007.

Bornemann, W. "Der erste Petrusbrief–eine Taufrede des Silvanus?" *ZNW* 19 (1919–20) 143–65.

Bornkamm, Günther. "The Authority to 'Bind' and 'Loose' in the Church in Matthew's Gospel." In *The Interpretation of Matthew*, edited by Graham Stanton, 83–97. IRT 3. Philadelphia, PA: Fortress, 1983.

Borrell, Agustí. *The Good News of Peter's Denial: A Narrative and Rhetorical Reading of Mark 14:54.66–72*. Atlanta, GA: Scholars, 1998.

Botterweck, Johannes, and Helmer Ringgren. *Theological Dictionary of the Old Testament*. 17 vols. Grand Rapids: Eerdmans, 1974–2021.

Bourke, M. M. "Peter in the Gospel of Luke." In *Peter in the New Testament: A Collaborative Assessment by Protestant and Roman Catholic Scholars*, edited by Raymond Brown et al., 109–28. Minneapolis, MN: Augsburg, 1973.

Bowes, William B. "Faith-Language, Jesus's Disciples, and Narrative Fulfillment in Luke-Acts." *JETS* 64.4 (2021) 767–84.

Boyarin, Daniel. "Beyond Judaisms: Metatron and the Divine Polymorphy of Ancient Judaism." *JSJ* 41.3 (2010) 323–65.

Bradley, K. R. *Slaves and Masters in the Roman Empire: A Study in Social Control*. Oxford: Oxford University Press, 1987.

Brettler, Marc. *God Is King: Understanding an Israelite Metaphor*. Sheffield: Sheffield Academic, 1989.

Brichto, Herbert Chanan. "On Slaughter and Sacrifice, Blood and Atonement." *HUCA* 47 (1976) 19–55.

Broadhead, Edwin. *Naming Jesus: Titular Christology in the Gospel of Mark*. Sheffield: Sheffield Academic, 1999.

Brooke, George. "Isaiah 40:3 and the Wilderness Community." In *New Qumran Texts and Studies: Proceedings of the First Meeting of the International Organization for Qumran Studies, Paris 1992*, edited by George Brooke, 117–32. Leiden: Brill, 1994.

Broughton, T. R. S. "Roman Asia Minor." In *An Economic Survey of Ancient Rome*, edited by Frank Tenney, 4:631–840. Paterson, NJ: Pageant, 1933.

Brown, Colin. *New International Dictionary of New Testament Theology*. 3 vols. Grand Rapids: Zondervan, 1977.

Brown, Jeannine. *The Gospel as Stories: A Narrative Approach to Matthew, Mark, Luke, and John*. Grand Rapids: Baker, 2020.

Brown, Raymond. *The Death of the Messiah from Gethsemane to the Grave: A Commentary on the Passion Narratives in the Four Gospels.* New York: Doubleday, 1994.
———. *The Gospel According to John xiii–xxi.* The Anchor Bible 29A. Garden City, NY: Doubleday, 1970.
Brown, Raymond, and John Meier. *Antioch and Rome: New Testament Cradles of Catholic Christianity.* New York: Paulist, 1983.
Brown, Raymond, et al. *Peter in the New Testament.* Minneapolis, MN: Augsburg, 1973.
Brown, Warren, et al. *Whatever Happened to the Soul? Scientific and Theological Portraits of Human Nature.* Minneapolis, MN: Fortress, 1998.
Brownlee, W. H. "Biblical Interpretation Among the Secretaries of the Dead Sea Scrolls." *BA* 14 (1951) 54–76.
———. *The Midrash Pesher of Habakkuk.* Missoula, MT: Society of Biblical Literature, 1979.
Bruce, F. F. *Commentary on the Book of Acts.* Grand Rapids: Eerdmans, 1979.
———. *Peter, Stephen, James, and John: Studies in Early Non-Pauline Christianity.* Grand Rapids: Eerdmans, 1980.
———. *The Speeches in the Book of Acts of the Apostles.* London: Tyndale, 1942.
———. "The Speeches in Acts—Thirty Years After." In *Reconciliation and Hope: New Testament Essays on Atonement and Eschatology Presented to L. L. Morris on his 60th Birthday*, edited by Robert Banks, 53–68. Carlisle: Paternoster, 1974.
Brueggemann, Walter. *A Pathway of Interpretation: The Old Testament for Pastors and Students.* Eugene, OR: Cascade, 2008.
———. *Theology of the Old Testament: Testimony, Dispute, Advocacy.* Minneapolis, MN: Fortress, 1997.
Büchler, Adolf. *Studies in Sin and Atonement: In the Rabbinic Literature of the First Century.* New York: KTAV, 1967.
Bultmann, Rudolf. "Bekenntris-und Lied fragmente im ersten Petrusbrief." In *Coniectanea Neotestamentica 11: In honorem Antonii Fridrichsen sexagenarii*, 1–14. Lund: Gleerup, 1947.
———. *Jesus Christ and Mythology.* New York: Scribner, 1958.
———. *History of the Synoptic Tradition.* New York: Harper & Row, 1963.
———. *Theology of the New Testament.* New York: Scribner, 1951.
Bultmann, Rudolf, et al. *Kerygma and Myth: A Theological Debate.* New York: Harper & Row, 1961.
Burkett, Delbert. *Theologie des Neuen Testaments.* Tübingen: Mohr-Paul Siebeck, 1948.
———. "The Transfiguration of Jesus (Mark 9:2–8): Epiphany or Apotheosis?" *JBL* 138.2 (2019) 413–32.
———. *The Son of Man Debate: A History and Evaluation.* SNTSMS 107. Cambridge: Cambridge University Press, 1999.
Butts, James. "The *Progymnasmata* of Theon the Sophist: A New Text with Translation and Commentary." PhD diss., Claremont Graduate School, 1987.
Bynum, Caroline Walker. *The Resurrection of the Body in Western Christianity, 200–1336.* New York: Columbia University Press, 1995.
Byrskog, Samuel. *Story as History-History as Story: The Gospel Tradition in the Context of Ancient Oral History.* Tübingen: Mohr, 2000.
Cadbury, Henry. "Acts and Eschatology." In *The Background of the New Testament and Its Eschatology*, edited by W. D. Davies and D. Daube, 300–321. Cambridge: Cambridge University Press, 1964.

———. "The Speeches in Acts." In *The Beginnings of Christianity: Part I, The Acts of the Apostles*, edited by J. Foakes Jackson and Kirsopp Lake, 1:402–26. 5 vols. Grand Rapids: Baker, 1979.
Callan, Terrance. "The Syntax of 2 Peter 1:1–7." *CBQ* 67.4 (2005) 632–40.
Calvin, John. *Calvin's Commentaries*. Grand Rapids: Baker, 1979.
———. *Institutes of the Christian Religion*. Philadelphia, PA: Presbyterian Board of Christian Education, 1936.
———. *Sermons on Deuteronomy*. Edinburgh: Banner of Truth, 1987.
Campbell, Barth. *Honor, Shame, and the Rhetoric of 1 Peter*. SBLDS 160. Atlanta, GA: Scholars, 1998.
Campbell, John K. *Honour, Family, and Patronage: A Study of Institutions and Moral Values in a Greek Mountain Community*. Oxford: Clarendon, 1964.
Caragounis, Chrys. *Peter and the Rock*. Berlin: Walter de Gruyter, 1990.
Carrington, Philip. *The Primitive Christian Catechism: A Study in the Epistles*. Cambridge: Cambridge University Press, 1940.
Carter, Warren. "Going All the Way? Honoring the Emperor and Sacrificing Wives and Slaves in 1 Peter 2.13–13.6." In *A Feminist Companion to the Catholic Epistles*, edited by Amy-Jill Levine and Maria Mayo Robbins, 14–33. London: T. & T. Clark, 2004.
———. *Households and Discipleship: A Study of Matthew 19–20*. Sheffield: JSOT, 1994.
Casel, Odo. "Die λογική θυσία der antiken Mystik in christlichliturgischer umdeutung." *JLW* 4 (1924) 37–47.
Casey, Maurice. "Aramaic Idiom and the Son of Man Problem: A Response to Owen and Shepherd." *JSNT* 25 (2002) 3–32.
———. *Aramaic Sources of Mark's Gospel*. SNTSMS 102. Cambridge: Cambridge University Press, 1998.
———. *The Solution to the "Son of Man" Problem*. London: T. & T. Clark, 2007.
———. *Son of Man: The Interpretation and Influence of Daniel 7*. London: SPCK, 1979.
A Century of Lawmaking for a New Nation: US Congressional Documents and Debates 1774–1875. Washington, DC: Congress, 1875.
Cerfaux, L. "Vestiges d'un florilège dans 1 Cor 1:18—3:24." *RHE* 27 (1931) 24–25.
Chalmers, Aaron. "Influence of Cognitive Biases on Biblical Interpretation." *BBR* 26.4 (2016) 467–80.
Chang, Andrew. "Second Peter 2:1 and the Extent of the Atonement." *BSac* 142 (1985) 55–56.
Charles, J. Daryl. *Virtue amidst Vice: The Catalog of Virtues in 2 Peter 1*. JSNTSup 150. Sheffield: Sheffield Academic, 1997.
Charlesworth, James. "Intertextuality: Isaiah 40:3 and the Serek ha-Yahad." In *The Quest for Context and Meaning: Studies in Biblical Intertextuality in Honor of James A. Sanders*, edited by Craig Evans and Shemaryahu Talmon, 197–224. Leiden: Brill, 1997.
Charue, A. *Les Epitres Catholiques*. Paris: La Sainte Bible. 1938.
Chase, Francis. "2 Peter." In *Hastings' Dictionary of the Bible*, edited by James Hastings, 3:809. 5 vols. Grand Rapids: Baker, 1994.
Chernus, Ira. "Visions of God in Merkabah Mysticism." *JSJ* 13 (1982) 123–46.
Chester, A., and R. P. Martin. *The Theology of the Letters of James, Peter and Jude*. Cambridge: Cambridge University Press, 1994.
Chilton, Bruce, and Craig Evans. *The Missions of James, Peter, and Paul: Tensions in Early Christianity*. Leiden: Brill, 2005.

Chilton, Bruce, and Jacob Neusner. *Classical Christianity and Rabbinic Judaism: Comparing Theologies*. Grand Rapids: Baker, 2004.
Chilton, Bruce, et al. *The Missing Jesus: Rabbinic Judaism and the New Testament*. Boston: Brill, 2002.
Christensen, Sean. "The Balch/Elliott Debate and the Hermeneutics of the Household Code." *TrinJ* 37 (2016) 173–93.
———. "Solidarity in Suffering and Glory: The Unifying Role of Psalm 34 in 1 Peter 3:10–12." *JETS* 58.2 (2015) 335–52.
Clerc, Michel. *De la condition des étrangers domiciles dans les cites grecques*. Toulouse: Universitaires du Midi Press, 2007.
Collins, John. *The Scepter and the Star: The Messiahs of the Dead Sea Scrolls and Other Ancient Literature*. New York: Doubleday, 1995.
———. "The Son of Man in First-Century Judaism." *NTS* 38 (1992) 448–66.
Conzelmann, Hans. *Acts of the Apostles*. Hermenia. Philadelphia, PA: Fortress, 1972.
———. *Die Kleineren Briefe des Apostels Paulus*. Edited by H. W. Beyer et al. Göttingen: Vandenhoeck & Ruprecht, 1962.
———. "History and Theology in the Passion Narratives." *Int* 24.2 (1970) 178–82.
———. *The Theology of St. Luke*. Philadelphia, PA: Fortress, 1961.
Cooper, Craig. *Politics of Orality*. Vol. 6, *Orality and Literacy in Ancient Greece*. Leiden: Brill, 2007.
Cooper, John. *Body, Soul, & Life Everlasting*. Grand Rapids: Eerdmans, 1989.
Corbo, Virgil. "The House at Capernaum." In *New Memoirs of Saint Peter by the Sea of Galilee*, edited by Virgil Corbo and Stanislaus Loffredda, 23–27. Jerusalem: Franciscan, 1969.
Cothenet, Edward. "Imitation du Christ." In *Dictionnaire de Spiritualité*, edited by Edward Cothenet et al., 7:1536–1601. Paris: Beaucresne, 1971.
Coults, John. "Ephesians 1:3–14 and 1 Peter 1:3–12." *NTS* 3 (1957) 115–27.
Cowley, A. E. *Aramaic Papyri of the Fifth Century B.C. Edited with Translation and Notes*. Oxford: Clarendon, 1923.
Cranfield, C. E. B. *The Gospel According to St. Mark*. Cambridge: Cambridge University Press, 1974.
Crawford, Matthew. "'Confessing God from a Good Conscience': 1 Peter 3:21 and Early Christian Baptismal Theology." *JTS* 67.1 (2016) 23–37.
Creed, J. M. *The Gospel According to St. Luke*. New York: Macmillan, 1930.
Crosby, Michael. *House of Disciples: Church, Economics and Justice in Matthew*. New York: Orbis, 1988.
Cross, Frank L. *1 Peter: A Paschal Liturgy*. London: A. R. Mowbray, 1954.
Crossan, John Dominic. *The Cross That Spoke*. San Francisco: Harper & Row, 1988.
Crouzel, Henri. "L'imitation et la 'suite' de Dieu du Christ dans les premiers siècles chrétiens, ansi que leurs sources gréco-romaines et hébraiques." *JAC* 21 (1978) 7–41.
Crum, J. M. C. *St. Mark's Gospel*. Cambridge: Heffer, 1936.
Cullmann, Oscar. *Christ and Time*. Philadelphia, PA: Westminster, 1964.
———. *The Christology of the New Testament*. London: SCM, 1963.
———. *Peter: Disciple, Apostle, Martyr*. Philadelphia, PA: Westminster, 1953.
Dahl, M. E. *The Resurrection of the Body*. London: SCM, 1962.
Dalton, W. J. *Christ's Proclamation to the Spirits: A Study of 1 Peter 3:18—4:6*. Rome: Pontifical Biblical Institute, 1989.

Daly, Robert. "The Soteriological Significant of the Sacrifice of Isaac." *CBQ* 39 (1977) 45–75.
Damgaard, Finn. *Rewriting Peter as an Intertextual Character in the Canonical Gospels.* London: Routledge, 2015.
Danker, F. *Benefactor Epigraphic Study of a Graeco-Roman and New Testament Semantic Field.* St. Louis: Clayton, 1982.
———. "1 Peter 1:24—2:17–A Consolatory Pericope." *ZNW* 58 (1967) 93–102.
———. "2 Peter 1: A Solemn Decree." *CBQ* 40 (1978) 65–72.
Daube, David. *The New Testament and Rabbinic Judaism.* London: University of London, 1956.
———. "Public Pronouncement and Private Explanation in the Gospels." *ExpTim* 57 (1945–46) 175–77.
———. "Rabbinic Methods of Interpretation and Hellenistic Rhetoric." *HUCA* 22 (1949) 239–64.
David, Carl Judson. *The Name and Way of the Lord: Old Testament Themes. New Testament Christology.* Sheffield: Sheffield, 1996.
Davids, Peter. *The First Epistle of Peter.* NICNT. Grand Rapids: Eerdmans, 1990.
———. "James." In *A Theology of James, Peter, and Jude: : A Biblical Theology of the New Testament*, 31–91. Grand Rapids: Zondervan, 2014.
———. *The Letters of 2 Peter and Jude.* The Pillar New Testament Commentary. Grand Rapids: Eerdmans, 2006.
———. "Rich and Poor." In *Dictionary of Jesus and the Gospel*, edited by Joel Green and Scot McKnight, 701–10. Downers Grove: InterVarsity, 1992.
———. "Textual Criticism of 1 Peter 3:10." Paper presented at Institute for Biblical Research, March, 2014.
———. *A Theology of James, Peter, and Jude: A Biblical Theology of the New Testament.* Grand Rapids: Zondervan, 2014.
Davies, Paul E. "Primitive Christology in 1 Peter." In *Festschrift to Honor F. Wilbur Gingrich*, edited by Eugene Barth and Ronald Cocroft, 115–22. Leiden: Brill, 1972.
Davies, W. D., and Dale C. Allison Jr. *The First Epistle of Peter.* NICNT. Grand Rapids: Eerdmans, 1990.
———. *The Gospel of Matthew.* 3 vols. ICC. Edinburgh: T. & T. Clark, 1991.
Dawsey, James. *Peter's Last Sermon: Identity and Discipleship in the Gospel of Mark.* Macon: Mercer University Press, 2010.
Dean-Otting, Mary. *Heavenly Journeys: A Study of the Motif in Hellenistic Jewish Literature.* New York: Lang, 1984.
De Boer, Willis P. *The Imitation of Paul: An Exegetical Study.* Kampen: J. H. Kok, 1962.
De Campos, Mateus. "Markan Epistemology and the Problem of Incomprehension." *JETS* 64.4 (2021) 74–66.
———. "The 'Sign from Heaven' (Mark 8,10–13)." *Bib* 98.2 (2017) 234–56.
Deissmann, Adolf. *Bible Studies.* Edinburgh: T. & T. Clark, 1901.
———. *Light from the Ancient East: The New Testament Illustrated by Recently Discovered Texts of the Graeco-Roman World.* Translated by Lionel Strachan, New York: Daron, 1927.
Demosthenes. *Demosthenes.* 7 vols. Translated by J. H. Vince et al. London: Heinemann, 1926–49.
De Saussure, Ferdinand. *Cours de linguistique Générale.* Paris: Payot, 1969.

Descartes, René. "Meditations on First Philosophy." In *Great Books of the Western World: Descartes, Spinoza*, edited by Robert Maynard Hutchins and Mortimer J. Adler, 31:69–103. Chicago: Encyclopaedia Britannica, 1952.
DeSilva, David. "1 Peter: Strategies for Counseling Individuals on the Way to a New Heritage." *ATJ* 32 (2000) 33–52.
Deterding, Paul. "Exodus Motifs in First Peter." *Concordia Journal* 7 (1981) 58–65.
deVilliers, J. L. "Joy in Suffering in 1 Peter." *Neot* 9 (1975) 70–80.
Dewey, Arthur. "A Re-Hearing of Romans 10:1–15." In *Orality and Textuality in Early Christian Literature*, edited by Joanna Dewey, 109–27. Atlanta, GA: Society of Biblical Literature, 1995.
Dewey, Joanna. *Orality and Textuality in Early Christian Literature*. Semia Studies. Atlanta, GA: Scholars, 1995.
Dibelius, Martin. *A Fresh Approach to the New Testament and Early Christian Literature*. London: Nicholson & Watson, 1937.
———. "The Speeches in Acts and Ancient Historiography." In *Studies in the Acts of the Apostles*, edited by H. Greeven, 138–85. New York: Scribner's, 1956.
Dihle, Albrecht. "The Gospels and Greek Biography." In *The Gospel and the Gospels*, edited by Peter Stuhlmacher, 361–86. Grand Rapids: Eerdmans, 1991.
Dill, Samuel. *Roman Society from Nero to Marcus Aurelius*. London: Macmillan, 1925.
Diodorus of Sicily. *The Library of History*. 12 vols. Cambridge: Harvard University Press, 1933–67.
Dix, Dom Gregory. *Jew and Greek: A Study in the Primitive Church*. London: Dacre, 1967.
Dodd, C. H. *According to the Scriptures*. London: Nisbet, 1952.
———. *The Apostolic Preaching and Its Developments*. New York: Harper, 1936.
———. "The Framework of the Gospel Narrative." *ExpTim* 43 (1931–32) 396–400.
Doering, Lutz. "Schwerpunkte und Tendenzen der neueren Petrus-Forschung." *BTZ* 19 (2002) 203–23.
Domeris, W. R. "The Office of Holy One." *Journal of Theology for Southern Africa* 54 (1968) 35–38.
Dossey, Lesley. "Wife Beating and Manliness in Late Antiquity." *Past and Present* 199 (2008) 3–40.
Douglas, J. D. *The New International Dictionary of the Christian Church*. Rev. ed. Grand Rapids: Zondervan, 1978.
Draper, Jonathan. *Orality, Literacy, and Colonialism in Antiquity*. Semia Studies. Atlanta, GA: Society of Biblical Literature, 2004.
Dubis, Mark. *Messianic Woes in First Peter: Suffering and Eschatology in 1 Peter 4:12–19*. Studies in Biblical Literature 33. New York: Lang, 2002.
Duchesne, Louis. *Histire ancienne de l'Englise*. Paris: A. Fontemoing et cie, 1910.
Dunn, James D. G. *Christianity in the Making*. Vol. 2, *Beginning from Jerusalem*. Grand Rapids: Eerdmans, 2009.
———. "Has the Canon a Continuing Function?" In *The Canon Debate*, edited by L. M. McDonald and J. A. Sanders, 558–79. Peabody, MA: Hendrickson, 2002.
———. *Jesus' Call to Discipleship*. Cambridge: Cambridge University Press, 1992.
———. *Jesus, Paul, and the Law: Studies in Mark and Galatians*. Louisville: Westminster/John Knox Press, 1990.
———. *Jesus Remembered*. Grand Rapids: Eerdmans, 2003.
———. *Jews and Christians: The Parting of the Ways, A.D. 70 to 135*. Grand Rapids: Eerdmans, 1992.

———. "The Messianic Secret in Mark." *TynBul* 21 (1970) 92–117.

———. *Paul and the Mosaic Law*. Grand Rapids: Eerdmans, 1996.

———. "Pharisees, Sinners, and Jesus." In *Jesus, Paul, and the Law: Studies in Mark and Galatians*, 61–88. Louisville: Westminster/John Knox, 1990.

———. "Q as Oral Tradition." In *The Written Gospel*, edited by Markus Bockmuehl and Donald A. Hagner, 45–69. Cambridge: Cambridge University Press, 2005.

———. *The Theology of Paul the Apostle*. Grand Rapids: Eerdmans, 1998.

———. *Unity and Diversity in the New Testament: An Inquiry into the Character of Earliest Christianity*. London: SCM, 1977.

Durham, John. *Exodus*. WBC 3. Waco: Word, 1987.

Ebright, Charles R. *The Petrine Epistles: A Critical Study of Authorship*. Cincinnati: Methodist Book Concern, 1917.

Edwards, Jonathan. *Freedom of the Will*. New Haven: Yale University Press, 1957.

———. *A Treatise Concerning Religious Affections*. New Haven: Yale University Press, 1959.

Ehrman, Bart. *Lost Scriptures: Books That Did Not Make It into the New Testament*. Oxford: Oxford University Press, 2005.

Eichrodt, Walter. *Theology of the Old Testament*. Philadelphia, PA: Westminster, 1961.

Eidersheim, Alfred. *Sketches of Jewish Social Life*. London: Religious Tract Society, 1876.

Eisenman, Robert. *James the Brother of Jesus*. New York: Viking, 1996.

Eisler, Robert. *The Messiah Jesus and John the Baptist: According to Flavius Josephus' Recently Rediscovered 'Capture of Jerusalem' and the Other Jewish and Christian Sources*. London: Methuen, 1931.

Elliger, Karl. *Leviticus*. HAT 4. Tübingen: Mohr, 1966.

Elliott, John. *1 Peter: A New Translation with Introduction and Commentary*. AB. New York: Doubleday, 2000.

———. "1 Peter, Its Situation and Strategy: A Discussion with David Balch." In *Perspectives on First Peter*, edited by Charles Talbert, 61–78. Macron: Mercer University, 1986.

———. *Conflict, Community, and Honor: 1 Peter in Social-Scientific Perspective*. Eugene, OR: Cascade, 2007.

———. "Elders as Leaders in 1 Peter and the Early Church." *CurTM* 28.6 (2001) 549–59.

———. *The Elect and the Holy: An Exegetical Examination of 1 Peter 2:4–10 and the Phrase βασίλειον ἱεράτευμα*. NovTSup 12. Leiden: Brill, 1966.

———. *A Home for the Homeless: A Sociological Exegesis of 1 Peter, Its Situation and Strategy*. Philadelphia, PA: Fortress, 1981.

———. "Ministry and Church Order in the NT: A Traditio-Historical Analysis (1 Pt 5, 1–5 & plls.)." *CBQ* 32.3 (1970) 367–91.

———. "The Rehabilitation of an Exegetical Step-Child: 1 Peter in Recent Research." *JBL* 95 (1976) 243–54.

Ellis, E. E. *The Gospel of Luke*. NCB. Grand Rapids: Eerdmans, 1974.

Ellul, Danielle. "Un exemple de cheminement rhétorique: 1 Pierre." *Revue d'hiustoire et de philosophie religieuses* 70 (1990/91) 17–34.

Eubank, Nathan. *Wages of Cross-Bearing and Debt of Sin: The Economy of Heaven in Matthew's Gospel*. Berlin: DeGruyter, 2013.

Evans, Craig. "A Fishing Boat, a House, and an Ossuary: What Can We Learn from the Artifacts?" In *The Missions of James, Peter, and Paul: Tensions in Early Christianity*, edited by Bruce Chilton and Craig Evans, 211–31. Leiden: Brill, 2005.

Farrar, Austin. *A Study in St. Mark*. London: Dacre, 1951.
Fay, Greg. "Introduction to Incomprehension: The Literary Structure of Mark 4:1–34." *CBQ* 51.1 (1989) 65–81
Feder, Yitzhaq. "On *Kuppuru, Kippēr* and Etymological Sins that Cannot be Wiped Away." *VT* 60 (2010) 535–45.
Feldmeier, Rinhard. *The First Letter of Peter: A Commentary on the Greek Text*. Waco: Baylor University Press, 2008.
Felix, Paul. "Penal Substitution in the New Testament: A Focused Look at First Peter." *TMSJ* 20.2 (2009) 171–97.
Ferda, Tucker. "The Ending of Mark and the Faithfulness of God: An Apocalyptic Resolution to Mark 16:8." *Journal of Theological Interpretation* 13.1 (2019) 36–52.
Fernadez, Pérez. "Rabbinic Text in the Exegesis of the New Testament." *The Review of Rabbinic Judaism* 7 (2004) 95–120.
Feuillet, A. "La coupe et le baptême de la passion (Mc, x, 35–40; Mt. xx, 20–23; Lc., xxii, 50)." *RB* 74 (1967) 356–91.
Filium, C. Gerald. *Corpus Scriptorum Ecclesiasticorum Latinorum*. New York: Johnson, 1972.
Filson, Floyd. "Partakers with Christ, Suffering in First Peter." *Int* 9 (1955) 410.
Finkel, Asher. *The Pharisees & the Teacher of Nazareth*. Leiden: Brill, 1964.
Finlan, Stephen. *The Background and Content of Paul's Cultic Atonement Metaphors*. Leiden: Brill, 2004.
Fiore, Benjamin. *The Function of Personal Example in the Socratic and Pastoral Epistles*. An. Bib. 105. Rome: Biblical Institute Press, 1986.
Fitzmyer, Joseph. "The Aramaic Qorban Inscription from Jebel Hallet et-Tûrî and Mk7:11/Mt 15:5." *JBL* 78 (1959) 60–65.
———. *The Gospel According to Luke (I–IX)*. Anchor Bible 28. New York: Doubleday, 1982.
———. "The Matthean Divorce Texts and Some New Palestinian Evidence." *Theological Studies* 37 (1976) 197–226.
———. "A Re-Study of an Elephantine Aramaic Marriage Contract (AP 15)." In *Near Eastern Studies in Honor of William Foxwell Albright*, edited by H. Goedicke, 137–68. Baltimore: Johns Hopkins University Press, 1971.
Flusser, David. *Jesus*. Jerusalem: Varda, 2014.
———. *Jesus' Jerusalem*. Jerusalem: Varda, 2013.
Foakes-Jackson, F. J. *Peter: Prince of Apostles*. London: Hodder & Stoughton, 1927.
Foakes-Jackson, F. J., and Kirsopp Lake, eds. *The Acts of the Apostles*. 5 vols. Grand Rapids: Baker, 1979.
Foley, John Miles. "Indigenous Poems, Colonialist Texts." In *Orality, Literacy, and Colonialism in Antiquity*, edited by Jonathan Draper, 28–31. Atlanta, GA: Society of Biblical Literature, 2004.
Ford, David F. "Paul Ricoeur: A Biblical Philosopher on Jesus." In *Jesus and Philosophy: New Essays*, edited by Paul Moser, 169–93. Cambridge: Cambridge University Press, 2009.
Fornara, Charles William. *The Nature of History in Ancient Greece and Rome*. Eidos Studies in Classical Kinds. Berkeley: University of California, 1983.
Foster, Paul. "Peter in Noncanonical Traditions." In *Peter in Early Christianity*, edited by Helen Bond and Larry Hurtado, 222–62. Grand Rapids: Eerdmans, 2015.
France, R. T. *The Gospel of Mark*. Grand Rapids: Eerdmans, 2002.

Francis, Fred. "The Form and Function of the Opening and Closing Paragraphs of James and 1 John." *Zeitschrift für die neutestamentliche Wissenschaft und die Kunde des Urchristentums* 61 (1970) 113–25.

Francotte, H. "De la condition des étrangers dans les cites grecques." *Musée* 7 (1903) 350–88.

Freedman, David, and David Miano. "People of the New Covenant." In *The Concept of the Covenant in the Second Temple Period*, edited by Stanley Porter and Jaqueline C. R. de Roo, 7–26. Leiden: Brill, 2003.

Freyne, Seán. *The Jesus Movement and Its Expansion: Meaning and Mission*. Grand Rapids: Eerdmans, 2014.

Funk, R. *A Greek Grammar of the New Testament and Other Early Christian Literature*. Chicago: University of Chicago Press, 1961.

Gammie, John. *Holiness in Israel*. Minneapolis, MN: Fortress, 1989.

Gane, Roy. *Cult and Character: Purification Offerings, Day of Atonement, and Theodicy*. Winona Lake, IN: Eisenbrauns, 2005.

———. "Private Preposition מן in Purification Offering Pericopes and the Changing Face of 'Dorian Gray.'" *JBL* 127 (2008) 209–22.

Garland, David. *Mark*. NIV Application Commentary. Downers Grove: InterVarsity, 1996.

Geddert, Timothy. "The Implied YHWH Christology of Mark's Gospel: Mark's Challenge to the Reader to 'Connect the Dots.'" *BBR* 25.3 (2015) 325–40.

Gelardini, Gabriella. "The Contest for a Royal Title: Herod Versus Jesus in the Gospel According to Mark (6,14–29; 15,6–15)." *Annali di Storia dell' Esegesi* 28.2 (2011) 93–106.

Gerhardsson, Bernard. *The Gospel Tradition*. Lund: Gleerup, 1986.

———. *Memory and Manuscript: Oral Tradition and the Written Transmission in Rabbinic Judaism and Early Christianity*. Lund: Gleerup, 1998.

Gese, Hartmut. "The Atonement." In *Essays on Biblical Theology*, 93–116. Minneapolis, MN: Fortress, 1981.

———. "Die Sühne." In *Zur biblischen Theologie Alttestamentliche Vorträge*, 85–106. Munich: Verlag, 1977.

Gibson, Craig. "Learning Greek History in the Ancient Classroom: The Evidence from the Treatises on Progymnasmata." *CP* 99 (2004) 103–29.

Gillman, Neil. *The Death of Death: Resurrection and Immortality in Jewish Thought*. Woodstock, VT: Jewish Lights Publishing, 2000.

Goguel, Maurice. *The Birth of Christianity*. Crows Nest, Australia: George Allen & Unwin, 1953.

Goldingay, John. *The Message of Isaiah 40–55: A Literary-Theological Commentary*. London: T. & T. Clark, 2005.

———. *Psalms*. Grand Rapids: Baker, 2008.

Goldingay, John, and David Payne. *Isaiah 40–55: A Critical and Exegetical Commentary*. London: Bloomsbury, 2014.

Goodspeed, E. J. "Enoch in 1 Peter 3:19." *JBL* 73 (1954) 84–92.

Goppelt, Leonhard. *A Commentary on 1 Peter*. Grand Rapids: Eerdmans, 1993.

———. *Der erste Petrusbrief*. Göttingen: Vandenhoeck & Ruprecht, 1978.

Goulder, Michael. *St. Paul versus St. Peter: A Tale of Two Missions*. Louisville: Westminster John Knox, 1994.

Grappe, Christian. *Images de Pierre aux deux premiers siècles*. Vol. 75, *Etudes d'historie et de philosophie religieuses*. Paris: Universitaires de France, 1995.

Grässer, Erich. "Der Hebräerbrief, 1938-63." *TRu* 30 (1964-65) 138-236.
Green, Edward Michael Banks. *2 Peter Reconsidered*. London: Tyndale, 1961.
———. *The Second Epistle of Peter and the Epistle of Jude*. Grand Rapids: Eerdmans, 1968.
Green, Gene. "'As for Prophecies, They will Come to an End': 2 Peter, Paul and Plutarch on 'the Obsolescence of Oracles.'" *JSNT* 82 (2002) 107-22.
———. *Jude, 2 Peter*. BECNT. Grand Rapids: Baker, 2008.
———. *Vox Petri: A Theology of Peter*. Eugene, OR: Cascade, 2020.
Green, Joel. *The Death of Jesus: Tradition and Interpretation in the Passion Narrative*. WUNT 2/33. Tübingen: J. C. B. Mohr, 1988.
———. "Embodying the Gospel: Two Exemplary Practices." *Journal of Spiritual Formation and Soul Care* 7 (2014) 11-21.
Green, Michael. *Saint Peter: A Biography*. New York: Scribner, 1995.
Greeven, H., ed. *Studies in the Acts of the Apostles*. New York: Scribner's, 1956.
Gregerman, Adam. "Critique of *Short Stories by Jesus*." A paper presented at the Society for Biblical Literature, November 22, 2015.
Grice, H. Paul. "Meaning." *Philosophical Review* 66 (1957) 377-88.
———. "Utterer's Meaning and Intentions." *Philosophical Review* 78 (1969) 147-77.
———. "Utterer's Meaning, Sentence-Meaning, Word-Meaning." In *The Philosophy of Language*, edited by J. R. Searle, 54-70. Oxford: Oxford University Press, 1977.
Grindheim, Sigurd. "Biblical Authority: What Is It Good For? Why the Apostles Insisted on a High View of Scripture." *JETS* 59.4 (2016) 791-803.
Gruenwald, Itamar. *Apocalyptic and Merkavah Mysticism*. Leiden: Brill, 1980.
Guarducci, Margherita. *La tomba di San Pietro: Une straordinario vicenda*. Milano: Saggi Boupiani, 2000.
Gubler, Marie-Louise. *Die Frühesten Deutungen des Todes Jesu: Eine motifgeschichtliche Darstellung aufrung der neuen exegetischen Forschung*. Orbis Biblicus et Orientalis 15. Freiburg: Universtatsverlag, 1977.
Guilbert, P. "The Message of Salvation in the Acts of the Apostles: Composition and Structure." *Lumen-Vitoria* 12 (1957) 406-17.
Gundry, Robert. *Mark: A Commentary on His Apology for the Cross*. Grand Rapids: Eerdmans, 1993.
———. *Peter: False Disciple and Apostate According to Saint Matthew*. Grand Rapids: Eerdmans, 2015.
———. *Soma in Biblical Theology: With Emphasis on Anthropology*. Grand Rapids: Zondervan, 1987.
———. *A Survey of the New Testament*. 4th ed. Grand Rapids: Zondervan, 2003.
Gurney, O. R. *Some Aspects of Hittite Religion*. London: Oxford University Press, 1977.
Guthrie, Donald. "The Development of the Idea of Canonical Pseudepigrapha in New Testament Criticism." In *The Authorship and Integrity of the New Testament: Some Recent Studies*, by Kurt Aland, 14-39. Theological Collections 4. London: SPCK, 1965.
———. *New Testament Introduction*. Downers Grove: InterVarsity, 1970.
———. "Tertullian and Pseudonymity." *EvT* 67 (1956) 341.
Gutiérrez, Gustavo. *A Theology of Liberation*. Maryknoll: Orbis, 1973.
Gutierrez, Pedro. *La Paternité spirituelle selon S. Paul*. Paris: Gabalda, 1968.
Hafemann, Scott. "'Divine Nature' in 2 Pet 1,4 within its Eschatological Context." *Bib* 94.1 (2013) 80-99.

———. "Salvation in Jude 5 and the Argument of 2 Peter 1:3–11." In *The Catholic Epistles and Apostolic Tradition*, edited by K. W. Niebuhr and R. W. Wall, 339–42, 480–82. Waco: Baylor, 2009.

Hägerland, Tobias. "Prophetic Forgiveness in Josephus and Mark." *Svensk exegetisk arsbok* 79 (2014) 125–39.

Hagner, Donald. *Matthew 14–28*. WBC 33B. Dallas: Word, 1995.

Halbwachs, Maurice. *Les cadres sociaux de la mémoire*. Paris: Alcan, 1925.

———. *On Collective Memory*. Edited by Lewis Coser, Chicago: University of Chicago Press, 1992.

Hallo, William, ed. *The Context of Scripture*. 3 vols. Leiden: Brill, 1997–2002.

Hanneken, Todd. "Moses Has His Interpreters: Understanding the Legal Exegesis in Acts 15 from the Precedent in Jubilees." *CBQ* 77.4 (2015) 686–706.

Harland, Philip A. *Associations, Synagogues, and Congregations: Claiming a Place in Ancient Mediterranean Society*. Minneapolis, MN: Fortress, 2003.

Harnack, *Die Chronologie der altchristlichen Literatur bis Eusebius*. Leipzig: J. C. Hinrichs, 1897.

Harris, J. Rendel. "A Further Note on the Use of Enoch in 1 Peter." *Expositor* 6 (1901) 346–49.

———. *Testimonies*. Cambridge: Cambridge University Press, 1916–20.

Harris, Laird, et al. *Theological Wordbook of the Old Testament*. Chicago: Moody, 1980.

Harris, Murray. *Jesus as God: The New Testament Use of Theos in Reference to Jesus*. Grand Rapids: Baker, 1992.

Harrison, James. "The Persecution of Christians from Nero to Hadrian." In *Into All the World: Emergent Christianity in its Jewish and Greco-Roman Context*, edited by Mark Harding and Alanna Nobbs, 266–300. Grand Rapids: Eerdmans, 2017.

Hartman, L. "Some Unorthodox Thoughts on the 'Household-Code Form.'" In *The Social World of Formative Christianity and Judaism*, edited by J. Neusner et al., 219–34. Philadelphia, PA: Fortress, 1988.

Harvey, A. E. *Jesus and the Constraints of History*. London: Duckworth, 1982.

Hastings, James, ed. *Hastings' Dictionary of the Bible*. Grand Rapids: Baker, 1994.

Hawthorne, Gerald, et al. *Dictionary of Paul and His Letters*. Downers Grove: InterVarsity, 1993.

Hauck, F. *Die Katholischen Briefe*. Göttingen: Vandenhoeck & Ruprecht, 1933.

Hayes, Richard. *Echoes of Scripture in the Gospels*. Waco: Baylor, 2017.

Helyer, Larry. *The Life and Witness of Peter*. Downers Grove: InterVarsity, 2012.

———. "The Necessity, Problems, and Promise of Second Temple Judaism for Discussions of New Testament Eschatology." *JETS* 47 (2004) 606–9.

Hemer, Colin J. *The Book of Acts in the Setting of Hellenistic History*. Winona Lake, IN: Eisenbrauns, 1990.

———. "The Speeches in Acts II: The Areopagus Address." *TynBul* 40 (1989) 239–59.

Hengel, Martin. *The Charismatic Leader and His Followers*. New York: Crossroad, 1981.

———. "Eye-Witness Memory and the Writing of the Gospels." In *The Written Gospel*, edited by Markus Bockmuehl and Donald A. Hagner, 70–96. Cambridge: Cambridge University Press, 2005.

———. *Saint Peter: The Underestimated Apostle*. Grand Rapids: Eerdmans, 2010.

———. *The Son of God: The Origin of Christology and the History of Jewish Hellenistic Religion*. London: SCM, 1976.

Hengel, Martin, and Daniel P. Bailey. "Effective History of Isaiah 53." In *The Suffering Servant: Isaiah 53 in Jewish and Christian Sources*, edited by Bernd Janowski and Peter Stuhlmacher, 75–146. Grand Rapids: Eerdmans, 2004.

Hennecke, Edgar. *New Testament Apocrypha*. 2 vols. Philadelphia, PA: Westminster, 1963–66.

Hermann, Johannes. *Die Idee der Sühne im Alten Testament: eine Ubersuchung über Gebrauch und Bedeutung des Wortes kipper*. Leipzig: Hinrichs, 1905.

Hewit, J. W. "The Use of Nails in the Crucifixion." *HTR* 25 (1932) 29–45.

Hicks, Robert. *Epicurus Principle Doctrines*. http://Classics.mit.edu/Epicurus/princdoc.html.

Hiebert, D. Edmund. "The Prophetic Foundation for the Christian Life: An Exposition of 2 Peter 1:19–21." *BSac* 141 (1984) 166.

Hillyer, Norman. *1 and 2 Peter, Jude*. New International Biblical Commentary 16. Peabody, MA: Hendrickson, 1992.

Himes, Paul. "Why Did Peter Change the Septuagint? A Reexamination of the Significance of the Use of τίθημι in 1 Peter 2:6." *BBR* 26.2 (2016) 227–44.

Hines, Paul. "Peter and the Prophetic Word: The Theology of Prophecy Traced through Peter's Sermons and Epistles." *BBR* 21 (2011) 227–41.

Hoag, Gary. *Wealth in Ancient Ephesus and the First Letter to Timothy: Fresh Insights from Ephesiaca by Xenophon of Ephesus*. Winona Lake, IN: Eisenbrauns, 2015.

Hobbes, Thomas. "Leviathan." In *The Great Books of the Western World: Machiavelli, Hobbes*, 23:39–283. Chicago: Encyclopaedia Britannica, 1952.

Hoffner, Harry A., Jr. "Hittite-Israelite Cultural Parallels." In *The Context of Scripture: Archival Documents from the Biblical World*, edited by William Hallo, xxix–xxxiv. Leiden: Brill, 2002.

Holdsworth, John. "The Sufferings in 1 Peter and 'Missionary Apocalyptic." *StudBib* 3 (1978) 226–31.

Hollaz, David. *Acromaticum Universam Theologiam Thetico-Polemicam Complectens*. Lipsiae: B.C. Breitkopfii, 1763.

Hollenbach, Paul. "Jesus, Demoniacs, and Public Authorities: A Socio-Historical Study." *JAAR* 49 (1981) 567–88.

Holtzmann, H. J. *Die Apostelgeschte. Hand-Commentar zum Neuen Testament* ½. Tübingen: J. C. B. Mohr, 1901.

Holzmeister, U. *Commentarius in Epistles SS. Petri et Iudae, Apostolorum*. Cursus Scripturae Sacrae 3/13. Paris: Lethielleux, 1937.

Hooker, Morna. *From Adam to Christ*. Cambridge: Cambridge University, 1990.

———. *Jesus and the Servant: The Influence of the Servant Concept of Deutero-Isaiah in the New Testament*. London: SPCK, 1959.

———. *The Son of Man in Mark: A Study of the Background of the Term "Son of Man" and Its Use in St. Mark's Gospel*. Montreal: McGill University, 1967.

———. "'Who Can This Be?' The Christology of Mark's Gospel." In *Contours of Christology in the New Testament*, edited by Richard Longenecker, 79–99. Grand Rapids: Eerdmans, 2005.

Horrell, David. "Between Conformity and Resistance: Beyond the Balch-Elliott Debate Towards a Postcolonial Reading of First Peter." In *Reading First Peter With New Eyes: Methodical Reassessments of the Letter of First Peter*, edited by Robert L. Webb and Betsy Bauman-Martin, 111–43. London: T. & T. Clark, 2007.

———. "The Label Χριστιανός: 1 Peter 4:16 and the Formation of Christian Identity." *JBL* 126.2 (2007) 361–81.

———. *The Social Ethos of the Corinthian Correspondence: Interests and Ideology from 1 Corinthians to 1 Clement*. Edinburgh: T. & T. Clark, 1996.

Horrell, David, et al. "Visuality, Vivid Description, and the Message of 1 Peter: The Significance of the Roaring Lion (1 Peter 5:8)." *JBL* 132.3 (2013) 697–716.

Horsley, G. H. R. "Speeches and Dialogue in Acts." *NTS* 32 (1986) 609–14.

Horsley, Richard. *Oral Performance, Popular Tradition, and Hidden Transcript in Q.* Semia Studies. Atlanta, GA: Society of Biblical Literature, 2007.

Horsley, Richard, et al. *Performing the Gospel: Orality, Memory, and Mark.* Minneapolis, MN: Fortress, 2006.

Hort, F. J. A. *The First Epistle of St. Peter 1:1—2:17.* London: Macmillan, 1898.

———. "A Note on the Words κοφίνους, σπυρίς, sarganh." *JTS* 10 (1909) 567–71.

Howard, V. "Did Jesus Speak About His Own Death?" *CBQ* 39 (1977) 515–27.

Howe, Bonie. "Review of *Reading First Peter with New Eyes: Methodological Reassessments of the Letter of First Peter*, edited by Robert Webb and Betsy Bauman-Martin, New York: T & T Clark, 2007." *RBL* 5 (2009) 3–4.

Huck, Albert. *Synopsis of the First Three Gospels.* Los Angeles: Hard, 2014.

Hugh of St. Victor. *On the Sacraments of the Christian Faith.* Translated by Roy Defarrari. Cambridge: The Catholic University of America, 1951.

Hughes, P. E. "The Blood of Jesus and His Heavenly Priesthood in Hebrews." *BSac* 131 (1973) 99–109.

Hummel, Reinhart. *Die Auseinandersetzung zwischen Kirche und Judentum im Matthäusevangelium.* BEvT 33. Munich: Kaiser, 1963.

Hunter, Archibald. *The Gospel according to John.* Cambridge Bible Commentary. Cambridge: Cambridge University Press, 1965.

Hurst, L. D. *The Epistle to the Hebrews: Its Background of Thought.* Cambridge: Cambridge University Press, 1990.

Hurtado, Larry. "Apostle Peter in Protestant Scholarship: Cullmann, Hengel, and Bockmuehl." In *Peter in Early Christianity*, edited by Helen Bond and Larry Hurtado, 1–15. Grand Rapids: Eerdmans, 2015.

———. "Christology in Acts: Jesus in Early Christian Belief and Early Christian Belief and Practice." In *Issues in Luke-Acts*, edited by Sean Adams and Michael Pahl, 217–37, Piscataway: Gorias, 2012.

———. *Lord Jesus Christ: Devotion to Jesus in Earliest Christianity.* Grand Rapids: Eerdmans, 2003.

Hurtado, Larry, and Paul Owen. *"Who Is the Son of Man?" The Latest Scholarship on a Puzzling Expression of the Historical Jesus.* London: T. & T. Clark, 2011.

Hutchison, John. "Servanthood: Jesus' Countercultural Call to Christian Leaders." *BSac* 166.1 (2009) 53–68.

Isaacs, Marie. *Sacred Space: An Approach to the Theology of the Epistle to the Hebrews.* Sheffield: Sheffield Academic, 1992.

Jacobs, Paul, and Hartmut Krienke. "Foreknowledge, Providence, Predestination." In *NIDNTT*, edited by Colin Brown, 1:693. Grand Rapids, 1975.

Jaffee, Martin. "The Oral-Cultural Context of the Talmud Yerushalmi: Greco-Roman Rhetorical Paedeia, Discipleship, and the Concept of Oral Torah." In *Transmitting Jewish Traditions: Orality, Textuality, and Cultural Diffusion*, edited by Yaakov Elman and Israel Gershoni, 27–73. New Haven: Yale University Press, 2000.

Janowski, Bernd. *Sühne als Heilsgeschehen: Stidien zur Sühnetheologie der Priesterschrift und zur Wurzel KPR im Alten Testament.* Neukirchen-Vluyn, Germany: Neukirchener Verlag, 1982.

Janowski, Bernd, and Peter Stuhlmacher. *The Suffering Servant: Isaiah 53 in Jewish and Christian Sources.* Grand Rapids: Eerdmans, 2004.

Jeremias, Jeremias. *The Eucharistic Words of Jesus*. London: SCM, 1966.
Jewett, Robert. *Romans*. Minneapolis, MN: Fortress, 2007.
Jobes, Karen. *1 Peter*. BECNT. Grand Rapids: Baker, 2005.
———. "Got Milk? Septuagint Psalm 33 and the Interpretation of 1 Peter 2:1–3." *WTJ* 63 (2002) 1–14.
———. "'O Taste and See': Septuagint Psalm 33 in 1 Peter." *Stone-Campbell Journal* 18 (2015) 241–51.
Johnson, Andrew. "Error and Epistemological Process in the Pentateuch and Mark's Gospel: A Biblical Theology of Knowing from Foundational Texts." PhD diss., University of St. Andrews, 2011.
Johnson, Luke Timothy. *Constructing Paul*. Grand Rapids: Eerdmans, 2020.
———. "Critique of *Short Stories by Jesus*." Paper presented at the Society for Biblical Literature, November 22, 2015.
———. "The Jesus of the Gospels and Philosophy." In *Jesus and Philosophy: New Essays*, edited by Paul Moser, 63–83. Cambridge: Cambridge University Press, 2009.
Jones, D. L. "The Christology of the Missionary Speeches in the Acts of the Apostles." PhD diss., Duke University, 1966.
Jones, M. R. *New Testament Apocrypha*. Berkeley: Apocryphile, 2004.
Juel, D. *Messiah and the Temple*. SBLDS 31. Missoula, MT: Scholars, 1977.
Julicher, Adolf. *Einleitung in das Neue Testament*. Tübingen: Mohr, 1894.
Justin Martyr. *Saint Justin Martyr: The First Apology, The Second Apology, Dialogue with Trypho, Exhortation to the Greeks, Discourse to the Greeks, The Monarchy; or the Rule of God*. Edited by Thomas B. Falls. New York: Christian Heritage, 1949.
Juza, Ryan. "Echoes of Sodom and Gomorrah on the Day of the Lord: Intertextuality and Tradition in 2 Peter 3:7–13." *BBR* 24.2 (2014) 227–45.
Kähler, "Zur Form- und Traditionsgeschichte von Matth. xvi. 17–19." *NTS* 23.1 (1974) 36–58.
Kalluveettil, P. *Declaration and Covenant: A Comprehensive Review of Covenant Formula from the Old Testament and Ancient Near East*. Rome: Pontifical Biblical Institute, 1982.
Kaminsky, Joel. "Israel's Election and the Other in Biblical, Second Temple, and Rabbinic Thought." In *The "Other" in Second Temple Judaism*, edited by Daniel Harlow et al., 17–30. Grand Rapids: Eerdmans, 2011.
Kant, Immanuel. "Critique of Practical Reason." In *Great Books of the Western World: Kant*, 42:291–364. Chicago: Encyclopaedia Britannica, 1952.
———. "Critique of Pure Reason." In *Great Books of the Western World: Kant*, 42:1–252. Chicago: Encyclopaedia Britannica, 1952.
———. *Religion within the Boundaries of Mere Reason*. Cambridge: Cambridge University Press, 1998.
Käsemann, Ernst. "An Apologia for Primitive Christian Eschatology." In *Essays on New Testament*, 169–95. London: Allenson, 1964.
———. "Eine Apologie der urchristlichen Eschatologie." *ZST* 49 (1952) 272–96.
Kautzsch, E., and A. E. Cowley. *Gesenius' Hebrew Grammar*. Oxford: Clarendon, 1976.
Keck, Leander. "Mark 3:7–12 and Mark's Christology." *JBL* 84 (1965) 349–59.
Keener, Craig. *1 Peter*. Grand Rapids: Baker, 2021.
———. *Acts: An Exegetical Commentary*. Grand Rapids: Baker, 2013.
———. *The Gospel of John: A Commentary*. Peabody, MA: Hendrickson, 2003.
———. *The Gospel of Matthew: A Socio-Rhetorical Commentary*. Grand Rapids: Eerdmans, 2009.

———. "Miracle Reports and the Argument from Analogy." *BBR* 25.4 (2015) 475–95.

———. *Miracles: The Credibility of the New Testament Accounts.* 2 vols. Grand Rapids: Baker, 2011.

Kelber, Werner. "The Case of the Gospels: Memory's Desire and the Limits of Historical Criticism." *Oral Tradition* 17 (2002) 55–86.

———. "The Generative Force of Memory: Early Christian Tradition as a Process of Remembering." *BTB* 36 (2006) 15–22.

Kelber, Werner, and Samuel Byrsog. *Jesus in Memory: Traditions in Oral and Scribal Perspectives.* Waco: Baylor University Press, 2009.

Kelly, J. N. D. *A Commentary on the Epistles of Peter and Jude.* Grand Rapids: Baker, 1969.

———. *Early Christian Doctrines.* San Francisco: HarperSanFrancisco, 1958.

Kendall, Robert. *Calvin and English Calvinism to 1649.* Oxford: Oxfor University Press, 1981.

Kennard, Douglas. *Biblical Covenantalism.* 3 vols. Eugene, OR: Wipf & Stock, 2015.

———. *A Biblical Theology of Hebrews.* Eugene, OR: Wipf & Stock, 2018.

———. *A Biblical Theology of the Book of Isaiah.* Eugene, OR: Wipf & Stock, 2020.

———. *The Classical Christian God.* Toronto Studies in Theology 86. Lewiston: Edwin Mellen, 2002.

———. "Covenant Pneumaticism." In *Biblical Covenantalism,* 3:30–161. Eugene, OR: Wipf & Stock, 2015.

———. *A Critical Realist's Theological Method: Returning the Bible and Biblical Theology to be the Framer for Theology and Science.* Eugene, OR: Wipf & Stock, 2013.

———. "The Doctrine of God in Petrine Theology." ThD diss., Dallas Theological Seminary, 1986.

———. *Epistemology and Logic in the New Testament.* Eugene, OR: Wipf & Stock, 2016.

———. "Form in the Epistles of Peter." In *Petrine Studies,* forthcoming. Eugene, OR: Wipf & Stock, 2022.

———. *The Gospel.* Eugene, OR: Wipf & Stock, 2017.

———. *Messiah Jesus: Christology in His Day and Ours.* New York: Lang, 2008.

———. "Petrine Redemption: Its Meaning and Extent." *JETS* 30.4 (1987) 399–405.

———. *Petrine Studies.* Eugene, OR: Wipf & Stock, 2022.

———. *Petrine Theology.* Eugene, OR: Wipf & Stock, 2022.

———. "The Recipients of the Petrine Epistles." In *Petrine Studies,* forthcoming. Eugene, OR: Wipf & Stock, 2022.

———. "The Reef of the O.T.: A Method for Doing Biblical Theology that Makes Sense for Wisdom Literature." *SwJT* 56 (2013) 227–57.

———. *The Relationship Between Epistemology, Hermeneutics, Biblical Theology and Contextualization.* Lewiston: Mellen, 1999.

Kennedy, George. *New Testament Interpretation through Rhetorical Criticism.* Chapel Hill: University of North Carolina Press, 1984.

Kertelege, Karl. *Die Wunder Jesu im Markusevangelium: Eine redaktionsgesgeschichtliche Untersuchung.* Munich: Kösel, 1970.

Kierkegaard, Søren. *Fear and Trembling.* Princeton: Princeton University Press, 1983.

Kim, Seyoon. "Jesus—The Son of God, the Stone, the Son of Man, and the Servant: The Role of Zechariah in the Self-Identification of Jesus." In *Tradition and Interpretation in the New Testament,* edited by Gerald Hawthorne with Otto Betz, 134–48. Grand Rapids: Eerdmans, 1987.

Kingsburry, Jack. *The Christology of Mark's Gospel.* Philadelphia, PA: Fortress, 1983.

Kirk, Alan. "Social and Cultural Memory." In *Memory, Tradition, and Text: Uses of the Past in Early Christianity*, edited by Alan Kirk and Tom Thatcher, 1–24. Semeia Studies 52. Atlanta, GA: Society of Biblical Literature, 2005.

Kirk, Alan, and Tom Thatcher. "Jesus Tradition as Social Memory." In *Memory, Tradition, and Text: Uses of the Past in Early Christianity*, edited by Alan Kirk and Tom Thatcher, 25–42. Semeia Studies 52. Atlanta, GA: Society of Biblical Literature, 2005.

———. *Memory, Tradition, and Text: Uses of the Past in Early Christianity*. Semeia Studies 52. Atlanta, GA: Society of Biblical Literature, 2005.

Kirk, J. R., and Stephen Young. "'I Will Set His Hand to the Sea': Psalm 88:26 LXX and Christology in Mark." *JBL* 133.2 (2014) 333–40.

Kistemaker, Simon. *Exposition of the Acts of the Apostles*. Grand Rapids: Baker, 1990.

———. *New Testament Commentary: Exposition of the Epistles of Peter and of the Epistle of Jude*. Grand Rapids: Baker, 1987.

Kittel, Gerhard, and Gerhard Friedrich. *Theological Dictionary of the New Testament*. 10 vols. Grand Rapids: Eerdmans, 1964–76.

Klassen, William. "The Sacred Kiss in the New Testament: An Example of Social Boundary Lines." *NTS* 39 (1993) 122–35.

Klauck, Hans-Josepf. *Ancient Letters and the New Testament: A Guide to Context and Exegesis*. Waco: Baylor University Press, 2006.

Klawans, Jonathan. *Impurity and Sin in Ancient Judaism*. Oxford: Oxford University Press, 2000.

Klijn, A. F. J. "The Study of Jewish Christianity." *NTS* 20 (1973–74) 419–31.

Klijn, A. F. J., and G. J. Reinink. *Patristic Evidence for Jewish-Christian Sects*. Leiden: Brill, 1973.

Knopf, R. *Die Briefe Petri und Judae*. Göttingen: Vandenhoeck & Ruprecht, 1912.

Koch, Dietrich-Alex. "The Quotations of Isaiah 8,14 and 28,16 in Romans 9,33 and 1Peter 2,6.8 as Test Case for Old Testament Quotations in the New Testament." *ZNW* 101.2 (2010) 223–40.

Kochenash, "Cornelius's Obeisance to Peter (Acts 10:25–26) and Judaea Capta Coins." *CBQ* 81.4 (2019) 627–40.

Koester, Craig R. *Hebrews: A New Translation with Introduction and Commentary*. Anchor Bible 36. New York: Doubleday, 2001.

Kolenkow, Bingham. "The Genre Testament and Forecasts of the Future in the Hellenistic Jewish Milieu." *JSJ* 6 (1975) 57–71.

Kraeling, E. G. *The Brooklyn Museum Aramaic Papyri: New Documents of the Fifth Century B.C. from the Jewish Colony at Elephantine*. New Haven: Yale University Press, 1953.

Kuhn, Karl. "The Kingdom Story through Speech and Theme in Luke 24 and the Acts of the Apostles" In *The Kingdom according to Luke and Acts: A Social, Literary, and Theological Introduction*, 147–78. Grand Rapids: Baker, 2015.

Kümmel, H. M. "Ersatzkönig und Sündenbock." *ZAW* 80 (1968) 289–318.

Künneth, Walter. *Theology of the Resurrection*. London: SCM, 1965.

Kurtz, Johann Heinrich. *Sacrificial Worship of the Old Testament*. Edinburgh: T. & T. Clark, 1863.

Kurz, William. "Narrative Models for Imitation in Luke-Acts." In *Greeks, Romans, and Christians*, edited by D. L. Balch, 171–89. Minneapolis, MN: Fortress, 1990.

Lacey, W. K. *The Family in Classical Greece*. London: Thames & Hudson, 1968.

Lackey, Jennifer, and Ernest Sosa. *The Epistemology of Testimony*. Oxford: Clarendon, 2006.

Lagrange, M. J. *Evangile selon Saint Luc*. Paris: Gabalda, 1948.

Lampe, G. W. H. "The Lucan Portrait of Christ." *NTS* 2 (1955/56) 160–75.

Lanzinger, Daniel. "Petrus und der Sigende Hahn: Eine Zeitgeschichtliche Anspielung in der markinischen Verlengnungsperikope (Mk 14,54. 66–72)." *ZNW* 109.1 (2018) 32–50.

Lapham, F. *Peter: The Myth, the Man and the Writings: A Study of Early Petrine Text and Tradition*. Sheffield: Sheffield Academic, 2003.

Lea, Thomas. "The Early Christian View of Pseudepigraphic Writings." *JETS* 27 (1984) 65–75.

Leaney, A. R. C. "1 Peter and the Passover: An Interpretation." *NTS* 10 (1964) 238–51.

———. *The Gospel According to St. Luke*. Black's New Testament Commentaries. London: A. & C. Black, 1967.

Lefkowitz, M., and M. Fant. *Womens' Life in Greece and Rome: A Source Book in Translation*. Baltimore: John Hopkins University, 1982.

Leitzmann, Hans. "Die Anfange des Glaubensbekenntnisses." In *Kleine Schriften*, 3:163–81. New York: Wentworth, 2019.

"Letter of the Emperor Claudius to the Alexandrians." https://www.csun.edu/~hcfll004/claualex.html.

Levine, Amy-Jill. *Short Stories by Jesus: The Enigmatic Parables of a Controversial Rabbi*. New York: HarperOne, 2014.

Levine, Baruch A. *In the Presence of the Lord: A Study of Cult and Some Terms in Ancient Israel*. Leiden: Brill, 1974.

———. *Leviticus*. JPS Torah Commentary. Philadelphia, PA: Jewish Publication Society, 1989.

Levine, Lee. *The Ancient Synagogue: The First Thousand Years*. New Haven: Yale University Press, 2000.

Liebengood, Kelley. *The Eschatology of 1 Peter: Considering the Influence of Zechariah 9–14*. New York: Cambridge University Press, 2014.

Lightfoot, John. *Apostolic Fathers*. Grand Rapids: Baker, 1981.

———. *A Commentary on the New Testament from the Talmud and Hebraica, Matthew—1 Corinthians*. 4 vols. Grand Rapids: Baker, 1979.

———. *St. Paul's Epistle to the Philippians*. London: Macmillan, 1881.

Lightfoot, Robert. *History and Interpretation in the Gospels*. London: Hodder & Stoughton, 1935.

Lim, Timothy. *Pesharim*. London: Sheffield, 2002.

Lincoln, Andrew T. *Paradise Now and Not Yet: Studies in the Role of the Heavenly Dimensions in Paul's Thought with Special Reference to His Eschatology*. Society for New Testament Studies Monograph 43. Cambridge: Cambridge University Press, 1981.

Lindars, Bernard. *New Testament Apologetic*. Philadelphia, PA: Westminster, 1961.

Lo, Jonathan. "Did Peter Really Say That? Revisiting the Petrine Speeches in Acts." In *Peter in Early Christianity*, edited by Helen Bond and Larry Hurtado, 62–75. Grand Rapids: Eerdmans, 2015.

Locke, John. "Concerning Human Understanding." In *Great Books of the Western World: Locke, Berkely, and Hume*, 20:85–402. Chicago: Encyclopaedia Britannica, 1952.

———. "A Discourse of Miracles." In *The Works of John Locke*, 9:256–65. London: C. & J. Rivington, 1824.

———. "The Reasonableness of Christianity." In *The Works of John Locke*, 6:21-71. London: C. & J. Rivington, 1824.

Lohse, Eduard. *Märtyrer und Gottesknecht: Untersuchungen zur urchistlichen Verkündigung vom sühntod Jesu Christi*. Forschungen zur Religion und Literature des Alten und Neuen Testaments 49. Göttingengen: Vandenhoeck & Ruprecht, 1963.

Longenecker, Richard N. *The Christology of Early Jewish Christianity Studies in Biblical Theology*. London: SCM, 1970.

Lossky, Vladimir. *In the Image and Likeness of God*. New York: St Vladimir's Seminary, 1974.

———. "Redemption and Deification." In *In the Image and Likeness of God*, 97-110. New York: St Vladimir's Seminary, 1974.

Love, Julian. "The First Epistle of Peter." *Int* 8 (1954) 82-83.

Luce, H. K. *The Gospel According to S. Luke*. Cambridge: Cambridge University Press, 1933.

Lund, Allan. "Zur Verbrennung der sogenanten *Chrestiani* (Tac. Ann. 15,44)." *ZRGG* 60.3 (2008) 253-61.

Lund, Oystein. *Way Metaphors and Way Topics in Isaiah 40-66*. Tübingen: Mohr Siebeck, 2007.

Luther, Martin. *Luther's Works*. Edited by E. Theodore Bachman. Philadelphia, PA: Fortress, 1960.

———. *Luther's Works*. Edited by Jaroslav Pelikan and Helmut Lehmann. Saint Louis: Concordia, 1955-2015.

Luz, Ulrich. "Das Geheimnismotiv und die markinische Christologie." *ZNW* 56 (1965) 9-30.

MacDonald, Dennis Ronald. "The Synoptic Problem and Literary Mimesis: The Case of the Frothing Demoniac." In *New Studies in the Synoptic Problem*, edited by P. Foster et al., 509-21. Leuven: Uitgeverij Peeters, 2011.

MacDonald, William. *True Discipleship*. Kansas City: Walterick, 1962.

Mackay, E. Anne. *Signs of Orality: The Oral Tradition and Its Influence in the Greek and Roman World*. Leiden: Brill, 1999.

Magness, J. Lee. *Sense and Absence: Structure and Suspicion in the Ending of Mark's Gospel*. Atlanta, GA: Scholars, 1981.

Maimonides, Moses. *Thirteen Principles of the Faith*. Brooklyn: Kol Menachem, 2008.

Manson, T. W. "The Life of Jesus: Some Tendencies in Present-Day Research." In *The Background of the New Testament and Its Eschatology: In Honor of C. H. Dodds*, edited by W. D. Davies and D. Daube, 211-21. New York: Cambridge University Press, 1956.

Marcus, Joel. "Mark 4:10-12 and Marcan Epistemology." *JBL* 103.4 (1984) 557-74.

———. *The Way of the Lord: Christological Exegesis of the Old Testament in the Gospel of Mark*. Louisville: Westminster/John Knox Press, 1992.

Marger, Martin N. *Race and Ethnic Relations: American and Global Perspectives*. Belmont, Wadsworth, 1991.

Markschies, Christoph. "Jesus Christ as a Man before God: Two Interpretive Models for Isaiah 53 in the Patristic Literature and Their Development." In *The Suffering Servant: Isaiah 53 in Jewish and Christian Sources*, edited by Bernd Janowski and Peter Stuhlmacher, 225-323. Grand Rapids: Eerdmans, 2004.

Marshall, I. H. *The Acts of the Apostles: An Introduction and Commentary*. Grand Rapids: Eerdmans, 1980.

———. *The Gospel of Luke: A Commentary on the Greek Text*. NIGTC. Grand Rapids: Eerdmans, 1978.

———. *The Pastoral Epistles*. ICC. Edinburgh: T. & T. Clark, 1999.

Martin, Martina. "It's My Perogative: Jesus Authority to Grant Forgiveness and Healing on Earth." *The Journal of Religious Thought* 59.1 (2006) 67–74.

Martin, Ralph P. "Aspects of Worship in the New Testament Church." In *Vox Evangelica II*, 6–32. London: Epworth, 1963.

———. *Mark, Evangelist and Theologian*. Grand Rapids: Zondervan, 1986.

———. *Vox Evangelica II: Biblical and Historical Essays*. London: Epworth, 1963.

Martin, Ralph, and Peter Davids. *Dictionary of the Later New Testament & Its Developments*. Downers Grove: InterVarsity, 1997.

Martin, Troy. *Metaphor and Composition in 1 Peter*. Society of Biblical Literature Dissertations Series 131. Atlanta, GA: Scholars, 1992.

———. "The Rehabilitation of a Rhetorical Step-Child: First Peter and Classical Rhetorical Criticism." In *Reading First Peter with New Eyes*, edited by Robert Webb and Betsy Bauman-Martin, 41–71. London: T. & T. Clark, 2007.

Martínez, Garcia, and J. Trebolle Barrera. *The People of the Dead Sea Scrolls*. Leiden: Brill, 1995.

Martyn, Louis. *Theological Issues in the Letters of Paul*. Edinburgh: T. & T. Clark, 1997.

Masterman, J. Howard. *The First Epistle of St. Peter*. London: Macmillan, 1900.

Mathetes. *Epistle to Diognetus*. Leiden: E. J. Brill, 1964.

Mayor, Joseph. *The Epistles of St. James: The Greek Text with Introduction, Notes and Comments*. Grand Rapids: Baker, 1978.

———. *The Epistles of St. Jude and the Second Epistle of St. Peter*. Minneapolis, MN: Klock & Klock, 1978.

McArthur, Harvey, and Robert Johnston. *They Also Taught in Parables*. Grand Rapids: Zondervan, 1990.

McCarthy, Dennis J. *Treaty and Covenant: A Study in Form in the Ancient Oriental Documents and in the Old Testament*. AnBib 21. Rome: Biblical Institute, 1981.

McCartney, Dan G. "Atonement in James, Peter and Jude." In *The Glory of the Atonement: Biblical, Historical & Practical Perspectives*, edited by Charles Hill and Frank James, 176–89. Downers Grove: InterVarsity, 2004.

McDonald, H. D. *The Christian View of Man*. Westchester: Crossway, 1981.

McDonald, L. M., and J. A. Sanders. *The Canon Debate*. Peabody, MA: Hendrickson, 2002.

McDonald, William. *True Discipleship*. Port Colborne, Ontario:Gospel Fplio, 1962.

McGrath, Alister E. *Iustitia Dei: A History of the Christian Doctrine of Justification*. Cambridge: Cambridge University Press, 1998.

McKenzie, John A. *Dictionary of the Bible*. New York: Macmillan, 1965.

McKnight, Scot. *Jesus and His Death: Historiography, the Historical Jesus, and Atonement Theory*. Waco: Baylor University Press, 2005.

———. *The King Jesus Gospel: The Original Good News Revisited*. Grand Rapids: Zondervan, 2011.

McNeile, Alan Hugh, and C. S. C. Williams. *An Introduction to the Study of the New Testament*. Oxford: Oxford University Press, 1953.

McPhee, Brian. "Walk, Don't Run: Jesus Water Walking Is Unparalleled in Greco-Roman Mythology." *JBL* 135.4 (2016) 763–77.

Meeks, Wayne. *The First Urban Christians: The Social World of the Apostle Paul*. New Haven: Yale University Press, 2003.

Meier, John. *A Marginal Jew: Rethinking the Historical Jesus*. Vol. 1, *The Roots of the Problem and the Person*. New York: Doubleday, 1991.
―――. *A Marginal Jew: Rethinking the Historical Jesus*. Vol. 2, *Mentor, Message, and Miracles*. New Haven: Yale University Press, 1994.
―――. *A Marginal Jew: Rethinking the Historical Jesus*. Vol. 5, *Parables*. New Haven: Yale University Press, 2016.
Melanchthon, Philip. *Corpus Reformatorum*. Vol. 21, *Loci Communes*. Edited by Karl Gottlieb Bretschneider. Berlin: C. A. Schwetschke, 1834.
Menard, Jacques E. "*Pais Theou* as a Messianic Title in the Book of Acts." *CBQ* 19 (1957) 83–92.
Mendenhahall, G. E. "Covenant Forms in Israelite Tradition." *BA* 17.3 (1954) 50–76.
―――. *Law and Covenant in Israel and the Ancient Near East*. Pittsburgh: The Biblical Colloquium, 1955.
Merkle, Benjamin L. *The Elder and Overseer: One Office in the Early Church*. New York: Peter Lang, 2003.
Metzger, Bruce. *A Textual Commentary on the Greek New Testament*. 2nd ed. Stuttgart: Deutsche Bibelgesellschaft, 2002.
Meye, Robert. *Jesus and the Twelve: Discipleship and Revelation in Mark's Gospel*. Grand Rapids: Eerdmans, 1968.
Meyendorff, John, et al. *The Primacy of Peter*. Leighton Buzzard, Bedfordshire: Faith, 1973.
Meyer, Eduard. *Ursprung und Anfänge des Christentums*. 3 vols. Sydney: Wentworth, 2018.
Meyers, Eric. *Galilee Through the Centuries: Confluence of Cultures*. Winona Lake, IN: Eisenbrauns, 1999.
Meyers, Eric, and Mark Chancey. *Alexander to Constantine*. Vol. 3, *Archeology of the Land of the Bible*. New Haven: Yale University Press, 2012.
Michaels, J. Ramsey. *1 Peter*. WBC 49. Waco: Word Biblical, 1988.
Miegge, Giovanni. *Gospel and Myth in the Thought of Rudolf Bultmann*. Richmond: John Knox Press, 1960.
Migne, J.-P. *Patrologiae cursus completus: Series Latina*. 221 vols. Paris: Imprimerie Catholique, 1844–64.
―――. *Patrologiae cursus completus: Series Graeca*. 161 vols. Paris: Imprimerie Catholique, 1857–66.
Milgrom, Jacob. "Israel's Sanctuary: 'The Priestly Picture of Dorian Gray.'" *RB* 83 (1976) 390–99.
―――. *Leviticus 1–16*. The Anchor Bible 3. New York: Doubleday, 1991.
―――. *Numbers*. The JPS Torah Commentary. Philadelphia, PA: The Jewish Publication Society, 1990.
―――. "The Preposition מִן in the חַטָּאת Pericopes." *JBL* 126 (2007) 161–63.
―――. *Studies in Levitical Terminology: The Encroacher and the Levite: The Term 'Aboda*. Berkeley: University of California, 1970.
Milik, Józef T. *Ten Years of Discovery in the Wilderness of Judea*. London: SCM, 1959.
Millauer, Helmut. *Leiden als Gnade: Eine Traditionsgeschichtliche Untersuchung zur Leidenstheologie des ersten Petrusbriefes*. Europäische Hochschulschriften. Reihe 23. Frankfurt: Lang, 1976.
Moffatt, James. *Introduction to the Literature of the New Testament*. New York: Scribner's, 1918.

Molina, Bruce, and Jerome Neyrey. *Calling Jesus Names: The Social Value of Labels in Matthew.* Foundations and Facets: Social Facets. Salem, OR: Polebridge, 1988.

Moloney, F. J. *The Johannine Son of Man.* Biblioteca di Scienze Religiose 14. Rome: LAS, 1976.

———. "The Johannine Son of Man Revisited." In *Theology and Christology in the Fourth Gospel: Essays by the Members of the SNTS Johannine Writing Seminar*, edited by G. Van Belle et al., 177–202. Biblothecha Ephemeridum Theologicarium Lovaniensium 434. Leuven: Leuven University, 2005.

Moo, Douglas. *A Biblical Theology of Paul and His Letters: The Gift of the New Realm in Christ.* Grand Rapids: Zondervan, 2021.

Moore, George F. "The Am Ha-ares (the People of the Land) and the Haberim (Associates)." In *The Beginnings of Christianity: Part I, The Acts of the Apostles*, edited by F. J. Foakes-Jackson and Kirsopp Lake, 1:439–45. 5 vols. Grand Rapids: Baker, 1979.

Morris, Leon. *The Gospel According to John.* Grand Rapids: Eerdmans, 1971.

———. *The Gospel According to St. Luke: An Introduction and Commentary.* Tyndale New Testament Commentaries. Grand Rapids: Eerdmans, 1974.

Moscicke, Hans. "The Gerasene Exorcism and Jesus' Eschatological Expulsion of Cosmic Powers: Echoes of Second Temple Scapegoat Traditions in Mark 5:1–20." *JSNT* 41.3 (2019) 363–83.

Moser, Paul. *The Elusive God: Reorienting Religious Epistemology.* Cambridge: Cambridge University Press, 2008.

———, ed. *Jesus and Philosophy: New Essays.* Cambridge: Cambridge University Press, 2009.

Moule, C. F. D. "The Nature and Purpose of 1 Peter." *NTS* 3 (1956–57) 1–11.

Moulton, James Hope, and George Milligan. *The Vocabulary of the Greek Testament: Illustrated from Papyri and Other Non-Literary Sources.* Peabody, MA: Hendrickson, 1997.

Mowinckel, Sigmund. *La décalogue.* Paris: Felix Alcan, 1927.

Müller, Morgens. *The Expression "Son of Man" and Development of Christology: A History of Interpretation.* London: Equinox, 2008.

Munck, J. "Discours d'adieu dans le Nouveau Testament et dans la Littérature biblique." In *Aux Sources de la Tradition Chrétienne*, edited by M. Maurice Goguel, 155–70. Neuchatel: Delachaux & Niestlé, 1959.

Murphy, Nancey. *Bodies and Souls, or Spiritual Bodies?* Cambridge: Cambridge University Press, 2006.

———. "Human Nature: Historical, Scientific, and Religious Issues." In *Whatever Happened to the Soul? Scientific and Theological Portraits of Human Nature*, edited by Warren Brown et al., 19–39. Minneapolis, MN: Fortress, 1998.

———. "Reductionism: How Did We Fall Into It and Can We Emerge From It?" In *Evolution and Emergence: Systems, Organisms, Persons*, edited by Nancey Murphy and William Stoeger, 19–39. Oxford: Oxford University Press, 2007.

Murphy, Nancey, and William Stoeger. *Evolution and Emergence: Systems, Organisms, Persons.* Oxford: Oxford University Press, 2007.

Mussner, Franz. "Ein Wortspiel in Mk 1,24?" *BZNF* 4 (1960) 285–86.

Myers, Alicia. *Characterizing Jesus: A Rhetorical Analysis on the Fourth Gospel's Use of Scripture in Its Presentation of Jesus.* London: T. & T. Clark, 2012.

Nagel, Norman. "Luther and the Priesthood of All Believers." *CTQ* 61.4 (1997) 283–84.

Neil, William. *The Acts of the Apostles*. NCB. Edinburgh: Oliphants, 1973.
Neusner, Jacob. *The Idea of Purity in Ancient Judaism*. Leiden: Brill, 1973.
———. *Sifre to Numbers: An American Translation and Explanation*. 2 vols. Brown Judaic Studies 118 and 119. Atlanta, GA: Scholars, 1986.
Neusner, Jacob, and Bruce Chilton. "Sanders Misunderstanding of Purity: Uncleanness as an Ontological, Not Moral-Eeschatological Category." In *Judaic Law from Jesus to the Mishnah*, edited by Jacob Neusner, 205–30. Atlanta, GA: Scholars, 1993.
Newton, M. *The Concept of Purity at Qumran and in the Letters of Paul*. Cambridge: Cambridge University Press, 1985.
Neyrey, Jerome. *2 Peter, Jude: A New Translation with Introduction and Commentary*. Anchor Bible 37C. New York: Doubleday, 1993.
———. "The Form and Background of the Polemic in 2 Peter." *JBL* 99 (1980) 407–31.
———. *The Social World of Luke-Acts: Models for Interpretation*. Peabody, MA: Hendrickson, 1991.
Nickelsburg, George. *Jewish Literature between the Bible and the Mishnah. A Historical and Literary Introduction*. Philadelphia, PA: Fortress, 1981.
———. *Resurrection, Immortality, and Eternal Life in Intertestamental Judaism*. Cambridge: Harvard University Press, 1972.
Niebecker, E. *Das allgemeine Priestertum der Gläubigen*. Paderborn: Schöningh, 1936.
Niebuhr, H. Richard. *Christ and Culture*. New York: Harper & Row, 1975.
Nineham, D. E. *Studies in the Gospels: Essays in Memory of R. H. Lightfoot*. Oxford: Basil Blackwell, 1955.
Noland, "Salvation-History and Eschatology." In *Witness to the Gospel: The Theology of Acts*, edited by I Howard Marshall and David Peterson, 63–82. Grand Rapids: Eerdmans, 1998.
Noonan, Benjamin. "On the Efficacy of the Atoning Sacrifices: A Biblical Theology of Sacrifice from Leviticus." *BBR* 31.3 (2021) 285–318.
Norden, Edward. *Die antike Kunstprosa vom Vi. Jahrhunddert V. Chr. Bis im Die Zeit Der Renaissance*. Sydney: Wentworth, 2018.
Novenson, Matthew V. "Why Are There Some Petrine Epistles Rather Than None?" In *Peter in Early Christianity*, edited by Helen Bond and Larry Hurtado, 146–57. Grand Rapids: Eerdmans, 2015.
Nygren, Anders. *Agape and Eros*. London: SCPK, 1957.
O'Brien, P. T. "Letters, Letter Forms." In *Dictionary of Paul and His Letters*, edited by Hawthorne et al., 550–53. Downers Grove: InterVarsity, 1993.
O'Conner, Daniel William. *Peter in Rome: The Literary, Liturgical, and the Archeological Evidence*. New York: Columbia University Press, 1969.
Oden, Thomas. *The Justification Reader*. Grand Rapids: Eerdmans, 2002.
Oliver, Nicholas. "The Fisherman as Expositor." *ExpTim* 28 (1917) 230.
Ortlund, Dane. "The Old Testament Background and Eschatological Significance of Jesus Walking on the Sea (Mark 6:45–52)." *Neot* 46.2 (2012) 325–26.
Oss, Douglas. "The Interpretation of the 'Stone' Passages by Peter and Paul: A Comparative Study." *JETS* 32.2 (1989) 181–200.
Oswalt, John. *The Book of Isaiah*. Grand Rapids: Eerdmans, 1988.
Otto, Rudolf. *The Idea of the Holy: An Inquiry into the Non-Rational Factor in the Idea of the Divine and Its Relation to the Rational*. Hamondsworth: Penguin, 1959.
Padilla, Osvaldo. "The Speeches in Acts: Historicity, Theology, and Genre." In *Issues in Luke-Acts: Selected Essays*, edited by Sean Adams and Michael Pahl, 171–94. Piscataway, NJ: Gorgias, 2012.

Pannenberg, Wolfhart. *Anthropology in Theological Perspective.* Philadelphia, PA: Westminster, 1985.

———. *Systematic Theology.* Grand Rapids: Eerdmanns, 1988.

Pao, David. *Acts and the Isaianic New Exodus.* Grand Rapids: Baker, 2000.

Parvis, Paul. "When Did Peter Become Bishop of Antioch?" In *Peter in Early Christianity,* edited by Helen Bond and Larry Hurtado, 263–72. Grand Rapids: Eerdmans, 2015.

Paschke, Boris A. "The Roman *ad bestias* Execution as a Possible Historical Background for 1 Peter 5.8." *JSNT* 28 (2006) 489–500.

Patai, Raphael. *The Messiah Texts: Jewish Legends of Three Thousand Years.* Detroit: Wayne State, 1979.

Pate, C. Marvin. *Communities of the Last Days: The Dead Sea Scrolls, the New Testament and the Story of Israel.* Downers Grove: InterVarsity, 2000.

Pate, C. Marvin, and Douglas Kennard. *Deliverance Now and Not Yet: The New Testament and the Great Tribulation.* New York: Lang, 2003.

Perdelwitz, R. *Die Mysterienreligion und das Problem des 1 Petrusbriefes.* Giessen: Alfred Töpelmann, 1911.

Perkins, Pheme. *Peter: Apostle for the Whole Church.* Minneapolis, MN: Fortress, 2000.

Perkins, William. *The Workes of That Famous and Worthy Minister of Christ in the University of Cambridge, Mr. William Perkins.* London: Legat, 1635.

Pierce, C. A. *Conscience in the New Testament.* London: SCM, 1955.

Pierce, Chad. *Spirits and the Proclamation of Christ: 1 Peter 3:18–22 in Light of Sin and Punishment Traditions in Early Jewish and Christian Literature.* Tübingen: Mohr Siebeck, 2011.

Pierce, Charles Sanders. *The Collected Papers of Charles Sanders Pierce.* Edited by Charles Hartshorne and Paul Weiss. Cambridge: Harvard University Press, 1966.

———. "The Fixation of Belief." *Popular Science Monthly* 12 (1877) 1–15.

———. "How to Make Our Ideas Clear." *Popular Science Monthly* 12 (1878) 286–302.

Pitre, Brant. *Jesus, the Tribulation, and the End of the Exile: Restoration Eschatology and the Origin of the Atonement.* Tübingen: Mohr Siebeck, 2005.

Plantinga, Alvin. *Knowledge and Christian Belief.* Grand Rapids: Eerdmans, 2015.

———. "Reason and Basic Belief in God." In *Faith and Rationality: Reason and Belief in God,* edited by Alvin Plantinga and Nicholas Woltersdorff, 16–93. Notre Dame: University of Notre Dame, 1983.

———. *Warrant and Proper Function.* New York: Oxford, 1993.

Plato. "Meno." In *Great Books of the Western World: Plato,* 7:115–41. Chicago: Encyclopaedia Britannica, 1952.

———. "Phaedo." In *Great Books of the Western World: Plato,* 7:174–90. Chicago: Encyclopaedia Britannica, 1952.

———. "Phaedrus." In *Great Books of the Western World: Plato,* 7:220–51. Chicago: Encyclopaedia Britannica, 1952.

———. "Timaeus." In *Great Books of the Western World: Plato,* 7:442–77. Chicago: Encyclopaedia Britannica, 1952.

Plummer, Alfred. *A Critical and Exegetical Commentary on the Gospel According to St. Luke.* ICC. Edinburgh: T. & T. Clark, 1896.

———. *The General Epistles of St. James and St. Jude.* The Expositor's Bible. London: Hodder & Stoughton, 1899.

Poland, Franz. *Geschichte des griechischen Vereinswesens.* Preis-schriften... der fürstlich Jablonowkischen Gesellschaft 38. Leipzig: Teubner, 1909.

Porten, Bezalel. *Archives from Elephantine*. Berkley, CA: University of California, 1968.
Porter, Stanley. "Thucydides 1.22.1 and Speeches in Acts: Is There a Thucydidean View?" *NovT* 2 (1990) 121–42.
———. "τοῦτο πρῶτον γινώσκοντες ὅτι in 2 Peter 1:20 and Hellenistic Epistolary Convention." *JBL* 127.1 (2008) 156–71.
Puech, Émile. "Une apocalypse messianique (4Q521)." *Revue de Qumrân* 15.4 (1992) 475–522.
Quenstedt, Johann Andreas. *Theologia didactio-polemica Polemica*. Wittenberg: Johanne Ludolph Quenstedt, 1685.
Raackam, Richard. *The Book of Acts in Its First Century Setting*. Grand Rapids: Eerdmans, 1995.
Rahner, Karl, and Herbert Vorgrimler. *Theological Dictionary*. New York: Herder & Herder, 1965.
Räisänen, Heikki. *Das "Messiasgheimnis" im Markusevangelium*. Helsinki: Länsi-Suomi, 1976.
Reeder, Caryn. "1 Peter 3:1–6: Biblical Authority and Battered Wives." *BBR* 25.4 (2015) 519–39.
Reese, Ruth A. *2 Peter & Jude*. Two Horizons New Testament Commentary. Grand Rapids: Eerdmans, 2007.
Reicke, Bo Ivar. *The Disobedient Spirits and Christian Baptism: A Study of 1 Pet. iii.19 and Its Context*. Kobenhaun: Ejnar Munksgaard, 1946.
———. *The Epistles of James, Peter and Jude*. Bijbel 37. Garden City, NY: Doubleday, 1964.
Reid, Thomas. *Thomas Reid: An Inquiry into the Human Mind on the Principles of Common Mind*. Edited by Derek Brookes. Edinburgh: Edinburgh University Press, 1997.
Reuschling, Wyndy. "The Means and End in 2 Peter 1:3–11: The Theological and Moral Significance of Theosis." *Journal of Theological Interpretation* 8.2 (2014) 275–86.
Reynolds, B. E. "The 'One Like a Son of Man' According to the Old Greek of Daniel 7.13–14." *Bib* 89 (2008) 70–80.
Rhee, Helen. *Loving the Poor, Saving the Rich: Wealth, Poverty, and Early Christian Formation*. Grand Rapids: Baker, 2012.
Rhetorica ad Herennium. Translated by H. Rackham. Cambridge: Harvard University Press, 1957.
Richards, G. C. "1 Peter 3:21." *JTS* 32 (1931) 77.
Richards, E. Randolf. "Silvanus Was Not Peter's Secretary: Theological Bias in Reading Bias in Interpreting διὰ Σιλουανοῦ ἔγραψα in 1 Pet 5:12." *JETS* 43 (2000) 417–32.
Richards E. Randolf, and Kevin Boyle. "Did Ancients Know the Testaments Were Pseudepigraphic? Implications for 2 Peter." *BBR* 30.3 (2020) 403–23.
Ricoeur, Paul. *Essays on Biblical Interpretation*. Minneapolis: Fortress, 1980.
———. *Memory, History, Forgetting*. Chicago: University of Chicago Press, 2004.
———. *Oneself as Another*. Chicago: The University of Chicago Press, 1992.
———. "Toward a Hermeneutic of the Idea of Revelation." In *Essays on Biblical Interpretation*, 73–118. Minneapolis: Fortress, 1980.
Ridderbos, Herman. *The Speeches of Peter in the Acts of the Apostles*. London: Tyndale, 1956.
Ridlehoover, Charles. "The Matthean Peter: as Archetype and Antitype." *JETS* 64.4 (2021) 729–44.

Riesenfeld, Herald. *Jesus Transfiguré: l'arriére-plan récit évangélique de la transfiguration de Notre-Seigneur.* Kobenhaven: Munksgaard, 1947.

Rigaux, Beda. *The Testimony of St. Mark.* Chicago: Franciscan Herald, 1966.

Robbins, Vernon. *Exploring the Texture of Texts: A Guide to Socio-Rhetorical Interpretation.* Valley Forge: Trinity, 1996.

———. *The Tapestry of Early Christian Discourse: Rhetoric, Society and Ideology.* London: Routledge, 1996.

Roberts, Alexander, and James Donaldson. *The Ante-Nicene Christian Library: Translations of the Fathers Down to A.D. 325.* 24 vols. Edinburgh: T. & T. Clark, 1866–72.

Roberts, R. C., and W. Jay Wood. *Intellectual Virtues: An Essay in Regulative Epistemology.* Oxford: Clarendon, 2007.

Robertson, A. T. *Grammar of the Greek New Testament in Light of Recent Research.* Nashville: Broadman Press, 1934.

———. "The Greek Article and the Deity of Christ." *The Expositor* 21 (1921) 185.

Robinson, J. A. T. *The Body: A Study in Pauline Theology.* London: SCM, 1952.

———. "The Most Primitive Christology of All?" *JThS* 97 (1956) 181–83.

Rogers, Richard. *Seven Treatises Leading and Guiding to True Happiness.* London: Man, 1610.

Rohrbaugh, Richard L. "The Pre-industrial City in Luke-Acts: Urban Social Relations." In *Social World of Luke-Acts: Models for Interpretation*, edited by Jerome Neyrey, 125–50. Peabody, MA: Hendrickson, 1991.

Rood, T. "Thucydides." In *Narrators, Narratees, and Narratives in Ancient Greek Literature*, edited by Irene de Jonge et al., 115–28. Leiden: Brill, 2004.

Rosenberg, Roy A. "Jesus, Isaac and the Suffering Servant." *JBL* 84 (1965) 381–88.

Roth, Martha. *Law Collections from Mesopotamia and Asia Minor.* Atlanta, GA: Society of Biblical Literature, 1997.

Rouwhorst, G. "Jewish Liturgical Traditions in Early Syriac Christianity." *VC* 51 (1997) 72–93.

Ruether, Rosemary Radford. *Introducing Redemption in Christian Feminism.* Sheffield: Sheffield Academic, 1998.

Russell, D. S. *Method and Message of Jewish Apocalyptic: 200 BC-AD 100.* Philadelphia, PA: Westminster, 1980.

Ryan, Jordon. *The Role of the Synagogue in the Aims of Jesus.* Minneapolis, MN: Fortress, 2017.

Sabourin, Leopold. "The Biblical Cloud." *BTB* 4 (1974) 290–311.

Saldarini, Anthony. *Matthew's Christian-Jewish Community.* Chicago: University of Chicago Press, 1994.

Saller, Richard. *Patriarchy, Property and Death in the Roman Family.* Cambridge: Cambridge University Press, 1994.

Sanday, William, and Arthur Headlam. *A Critical and Exegetical Commentary on the Epistle to the Romans.* Edinburgh: T. & T. Clark, 1902.

Sanders, E. P. *Jesus and Judaism.* Philadelphia, PA: Fortress, 1985.

———. *Jewish Law from Jesus to the Mishnah.* London: SCM, 1990.

———. *Judaism: Practice and Belief 63 B.C.E.–66 C.E.* London: SCM, 1992.

———. *Paul and Palestinian Judaism.* Philadelphia, PA: Fortress, 1977.

———. *Paul, the Law, and the Jewish People.* Minneapolis, MN: Fortress, 1983.

Sanders, Jack T. *The Jews in Luke-Acts.* Philadelphia, PA: Fortress, 1987.

———. "The Pharisees in Luke-Acts." In *The Living Text: Essays in Honor of Ernest W. Saunders*, edited by Dennis E. Groh and Robert Jewett, 141–88. Lanham: University Press, 1985.

Sandmel, David. "Critique of *Short Stories by Jesus*." Paper presented at the Society for Biblical Literature, November 22, 2015.

Santos, Narry. "The New Family of Jesus and the Relativization of the Natural Family: An Exposition on Honor and Shame (Mark 1:16–20; 2:13–14; 3:13–35)." *RevExp* 115.4 (2018) 542–601.

Sapp, David A. "LXX, 1QIsa, and MT Versions of Isaiah 53 and the Christian Doctrine of Atonement." In *Jesus and the Suffering Servant: Isaiah 53 and Christian Origins*, by William Bellinger and William R. Farmer, 170–92. Atlanta, GA: Trinity, 1998.

Sawyer, John. *The Fifth Gospel: Isaiah in the History of Christianity*. Cambridge: Cambridge University Press, 2000.

Schafer, Peter. *Kehhalot-Studien*. Tübingen: Mohr Siebeck, 1988.

Schaff, Philip. *History of the Christian Church*. Peabody, MA: Hendrickson, 1996.

———. *A Select Library of the Nicene and Post-Nicene Fathers of the Christian Church*. Grand Rapids: Eerdmans, 1994.

Schenker, Adrian. "kōper et expiation." *Bib* 63 (1982) 32–46.

Schlatter, Adolf. *New Testament Theology*. Grand Rapids: Baker, 1997.

Schleiermacher, Fredrich. *The Life of Jesus*. Philadelphia, PA: Fortress, 1975.

———. "Uber die Zeugnisse des Papias." In *Theologisches Studien U. Kritiken*. Philadelphia, PA: Sunday School Times, 1887.

Schmidt, Thomas. *Hostility to Wealth in the Synoptic Gospels*. Ottawa: UNKNO, 1987.

Schnelle, Udo. *Theology of the New Testament*. Grand Rapids: Baker, 2007.

Schoedinger, Andrew. *Readings in Medieval Philosophy*. New York: Oxford University Press, 1996.

Schoeps, Hans-Joachim. *Jewish Christianity: Factual Disputes in the Early Church*. Philadelphia, PA: Fortress, 1969.

———. *Paul: The Theology of the Apostle in the Light of Jewish Religious History*. Translated by Harold Knight. Philadelphia, PA: Westminster, 1961.

———. *Theologie und Geschichte des Judenchristentums*. Tübingen: Mohr, 1949.

Schrange, W. "Zur Ethik der NT Haustafeln." *NTS* 21 (1974) 1–22.

Schreiner, Thomas. *1, 2 Peter, Jude*. NAC 37. Nashville: Broadman & Holman, 2003.

Schreuer, Adiel. "Midrash, Theology, and History: Two Powers in Heaven Revisited." *JSJ* 39 (2008) 230–54.

Schubert, Paul. "The Final Cycle of Speeches in the Book of Acts." *JBL* 87 (1968) 1–16.

Schultz, Anselm. *Nachfolgen und Nachahmen. Studien über das Verhältnis der neutestamentlichen Jüngerschaft zur ur christlichen Vorbildethink*. SANT 6. Munich: Kösel-Verlag, 1962.

Schürer, Emil. *The History of the Jewish People in the Age of Jesus Christ (175 BC–AD 135)*. Revised and edited by M. Black et al. 1973. Rev. ed. Edinburgh: T. & T. Clark, 1987.

Schürmann, Heinz. *Das Lukasevangelium*, Vol. 1. Herders theologischer Kommentar zum Neuen Testament 3. Freiberg: Herder, 1969.

Schutter, W. L. "1 Peter 4.17, Ezekiel 9.6, and Apocalyptic Hermeneutics." In *SBL Seminar Papers*, 276–84. SBLSP 26. Atlanta, GA: Scholars, 1987.

———. *Hermeneutic and Composition in First Peter*. WUNT 2. Tübingen: Mohr [Siebeck], 1989.

Schweitzer, Albert. *Quest for the Historical Jesus: A Critical Study of its Progress from Reimarus to Wrede*. London: A. & C. Black, 1906, 1954.

Schweizer, Eduard. "Concerning the Speeches in Acts." In *Studies in Luke–Acts*, edited by L. E. Keck and J. L. Martyn, 208–16. London: SPCK, 1968.
———. *The Good News According to Mark*. Richmond: Knox, 1970.
———. *Lordship and Discipleship*. SBT 28. London: SCM Press, 1960.
Scott, James C. *Domination and the Arts of Resistance: Hidden Transcripts*. New Haven: Yale University Press, 1990.
———. *Weapons of the Weak: Everyday Forms of Peasant Resistance*. New Haven: Yale University Press, 1985.
Searle, John. *Speech Acts*. Cambridge: Cambridge University Press, 1970.
Seeley, David. *The Noble Death: Greco-Roman Martyrology and Paul's Concept of Salvation*. JSNTSup 28. Sheffield: JSOT, 1990.
Segal, Alan. "Hellinistic Magic: Some Questions of Definition." In *Studies in Gnosticism and Hellenistic Religions: Giles Quispel Festschrift*, edited by R. van den Broek and M. J. Vermaseren, 349–75. Leiden: Brill, 1981.
———. *The Two Powers in Heaven: Early Rabbinic Reports about Christianity and Gnosticism*. Leiden: Brill, 1977.
Segovia, Fernando. *Discipleship in the New Testament: 1982 Marquette University Symposium "Call and Discipleship: New Testament Perspectives."* Philadelphia, PA: Fortress, 1985.
Selwyn, Edward G. "Eschatology in 1 Peter." In *The Background of the New Testament and Its Eschatology*, edited by W. D. Davies and D. Daube, 394–401. Cambridge: Cambridge University Press, 1964.
———. *The First Epistle of St. Peter*. Grand Rapids: Baker, 1981.
———. "The Problem of the Authorship of 1 Peter." *ExpTim* 60 (1948) 257–58.
Seneca. *Ad Lucilium Epistulae Morales*. Translated by R. M. Gummere. LCL. Cambridge: Harvard University Press, 1947.
Senior, Donald. *The Passion of Jesus in Matthew*. Wilmington: Michael Glazier, 1985.
Sevenster, J. N. *Paul and Seneca*. NovTSup 4. Leiden: Brill, 1961.
Sheeley, Steven. *Narrative Asides in Luke-Acts*. Sheffield: Sheffield Academic, 1992.
Sh'muel, Y'huda Ibn. *Midr'she G'ula*. Jerusalem: Mosad Bialik-Massada, 1954.
Sholem, Gershom. *Jewish Gnosticism, Merkabah Mysticism, and Talmudic Tradition*. New York: Jewish Publication Society of America, 1960.
Sibley, Jim. "You Talkin' to Me? 1 Peter 2:4–10 and a Theology of Israel." *SwJT* 59.1 (2016) 59–75.
Silberman, Lou. *Orality, Aurality and Biblical Narrative*. Semia Studies. Atlanta, GA: Scholars, 1987.
Silius Italicus. *Punica*. LCL. Translated by J. D. Duff. Cambridge: Harvard University Press, 1949.
Simon, Ulrich. *A Theology of Salvation: A Commentary on Isaiah 40–55*. London: SPCK, 1953.
Sjöberg, Erik. *Der Menschensohn im ältiopischen Henochbuch*. Lund: Gleerup, 1946.
Skarsaune, Oskar, and Reidar Hvalvik. *Jewish Believers in Jesus: The Early Centuries*. Peabody, MA: Hendrickson, 2007.
Skehan, P. W. "A Note on 2 Peter 2,13." *Bib* 41 (1960) 69–71.
Sklar, Jay. "Sin and Atonement: Lessons from the Pentateuch." *BBR* 22 (2012) 472–89.
———. "Sin and Atonement: What the Pentateuch Teaches Us." Paper presented for Institute for Biblical Research, November 20, 2010.
———. *Sin, Impurity, Sacrifice, Atonement: The Priestly Conceptions*. Sheffield: Sheffield Phoenix, 2005.

Slater, T. B. "One Like a Son of Man in First Century CE Judaism." *NTS* 41 (1995) 183-98.
Sleeper, Freeman. "Political Responsibility According to 1 Peter." *NovT* 10 (1968) 281-85.
Smith, Clyde. "Laodicea, Canons of." In *The New International Dictionary of the Christian Church*, edited by J. D. Douglas, 578. Grand Rapids: Zondervan, 1978.
Smith, Morton. *Jesus the Magician*. San Francisco: Harper & Row, 1978.
Smith, Terence. *Petrine Controversies in Early Christianity: Attitudes towards Peter in Christian Writings of the First Two Centuries*. Tübingen: J. C. B. Mohr, 1985.
Snodgrass, Klyne. "From Allegorizing to Allegorizing: A History of the Interpretation of the Parables of Jesus." In *The Historical Jesus in Recent Research*, edited by James Dunn and Scot McKnight, 248-68. Winona Lake, IN: Eisenbrauns, 2005.
Snyder, John Ivan. *The Promise of His Coming: The Eschatology of 2 Peter*. San Mateo, CA: Western, 1986.
Snyder, Graydon F. "Survey and 'New' Thesis on the Bones of Peter." *BA* 32.1 (1969) 1-24.
Soards, Marion L. *The Speeches in Acts: Their Content, Context, and Concerns*. Louisville: Westminster, 1994.
Soden, Herman von. *Urchristliche Literaturgeschichte in Die Schriften des Neuen Testaments*. Berlin: Alexander Duncker, 1905.
Spicq, Ceslas. *L'Epitre aux Hebreux*. Paris: Gabalda, 1952.
Stamm, Johann Jakob. *Erlösen und Vergeben im alten Testament: Eine begriffsgeschichtliche Untersuchung*. Bern: Francke, 1940.
Stanley, David. "The Conception of Salvation in Primitive Christian Preaching." *CBQ* 18 (1956) 231-54.
Starr, James. *Sharers in Divine Nature: 2 Peter 1:4 in Its Hellenistic Context*. ConB 33. Stockholm: Almqvist & Wiksell, 2000.
Stauffer, Ethelbert. *Jesus and His Story*. Translated by Richard and Clara Winston. New York: Knopf, 1960.
Stegman, Thomas. "'The Spirit of Wisdom and Understanding': Epistemology in Luke-Acts." In *The Bible and Epistemology: Biblical Soundings on the Knowledge of God*, edited by Mary Healy and Robin Parry, 90-94. Milton Keynes: Paternoster, 2007.
Stendahl, Krister. *The School of St. Matthew & Its Use of the Old Testament*. Lund: C. W. K. Gleerup, 1954.
Stern, Ephraim. *New Encyclopedia of Archeological Excavations in the Holy Land*. Jerusalem: Carta, 1993.
Stibbs, Alan M. *The First Epistle General of Peter*. TNTC. Grand Rapids: Eerdmans, 1959.
Stobel, Albert. "Das Aposteldekratt als Folge des antiechenischen Strettes." In *Kontinutat und Erdenherit*, edited by G. Muller and H. Strenger, 81-104. Freeberg: Verlag Herder GmbH, 1981,
Stock, Augustine. "Is Matthew's Presentation of Peter Ironic?" *BTB* 17.2 (1987) 64-69.
———. *The Way in the Wilderness: Wilderness and Moses Themes in Old Testament and New*. Collegeville: Liturgical, 1969.
Strack, Herman L., and Paul Billerbeck. *Kommentar zum Neuen Testament aus Talmud und Midrash*. München: Beck, 1978-83.
Strack, Max. "Die Müllerinnung in Alexandrien." *ZNW* 4 (1903) 213-34.
Strange, James. "Ancient Texts, Archeology as Text, and the Problem of the First Century Synagogue." In *Evolution of the Synagogue: Problems and Progress*, edited by Howard Clark Kee and Lynn Cohick, 27-45. Harrisburg: Brill, 1999.

Strange, James, and Hershel Shanks. "Has the House Where Jesus Stayed in Capernaum Been Found?" *BAR* 8 (1982) 30–32.

Strauss, David. *The Life of Jesus Critically Examined.* London: Chapman, 1846.

Strecker, Georg. "Appendix 1: On the Problem of Jewish Christianity." In *Orthodoxy and Heresy in Earliest Christianity*, by Walter Bauer, 241–85. Minneapolis, MN: Fortress, 1971.

———. *Das Judenchristentum in den Pseudoklementinen.* TU 70, no. 2. Berlin: Akademie, 1981.

———. "The Kerygmata Petrou." In *The New Testament Apocrypha*, edited by Edward Hennecke and Wilhelm Schneemelcher, 2:102–27. Philadelphia, PA: Westminster, 1965.

Streeter, Burnett H. *The Primitive Church.* New York: Macmillan, 1929.

Stuhlmacher, Peter. *The Gospel and the Gospels.* Grand Rapids: Eerdmans, 1991.

Stuhlmueller, Carroll. "Yahweh-King and Deutero-Isaiah." *BR* 15 (1970) 32–45.

Swinburne, Richard. *The Evolution of the Soul.* Oxford: Clarendon, 1986.

Tacitus. *Ann.* Translated by John Jackson. LCL. Cambridge: Harvard University Press, 1951.

Talbert, Charles. *Matthew.* Grand Rapids: Baker, 2010.

———. *Perspectives on First Peter.* Macon: Mercer University Press, 1986.

Talbert, G. W. "Biographies of Philosophers and Rulers as Instruments of Religious Propaganda in Mediterranean Antiquity." *ANRW* 2.16.2 (1978) 1619–51.

———. *Learning Through Suffering. The Educational Value of Suffering in the New Testament and Its Milieu.* Collegeville: Liturgical Press, 1991.

Taylor, J. E. "The Phenomenon of Early Jewish Christianity: Reality or Scholarly Invention." *VC* 44 (1990) 313–34.

Taylor, R. O. P. *The Groundwork of the Gospels.* Oxford: Basil Blackwell, 1946.

Tenney, Merrill. "Some Possible Parallels Between 1 Peter and John." In *New Dimensions in New Testament Study*, edited by Richard Longenecker and Merrill Tenney, 370–77. Grand Rapids: Zondervan, 1974.

Tertullian. *The Writings of Quintus Sept. Flor. Tertullianus.* Edited by Richard Ellmann. Kila: Kessinger, 1869–70.

Teugels, Lieve M. "Consolation and Composition in a Rabbinic Homily on Isaiah 40: Pesiqta' de Rav Kahana' 16." In *Studies in the Book of Isaiah*, edited by J. Van Ruiten and M. Vervenne, 433–46. Leuven: Leuven University Press, 1997.

Thatcher, Tom. *Jesus, the Voice, and the Text: Beyond the Oral and Written Gospel.* Waco: Baylor University Press, 2008.

———. "Why John Wrote a Gospel: Memory and History in an Early Christian Community." In *Memory, Tradition, and Text: Uses of the Past in Early Christianity*, edited by Alan Kirk and Tom Thatcher, 79–98. Semeia Studies 52. Atlanta, GA: Society of Biblical Literature, 2005.

Thayer, Joseph. *A Greek-English Lexicon of the New Testament: Coded with Strong's Concordance Numbers.* Carol Stream: Tyndale, 1995.

Theissen, Gerd. *Lokalkolorit und Zeitgeschichte in den Evangelien.* NTOA 8. Göttingen: Universitatsverlag Freiburg Vandenhoeck Ruprecht, 1989.

Theissen, Gerd, and Annette Merz. *The Historical Jesus: A Comprehensive Guide.* Minneapolis, MN: Fortress, 1998.

Thiselton, Anthony. *The First Epistle to the Corinthians.* Grand Rapids: Eerdmans, 2000.

Thomas, John. *Footwashing in John 13 and the Johannine Community.* JSNTSup 61. Sheffield: Sheffield Academic Press, 1991.

Thornton, T. D. G. "1 Peter, a Pascal Liturgy?" *JTS* 12 (1961) 17-26.
Thurén, Lauri. *Argument and Theology in 1 Peter: The Origins of Christian Paraenesis*, Sheffield: Sheffield Academic, 1995.
———. *The Rhetorical Strategy of 1 Peter, with Special Regard to Ambiguous Expressions*. Åbo, Findland: Åbo Academy Press, 1990.
Tillich, Paul. *Systematic Theology*. Chicago: University of Chicago, 1963.
Tite, Philip. "The Compositional Function of the Petrine Prescript: A Look at 1 Pet 1:1-3." *JETS* 39 (1996) 47-56.
———. "Nurslings, Milk and Moral Development in Greco-Roman Context: A Reappraisal of the Paraenetic Utilization of Metaphor in 1 Peter 2.1-3." *JSNT* 31.4 (2009) 371-400.
Tödt, H. E. *The Son of Man in the Synoptic Tradition*. Translated by D. M. Barton, London: SCM, 1965.
Torrance, T. F. *The Royal Priesthood*. Edinburgh: T. & T. Clark, 1993.
Tosato, Angelo. "The Law of Leviticus 18:18: A Reexamination." *CBQ* 46 (1984) 199-214.
Toussaint, Stanley. *Behold the King: A Study of Matthew*. Portland: Multnomah, 1980.
Towner, Philip H. "Households and Household Codes." In *Dictionary of Paul and His Letters*, edited by Gerald Hawthorne et al., 417-19. Downers Grove: InterVarsity, 1993.
Tracy, Steven. "Domestic Violence in the Church and Redemptive Suffering in 1 Peter." *CTJ* 41 (2006) 279-96.
Treggiari, Susan. *Roman Marriage: Iusti coniures from the Time of Cicero to the Time of Ulpian*. Oxford: Clarendon, 1991.
Trites, Allison. *The New Testament Concept of Witness*. Cambridge: Cambridge University Press, 1977.
Trompf, G. W. *The Idea of Historical Recurrence in Western Thought: From Antiquity to the Reformation*. Berkeley: University of California Press, 1979.
Tuckett, C. M. *The Messianic Secret*. Issues in Religion and Theology 1. London: SPCK, 1983.
Twelftree, Graham. *The Miracle Worker*. Downers Grove: InterVarsity, 1999.
Tyson, Joseph B. "Blindness of the Disciples in Mark." *JBL* 80.3 (1961) 261-68.
Tzaferis, Vassilios. "Capernaum." In *New Encyclopedia of Archeological Excavations in the Holy Land*, edited by Ephraim Stern, 1:201-95. 4 vols. Jerusalem: Carta, 1993.
Van Brock, N. "Substitution rituelle." *RHA* 17.65 (1959) 117-46.
VanderKam, James, and Peter Flint. *The Meaning of the Dead Sea Scrolls: Their Significance for Understanding the Bible, Judaism, Jesus, and Christianity*. San Francisco: HarperSanFrancisco, 2002.
VanGemeren, Willem. *New International Dictionary of Old Testament Theology and Exegesis*. 5 vols. Grand Rapids: Zondervan, 1997.
Van Gulick, Robert. "Reduction, Emergence, and the Mind/Body Problem: A Philosophic Overview." In *Evolution and Emergence: Systems, Organisms, Persons*, edited by Nancey Murphy and William Stoeger, 40-73. Oxford: Oxford University Press, 2007.
Van Kooten, George. *Paul's Anthropology in Context: The Image of God, and Tripartite Man in Ancient Judaism, Ancient Philosophy and Early Christianity*. Tübingen: Mohr Siebeck, 2008.
Van Unnik, W. C. "Christianity According to Peter." *ExpTim* 68 (1956) 79-83.
———. "The Teaching of Good Works in 1 Peter." *NTS* 1 (1954) 95-109.

Van Voorst, Robert E. *The Ascents of James: History and Theology of a Jewish-Christian Community.* SBLDS 112. Atlanta, GA: Scholars, 1989.

Varma, Ashish. "Jews and Gentiles Together in Christ? The Jerusalem Council on Racial Reconciliation." *ExAud* 33 (2017) 153–74.

Velasco, Jesus Maria, and Leopald Sabourin. "Jewish Christianity of the First Centuries." *BTB* 6 (1976) 5–26.

Vermes, Geza. *Jesus the Jew: A Historian's Reading of the Gospels.* Philadelphia, PA: Fortress, 1981.

———. "Qumran Forum Miscellanea I." *JJS* 43 (1992) 303–4.

———. *Scripture and Tradition in Judaism: Haggadic Studies in Studia Post-Biblica.* Leiden: Brill, 1961.

Verner, David. *The Household of God: The Social World of the Pastoral Epistles.* Chico: Scholars, 1983.

Volf, Miraoslav. "Soft Difference: Theological Reflections on the Relation between Church and Culture in 1 Peter." *ExAud* 10 (1994) 16–21.

Von Harnack, Adolf. *Die Chronologie der altchristlichen literatur bis Eusebius.* Leipzig: J. C. Hinrichs, 1904.

———. *Die Chronologie der altchristlichen Litteratur bis Irenäus.* Leipzig: Hinrichs, 1897.

Von Hefele, Karl. *Histoire des concilesd'après les documents originaux: 755–870.* Charleston, SC: Nabu, 2011.

Von Rad, Gerhard. *Old Testament Theology.* New York: Harper & Row, 1962–65.

Von Soden, Herman. *Die Brief des Petrus, Jakobus, Judas.* Freiburg: J. C. B. Mohr, 1891.

Vrba, Carl Franz, and Joseph Zycha. *Sanct Aureli Augustini De peccatorum meritis et remissione et de baptismo parvulorum ad Marcellinum libri tres.* Vindobonae: F. Tempsky, 1913.

Wachsman, Shelley. "The Galilee Boat 2,000 Year-Old Hull Recovered Intact." *BAR* 14.5 (1988) 18–33.

Wainwright, William. "Obedience and Responsibility." In *The Wisdom of the Christian Faith*, edited by Paul Moser and Michael McFall, 58–76. Cambridge: Cambridge University Press, 2012.

Waldis, Joseph. *Sprache und stil der grossen Griechischen Inschrift von Nemrud-Dagh in Kommagen.* Zürich: Koine-Forschung, 1920.

Wallace, Daniel. *Greek Grammar Beyond the Basics: An Exegetical Syntax of the New Testament.* Grand Rapids: Zondervan, 1996.

Walls, Andrew. "The Canon of the New Testament." In *The Expositor's Bible Commentary*, edited by Frank Gaebelein, 1:631–44. Grand Rapids: Zondervan, 1979.

———. "Papias and Oral Tradition." *VC* 21 (1967) 137–40.

Waltke, Bruce. *The Book of Proverbs.* Grand Rapids: Eerdmans, 2004.

Waltke, Bruce, and M. O'Connar. *An Introduction to Biblical Hebrew Syntax.* Winona Lake, IN: Eisenbrauns, 1990.

Walton, John, and Brent Sandy. *The Lost World of Scripture: Ancient Literary Culture and Biblical Authority.* Downers Grove: InterVarsity, 2013.

Wand, J. W. C. *The General Epistles of St. Peter and St. Jude.* London: Methuen, 1934.

Watson, D. E. *Invention, Arrangement, and Style: Rhetorical Criticism of Jude and 2 Peter.* Atlanta, GA: Scholars, 1988.

Watts, John. *Isaiah 1–33.* WBC 24. Nashville: Thomas Nelson, 2000.

———. *Isaiah 34–66.* WBC 25. Nashville: Thomas Nelson, 2005.

Webb, Robert. "Intertexture and Rhetorical Strategy in First Peter's Apocalyptic Discourse: A Study in Sociorhetorical Interpretation." In *Reading First Peter with New Eyes*, edited by Robert Webb and Betsy Bauman-Martin, 72–110. London: T. & T. Clark, 2007.

Webb, Robert, and Betsy Bauman-Martin. *Reading First Peter with New Eyes: Methodological Reassessments of the Letter of First Peter*. London: T. & T. Clark, 2007.

Weidinger, Karl. *Die Haustetafeld, ein Stück urchristlicher Paränese*. Leipzig: Hinrichs, 1928.

Weidner, E. F. *Politische Dokumente aus Kleinasien: Die Staatsverträge in akkadischer Sprache aus dem Archiv von Boghazköi-Studien 8–9*. Leipzig: Hinrichs, 1923.

Weinfeld, Moshe. "The Covenant Grant in the Old Testament and in the Ancient Near East." In *Essential Papers on Israel and the Ancient Near East*, edited by F. E. Greenspahn, 69–102. New York: New York University Press, 1991.

Weiss, Johannes. *Das Alteste Evangelium, ein Beitrag zum Verstandis des Markusevangeliums und der altesten evangelischen Uberleifurung*. Whitefish, MT: Kessinger, 2010.

———. *Das Urchristentum*. Sydney: Wentworth, 2016.

———. *Die Predigt Jesu vom Reiche Gottes*. Göttingen: Vandenhoeck & Ruprecht, 1892.

———. *Jesus' Proclamation of the Kingdom of God*. Translated and edited by R. H. Hiers and D. L. Holland. London: SCM, 1971.

Wendling, Emil. *Ur-Marcus, Versuch einer Wiederherstueling der altesten Mitteilungen uber das Leben Jesus, und Die Enstehung des Marcusevangeliums, philogische Untersuchunger*. Tubingen: Mohr, 1905.

Westphal, Merold. "Taking St. Paul Seriously: Sin as an Epistemological Category." In *Christian Philosophy*, edited by Thomas Flint, 200–226. Notre Dame: University of Notre Dame Press, 1990.

White, Aaron. "The Apostolic Preaching of the Lord Jesus: Seeing the Speeches in Acts as a Coherent Series of Sermons." *Presbyterian* 44.2 (2018) 33–51.

Wilde, Oscar. *The Picture of Dorian Gray*. Philadelphia, PA: Ivers, 1890.

Wilken, Robert. *The Christians as the Romans Saw Them*. New Haven: Yale, 1984.

Willard, Dallas. *The Spirit of the Disciplines: Understanding How God Changes Lives*. San Francisco: HarperSanFrancisco, 1988.

Williams, Margaret H. "From Shimon to Petros: Petrine Nomenclature in the Light of Contemporary Onomastic Practices." In *Peter in Early Christianity*, edited by Helen Bond and Larry Hurtado, 30–45. Grand Rapids: Eerdmans, 2015.

Williams, David J. *Acts*. NIBCNT. Peabody, MA: Hendrickson, 1990.

Williams, Jocelyn. "A Case Study in Intertextuality: The Place of Isaiah in the 'Stone' Sayings of 1 Peter 2." *RTR* 66.1 (2007) 37–55.

Williams, Prescott. "The Poems About Incomparable Yahweh's Servant in Isaiah 40–55." *SwJT* 11 (1968) 73–87.

Williams, Travis. "The Divinity and Humanity of Caesar in 1 Peter 2,13." *ZNW* 105.1 (2014) 131–47.

Wilson, B. R. *Magic and the Millennium: A Sociological Study of Religious Movements of Protest Among Tribal and Third-World Peoples*. London: Heinemann, 1973.

Wilson, Jan. *Mesopotamia*. Herstellung: Verlag Butzon & Bercker Kevelaer, 1994.

Windisch, Hans, and H. Preisker. *Die katholische Briefe*. Tübingen: J. C. B. Mohr-Paul Siebeck, 1951.

Witherington, Ben, III. *The Acts of the Apostles: A Socio-Rhetorical Commentary*. Grand Rapids: Eerdmans, 1998.

———. *The Indelible Image: The Theological and Ethical Thought World of the New Testament*. Vol. 1, *The Individual Witnesses*. Downers Grove: InterVarsity, 2009.

Woan, Sue. "The Psalms in 1 Peter." In *The Psalms in the New Testament*, edited by Steve Moyise and Maarten Menken, 213–29. London: T. & T. Clark, 2004.

Wolff, Hans Walter. *Anthropology of the Old Testament*. Philadelphia, PA: Fortress, 1974.

Wolters, Al. "'Partners of the Deity': A Covenantal Reading of 2 Peter 1:4." *CTJ* 25 (1990) 28–46.

———. "Postscript to 'Partners of the Deity.'" *CTJ* 26 (1990) 418–20.

———. "Worldview and Textual Criticism in 2 Peter 3:10." *WTJ* 49 (1987) 405–13.

Wood, Jay. *Epistemology: Becoming Intellectually Virtuous*. Downers Grove: InterVarsity, 1998.

Wood, J. Edwin. "Isaac Typology in the New Testament." *NTS* 14 (1968) 583–89.

Wrede, William. *The Messianic Secret*. London: Clarke, 1971.

Wright, David P. *The Disposal of Impurity: Elimination Rites in the Bible and in Hittite and Mesopotamian Literature*. SBLDS 101. Atlanta, GA: Scholars, 1987.

Wright, N. T. *Following Jesus: Biblical Reflections on Discipleship*. Grand Rapids: Eerdmans, 1994.

———. *Jesus and the Victory of God*. Minneapolis, MN: Fortress, 1996.

———. *The New Testament and the People of God*. Minneapolis, MN: Fortress, 1992.

———. *Paul and the Faithfulness of God*. Minneapolis: Fortress, 2013.

———. *The Resurrection of the Son of God*. Minneapolis, MN: Fortress, 2003.

———. *What Saint Paul Really Said: Was Paul of Tarsus the Real Founder of Christianity?* Grand Rapids: Eerdmans, 1997.

Young, Edward. *The Book of Isaiah: The English Text, with Introduction, Exposition, and Notes*. Grand Rapids: Eerdmans, 1969–72.

Zacharias, Daniel. "Old Greek Daniel 7:13–14 and Matthew's Son of Man." *BBR* 21 (2011) 454–55.

Zehnle, R. F. *Peter's Pentecost Discourse: Tradition and Lukan Reinterpretation in Peter's Speeches of Acts 2 and 3*. Nashville: Abingdon, 1971.

Ziegler, Joseph, and Oliver Munnich. *Susanna-Daniel-Bel et Draco. Editio secunda: Versionis juxta LXX interpretes textum plane novum constituit Oliver Munnich*. Vetus Testamentum Graecum 16/2. Göttingham: Vandenhoeck & Ruprecht, 1999.

Zimmerli, Walter. *Ezekiel 2: A Commentary on the Book of the Prophet Ezekiel Chapters 25–48*. Hermeneia. Philadelphia, PA: Fortress, 1983.

Zzaan, J. de. "The Use of the Greek Language in Acts." In *The Beginnings of Christianity: Part I, The Acts of the Apostles: Prolegomena II: Criticism*, edited by F. J. Foakes-Jackson and Kirsopp Lake, 2:30–65. 5 vols. London: Macmillan, 1922.

Subject Index

Adoption, 26
Angel, 13, 15
Anointing Christ, 15, 23, 32, 35
Anthropomorphism, 18
Apologetics, 195–206
Apostle, 146–48, 163
Assurance, 174–75
Atonement, 43–45, 85–122

Baptism, 133–35, 157
Biography, 9
Born again, 172–74

Call, 151–52
Christ or Messiah, 22–57
Church, 12, 176–214
Collective Memory, 5–7
Coming of the Lord, 254–82
Confession, 143
Conscience, 76–77, 135, 195–200
Covenant, 11–12, 177–79
Creator, 11–12

Daughter of Voice, 32, 35, 144
Deification, 35, 167–70
Demons, 33, 225–26, 228–35
Descent to Hell, 235–39
Determinism, 16–18, 46–47
Discipleship, 125, 137–61, 171–72
Divine Nature, 111–12
Domestic Violence, 200–201

Election, 18, 183
Elders, 201–14
Elijah, 34–35, 139–41
Elohim, 11–12
Epistemology, 9
Eschatology, 13, 49, 254–82
Eternity, 16
Ethical issues, 9
Eucharist, 108, 159–61
Everlasting, 16
Exodus, 12, 47–49, 108–13, 137–75

Faith/Faithfulness, 171–72
False Teachers, 240–53
Flock of God, 162–63, 176
Foreknowledge, 16, 18
Forgiveness, 95–96, 140–42, 160–61, 172

Gentiles, 9, 12
Glory, 14, 20, 35
God, 11–21, 51–57
Gospel, 61–62, 123–36
Guardian, 14, 47

Healing, 33, 111, 134
Heart, 69, 73–74
Hermeneutics, 64–65
Holy, 14–15, 86–87
Holy Spirit, 13, 15, 36, 51–63, 69–72, 143–44, 172, 271
House Code, 81–83, 197–206

SUBJECT INDEX

Household of God, 82–84, 176–214
Humanity, 66–84

Jesus, 22

Kingship, 13
Know, 171–72

Loosed/bound, 214
Lord, 11–12, 22–25, 40–42, 54, 136
Love, 39–40, 163, 171–73

Marriage, 199–201, 205–6
Master, 22–25, 40–42, 54, 114
Mercy, 12, 183
Merkabah Mysticism, 103
Messianic secret, 24–25
Mimetic Atonement, 85, 97, 103–8, 118–22, 155, 157–59
Mind, 74–75

New Birth, 166

Obedience, 87, 197–98
Omniscience, 15–16

Passover, 108, 159–61
Patriarchy/patronage, 82–83, 193–202
Penal Atonement, 88–92, 102–3, 132
Perichoresis, 168
Peter as Apostle, 1–2
Peter of Faith, 2–3
Peter as Foundation, 1–2
Peter as Pope, 2–3
Petrine theology, 3–10
Prayer, 13–15, 19–20, 105–6, 122, 125, 134–36
Priesthood of believers, 183–84, 188–91
Primacy of Peter, 1–3
Prince of Life, 43
Prophecy, 12, 62–65
Purification, 85–108

Ransom, 158–59
Redemption, 88–89, 108–18, 166
Relationship, 77–84
Repentance, 132–36
Resurrection, 39
Rhetorical Criticism, 37–40

Righteousness, 20, 203
Rock, 35, 190–92

Sacrifice, 191–93, 207
Salvation, 15, 111, 135–36
Sanctification, 14, 55–56, 85–108, 189–91
Satan, 15, 161–62, 225–39
Scribe, 37–39, 64–65
Scripture, 65
Self-control, 172–73
Servant of Lord, 99–106
Serving, 157–58, 214
Shepherd, 14, 47–49, 162–63
Sin/Guilt Offering, 85–106
Slave, 193–94, 199–201
Son of God, 29, 35, 42–43
Son of Man, 26–31, 36, 49
Soul, 67–69
Spirit, 69–72
Sovereignty, 12–13, 18–20, 49
Submission, 197–98
Substitutionary Atonement, 85–108, 132, 157–59
Suffering, 215–24
Supercession, 176–82
Synagogue to church, 207–14
Synergism, 168

Tabernacles, 35
Tax, 38
Temptation, 161–62
Theosis, 167–75
Transcendence, 14–15
Trinity, 51–57
Two Powers, 13, 27, 51–57
Two Ways, 112, 126, 135–75

Vicarious Atonement, 85–108, 132, 157–59
Virtues, 112–14, 137–75

Will, God's, 18–19
Will, Human, 18–19, 76
Witness, 5–6
Word, God's, 12, 61–65
Works, 80–81, 195–205

Yahweh, 11–12

Author Index

Abbot, E, 71
Abegg, M, 29
Achtemeier, P, 185–86
Adams, E, 27, 77–78, 176, 193, 196
Aeschines, 199
Akiva, Rab, 28, 40, 266
Aland, B, 276
Allison, G, 37, 54, 63–64, 119, 141, 148–49, 153, 270–73
Altereatio, 225
Althaus, P, 193
Ambrose, 91
Anderson, R, 67
Andreas of Caesarea, 265
Anselm, 16
Appian, 142
Aquila, 46
Aquinas, 16–17, 69–70, 72, 75, 167
Archer, 67
Aristeas, 40
Aristides, 54, 106, 112, 200, 203
Aristotle, 5, 69, 75, 81, 171, 173, 197, 200–201, 209, 243, 245
Arius Didymus, 81
Arnobius, 228
Arrian, 53, 145
Artapanus, 145
Artemidorus, 199
Assmann, J, 7
Athanasius, 167
Augustine, 16, 68, 70, 72, 75, 90, 115, 167, 225, 231

Aulén, G, 225
Aune, D, 142, 228
Aurelius, M, 197
Averbeck, 88
Avi-Yonah, 160

Bahr, G, 160
Bailey, D, 101
Bailey, K, 7
Balch, D, 80–82, 193–94, 197–98, 200, 205
Balentine, S, 86
Baley, D, 90
Barnet, P, 262
Barrie, J, 3
Barth, K, 69
Barton, S, 147
Bauckham, R, 6–7, 25, 51–52, 111, 113, 124, 168–69, 173, 207, 222, 245, 248, 255
Bauernfeind, 110
Bauman-Martin8, 181
Baumgärtel, 69–70, 73
Baur, F, 4–5
Beale, G, 3
Beare, F, 3, 62, 190, 217, 220
Beasley-Murray, 51
Beck, B, 119
Beckman, G, 91, 179–80
Bede, 198
Bellinger, W, 100
Bengel, J, 109–10

Berger, P, 77, 176, 193, 196, 205
Berkeley, G, 74–75
Bermejo-Rubio, 157
Bertram, 242
Best, E, 57–58, 87, 147, 154, 184–85, 189, 217
Bettenson, H, 167
Betz, H, 100, 150
Beyer, 221
Beyreuther, 203
Bietenhard, 23, 128
Bigg, C, 32, 55–56, 87, 107, 169, 190, 252
Billerbeck, P, 100, 274
Blaising, C, 122
Blass, F, 184, 203
Blinzer, J, 184–85, 189
Blue, B, 210, 211
Bochmuehl, M, 5, 7, 34
Bock, D, 8, 116, 119, 160, 227, 230, 232, 245, 257
Boda, M, 86
Boethius, 16
Bond, H, 124
Bonhoeffer, D, 155
Bonner, C, 235
Bonsirven, J, 223
Boomershine, 7
Borg, M, 259
Boring, M, 8
Bornkamm, G, 154
Botterweck, 67
Bourke, M, 162
Bowes, W, 172
Bowling, 73
Boyarin, D, 27
Bradley, K, 199
Bratsiotis, 73
Braumann, 256
Brettler, M, 47
Brichto, H, 88
Broadhead, E, 29, 33
Brooke, G, 138–39
Broughton, T, 186
Brown, C, 67, 71, 76, 256
Brown, W, 69, 72, 75
Brownlee, W, 63
Bruce, F, 43, 127, 132, 135–36, 254
Büchler, A, 95

Büchsel, 109
Bultmann, R, 3, 73, 222, 234
Burkett, D, 27–28, 35
Bynum, C, 279
Byrsog, S, 7

Cadbury, H, 127, 254
Callan, T, 112
Calvin, J, 73–74, 111, 113, 168
Campbell, J, 82
Caragounis, C, 35, 153
Carter, W, 205
Casel, O, 192–93
Casey, M, 26–27
Cassiodorus, 167
Cassius Dio, 112, 186
Celsus, 187
Cerfaux, L, 184
Chancey, M, 210
Chang, A, 115
Charles J, 170–71
Charlesworth, 139
Chernus, I, 104
Chester, A, 255
Chilton, B, 14, 97
Christensen, S, 81, 193–94, 196–97, 200
Chrysostom, 1, 124, 196, 199–200, 205
Cicero, 89, 171, 186, 198–99, 205, 242–43, 276
Cisholm, 73
Claudius, 53, 209
Clement Alex, 7, 49, 81, 142, 197, 201, 205–6, 222, 236–37, 242, 246, 247
Clement Rom, 1, 81, 112, 142, 148, 163, 167, 171–73, 194, 200, 207, 211, 241, 265
Collins, J, 29–30
Conzelmann, 24, 73, 126, 222
Cooper, J, 67
Coppes, 76
Cothenet, E, 124, 145
Cowley, A, 138
Crawford, M, 135
Crosby, M, 147
Crouzel, H, 124, 145
Cullmann, O, 16, 23, 99, 128, 154, 254
Cyprian, 1, 81, 197, 201, 221

Cyril of Alex, 1, 90, 135
Cyril of Jerusalem, 225

Dahl, M, 73
Dalton, W, 51, 237
Daly, R, 99-100
Damgaard, F, 153
Danker, F, 168, 171-72, 174, 181
Daube, D, 38, 148
David, C, 138
Davids, P, 3-4, 8, 11, 51-52, 55, 77-78, 87, 107, 250, 276
Davies, P, 22, 54, 63-64, 119, 141, 148-49, 153, 270-71, 273
Dean-Otting, 104
De Boer, 124, 145
Deismann, A, 23, 25, 51, 53, 109, 128, 171-72, 209
Demosthenes, 6, 177
De Saussure, F, 88
Descartes, 69-70, 72, 75
DeSilva, D, 201, 216
DeVilliers, J, 218, 220, 222
Dewey, A, 6-7
Dibelius, M, 125, 127
Didymus, A, 2, 197-98, 201, 276
Dilhe, A, 68, 123, 278
Dill, S, 187
Dio Cassius, 157, 197, 227, 258, 261, 268
Dio Chrysostom, 82
Diodorus of Sicily, 244
Dionysius, 53, 124, 145, 171, 209
Dix, D, 254
Dodd, C, 127
Doering, L, 5
Domeris, W, 229
Dossey, L, 191
Draper, J, 7
Dubis, M, 255
Dunn, J, 5, 7-8, 24-25, 67-69, 71, 73-75, 150
Durham, J, 179

Edwards, J, 17, 107, 113, 174
Eichrodt, W, 47, 74
Eisenman, R, 8
Eisler, R, 267
Elinger, K, 88

Elliott, J, 3-4, 8, 44, 51, 55-56, 80-83, 176-77, 180, 182-83, 186-91, 193, 197-200, 205, 211-12
Ellis, E, 63, 231
Ephrem, 259
Epictetus, 85, 103, 133, 203
Epicurus, 242-43
Epiderxis, 225
Epiphanius, 1, 140, 152, 156, 268
Euripides, 157, 200
Eusebius, 6-7, 90, 120, 124, 157, 206-7, 222, 242, 244, 261-63, 266-69, 276

Fant, M, 200
Feder, Y, 88
Felix, P, 89
Feuillict, A, 120, 157
Filson, F, 215
Finlan, S, 90
Fiore, B, 124, 145
Fitzmyer, J, 100
Flint, P, 30
Foakes-Jackson, 2
Fornara, C, 124, 145
Francis, F, 51, 53
Fredericks, 67-68, 76
Freedman, D, 26
Friedrich, 67
Funk, R, 137

Gamaliel, 279
Gammie, J, 14, 87, 95
Gane, R, 86, 95-96
Gärtner, 216-17
Geddert, T, 32
Gelardini, G, 23, 41
Gellius, A, 205, 227
Gese, H, 88
Gilchrist, 75
Gillman, N, 279
Goguel, M, 242
Goldingay, J, 36, 45, 48, 139, 159
Goodspeed, E, 236
Goppelt, L, 3, 199
Gorgias, 6
Goulder, M, 5
Grappe, C, 5

Grässer, 164
Green, G, 3–4, 8–10, 49, 171, 243
Gregory Nazianzus, 124, 225
Gregory Nyssa, 167
Grundmann, 203, 219
Gubler, M, 99–100
Guilbert, P, 126
Gundry, R, 73, 119, 122, 155, 159, 162, 269
Gurney, O, 98
Gutierrez, P, 124, 145, 225

Hafemann, S, 167–70
Hägerland, T, 141
Hahn, 76, 82
Halbwachs, M, 7
Hanck, 195
Hanse, 166
Haarbeck, 218
Harder, 109, 116
Harland, P, 81, 194, 197–98
Harris, J, 236
Harris, L, 67
Harris, M, 25
Hartman, L, 81, 197
Hayes, R, 25
Headlam, A, 91
Hegel, G, 4–5
Helmer, C, 127
Helyer, L, 2, 4, 8–9, 181, 184, 274
Hemer, C, 127
Hengel, , M, 2, 8, 25, 101, 146, 206
Heraclitus, 6
Hermann, J, 88
Hermas, , 173, 247
Herodotus, 174
Herostratus, 172
Hicks, R, 243
Hierocles, 174
Hilary, 225
Hillel, 64, 152
Himes, P, 44
Hippolytus, 136, 236, 247, 253
Hobbes, T, 74
Hoffner, H, 91, 98, 179–80
Holdsworth, J, 220
Hollaz, D, 236
Hollenbach, P, 227, 230

Holtzmann, H, 16, 131
Holzmeister, 190
Homer, 47, 54
Hooker, M, 28, 32, 100, 167
Horrell, D, 78, 81, 186, 197, 227
Horsley, 6
Hort, F, 188, 192
Howard, V, 120, 157
Howe, B, 8
Hutchison, J, 157
Hughes, P, 110
Hugh of St Victor, 167
Hummel, R, 153
Hunter, A, 161
Hurst, L, 164
Hurtado, L, 2, 27

Ignatius, 2, 49, 57–58, 124, 174, 186, 207, 212, 214, 222, 236
Irenaeus, 6, 120, 124, 136, 157, 167, 192, 225–26, 233, 236, 250, 253, 274
Isaacs, M, 104
Isocrates, 82

Jacob, 68
Jacobs, P, 16, 131
Jaffee, M, 7
Janowski, B, 88
Jeremias, J, 160
Jerome, 115, 124, 138, 141, 221, 267
Jewett, R, 110
Jobes, K, 51, 55, 62, 107, 199–201, 215
Johanan ben Zacchai, 148
Johnson, L, 8
Jones, D, 126
Josephus, 5, 31–33, 37–40, 53, 77, 81–82, 105, 109, 133, 140–42, 144–45, 147, 169–72, 174, 186, 196, 198–201, 203–4, 208–12, 214, 230–31, 235, 248, 257–58, 260–63, 265–69, 272, 279–81
Joshua, Rab, 92
Julian, 205
Justin Martyr, 67, 90, 115–16, 135–36, 148, 192, 228, 230–31, 236, 253, 261, 265–66
Juvenal, 199, 210
Juza, R, 275

Kähler, 153
Kalluveettil, 26
Kaminsky, J, 92
Kamlah, 71
Kant, I, 14–15, 24
Käsemann, E, 168, 170, 254
Kautzsch, E, 138
Keck, L, 32
Keener, C, 36, 55, 141, 144, 152, 159, 197–200, 209, 223
Kelber, W, 6–7
Kelley, J, 1, 51, 62, 135
Kendall, R, 113
Kennard, D, 5, 7–12, 14, 17, 20, 25, 29, 37, 42, 47, 50–53, 55, 59, 64, 66, 75–77, 80, 85, 89, 92, 96, 99, 101, 103–4, 106–7, 113, 119–20, 122, 124–25, 127, 129, 131–33, 136–37, 140, 145, 152, 155, 157, 159, 164–65, 176, 178, 182, 185–86, 189, 195, 198, 201, 216, 218–20, 225–26, 243, 250, 253, 256–57, 277
Kennedy, G, 127
Kerteledge, K, 33
Kim, S, 44
Kingsburry, J, 25
Kirk, A, 7, 34, 54–55
Kistmacher, S, 51, 55, 107
Kittel, 67
Klauck, H, 51, 53
Klawans, J, 92
Kleinknect, 71
Koch, D, 45
Koester, C, 104
Kornfeld, 14
Köster, 116
Krienke, H, 16, 131
Kuhn, K, 127
Kümmel, H, 98
Kurtz, J, 88, 124, 145

Lac, 73
Lacey, W, 177
Lactantius, 207, 221–22
Laertius, D, 242–43
Lampe, G, 135
Lang, 219

Lefkowitz, M, 200
Leo the Great, 91, 167
Levine, B, 86, 208, 213
Libanius, 200
Liebengood, K, 256
Lightfoot, J, 64, 120, 154, 157, 209–10
Lincoln, A, 104
Lindars, B, 63
Livy, 142, 205
Longenecker, 100
Lossky, V, 167
Love, J, 49
Luce, H, 147
Lucian, 112, 145, 157, 186, 199–200, 205, 234
Luckmann, T, 77, 176
Lucretius, 276
Lund, O, 137
Luther, M, 3, 89, 125–26, 188–89, 193, 225
Luz, U, 24

Mackay, E, 6
Maimondes, 30
Manson, T, 24
Markschies, C, 90
Marshall, I, 76, 82, 115, 160
Martial, 199, 227
Martin, R, 141, 164, 255
Martyn, L, 225
Masterman, J, 164
Mathetes, 66–67
Matthew of Aquasparta, 167
Maunder, C, 167
Maurer, 76, 82
Maximus, 1
Mayor, J, 168
McCarthy, D, 178–79
McCartney, D, 89
McDonald, H, 73, 75–76
McDonald, W, 155
McGrath, A, 89
McKenzie, J, 67
McKnight, S, 120, 157
McPhee, B, 34, 55
Meeks, W, 177, 187, 200, 209
Meier, J, 140, 142, 231, 233
Melanchthon, 89

AUTHOR INDEX

Menard, J, 100
Mendenhall, G, 179
Merkle, B, 209
Merz, A, 142
Metzger, B, 276
Meye, R, 146
Meyendorff, J, 2
Meyers, E, 210
Michaels, J, 55, 107, 216–17
Milano, D, 26
Milgrom, J, 86, 88–89, 93–94, 96–98
Millauer, H, 255
Milligan, 109, 196
Minucius Felix, 186
Moffatt, J, 164
Molina, B, 38
Moloney, F, 27
Moo, D, 8
Morris, L, 162
Moscicke, H, 228
Motyer, 73
Moulton, 109, 196
Mowinckel, S, 179
Müller, M, 27
Munnich, O, 28
Murphy, N, 67, 69, 72, 75
Musonius Rufus, 81
Mussener, F, 33

Nagel, N, 189
Nathan, Rab, 106
Nazianzen, 90–91
Neusner, J, 14, 97, 106, 231
Neyrey, J, 38, 242–45, 247–49, 276
Nickelsberg, 103, 122, 158
Niebecker, E, 190
Niebuhr, H, 78, 176, 196
Noonan, B, 97

O'Connar, M, 138
Oden, T, 90
Oepke, A, 277
Origen, 68, 70, 72, 90, 124, 169, 177, 187, 205, 236, 242, 246, 278
Ortand, D, 34, 55
Oss, D, 44
Oswalt, , J, 73, 102–3
Otto, R, 14
Owen, P, 27

Palamas, 2
Pannenberg, 68, 70
Pao, D, 139, 163
Papias, 6, 252
Paschke, B, 227
Patai, R, 30
Pate, M, 20, 28–29, 42, 85, 99, 103–4, 119–20, 124, 131, 133, 145, 157, 159, 219–20, 256–57
Payne, 69, 71, 139
Perkins, P, 2, 7
Perkins, W, 113
Philstratus, 235
Philo, 5, 36, 39–40, 48, 76–77, 81–82, 94, 105–6, 124, 145–47, 169–70, 172–74, 178, 184–85, 196, 198–99, 201, 203, 206, 208–10, 212, 225, 228, 243, 248–50, 263, 271, 276
Photius, 2
Pierce, C, 76, 137
Pilate, 33
Pindar, 6
Pitre, B, 273
Plantinga, A, 176
Plato, 5–6, 66, 68, 70, 72, 75, 169, 173
Plautus, 199
Pliny, 149, 265
Plummer, A, 160, 242
Plutarch, 6, 53, 82, 85, 103, 124, 141, 145, 157, 169, 174, 199–201, 206, 242–44
Poland, F, 177, 187
Pollio, V, 199
Polybius, 171, 243
Polycarp, 81, 142, 173, 200, 207, 211–12
Porphyry, 206
Porten, B, 105–6
Porter, S, 127
Puetch, E, 30

Quell, 11
Quenstedt, J, 236
Quintilian, 124, 145, 171, 199, 206

Rabab, Rabbi, 97
Rahner, K, 67
Räisänen, H, 25
Rashi, 94

Reeder, C, 201
Reese, R, 168
Reicke, B, 135, 197, 137
Rengstorf, 13, 24
Reuschling, W, 170
Reynolds, B, 30
Richards, G, 135
Ricoeur, P, 7
Ridderbos, H, 127
Ridlehoover, 155, 162
Riesenfeld, H, 99–100
Ringgren, 67
Robertson, J, 52, 56
Robinson, J, 24
Rogers, R, 113
Rohrbaugh, R, 159–60
Rosenberg, R, 99–100
Roth, M, 91
Ruether, R, 225
Rufus, M, 197, 201, 205
Russell, D, 16
Ryan, J, 212–13

Sabourin, L, 27
Saller, R, 199
Sallust, 198
Sanday, W, 91
Sanders, E, 120, 157
Sandy, B, 7
Santos, N, 139, 156
Sawyer, P, 138
Schafer, P, 104
Schaff, P, 2, 91
Schenker, A, 88
Schillebececkx7
Schlatter, A, 3
Schleiermacher, 24
Schnelle, U, 3
Schoeps, H, 99, 101
Schrange, W, 81, 197
Schreiner, T, 168
Schrenk, 76
Schubert, P, 127
Schultz, A, 150, 195
Schürer, E, 263
Schürmann, H, 147
Schutter, W, 185
Schweitzer, A, 24, 119, 259, 269
Schweizer, E, 35, 127, 153

Scott, J, 81, 197
Scotus, S, 167
Seebass, 67
Seeley, 85, 103, 119
Seeseman, 218
Segal, A, 13, 27, 53, 228
Segovia, F, 145, 150
Selwyn, E, 55, 57–58, 107, 184, 217, 222, 254
Seneca, 6, 56, 85, 103, 119, 169, 171, 173, 199
Septimus Geta, 123
Sevenster, J, 199
Shammai, 152
Sholem, G, 104
Sibley, J, 181
Siculus, D, 171, 174, 209
Silberman, L, 7
Silius Italicus, 119, 205
Simon, U, 137
Sjöberg, E, 103
Skehan, 252
Sklar, J, 86, 88
Slater, T, 27
Sleeper, F, 197
Smith, T, 168, 228
Snyder, J, 255
Soads, M, 127–28
Socrates, 173
Song, 73–74
Sophicles, 6
Stamm, J, 88
Stanley, D, 126
Starr, J, 168
Stauffer, 52, 161
Stendahl, K, 63
Stibbs, A, 184, 217
Stock, A, 137, 162
Strabo, 149, 184
Strack, H, 100, 209, 274
Strange, J, 210
Strathmann, 111
Strauss, D, 24
Stuhlmacher, 125
Stuhlmueller, 47
Suetonius, 23, 128, 263
Swinburne, 69
Symmachus, 46

Tacitus, 38, 85, 103, 145, 186, 199, 262, 265
Talbert, C, 124, 145
Tertullian, 33, 68, 70, 81, 124, 135, 197, 199, 201, 205, 207, 221–22, 225
Teugels, L, 139
Thacher, T, 7
Theissen, G, 142, 267
Themistius, 261
Theodoret, 1, 90, 124
Theodosius, 221
Theodotion, 46
Theodotos, 212
Theophrates, 245
Thomas, J, 159
Thorton, T, 218
Tillich, P, 70–71, 75
Tite, P, 62
Torrance, T, 189, 193
Tracy, S, 199
Trites, A, 5
Trompf, G, 124, 145
Tuckett, C, 24
Twelftree, G, 231

Valerius, 81, 197, 199–201
Van Brock, N, 98
VanGemeren, 67
Van Gulick, 69, 75
Van Kooten, 67
VanderKamm, 30
VanPelt, 69, 71
Van Unnik, 198, 204
Varro, 149, 199
Vermes, G, 30, 99–100
Verner, D, 177
Volf, M, 185
Von Harnack, 51
Von Martiz, 25
Vorgrimler, H, 67

Wallace, D, 18, 47, 52, 56, 229
Waltke, 67–68, 138
Walton, J, 7
Watts, J, 138
Webb, R, 8, 279
Weidner, E, 26
Weidinger, 81, 197
Weinfeld, M, 26
Weiss, J, 24, 259
White, A, 127
Wilde, O, 86
Wilken, R, 186
Willard, D, 150
Williams, C, 153
Williams, J, 44
Williams, P, 101
Williams, T, 23
Wilson, J, 14, 75
Wilson, R, 78, 176, 196
Witherington, 56, 58, 133
Woan, S, 199
Wolff, H, 67–69, 71, 73
Wolters, A, 168, 276
Wood, J E, 99–100
Wrede, W, 24
Wright, D, 98
Wright, N, 7–8, 28, 37, 49, 125, 140, 258–59, 262–63, 272, 279

Xenophon, 47, 199, 201, 205, 243, 247

Young, E, 44
Young, S, 34, 54–55

Zacharias, D, 27–28
Zehnle, R, 127
Ziegler, J, 28

Scripture Index

OLD TESTAMENT

Genesis

1	11, 67
1–2	276
2:7	67
2:17	91
3:4	243
5:5–31	91
8:21	192
9:4–10	67
12:2–8	13, 24–25, 42
15:18–21	25
18:12	200
18:28	81, 203
19:3–16	81, 203
35:2	86
48:15	47
49:24	47

Exodus

3:6	39, 281
3:14–18	12–13, 54, 209
3:20	25
4:29	209
6:6	110
12–19	226
12:1—13:16	108, 165, 209
13:21	139
14:10—15:21	34, 42, 55, 71, 139
15:13	47
17:1–8	42, 209
18:12	209
19-Lev 27	179
19:4–7	3, 178, 180, 183–84, 188, 190, 209
19:12–16	178
20:1—24:8	108, 179
20:11–12	25
21:29–30	90, 96
22:16–26	42
23:2	68
23:19	180
23:22	188
24:1–11	18, 55, 59, 85, 91–92, 95, 99, 102, 165, 209
29:21	87
29:35–37	93, 108
30:10–16	88, 96, 108
32:30–40	89, 179
33:9–14	25, 139, 146
34:6–7	95
34:26	180
36:1–4	209
40:34–38	103, 184

Leviticus

1–7	90
1:3–13	192
2:2–12	93, 192
3–4	209
3:5–16	192
4:2–31	85, 93, 95, 97, 192, 209
5:1–25	85–86, 95–96, 98, 103, 143, 192
6:1–17	86, 95, 97
8:15	93
9:1	209
10:17	95, 98, 103
11:22–45	53, 98–99
12:2–8	92, 95
12:8	94
13:3–14	177
14:12–28	97
15:2–33	92, 95–96, 99
16	85–86, 88, 90, 93, 95, 98–99, 102–3, 143
17:11–16	89, 96, 98, 103
19:2–22	53, 86, 97
20:2–26	53, 86, 98, 103, 177
23:29–30	86
24:1–23	86
25:25–49	109
26	178
26:40	143

Numbers

1:53	53
3:11–51	109
4:15–20	86
5:6–8	97–98, 143
5:58	86
6:12	97
8:19	89
9:13	98, 103
10:10	273
11:2–11	86
11:24–30	209
12:3	86
14:7	209
14:14–19	86, 139
14:34	98, 103
15:22–36	85–86, 94–95
16:21–25	86, 209
16:46–47	96
18:19–23	89, 97
19:2–20	94–95, 99
20:6	86
21:7	86
22–25	250
22:23–32	175, 249
24:8	161
24:17	256
25:8–11	121
25:11–13	96
27:17	48
28:6–12	89, 192
29:17	95
31:50	96

Deuteronomy

	179
4:20	180
5:14	25
5:1–23	5, 209
6:4–5	68
7:6–8	108, 177, 180
9:6	108
10:15	180
12:10	25
12:12	68
17:6	5
18:15	11
19:15–18	5
21:1–9	88, 95
21:22	132
23:10	92
25:14	25
27:1	209
28:3–11	25
28:15—29:29	99, 178
29:10–19	161, 209
31:9–28	209
32:43	96

Scripture Index

Joshua

1:5	25
6:5	273
21:44	25
22:4	25
22:17	86
23:1	25
24	179

1 Samuel

3:14	96
15:1–17	32
16:3	32
16:12–13	32

2 Samuel

5:2	48
7:7–18	11, 25–26, 29, 41, 128, 180, 184
15:1–17	25
16:3–13	25
21:3–6	89, 96
22:4–18	120, 157

1 Kings

1:2–34	227, 230, 273
6:1	180
8:22	210
11:4–18	26
11:33	26
14:8	26
15:3–11	26
22:17	48

2 Kings

6:16–17	71
8:19	26

1 Chronicles

11:2	48
13:2–4	213
17:8–14	25–26, 184
21:7	26
22:10	26
29:1–20	213

2 Chronicles

1:3–5	213
6:3	213
7:17	26
11:17	26
20:5–14	213
29:2–31	26, 193
29:28–38	213
34:2–3	26
35:4–15	

Nehemiah

9:2–3	143
12:45	108

Job

9:8	34, 54
14:12	144
22:11	120, 157
38:16–17	34, 55, 154

Psalms

2:1–2	12, 20, 43, 132
2:7	26
2:12	43, 132
3:2	68
6:3	68
8:4	27
9:13	154
11:6	120
16:8–9	12, 73–74
18:4–17	120, 157
21:26	213
22:26	74
23:1–4	48
28:9	48
31:4	47
32:6	120, 157
34	18, 194–95, 198, 204, 213
39:9	213
41:9	161
42:7	120, 157
44:12	47
48:15	47
49:8–9	89

Psalms (cont.)

51:9	93
51:17	105, 192
54:4	68
65:3	95
65:7	34
69:1–17	120, 157
73:26	74
74:1–2	47–48, 108
75:8	120
77:15	108
77:20–21	47–48
78:14, 52	47
78:38	95–96
78:52	48
78:70–72	48
79:9	95–96
79:13	47–48
80:1	47–48
81:3	273
84:2	74
88:6	213
88:26	34
89:3–37	26, 34
90:1	208
93:3–4	34, 54
95:7	47
100:3	47–48
102:26	144
106:8–9	34, 54
106:32	213
106:38–39	87
107:18–32	34, 54–55, 154, 192
110	53
110:1	12, 23, 27, 36, 40–41, 53–54, 128, 136, 279
118:22–26	36, 44–45, 138, 159
118:27–29	45
118:34	109
119:89–160	271
124:1–5	120, 157
132:10–12	26
139:7	56, 58
141:2	105
144:7–11	120, 157
149:1	213

Proverbs

3:34	21
6:34–35	88
10:5	82
10:12	207
11:31	204
16:6	97, 106
17:9	207
18:3	82
20:21	203
26:11	117

Isaiah

5:13–14	265
6:7	95–96
6:9–10	17, 149
7:9	171
8:12–14	17–18, 44, 46, 195
9:6	53, 264
11:1–5	22, 30, 56, 58, 144, 277
12:2	171
13:6–16	265
13:8	260
13:10	37, 272
14:30	48
15:5	268
19:3	69
22:14	96
24:5	87
24:18–23	37, 272
26:3–4	171
26:17–18	260
27:9	95–96
27:12–13	273
28:16–18	44, 96, 191
29:6	265
34:4–23	37, 48, 272
35:3–6	225
35:10	154
37:4–17	11
40:1–31	137–39, 143
40:2	101

40:3–5	124, 138, 143–44
40:6–8	61, 138, 271
40:27	101
40:11	47–48
41:15–16	138
42:1–4	99, 101
42:16	139
42:19	101
43:9–10	99, 138
43:20	180
44:22–24	109
45:15	270
47:11	89, 96
49:1–8	99, 101
49:9–13	47–48, 101, 138
49:18	11
49:25	225
50:10–11	101
51:9–10	34, 54
51:17–23	68, 102, 120
52:2–3	110, 225
52:13	131
52:13—53:12	85, 99–106, 157
52:14–15	101–2, 107
53:1	102
53:4	102
53:4–6	103, 107, 225
53:6	14
53:9	101, 103, 107
53:10–12	43, 102–3, 132, 161
54:1–17	102
55:10–11	271
56:7	210
60–63	277
60:15–17	270
61:1–2	32, 225
63:10–11	47–48, 58
64:1	144
66:7–9	260
66:16	264
66:24	144

Jeremiah

2:7	87
3:9	87
4:5	273
4:24	265
4:31	260
6:24	260
7:11	180
13:12	260
13:15–17	47–48
13:17	48
15:2	264
15:9	68
16:15–16	268, 278
22:23	260
23:1–8	30, 48, 144, 278
24:6	278
25:15–27	120
31:10	47–48
31:31–33	55, 107, 161
33:15	30, 144
49:8	268
49:12	120
49:22	260
50:43	260
51:7	120

Ezekiel

1:1–28	104, 144
2:1	27
5:17	264
7:16	268
11:16	208
11:22–25	104
14:13	264
16:55	278
24:13	86
26:25	93
32:7	37, 272
34:11–17	47–48
34:23	48
36:22–37	55, 107, 144, 177
37:24	47
38:19–20	265
39:18	48
43:7–8	99
43:20–26	93, 95–96
44:27	96
45:6	177
45:15–20	96

Daniel

2	31, 115
2:28–44	273
3:8	115
6:33	115
7	31
7:13–14	27–28, 36–37, 40, 53, 271
7:15	69
7:17–27	28
8:13	266, 268–69
9:24–27	118, 259, 266–69
10:20–21	71
11	259
11:31	266–69
12:2	38
12:11	266–69

Hosea

1:6–23	187
2:6	144
2:21–23	21, 144
4:16	47
5:3	87
6:6	106
6:10	87
13:13–14	109, 260

Joel

2:1	273
2:2–18	58
2:10	37, 265, 272, 275
2:28–32	36, 59, 63, 133, 144, 271
2:31	37, 272
3:1–5	144
3:15	37, 272

Amos

2:15–16	268
5:20–24	37, 86, 272
8:9	37, 272
9:11	30

Jonah

1:1–16	34, 55

Micah

2:12	47
4:6–8	33, 47
4:9–10	260
4:13	270
5:4	48
5:5	264
7:14	48
7:18–20	95

Nahum

1:15	264
3:18	268

Habakkuk

3:3–6	265

Haggai

2:6	265

Zephaniah

1:15–16	37, 272–73
3:19	47

Zechariah

3:8	30
4:7–10	26
6:12	30
9–14	256
9:1–9	36, 144, 159
9:10	264
9:14	271, 273
9:16	47–48
10:3	47–48
12:1	69
12:10–11	101
13:2	228
13:7	48
14:5	265, 268
14:16	35

SCRIPTURE INDEX   337

Malachi

4:1–6   140, 143–44, 278

NEW TESTAMENT

Matthew

1:1–18	32
2:3–12	143
2:9–11	32
2:23	22
3:1–17	140, 144, 147
3:3	139, 143–44
3:7	270
3:12	270
3:16	32
4:8–22	151
4:17–19	147, 150
4:23–24	33, 123, 147
5:1–3	71, 146
5:1–12	171, 223
5:13–15	149, 228
5:17	103
6:33	146
7:13–23	163, 241
7:15	262
7:17–18	149
8:2–4	5, 33, 88, 92
8:13	33
8:16	238
8:19–22	152
8:21	148, 150
8:23	150
8:28–34	229
8:29	33, 228
9:6–9	33, 152
9:18–23	33, 88, 92, 150
9:27–31	33, 230
9:32–35	33, 123, 147, 226, 230
9:37	146
10:1–4	1, 147, 152, 234
10:1–42	148
10:7–8	88, 92, 147, 234–35
10:17–18	212
10:19	266
10:32–33	129, 244
10:35–39	119, 122, 147, 156, 158
11:1–2	146
11:5	33, 88, 92
11:7–15	140, 143
12:1–2	150
12:9–13	214
12:22	33
12:22–45	230
12:28	32
12:31–32	232
12:38–42	233
12:43–45	233, 238
12:46–50	147, 156
13:1–23	148–49
13:10	146
13:16	153
13:30–38	214, 273
13:36	146
13:41–45	149, 214, 272–73
13:49–50	273
13:52	146
14:1–12	140, 238
14:24–33	34
14:28	1
15:15	1
15:21–28	233
15:30–33	33
16	63
16:1–12	232
16:4	153
16:8	214
16:15–28	155
16:16–20	1, 11, 23, 35, 64–65, 103, 153–54, 187, 191, 213–14
16:21	100, 103, 118
16:22–23	65, 155, 162, 227
16:24–27	119, 122, 158, 272
16:28—17:9	35
17:1	1
17:10–13	140, 234
17:11	278
17:12–23	118, 234
17:18	33
17:20	235
17:27	247

Matthew (cont.)

17:30	235
18:1	161
18:7–9	149, 266
18:12–19	214
18:15–35	141, 213
18:16	5
18:18	64–65, 154, 214
18:21	1
19:16–30	152
19:21–22	152
19:27–29	147, 156
20:18–25	118–19, 122, 161
20:21–28	103, 120, 157–58
20:28–34	125
20:34	33
21:5	36, 159
21:14–15	33
21:25–32	143
21:42	129
22–23	265
22:15–46	38–40, 68, 146
22:23–33	279–80
22:50	69
23:1—24:1	257
23:2–6	210
23:30	170
23:34	212
23:38	259
24:1–2	259
24:3	257, 259
24:5	260
24:6–7	262, 264
24:8	260
24:9	265–66
24:10–13	266
24:14	123, 148, 266, 270
24:15	266, 268
24:15–19	268–69
24:21–24	262, 270
24:23–24	260, 270
24:25–26	270
24:27–30	36–37, 271–72
24:30	27
24:30—25:46	259
24:31	270
24:32–35	271–72
24:36–39	273
24:39–41	273
24:42	274
24:42–40	274
24:44	273
24:51	273
25:10–13	273
25:30	273
25:31	272
25:35	207
25:41	251
25:46	251
26:6	33
26:13	123
26:14–25	161
26:20–29	159–60
26:24–25	136
26:30–34	162, 226
26:35	1
26:37	1, 120, 148
26:40	1
26:57—27:10	265
26:61	40
26:63	40
26:64	27
26:70–74	172, 244
27:5	257
27:11	40
27:11–66	265
27:32–57	41, 146, 264
28:18–20	134, 146–48

Mark

	22
1:1–4	12, 32, 123, 137–39, 143–45
1:2–11	140, 144–45
1:5–8	133
1:10–13	15, 23, 32, 145, 148, 227
1:11–13	13, 53, 148
1:14–17	32, 108, 123–24, 125, 145, 147, 150
1:16–21	145, 151, 214
1:22	32, 214
1:23–25	22, 33, 69, 214, 228–29, 238
1:26–28	25, 69, 214, 228–29, 238

SCRIPTURE INDEX

1:29	151	5:36	22
1:34	24, 228	5:37	1
1:35	125, 156	5:42	88, 92
1:38–39	33, 238	6:1	150
1:40	88, 92	6:4	22
1:41	33	6:7–13	33, 125, 228, 234
1:44–45	24, 33, 88, 92	6:14–15	34
2:5	22, 125, 141, 171–72	6:14–29	140, 143, 146
		6:27	238
2:6–8	74	6:30	13
2:7	25	6:45–52	34, 54, 125, 156
2:12	33, 230	6:50	13
2:13	152	6:52	74
2:14	124–25, 145, 152	7:3	211
2:17	81, 202	7:17	146
2:18	146	7:24–30	233
2:19	22	7:35–37	24, 33
2:27—3:6	34, 214	8:11–21	232–33
3:7	22, 150	8:22–25	33
3:10–14	24, 33, 69, 143, 228, 238	8:25–27	33, 153
		8:28	34, 153
3:13–19	1, 33, 147, 152	8:29	1, 35, 125, 153, 191
3:15	147, 228, 234		
3:18	263	8:30	24
3:20–30	230	8:31	100, 103, 118, 198, 209
3:22–23	226–27		
3:27	226–27	8:33–38	85, 118–19, 122, 123–25, 145, 155, 158, 218, 226
3:28–29	232		
3:31–35	125, 145, 147, 156		
4:3–20	148, 156	8:36–37	68
4:10–11	125, 145–46	8:42–45	122
4:10–25	149	9:1–10	35
4:12	17, 46, 143	9:2	1, 22, 53, 148
4:15	74, 227	9:3	14
4:20	232	9:5	1
4:26–30	145	9:7	13–14
4:34	146	9:9	24
4:35–41	54, 171	9:12	103, 118, 198, 277
4:41	25, 34	9:14–29	228, 234–35
5:1–20	228–29	9:25–26	33, 228
5:2–8	69, 238	9:31	103, 118, 198
5:7	33, 228	9:33–34	161
5:8	229	9:35–41	125
5:9	198, 225	9:38	231, 235
5:15	22, 76, 225	9:39–40	32, 235
5:29–30	22, 111	9:47	145, 174
5:34	88, 92, 172	9:49–50	235
5:35–41	33	10:12–25	145, 173, 202

Mark (cont.)

10:17	81
10:17–30	152
10:18	25, 81
10:21–27	22, 152, 174
10:28–31	1, 145, 147
10:33–45	82, 85, 103, 118–20, 125, 156–58, 161, 212, 214, 223
10:46–52	33, 150
10:49	22
10:52	172
11:1–33	159
11:7	22
11:9–10	36, 138, 159
11:16–17	180
11:18	36, 145, 159
11:22	172
11:23–25	74, 125, 141, 159
11:27—12:2	36–37, 209
11:29	22
11:30–37	143, 145
11:38	22
12	265
12:1–12	45
12:10–11	36
12:12	159
12:13–44	37–40, 159
12:18–27	279–81
12:25	69
12:30	68, 74
12:31–35	22, 74
12:35–37	13, 41, 53
12:36	12, 23, 36, 54, 136, 279
12:37	25, 36
12:40—13:2	259
13	257
13:3	1, 259
13:4	259, 264
13:5–6	145, 260
13:7–8	262
13:8	260, 264
13:9–13	125, 212, 265–66
13:10	123, 148, 270
13:14	266, 268
13:14–17	268–69
13:20	270
13:21–23	270
13:22	270
13:24–25	37, 272, 276
13:26	27, 36–37, 49, 271–72, 276
13:26–32	272
13:27	36, 49, 226, 270
13:32–37	156, 226, 273–74
14:3	33
14:9	123
14:10–21	161
14:17–31	159
14:21	28, 136
14:22–25	122, 145, 160
14:27–31	162
14:32–41	68, 120, 122, 125, 148, 156
14:53—15:37	198, 265
14:58	40
14:61	25, 40
14:62	27, 28
14:66–72	195
14:68	172, 244
14:70	244
15	131
15:2–32	40–41, 209
15:14	76
15:15	22, 91, 107
15:21–39	41, 209
15:26	91, 107
15:29	40
15:37–39	69, 257
15:43	125, 145
16:6	22
16:15	123

Luke

1:1–71	32, 71, 108, 121, 124, 140, 144, 166
2:11	32
2:14–15	53, 143
2:22–24	93, 108
2:35	68
2:38	108, 121
3:1–22	140, 144
3:3–6	133, 139, 143
3:7	270
3:17	270

3:19–20	143	9:44	118
3:22	32	9:49	151, 231
3:23–34	124	9:57–62	152, 155
4:1	144	10:17–20	235, 238
4:13	220	10:23	153
4:16–21	212–13	11:1	146
4:18–20	32–33	11:5	207
4:31	229	11:14–15	33, 226, 230
4:41	33, 228	11:14–32	230
5:1–11	151	11:20	32, 231
5:5	151	11:22	226
5:8	23	11:23–26	233, 235, 238
5:10	170	11:28	232
5:12	88, 92	11:33	149
5:13	33	12:3	238
5:14	108	12:9	129, 244
5:24–26	33	12:11–12	212
5:27–28	152	12:52–53	147
5:30	146	13:1	263
6:6–10	214	13:10	33
6:12–16	1, 147, 152	14:12–14	207
7:5	210	14:15–24	115
7:10–15	33, 88, 92, 150, 234	14:15–35	156
		14:26–27	119, 147, 156
7:18–19	146, 228	16:8	194
7:20–21	228	16:16	143
7:22–23	33, 88, 92, 228	16:19–31	281
7:25	184	17:13–17	33, 88, 92, 151
7:29–33	143	17:25	118
7:44–47	207	17:26–35	268–69, 273
8:5–20	148–49, 156	18:18–30	152
8:21	147	18:22–23	152
8:24	151	18:28–30	147
8:26–39	229	18:31–33	103
8:28	33	18:31	118
8:30	226	18:42–43	33
8:41–42	210, 234	19:44	357
8:45–51	33, 151	20	265
9:2	147	20:6	143
9:6–9	140, 148	20:19–44	38–40, 280
9:20	35, 153	20:45—21:7	257, 259
9:20–27	103, 118–19, 122, 155, 158	20:67	40
		20:70	40
9:27–36	35	21:6–7	259
9:28	1, 148	21:8	260
9:33	151	21:9–10	262
9:38–39	234	21:11	264
9:42	33	21:11–66	265

Luke (cont.)

21:12	212, 265
21:13–15	266
21:16–17	265–66
21:18–20	266–67
21:20–23	268–69
21:23	265
21:25–32	37, 272
21:27	27, 36–37, 271
21:33	271
21:34–36	274
21:37	259
22:14–34	159–61
22:20	122, 161
22:22	118, 136
22:28	122
22:31–34	162, 227
22:34–61	129, 163, 172
22:37	103
22:47–71	265
22:57	244
22:69	27
23:2–3	40
23:11–12	34
23:19–25	263
23:28–31	264
23:33–49	41, 69, 257
24:21	108, 121
24:47–49	5, 148–49

John

1	11, 144
1:22–27	139, 143
1:29	90
1:35	22, 146
1:36	90
1:37	146
1:40–44	150–51, 153
2:2–4	150, 152
2:11–22	152
2:19	40, 257
3:3–5	72, 152
3:6–8	71–72
3:10	152
3:16–18	71
3:19	194
3:22	150
3:25	146
4:48	152
5:8–11	33
5:33	144
6:16–21	34
6:68	1
7:6–8	152
7:20	230
8:12	194
8:48–52	230
9:1–11	214
9:2	146
9:5	194
9:11	33
9:13–34	212, 214
9:28–29	146
10:20	230
10:41	144
11:14	230
11:43–44	33, 88
12:16	152
12:20–25	122, 158
12:36	194
12:42	214
13:1—16:33	159
13:14–16	147
13:18–30	161
13:27	136
13:36–38	162
14:30	227
15:12	162
16:17–29	146
17:12	161
18:1	150
18:25–27	244
18:29–33	40
19:7–9	40
19:12	186
19:19–21	41
20:23	154
20:29	153
21:15–17	153, 162–63, 212, 214

Acts

1	22
1:5	59
1:6–7	23, 36, 49, 271, 273–74

SCRIPTURE INDEX 343

1:8	5, 19, 36, 60, 148, 202, 271	2:36	12–13, 41–43, 53, 63, 128, 132–33, 172, 180, 257
1:11	271	2:37	172
1:13–15	1, 147, 163, 210, 213	2:38	15, 42, 57–60, 79, 126, 129, 134, 144, 172–73
1:16	15, 58, 63, 210, 244		
1:16–20	72, 109, 136	2:39	12–13
1:17–25	161, 166	2:40	79
1:20–22	59, 62–63	2:41	68, 126
1:24	19, 74, 134	2:42	211
1:25–26	59, 136	2:44	163
2:1–21	36, 163	2:46	210
2:2	58, 71	2:47	12, 214
2:4	15, 58–60, 71	3	128–29
2:8–11	270	3:4	1
2:14	1, 61	3:6	134
2:14–40	128, 130, 132–33	3:12	1, 128
2:16–38	41–42, 62–63, 132–33, 144, 221, 257	3:12–26	42–43, 79, 128–30
		3:13–17	131–32, 244, 275
		3:14	15, 20, 33
2:17	12, 57–59, 73, 86, 132–33, 221	3:15	12, 33, 91, 135, 216
2:18	13, 57–59, 63, 132–33	3:16	172, 216
		3:17	117, 172, 198, 216, 243
2:19–21	11–13, 32, 37, 111, 132–33, 272–73	3:18	12, 23, 33, 62, 129, 216, 259, 275
2:22	32–33, 132–33		
2:23–24	12–13, 17–18, 20, 46, 68, 76, 91, 129, 131–33, 188, 236	3:19–20	10, 49, 126, 129, 136, 166, 172, 180, 259, 275, 277–78
2:25	12–13, 20, 132–33	3:21	15, 49, 62, 129, 136, 172, 180, 259, 275–78
2:25–31	62, 73–74, 132–33, 172		
2:27	15, 68	3:22–26	11–13, 62, 87, 131–32, 136, 166, 180, 259, 277–79
2:30	11, 26, 41–42, 59, 62, 128, 257, 275		
2:31	42, 275	4	265
2:32	12, 63, 132–33, 275	4:1–12	163, 222
		4:1–22	195, 266
2:33	15, 42–43, 59, 63, 132–33, 135, 257, 275	4:8	1, 15, 57, 59, 144
		4:8–12	128, 130
		4:9	42, 58, 129, 202
2:34–35	12–13, 23, 41–43, 54, 63, 128, 132–33, 136, 172, 257, 275, 279	4:10	12, 79, 129, 131, 134, 202
		4:12	33, 42, 79, 125, 129, 134
		4:19–20	12, 18–20, 198, 202

Acts (cont.)

4:21	136, 279
4:23	207
4:24–31	11–14, 19–20, 23–24, 43, 91, 132, 211, 213, 224
4:30	15, 20, 211, 224
4:31	12, 20, 57–58, 144, 211, 224, 265
4:32	68
4:32–37	79, 211
5:1–8	1, 15, 19, 58, 60, 136, 213, 250
5:2	76, 173
5:3–4	74, 144, 173, 227
5:9–11	13, 15, 19, 23, 136, 250
5:12–42	163, 195, 222, 265–66
5:16	235
5:19–23	226, 238
5:25	109
5:29	19, 60, 192, 198, 202
5:30	132, 192, 202
5:31	12, 42, 126, 135, 166, 192, 202
5:32	15, 60, 174, 192
5:40	136, 202, 216, 279
5:41	134, 223
5:42	210
6:1	163, 264
6:1–5	214
6:2	12
6:4	211
6:7	171
6:8—8:3	163, 210, 216, 265
6:14	257
7:22–26	266
7:38	213
7:54–60	119, 136, 279
7:56	36, 271
7:59	69
7:60—8:1	266
8:7	235
8:11	61
8:12	72, 126
8:12–17	134
8:13	115
8:15–19	15, 57–58, 144, 212, 250
8:20	1, 59, 115, 136, 212, 213, 235, 250–51, 253
8:21	12, 213, 235, 250, 253
8:22	74, 213, 221, 235, 250, 253
8:23	115, 213, 235, 250, 253
8:24	13, 72, 213, 235, 250, 253
8:31	211
8:32–35	103
9:1	163
9:2	126, 163–64, 241, 265
9:4–7	36, 271
9:10–26	163, 216
9:32	14
9:38	163
9:42–43	14, 207
10:2	187
10:3–7	226
10:6–30	177
10:9—11:18	1, 163
10:12	15
10:19	58
10:22	12, 21
10:22–43	195
10:24–25	173
10:28	96
10:28–43	130
10:30–33	12, 226
10:34–35	20, 92
10:34–43	128
10:36	257
10:37–39	23, 32–33, 54, 57–58, 61, 91–92, 129, 131, 226–27, 235
10:40	12
10:40–48	92, 96, 126
10:42–43	49, 54, 59, 126, 129, 134, 171–73

10:44–48	15, 59, 129, 134, 144, 164, 173, 210, 257
11:1	12
11:1–18	164
11:2–3	92, 96
11:2–18	213
11:11	61, 177
11:12–14	177, 187
11:14–18	15, 57–60, 92, 126, 134, 144, 172
11:19	163
11:26	163, 186
11:27	211
11:28–29	264
12	265
12:1–17	20, 71, 119–20, 216, 222
12:1–3	136, 266, 279
12:4	76
12:5–19	224, 226
12:7–11	198, 202
12:12	76, 157, 207, 210, 213
13:8–11	235
13:10	126, 163–64, 241
13:15	212
13:29	132
13:45	265
14:2–5	265
14:5	216
14:16	76
14:19–28	163, 216, 265
14:53	211
15:1	211
15:4	214
15:1–30	213
15:7	1, 12, 125, 171–72
15:7–11	79, 96, 164, 172
15:8	15, 59, 144
15:9	74, 172
15:10	218
15:11	21
15:19–29	164
15:21–22	211–12, 214
16:1	163
16:6–7	58
16:11–18	205
16:13	207, 210–11
16:15	187
16:16	210–11, 235
16:17	126, 163–64, 235, 241
16:18–19	235
16:19–34	163, 187, 216
16:22–40	238
16:40	207, 210–11
17:5–9	265
17:34	205
18:1–8	187, 205
18:6	265
18:12–17	265
18:25–26	126, 163–64, 241
19:9	126, 163–64, 241
19:12	235
19:13–20	231, 235
19:19	163, 241
19:23–41	163, 186, 216, 241
20:7–8	210
20:17	211
20:24	125
20:33	212
21:24	108
21:27—23:16	265
21:30—26:32	163
21:38	262
22:4	126, 163–64, 238, 241
23:1	76, 82
23:1—26:10	238
23:6–7	279
23:11–21	216
24:5–9	265
24:14–22	126, 163–64, 241
24:18	108
26:18	194
26:28	186
27:15–17	62
28:1	211

Romans

1:1–9	71, 190
2:15	76
3:24	108, 166
3:25	90
5	270

Romans (cont.)

5:1–5	171
6:23	91
7:5	73
7:6–14	190
8:4–7	73
8:17–25	270
8:23	108, 166
10:7	236
10:14	238
10:16	103
11:26–29	4
11:36	53
12:1	192
12:13	207
13–14	214
13:1–7	197
13:6	112
14:1	190
15:21	103
15:27–30	190
15:44–46	190
16:1	214
16:15	207, 210

1 Corinthians

1:9–11	190
1:21	238
2:13–15	190
3:1–2	62, 190
5:5	217
6:4	211
6:18–22	211
6:20	109, 114
7:4	173
7:17	214
7:23	109, 114
7:34	71
8:7	171
9:5	206
9:7–14	212
9:25	173
9:27	238
10:18	170
10:32	214
11:16	214
11:23–26	160

14:3	190
14:12	211
14:26–33	211
14:34–35	200
15:3–4	190
16:19	207, 210

2 Corinthians

2:14–17	226
4:2	76
4:7—5:21	270
5:3–5	73, 112
6:6–7	171
7:11	112
8–10	214
9:10	171
12:13–18	212

Galatians

1:4–5	53
2:7	5
2:9–10	1, 112
3:25	206
4:8–12	239
4:26	104
5:19–21	73
5:22–26	171, 173
6:1	190

Ephesians

1:7–14	108, 166
2:2–3	169, 227
3:21	53
4:8–13	226, 236
5:8	194
5:13–19	190, 211
5:22—6:9	200–201, 205
6:14–17	171

Colossians

1:9	190
1:12–13	194
3:12–14	171
3:16–17	211
3:18—4:1	201, 205
4:15	207, 210

Philippians

2:6–7	169
4:8	171
4:18	192
4:20	53

1 Thessalonians

1:5	194
4:4	205
5:3	262

2 Thessalonians

1:9	251
2:1–12	266
2:3	161

1 Timothy

1:4	76, 82
1:17	53
1:19	76, 82
2–3	207
2:1–12	195, 197, 199
2:8	76, 211
3:1–7	211
3:2–3	171
3:8–13	214
3:16	69
5:1—6:2	207, 211
5:17–22	211–12
5:23	68
6:9	220
6:11	171, 173

2 Timothy

3:10	171

Titus

1–2	207
1:7–8	171, 212
2:2–10	201, 211
3:1–2	171, 197
3:3	173

Hebrews

1–2	164
1:4–14	164
2:11–14	164
2:9–18	164
3–4	226
3:6	165
3:8–9	220
3:12	113
4:1	165
4:12	165
5:2	165
5:7	122
7:1–2	165
7:4—10:18	190
7:26–27	95
9:2–28	85–86, 90, 92, 95–96, 98–99, 102
9:7	165
10:10	164
10:30	165
10:33	170
11:1–30	165
12:1	165
12:7–9	165
12:12	104
12:23	214
12:24	164
13:2	207
13:5	193
13:10	165

James

1:2	222
2:2	210, 214
3:7	169
3:17–18	171
4:4	76
5:13–15	210, 212

1 Peter

1:1	3, 11, 22, 51, 17–18, 32, 55, 117, 164, 166, 169, 180, 185, 190–91

1 Peter (*cont.*)

1:2–3	11–14, 18, 21, 32, 55–56, 58–59, 72, 87, 90–92, 95, 99, 102, 108–9, 117, 166, 169, 173, 180, 187, 190–92, 197, 279
1:3–5	11–12, 17, 19, 49, 56, 61, 72, 80, 102, 108, 111, 117, 164, 166, 169, 172–73, 191, 195, 279
1:3–12	20, 55–56, 187
1:6	85, 111, 164, 215, 218, 222–23
1:7–8	37, 49, 56, 82–83, 85, 111, 164, 172, 174, 196, 215, 217, 219, 222–23
1:9	14, 68, 85, 102, 111, 115, 172, 180, 223, 280
1:10	21, 57–58, 62, 115, 164, 191, 280
1:11	14, 19, 23, 37, 57–58, 62, 164, 191, 215, 217, 272, 280
1:12	57–58, 85, 123, 164, 191–92, 203, 226, 280
1:13	156, 165, 173, 277, 280
1:14	78–80, 110, 117, 165, 172–73, 243, 252
1:14–16	14–15, 53, 95, 99, 113, 156, 192, 215, 277
1:17	13, 15, 19–20, 113, 165, 177, 185, 195, 203
1:18	79, 85, 89–90, 95, 108–10, 113–15, 117, 122, 164–65, 169, 246
1:19	23, 61, 85, 89–90, 95, 109, 113–14, 122, 164–66, 277
1:20	12, 18, 122, 164, 191, 257, 280
1:21	14, 62, 109, 122, 164, 171–72, 280
1:22	12, 72, 74, 103, 108, 122, 164–65, 174
1:23	12, 61, 72, 80, 108, 122–23, 138, 164–66, 174, 191
1:24	14, 61, 72–73, 102, 108, 122–23, 138, 164, 166, 174, 191
1:25	13, 61, 72, 108, 122–23, 138, 166, 174, 191
2:1–2	62, 101, 110, 221, 280
2:3	13, 61
2:4–10	3, 44–47, 83, 153, 182–83, 187–88, 190–91, 214
2:4	12, 18, 165, 191, 219
2:5	86, 147, 165, 182–85, 187–88, 190–93, 196, 213, 223
2:6–7	18, 129, 165, 187–88, 191, 194, 213, 219
2:8	18, 62, 191, 194, 213
2:9–10	12, 18, 21, 73, 80, 82, 165, 177, 182–85, 187–88, 190, 192–96
2:11	82, 177, 198, 221
2:12	12, 14, 186, 190, 193–94, 196, 198, 203–4, 214, 216, 221–23, 227
2:13	13, 194, 196–97, 199
2:14	166, 190, 194, 196, 199, 203, 221

2:15	12, 78, 81, 83, 117, 172, 192–94, 196, 198–99, 203–4, 216, 243	3:10	204, 221, 224
		3:11	203, 221, 224
		3:12	12–13, 18–19, 21, 81, 203–4, 221, 224
2:16	12, 86, 192, 194, 196–99, 221	3:13	204
2:17	12, 19, 82, 84, 194–95, 197, 199, 203	3:14	20, 193, 195, 202, 215, 217, 221, 223
		3:15	13, 15, 74, 83, 172, 193–95, 203, 216, 280
2:18	80, 86, 194, 197–99, 203–4, 216, 221, 223	3:16	23, 76–78, 81–83, 190–91, 193–96, 198, 214, 216, 221, 227
2:18–24	104, 203–4, 216, 221, 223		
2:19	77, 81, 85, 194, 196, 199, 203–4, 215–18, 221–23	3:17	12, 193, 203–4, 215, 217, 221
2:20	81, 83, 85, 193–94, 203–4, 215–17, 221–23	3:18	69, 73, 81, 91, 96, 108, 203, 216, 221, 226, 236, 280
2:21	23, 41, 81, 83, 85, 97, 173, 193, 200, 203–4, 215–17, 221–23	3:18–22	10, 12, 20, 49, 68, 76–77, 81–82, 111, 126, 135, 196–97, 226, 236–39, 257, 280
2:22	81, 85, 97, 173, 193, 200, 203–4, 215, 221–23	4:1	23, 73, 215–17, 223
2:23–25	14, 20, 40, 49, 78, 80–81, 85, 90–91, 97–98, 103, 110, 131, 165, 173, 193, 200, 203–4, 215–17, 221–24	4:1–7	173
		4:2	12, 217, 247
		4:2–16	186
		4:3	73, 78–79, 110, 186, 216, 246–47
		4:4	78–79, 110, 186, 216
3:1	78, 83, 190, 193–94, 196–97, 200, 204, 214, 223	4:5	19–20
		4:6	12, 20, 69, 73, 108, 135, 203, 224, 236–39, 280–81
3:2	190, 194, 200		
3:3	73, 200	4:7	156, 224, 246, 257, 280
3:4	18, 69, 71, 74, 192, 195, 200	4:8	174, 207, 246
3:5	190, 197, 200	4:9	165
3:6	23, 200, 202–4, 216	4:10	12, 21, 59, 81, 172, 203, 208, 214
3:7	21, 82–83, 201, 205–6, 224, 280	4:11	12, 20, 37, 171, 185, 208, 257, 272
3:8–12	83, 192–93, 196, 199, 207	4:12–18	180, 185, 219–20
3:9	200, 204, 215–16, 221, 227, 280		

1 Peter (cont.)

4:13–14	23, 57, 60, 111, 192, 215, 218–20, 223, 227, 246, 280
4:15	215, 217, 219–21, 223
4:16	12, 196, 204, 219–21, 223
4:17–19	12, 15, 20–21, 111, 117, 177, 182, 187, 203–4, 215, 217, 223–24
4:18	280
5:1	23, 37, 212, 217, 272, 280
5:2	14, 201, 209, 212, 249
5:3	201, 209, 211–12
5:4	14, 163, 211–12, 280
5:5	21, 197, 201, 207, 209, 211–13, 227
5:6–7	11, 19, 207, 224, 227, 280
5:8	198, 226–27, 274
5:9	156, 215, 218, 220
5:10	12, 37, 185, 215, 217, 223, 272, 280
5:11	20, 37, 185, 272
5:12	12, 21, 65, 185
5:13	187

2 Peter

	4, 22, 51
1:1	20, 42, 46, 52–53, 71, 112, 166, 168–72, 212
1:1–11	164, 180, 226
1:2	11, 13, 21, 52–53, 111–12, 166, 168–70, 172
1:2–7	114
1:3–5	46, 52, 71, 79, 112, 117, 166, 168–72, 174
1:3–15	64–65, 72, 80, 111–12, 135, 167, 255
1:4	167–70, 245, 247–48, 251
1:5–6	166, 277
1:7	174
1:8	113–14, 117, 172, 174
1:9	59, 72, 87, 91–92, 95–96, 108, 113–14, 117, 172, 174–75
1:10	14, 113–14, 117, 172, 174
1:11	19, 35, 37, 49, 52, 113–14, 117, 171–72, 174–75, 185, 187, 257, 277
1:13	20
1:13–15	73, 168–69, 222, 255
1:16	19, 35, 37, 49, 62–63, 255, 257, 271–72, 274
1:17	11, 13–15, 35, 52–53, 59, 62, 168–69, 172, 255, 272, 274
1:18	15, 35, 37, 62, 115, 168, 255, 274
1:19	14–15, 35, 37, 61–62, 74, 115, 168, 255, 272, 274
1:20	62–63, 115, 255
1:21	12, 15, 52, 57–58, 62–63, 76, 115, 168–69, 255
1:22	108, 115
2:1	13, 23, 72, 85, 109–10, 115, 240–42, 244–47, 251, 262, 266
2:1–22	111, 135, 241, 255
2:2	13, 163, 241, 246–47
2:2–9	113
2:3	61, 241, 244, 249, 251

2:4–6	19, 64, 175, 238, 241, 251–52, 273		244–45, 256, 273, 275–77
2:5	15, 19, 21, 79–80, 114	3:8–10	13, 23, 64, 117, 241, 274, 276
2:6–7	19, 21, 64, 79–80, 114, 175, 241, 247, 251–52	3:9	275
		3:10–13	15, 21, 256, 275–77
2:8–9	15, 19, 21, 23, 64, 79–81, 114, 117, 175, 203, 219–20, 229, 241, 247, 251–52	3:12	219, 256, 275–77
		3:13–14	64, 275, 277
		3:15	23, 64, 111, 117, 275
2:10–11	13, 19, 21, 23, 73, 114, 117, 241–43, 246–47	3:16–17	64–65, 175, 240, 242–44, 255
		3:18	11, 20–21, 174–75, 255
2:12	80, 115, 172, 242–43, 245, 248, 251–52		
		1 John	
2:13	20–21, 242, 246–47, 252, 277	2:18–23	266
2:14	68, 95, 242–43, 247, 249, 252	**2 John**	
		1	211
2:15	163, 175, 241–42, 249–50, 252	**3 John**	
2:16	62, 116, 242, 246, 250, 251, 272	1	211
		5–8	207
2:17	245, 252		
2:18–22	72–73, 114, 116, 242–43, 245–46, 247, 272	**Jude**	
			114
2:19	80, 245–46, 248, 251	3	240
		3–23	111
2:20–22	113, 117, 172, 233, 248–49, 251	4	114, 240, 246–47
		5	252
2:21	20, 117, 163, 172, 241, 248	6	238, 251–52
		7	73, 252, 273
2:25	165	8	246–47
3:1–2	15, 42, 61–62, 65, 241–42, 255	9	251
		10	243
3:3–15	113, 175, 216, 255, 276	11	175, 249
		12	245
3:3–4	63, 114, 241–42, 245, 247, 256	15–16	246–47, 249, 251
		18	245, 247
3:5–7	11–12, 15, 114, 219, 241–42,	19	246
		22–23	240
		24–25	53, 112

Revelations

1:6	184
1:17–25	161, 236, 239
2:1–18	212
3:1–14	212
3:12	104
5:2	238
5:9–10	114, 184
5:13	53
6:4	264
6:5–8	264
6:12–13	37, 272, 276
6:18–12	265
7:12	53
8:3–4	193
8:5	265
8:12	37, 272
9:27	268–69
11:8	190
11:13–19	265
12	264
13:11–17	262
14:3–4	114
14:15–19	272
16:1—18:6	120
16:18	265
18:8	264
19	264
19:11–16	37, 271
20:1–7	238, 264
21:2–10	104

www.ingramcontent.com/pod-product-compliance
Lightning Source LLC
Chambersburg PA
CBHW071146300426
44113CB00009B/1104